P9-DMM-676

Photographic Imaging Techniques in C++ for Windows® and Windows NT™

CRAIG A. LINDLEY

John Wiley & Sons, Inc.

New York • Chichester
Brisbane • Toronto • Singapore

To HH, you know who you are!

Trademarks and Copyrights

Apple and Macintosh are registered trademarks of Apple Computer.
IBM, IBM Enhanced Graphics Adapter, PCJr, PC/AT, PC/XT, PS/2, PCDOS, OS/2, and
    AIX are registered trademarks of International Business Machines Corporation.
HiCOLOR is a registered trademark of Sierra Semiconductor.
Intel is a registered trademark of Intel Corporation, Delaware.
Microsoft, Microsoft C, MSDOS, MASM, Windows, Windows/386, Windows 95, and
    Visual C++ are registered trademarks of Microsoft Corporation.
Motorola is a registered trademark of Motorola Corporation.
TARGA is a registered trademark of Truevision, Inc.
Turbo C and Borland C++ are registered trademarks of Borland International.
All other trademarks are the property of their respective owners.

Publisher: Katherine Schowalter
Senior Editor: Diane D. Cerra
Assistant Managing Editor: Angela Murphy
Text Design & Composition: North Market Street Graphics

Designations used by companies to distinguish their products are often claimed as
trademarks. In all instances where John Wiley & Sons, Inc. is aware of a claim, the
product names appear in initial capital or all capital letters. Readers, however, should
contact the appropriate companies for more complete information regarding trademarks and registration.

This text is printed on acid-free paper.

Copyright © 1995 by John Wiley & Sons, Inc.

All rights reserved. Published simultaneously in Canada.

This publication is designed to provide accurate and authoritative information in
regard to the subject matter covered. It is sold with the understanding that the publisher is not engaged in rendering legal, accounting, or other professional service. If
legal advice or other expert assistance is required, the services of a competent professional person should be sought.

Reproduction or translation of any part of this work beyond that permitted by section
107 or 108 of the 1976 United States Copyright Act without the permission of the copyright owner is unlawful. Requests for permission or further information should be
addressed to the Permissions Department, John Wiley & Sons, Inc.

Library of Congress Cataloging-in-Publication Data:

Lindley, Craig A.
    Photographic imaging techniques in C/C++ for Windows and Windows
NT / Craig Lindley.
        p.   cm.
    Includes index.
    ISBN 0-471-11568-1 (paper/disk : acid-free paper)
    1. Windows (Computer programs)   2. Microsoft Windows NT.   3. C
(Computer program language)   4. C++ (Computer program language)
5. Computer graphics.   I. Title.
QA76.76.W56.L54   1995
006'.76—dc20   94-49718

Printed in the United States of America
10 9 8 7 6 5 4 3 2 1

C O N T E N T S

Four pages of full-color illustrations follow page 176.

F I G U R E S

vii

P R O G R A M   L I S T I N G S

P R E F A C E

If you are using or contemplating using photographic imaging in a professional Windows application, you need this book!

This is not just another book on Windows programming. The entire focus of this book is on the photographic imaging techniques required for professional Windows application programs. Why is this important? Because just about every Windows program written these days includes some form of imaging. Remember the old adage "A picture is worth a thousand words"? This statement is truer today in our culturally rich society than it has ever been. People do not have the time nor the inclination to read a lot of text and in some cases cannot read the language of the text or cannot read period. Images in many cases can convey the same information in a universally understandable way while requiring very little effort on the part of the receiver of the information. Whether we like or agree with this societal trend is unimportant; what is important is to be able to convey information to as many people as possible in the least amount of time. Images assist greatly with this process.

In a nutshell, the purpose of this book is to give software developers a very complete set of tools (in the form of C++ classes) for adding imaging to any Windows application. Imaging can be added to an application program very quickly and with minimal effort using the software provided. This book and the accompanying software are the result of my experiences building professional Windows imaging applications for the last four years. All of the algorithms and techniques presented here are used in a professional imaging application currently on the market.

What You Get

In addition to a full discussion of the various imaging techniques in the text, full source code to everything in this book is provided on a companion disc in the form of reusable C++ classes. The object-oriented nature of these classes allows them to be easily incorporated into imaging programs of your own design. In addition, two powerful imaging programs are included that are well worth what you paid for this book.

Audience

This book is intended for the intermediate to advanced programmer/hobbyist interested in Windows imaging. The level of discussion assumes a basic knowledge of C, C++, and Windows. No attempt is made herein to teach basic Windows programming techniques or C++, although a novice can probably learn a lot from studying the fully commented source code provided. Most Windows concepts specific to imaging, regardless of level, are discussed to help and encourage imaging novices.

Content Summary

Chapter 1 lays the foundation for the information presented. You will find discussions about incorporating imaging into application programs, about what differentiates a professional imaging application from an amateur one, about some of the differences in Win16 and Win32 programming for imaging applications, and about an imaging system architecture that can be used as a model for adding imaging to any Windows application program. Last, but certainly not least, you will be introduced to the TestApp program, which is a fully capable, Windows-based, photographic image processing program. TestApp, with its full source code, is provided for numerous reasons including:

1. Because it is an example of the imaging architecture presented.
2. Because TestApp is a powerful imaging tool that readers will find useful in and of itself.
3. Because of its object-oriented nature, TestApp can easily be extended in any of many directions. TestApp's code could be the foundation from which many different professional photographic imaging application programs spring.
4. Because TestApp is a convenient platform for testing new image processing algorithms and techniques. Since it already has the framework in place for loading, displaying, and printing image files, you can easily hook in a new algorithm for testing. In this sense, you can think of TestApp as providing the scaffolding needed to support new image processing ideas during development and test.
5. Because TestApp uses and demonstrates the imaging concepts presented throughout this book. Because you can step through the code with a debugger if you need to, you can see exactly how the algorithms and techniques work line by line. Nothing is hidden from view and there is nothing you cannot change if you desire to.

Chapter 2 presents background information that will be needed by people who have never attempted imaging before. Windows concepts *important to imaging* such as device contexts, coordinate systems, mapping modes, palette management, and device independent bitmaps will be given appropriate discussions. Building and using Windows DLLs are also described because of the applicability to the code in this book. You should note that a general discussion of Windows programming and programming practices is not provided in this chapter because these topics can be found in any number of Windows programming books. Since this book is targeted at the intermediate to advanced programmer/hobbyist, most elementary Windows concepts should be second nature by this time. I won't waste your time nor waste paper rehashing basic techniques that can be found in many other sources. What I hope I have done is to provide information about using imaging in Windows that is difficult, if not impossible, to come by otherwise.

Chapter 3 presents a vendor neutral class library for encapsulation of the Windows common dialog boxes useful in imaging applications. This discussion is given a full chapter because of the importance I place on uniformity in user interface design and therefore on the use of the common dialog boxes. Also, why rewrite the common dialog box code when you can reuse code written by and maintained by others (Microsoft)? In addition to providing a C++ interface to the common dialog box code, many of the provided classes greatly extend the base functionality; for example, the printer common dialog box code is vastly extended to report detailed information about the currently selected printer. Information that is required to support *What You See Is What You Get* (WYSIWYG) printing. The TestApp program of Chapter 1 and much of the other code here make extensive use of the common dialog box classes developed in this chapter.

Chapter 4 presents an architecture for reading and writing graphic image files. A class library is developed that supports monochrome, palettized, and true color images in BMP, GIF, and TIF file formats. The Compand class is structured in such a way that it can easily be extended to other graphic file formats. Use of the Compand class in an application program for reading and writing graphic image files is simplicity itself, since the Compand code is self-contained in a Windows DLL that we will build.

Chapter 5 discusses the rather arcane topic of color reduction. Color reduction is required whenever a color image must be displayed on an output device with limited color capability. Displaying a true color image (16.7 million color possibilities) on a SuperVGA graphics adapter only capable of 256 colors is one example. The color reduction techniques presented and implemented in this chapter include Median Cut Color Quantization and Uniform Quantization with Dithering. These very different and rather complicated color reduction techniques will be discussed fully. C++ classes are developed for both techniques to make their application as simple as possible. In fact, these classes can be used without understanding the underlying processes involved.

Chapter 6 discusses how images are displayed within the Windows environment. The discussion in this chapter draws on the information presented in many of the previous chapters. A C++ class called Display that simplifies the image display process for the programmer is developed. Many important image display topics including image panning, image zooming, displaying an image to scale, displaying an image to fit within a window, and displaying an image with its aspect ratio maintained are described in this chapter. These techniques, not surprisingly, are also supported by the Display class. By using the Display class, a programmer can forget about the complexities of the DIB format as required for image display.

Chapter 7 does for printing what Chapter 6 did for image display within a window. The discussion details how printing in Windows is traditionally performed and goes on to present a class called PrintOp that drastically simplifies the page layout and printing processes for the programmer. The PrintOp class provides printing and print previewing facilities for user-defined layouts containing images, text, and graphic elements. A lot of the discussion focuses on what is required for WYSIWYG page layout.

Chapter 8 describes image acquisition from TWAIN compliant devices. TWAIN is an industry standard in the Windows and Macintosh environments for control of raster-generating devices. Most image scanners (and some video digitizer boards) shipped today come with a TWAIN driver. This allows these devices to be controlled within an imaging application program by the code presented in this chapter. A class called Twain, implemented as a Windows DLL, is developed for control of and acquisition from TWAIN compliant devices.

Chapter 9 describes a great many image-processing algorithms that can be applied to photographic images. Algorithms are included for image cropping, rotation, flipping, copying images to and from the clipboard, brightness and contrast enhancement, filtering, sharpening, softening, edge enhancement, color reduction, conversion of color images to gray scale, and so on. Although the discussion is kept on the practical side, some theoretical discourse can be found in this chapter as well.

Chapter 10 ends the discussion with the presentation of three concepts important to most professional imaging applications. These are:

- Image cacheing as required for high-performance display and redisplay of images
- Generation and use of thumbnail images
- Annotation of images with textual and/or graphic information

Again, there are not only discussions of these concepts but complete classes and/or code segments implementing these techniques that can be used in your application programs. Another example program called CacheTst is developed here that illustrates the three concepts presented. CacheTst, like TestApp of Chapter 1, is useful as a stand-alone imaging tool in addition to its uses for illustration purposes.

Within this preface, I think it is also important to tell you what is not covered here. At the time this book was written, there was not enough stable information about the new Win32 color matching API (ICMAPI) to provide a meaningful discussion. This is one topic area that deserves coverage in a book such as this and will be covered if there is a second edition. OpenGL is not covered either because the focus of the book is photographic imaging as opposed to two-dimensional or three-dimensional imaging. I am sure a lot of information will become available about these and other interesting Windows 95 features when Windows 95 is closer to release.

I truly hope you find the information and code provided in this book to be usable in your programming endeavors. If I can help to prevent you from reinventing the wheel, I have accomplished my goals. Good luck and have fun with Windows imaging!

Acknowledgments

First and foremost, I have to again acknowledge the contribution that my wife Heather made to this book. This is the fourth book of mine she has had to proofread, and she did so without complaint. Somehow she managed to squeeze the critique and proofreading of these 10 chapters in between gardening, weaving, reading, and pampering me. I could not have done this book without her help and support.

I would also like to thank Diane Cerra of John Wiley & Sons for helping me with the business of book publishing and for convincing me that the industry really needs a book like this one and to the gang at Enhanced Data Technology for providing me with the opportunity to write another book.

All images within this book were designed and rendered by me on my IBM compatible PC in my messy little office in the mountains of Colorado. Each image is truly an original that no one would probably want to claim except me.

Important Note

No patent liability is assumed with respect to the use of the information contained herein. While every precaution has been taken in the preparation of this book, the publisher and author assume no responsibility for errors or omissions. Neither is a liability assumed for damages resulting from the use of the information contained herein.

CRAIG A. LINDLEY

Manitou Springs, Colorado

Basic Information

In this chapter you will learn about:

- Imaging in Professional Applications
- Imaging System Architecture
- Programming Considerations for 16-bit and 32-bit Operation
- Computer Requirements
- The TestApp Imaging Example Program

Introduction

Where do we begin? On such a long journey, in which direction do we place our first step? Windows imaging comprises a large subject domain, and many topics will need to be covered before a complete, cogent picture of imaging technology for the Windows platform can be painted. As is usual for Chapter 1 of any technical book, I will devote time and space to describing some important, although sometimes mundane, aspects of imaging. If you are an imaging expert, you may be able to skip the information contained in this chapter without any ill effects and move on to the chapters with more meat. I highly recommend, however, that you read this chapter because it contains little gems of wisdom that you may not have thought of before and may even save you some time and energy in developing your own imaging applications in the future. Be assured, I will try to get through all of the introductory information contained in this chapter as quickly as possible so that we can get to the fun stuff ASAP.

As mentioned in the preface, this book does not try to teach either Windows or C/C++ programming. The stated purpose of this book is to teach imaging concepts and how to apply them. A generalized coverage of computer programming will not be provided because a working knowledge of Windows, C, and C++ is an expected pre-requisite. Therefore, only the aspects of the programming languages that are unique to an implementation will be discussed in any depth. See the list of books provided in Appendix B, "Further Reading" for more information on programming in Windows, C, and C++.

Note: Throughout these discussions, references are made to the many program files. To find out where on the companion disc these files reside, please consult Appendix A. Most files on the companion disc are compressed to save space and therefore must be decompressed before they can be used. Instructions for decompressing the files are also found in Appendix A.

Imaging in Professional Applications

Anyone with a little Windows programming expertise can add a bit of imaging to an application program. One can easily draw a bitmap here or an icon there. Windows makes this pretty easy to do actually. However, one cannot approach building an image extensive application in the same ad hoc manner and expect the results to be credible. Imaging must be correctly architected into an application program for max-imum effectiveness. Maximum imaging software effectiveness in this context can be defined as running in a great many varied environments, running with as little mem-ory as possible, reacting quickly to user requests and reading, writing, processing, and displaying images in a timely manner. Probably the most important of these cri-teria is the first; that is, imaging software must understand and react to the environ-ment on which it is being run if it is going to be usable on a large number of computers. The device independence nature of Windows is great, but there is still a lot of work for the programmer to do to make imaging happen on a wide variety of different computer equipment. The following are the most important environmental factors that must be taken into consideration for effective imaging software:

- The amount of memory available to the imaging software. This includes both the physical semiconductor memory (RAM) and virtual memory.
- The resolution and the number of colors supported by the VGA display device. Note: A VGA display device with 256-color capability is assumed throughout this book. There is no reason for anyone to attempt photographic quality imag-ing on 16-color VGA, EGA, or older types of displays.
- The color capabilities of an attached printer.
- The bandwidth of the medium delivering the image data to the computer. Are images being read off a local hard disk, from a CD-ROM or being delivered over a network?
- The most common graphics file types used by the host computer and its appli-cation programs.

When imaging software understands the environment in which it is being run and adapts itself accordingly, it will be considered robust and professional by its users. Imaging software that forces users to run in only one video mode, only use printer X, or requires an inordinate amount of memory, or is extremely sluggish in processing user requests will be considered amateurish to users (and software review-ers and you know what that means). To help your imaging software appear as profes-sional as possible, the following guidelines are proposed:

- Use memory efficiently. Only make copies of image data and image palette data when necessary and dispose of them as quickly as possible. Do not allow these copies to remain in memory any longer than necessary. Keeping memory as uncluttered as possible will mean less use of virtual memory which will help your application run faster. Remember, virtual memory is convenient but slow, especially when handling large images.
- Make your software display images on any VGA graphics adapter regardless of its capabilities. For example, if a true color image is to be displayed and the display adapter is running in 256-color mode, the imaging software should either quantize the image colors down to 256 or use a dithering technique to display the image to the user.
- Code your imaging applications as efficiently as possible for maximum speed. Use compiler optimization as much as possible to speed up the code.
- Make extensive use of the Windows common dialog boxes in your imaging software. Window users are already familiar with how to use these items and will feel more comfortable with your software because of the familiarity. This is so important that Chapter 3 of this book is devoted to discussion of the common dialog boxes.
- Work with the most common graphic file formats used in the environment. For the Windows environment, this means BMP, TIF, GIF at the very least. The list, however, could go on and on.
- Support various image data compression methods. This is extremely important when working with scanned images where file sizes can be enormous.
- Design with extendability, maintainability, and revisability in mind. In this day and age, it is no longer acceptable to write throwaway code. Imaging software should be written for reuse and C++ is great for this. It should be noted that writing code for extendability, maintainability, and revisibility can have adverse effects on performance. The highest performance code, in most cases, is not portable at all and is very hard to maintain. Some intuitive trade-offs must be made in trying to balance performance with code longevity.

Most of the software presented here were written with the previously listed guidelines in mind. I, however, cannot honestly say that every piece of code in this book meets all of the guidelines. Any software development effort of any magnitude requires juggling of functional requirements, implementation issues, time constraints, and other factors. The code presented here is no different. A programmer must do what he or she can in the time allotted for the development. In a perfect world, things would be different.

Imaging System Architecture

Most new Windows programs use photographic image display in some form or another. With all of the multimedia hype that abounds, it would be unthinkable not to. Word processors, database programs, telecommunication programs, paint programs, and most other new applications place heavy emphasis on their imaging capabilities. Imaging in a spreadsheet, who would have thought it? As described in the previous section, adding imaging to an application is not a trivial undertaking. Quite a bit of architectural planning and behind-the-scenes programming effort is required to provide effective imaging. The purpose of the discussion in this section is to describe a workable architecture for adding imaging to an application program.

The architecture of the imaging system described throughout this book is shown in Figure 1.1. This combination of hardware devices and software drivers shown in the block diagram could probably be used to describe the imaging architecture of most applications at a very high level. Notice how the diagram is broken up into three major sections: Input, Processing, and Output. Each of these sections of the block diagram will be described subsequently.

Image Input

Image input can come from a variety of sources, such as graphic image files, video-digitizing devices, electronic cameras, and scanners. Many of these sources are governed by standards and specifications, while others require custom software for interface. A bit of advice: If a standard exists for interface to a class of devices, use it instead of inventing a proprietary interface of your own. Further, if the vendor of the imaging equipment you would like to use doesn't support the applicable standards, find another vendor if possible. Whenever you must write custom software for interfacing to a unique piece of imaging equipment, you are at the mercy of the vendor for keeping the software interface consistent. It is possible and probable that a minor change to the

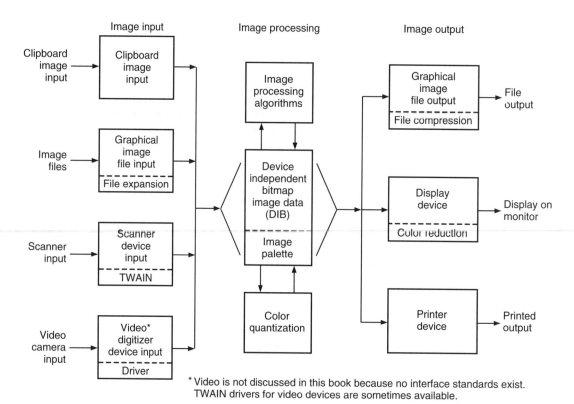

*Video is not discussed in this book because no interface standards exist. TWAIN drivers for video devices are sometimes available.

FIGURE 1.1 Imaging system architecture block diagram.

vendor's software will break the software you have developed. This will make you look bad in the eyes of your customers, even though the fault may not be your own.

The processing of graphic image files for image input will be discussed in Chapter 4. Chapter 4 also provides a description of image compression and expansion along with a quick look at graphic file formats. Chapter 8 will discuss TWAIN and image acquisition from TWAIN compatible devices in detail. Input from video devices is not described in this book because no standard exists that I am aware of that would allow me to write code that would be portable to more than one video-digitizing device. This is unfortunate because I would have liked to include video imaging in this book. I could have included code for accessing a specific video digitizer device but you would have to have the exact same board (with the exact same revision level) to make the code run. This would have been unfair to you readers. Luckily, TWAIN compatible drivers (called TWAIN Sources) will shortly become available for certain video digitizer devices. This will allow the acquisition of still video images using the TWAIN code provided in this book.

As images are input into this imaging system, they are converted into an internal format so that they can be manipulated expediently and uniformly. The internal format used in this book is the Windows device-independent bitmap (DIB) format. The DIB format will be discussed extensively. Device-dependent bitmap (DDB) format will not be because it offers few advantages and many disadvantages for manipulation of bitmap images. Support for DDB has been obsoleted in Win32, and for good reason. For now, just understand that the internal DIB format consists of a block of memory containing the image raster data and a palette (if required) used to further define the image data.

Image Processing

With the images in the DIB internal format, they can be processed. Many forms of image processing will be discussed including rotation, flipping, cropping, brightness and contrast enhancement, color quantization, edge detection, filtering, various forms of convolution, and so on (see Chapter 9). Some of these processing algorithms affect the image's raster data, some affect just the data contained in the palette, and some affect both the raster data and the palette. The important thing to note here is that it is much easier to manipulate image data when it is in a standard internal format than when it is in a multitude of proprietary or device-dependent formats.

When processing image data, one has to take into account the amount of data in a typical image. Take, for example, a 640×480 256-color image. Each pixel of this image requires a single byte of memory for storage. This means that the image will require 307,200 bytes when uncompressed in memory. This same resolution image in true color format (24 bits per pixel [BPP], three bytes per pixel) requires three times that or 921,600 bytes. The memory required for scanned images makes these numbers pale in comparison. Consider a 4- × 6-inch photograph scanned in true color format at 500 dots per inch (DPI). This results in an image that is over 15 megabytes in size. An 8.5- × 11-inch image at the same resolution is about 70 megabytes. Obviously, a programmer dealing with images must not be afraid to cross the dreaded 64K segment boundary limits imposed on DOS and 16-bit Windows programs. The flat address space of Win32 is a blessing with its lack of 64K segments when processing huge images such as these.

Image Output

Image output can consist of writing a new graphic image file that contains the results of image processing, writing the image to a film recorder, the display of the image on a computer's monitor or output to a printer or other device. Windows' device independence helps when outputting an image to a device, but there is still plenty for the programmer to contemplate to obtain high-quality image output. The display of images will be addressed in Chapter 6 based on some of the information in Chapter 5. Image printing will be described in Chapter 7.

The architecture presented in this chapter has been in use for over two and a half years in imaging products of my own design. During this period, the capabilities of these imaging products have steadily evolved. Fortunately, this architecture (based on the block diagram in Figure 1.1) has served me well. One of the most important things I learned from this experience is to keep the block diagram intact; that is, to keep the blocks delineated as shown on the diagram instead of adding or changing code that would blur where one block ends and the next begins. Many times it would have been expedient to compromise this architecture, but looking back, it would have been a real mistake in terms of longevity and maintenance of the code.

Programming Considerations for 16-bit and 32-bit Operation

First, there was DOS and if you wanted to write a program, you generally did it in assembler language. People who began their programming career at this point in the evolution of personal computing patted themselves on the back when they got their first DOS/assembler program to finally run.

A seemingly short period of time went by, and the software gurus said that life was too short to use assembler language for programming. High-level languages then became the rage. If you were like me, you learned a handful of high-level languages during this period including FORTH, Pascal, FORTRAN, and maybe C. We again patted ourselves on the back for a job well done. We could in fact write programs faster using a high-level language. Even though we were initially skeptical about having to learn a new programming paradigm, in the long run it turned out to be worth the effort expended.

Well, DOS had problems of its own, and the powers that be said that DOS programs would never be easy enough to use for people, shall we say, with less than our technical prowess. The gurus went back to work and determined that only a graphical user interface that uses pictures to communicate with the user instead of a command line, would ever be understandable to mere mortals. Hence, Windows was born. Most of us real programmers tried to ignore Windows in its first incarnations in the hope that it would go away. After all, we now had DOS programming down pat and were hesitant to learn something new.

Guess what? Windows did not go away. However, it took a long time and many revisions for it to become a stable and therefore usable programming environment. We said well now that Windows has finally arrived, how hard can it be to learn how to program in it? Boy, were we mistaken. Programming in Windows was a major paradigm shift from what we learned programming DOS applications. What were messages, message loops, and event-driven programming all about anyway? Being the real programmers that we are, we buckled down and in a month or two had our first Windows program up and running. Major pats on the back were in order for our newest and most difficult programming transition to date. Hot damn, time to update the resume, I can now program in Windows.

Back on the language front, the C programming language was all the rage. That was okay with us because we had made that transition a long time ago. Weren't we forward thinking? With the C language and Windows under our belts so to speak, we were equipped for some major programming. And programming we did until it became apparent that this new concept of object-oriented programming was not going to go away anytime soon. We were told that we could not possibly write programs as complex as we had been doing without using object-oriented techniques. It just was not possible. At the same time, some guy named Bjourn started talking about a new version of C to be called C++. Who would name a programming language C++ anyway?

Back to the books we went yet again. (Do you ever wonder why so many computer programmers burn out and change careers?) After all, we knew the C language quite well. How hard could this C++ be? After a brief, yearlong study of C++, I felt that I had mastered enough of the language to write a program. It was not that C++ was so difficult in itself; the problem was that object-oriented techniques had to be learned at the same time. Otherwise, I would just be writing C code using the C++ language, with not much benefit there. I now proudly proclaim that I can spell data encapsulation as well as use it. After a two and a half year encounter with C++, I still am not fluent in its use, and it is constantly evolving, pushing my goal of C++ guru farther and farther away.

With the arrival of Windows 3.1, Windows programming became a lot of fun for us initiated. It was unfortunate, however, that writing the classic "Hello World" program took 80+ lines of C code. If you wanted to write a program more involved than "Hello World," you needed your C or C++ files, your header files, your resource files, make files, LIB files, DEF files, and all that. But we understood this; that's why they paid us the big bucks. But alas writing a Windows program took too long to do. There had to be a better way.

Enter C++ class libraries. These libraries were supposedly written by experts using all of the object-oriented techniques offered by C++. We were supposed to immediately use these class libraries to speed our program development, to save us from mundane programming chores, and to cure all of the other software development ills that existed at that time. Can you say steep learning curve? I knew you could. How was a real programmer supposed to use something that they didn't write? What if there was a bug in the class library, how could it be fixed? Having gotten over the class library learning curve (remember you must learn about the libraries from both software big boys: Microsoft and Borland. Surprise, surprise, they are not compatible in any way, shape, or form. Don't you just love this business?), I have come to appreciate their utility and importance for rapid software development.

Well, time has a way of making one forget about past programming pain. At this point, we knew Windows programming, C, and C++ were like a second language to us, and class libraries were finally proving their merit. By the time we had gotten to this point, our elbow was sore from patting ourselves on the back so much. Yes, we had accomplished a lot; but wait, what is this stuff about 32-bit programming?

This brings us to the present. Now it is time to learn about 32-bit Windows programming, the new end all, be all programming environment. I can see it now, endless late nights fighting with the code trying to get "Hello World" to run successfully.

It can't be happening again, it just can't be. But wait, am I dreaming? I must have missed something. Could it really be that programming in 32-bit mode is easier than programming in 16-bit mode? Where have all my segments gone, long time passing? What do you mean I don't need huge pointers to access by image data? *I cannot function without my segments!* Or can I?

The purpose of this long diatribe is to let you know that programming with Win32 can be a lot easier than with Win16, especially where accessing large data items, such as images, are concerned. To make things even better, most Win16 code is directly portable to the Win32 environment. The most the ported code needs is only a tweak here and there to make it compile and run. The icing on the cake is that the ported code is almost certain to run faster than the equivalent 16-bit code.

This is not to say that Win32 does not offer anything new for the programmer. There are lots of cool new stuff (true multitasking, processes, threads, intertask communication, memory-mapped files, security, simplified networking, the color matching API and more) that you can learn at your own pace. The thing is you won't need to know all about the new stuff before you can begin programming in the new environment. Switching from 16- to 32-bit Windows programming may be one of the less traumatic transitions in your programming career.

To learn about porting your 16-bit Windows 3.X code to Win32 for use with Windows 95 and/or Windows NT, I suggest reading the following articles:

1. "At Last—Write Bona Fide 32-bit Programs That Run on Windows 3.1 Using Win32s" by Andrew Schulman in the April 1993 issue of *Microsoft Systems Journal.*
2. "Porting Your 16-bit Applications to Windows NT without Ripping Your Hair Out" by Scot Gellock in the August 1993 issue of *Microsoft Systems Journal.*
3. "Slay the Porting Beasties: Dave's Top Ten Tips for Migrating to Windows NT" by Dave Edson in the September 1993 issue of *Microsoft System Journal.*
4. "Seventeen Techniques for Preparing Your 16-bit Applications for Chicago" by Dave Edson in the February 1994 issue of *Microsoft System Journal.*

The most important porting concepts detailed in these articles are summarized as follows:

• The integer data type (int) for C and Windows has changed from a 16-bit value to a 32-bit value. This affects the following types:

Type	Number of Bits Win16	Range of Values Win16	Number of Bits Win32	Range of Values Win32
int	16	−32,768 to 32,767	32	−2,147,483,648 to 2,147,483,647
unsigned int	16	0 to 65,535	32	0 to 4,294,967,295
HANDLE	16	0 to 65,535	32	0 to 4,294,967,295
UINT	16	0 to 65,535	32	0 to 4,294,967,295

Note, the lengthening of HANDLE affects all flavors of Window handles including HWND, HMODULE, HCURSOR, and so on. This change in the definition of an integer also means that most of the Win16 API functions that use integer parameters have now been widened to 32 bits for Win32.

- The STRICT compiler directive should be defined when porting 16-bit to 32-bit code. This will allow the compiler to help you find problems in the ported code that need to be addressed.
- The keyword HUGE is no longer needed for Win32 programming. In fact, Microsoft's Visual C++ 2.0 considers it an illegal keyword. The FAR designation is also obsolete.
- A tool provided as part of the Windows 95 SDK called "porttool.exe" can be used to point out areas of your code that need attention. Please note that PORTTOOL is not foolproof; in fact, it is almost brain-dead. It should only be used to perform a first pass port of your code. You should review all changes that PORTTOOL suggests before allowing changes to be made to your source.
- One subtle problem you will have to face when porting your code has to do with the alignment of data within a structure. In 16-bit Windows, data within structures were assumed to be BYTE packed. In Win32, data within a structure are naturally aligned. By that I mean that data within a structure reside on a boundary the size of itself. The following table shows the default alignment in Win32 for various data types.

Data Type	*Alignment*
char and BYTE	Aligns on byte boundary
short and WORD (16-bit)	Aligns on even byte boundary
ints, longs and DWORD (32-bit)	Aligns on 32-bit boundary
float	Aligns on 32-bit boundary
double	Aligns on 64-bit boundary
structures	Aligns on boundary of the data type with the largest boundary requirement

This alignment issue can have serious consequences when porting code that reads data from files. Graphic image files are a keen example of where problems can and do occur. Any structure (defining the content of a graphic image file) that mixes data types and was written to disk in BYTE packed format under Win16 will not be readable within Win32 without special consideration. We will have to deal squarely with this issue in Chapter 4 when we talk about graphic file I/O. Note that in most programming environments, you can force the compiler to generate packed structures if you so desire. This will certainly get you past the structure alignment problem, but it will have a performance impact on the code.

- The return type and various parameters of Windows procedures have been changed.
- Many of the parameters passed in wParam and lParam for various Windows messages have been changed. This includes the venerable WM_COMMAND message that just about every Windows program uses.

- A small number of Windows messages have vanished. Some have been replaced with messages new to Win32.
- Some API calls were dropped from Win32 and are considered illegal by the compiler. Most of these have to do with memory management, which is vastly different under Win32. Other API calls get mapped to white space by the compiler and have no effect on a Win32 program.

Of course, one advantage of porting code to Win32 is that the resultant application should run unchanged on all processor versions of Windows NT and Windows 95.

Computer Requirements for Imaging Software Use

To run any serious imaging software, such as those provided here, on a PC requires a computer with a lot of processing power and a lot of free resources (read that memory and free hard disk space). With the falling price of computer hardware, this is not as serious a problem as it once was. Computers that meet the minimum requirements for imaging can be purchased off the shelf for under $1800 at the time of this writing. In fact, most computers that can be purchased at the neighborhood appliance store meet the majority of the requirements. As is usually the case, more is better in terms of processor speed, memory, and disk space. For these reasons, the computer requirement list that follows is broken up into two sections: minimum computer requirements and recommended computer requirements. If the computer you are using for your imaging software falls somewhere between these sets of requirements, you are set. If not, it may be time to upgrade your existing computer or bite the bullet and buy a new one.

Minimum Computer Requirements

- A 386 or 486 processor running at 20 MHz or faster
- Windows 3.1 running in enhanced 386 mode for 16-bit operation or Windows 95 for 32-bit operation. Running in 32-bit mode on Windows 3.1 using Win32s is also possible.
- At least 6Mb of RAM
- A VGA graphics adapter capable of at least 640×480 resolution with 256 colors. This also means an analog monitor for VGA display.
- At least 10Mb of free disk space
- At least 15Mb of virtual memory configured as *permanent* if possible. If you are not sure how to configure virtual memory, consult your Windows documentation.
- A black-and-white laser printer similar to the Hewlett-Packard IIIP or equivalent

Recommended Computer Requirements

- A 486 or Pentium processor running at 66 MHz or faster
- Windows 95 or Windows NT. The speed of imaging software running in 32-bit mode is quite a bit faster, given the same processor speed, than when running in 16-bit mode.
- 16Mb of RAM or more if you will be scanning very large images

- A VGA graphics adapter capable of at least 800×600 resolution with 64K colors
- At least 50Mb of free disk space
- At least 50Mb of virtual memory
- A color printer with true color capability. A Hewlett-Packard 1200C, or Epson Color Stylus are excellent choices as are most other modern true color printers.

Computer Requirements for Developing Imaging Software

To use the software provided here in imaging applications of your own, you will need a computer capable of compiling, linking, and running the software in the target environment; that is, running Windows 3.1 for 16-bit development and running Win32s under Windows 3.1, Windows 95, or Windows NT for 32-bit development and execution. The computers used during the development of the code for this book were as follows:

For 16-bit code development I used
- 486 processor running at 33 MHz
- 8MB of RAM
- A SuperVGA card capable of 640×480 at 256 and 64K colors
- DOS 6.2 and Windows 3.1
- Borland C++ version 4.0. All code was developed using the integrated development environment (IDE) using project files to control the build process.
- 50Mb of free disk space after all tools were loaded

For 32-bit code development I used
- 486 processor running at 33 MHz
- 24Mb of RAM
- A SuperVGA card capable of 640×480 at 256 and 64K colors
- Win32s for Windows 3.1 operation and Windows 95 (actually Chicago Beta 1 version) for Win32 operation
- Borland C++ 4.0 for Win32s development and Microsoft Visual C++ version 2.0 for Windows 95 development. All code was developed using the visual C++ environments.
- 100Mb of free disk space after all tools were loaded

The incredible amount of RAM required for 32-bit code development was necessary for running Visual C++, not for running Windows 95. Windows 95, by itself, runs quite well on an 8Mb machine. I hope by the time Visual C++ version 2.0 has its commercial release that it can run in much less RAM. As it stands now, a "Hello World" program written in Visual C++ will not even compile, much less link or run in a machine with only 8Mb of RAM. Is there something wrong with this picture or is it just me?

Because I prefer the Borland C++ development environment, I do most of my code development in that environment using the Borland tools. All of the code presented here (16-bit and 32-bit applications and Dynamic Link Library [DLL]) were developed using the Borland IDE. I only use Microsoft Visual C++ when I am forced to because of its enormous appetite for RAM, its slow compilation performance, and because it was a prerelease version that was not quite ready for prime time.

The TestApp Imaging Program

When I began this book project, I decided I wanted to incorporate almost all of the imaging techniques discussed into a single test application program for demonstration purposes. Further, I wanted the test application program to be a useful imaging tool in itself, not just some kludge. The result of this effort is the TestApp program presented here but described throughout the whole book. Besides being a demonstration vehicle for the code and concepts in this book and in addition to being a convenient platform for implementing new image processing algorithms, the TestApp program provides much of the useful functionality of commercial photo manipulation software. The TestApp program lacks the user interface bells and whistles that professional imaging software would have. These were intentionally left out to prevent confusion between core topics and algorithms being discussed.

With the TestApp program, you can load images from graphics files for display, scan in images from a TWAIN compliant device such as a scanner, process the images with various image processing algorithms, convert the images from true color to palettized formats, save the processed images in graphics files, do graphics file conversions, display images on the screen, and even print them out in full color (if you have a color printer, of course). The complete list of features of the TestApp program will be provided shortly. The TestApp program itself is worth the price you paid for this book. As an added bonus, you get the complete source code to the program for use within your imaging programs. Is this a good deal or what?

The TestApp program is written using the Multiple Document Interface (MDI) popular with a lot of Windows programs. This means that multiple images can be open at one time, and you can pick and choose which image to manipulate by clicking on it with a mouse. The main window of the TestApp program is shown in Figure 1.2.

TestApp Program Features

The TestApp program uses the code described throughout this book to implement the following features:

- Multiple Document Interface (MDI) allowing the viewing of multiple images side by side. This is useful for inspecting images before and after image processing has occurred.
- Reading and writing most BMP, GIF, and TIF graphic image files in monochrome, palettized, and true color formats
- The ability to acquire images from most TWAIN compliant imaging devices including scanners and video digitizers
- The concepts of WYSIWYG printing and print previewing for images and text
- The ability to copy and paste images to/from the clipboard
- Three different image viewing modes: display image to scale, display image to fit window, and display image to fit window while keeping aspect ratio correct
- Image duplication. The ability to quickly make a copy of an image displayed in a window to facilitate image processing
- 2×, 4×, and 8× image zooming
- Display of image information and specifications
- The ability to adjust the brightness and/or contrast of an image

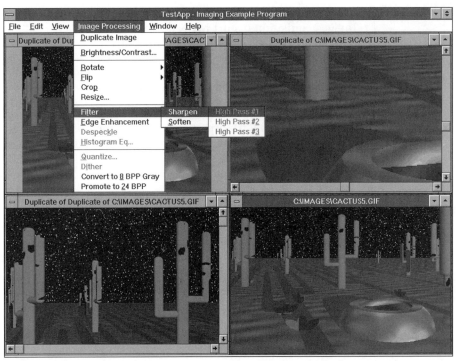

FIGURE 1.2 TestApp screen shot.

- The ability to flip and/or rotate images
- Image cropping
- Image resizing. Resize image up to ±500%
- Image filtering. Three different varieties of high-pass and low-pass filtering are available for sharpening and softening images.
- Image edge enhancements. Selectively enhanced image edges in eight different orientations
- Image despeckling for cleanup of noisy images
- Histogram equalization. A method of automatic image contrast adjustment
- Support for both Median Cut Color Quantization and Uniform Quantization with Dithering
- Ability to convert images to gray scale
- Ability to promote palettized images to 24 bits per pixel

The implementation of most of these features is described in Chapter 9 in the discussion of the TProcessImage class. The discussion of many of the salient points is spread throughout the book.

TestApp Program Architecture

The TestApp program is the embodiment of the imaging system architecture described earlier in this chapter and shown in Figure 1.1. TestApp has subsystems, shown as blocks on the block diagram, for:

- Input and output of graphic image files
- Image acquisition from TWAIN devices
- Exchanging images via Windows clipboard
- Displaying image data
- Printing image data
- Processing of image data in DIB format

It is important to understand that all subsystems within the TestApp program deal directly with images in DIB format just as shown on the block diagram. The consistency of this approach was rigorously enforced during TestApp's development. You will see in the discussions throughout how important choosing and sticking to an architecture is for the development of imaging programs (actually any software).

Image Descriptors

Throughout the TestApp program and this book in general, IMAGEDESCRIPTOR and IMAGEDESCRIPTOREXT data structures are used for management of images and image data. The definition of these structures are shown for your inspection:

```
// This structure is used for describing an image.
typedef struct _IMAGEDESCRIPTOR {
  WORD Width;
  WORD Height;
  DWORD RasterSize;
  WORD BPP;
  WORD Colors;
  HGLOBAL hImageData;
  RGBCOLOR Palette [256];
} IMAGEDESCRIPTOR, * LPIMAGEDESCRIPTOR;

// Define an extended image descriptor type
typedef struct _IMAGEDESCRIPTOREXT {
  IMAGEDESCRIPTOR ImgDesc;
  BYTE huge *lpImageData;
} IMAGEDESCRIPTOREXT, * LPIMAGEDESCRIPTOREXT;
```

An IMAGEDESCRIPTOR contains all of the information necessary to completely define an image. The Width and Height members contain the dimension of the contained image in pixels. RasterSize is the amount of memory required for storage of the raster data, taking into consideration all padding that may be required (see Chapter 2). Bits per pixel (BPP) describe the bit depth of the image. A 256-color image, for example, would have a BPP value of eight, while a true color image would have 24 BPP. Colors contain a count of the number of colors actually used in the image. For 256-color images, this entry would equal 256. By convention, for true color images, Color equals zero. Moving right along, hImageData is a handle to a block of memory that contains the image raster data. Finally, Palette is an array of 256 RGBCOLOR entries, each with a BYTE of Red, Green, and Blue color data, which contains the palette for display of the image. As you can see, an IMAGEDESCRIPTOR data structure not only describes an image, it contains the image data and palette as well.

In most instances, a pointer to the image data contained within the IMAGE-DESCRIPTOR structure is required for manipulation of the data. For this reason, an IMAGEDESCRIPTOREXT structure is defined to extend the information contained in an IMAGEDESCRIPTOR by the addition of a pointer to the image data. Of course, the pointer is initialized by calling **GlobalLock** on the hImageData entry within the IMAGEDESCRIPTOR. By maintaining an IMAGEDESCRIPTOREXT structure within each MDI child window, the TestApp program can keep track of all of the information it needs about the image to be processed and/or displayed. As image parameters change as a result of the application of some form of image processing to the image displayed within an MDI child window, the information contained in the corresponding IMAGEDESCRIPTOR is updated. That way, the IMAGEDESCRIPTOR always contains valid information about the image in the window. Extensive use of the IMAGEDESCRIPTOR concept is made not only in the TestApp program but also in the TWAIN code of Chapter 8 and the cacheing code of Chapter 10.

The TestApp program is too large and consists of too many files to list here. Of course, all of the files that make up the program can be found on the companion disk along with an executable version called "testapp.exe" for immediate use and experimentation. Understanding of how TestApp works should be easily achieved once you look at the files that make it up. The short discussions to follow detail some of the less obvious, but nevertheless important, points of TestApp's implementation to help clarify how the program works.

The MDI Child Windows

As mentioned, TestApp is an MDI application with most of the intelligence within the program contained in the MDI child window class (see the files "tappchil.hpp" and "tappchil.cpp"). The important things to notice about the child window class are that:

- Each instance of the child window class (each child window) contains an IMAGEDESCRIPTOREXT structure for maintaining the specifications for the image the child window is to display.
- Each instance of the child window class (each child window) contains a MENU-UPDATE structure for maintaining information required for main menu updates. See the MENUUPDATE discussion later in this chapter for information.
- Three different constructors exist for the child window class. The first constructor is used whenever an image read from a graphic image file is to be displayed. The second is used whenever a scanned image is to be displayed or an image is pasted from the clipboard. The third and final constructor is used when it is necessary to clone and copy a child window for display.

Image Processing Functions

All image processing operations offered by the TestApp program are provided directly or indirectly by the TProcessImage class described in length in Chapter 9. Each image processing operation operates on an image contained in a specific child window (the child window that currently has input focus). After an image undergoes image processing, the IMAGEDESCRIPTOREXT structure and the MENUUPDATE structure within the child window may, and probably will, be updated to reflect current image specifications and parameters.

Handling the Main MDI Window Menu

Because an MDI program only has one menu available at a time, a mechanism must be put in place to change menu states, depending on which child window has input focus.

In other words, the states of various menu operations may change dynamically, depending on which child window is active (has user attention). To complicate matters further, many of the image processing algorithms will only work on images with certain attributes or when displayed in certain modes. The main menu must have certain menu picks enabled or disabled, depending on the type of image present in the child window. As an example, image cropping is only available when the view mode is "display image to fit." Another example is that image sharpening is only available on 24 BPP true color images. For palettized images, the image sharpening options are grayed.

Main menu updates are handled by cooperation between code in the MDI child window and code in the MDI client window (which manages the main MDI window menu). For more information about MDI, please consult the documentation that came with your development environment or just about any of the Windows books listed in Appendix B.

Whenever a child window is given input focus and/or whenever a parameter of the image contained within the child window changes, a MENUUPDATE structure, as defined later, is sent from the active child window to the MDI client window. This structure contains all of the information necessary to bring the main MDI menu into compliance with the state of the image within the child window. The child window contains and maintains all of its own state information within a MENUUPDATE structure and broadcasts the structure to the MDI client window as necessary. That way, the MDI client window does not need to know or maintain any information about the one or more child windows it is currently managing. The MDI client will have the local MENUUPDATE structure it maintains, updated automatically. The client window just needs to set the various menu selections in accordance with the information contained within its MENUUPDATE structure (the processes for doing this is, of course, different in the Borland and Microsoft environments). In any case, menu items will be enabled or disabled, checked or unchecked as a result of the contents of the client windows MENUUPDATE data structure.

```
// This structure is passed from child window to MDI client with information
// about the image. This information is used to update the main menu.
typedef struct _MENUUPDATE {
  BOOL MUDisplayToScaleEnable;
  BOOL MUDisplayToScaleChecked;
  BOOL MUDisplayToFitEnable;
  BOOL MUDisplayToFitChecked;
  BOOL MUDisplayToFitAspectEnable;
  BOOL MUDisplayToFitAspectChecked;
  BOOL MUNormalEnable;
  BOOL MUNormalChecked;
  BOOL MUZoom2xEnable;
  BOOL MUZoom2xChecked;
  BOOL MUZoom4xEnable;
  BOOL MUZoom4xChecked;
  BOOL MUZoom8xEnable;
  BOOL MUZoom8xChecked;
  WORD MUBPP;
} MENUUPDATE;
```

As you can see, the MENUUPDATE structure contains a series of Boolean values and that the names of the entries in the structure define the menu selections they control. Notice also that a pair of Boolean values is associated with each entry. The "enable" entry determines if the corresponding menu item should be enabled (TRUE) or disabled (FALSE). The "checked" entry controls whether the corresponding menu item is checked (TRUE) or not checked (FALSE). As you investigate the child window code ("tappchil.cpp"), you will see which operations affect the MENUUPDATE structure. You will also see that a function called **SendMenuUpdateToClient** is called within the child window code to perform the broadcast of the MENUUPDATE structure to the MDI client window.

Miscellaneous TestApp Notes

Because the TestApp program makes use of the Display class (described in depth in Chapter 6), it will automatically display images in whatever format appropriate, given the available display hardware and Windows video mode. In other words, it will adjust the display images as required for the computer on which it runs. A true color image displayed while in a 256-color video mode will be dithered, for example.

Another aspect of the TestApp program that needs mentioning is WM_PALETTE-CHANGED message propagation and processing. Although a complete discussion of how Windows manages colors (and color palettes) for color intensive application is provided in Chapter 2, the topic of color management must at least be mentioned here in the context of the TestApp program. As you may or may not be aware, Windows sends a WM_PALETTECHANGED message to all top level windows whenever the window with input focus realizes its palette. This message is sent to all top level windows and enables all windows without focus that use a color palette to realize their logical palettes (as background palettes) and update their client areas appropriately. In the TestApp program, images are displayed in child windows that are not top level windows and therefore do not receive a WM_PALETTECHANGED message when one is sent. In other words, when an image is displayed and its palette is realized in the child window with input focus, Windows will generate a WM_PALETTECHANGED message, but the message will only be received by top level windows. As a result, special code was put in place in the TestApp program for propagating the WM_PALETTE-CHANGED message from the top level window down to each of the child windows so that they can react accordingly. As this message is received by each child window, the child will only realize its own palette if it was not the child window that caused the system palette to change in the first place. This prevents infinite loops of palette updates from occurring.

Finally, the TestApp program uses "compand.dll" (described in Chapter 4) for reading and writing graphic image files and "mytwain.dll" (described in Chapter 8) for interface to TWAIN compatible devices. Both of these DLLs must be available (in the same directory as the TestApp program or on the path) whenever the TestApp program is run.

Possible TestApp Extensions

As functional as the TestApp program is, many additional features and functions could be added to make it yet more usable. In fact, many additions would be necessary to convert TestApp into a full-fledged professional imaging application program. Possible feature enhancements could include:

- Enhancing the user interface with toolbars and possibly a status bar
- Addition of context-sensitive help

- Addition of object linking and embedding (OLE) server support for providing image manipulation facilities to word processors and other OLE client application programs
- Addition of more image processing capabilities such as pixelizing, posterizing, gamma correction, and so on
- Integrated layout of pages for printing images and/or textual data
- Replacement of the Compand DLL with a more complete graphic image file library for support of more varieties of images.

Which and how many features you want to add to the TestApp program is entirely up to you.

Conclusions

In this first chapter, a lot of preliminary information has been presented to prepare you for the remainder of the book. The most important information to take with you from this chapter is the idea of designing and using an architecture for adding imaging to your application programs. Ad hoc code development where imaging is concerned will result in an end product that you will never be proud of and that your customers will be hesitant to use. In addition, lack of a sound imaging architecture will lengthen your code development schedule and increase chances of introducing serious bugs in your code. The imaging architecture presented is simple yet remarkably effective. It has served me well in the past and will presumably serve me well into the future.

To show how an imaging application program can be built on the architecture presented, the TestApp imaging example program was also described. This program really has three main goals. The first is as an example of using the imaging architecture presented, the second is as a platform for experimenting with new image processing algorithms, and third, as a tool for image manipulation.

With the description of the imaging architecture complete, Chapter 2 provides information about Windows imaging concepts and techniques that are required to put the imaging architecture to use in the Windows environment. Stay tuned.

Windows Background

In this chapter you will learn about:
- The difference between palettized and true color images
- Device contexts
- Windows coordinates systems
- Mapping modes
- How to query and understand device capabilities
- Bitmap images in Windows
- Windows treatment of color on color-limited systems
- Building and using Windows DLLs
- Helpful imaging hints

Introduction

The discussion here will focus on using Windows as a photographic imaging environment. To use Windows in this fashion requires first an understanding of basic Windows programming techniques and then an understanding of the numerous and somewhat arcane details that make photographic imaging possible. As stated in the Preface, it is not the purpose of this book to teach basic Windows programming skills, and for that reason a general discussion of Windows programming will not be provided. Instead, the discussion will concentrate on those topics of Windows programming that are necessary to the full understanding and application of the imaging ideas and concepts described later. When it is important to our discussion of imaging, basic Windows topics will be brought up and discussed to point out some important and/or interesting detail that may have been glossed over in other Windows programming books. Differences in programming required for the Win16 and Win32 environments will also be presented.

Because much of the information in this chapter will already be somewhat familiar to many Windows programmers, the discussions have intentionally been kept short and concise. A collection of hints that effectively summarizes the important imaging-related concepts is given at the end. Experienced programmers who may be inclined to skip reading this chapter are advised to refer to the hints before moving on to the more advanced imaging topics spread throughout this book. It is recommended, however, that everyone read this chapter if for no other reason than review.

Image Types

Before jumping into a discussion of how Windows treats images, we must first define what types of images we are referring to. Fundamentally, there are two unique types of images that must be supported in professional imaging applications: true color and palettized. True color images have 24 bits of color information available per pixel: one byte (8 bits) each of red, green, and blue. The ratio of red to green to blue determines the color of the pixel when it is displayed or printed. In all, there are 2^{24} bits of color information resulting in 16.7 million color possibilities for a true color pixel. True color images do not have and do not need a palette for their display. True color data completely describe the image it contains.

Palettized images, on the other hand, use a limited collection of colors for display. Two-color (black and white), 4-color, 16-color, and 256-color images are examples of palettized images. To display a palettized image requires image data and a palette. The 256-color images use a palette consisting of 256 entries with each entry containing an RGB value. Each pixel in a palettized image is an index into the palette. The image data do not actually contain any color information at all; for example, if a pixel's value is 24, that pixel should be displayed using the RGB values in the 25th palette entry (palette entries are numbered from zero).

The software palette to be used to display an image must be translated into a hardware palette for the display hardware before an image can be displayed. This, of course, is done automatically behind the scenes by the Windows Palette Manager (described later in this chapter). At the VGA hardware level, each palette entry is referred to as a color register. Each color register has only six bits available for each of the three color components R, G, and B. Since each color register contains 18 bits of color information total, 2^{18} unique colors can be represented for a total of 262,144 color possibilities. Said another way, a 256-color palettized image contains at most 256 colors. Each of those colors, however, can be picked from a total of 262,144 unique possibilities.

Device Contexts

All imaging operations within Windows take place through a device context. A device context is the link between your application program, a device driver, and an output device. All device-independent GDI calls made by an application program are passed through the device context to the device driver where they are converted into device-dependent actions. In effect, application programs draw on the device context, and the resultant output appears on a device. Windows provides four unique types of device contexts for use within application programs. They are:

1. Display device contexts that support GDI drawing and/or imaging operations on a video device
2. Printer device contexts that support GDI drawing and/or imaging operations on printers or plotters
3. Memory (also referred to as compatible) device contexts that support GDI drawing and/or imaging operations on bitmaps
4. Information device contexts that are used to retrieve device-specific information.

Display Device Contexts

An application program obtains a display device context identifying the window in which output will appear by calling either the **BeginPaint** or **GetDC** Windows functions. Actually, these functions do not return a device context but, instead, return a handle to a device context by way of which all operations are performed. In actuality, three different types of display device contexts (class, common, and private) can be returned depending on how the window class was registered. (A discussion of the different types of display device contexts is not important to us here and will not be pursued. See the discussion in almost any basic Windows programming book for more details.) With a handle to a device context for output, an application program calls GDI functions (passing the handle) to draw on the device context and therefore on the window. When the application is finished drawing, it must release the device context by calling either the **EndPaint** or **ReleaseDC** Windows functions.

An application program can obtain a device context for the client portion of a window, the whole window, or the whole screen. Armed with these device contexts, an application program can write anywhere within the client area of the window (the most common drawing operation), anywhere on a window including the nonclient areas (title bar, etc.), or anywhere on the screen, respectively. The use of display device contexts is illustrated extensively in Chapter 6.

Printer Device Contexts

Windows provides a printer device context that is used for drawing on a printer type output device regardless of its technology. In other words, a printer device context is usable with a dot matrix printer, ink jet printer, laser printer, and/or plotter. An application creates a printer device context by calling the **CreateDC** function and supplying the appropriate arguments (see help for the **CreateDC** function). When an application has finished printing, the printer device context is deleted by calling **DeleteDC.** Note: an application program must delete, rather than release, a printer device context when it is finished. The use of printer display device contexts is illustrated in both Chapters 3 and 7.

Memory Device Contexts

An application program creates a memory device context by calling the **Create-CompatibleDC** function and supplying a handle that identifies a device context for a particular device. Windows then supplies a bitmap having the same (compatible) color format as the specified device but with dimensions of only one pixel by one pixel. The same color format implies the same number of bits per pixel and same number of color planes. Before the application program can begin drawing on the memory context, it must select a bitmap with the appropriate width and height into the device context by calling the **SelectObject** function. Once the new bitmap is selected into the memory device context, an application can begin using the device context to store and/or manipulate images. See Chapter 10 for an example of the use of memory device contexts for merging images and text.

One serious limitation of memory device contexts is that they must be compatible with an actual physical device on the computer for which they are created. In other words, you cannot create a memory context of arbitrary bit depth. This is true in Windows 3.1 and Windows 95. This makes it impossible, for example, to create a 24-bit-per-pixel memory context on a computer running in a 256-color video mode. One ramification of this limitation is that text cannot be merged with a true color (24 BPP) image on a computer running in 256-color mode. While this may not sound like much of a limitation, I have personally confronted this problem many times in my imaging software. You may or may not ever have to face this problem in your imaging application programs. Hopefully, future versions of Windows will provide a means for creating a user device context to circumvent just such problems.

Informational Device Contexts

Windows supports an information device context used to retrieve device data. An application can call the **CreateIC** function to create an information device context for a particular device and then call the **GetObject** and/or the **GetCurrentObject** (new for Win32) functions to retrieve the pen, brush, palette, font, path, or bitmap attributes of the corresponding device. Information device contexts require far less overhead than device contexts and are therefore much faster in operation. After an application finishes retrieving data by using an information device context, it should call the **DeleteDC** function to get rid of it. I cannot point you to an example of the use of information device context anywhere in this book, I don't generally use them.

Now that you have a feeling for the types of device contexts that can exist, we will move on to what is actually contained in a device context. You can think of a device context (DC) as a collection of graphic objects (with their associated attributes) and the graphic modes that affect output for a specified device. A DC identifies the pen, brush, palette, font, path, and bitmap graphics object currently in effect along with the mapping mode in which drawing will take place in addition to the area on the device available for output (referred to as the clipping region). The following table shows most of the content of a typical DC with assigned default values.

Device Context Attribute	*Default Value*
Background color	White
Background mode	OPAQUE
Bitmap	No Default
Brush	WHITE_BRUSH
Brush origin	0,0
Clipping region	Whole display surface
Color palette	DEFAULT_PALETTE

Device Context Attribute	Default Value
Current pen position	0,0
Drawing mode	R2_COPYPEN
Font	SYSTEM_FONT
Intercharacter spacing	0 extra spaces
Mapping mode	MM_TEXT
Pen	BLACK_PEN
Polygon filling mode	ALTERNATE
Stretching mode	BLACKONWHITE
Text color	Black
Viewport extent	1,1
Viewport origin	0,0
Window extent	1,1
Window origin	0,0

Many Windows GDI functions exist for altering the values contained in the DC and therefore how drawing operations take place on the target device.

Windows Coordinate Systems and Transformations

Prior to Win32, programmers had only two coordinate systems to worry about: device coordinates that allowed working with the individual pixels on a physical device and logical coordinates that allowed operations in physical units such as inches, millimeters, twips, or other user-defined units. All device and logical coordinates values were limited by the use of a 16-bit signed integer to the range −32,768 to +32,767 (which I am sure seemed like reasonable values at the time). This two-coordinate system was complicated by the fact that certain functions within the Windows API use and/or return device coordinates and some use and/or return logical coordinates. Some functions even accept one type of coordinate (such as the **DPtoLP** and **LPtoDP** functions) and return the other. To make matters worse, those functions that use and/or return device coordinates might expect screen, window, or client area coordinates for proper operation. Are you confused yet? Don't feel bad, it has always been a problem keeping the coordinate systems straight, especially in imaging programs where you are trying to achieve WYSIWYG performance.

Well, things just got worse (or more flexible depending on your point of view) in Win32 as embodied in Windows 95. Now, there are four coordinate spaces in which an application can work. They are world coordinates, page coordinates, device coordinate, and physical coordinates. Both the world and page coordinate spaces are considered logical spaces in Win32. The range of coordinate values has also been increased by the use of 32-bit integer values. This was deemed necessary because of the size and resolution of images that are being produced on modern scanning equipment and processed on a PC under Windows. The valid range of logical values in both the X and Y directions is from −2,147,483,648 to +2,147,483,647. Device coordinates have a range in both the X and Y directions from −67,108,864 to +67,108,863, which represents a hell of a lot of pixels for a device to have. There is not much chance these numbers will need to be enlarged any time soon. That was probably the idea.

When Windows needs to produce output, it maps all drawing operations from one coordinate space to another until output appears on a physical device. The order of mapping is from world space to page space to device space to the actual physical output device. World coordinate space can only be used when an application program calls the new Win32 function **SetGraphicsMode** specifying the GM_ADVANCED parameter that enables the use of world coordinate space. If world coordinate space is not used, coordinate mapping starts at page space instead of world space and proceeds down to the physical output device. Additionally, when world coordinate space is not used, Win32 coordinate space mapping is equivalent to that in Windows 3.1. The **SetGraphicsMode** function can also be used to change graphics mode back to being Windows 3.1 compatible by specifying a parameter of GM_COMPATIBLE.

You may now be asking yourself why you would complicate matters by using world coordinate space for your application programs. The answer is that Win32 provides some interesting two-dimensional transformations that can be applied to graphics operations (within a device context) without needing your assistance. These two-dimensional transformations include translation, scaling, rotation, sheering, and reflection. (Which of these transformations will be supported in Windows 95 is still in question.) For the sake of understanding, the various transformations are defined as follows:

Transformation	*Description*
Translation	A transformation that shifts an object farther from or closer to the coordinate systems origin
Scaling	A transformation that alters the size of an object
Rotation	A transformation that rotates an object with respect to the coordinate systems origin
Sheering	A transformation that alters the apparent length and orientation of vertical or horizontal lines in an object
Reflection	A transformation that creates a mirror image of an object

Once a transformation is set up, it will automatically be applied to all graphics operation within the device context. Transformations are specified in terms of a three-by-three matrix such as:

$$\begin{vmatrix} eM11 & eM12 & 0 \\ eM21 & eM22 & 0 \\ eDx & eDy & 1 \end{vmatrix}$$

the coefficients of which are stored in an XFORM structure of the form:

```
typedef struct {
    float eM11;
    float eM12;
    float eM21;
    float eM22;
    float eDx;
    float eDy;
}   XFORM;
```

For any coordinate (x, y) in world space, the transformed coordinate in page space (x', y') can be determined by application of the following formulae:

$$x' = x * eM11 + y * eM21 + eDx,$$
$$y' = x * eM12 + y * eM22 + eDy,$$

Once a transformation is properly set up, Windows will automatically perform these calculations for you whenever world coordinates are to be transformed to page coordinates. The values stored in a XFORM structure depend on the type of transformation to be applied. The following table shows which matrix coefficients play a part in which transformations.

Coefficient	*Translation*	*Scaling*	*Rotation*	*Sheering*	*Reflection*
eM11		Horizontal scaling component	Cosine of rotation angle		Horizontal reflection component
eM12			Sine of rotation angle	Horizontal proportionality constant	
eM21			Negative sine of rotation angle	Vertical proportionality constant	
eM22		Vertical scaling component	Cosine of rotation angle		Vertical reflection component
eDx	Horizontal translation component				
eDy	Vertical translation component				

You can consult any good mathematics book for information on matrix manipulations if you require further information on world to page coordinate space transformations.

Page space to device space conversions do not require the use of matrices. Instead, the ratios of width and height of the two rectangular areas defined by a *window*, and its *viewport* are used to perform the required conversions. A viewport defines the portion (in what part of an on-screen window or on which part of a printed page) of a physical display device on which information will be displayed. The viewport origin defines where on the output device the information will be displayed and the viewport extents define how big the display area will be. Viewport parameters are specified in terms of pixels.

A *window*, when used in the same context as a viewport, does not refer to a window on the screen. Instead, it represents a portion of an item (an image for example) that will be displayed within the viewport. The window origin and the window extents are both specified in logical coordinates (which may be the same as device coordinates depending on the mapping mode currently in effect within the device context).

In the case of an image, if the window origin coincides with the origin of the image and if the window extents are specified as the width and the height of the image in logical coordinates, the complete image will be displayed within the defined viewport. By clever manipulation of both the viewport and the window, any or all of an image can be displayed at any location and at any size on any display device. In other words, Windows provides maximum flexibility for image display by the use of the various coordinate mapping methods.

Windows Mapping Modes

A mapping mode applied to a device context defines the unit of measure used for drawing operations and, in addition, defines the orientation of the X and Y axes. In this book, only three of the eight possible mapping modes are used. They are the MM_TEXT, MM_LOENGLISH, and the MM_ISOTROPIC mapping modes. Since the MM_TEXT mapping mode is the default for a device context, it is the mode used by all of the code presented in this book unless the **SetMapMode** function is called to change the mapping mode for a specified device context. The MM_LOENGLISH mapping mode is used extensively in Chapter 7 for page layout purposes. This allows images, graphics, and text to be placed anywhere on a printed page with .01-inch resolution. The MM_ISOTROPIC mapping mode is also used in Chapter 7 for implementing print preview. This mapping mode allows the presentation of a scaled down version of a printed page to be displayed on the screen in perfect scale.

For reference, a short description of all of the available mapping modes follows. Please consult any basic Windows programming book and/or help in your programming environment for further details.

Mapping Mode	Description
MM_ANISOTROPIC	Logical units are mapped to arbitrary units with arbitrary scaled axes. In other words, the programmer can specify the origin, units, orientation of the axes and the scaling desired.
MM_HIENGLISH	Each logical unit represents .001 inch. The positive X axis is to the right and the positive Y axis is up. Origin is the upper left.
MM_HIMETRIC	Each logical unit represents .01 millimeter. The positive X axis is to the right and the positive Y axis is up. Origin is the upper left.
MM_ISOTROPIC	Logical units are mapped to arbitrary units with equally scaled axes; that is, one unit along the X axis is equal to one unit along the Y axis.
MM_LOENGLISH	Each logical unit represents .01 inch. The positive X axis is to the right and the positive Y axis is up. Origin is the upper left.
MM_LOMETRIC	Each logical unit represents .1 millimeter. The positive X axis is to the right and the positive Y axis is up. Origin is the upper left.
MM_TEXT	Each logical unit is mapped to one device pixel the size of which varies from device to device. The positive X axis is to the right while the positive Y axis is down. Origin is the upper left.
MM_TWIPS	Each logical unit is mapped to $\frac{1}{20}$ of a printer's point or $\frac{1}{1440}$ inch (referred to as a twip). Positive X axis is to the right and the positive Y axis is up. Origin is the upper left.

The MM_TEXT mode allows application programs to operate at the pixel level for a device and is therefore device-dependent because pixel sizes can and do differ from device to device. The MM_HIENGLISH, MM_HIMETRIC, MM_LOENGLISH, MM_LOMETRIC, and MM_TWIPS modes are useful for applications needing to draw in actual physical units such as inches or millimeters. These mapping modes are device-independent, meaning that applications that use these mapping modes can send output to any device knowing that the size and placement of displayed (and/or printed) items will be maintained.

The MM_ISOTROPIC mode ensures a 1:1 aspect ratio (where a circle remains a circle when displayed), whereas the MM_ANISOTROPIC mode allows the X and Y coordinate scaling to be adjusted independently, in which case a circle can very easily become an ellipse and vice versa.

Understanding Device Capabilities

As suggested in Chapter 1, it is important for imaging software to ascertain the capabilities of the output device(s) (display and/or printer) it will be dealing with. Armed with this information, the imaging software can adapt to the best of its ability and provide the user with the best possible image output. Given a handle to a device context (as described previously), certain attributes of the device to which the context belongs can be queried using the Windows' function **GetDeviceCaps.** In addition to a handle to a device context, **GetDeviceCaps** requires a capability identifier that identifies the information requested by the software. The integer return value contains the capability information requested. Some capabilities are returned as integer values and some are returned as bit flags. The capabilities used in this book are as follows:

Capability	*Description*
HORZSIZE	Width of device in millimeters
VERTSIZE	Height of device in millimeters
HORZRES	Width of device in pixels
VERTRES	Height of device in pixels
LOGPIXELSX	Number of pixels per logical inch along the device width
LOGPIXELSY	Number of pixels per logical inch along the device height
BITSPIXEL	Number of adjacent color bits for each pixel
PLANES	Number of color planes

Most of the preceding capabilities have obvious meanings because they represent some physical characteristic of an actual output device. The two entries, LOGPIXELSX and LOGPIXELSY, are a little bit different. These entries represent an idealized resolution of the output device to be used for the output of text. For printers, the LOGPIXEL values represent the actual resolution of the printer such as 300 dots per inch (DPI). However, for video displays, the LOGPIXEL values are inflated to make text display larger than it ordinarily would. This is done to take into consideration the distance from which we typically read printed output versus the typical distance we view the monitor screen from. A 10-point font (10/72 inch) is fine for printed output but appears very small when displayed on the screen. Logical scaling enlarges on-screen fonts to make them easier to read.

The following code segment below produces a 10-point Arial font specification, given a handle to a device context. This code is suitable for WYSIWYG applications because it will produce a scaled font for display devices and an unscaled font when used in conjunction with a printer.

```
// The lfHeight member of the LOGFONT structure is calculated from the required
// point size and the logical resolution of the output device.hDC is the handle
// to a device context for the output device.

LOGFONT Font;
memset (&Font, 0, sizeof (LOGFONT));    // Clear the structure

int LogPixelsY = GetDeviceCaps (hDC, LOGPIXELSY);
// Create a 10 point Arial font. A point is 1/72". The round function rounds
// its first parameter value up or down to the closest second parameter.
int LogSize = round (10 * LogPixelsY, 72) / 72;

Font.lfHeight = -1 * LogSize;
Font.lfWeight = 400;
Font.lfOutPrecision = 3;
Font.lfClipPrecision = 2;
Font.lfQuality       = 1;
Font.lfPitchAndFamily = 0x22;
lstrcpy ((LPSTR) &Font.lfFaceName, "Arial");
```

To give you an idea of how much scaling is performed, consider the following capability values extracted from the computer on which I am writing this book. As you can see, the video display mode being used is 640 × 480, 256 colors.

Capability	*Value*
HORZSIZE	208 mm
VERTSIZE	156 mm
HORZRES	640
VERTRES	480
LOGPIXELSX	96
LOGPIXELSY	96
BITSPIXEL	8
PLANES	1

The width of the display is estimated to be 208 mm or approximately 8.19 inches. Given the horizontal resolution of 640 pixels, the physical resolution in pixels per inch is 78.15. Note that **LOGPIXELSX** indicates 96 pixels per logical inch. This means that a logical inch is approximately 23 percent larger than a physical inch. With this scaling, a 10-point font would then appear as large on screen as a 12.3-point font on a printed page. It is important to keep the idea of on-screen scaling in mind when attempting to provide WYSIWYG capabilities on screen as in the previous code segment. If you key your size and placement calculation off pixels per logical inch instead of pixels per physical inch, everything will scale correctly. If you mix and match logical and physical measures, on-screen WYSIWYG will not be possible.

Another important item of information to glean from the capability values presented earlier is that the logical and physical resolutions are the same in the horizontal and vertical directions. In other words,

$$\frac{\text{HORZRES}}{\text{HORZSIZE}} = \frac{\text{VERTRES}}{\text{VERTSIZE}}$$

and

$$\text{LOGPIXELSX} = \text{LOGPIXELSY}$$

This fact is true for most modern output devices and indicates that the height and width of each pixel represent the same physical distance; that is, the pixels are square. All SuperVGA video display modes as well as most printers exhibit square pixels. This is extremely important when attempting to display images with proper aspect ratio. Older PC video display standards, such as EGA, did not have square pixels so that special care was needed to prevent distortion of the aspect ratio of the displayed images. All of the software in this book, however, assumes the presence of square pixels. This mandates the use of a SuperVGA video mode with at least 640×480 resolution, 256 colors or greater.

Many other capabilities, in addition to those listed in the previous table, exist and may need to be queried from time to time. In general, information concerning device technology, physical display size and resolution, color capabilities, color-palette capabilities, available drawing objects, clipping capabilities, raster capabilities, curve drawing capabilities, line drawing capabilities, polygon drawing capabilities, and text capabilities of the device can be determined using the **GetDeviceCaps** function. Consult the online help in your programming environment for more information

The code segment that follows ascertains information about the resolution, size, and the number of colors supported by the current display device (the screen).

```
HDC hDC = GetDC (NULL) ; // Get device context for screen

int WidthInPixels = GetDeviceCaps (hDC, HORZRES);
int HeightInPixels = GetDeviceCaps (hDC, VERTRES);
int WidthInMM = GetDeviceCaps (hDC, HORZSIZE);
int HeightInMM = GetDeviceCaps (hDC, VERTSIZE);
int BitsPerPixel = GetDeviceCaps (hDC, BITSPIXEL);

// Now derive values from device specifications. Namely, the resolution of display
// in pixels/mm, whether the display is true color capable and if not, the number
// of colors supported by the display.
float PixelsPerMM = (float) WidthInPixels / (float) WidthInMM;
BOOL TrueColorCapable = (BitsPerPixel > 8);
int NumberOfColors;

if (TrueColorCapable)
   NumberOfColors = 0;          // Default is 0 for true color images
else
   NumberOfColors = 1 << BitsPerPixel;

ReleaseDC (NULL, hDC);          // Give device context back
```

As you can see, the **GetDeviceCaps** function can provide a good deal of information about an output device by querying its device context. As shown earlier, some of the capability information is useful directly by imaging software, and some requires further manipulation to extract. At the risk of getting way ahead of myself, there is another important thing to note from this code segment; that is, as long as the display device reports more than eight bits per pixel, it can be considered true color capable. By this I mean that true color image data can be passed directly to the display device without needing preprocessing by the application software. Much more discussion of true color images and true color image display will be found later in this chapter and in Chapters 5 and 6.

Of course, the same information could just as easily have been requested for a printer as long as a device context for the printer was available. See Chapters 3 and 7 for information on obtaining printer device contexts.

Windows provides other means as well as for gathering additional information about printers. This is necessary because there is a lot more to know about printers than about display graphics adapters, different paper sizes, feed bins, and so on. Given that the name of a printer is known as well as the port to which it is connected, the function, **DeviceCapabilities** can be used to gather extensive information about the printer. Again, see help on this function for more information.

Bit-mapped Images in Windows

Early on in Windows evolution, images were stored as device-dependent bitmaps or DDBs. These bitmaps were *device-dependent* because the image data mimicked the physical layout of the device on which the images were produced. If the image-producing device had multiple planes of color information and/or multiple bits per pixel, the DDB data reflected the same organization. This was okay in the old days because there were very few video display standards (CGA and EGA) in use. Unfortunately, the DDB structures had no way of conveying important information such as the resolution of the image-producing device or information regarding the aspect ratio of the image. As more and different video standards evolved (VGA, XGA, PGA, SuperVGA, etc.) it became painfully apparent that DDBs needed to give way to a more complete and flexible method of defining images that did not have hardware dependencies built in. In response to this need, Microsoft came up with DIBs or *device-independent* bitmaps in version 3.0 of Windows. The DIBs solved the problems with DDBs and to this day continues to be a viable technique for manipulation of images in the Windows environment. Certain extensions to the DIB format have been proposed for image color matching (ICM) and JPEG compression, but these are still sometime in the future. It is still up in the air whether Windows 95 will have these DIB extensions.

Since DDBs are a relic of the past, they are not discussed. I personally have never needed to use one. The DIB format, however, being as important to Windows imaging as it is, is given the following detailed description. Please note that the Windows BMP file format is an encapsulation of a DIB and is discussed at length in Chapter 4 where graphic file I/O is examined.

The DIB Format

The DIB format defines all characteristics of an image that are necessary for display of an image on an arbitrary output device. In contrast to a DDB, a DIB does not contain any information specific to the hardware on which the contained image was generated. Notice how the focus has shifted away from the image acquisition device to the device on which the image is to be displayed. A DIB consists of three distinct parts:

1. An informational header containing all pertinent parameters for the contained image
2. Color information used for display of the image
3. Image raster data in a specified format

The best way to describe the DIB format is by describing the data structures that define it. The first two items from the previous list are contained in a BITMAPINFO structure that is defined as follows:

```
typedef struct {
    BITMAPINFOHEADER bmiHeader;
    RGBQUAD bmiColors [1];
} BITMAPINFO;
```

The **BITMAPINFO** structure fully defines the dimensions and color information for a device-independent bitmap. The **BITMAPINFOHEADER** specifies information about the dimensions and color format of a DIB and is followed within the BITMAP-INFO structure by an array of RGBQUAD structures that define the colors used in the DIB. The definitions of the **BITMAPINFOHEADER** and RGBQUAD structures follow:

```
typedef struct {
    DWORD    biSize;
    LONG     biWidth;
    LONG     biHeight;
    WORD     biPlanes;
    WORD     biBitCount;
    DWORD    biCompression;
    DWORD    biSizeImage;
    LONG     biXPelsPerMeter;
    LONG     biYPelsPerMeter;
    DWORD    biClrUsed;
    DWORD    biClrImportant;
} BITMAPINFOHEADER;
```

The definitions of the members of the **BITMAPINFOHEADER** are as follows:

- The biSize member specifies the sizes in bytes of the BITMAPINFOHEADER structure. This field is included within this structure (and many other Windows structures) to help with structure version control. It is assumed that different versions of this structure will be of different sizes and that newer versions will probably be larger than older versions. The assumption is also made that all new fields added to the structure will be added at the end of the structure and can therefore be ignored if necessary if they are not understood by code manipulating the DIB. By checking the number in the biSize field against the size of the **BITMAPINFOHEADER** structure a program understands, the program can determine if it can process the DIB or not.
- The biWidth member specifies the width, in pixels, of the bitmap.

- The biHeight member specifies the height of the bitmap, in pixels. In Win32, if this member is negative, then the origin of the image is assumed to be at the upper left instead of the lower left, and the image height in pixels is the absolute value of biHeight.
- The biPlanes member must always be set to one and specifies the number of color planes for the target device. This is one method by which DIBs remain device-independent. The target device is always assumed to have just a single plane of color information.
- The biBitCount member specifies the number of bits per pixel (BPP) used by the image contained in the DIB. This entry must have one of the following values: 1, 4, 8, 16 (Win32 only), or 24. If biBitCount is equal to one, the bitmap is monochrome and therefore bmiColors must contain two entries (usually black and white). Under these conditions, each bit of the bitmap data represents a single pixel. If the bit is zero, the pixel is displayed with the color of the first entry in the bmiColors table. If the bit is a one, the pixel has the color of the second table entry.

  If biBitCount is equal to four, the DIB uses a maximum of 16 colors. bmiColors would therefore contain 16 entries numbered 0 through 15 with the color of each pixel represented by a four-bit index into bmiColors. With biBitCount equal to four, each byte of image raster data contains two pixels. For example, if the first byte in the bitmap is 0x7F, the first pixel would be drawn in the color of the seventh bmiColors table entry, and the second pixel would be drawn with the color of the fifteenth table entry.

  If biBitCount is eight, the DIB uses a maximum of 256 colors and bmiColors contains 256 entries. In this case, each byte in the DIB image data contains a single pixel.

  Under Win32, if biBitCount is 16, the DIB contains a maximum of 2^{16} or 65,536 colors. bmiColors would contain just three DWORD entries that describe the mask to be applied to the pixel data for the red, green, and blue color components, respectively; that is, which bits of the image data represent the red component of the pixel, which bits represent the green component of the pixel, and so on. With biBitCount equal to 16, each WORD of the DIB image data would represent a single pixel.

  If biBitCount is 24, the DIB contains a maximum of 2^{24} or 16.7 million colors. bmiColors in this case has zero entries and each three-byte sequence in the DIB image data would represent a single pixel's value in *BGR* (blue followed by green followed by red) not RGB format as one might expect.
- The biCompression member is usually set to BI_RGB and indicates no compression of the image data. Note: The DIB format does allows for image data compression of four- and eight-bit images, but compression is rarely used so that it can be usually be ignored. Extensions to the DIB format for JPEG compression may change this fact. The code presented in Chapter 4 for reading BMP files (which are encapsulations of DIB images) will put out an error message if a compressed DIB is detected.
- The biSizeImage member that specifies the size, in bytes, of the image's raster data. It is valid to set this member to zero if the DIB is in the BI_RGB format (uncompressed). If this member is non-zero, it must reflect the size of the image raster data, taking into consideration any and all padding required to align each row of image data to a double word boundary.

- biXPelsPerMeter specifies the horizontal resolution, in pixels per meter, of the target device for the DIB. An application can use this value to select a bitmap that best matches the characteristics of the current output device. However few, if any, applications ever set this member; its value is typically zero.
- biYPelsPerMeter specifies the vertical resolution, in pixels per meter, of the target device for the DIB. See the previous description of biXPelsPerMeter.
- The biClrUsed member specifies the number of color indices in the color table that are actually used by the DIB image. If biClrUsed is zero, the bitmap uses the maximum number of colors defined by the value 1 << biBitCount. If biClrUsed is non-zero, it specifies the actual number of colors needed for display if the biBitCount member is less than 24. If biBitCount is 24, biClrUsed (which can and is usually zero) specifies the size of the reference color table used to optimize performance of Windows color palettes. If the DIB is a *packed bitmap* in which the DIB image data immediately follows the BITMAP-INFO header, the biClrUsed member must be set to zero or to the actual number of colors in the color table.
- The biClrImportant member specifies the number of color indexes that are considered important for displaying the DIB image. If this value is zero, as it usually is, all colors are considered important.

The bmiColors portion of the BITMAPINFO structure is made up of an array of zero or more RGBQUAD entries. An RGBQUAD structure is defined by Windows as:

```
typedef struct {
    BYTE rgbBlue;
    BYTE rgbGreen;
    BYTE rgbRed;
    BYTE rgbReserved;
} RGBQUAD;
```

and describes a color consisting of the relative intensities of red, green, and blue all in the range of 0 to 255. The rgbReserved member of an RGBQUAD structure must always be set to zero. The RGBQUAD entries in the bmiColors table should appear in order of importance, from most important to least important. Alternatively, the bmiColors member can be an array of 16-bit unsigned integers that specify an index into the currently realized logical palette instead of explicit RGB values. In this case, an application using the DIB must call DIB functions with the wUsage parameter set to DIB_PAL_COLORS instead of the more typical DIB_RGB_COLORS. This technique is never used in the code in this book, however, because it would make the DIBs non-portable between application programs running on different computers (because the system palettes would most likely be different). The BITMAPINFO structure may not contain any bmiColor entries if the DIB describes a true color image.

As mentioned, a DIB is considered a packed bitmap if the DIB image raster data immediately follows the BITMAPINFO header. A packed bitmap is not a requirement for using DIB images in an application program. The BITMAPINFO header and the image raster data can reside sequentially in memory or not; it really does not matter. What does matter is the organization of the raster data that must be in the format described in the BITMAPINFOHEADER. If the image is described as a 16-color image, then each byte of image data must contain two pixel values. If the BITMAPINFO-HEADER describes a true color image, the data must consist of three bytes of pixel information stored in BGR format. If the image raster data does not match its description in the DIB, one of two things will happen. Either the image will display as garbage or more likely, your machine will crash and burn. Keep this fact in mind as you manipulate DIB image data in your imaging programs.

Regardless of the organization of the image's raster data, each row of the image data must be zero padded to a double word or four-byte boundary. The following macro can be used for forcing double-word alignment if used for calculating an address or can aid in figuring out the number of bytes per line of image raster data:

```
#define ALIGN_DWORD (x) ((((x) + 3)/4) * 4)
```

You will see this macro used extensively in the code provided in this book. Can you say "almost every listing"? I knew you could.

It is very important to keep the concepts of the width of an image in pixels and the number of data bytes that make up a row of image data straight. These two values are only very rarely the same because of the image data alignment requirements. Confusing these quantities can cause no end to grief for beginning imaging programmers. The rather lengthy code segment that follows calculates the amount of memory required for storage of an image's raster data given the number of bits per pixel (BPP) of the image and its width and height values in pixels:

```
DWORD BytesPerLine;

// Calculate BytesPerLine given bits per pixel (BPP) and width of image
switch (BPP) {
    case 1:
        BytesPerLine = (Width+7)/8; // Exactly 8 pixels in each byte
        break;

    case 2:
        BytesPerLine = (Width+3)/4; // Exactly 4 pixels in each byte
        break;

    case 4:
        BytesPerLine = (Width+1)/2; // Exactly two pixels in each byte
        break;

    case 8:
        BytesPerLine = Width;       // Exactly one pixel in each byte
        break;

    case 24:
        BytesPerLine = Width * 3;   // Exactly three bytes per pixel
        break;
}

// Align to double word boundary
BytesPerLine = ALIGN_DWORD (BytesPerLine);

DWORD RasterSize = BytesPerLine * (DWORD) Height;
```

It is very important to understand these calculations. If your calculations of image raster size do not take data alignment requirements into consideration, your Windows imaging programs are destined to fail.

The final, and probably most important, item of information to convey about image raster data in DIB format is the way in which the raster data is stored in memory. Under Win16, Microsoft specified that the origin of an image was at its lower left making the image data appear in memory upside down; that is, the bottom row of an image is stored at the lowest memory address, whereas the first row of image data is stored at the highest address. The implications of the DIB image data storage requirements come into sharp focus when you are called on to exchange the DIB image data with the outside world. Consider the task of writing 24 BPP image data to a TIF graphics file. For other applications to understand the TIF file you write, the origin of the image data must be translated from the lower left to the upper left corner; that is, the data must be read from memory last row first. The pixel data must also be converted from BGR to RGB format for incorporation into the TIF file. Windows BMP files do not have these data conversion requirements because they contain DIB format image data, and therefore no conversions are necessary.

Under Win32, the origin of an image can be specified as being either in the upper or lower left corner, depending on the sign of the biHeight member of the BITMAP-INFOHEADER structure. Although this elevates one of the problems involved in exchanging DIB images in the real world, it does not solve all of the problems.

Windows Treatment of Color

As one would suspect, the quality of displayed photographic images improves with the availability of more colors for display. In fact, the human eye is more sensitive to color aberrations caused by limited color display than to image artifacts caused by display at low spatial resolution. At an absolute minimum, 256 colors are required for display of photographic type images. Most modern Super VGA cards are capable of 256-color display in resolutions of up to $1,024 \times 768$, which requires at least 1Mb of video memory. Many of the newest SuperVGA cards also have true color capability (16.7 million colors) at 640×480 and 64K colors at resolutions up to 800×600. Of course, if money is no object, a true color display card that will run at any resolution you desire can be purchased.

In 256-color graphics modes, Windows employs a *palette manager* as the interface between the display hardware and color-intensive application programs. In 256-color modes, Windows has 256 colors available for simultaneous display. Although this might seem like a lot of colors for many programs, 256 colors is hardly sufficient for display of photographic images. To make matters even worse, except in special cases, Windows reserves 20 colors for its own use in painting window components such as title bars and backgrounds. This doesn't leave many colors for displaying images.

The palette manager uses the notion of foreground and background palettes to manage the use of on-screen colors. Only one foreground image (with foreground palette) can exist at a time, whereas many background images (with background palettes) can exist simultaneously. The image that is considered foreground exists in the window that has input focus. Only one window at a time can have input focus and hence the constraint on one foreground image and associated palette.

When Windows is asked to display a 256-color foreground image, the palette manager looks into the system palette to see how many of the colors specified in the foreground image's (logical) palette can fit into the empty slots in the system palette. 236 of the colors are always able to fit, but that leaves 20 colors in the image unaccounted for. Next, the palette manager searches for the closest match for the unresolved 20 colors in the image to the reserved colors in the system palette. The palette manager will use the closest colors it finds in the system palette for displaying the 20 remaining image colors. The foreground image is given the highest priority for colors for display, but color distortion may still be present if there is a sufficient mismatch between the required image colors and the colors the palette manager provides.

Whenever the palette for the foreground image is realized (see help for the **RealizePalette** function for more information), Windows sends out a WM_PALET-TECHANGED message to all top level windows, indicating the system palette has changed. This gives the background images the opportunity to repaint themselves so that they match the colors in the system palette as closely as possible.

A background image should realize its palette whenever it receives a WM_PALETTECHANGED message. In the case of a background image, the palette manager will attempt to match the colors in the background image's palette as closely as possible to those in the system palette. This match will be poor at best if there is a substantial difference in the palettes of the foreground and background image. A poor match manifests itself in off colors in displayed background images. Note: None of the entries in the system palette will be swapped out to make room for the colors in the images palette because the image is a background palette.

As soon as the focus is changed to a window that contains a background image, the image becomes the foreground image, and the palette manager will display it to the best of its ability. Instantly, the colors of the image will snap in. The generation of the WM_PALETTECHANGED message will cause all other images to be repainted, and the previous foreground image will be relegated to a background image.

In 32K, 64K, or true color graphics modes, the palette manager and the system palette operate quite differently. In these modes, the RGB value that represents the color to be displayed is passed directly to the hardware for display. In true color modes, the eight bits of red, green, and blue data are written directly to the hardware and show up as one of 16.7 million colors on an attached analog monitor. Five bits of red, five bits of green, and five bits of blue are typically available in 32K colors modes (2^{15} is 32,768 colors). The RGB component values in the range of 0 to 255 are shifted to the right three bits and then sent off to the hardware. This results in one of 32,768 unique displayable colors. The 64K color modes operate very much the same as 32K color modes except that the green component is usually given six instead of five bits. Green is given the most color resolution because the human eye is more sensitive to green than to any other color.

When a 256-color image is displayed in a 32K, 64K, or true color graphics mode, the palette manager looks up the RGB values of each palette entry and sends them to the hardware. If the image to be displayed is true color (24 BPP), the palette manager is not involved; Windows sends the RGB pixel values directly to the hardware for display.

As flexible as the Windows imaging subsystem sounds, it was designed when 256-color modes were thought to be the end all for imaging systems. Fortunately (or unfortunately depending on your perspective), technology has marched on, and modern graphic applications now support the manipulation and display of true color images. Manipulation of true color image data is relatively easy; data are data. Display of true color images on computers with only 256-color capability, however, takes a bit of doing.

You can ask Windows to display a true color image for you while operating in a 256-color mode, but you will be disappointed with the result. The first problem is that a 640 × 480 true color image will require about 2.5 minutes on a 33-MHz 486 to display. Second, the displayed results are usually terrible. The problem is that Windows attempts to match each RGB pixel value in the image to the colors available in the system palette but does not attempt any type of error diffusion to improve the image quality (see Chapter 5). Error is defined as the difference between the pixel's RGB color value and the RGB color actually used for display of the pixel. Error diffusion processes divide up the error and use it to modify the adjoining pixel values to improve the image quality. Error diffusion greatly increases the quality of the displayed image.

Depending on the situation, I use two very different techniques for display of true color images when operating in a 256-color graphics mode:

1. Median cut color quantization is a technique that extracts the most important 256 colors from an image. These colors are combined together into a palette with which to display the image. I use this technique when I want to permanently convert a true color image to 256-color format.
2. Uniform quantization with dithering is a technique that renders images against a fixed, wide range palette and uses a modified Floyd-Steinberg error diffusion technique to diffuse the introduced error. I use this technique when I want to leave the image in its true color form but display it on a 256-color device.

Both of these color reduction techniques are discussed at length in Chapter 5. The problem, of course, with both techniques is performance. Neither technique is very fast (because both are implemented in C++ in this book), but they work. If image display is too slow, it can always be sped up by changing video modes to true color or 64K color modes. Then, because the hardware is capable of displaying true color data directly, the color reduction techniques are not required, and display of images occur much faster.

Building and Using Windows DLLs

Because much of the code presented in this book is in the form of Windows DLLs, a short discussion of DLL basics is provided here for those readers not intimately familiar with them. To the uninitiated, DLLs can seem a bit arcane, but as you will see, they are nothing to be afraid of. Once you understand the advantages of using DLLs in your application programs and how to build and use them, you'll use them for just about everything. In fact, the developers of Windows used DLLs extensively for implementing the Windows API. Major portions of Windows are contained in the USER, KERNEL, and GDI DLLs.

A DLL is a file (which usually has a ".dll" file extension) containing executable code and/or resources (such as fonts, bitmaps, text strings, etc.) that is dynamically loaded by the operating system and linked to an application program at runtime. The executable code and/or resources encapsulated within a DLL can be accessed within any programming environment that supports DLLs. The programming language used to build a DLL is not significant to the calling program. A DLL written in C can be used by an application program written in Visual Basic, for example. What is important is the interface the DLL defines for an application to use. Functions within a DLL must be exported by the DLL for use by an application program. Application programs must also take some steps to make the exported DLL functions available for its use.

Some of the benefits of using DLLs as part of an application program are:

1. Code modularization. When DLLs are designed into an application program, they tend to perform a single or limited number of closely related functions. Rarely are DLLs used for big chunks of unrelated code.
2. Well-defined interfaces. The DLLs by definition must provide a well-defined interface for application programs to use. Since an application program can only interact with a DLL through its interface, there is complete isolation between the application's code and the code implementing the DLL functions. There can be no name space conflicts, variable name conflicts, clobbering of global variables, or other problems that can plague large monolithic application programs.
3. Memory usage. Since code and/or resources contained in a DLL are loaded only when required, runtime memory requirements of an application program using DLLs can be lower.
4. Reduced program build times. With application code segmented into one or more DLLs, the code contained within a single DLL can be worked on without having to completely recompile and link the entire application program every time a small change is made. This speeds the edit, compile, link, and debug cycle typical in code development.

Unlike application programs, DLLs do not have their own stack. Instead, they use the stack of the process that calls them. Therefore, all automatic and local variables used within a DLL are placed on the stack of the calling application. Under Win16, DLLs can have a maximum of 64K of space for the local heap that a DLL can maintain for itself. Of course, under Win32 the segment limit is lifted. The initial size of the local heap is specified within the module definition file ("dllname.def") that all DLLs require.

When an application program requests a function contained within a DLL, Windows first checks to see if the DLL has already been loaded into memory. If not previously loaded, Windows will allocate memory for the DLL and load it into memory. The DLLs' module name, specified within the module definition file, is saved so that Windows will know the DLL has been loaded. Any subsequent access to functions within the DLL will not require the DLL to be loaded from disk. If Windows determines that the DLL is already resident in memory as a result of being loaded by another application, the usage count maintained by Windows for the DLL will be incremented because more than one application program is using the same DLL. When Windows determines that no applications are using a DLL, it will unload it from memory. The usage count for a DLL will be decremented by one each time an application that was using a DLL terminates. If two application programs were using a DLL and one terminates, the DLL will remain in memory until the other application terminates (causing the usage count to go to zero). At that time, Windows will unload the DLL.

When access to a DLL is first requested by an application program, a function within the DLL called **LibMain** under Win16 and **DLLEntryPoint** in Win32 (actually the name DLLEntryPoint is just a place holder for the DLL's actual entry point function, which is specified during the linking process) will be called to initialize the code within the DLL. Parameters passed to these functions indicate to the DLL whether this is the first application requesting its services or whether a new application is making the request. Special coding is required if the DLL needs to limit itself to a single application's use or if special preparations are required for supporting more than one application at a time. It is very important to understand that Windows does not provide much help (Win32 provides more help than Win16) to a DLL code developer in coping with the possibility of use by multiple applications simultaneously. That responsibility falls squarely on the shoulders of the developer. If multiple applications must be supported simultaneously by a DLL, the idea of task local storage is generally used; that is, state information about each possible application or task that may use the DLL must be stored on the local heap and referenced whenever an application makes a request of the DLL. To support task local storage, the functions in the DLL require a handle, identifying the application requesting the function, in addition to any other parameters the functions may require. The handle is used to identify the state information stored on the heap for a specific application so that the requested function can function in the context of the calling application. Under Win16, the programmer must implement the task local storage concept directly if support of multiple applications is desirable. Under Win32, there are functions for implementing thread local storage (TLS) designed just for this purpose. See the Win32 documentation for information on TLS.

Just as **LibMain** is called in Win16 when a DLL is first accessed by an application program, the functions **WEP** for Win16 and **DLLEntryPoint** in Win32 are called just before a DLL is unloaded from memory. Code placed within these functions can be used to free memory or clean up any resources used by the DLL before it unloads. Use of these functions is entirely optional. If there is nothing that needs to be done before the DLL unloads, the use of these functions for cleanup are unnecessary.

There are two methods with which an application program can request a connection to a DLL in preparation for using the services it provides. The first method is by explicitly loading the DLL into memory by calling the Windows API function **LoadLibrary** specifying the DLL name as a parameter. After the DLL has been loaded, the function **GetProcAddress** is called (with the DLL instance handle returned from the previous **LoadLibrary** call and a pointer to a function name string as parameters) and returns a far pointer to the entry point of the specified function. The function within the DLL can then be accessed via the returned pointer. When access to the DLL is no longer required, **FreeLibrary** is called to unload the DLL.

The other, and possibly the more common, method for accessing functions within a DLL is to link the application program with the import library generated from the DLL by the "implib.exe" tool provided in all Window's development environments. With the application and DLL connected in this manner, Windows will automatically and transparently take care of loading the DLL into memory when required by the application program, will make all the appropriate calls to **GetProcAddress** for each DLL function used by the application, and will even unload the DLL when it is no longer needed. In fact, this is how programs are given access to the Windows API, whose functions are all contained in DLLs, without having to call **GetProcAddress** for each API function we want to use.

A benefit for developers of using the statically linked technique is that if the application program crashes, a typical occurrence during program development, the DLL will usually be unloaded from memory automatically. If a DLL is explicitly loaded by an application as in the previous method and the application crashes, the DLL will usually remain in memory and necessitate having to get out of Windows and then going back in to continue working on the application.

DLLs are typically written in the C and provide an interface for each function within the DLL needed by a calling application. As mentioned, all interface functions must be exported by the DLL and in addition must be declared FAR in Win16 DLLs. In this book, however, the interface between DLLs and application programs are in the form of C++ classes instead of separate C functions. As you might expect, this has different ramifications, depending on whether Win16 or Win32 is being used and whether Borland or Microsoft development tools are being employed. Another complication arises because a single interface definition file is being used for both building the DLL and for defining the interface to the DLL for the application program. To see how these complexities were managed within the code in this book, see Chapter 4 and the discussion of the Compand DLL, Chapter 8 and the discussion of the MyTwain DLL, and Chapter 10 and the discussion of the Cache DLL.

Helpful Imaging Hints

Please keep the following in mind while implementing imaging in your application programs. Most of these items have been discussed in this chapter.

- If possible, use the CS_BYTEALIGNWINDOW style when registering window classes that will be used for image display. Aligning a window on a byte boundary allows for faster bit-bliting operations which are the means by which imaging is performed in the Windows environment.
- Each row of image data in DIB format must be zero padded to a long word (four-byte) boundary, that is, to a data address evenly divisible by four. If this rule is not followed to the letter, Windows will complain in subtle and not so subtle ways (read that UAE). In some cases, images without double word alignment will display okay but will cause printer drivers to blow up when an attempt is made to print the image. The moral here is to always make sure of the alignment of the image data.
- The width of an image in pixels and the number of data bytes that make up a row of image data are very rarely the same because of data alignment requirements.
- True color image data stored in DIB format is stored in BGR order, not RGB as one would expect.
- When processing DIB image data, be sure to skip the processing of any padding bytes added at the end of a row of image data for alignment purposes.
- In the Win16 environment, *huge* pointers must be used to access image data larger than 64K in size. Also huge memory move functions such as **hmemcpy** are available for moving image data around in memory. There is no such thing as huge pointers or huge memory functions in Win32 since all pointers can access up to two gigabytes of memory and because the 32-bit C library functions can by definition move blocks of memory larger than 64K in size.
- Images in DIB format under Win16 have their origin at the lower left of the image making the image appear in memory upside down. Under Win32, an image's origin can be specified as either in the upper or lower left of the image.
- Some image processing operations applied to DIB images are applied only to the image's raster data, only to the image's palette, or to both the data and the

palette depending on whether the image is true color or palettized. Examples of image processing algorithms can be found in Chapter 9.

Conclusions

There is quite a lot to understand about Windows before you can successfully add imaging to your application programs. Imaging adds another dimension of complexity and a new learning curve on top of that required for general Windows programming. This chapter has not attempted to explain basic concepts that should by now be second nature to almost all Windows programmers. Instead, the discussion was focused on the more subtle details of Windows programming that need to be understood for successful imaging to occur. As a wise person once said (and subsequently amended by me), "Heaven and/or hell is in the details." The helpful imaging hints given earlier summarizes most of the important concepts (the details) presented in this chapter. When you fully understand these hints and have committed them to memory, your experiences with Windows imaging will be much more pleasant and productive.

Chapter 3 continues with the discussion of Windows specific concepts that can be used in imaging applications. The discussion of imaging specific topics begins in Chapter 4 and continues throughout the book.

3

Using Common Dialog Boxes for Imaging Applications

In this chapter you will learn about:

- What common dialog boxes are
- The common dialog boxes available in the Windows environment
- Why common dialog boxes should be used in application programs
- How to encapsulate the common dialog boxes into a C++ class
- Extensions to common dialog boxes useful in imaging programs

Introduction

The common dialog boxes are a group of prepackaged dialog boxes defined and developed by Microsoft to perform tasks common to most application programs. Microsoft hoped that application developers would use the common dialog boxes in their applications, instead of developing their own equivalents because it helps speed program development. For the end user, the use of common dialog boxes in an application program is advantageous because they have become accustomed to their appearance by seeing them in various programs and feel comfortable using them. Readers who may not be familiar with the term common dialog box have probably used them in various Windows application programs without knowing it. The little bit of familiarity provided by the common dialog boxes is comforting when using a new program for the first time. At least you know how to perform some of the simple things.

The common dialog boxes that are currently defined in the Windows 3.1 and Windows 95 environments include:

1. File Open Dialog
2. File Save Dialog
3. Find and Replace Dialog
4. Color Selection Dialog
5. Font Selection Dialog
6. Print Dialog
7. Print Setup Dialog

Even though all of the common dialog boxes available in Windows 95 are also available in Windows 3.1, there are substantial differences in the look and feel of the common dialog boxes between these two versions of Windows. Note: All screen shots of the dialog boxes shown in this chapter are taken from Windows 3.1.

Like most add-on functionality in the Windows environment, the common dialog boxes are contained in dynamic link libraries (DLLs). In the 16-bit environment, the library is called "commdlg.dll"; in the 32-bit environment, the library is called "comdlg32.dll." These DLLs are loaded automatically by the system whenever they are needed. The programmer does not need to load them explicitly to use the common dialog boxes they contain.

A programmer can access the common dialog boxes in different ways: (1) by calling the common dialog box API, provided by Windows, directly; (2) by using the support for the common dialog boxes built into a class library such as Borland's Object Windows Library (OWL) or Microsoft's Foundation Classes (MFC); and (3) by using the C++ class code contained in this chapter. Although all three of these access methods result in access to the use of the common dialog boxes, I believe the third method is the best because the code provided in this chapter is easy to use, is portable between the Borland and Microsoft environments, and provides many extensions not available otherwise. The class library approach to accessing the common dialog boxes is definitely nonportable between the major code development environments. Direct usage of the common dialog boxes API in your application is not recommended either because it results in having too much repeated code in your application and in having to relearn the use of the common dialog box functions and structures every time you need to use them. As you shall see in a minute, using the C++ code will only require a couple of lines of code in your application every time you need to access any one of the common dialog boxes.

It might seem strange to have a chapter dedicated to the common dialog boxes in a book on imaging. However, when you stop to consider just what functions the common dialog boxes perform, you'll begin to understand why they are important to imaging programs and therefore why they deserve discussion here. There is only one of the common dialog boxes not usually needed by imaging software. It is the common dialog box used for text find and replace. Otherwise, imaging software (all Windows software for that matter) always has the need to load and save files by filename, to select a color for painting an image, to select a font for annotation of an image, or to set up a printer for hard copy output. It is wise for imaging software developers to use the common dialog boxes in their programs for two reasons: the familiarity of users with the common dialog boxes and the ability to leverage the work Microsoft did to develop the dialog boxes in the first place. This is work you won't have to repeat and code you won't have to maintain but can readily take advantage of. It is important to note that Microsoft even built in ways for programmers to customize the look and operation of the dialog boxes to a certain extent through the use of hook functions.

Unfortunately, Microsoft chose to change the appearance and the operation of the common dialog boxes for Windows 95 from that in Windows 3.1. While it could be argued that the changes made increased the usability of the dialog boxes, it can also be argued that they have lost the familiarity to Windows 3.1 users. Of course, the complete user interface shell for Windows 95 changed so that a change to the common dialog boxes is just a minor adjustment for users to make. It could also be that Microsoft felt some pressure from other companies such as Symantec whose Norton Desktop for Windows substantially increased the functionality of the common dialog boxes in a backward compatible fashion. Symantec did this by replacing the standard DLL (thereby making the standard common dialog boxes inaccessible to all application program) with one of their own making when the Norton Desktop application is installed. Some of the functionality provided by the Norton Desktop common dialog boxes have been incorporated into the common dialog boxes in Windows 95.

In this chapter, a group of common dialog box classes that encapsulate the common dialog box API will be presented. I will substantially extend the functionality of the printer setup common dialog box to allow it to return more information about the currently selected printer. Information that will come in handy when printing is taken up in Chapter 7. The result of the encapsulation makes the common dialog boxes very easy to understand and use.

Accessing the Common Dialog Box API

Four steps are required for directly accessing the standard Windows API for the common dialog boxes. The first is that the application program must include the file "commdlg.h" that contains the function prototypes and structure definitions required for using them. Next, an instance of a structure must be declared and initialized with the proper values. Which structure and what values depend on which dialog box is going to be used. Values stored in the structure can result in default values being presented to the user or in constraining some choices the user might have when interacting with the common dialog box. A call is then made to a function in the API for the dialog box desired. Parameters to the common dialog box API functions generally include a pointer to the initialized structure, which gives the API function some idea of what you are trying to accomplish. When the API function is called, the dialog box becomes visible to the user, and the user interacts with the controls provided in the dialog box. When the dialog box is dismissed, control returns to the programmer. User choices are stored in fields of the structure originally passed to the API function. The appropriate values are extracted from the structure and acted upon by the remainder of the program. If an error occurs when the API function was called, another function is called to ascertain why. This function, called **CommDlgExtendedError,** returns an error code that can be used to inform the user what failed.

The Common Dialog Box Classes

In all, six classes are defined for support of the common dialog boxes presented here. The class interface definitions shown in Listing 3.1 represent the file "cdialog.hpp".

Figures 3.1 through 3.4 provide short descriptions of what each member function of each class does. Only five of the six classes are meant for external use. One of the classes, FileDialog, is a base class for the OpenFileDialog and the SaveFileDialog classes and should never be instantiated directly. The code for the common dialog box classes is contained in the file "cdialogs.cpp" and is shown in Listing 3.2. Please refer to Listing 3.1 and Listing 3.2 during the discussion of the common dialog box classes.

Listing 3.1 Common dialog box class interface definitions.

```
/************************************************************/
/***                   "cdialogs.hpp"                  ***/
/***          Common Dialog Box Class Definitions      ***/
/***                     written by                    ***/
/***                  Craig A. Lindley                  ***/
/***                                                   ***/
/***      Revision: 2.0     Last Update: 11/11/94      ***/
/************************************************************/

// Copyright (c) 1995 John Wiley & Sons, Inc. All rights reserved.

#ifndef CDIALOGS_HPP
#define CDIALOGS_HPP

#ifndef WIN32
#include <print.h>
#endif

#ifndef LPOFNHOOKPROC
typedef UINT (WINAPI *LPOFNHOOKPROC) (HWND, UINT, WPARAM, LPARAM);
#endif

#include <commdlg.h>

#define MAXDIALOGBOXNAMELENGTH 80

// Base Class Defintion
class FileDialog {
  protected:
  // Protected data
    OPENFILENAME ofn;
    char DialogBoxName[MAXDIALOGBOXNAMELENGTH+1];
    char PathName[260];
    char FileName[255];
    char FilterStr[256];
    char TempFilterStr[256];
    WORD FilterIndex;
    DWORD DialogFlags;
    FARPROC lpfnHookProcAddress;

  public:
    FileDialog();

    void ClearFileName(void);
    void SetFileName(LPSTR TheFileName);
     void SetHookFunction(FARPROC lpfnHookProcAdr);
    LPSTR GetFileNamePtr(void);
```

```
      LPSTR GetPathNamePtr(void);
      void ClearFilterStr(void);
      void AddToFilter(LPSTR TheFilterStr);
      void SetFlags(DWORD TheFlags);
      void SetDialogBoxName(LPSTR DialogBoxName);
};

// Open File Dialog Class
class OpenFileDialog: public FileDialog {
  public:
    OpenFileDialog(void);
    BOOL DoDialog(HWND hWindow);
};

// Save File Dialog Class
class SaveFileDialog: public FileDialog {
  public:
    SaveFileDialog(void);
    BOOL DoDialog(HWND hWindow);
};

// Select Color Dialog Class
class SelectColorDialog {
  private:
    CHOOSECOLOR CC;
    COLORREF BlackColor;
    COLORREF CustomColors[16];
    COLORREF CurrentColor;
    DWORD CurrentFlags;

  public:
    SelectColorDialog(void);
    void SetSelectedColor(COLORREF Color);
    void ClearCustomColors(void);
    void SetFlags(DWORD TheFlags);
    COLORREF GetColor(void);
     void SetCustomColor(WORD Index, COLORREF Color);
     COLORREF GetCustomColor(WORD Index);
     BOOL DoDialog(HWND hWindow);
};

// Select Font Dialog Class
#define DBCHARACTERISTICS (CF_EFFECTS | CF_USESTYLE | CF_ANSIONLY |
  CF_INITTOLOGFONTSTRUCT | CF_FORCEFONTEXIST)
#define SELSCNFONTS         (DBCHARACTERISTICS | CF_SCREENFONTS)
#define SELPRTFONTS         (DBCHARACTERISTICS | CF_PRINTERFONTS)
#define SELCOMMONFONTS      (DBCHARACTERISTICS | CF_WYSIWYG | CF_BOTH |
  CF_SCALABLEONLY)

class SelectFontDialog {
  private:
    LOGFONT LF;
    CHOOSEFONT CF;
    DWORD CurrentFlags;
    HDC    CurrentHDC;
```

```
      COLORREF CurrentColor;
      WORD CurrentFontType;
      char FontStyleDesc[LF_FACESIZE];

  public:
      SelectFontDialog(void);
      void SetSelectedFont(LOGFONT Font);
      void CopyandSetSelectedFont(LPLOGFONT FontPtr);
      void SetFlags(DWORD TheFlags)          { CurrentFlags = TheFlags; }
      DWORD GetFlags(void)                   { return CurrentFlags; }
      void SetFontHDC(HDC hDC)               { CurrentHDC = hDC; }
      void SetFontType(WORD TheFontType);
      LOGFONT GetFont(void);
      void SetFontStyle(LPSTR StyleDesc);
      LPSTR GetFontStyle(void);
      void SetFontColor(COLORREF Color);
      COLORREF GetFontColor(void);
      void ShowScreenFontsOnly(void)         { CurrentFlags = SELSCNFONTS; }
      void ShowPrinterFontsOnly(void)        { CurrentFlags = SELPRTFONTS; }
      void ShowCommonFontsOnly(void)         { CurrentFlags = SELCOMMONFONTS; }

      BOOL DoDialog(HWND hWindow);
};

// Print Dialog Box Class
class PrintDialog {
  private:
      PRINTDLG PD;
      DWORD PrinterFlags;
      HGLOBAL hGlobalDEVMODE;
      HGLOBAL hGlobalDEVNAMES;
      HINSTANCE hPrintDriver;
      LPFNDEVCAPS DeviceCapabilities;
      BOOL  FirstTimeInit;
      char  PrinterName[CCHDEVICENAME];
      char  PortName[10];
      char  DriverNameWExt[255];
      char  DriverNameWOExt[255];
      HDC         PrinterDC;
      WORD  Orientation;
      WORD  PaperType;
      WORD  PaperWidth;
      WORD  PaperLength;

      // Get DEVMODE info function
      BOOL  GetPrinterInfo(void);

  public:
      PrintDialog();
      ~PrintDialog();
      void        SetFlags(DWORD PrtFlags);
      DWORD       GetFlags(void);
      void        SelectPrintSetupDialog(void);
      void        SelectPrintDialog(void);
```

```
HDC        GetPrtHDC(void);
LPSTR      GetPrinterName(void);
LPSTR      GetPortName(void);
DWORD      GetPrinterCapabilities(WORD Capability, LPSTR lpszOutput);
int        GetPaperOrientation(void);
int        GetPaperType(void);
int        GetPaperWidthinMM(void);
int        GetPaperLengthinMM(void);
BOOL       SetPaperOrientation(short Orientation);
 BOOL      SetPaperType(short Type);
BOOL       GetPrinterInformation(void);

BOOL DoDialog(HWND hWindow);
};

#endif
```

Listing 3.2 Common dialog box class functions.

```
/**********************************************************/
/***                  "cdialogs.cpp"                   ***/
/***         Common Dialog Box Class Functions         ***/
/***                   written by                      ***/
/***                Craig A. Lindley                   ***/
/***                                                   ***/
/***      Revision: 2.0    Last Update: 11/11/94       ***/
/**********************************************************/

// Copyright (c) 1995 John Wiley & Sons, Inc. All rights reserved.

#include <stdio.h>
#include <stdlib.h>
#include <string.h>
#include <windows.h>
#include <cderr.h>                  // Common dialog box errors
#include "cdialogs.hpp"

#ifdef _WIN32_
// Necessary because this function does not exist in Win32 API
LPSTR lstrcpyn(LPSTR lpszString1, LPCSTR lpszString2, int cChars) {

  if (lstrlen(lpszString2) <= cChars) {// If String2 shorter than cChars
    // Go ahead and copy String2 to String1 storage
    return lstrcpy(lpszString1, lpszString2);
  } else {                                // String2 longer than cChars
    LPSTR lpS1 = lpszString1;
    LPSTR lpS2 = (LPSTR) lpszString2;
    char S2Char = *lpS2++;
    while(S2Char && cChars--) {
      *lpS1++ = S2Char;
      S2Char = *lpS2++;
    }
    *lpS1 = '\0';
    return lpszString1;
  }
}
#endif
```

```
// A message box with printf capability used throughout this file
void PrintfMsgBox(char *szCaption, char *szFormat, ...)  {
  char szBuffer[256];
  char *pArguments;

  pArguments = (char *) &szFormat + sizeof(szFormat);
  vsprintf(szBuffer, szFormat, pArguments);
  MessageBox(NULL, szBuffer, szCaption, MB_OK | MB_TASKMODAL);
}

// Check the Window's version
BOOL IsCorrectWinVersion(void) {

  DWORD Version = GetVersion();
  BYTE MajRev = LOBYTE(LOWORD(Version));
  BYTE MinRev = HIBYTE(LOWORD(Version));

  // Make sure we are Windows 3.1 of newer
  if (MajRev < 3)
    return FALSE;
  if ((MajRev == 3) && (MinRev < 10))
    return FALSE;

  return TRUE;
}

// Constructor and destructor for base dialog class
FileDialog::FileDialog(void) {
  memset(&ofn,                0, sizeof(OPENFILENAME));
  memset(&PathName,           0, sizeof(PathName));
  memset(&FileName,           0, sizeof(FileName));
  memset(&FilterStr,          0, sizeof(FilterStr));
  memset(&DialogBoxName,      0, sizeof(DialogBoxName));
  FilterIndex = 0;
  lpfnHookProcAddress = NULL;
}

// Set the flags for the open file dialog box
void FileDialog::SetFlags(DWORD TheFlags)  {

  DialogFlags = TheFlags;
}

// Set the dialog box name
void FileDialog::SetDialogBoxName(LPSTR DlgBoxName)  {
  lstrcpyn((LPSTR) DialogBoxName, DlgBoxName, MAXDIALOGBOXNAMELENGTH);
}

// This function clears out the FileName stored in the object
void FileDialog::ClearFileName(void)  {
  memset(&FileName, 0, sizeof(FileName));
}

void FileDialog::SetFileName(LPSTR TheFileName)  {
  lstrcpy((LPSTR) FileName, TheFileName);
}
```

```
// This function clears out the Filter string stored in the object
void FileDialog::ClearFilterStr(void) {
  memset(&FilterStr, 0, sizeof(FilterStr));
}


void FileDialog::AddToFilter(LPSTR FilterSpec) {
  lstrcat((LPSTR) FilterStr, FilterSpec);
}


// This function sets up the hook function procedure address
void FileDialog::SetHookFunction(FARPROC lpfnHookProcAdr) {
  lpfnHookProcAddress = lpfnHookProcAdr;
}


// This function returns a ptr to the user picked filename
LPSTR FileDialog::GetFileNamePtr(void) {
  return (LPSTR) ofn.lpstrFileTitle;
}


// This function returns a ptr to the user picked filename
LPSTR FileDialog::GetPathNamePtr(void) {
  return (LPSTR) ofn.lpstrFile;
}


// Open File Dialog Box Class functions

// Constructor for the Open File Dialog Class
OpenFileDialog::OpenFileDialog() {
  if(!IsCorrectWinVersion()) {
    PrintfMsgBox("Error", "This dialog box requires Windows 3.1 or newer");
    exit(-1);
  }
  // Set default for flags
  DialogFlags = OFN_FILEMUSTEXIST | OFN_HIDEREADONLY | OFN_PATHMUSTEXIST;
  FilterIndex = 1;
  SetDialogBoxName((LPSTR) "Open File Dialog Box");
}


// This function does the actual dialog box
BOOL OpenFileDialog::DoDialog(HWND hWindow) {

  /*
  We make a copy of the filter string so our original ASCII version
  is untouched. That way we can AddToFilter at any time with problem
  */
  strcpy(TempFilterStr, FilterStr);
  // Get length of filter string
  WORD FilterLen = (WORD) strlen(TempFilterStr);
  // Get last char of filter string - this is the delimiter
  char cLastChar = TempFilterStr[FilterLen-1];
  // Everywhere delimiter is found replace with a zero
  for (WORD Index = 0; TempFilterStr[Index] != '\0'; Index++) {
    if (TempFilterStr[Index] == cLastChar)
      TempFilterStr[Index] = '\0';
  }
  // Filter string is now properly formatted
```

```
    memset(&ofn, 0, sizeof(OPENFILENAME));
    ofn.lStructSize        =  sizeof(OPENFILENAME);
    ofn.hwndOwner          =  hWindow;
    ofn.Flags              =  DialogFlags;
    ofn.nFilterIndex       =  FilterIndex;
    ofn.lpfnHook = (LPOFNHOOKPROC) lpfnHookProcAddress;

    strcpy(PathName, FileName);
    ofn.lpstrFile          =  (LPSTR) PathName;
    ofn.nMaxFile           =  sizeof(PathName);
    ofn.lpstrFileTitle     =  (LPSTR) FileName;
    ofn.nMaxFileTitle      =  sizeof(FileName);
    ofn.lpstrFilter        =  (LPSTR) TempFilterStr;
    ofn.lpstrTitle         =  (LPSTR) DialogBoxName;

  if (GetOpenFileName((LPOPENFILENAME) &ofn) != TRUE) {
    DWORD ErrVal = CommDlgExtendedError();
    if (ErrVal != 0)          // Error = 0 is user cancel
      PrintfMsgBox("Open File Dialog Error", "Error #: 0x%1x", ErrVal);
    return FALSE;
  } else {
    FilterIndex = (WORD) ofn.nFilterIndex;
    return TRUE;
  }
}


// Save File Dialog Box Class functions

// Constructor for the Save File Dialog Class
SaveFileDialog::SaveFileDialog() {
  if(!IsCorrectWinVersion()) {
    PrintfMsgBox("Error", "This dialog box requires Windows 3.1 or newer");
    exit(-1);
  }
  // Set default for flags
  DialogFlags = OFN_OVERWRITEPROMPT | OFN_PATHMUSTEXIST | OFN_HIDEREADONLY;
  FilterIndex = 1;
  SetDialogBoxName((LPSTR) "Save As File Dialog Box");
}


// This function does the actual dialog box
BOOL SaveFileDialog::DoDialog(HWND hWindow)  {

  /*
  We make a copy of the filter string so our original ASCII version
  is untouched. That way we can AddToFilter at any time with problem
  */
  strcpy(TempFilterStr, FilterStr);
  // Get length of filter string
  WORD FilterLen = (WORD) strlen(TempFilterStr);
  // Get last char of filter string - this is the delimiter
  char cLastChar = TempFilterStr[FilterLen-1];
  // Everywhere delimiter is found replace with a zero
  for (WORD Index = 0; TempFilterStr[Index] != '\0'; Index++)  {
```

```
      if (TempFilterStr[Index] == cLastChar)
        TempFilterStr[Index] = '\0';
  }
  // Filter string is now properly formatted

  memset(&ofn, 0, sizeof(OPENFILENAME));
  ofn.lStructSize  = sizeof(OPENFILENAME);
  ofn.hwndOwner    = hWindow;
  ofn.Flags        = DialogFlags;
  ofn.nFilterIndex = FilterIndex;
  ofn.lpfnHook = (LPOFNHOOKPROC) lpfnHookProcAddress;

  strcpy(PathName, FileName);
  ofn.lpstrFile      = (LPSTR) PathName;
  ofn.nMaxFile       = sizeof(PathName);
  ofn.lpstrFileTitle = (LPSTR) FileName;
  ofn.nMaxFileTitle  = sizeof(FileName);
  ofn.lpstrFilter    = (LPSTR) TempFilterStr;
  ofn.lpstrTitle     = (LPSTR) DialogBoxName;

  if (GetSaveFileName((LPOPENFILENAME) &ofn) != TRUE)  {
    DWORD ErrVal = CommDlgExtendedError();
    if (ErrVal != 0) // Error = 0 is user cancel
      PrintfMsgBox("Save File Dialog Error", "Error #: 0x%1x", ErrVal);
    return FALSE;
  } else {
    FilterIndex = (WORD) ofn.nFilterIndex;
    return TRUE;
  }
}


// The Color Select Dialog Box Class
SelectColorDialog::SelectColorDialog()  {

  ClearCustomColors();
  BlackColor = RGB(0, 0, 0);
  CurrentColor = BlackColor;
  CurrentFlags = CC_RGBINIT | CC_PREVENTFULLOPEN;
}


// Set the color the dialog box will come up with
void SelectColorDialog::SetSelectedColor(COLORREF Color)  {

  CurrentColor = Color;
}


// This function sets all custom colors to white
void SelectColorDialog::ClearCustomColors(void)  {
  WORD Index;

  for (Index=0; Index < 16; Index++)
    CustomColors[Index] = RGB(255, 255, 255);
}

void SelectColorDialog::SetFlags(DWORD TheFlags)  {
```

```
    CurrentFlags = TheFlags;
}


// Get the current color
COLORREF SelectColorDialog::GetColor(void)  {
  return CurrentColor;
}


// Set a custom color
void SelectColorDialog::SetCustomColor(WORD Index, COLORREF Color) {

  CustomColors[Index] = Color;
}


// Get a custom color
COLORREF SelectColorDialog::GetCustomColor(WORD Index) {

  return CustomColors[Index];
}


// This function does the actual dialog box
BOOL SelectColorDialog::DoDialog(HWND hWindow) {

  memset(&CC, 0, sizeof(CHOOSECOLOR));
  CC.lStructSize   = sizeof(CHOOSECOLOR);
  CC.hwndOwner     = hWindow;
  CC.Flags         = CurrentFlags;
  CC.rgbResult     = CurrentColor;
  CC.lpCustColors  = (COLORREF FAR *) CustomColors;

  if (ChooseColor((CHOOSECOLOR FAR *) &CC) != TRUE) {
    DWORD ErrVal = CommDlgExtendedError();
    if (ErrVal != 0)          // Error = 0 is user cancel
      PrintfMsgBox("Select Color Dialog Error", "Error #: 0x%lx", ErrVal);
    return FALSE;
  } else {
    CurrentColor = CC.rgbResult;
    // Save the custom colors configured by the user
    memcpy((LPSTR)CustomColors, CC.lpCustColors, 16 * sizeof(COLORREF));
    return TRUE;
  }
}

// The Font Select Dialog Box Class
SelectFontDialog::SelectFontDialog()  {

  memset(&LF, 0, sizeof(LOGFONT));
  memset(&FontStyleDesc, 0, LF_FACESIZE);
  CurrentFlags = SELSCNFONTS;
  CurrentColor = RGB(0, 0, 0);
  CurrentFontType = SCREEN_FONTTYPE;
}
```

```
// This function returns the color to be used with the font
COLORREF SelectFontDialog::GetFontColor(void)  {
  return CurrentColor;
}


// This function sets the font color
void SelectFontDialog::SetFontColor(COLORREF Color) {

  CurrentColor = Color;
}


// This function sets the FontStyle data member
void SelectFontDialog::SetFontStyle(LPSTR StyleDesc)  {

  lstrcpyn(FontStyleDesc, StyleDesc, LF_FACESIZE);
}


// This function returns a ptr to the FontStyle
LPSTR SelectFontDialog::GetFontStyle(void) {

  return &FontStyleDesc[0];
}

// This function sets the current font
void SelectFontDialog::SetSelectedFont(LOGFONT Font) {

  LF = Font;
}

// This function sets the current font
void SelectFontDialog::CopyandSetSelectedFont(LPLOGFONT FontPtr) {

  memcpy((LPSTR) &LF, FontPtr, sizeof(LOGFONT));
}


void SelectFontDialog::SetFontType(WORD TheFontType) {

  CurrentFontType = TheFontType;
}
```

```
// This function returns the LOGFONT structure describing the current font
LOGFONT SelectFontDialog::GetFont(void) {

  return LF;
}

// This function does the actual dialog box
BOOL SelectFontDialog::DoDialog(HWND hWindow) {

  memset(&CF, 0, sizeof(CHOOSEFONT));
  CF.lStructSize  = sizeof(CHOOSEFONT);
  CF.hwndOwner    = hWindow;
  CF.hDC          = CurrentHDC;
  CF.lpLogFont    = (LPLOGFONT) &LF;
```

```
    CF.Flags       = CurrentFlags;
    CF.rgbColors   = CurrentColor;
    CF.nFontType   = CurrentFontType;
    CF.lpszStyle   = (LPSTR) FontStyleDesc;

  if (ChooseFont((CHOOSEFONT FAR *) &CF) != TRUE) {
    DWORD ErrVal = CommDlgExtendedError();
    if (ErrVal != 0)               // Error = 0 is user cancel
      PrintfMsgBox("Select Font Dialog Error", "Error #: 0x%lx", ErrVal);
    return FALSE;
  } else {
    CurrentColor = CF.rgbColors;
    return TRUE;
  }
}


// Printer Dialog Box Class functions

// Constructor for the Printer Dialog Class
PrintDialog::PrintDialog() {

FirstTimeInit = TRUE;          // TRUE until dialog box used

if (!IsCorrectWinVersion()) {
  PrintfMsgBox("Error", "This dialog box requires Windows 3.1 or newer");
  exit(-1);
}
// Set default for flags
PrinterFlags = (DWORD) PD_HIDEPRINTTOFILE | (DWORD) PD_NOPAGENUMS;
// Clear misc info string storage
memset(PrinterName,    0, sizeof(PrinterName));
memset(PortName,       0, sizeof(PortName));
memset(DriverNameWExt,  0, sizeof(DriverNameWExt));
memset(DriverNameWOExt, 0, sizeof(DriverNameWOExt));

Orientation     = 0;
PaperType       = 0;
PaperWidth      = 0;
PaperLength     = 0;
hPrintDriver    = 0;           // Handle to print driver library
PrinterDC       = 0;
}


PrintDialog::~PrintDialog() {

  if (PrinterDC) DeleteDC(PrinterDC);
  if (PD.hDevMode) GlobalFree(PD.hDevMode);
  if (PD.hDevNames) GlobalFree(PD.hDevNames);
  if ((UINT) hPrintDriver >= 32)  // If device driver was previously loaded
                                  successfully
    FreeLibrary(hPrintDriver);    // free it now
}

// Set the printer flags
void PrintDialog::SetFlags(DWORD PrtFlags) {
```

```
    PrinterFlags = PrtFlags;
}


// Get the printer flags
DWORD PrintDialog::GetFlags(void) {

  return PrinterFlags;
}

// Select printer setup dialog
void PrintDialog::SelectPrintSetupDialog(void) {

  PrinterFlags |= PD_PRINTSETUP;
}

// Select print dialog
void PrintDialog::SelectPrintDialog(void) {

  PrinterFlags &= ~PD_PRINTSETUP;
}

// Copies printer's info from DEVMODE structure to local storage
BOOL PrintDialog::GetPrinterInfo(void) {

  if (PD.hDevMode == NULL)        // If no printer selected
    return FALSE;                 // return FALSE
  // Try to lock down the DEVMODE structure
  LPDEVMODE Ptr = (LPDEVMODE) GlobalLock(PD.hDevMode);
  if (Ptr == NULL)                // return FALSE on failure
    return FALSE;
  // Now that we have a ptr to the DEVMODE structure, get the required info
  lstrcpyn(PrinterName, (LPSTR) &Ptr->dmDeviceName, CCHDEVICENAME);
  Orientation = Ptr->dmOrientation;

  PaperType   = Ptr->dmPaperSize;     // This integer identifies a paper size
                                      //    (its an index)
  PaperWidth  = Ptr->dmPaperWidth;    // These dimensions in mms
  PaperLength = Ptr->dmPaperLength;
  // Unlock DEVMODE structure
  GlobalUnlock(PD.hDevMode);

  // Now attempt to access DEVNAMES structure. This is complicated by the fact
  // that if a user chooses cancel from the print setup dialog box, the
  // PD.hDevNames value goes to zero. We cannot let that situation mess up the
  // information we already have about the selected printer so we do not try to
  // process the DevNames structure. We return a true value even if hDevNames
  // is NULL.

  if (PD.hDevNames != NULL) {     // If this structure is valid
    // Try to lock down the DEVNAMES structure
    LPDEVNAMES NPtr = (LPDEVNAMES) GlobalLock(PD.hDevNames);
    if (NPtr == NULL)             // return FALSE on failure
      return FALSE;
    // Now that we have a ptr to the DEVNAMES structure, get the required info
```

```
      // Get a pointer to the output device name (i.e. port)
      LPSTR StrPtr = (LPSTR)((LPSTR) NPtr + NPtr->wOutputOffset);
      lstrcpy(PortName, StrPtr);     // Copy port name to local storage

      StrPtr = (LPSTR)((LPSTR) NPtr + NPtr->wDriverOffset);
      lstrcpy(DriverNameWOExt, StrPtr);  // Copy driver filename to local storage
      lstrcpy(DriverNameWExt,  StrPtr);  // Copy driver filename to local storage
      lstrcat(DriverNameWExt, ".DRV");   // Append extension to one copy
      // Unlock DEVNAMES structure
      GlobalUnlock(PD.hDevNames);
   }
   return TRUE;                         // Sweet success
}


// Externally available function for getting info on current printer
BOOL PrintDialog::GetPrinterInformation(void) {

   if (FirstTimeInit) {               // If printer has yet to be queried
      DWORD Flags = GetFlags();       // Get the default flags
      SetFlags(PD_RETURNDEFAULT);     // Set the flags to invisibley execute
                                      //    dialog box
      DoDialog(NULL);
      SetFlags(Flags);               // Put flags back
   }
   return (GetPrinterInfo());         // Copy info about printer to local storage
}


BOOL PrintDialog::SetPaperOrientation(short Orientation) {

   if (FirstTimeInit) {               // If printer not initialized
      if (!GetPrinterInformation())   // Get printer information
         return FALSE;
   }
   if (PD.hDevMode == NULL)          // If no printer selected
      return FALSE;                  // return FALSE
   // Try to lock down the DEVMODE structure
   LPDEVMODE Ptr = (LPDEVMODE) GlobalLock(PD.hDevMode);
   if (Ptr == NULL)                  // return FALSE on failure
      return FALSE;
   // Now that we have a ptr to the DEVMODE structure, set the required info
   Ptr->dmOrientation = Orientation;
   if (PrinterDC)                    // If HDC for printer already existed, delete
                                     //    it
      DeleteDC(PrinterDC);
   // Request a new printer DC with revised characteristics
   PrinterDC = CreateDC(DriverNameWOExt, PrinterName, PortName, Ptr);
   // Unlock DEVMODE structure
   GlobalUnlock(PD.hDevMode);
   return (PrinterDC != NULL);
}


BOOL PrintDialog::SetPaperType(short Type) {

   if (FirstTimeInit) {                   // If printer not initializes
      if (!GetPrinterInformation())       // Get printer information
```

```
        return FALSE;
    }
    if (PD.hDevMode == NULL)              // If no printer selected
      return FALSE;                       // return FALSE
    // Try to lock down the DEVMODE structure
    LPDEVMODE Ptr = (LPDEVMODE) GlobalLock(PD.hDevMode);
    if (Ptr == NULL)                      // return FALSE on failure
      return FALSE;
    // Now that we have a ptr to the DEVMODE structure, set the required info
    Ptr->dmPaperSize = Type;
    if (PrinterDC)                        // If HDC for printer already existed,
                                          //   delete it
      DeleteDC(PrinterDC);
    // Request a new printer DC with revised characteristics
    PrinterDC = CreateDC(DriverNameWOExt, PrinterName, PortName, Ptr);
    // Unlock DEVMODE structure
    GlobalUnlock(PD.hDevMode);
    return (PrinterDC != NULL);
}


HDC PrintDialog::GetPrtHDC(void) {

    if (PrinterDC)                        // If a printer DC already exists
      return PrinterDC;                   // return it
    else {                                // Otherwise, we must create one
      if (FirstTimeInit) {                // If printer not initializes
        if (!GetPrinterInformation())     // Get printer information
          return NULL;
      }
      if (PD.hDevMode == NULL)            // If no printer selected
        return NULL;                      // return NULL
      // Try to lock down the DEVMODE structure
      LPDEVMODE Ptr = (LPDEVMODE) GlobalLock(PD.hDevMode);
      if (Ptr == NULL)                    // return NULL on failure
        return NULL;
      if (PrinterDC)                      // If HDC for printer already existed,
                                          //   delete it
        DeleteDC(PrinterDC);
      // Now that we have a ptr to the DEVMODE structure, we can create a DC
      PrinterDC = CreateDC(DriverNameWOExt, PrinterName, PortName, Ptr);
      // Unlock DEVMODE structure
      GlobalUnlock(PD.hDevMode);
      return (PrinterDC);
    }
}


// Returns a ptr to the name of the printer
LPSTR PrintDialog::GetPrinterName(void) {

    if (!GetPrinterInfo())
      return NULL;
    return PrinterName;
}
```

```
// Returns a ptr to the name of the port to which the printer is connected
LPSTR PrintDialog::GetPortName(void) {

  if (!GetPrinterInfo())
    return NULL;
  return PortName;
}


// Returns either DMORIENT_PORTRAIT or DMORIENT_LANDSCAPE
int PrintDialog::GetPaperOrientation(void) {
  if (!GetPrinterInfo())
    return -1;
  return Orientation;
}


// Return an integer which represents the paper type (size). See DEVMODE for
   constants
int PrintDialog::GetPaperType(void) {
  if (!GetPrinterInfo())
    return -1;
  return PaperType;
}


// Return the width of the selected paper
int PrintDialog::GetPaperWidthinMM(void) {
  if (!GetPrinterInfo())
    return -1;
  return PaperWidth;
}


// Return the length of the selected paper
int PrintDialog::GetPaperLengthinMM(void) {
  if (!GetPrinterInfo())
    return -1;
  return PaperLength;
}


// This function returns the specified capabilities of the current printer
DWORD PrintDialog::GetPrinterCapabilities(WORD Capability, LPSTR lpszOutput) {

  return (DeviceCapabilities(PrinterName, PortName, Capability, lpszOutput,
    NULL));
}


// This function does the actual dialog box. After successful completion
// of dialog box execution a new printer context is established.
BOOL PrintDialog::DoDialog(HWND hWindow) {

  memset(&PD, 0, sizeof(PRINTDLG));
  PD.lStructSize  = sizeof(PRINTDLG);
  PD.hwndOwner    = hWindow;
  PD.Flags        = PrinterFlags;
  PD.nCopies      = 1;
```

```
        if (!FirstTimeInit) {
          PD.hDevMode    = hGlobalDEVMODE;
          PD.hDevNames   = hGlobalDEVNAMES;
        }
        if (PrintDlg((LPPRINTDLG) &PD) != TRUE) {
          DWORD ErrVal = CommDlgExtendedError();
          // If an error occurred and it is not User Cancel (ErrVal = 0)
          // and it is not No Default Printer then output error message
          if (ErrVal != 0 && ErrVal != PDERR_NODEFAULTPRN)
            PrintfMsgBox("Printer Dialog Error", "Error #: 0x%lx", ErrVal);
          return FALSE;
        } else {
          if (FirstTimeInit)                  // Reset flag
            FirstTimeInit = FALSE;

          // Save handle to the DEVMODE structure
          hGlobalDEVMODE = PD.hDevMode;       // Save handle for reuse
          hGlobalDEVNAMES = PD.hDevNames;     // Ditto

          // If a current print DC exists, delete it
          if (PrinterDC) {
            DeleteDC(PrinterDC);
            PrinterDC = 0;
          }

          // Get the general printer info into local storage
          if (!GetPrinterInfo())
            return FALSE;

          // If a print driver was already loaded, free it.
          if (hPrintDriver != NULL)
            FreeLibrary(hPrintDriver);

          // Load the new printer driver
          hPrintDriver = LoadLibrary(DriverNameWExt);

          // Check for successful load of driver
          if (hPrintDriver == NULL) {   // Check for successful load
            PrintfMsgBox("Printer Dialog Error", "Print driver load error");
            return FALSE;
```

```
          }
          // When we get here, the driver has been loaded successfully.
          // Get entry point into the driver
          DeviceCapabilities = (LPFNDEVCAPS) GetProcAddress(hPrintDriver,
            "DeviceCapabilities");
          if (DeviceCapabilities == NULL)
            return FALSE;

          // Verify print driver of selected printer is 3.1 level.
          if (GetPrinterCapabilities(DC_VERSION, NULL) < 0x30A)
            PrintfMsgBox("User Advisory",
              "The driver for the selected printer is outdated. "
              "As a result this printer will not work correctly with this program. "
```

```
        "Please contact the printer manufacturer for a Windows 3.1 print driver.");

    return TRUE;
  }
}
```

All of the classes are used in basically the same manner. First, the application program must include the interface class definition in the application program by including the file "cdialog.hpp". Second, an instance of the appropriate dialog box class must be instantiated. None of the common dialog box class constructors require any parameters. Next, some of the member functions of the class may need to be called to configure the dialog box for the application. Finally, a call to the member function **DoDialog** is made passing the handle of the parent window. This causes the dialog box to be made visible and allows interaction with the user. After a return from the **DoDialog** function, calls to other class member functions may need to be made to retrieve the user's inputs. As an example, consider the following use of the Open File dialog box:

```
#include "cdialog.hpp"        // Include the class definitions
OpenFileDialog * OFD;         // Declare a pointer to the class

OFD = new OpenFileDialog;     // Instantiate an object of the class
// Add All files, BMP files, GIF files, and TIF Files to the filter string
OFD->AddToFilter("All Files|*.*|BMP Files|*.bmp|GIF Files|*.gif|");
OFD->AddToFilter("TIF Files|*.tif|");
// Give the Open File dialog box an appropriate name
OFD->SetDialogBoxName("Select a Graphic Image File");
// Make it visible to the user for interaction
if (OFD->DoDialog(HWindow))  {
        // If we get here, all is well, save the path and filename of the file
          to be opened
        lstrcpy(PathandFileName, OFD->GetPathNamePtr());
        .
        .
        .
}
  .
  .
  .
delete OFD;  // Delete the Open Dialog box object
```

This code segment illustrates how easy it is to use the Open File dialog box class. Notice that the programmer does not need to declare instances of any of the common dialog box structures or configure any of the structure elements directly. From the discussion earlier, it should be obvious what each line of code does. The only nonobvious function call is probably **AddToFilter.** The strings passed to this function determine the file types that will be presented to the user for selection; that is, the file types can be selected using the drop-down list box in the lower part of the Open File common dialog box. See Figure 3.5. The filter string is made up of three individual elements. Consider the first entry in the filter string "All Files|*.*|" for purposes of discussion. The first element is the substring "All Files". This is the ASCII text that will be listed in the drop-

---

The FileDialog class

Purpose

This class functions as a base class for the OpenFileDialog and SaveFileDialog classes. This class should probably never be instantiated on its own, although nothing will prohibit a programmer from doing so.

Member Functions

FileDialog.   This is the class constructor. It initialized all storage areas and variables of the class to zero. Within this class are storage areas for the OPENFILENAME structure, the path name of a selected file, the filename of a selected file, the filter strings for the dialog box, and the title to be given to the dialog box. Other miscellaneous class variables are also initialized.

ClearFileName.   When called, this function clears out the filename stored in the FileDialog object.

SetFileName.   This function is called to store a default filename that is to be used when the common dialog box is made visible. In most cases, this is the filename you would like the user to select.

SetHookFunction.   This function is called when the address of a hook function for a dialog box must be stored. Hook functions allow programmers to preprocess messages generated by the common dialog boxes in response to user actions. For example, a "Help" button within a dialog box is implemented by way of a hook function that traps the message generated whenever the help button is clicked and calls a programmer supplied function whose address is specified by this function call.

GetFileNamePtr.   This function is called after the dialog box has been made visible to retrieve a pointer to the filename selected by the user.

GetPathNamePtr.   This function is called after the dialog box has been made visible to retrieve a pointer to the path and filename of the file selected by the user.

ClearFilterString.   Calling this function clears the filter string stored within this class object. Since calls to **AddToFilter** are cumulative, it is necessary to call this function to begin building a new filter string from scratch.

AddToFilter.   This function adds the specified filter string passed in as a parameter to the filter string stored with this class object. Filter strings consist of an ASCII string to be displayed in the common dialog box for filter selection, a "|" delimiter followed by the filter specification. See text for details.

SetFlags.   The Open File and the Save File dialog boxes are controlled, in part, by a series of control flags contained in a DWORD variable. These flags are defined in the Windows include file "commdlg.h". This class, which is the base class for both of these common dialog boxes, maintains a copy of the control flags. This function, **SetFlags,** is called whenever the control flag variable must be altered.

SetDialogBoxName.   This function is called with a string as a parameter to set the name to be given to the open file or save file dialog boxes. This name will become the caption of the dialog box when it is made visible.

FIGURE 3.1 The FileDialog, the OpenFileDialog, and the SaveFileDialog classes.

The OpenFileDialog and SaveFileDialog classes

Purpose

The purpose of these classes is to provide easy use and access to the Open File and the Save File common dialog boxes to an application program. An instance of the OpenFileDialog class would be used when a program needs to ask the user which file to open. In the same vein, the SaveFileDialog box class would be used when a program needed to ask the user for a filename for storage of some sort of program information, an image for example.

Example usage of the OpenFileDialog class is given in the text. The SaveFileDialog class is used almost exactly the same way. Both of these classes inherit the FileDialog class that provides much of their functionality. Only two member functions are defined for each class. They are detailed below.

Member Functions

OpenFileDialog/SaveFileDialog.   These are the class constructors that are called whenever objects of these classes are instantiated. The first function performed by the constructors is to call the function **IsCorrectWinVersion** that verifies that Windows 3.1 or newer is running. This is necessary because older versions of Windows did not include the common dialog box DLL, which means that the OpenFileDialog and the SaveFileDialog classes cannot be used. It is assumed that all versions of Windows, 3.1 and newer, will provide the dialog box DLL, and therefore this class can be used. If you would like to use these common dialog box classes with Windows 3.0, you must change or remove the calls to **IsCorrect-WinVersion** and load the common dialog box DLL yourself.

The next function performed by both of the class constructors is to set the control flags in their respective base classes as appropriate for their use. The control flag for the OpenFileDialog class is set so that only files that exist will be shown to the user, that files tagged as read only will not be shown, and that only paths that exist can be entered by the user. The control flag for the SaveFileDialog class is set so that the dialog box will issue a message asking to overwrite the selected file whenever the user selects a filename that already exists, that only paths that exist can be selected by the user for saving a file, and that files that are marked read only will not be shown to the user. The FilterIndex variable is then set to one in both constructors, indicating that the first filter in the filter string should be selected when the respective dialog box becomes visible. Finally, the default name "Open File Dialog Box" is assigned to the open file dialog box, and similarly the default name "Save As File Dialog Box" is assigned to the save file dialog box. Of course, the filter index and the names given to the dialog boxes can be overridden anytime after the object of the class has been instantiated.

DoDialog.   When this function is called, the appropriate dialog box becomes visible to the user. Before that happens, however, a certain amount of setup is required. Namely, the filter string is parsed and the OPENFILENAME structure is initialized

FIGURE 3.1 (*Continued*)

with the appropriate variables from the object. The call is then made to the common dialog box API function **GetOpenFileName** or **GetSaveFileName** to display the dialog box. Both functions return TRUE if the user closed down the dialog box by clicking the okay button and FALSE if the user canceled the dialog box or an error occurred. A call is made to another API function, **GetDlgExtendedError,** to determine the cause of the error if an error is indicated. An error code other than zero (which indicates the user canceled) will cause a message box to be displayed, which will indicate the error condition. The meaning of the error code can be ascertained by looking in the Windows include file "cderr.h". Since common dialog box errors are a rare occurrence, no attempt was made to give the user an error message in English. The condition that caused the error is probably out of the user's capability to remedy anyway.

The information returned in the OPENFILENAME structure is retained within the class object and will be available for reuse the next time **DoDialog** is called. This means that if an instance of the OpenFileDialog class or the SaveFileDialog class is declared globally in an application program, each time it is used it will remember the parameters it had the previous time it was used such as which directory was selected and so on. If an instance of these classes is declared just when it is needed and disposed of after it is used, no historical information will be retained between invocations.

FIGURE 3.1 (*Continued*)

The SelectColorDialog class

Purpose
The purpose of this class is to provide easy use and access to the ChooseColor common dialog box in an application program. This class would be used within a program when the user is required to select a color appropriate for some use such as selecting the color of text, for example. An example of the use of the SelectColorDialog class is shown in the example program in Listing 3.3. Instantiation and invocation of this class are very similar to that shown in the text for the OpenFileDialog class.

Member Functions
SelectColorDialog.   This is the class constructor that is called whenever an object of this class is instantiated. The actions performed by this constructor are to set each of the 16 possible custom colors to white (RGB value 255, 255, 255), to set the default color to black, to set flags in the CurrentFlags class variable so that the default color is highlighted when the dialog box becomes visible, and to prevent selection of custom colors by the user. In other words, user access to the custom color definition functionality provided by the ChooseColor dialog box will be blocked. As described earlier, any of the characteristics put in place by the execution of the class constructor can be overridden anytime after the constructor has

FIGURE 3.2 The SelectColorDialog class.

been run. The other member functions of this class provide the programmer with the tools to do so.

SetSelectedColor.   This function is called, with a COLORREF as a parameter, to select the color to be the highlighted color when the dialog box is visible.

ClearCustomColors.   This function initializes the 16 possible custom colors to white, thereby clearing the definitions of all custom colors.

SetCustomColor.   This function sets the custom color entry specified by an index to the color specified by the COLORREF. Sixteen custom colors are allowed, therefore valid index values are 0 to 15.

GetCustomColor.   This function returns the COLORREF of the custom color specified by an index.

SetFlags.   The functionality offered by the ChooseColor common dialog box is controlled, in part, by a series of control flags contained in a DWORD variable. These flags are defined in the Windows include file "commdlg.h". The SelectColorDialog class maintains a copy of the control flags. This function, **SetFlags,** is called whenever the control flag class variable must be altered.

GetColor.   This function is typically called after the select color dialog box has been dismissed to retrieve the color selected by the user. The value is returned to the calling program as a COLORREF variable.

DoDialog.   This function causes the ChooseColor common dialog box to be displayed for interaction with the user. Before being made visible, the CHOOSE-COLOR structure within the class is initialized with the appropriate class variables. The call to **ChooseColor,** causes the dialog box to be presented to the user. Error conditions returned from the **ChooseColor** function call are processed as described for the OpenFileDialog box class discussed previously. If no errors are detected, the value of certain class variables are extracted from the CHOOSE-COLOR structure and stored in the class, specifically, CC.rgbResult, which indicates the color selected by the user and CC.lpCustColors, which points at the custom colors configured by the user, if any.

FIGURE 3.2 (*Continued*)

down list box for selection by the user. The vertical bar, the second element, is a delimiter that separates the displayed ASCII string from the third element, which is the filter to be applied to the filenames available to the user for selection. In this case, when "All Files" is selected, all files in the current directory will be displayed because the filter applied is "*.*". In total two calls are made to **AddToFilter** for a total of four file types that can be selected: All files, BMP files, GIF files, and TIF files. When GIF files is selected, for example, only files with a ".GIF" file extension will be listed and therefore be available to the user for selection.

A portion of the short driver program to exercise all of the common dialog box classes provided is shown in Listing 3.3. This program has no utility other than to allow each of the supported common dialog boxes to be displayed and to show typical code sequences associated with their calls. All of the screen shots shown in Figures 3.5 to 3.10 were made using the driver program.

The SelectFontDialog class

Purpose

The purpose of this class is to provide easy use and access to the ChooseFont common dialog box in an application program. This class is used whenever a user needs to specify a new font for use within a program. An example of the use of the SelectFontDialog class is shown in the example program in Listing 3.3. Instantiation and invocation of this class are very similar to that shown in the text for the OpenFileDialog class. This class contains more member functions than any of the previously discussed classes because the control of fonts in the Windows environment is a more complicated endeavor than just selecting a filename. Most of the member functions are one liners, however.

Because the functionality inherent in the ChooseFont common dialog box is much more complex than any of the common dialogs discussed previously, it eludes me why any programmer would want to develop their own version of a ChooseFont dialog box instead of using the one provided by Windows.

Member Functions

SelectFontDialog.   This is the constructor for the SelectFontDialog class. Its purpose is to initialize class variables to appropriate initial values before a select font dialog box can be used. The class variables are initialized so that only screen fonts will be displayed and therefore selectable by the user, and the current font color will be black.

SetSelectedFont.   When this function is called with a logical font structure as a parameter, the specified font will be used as the default selection offered the user when the ChooseFont common dialog box is subsequently displayed.

CopyandSetSelectedFont.   This function is identical to the earlier function except that it accepts a pointer to a logical font as a parameter instead of an actual logical font structure.

SetFlags.   The functionality offered by the ChooseFont common dialog box is controlled, in part, by a series of control flags contained in a DWORD variable. These flags are defined in the Windows include file "commdlg.h". **SetFlags** is called whenever the control flag class variable must be altered. The ChooseFont common dialog box has a great number of flags that control its operation. To help simplify the task of choosing the correct flags to set for some common situations, a series of defines are defined in Listing 3.1. The first define **DBCHARACTERISTICS, OR**s together many of the flags I commonly use. Specifically, these combined flags turn on effects selection (strike out, underline, and color selection) for the user, allow the dialog box to be initialized by specifying a font style, allow only the display for selection of ANSI fonts, and allow selection of only those fonts that currently exist on the system. The second define, SELSCNTFONTS, combines the flags specified in DBCHARACTERISTICS with a flag that causes only screen fonts to be shown to the user. A similar define SELPRTFONTS only allows printer supported fonts to be displayed. The final define, SELCOMMONFONTS, causes fonts that are available on both the screen and the printer to be displayed as long as they are scalable and support What You See Is What You Get (WYSIWYG) usage.

FIGURE 3.3 The SelectFontDialog class.

GetFlags. This function returns the current value of the class control flag variable. This function is used whenever a single bit of the control flag variable must be altered. The current value of the flag variable is first fetched with this function, any of the bits can then be modified by ANDing and ORing the appropriate values, and the result can be set back into the control flag variable by calling **SetFlags.**

SetFontHDC. This function is used to set the device context that the ChooseFont common dialog box should access. For example, if the need arises to select the fonts available for a certain printer, the device context for the printer must be setup before the ChooseFont dialog box is called. Please note that the mapping mode (see Chapter 2) in effect for the device context at the time the ChooseFont dialog box is used affects the values returned for the selected font. Specifically, the entries in the LOGFONT structure dealing with size will be returned in logical units appropriate to the mapping mode and not in device pixels as one might expect.

SetFontType. This function determines what types of fonts will be made available to the user for selection. The font type is the only parameter to this function. Available font types are GDI simulated fonts, printer fonts, or screen fonts. See the font overview in the help system for more information about font types.

GetFont. This function returns the logical font structure (LOGFONT) of the font selected and configured by the user during interaction with the ChooseFont common dialog box.

SetFontStyle. This function accepts a pointer to a string that sets the font style. Font style strings include Regular, Italic, Bold, and Bold Italic. Note, the CF_USESTYLE bit in the control flags must be set for a style string to have any affect.

GetFontStyle. After the user has interacted with the ChooseFont dialog box, this function can be called to return a pointer to a font style string. Font style strings are shown earlier.

SetFontColor. This function sets the color of the font presented to the user in the ChooseFont common dialog box to the value of the COLORREF passed in as a parameter.

GetFontColor. This function returns the color to be assigned to the font selected by the user. A COLORREF value describes the selected color.

ShowScreenFontsOnly. Execution of this function sets the control flags to SEL-SCNFONTS, which allows only those fonts destined for the screen to be presented to the user for selection.

ShowPrinterFontsOnly. Execution of this function sets the control flags to SEL-PRTFONTS, which allows only those fonts usable on the printer to be presented to the user.

ShowCommonFontsOnly. Execution of this function sets the control flags to SEL-COMMONFONTS, which allows only those fonts available for both the screen and the printer to be presented to the user for selection.

DoDialog. This function caused the ChooseFonts common dialog box to be presented to the user for font selection. The appearance of this dialog box is controlled by a set of flags, a font type, and a font style descriptor that are maintained within the SelectFontDialog class and have been previously discussed. Before being made visible, the CHOOSEFONT structure within the class is initialized with these class

FIGURE 3.3 (*Continued*)

variables. The call to **ChooseFont,** causes the dialog box to be presented to the user. Error conditions returned from this function call are processed using the **CommDlgExtendedError** function as described for the OpenFileDialog box class discussed earlier. If no errors are indicated, the value of CF.rgbColors, which indicates the color of the font selected by the user, is extracted from the CHOOSEFONT structure and stored in the CurrentColor class variable for inspection of the calling program.

FIGURE 3.3 (*Continued*)

The PrintDialog class

Purpose

The PrintDialog class provides access to the PrintDlg common dialog box in addition to providing additional functionality of its own. This class can be used in an application program for printer selection, printer configuration, printing control, and page setup. An example of the use of the PrintDialog class is shown in the example program in Listing 3.3. The PrintDialog class is the most complicated class presented in this chapter. It contains the most member functions, and the member functions are more complicated than in the other classes presented. See the text for a discussion of how and why the PrintDialog class extended the PrintDlg common dialog box API.

Member Functions

PrintDialog.   This is the constructor for the PrintDialog class. It does not require any parameters. The first operation performed by this constructor is to verify that it is being run on a machine running Windows 3.1 or newer. This is necessary because earlier versions of Windows did not have common dialog box support built in. After checking the Windows version, the constructor proceeds to initialize various class variables to appropriate initial values. This is necessary before the PrintDlg dialog box can be used. All storage for a printer name, a printer port, and a device driver name is initialized to zeros or NULL strings.

~PrintDialog.   This is the destructor for the PrintDialog class. It performs various cleanup tasks that are necessary before the class can be destructed. Specifically, it deletes any printer device context that exists, it frees memory associated with certain structures maintained by the PrintDialog class, and it unloads the print driver for the currently selected printer if one had been loaded.

SetFlags.   The PrintDialog functionality is controlled in part by a series of flags contained in the DWORD class variable, PrinterFlags. These flags are defined in the Windows include file "commdlg.h". This function, **SetFlags,** is called whenever the control flag variable must be altered.

GetFlags.   Execution of this function returns the current value of the control flag variable, PrinterFlags.

FIGURE 3.4 The PrintDialog class.

SelectPrintSetupDialog. The only purpose of this function is to set the PD_PRINTSETUP bit in PrinterFlags. The result is that the print setup dialog box will be presented to the user whenever the **DoDialog** function is called instead of the print dialog box. See Figure 3.9.

SelectPrintDialog. The only purpose of this function is to reset the PD_PRINTSETUP bit in PrinterFlags. The result is that the print dialog box will be presented to the user whenever the **DoDialog** function is called instead of the print setup dialog box. See Figure 3.10.

GetPrtHDC. This function returns a device context to be associated with the currently selected printer. It does this by calling the Windows function **CreateDC** and passing it the name of the device driver associated with the current printer, the name of the printer, the port number the printer is attached to, and a pointer to a DEVMODE structure that contains device-specific initialization information for the print driver. The device context returned from **CreateDC** is returned by this function. This device context is used to draw text and graphics on the currently selected printer.

GetPrinterName. This function returns a zero terminated ASCII string that contains the name of the current printer.

GetPortName. This function returns a zero terminated ASCII string that contains the port the current printer is connected to. Typical strings are COM1:, LPT1:, and so on.

GetPrinterCapabilities. This function is used to retrieve information about the various capabilities of the current printer. A constant that defines which capability is to be queried (defined as DC_XXXXXX in windefs.h where XXXX is the capability being queried) and a pointer to an output buffer is passed to this function. Device capabilities are further defined in help for the Windows **DeviceCapabilities** function and are also discussed in Chapter 2. The information returned depends on the capability queried. Capability information is returned both in the return value from the function call and as information stored in the output buffer. An example of the use of this function to obtain the version number of the current print driver can be seen in the implementation of the **DoDialog** function in Listing 3.2.

GetPaperOrientation. This function calls the private class function **GetPrinterInfo** to retrieve the orientation value stored in the DEVMODE structure associated with the current printer. Orientation values returned are either DMORIENT_PORTRAIT (1) or DMORIENT_LANDSCAPE (2).

GetPaperType. This function calls the private class function **GetPrinterInfo** to retrieve the paper size value stored in the DEVMODE structure associated with the current printer. Paper size is really the index into the paper size array for the paper currently selected for use on the current printer. This function therefore returns the paper size index.

GetPaperWidthinMM. This function calls the private class function **GetPrinterInfo** to retrieve the paper width value (specified in tenth of a millimeter) stored in the DEVMODE structure associated with the current printer.

GetPaperLengthinMM. This function calls the private class function **GetPrinterInfo** to retrieve the paper length value (specified in tenth of a millimeter) stored in the DEVMODE structure associated with the current printer.

FIGURE 3.4 (*Continued*)

SetPaperOrientation. This function accepts a paper orientation as a parameter and creates a new device context for the printer incorporating the specified orientation. The next call to **GetPrtHDC** will return the new device context.

SetPaperType. This function accepts a paper size identifier as a parameter and creates a new device context for the printer incorporating the specified paper size. The next call to **GetPrtHDC** will return the new device context.

GetPrinterInformation. This function, when called, fills the instance of the Print-Dialog class with information about the default system printer. It does this by invisibly executing the print setup dialog box which causes the DEVMODE and DEVNAME structures for the default printer to be returned. The subsequent call to **GetPrinterInfo** within this function causes the specifics of the default printer to be parsed out of these data structures and stored in class variables.

DoDialog. This function causes the Windows PrintDlg API function to be executed. The user may be presented with the print dialog box, the print setup dialog box, or no dialog box at all depending on the PrintFlags. Before calling PrintDlg, a PRINT-DLG structure within the class is initialized with the appropriate class variables. Any error in the execution of the PrintDlg function will cause a Boolean FALSE to be returned. Error conditions are processed using the **CommDlgExtendedError** function as described for the OpenFileDialog box class earlier. If no errors are detected, any existing printer device context is deleted, information on the selected printer is loaded into the class variables by a call to **GetPrintInfo,** any previously loaded print driver is unloaded, the print driver for the newly selected printer is loaded, and the "DeviceCapabilities" entry point is extracted from the printer driver and stored. Finally, the **GetPrinterCapabilities** function is called to verify that the print driver is version 3.10 or newer. If the print driver is older, a warning message will be output to the user in a message box.

FIGURE 3.4 (*Continued*)

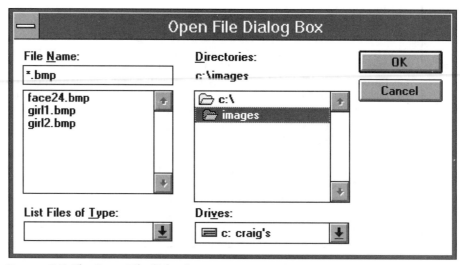

FIGURE 3.5 The Open File dialog box.

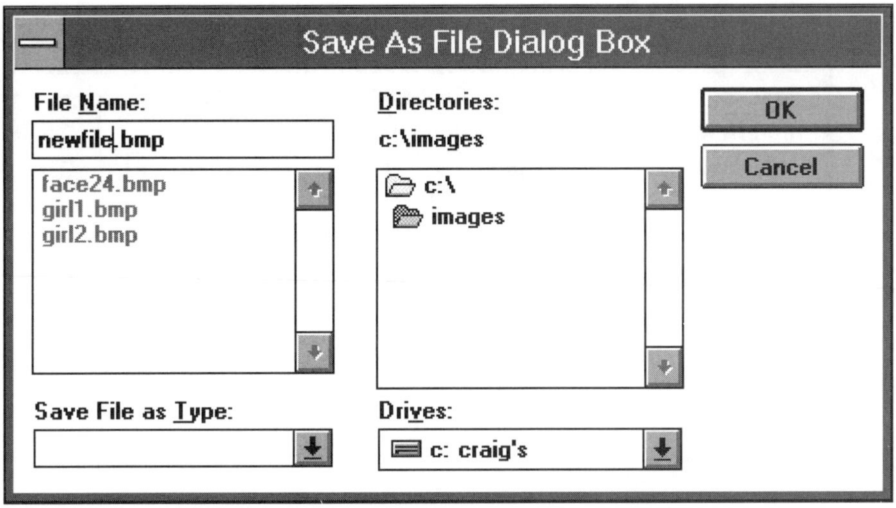

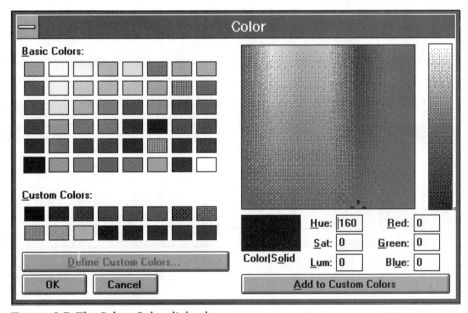

FIGURE 3.6 The Save File dialog box.

FIGURE 3.7 The Select Color dialog box.

Listing 3.3 Driver program for common dialog box classes.

Note: This is only one of the files required for the driver program. All others are available on the companion disc.

```
// Copyright (c) 1995 John Wiley & Sons, Inc. All rights reserved.

/*  Project testapp
    SUBSYSTEM:    testapp.exe Application
```

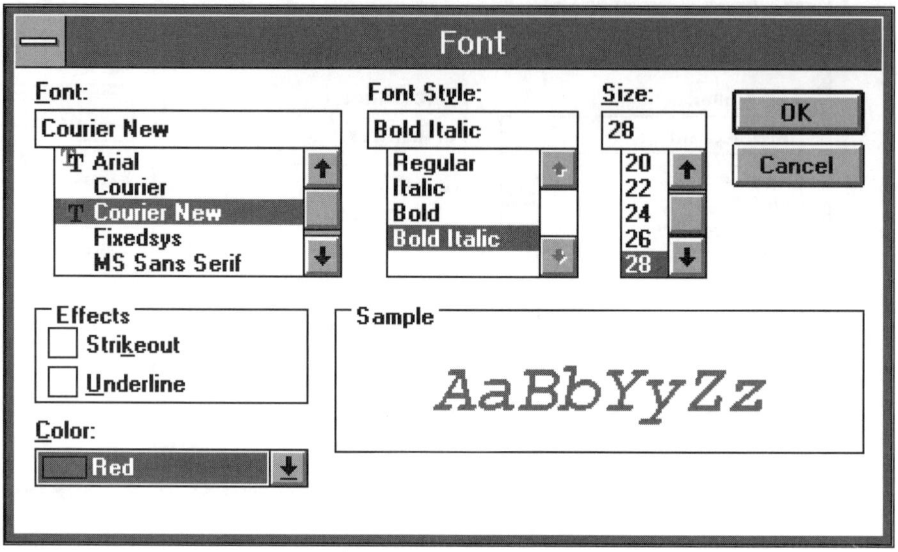

FIGURE 3.8 The Select Font dialog box.

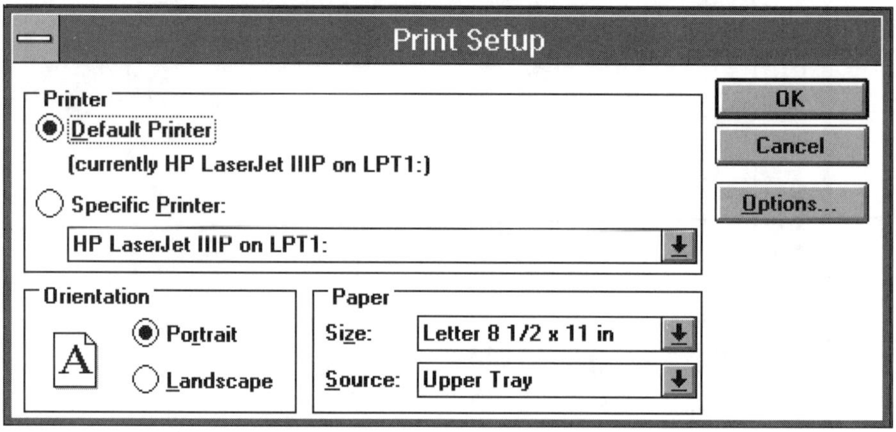

FIGURE 3.9 The Print Setup dialog box.

```
FILE:        tstppapp.cpp
AUTHOR:      Craig A. Lindley

OVERVIEW
========
Source file for implementation of testappApp (TApplication).
*/

#include <owl\owlpch.h>
#pragma hdrstop
```

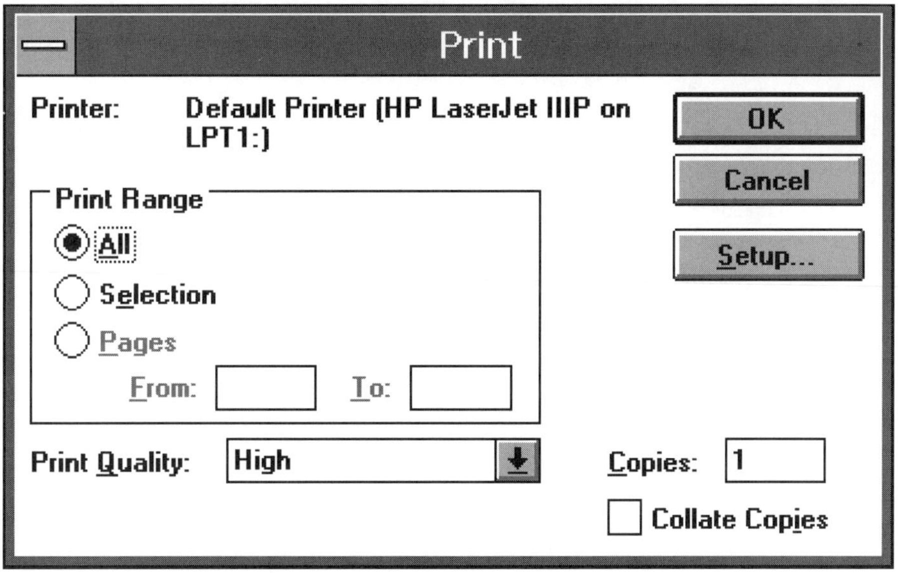

FIGURE 3.10 The Print dialog box.

```
#include "cdialogs.hpp"
#include "tstppapp.h"
#include "tstppabd.h"                              // Definition of about dialog.

//{{testappApp Implementation}}

//
// Build a response table for all messages/commands handled
// by the application.
//
DEFINE_RESPONSE_TABLE1(testappApp, TApplication)
//{{testappAppRSP_TBL_BEGIN}}
    EV_COMMAND(CM_OPENFILEDIALOG, CmOpenFileDialog),
    EV_COMMAND(CM_SAVEFILEDIALOG, CmSaveFileDialog),
    EV_COMMAND(CM_SELECTCOLORDIALOG, CmSelectColorDialog),
    EV_COMMAND(CM_SELECTCUSTOMCOLORDIALOG, CmSelectCustomColorDialog),
    EV_COMMAND(CM_SELECTFONTDIALOG, CmSelectFontDialog),
    EV_COMMAND(CM_PRINTSETUPDIALOG, CmPrintSetupDialog),
    EV_COMMAND(CM_PRINTDIALOG, CmPrintDialog),
    EV_COMMAND(CM_HELPABOUT, CmHelpAbout),
//{{testappAppRSP_TBL_END}}
END_RESPONSE_TABLE;

//
// FrameWindow must be derived to override Paint for Preview and Print.
//
class SDIDecFrame : public TDecoratedFrame {
public:
    SDIDecFrame (TWindow *parent, const char far *title, TWindow *clientWnd, BOOL
trackMenuSelection = FALSE, TModule *module = 0) :
```

```
                      TDecoratedFrame(parent, title, clientWnd, trackMenuSelection, module)
        {   }
     ~SDIDecFrame ()
        {   }
};


//////////////////////////////////////////////////////////
// testappApp
// =====
//
testappApp::testappApp () : TApplication("Common Dialog Test Application")
{

}

testappApp::~testappApp ()
{
    // INSERT>> Your destructor code here.

}


//////////////////////////////////////////////////////////
// testappApp
// =====
// Application intialization.
//
void testappApp::InitMainWindow ()
{
    Client = new TWindow(0, "");
    SDIDecFrame *frame = new SDIDecFrame(0, GetName(), Client, FALSE);

    nCmdShow = nCmdShow != SW_SHOWMINIMIZED ? SW_SHOWNORMAL : nCmdShow;

    //
    // Assign ICON w/ this application.
    //
    frame->SetIcon(this, IDI_SDIAPPLICATION);

    //
    // Menu associated with window and accelerator table associated with table.
    //
    frame->AssignMenu("TestAppMenu");

    MainWindow = frame;

    //
    // Windows 3-D controls.
    //
    EnableCtl3d(TRUE);
}

// Do the open file dialog box
void testappApp::CmOpenFileDialog(void) {
```

```
 OpenFileDialog OFD;
 OFD.DoDialog(MainWindow->HWindow);
}

// Do the save file dialog box
void testappApp::CmSaveFileDialog(void) {

  SaveFileDialog SFD;
  SFD.DoDialog(MainWindow->HWindow);
}

// Do the select color dialog

void testappApp::CmSelectColorDialog(void) {

  SelectColorDialog SCD;
  SCD.DoDialog(MainWindow->HWindow);
}

// Do the select custom color dialog
void testappApp::CmSelectCustomColorDialog(void) {

  SelectColorDialog SCD;
  SCD.SetFlags(CC_RGBINIT);

  // Set the custom colors
  SCD.SetCustomColor(0,   RGB(  0, 0, 0));
  SCD.SetCustomColor(1,   RGB( 51, 0, 0));
  SCD.SetCustomColor(2,   RGB(102, 0, 0));
  SCD.SetCustomColor(3,   RGB(153, 0, 0));
  SCD.SetCustomColor(4,   RGB(204, 0, 0));
  SCD.SetCustomColor(5,   RGB(255, 0, 0));

  SCD.SetCustomColor(6,   RGB(0,  51, 0));
  SCD.SetCustomColor(7,   RGB(0, 102, 0));
  SCD.SetCustomColor(8,   RGB(0, 153, 0));
  SCD.SetCustomColor(9,   RGB(0, 204, 0));
  SCD.SetCustomColor(10, RGB(0, 255, 0));

  SCD.SetCustomColor(11, RGB(0, 0,  51));
  SCD.SetCustomColor(12, RGB(0, 0, 102));
  SCD.SetCustomColor(13, RGB(0, 0, 153));
  SCD.SetCustomColor(14, RGB(0, 0, 204));
  SCD.SetCustomColor(15, RGB(0, 0, 255));

  SCD.DoDialog(MainWindow->HWindow);
}

// Do the select color dialog
void testappApp::CmSelectFontDialog(void) {

  SelectFontDialog SFD;
  SFD.DoDialog(MainWindow->HWindow);
}
```

```
// Do the select print setup dialog box
void testappApp::CmPrintSetupDialog(void) {
  PrintDialog PD;
  PD.SelectPrintSetupDialog();
  PD.DoDialog(MainWindow->HWindow);
}

// Do the select print dialog box
void testappApp::CmPrintDialog(void) {
  PrintDialog PD;
  PD.DoDialog(MainWindow->HWindow);
}

// Do the about box
void testappApp::CmHelpAbout(void) {

  // Show the modal dialog.
  testappAboutDlg(MainWindow).Execute();
}

int OwlMain (int , char* []) {
  testappApp App;
  int result;
  result = App.Run();

  return result;
}
```

Extensions to the PrintDlg Common Dialog Box Functionality

With the exception of the PrintDialog class, the common dialog box classes presented here are straightforward encapsulations of the functionality provided by the Windows common dialog box API. The PrintDialog class however, extends the functionality provided by the Windows PrintDlg API function. These extensions have to do with management of printer selection, management of printer device contexts, retrieval of printer capabilities, and the retrieval of printer names and port assignments. The functionality provided by these extensions are always required whenever printing is performed in professional Windows application programs. Someone else might have included the extension functions into classes dealing directly with printing, but I chose to place them here in the class dealing with selection of printers.

To understand how the extensions work, one must understand the DEVMODE and DEVNAMES structures returned by the PrintDlg common dialog box function in the PRINTDLG structure. As you may recall, the PRINTDLG structure contains information Windows uses to initialize the Print Setup dialog box presented to the user for printer selection. After the user selects a printer and closes the dialog box, information concerning the user defined print parameters is returned in the PRINTDLG structure. One member of the PRINTDLG structure, hDevMode, contains a handle to an initialized DEVMODE structure stored in memory. A DEVMODE structure contains information about a printer driver's initialization and environment data. From the DEVMODE structure, the orientation of the selected paper, an identifier indicating the dimensions of the selected paper and the width and length of the selected paper can be extracted. Many other items of information about the selected printer could also be extracted from this structure but are unneeded by the programs in this book. Note: The Win32 version of the DEVMODE structure is substantially different from the Win16 version. Much more information is contained in the DEVMODE structure in the Win32 environment.

A handle to a DEVNAMES structure is also returned in PRINTDLG. A DEV-NAMES structure contains strings that identify the print driver name, the name of the printer, and the name of the output port assigned for the selected printer. These items are used in creating a device context for the selected printer using the Windows **CreateDC** function.

Figure 3.4 has a short description of each of the functions provided in the PrintDialog class. How these functions are implemented can be seen in Listing 3.2. For more information about the contents of the PRINTDLG, DEVMODE, and DEV-NAMES structures, consult help in your programming environment.

Conclusions

In this chapter, you have been exposed to the common dialog box functions provided by Windows and to the common dialog box classes I wrote that encapsulate the common dialog box API provided by Windows. It is hoped that the reasons for using the extended common dialog box classes provided are obvious. Besides being portable to various programming environments, the classes are much easier to understand and to use than some of the vendor-provided classes. Lastly, the functionality provided by the class PrintDialog greatly extends the power of PrintDlg by incorporating many functions that are required whenever WYSIWYG printing is to be performed.

An Architecture for Graphic Image File I/O

In this chapter you will learn about:
- Storage requirements of bit-mapped images
- Graphic image file types and image compression
- The graphic image file library class hierarchy supporting BMP (and THM), GIF, and TIF files
- The BMP graphic file format
- Using the graphic image file library

Introduction

Access to graphic image files is a necessity for all imaging application programs. Regardless of how images are acquired (from a video digitizer, drawn in a paint program, produced by a ray tracer, output from a CAD program or input from a scanner), the images must be saved in some sort of graphic file format for manipulation, use, and exchange. Many different graphic file formats are in use today, too many even to list exhaustively. Examples in the PC world include PCX, IMG, BMP, GIF, WMF, JPEG in JFIF, TGA, TIF, and so on. Whole books have been written devoted solely to understanding the formats of these file and how to read and write them. Some of these books are listed in Appendix B "Further Reading."

Professional imaging applications must support the majority of the graphic file formats in use in industry today for the application to be considered complete. To further complicate matters, many of these formats allow monochrome, palettized, and true color image variations each compressed with different algorithms including run length encoding, LZW compression, discrete cosine transforms, and so on. In addition, most applications must both read and write these file formats. The net result is hundreds of different graphic file permutations that must be taken into consideration.

If you are planning to develop a professional imaging application, my advice to you is to buy a library of graphics file functions instead of developing your own. There are many products on the market that are very complete (and very high performance) libraries of functions for reading, writing, and manipulation of graphic image files. These libraries come in a variety of formats such as object files for direct linking into your application or DLLs for use in the Windows environment. Keep in mind that reading and writing graphic image files is just one relatively small facet of your imaging application, whereas it is the bread and butter for the companies that provide the function libraries. Ask yourself this question, "Whose function library is going to be more complete, yours or theirs?" Also, how much software development can you or your company afford to do for the $500 to $2,000 these companies charge for a royalty free license? I think the answers to these questions are obvious.

If you decide to develop your own library (as was done in this chapter), an object-oriented approach is suggested. The processing of graphics files maps very well into C++ object schema; in fact, it is almost a textbook example. In the approach taken here, a base class called Image was developed that contains all of the data and functions common to all types of graphics files for reading and writing disk files, allocating memory for images, recording image information, and so on. Each specific type of graphics file, such as BMP (and THM), GIF, and TIF inherits Image. Additionally, a manager class was created, called *Compand* (for image *Comp*ressor/Exp*and*er), which instantiates the proper type of graphic file object (referred to as a *Codec*) needed to read or write an image file of the required type. This has turned out to be a very clean approach to take. All of the code for the graphic file library is contained within a single DLL with a C++ interface. This makes the application code more maintainable because all of the code required to read and write graphic image files is modularized and segregated into a separate DLL and therefore is not mixed in with and mixed up with the application's code.

This chapter focuses more on describing the architecture for a graphic file library than it does on implementing all useful file formats. The library is designed in accordance with the imaging system architecture described in Chapter 1 in that it reads and writes image data in DIB format; that is, an image's data in DIB format and its accompanying palette are required to write a graphic image file. Conversely, reading a graphic image file results in a block of memory containing the image in DIB format and a palette for image display.

As mentioned in Chapter 2, the DIB format (under Win16) places the origin of the image at the lower left corner of the image data, resulting in an inverted raster format (the bottom of an image is located at a lower address in memory). For this reason, most image file formats require the inversion of the raster data when reading and writing the data from/to a file. While Win32 does not force the origin to the lower left corner of the raster data as does Win16, images are handled the same way under Win32 for compatibility reasons.

In terms of code, this chapter provides a simple yet general purpose, extremely easy to use graphic file library implemented in the form of a Windows DLL (dynamic link library) that can read and write BMP (Windows standard), THM (used for thumbnail images as described in Chapter 10), GIF, and TIF image files in monochrome, palettized, and true color formats (except GIF, which does not support true color). Note: THM files are my own invention and are 256-color BMP files with a ".THM" file extension instead of a ".BMP" file extension so that they can be uniquely identified.

For brevity sake, not all of the code that makes up the graphic file library appears in this chapter. A discussion of the BMP file format and all of the BMP code will be shown to give you an idea of how the graphic file library works. There will not be any discussion of the GIF or TIF file formats in this chapter. If you desire information on these and other graphic file formats, please consult the books *Practical Image Processing in C* and *Practical Ray Tracing in C,* both published by John Wiley & Sons, Inc., New York, N.Y. If you are interested in detailed specifications of the various file formats, they are typically available for download from major bulletin boards, CompuServe, and/or Internet. Of course, all of the code for support of BMP, THM, GIF, and TIF files is provided on the companion disk for your viewing pleasure and use. See Appendix A.

Indeed, the support of BMP, GIF, and TIF image files is a small subset of the graphic file formats in use today. However, this library was designed to be easily extendible so that any other graphic file formats you desire can be added. If you are interested in an extended version of this library (based on the same architecture) that supports PCX, IMG, and JPEG in addition to BMP, GIF, and TIF, contact the author directly for details.

Two important facts about the graphic file library presented in this chapter are:

1. The code can only process graphic image files that have the correct filename extension for the graphic file type; for example, BMP files must have a ".BMP" extension, THM files must have a ".THM" extension, GIF files must have a ".GIF" extension, and TIF files must have a ".TIF" filename extension. In other words, automatic recognition of the image file types is not supported.
2. The code in its present form does not support the reading or writing of compressed BMP files.

Keep these facts in mind if you decide to use the code presented.

Storage Requirements of Bit-Mapped Images

When adding imaging capability to an application program, two important factors come into play:

1. The size and number of the image files needing to be stored on disk
2. The amount of memory required for manipulation of the images once they are in memory

A desktop flatbed scanner, for example, is capable of generating image files of extreme size. To give you an idea of just how big image files can become, two tables are provided. These tables record approximate uncompressed image sizes for various numbers of bits per pixel (BPP) and various resolutions from 72 to 1,200 dots per inch (DPI). Each table assumes a constant document size. The first table gives image sizes, in bytes, for a scanned 4- × 5-inch photograph. The second table shows the sizes when a full 8.5- × 11-inch page is scanned. The numbers are amazing, aren't they? Note: The actual size of the images if they were to be stored on disk would probably be larger than what is shown here because each graphic image file format contains overhead information that must be stored in the file in addition to the image raster data.

For a 4- × 5-inch color photograph:

Resolution in DPI	1 BPP	4 BPP	8 BPP	24 BPP
72	12,960	51,840	103,680	311,040
100	25,000	100,000	200,000	600,000
150	56,250	225,000	450,000	1,350,000
300	225,000	900,000	1,800,000	5,400,000
500	625,000	2,500,000	5,000,000	15,000,000
600	900,000	3,600,000	7,200,000	21,600,000
1200	3,600,000	14,400,000	28,800,000	86,400,000

For an 8.5- × 11-inch full page:

Resolution in DPI	1 BPP	4 BPP	8 BPP	24 BPP
72	60,588	242,352	484,704	1,454,112
100	116,875	467,500	935,000	2,805,000
150	262,969	1,051,875	2,103,750	6,311,250
300	1,051,875	4,207,500	8,415,000	25,245,000
500	2,921,875	11,687,500	23,375,000	70,125,000
600	4,207,500	16,830,000	33,660,000	100,980,000
1200	16,830,000	67,320,000	134,640,000	403,920,000

From these tables, you can see why scanning at the correct resolution for a specific application is important (said another way, why scanning at a resolution too high for an application can be detrimental) and why image file compression is required for storing scanned images. Another bit of information to glean from these tables is the quantity of image information that must be processed within an application when high-resolution true color (24 BPP) images are manipulated and displayed. Given the amount of data needing manipulation, you can appreciate why many image processing algorithms applied to images appear to be slow.

Graphic Image File Types and Image Compression

Given how large graphic image files can be (and the situation will only get worse), some form of image data compression is usually required for storing images. Even with the cost of large hard disk drives plummeting, it doesn't take too many uncompressed images to fill up even the largest drive. The 650Mb available on a typical CD-ROM can just as quickly be eaten up if high resolution uncompressed images are stored onto it. Given that image compression is a must, a decision must be made on which type of image compression to use for specific applications. This decision must be based on a couple of different factors including:

- The fidelity requirements of the image after compression and subsequent expansion. Some compression techniques, such as JPEG, use a lossy compression process (using a discrete cosine transform) that actually discards some of the (less visible, high frequency) image data as part of the compression process. This data is not recoverable later when the image is expanded; it has been lost. The loss in image fidelity must be traded off against the incredible amounts of compression JPEG can offer. It is not uncommon to achieve a compression ratio of 50:1. Lossless compression schemes, in contrast, retain all of the image data so there is no degradation of image fidelity but have much lower compression ratios; 5:1 is typical.
- Speed of image data access. This really means how fast images can be compressed and how fast they can be later expanded. Some compression schemes are much faster than others with lossless methods generally faster than lossy methods. The JPEG compression/expansion, implemented entirely in software, for example, takes a considerable amount of time for high-resolution images. Other compression/expansion algorithms are not balanced in terms of processing requirements. A certain fractal image compression method, for example, takes a considerable amount of time to compress an image of reasonable size (3 to 4 minutes) but is blazing fast when decompressing (3 to 4 seconds).

As you can appreciate, these two goals (maximum image compression versus speed of image data access) are somewhat mutually exclusive. Unless you have some blatant, overriding requirement to minimize image storage at all cost with the image access time a secondary concern, it can sometimes be difficult to choose which compression technique to use.

Fortunately (or unfortunately depending on your perspective), with the simple graphic image file library presented in this chapter, you do not have to make choices of which compression techniques to use because the choice has been made for you. If you use the graphic library to write BMP files, no image compression is performed. Similarly, a lossless compression technique called *LZW* is used whenever GIF or TIF files are written. LZW provides moderate image compression without too much processing overhead to slow it down. For information on how LZW works its magic, see the books cited in the introduction to this chapter and listed in Appendix B "Further Reading."

The Graphic Image File Library Class Hierarchy

All of the classes that play a part in reading and writing graphic image files are shown pictorially in Figure 4.1. The important things to notice on this diagram are that:

1. All of the code for reading and writing graphic image files is contained in a single DLL called "compand.dll."
2. All interface between the Compand DLL and an application program is through the very well-defined and controlled C++ Compand class interface. An application never interacts with any other portion of the graphics code either directly or indirectly. Further, an application program never has to deal directly with image files, only with an object of the Compand class.

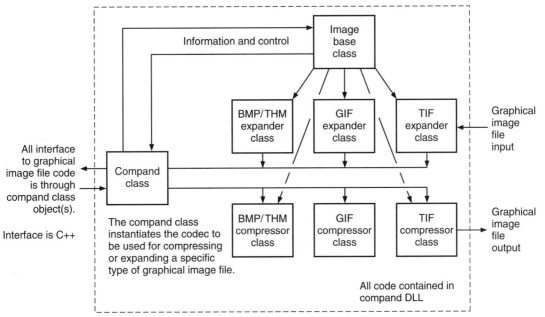

FIGURE 4.1 The Compand class organization.

3. The Compand class instantiates an appropriate Codec (Coder/Decoder) for processing the type of graphic file requested by the application program. Only one Codec is ever instantiated by the Compand class at one time. Codecs exist for reading and writing BMP (and THM) files, GIF files, and TIF files.

4. All Codecs inherent the Image base class. Execution of code within a Codec is through virtual functions in the base class. The base class controls the memory for the image raster data and image palette.

5. Although only three file formats are currently supported, others could be added using the architecture illustrated.

For your reference, Figure 4.2 describes the member functions of the Compand class and Listings 4.1 and 4.2 show the code. A careful inspection of Listing 4.2 should give you a complete understanding of the architecture used in this graphic image file library.

Listing 4.1 The Compand class interface definition.

```
/**********************************************************/
/***                   "compand.hpp"                 ***/
/***      Compressor/Expander Class Definition File  ***/
/***                   written by                    ***/
/***                Craig A. Lindley                 ***/
/***                                                 ***/
/***      Revision: 2.0    Last Update: 11/11/94     ***/
/**********************************************************/

// Copyright (c) 1995 John Wiley & Sons, Inc. All rights reserved.
```

```
    // Check to see if this file already included
    #ifndef COMPAND_HPP
    #define COMPAND_HPP
    #include "image.hpp"        // This must always be available

    #ifndef __WIN32__           // If 16 bit code

    #ifdef __DLL__
    #  define EXPORT _export
    #else
    #  define EXPORT huge
    #endif

    #else                       // If 32 bit code

    #ifdef __DLL__
    #  define EXPORT _export
    #else
    #  define EXPORT
    #endif

    #endif

    // Misc type defintions
    enum CompandOp    {NOOP, COMPRESS, EXPAND, VERIFY};
    enum CompandType {NOTYPE, SAMETYPE, BMPTYPE, THMTYPE, TIFTYPE, GIFTYPE};

    // class __declspec(dllexport) Compand {
    class EXPORT Compand {
      private:
        // Private data
        CompandOp CompanderOp;
        CompandType CompanderType;
        ImgType ImageType;
        BOOL CompanderInitialized;
        BOOL ImageExpanded;
        WORD CompressionQuality;
        Image *Codec;               // Ptr to compander type

        // Private member functions
        void DoOp(void);

      public:
        FAR Compand(void);
         virtual FAR ~Compand(void);
        // This is the initialization for compression
        BOOL FAR InitCompressor(CompandType CompType, LPSTR Filename, WORD Width,
                        WORD Height, WORD BitsPerPixel, WORD NumOfColors,
                        BYTE huge *RasterDataPtr,
                        RGBCOLOR *PalettePtr);
        // This is the initialization for expansion
        BOOL FAR InitExpander(LPSTR Filename);
        CompandType FAR GetCompressionType(void) { return CompanderType; }
        BOOL FAR DoCompression(void);
        BOOL FAR DoExpansion(void);
        BYTE huge * FAR GetDataPtr(void);
```

```
    RGBCOLOR * FAR GetPalettePtr(void);
    WORD FAR GetWidth(void);
    WORD FAR GetHeight(void);
    WORD FAR GetColors(void);
    WORD FAR GetBitsPerPixel(void);
    void FAR DisposeOfImage(void);
    void FAR SetCompressionQuality(WORD Quality) { CompressionQuality =
      Quality; }
    void FAR SetImageType(ImgType Type) { ImageType = Type; }

    CompandType FAR FileTypeFromName(LPSTR FileName);
    BOOL FAR FileNameFromType(LPSTR FileName, CompandType Type);

  int FAR GetError(void);
};

#endif
```

Listing 4.2 The Compand class member functions.

```
/*************************************************************/
/***                   "compand.cpp"                  ***/
/***         Compressor/Expander Class Functions      ***/
/***                   written by                     ***/
/***                 Craig A. Lindley                 ***/
/***                                                  ***/
/***       Revision: 2.0     Last Update: 11/11/94    ***/
/*************************************************************/

// Copyright (c) 1995 John Wiley & Sons, Inc. All rights reserved.

#include <windows.h>
#include <io.h>
#include <string.h>
#include "compand.hpp"
#include "bmp.hpp"
#include "gif.hpp"
#include "tif.hpp"
#include "defines.h"

/*
The compand class works with many graphic file formats. Monochrome, 16 color, 256
color and true color images are supported. Images can be of any
spatial resolution.
*/

static HANDLE DLLInstance;

Compand::Compand(void) {

  CompanderInitialized = FALSE;
  Codec = NULL;
  CompanderType = NOTYPE;
  CompanderOp   = NOOP;
  ImageExpanded = FALSE;
  ImageType = NOIMAGE;
```

The Compand Class

Purpose

The Compand (*Comp*ressor/Exp*and*er) class manages the interaction between an application program and the code for performing reading and writing of graphics files. Use of the Compand class isolates a programmer from the intricacies of the graphics file code. The Compand class instantiates and manages an object of the type required to compress or expand a graphics image file. When used for writing graphics files, a Compand object gets the image parameters from the calling application (including a pointer to the DIB image data in memory) and stores the image as a file according to the specified parameters. When used for reading graphics files, a Compand object reads the specified graphics file and converts it into DIB format in memory it owns. An application program then queries the Compand object for the image specifications and the image data. In any case, memory allocated by a Compand object is released when the object goes out of scope.

Member Functions

Compand.   This is the class constructor that is executed when an object of the Compand class is instantiated. Its function is to initialize class variables as required for correct operation of the Compand object. Codec, the most important class variable, is a pointer to an object derived from the Image class that will actually perform the image compression or expansion. It must be initialized to NULL within the constructor for proper operation.

~Compand.   This is the class destructor. Its only function is to delete the Codec if a Codec has been instantiated.

InitCompressor.   This member function of the Compand class must be called with all of the parameters describing an image before the image can be compressed and stored on disk. The call to this function must occur after the Compand object is instantiated but before the call to **DoCompression** is made. Parameters to this function include a specifier for the type of graphics file to produce, the filename to be assigned to the graphics file, and the image parameters (including the width in pixels, the height in pixels, the number of BPP, and the number of image colors). The final parameter is a pointer to the image's raster data in DIB format. This function returns Boolean TRUE if successful and FALSE if not. If this function is successful, a Codec is assigned for compression of the image.

InitExpander.   This member function is called when a Compand object is to be used for expanding a graphics file. This function is passed a filename (actually path and filename) of the graphics file to be expanded. This function returns Boolean TRUE if successful and FALSE if not. If this function is successful, the image file has been located, and a Codec has been assigned for expansion of the image.

GetCompressionType.   This in-line member function returns the type of image being managed by the Compand object. Valid types include NOTYPE (meaning an unsupported or unknown file type), BMPTYPE, THMTYPE, TIFTYPE, and GIFTYPE.

DoCompression.   This member function is called (with no parameters) to perform the actual image compression (and storage) process. All parameters for the compression were stored away during the execution of the **InitCompressor** function

FIGURE 4.2 The Compand class.

described earlier. This function returns Boolean TRUE if the image was successfully compressed and stored and FALSE if not.

DoExpansion. This member function is called (with no parameters) to perform expansion of an image from a disk file (or other storage medium). The filename of the image to be expanded was stored away during the execution of the **InitExpander** function described earlier. This function returns Boolean TRUE if the image was successfully expanded by the Compand object and FALSE if an error occurred during expansion.

GetDataPtr. This function returns a pointer to the just expanded image's raster data. The pointer returned is huge in Win16 and a regular 32 bit pointer in Win32. All rows of the raster data to which this pointer points are aligned and zero padded to a double word boundary.

GetPalettePtr. This function returns a pointer to the just expanded image's palette. Palette in this context is an array of RGBCOLOR entries, not a logical palette as required by Windows.

GetWidth. This function returns the width of an expanded image in pixels.

GetHeight. This function returns the height of an expanded image in pixels.

GetColors. This function returns the number of colors in an expanded palettized image or zero for true color, 24 BPP images.

GetBitsPerPixel. This function returns the number of bits per pixel used in the expanded image. An image with 8 BPP would return eight, for example.

DisposeOfImage. Whenever this function is called, the memory allocated for an image managed by a Compand object is freed.

SetCompressionQuality. This function is used to specify a level of compression to be applied to an image's raster data during the image file compression process. However, none of the graphic file formats supported in this book support variable compression. This function is included for future functionality enhancements such as managing JPEG file compression.

SetImageType. This function sets the type of image managed by the Compand object. Valid types include NOIMAGE, MONOCHROME, PALETTECOLOR, and TRUECOLOR. This function is typically called just before an image is compressed into a file.

FileTypeFromName. This function determines and returns the type of graphics file contained in the specified filename. Valid return types include NOTYPE (meaning an unsupported or unknown file type or a filename with no extension), BMPTYPE, THMTYPE, TIFTYPE, and GIFTYPE. As mentioned in the text, all graphic files processed by the Compand class must have file extensions that are valid for the file type. For example, a BMP file called "MYFILE" would return NOTYPE from this function because it does not have a ".BMP" file extension.

FileNameFromType. This function adds the proper extension for the specified file type onto a filename passed as a parameter; for example, if BMPTYPE is specified and the filename is "MYFILE.XXX", a call to this function will change the filename to "MYFILE.BMP". Note: *The storage area containing the original filename must be large enough to accommodate the addition of the file extension to the filename.*

GetError. If an error occurs during image compression or expansion, this function can be called to ascertain the cause. All possible error codes are described in the file "errors.h" and shown in Figure 4.5.

FIGURE 4.2 *(Continued)*

```
          CompressionQuality = 50;          // Default quality level
        }

        Compand::~Compand(void) {

          // Release the codec class on exit
          if (Codec != NULL)
            delete Codec;
        }

        // This is the initialization for the expander function. NOTE: the expander
        // is capable of reading more graphic file formats then the compressor
        // can write.

        BOOL Compand::InitExpander(LPSTR FileName) {
          if (Codec != NULL) {                // If a previous codec exists
            DisposeOfImage();                 // Free expansion buffer
            delete Codec;                     // free it and reinitialized
            Codec = NULL;                     // the pertinent variables
            CompanderInitialized = FALSE;
            CompanderType = NOTYPE;
            CompanderOp   = NOOP;
        }

        strupr(FileName);                     // All chars to upper case
        // Check file extension for file type
        if ((strstr(FileName,(LPSTR) ".GIF") == NULL) &&
            (strstr(FileName,(LPSTR) ".BMP") == NULL) &&
            (strstr(FileName,(LPSTR) ".THM") == NULL) &&
            (strstr(FileName,(LPSTR) ".TIF") == NULL))
          return FALSE;                       // Unsupported file type

        if (access(FileName, 0) != 0)   // Does specified file exist ?
          return FALSE;                       // Return if not

        if (strstr(FileName,(LPSTR) ".GIF")) {   // Its a GIF image file
          Codec = new ExpandGIF(FileName);
          CompanderType = GIFTYPE;
        } else

        if (strstr(FileName,(LPSTR) ".BMP") ||   // Its a BMP image file
            strstr(FileName,(LPSTR) ".THM")) {   // or a THM file
          Codec = new ExpandBMP(FileName);
          CompanderType = BMPTYPE;
        } else

        if (strstr(FileName,(LPSTR) ".TIF")) {   // Its a TIF image file
            Codec = new ExpandTIF(FileName);
            CompanderType = TIFTYPE;
        }

        CompanderOp = EXPAND;
        CompanderInitialized = TRUE;
        return TRUE;
        }
```

```
// This is the initialization for the compression function. NOTE: The
// filename passed in will have the extension truncated and replaced
// with extension specifying the compression used.
BOOL Compand::InitCompressor(CompandType CompType, LPSTR FileName, WORD Width,
                WORD Height, WORD BitsPerPixel, WORD NumOfColors,
                                            BYTE huge *RasterDataPtr,
                RGBCOLOR *PalettePtr) {

LPSTR ExtPtr;
/*
Remove any specified file extensions provided. Compressor
will append the proper extension and return it to the application.
*/
strupr(FileName);       // All chars to upper case
if ((ExtPtr = strchr(FileName,'.')) != NULL)
     *ExtPtr = '\0';

if (Codec !=NULL) {             // If a previous codec exists
  delete Codec;                 // free it and reinitialized
  Codec = NULL;                 // the pertinent variables
  CompanderInitialized = FALSE;
  CompanderType = NOTYPE;
  CompanderOp = NOOP;
}
switch(CompType)  {             // Determine type of compression

  case BMPTYPE:
  case THMTYPE:
    Codec = new
              CompressBMP(FileName, (CompType == BMPTYPE),
RasterDataPtr,PalettePtr,Width,Height,BitsPerPixel,NumOfColors);
     break;
       case GIFTYPE:
            Codec = new

CompressGIF(FileName,RasterDataPtr,PalettePtr,Width,Height,BitsPerPixel,Num
  OfColors); break;

     case TIFTYPE:
    Codec = new
      CompressTIF(FileName,RasterDataPtr,PalettePtr,Width,Height,
        BitsPerPixel,NumOfColors); break;

     case NOTYPE:
     case SAMETYPE:
     default:
           return FALSE;
  }
  // If we get here all is well
  CompanderOp = COMPRESS;         // The operation is compression
  CompanderType = CompType;       // Save the compression type
  CompanderInitialized = TRUE;    // Indicate initialization has/is happening
  return TRUE;
}
```

```
BOOL Compand::DoCompression(void)   {
  BOOL Result = FALSE;

  if ((!CompanderInitialized) || (CompanderOp==EXPAND))
    return Result;

  Result = Codec->CompressImage(CompressionQuality, ImageType);
  CompanderInitialized = FALSE;    // Force reinit
  return(Result);
}

BOOL Compand::DoExpansion(void) {
  BOOL Result = FALSE;

  if ((!CompanderInitialized) || (CompanderOp==COMPRESS))
    return Result;

  Result = Codec->ExpandImage();
  ImageExpanded = TRUE;                 // Indicate image has been expanded
  CompanderInitialized = FALSE;    // Force reinit
  return(Result);
}

// Return a huge pointer to the raster data
BYTE huge *Compand::GetDataPtr(void) {

  return(Codec->GetImageDataPtr());
}

// Return a huge pointer to the palette data
RGBCOLOR *Compand::GetPalettePtr(void) {

  return (Codec->GetImagePalettePtr());
}

void Compand::DisposeOfImage(void) {

  if (ImageExpanded) {
    Codec->DeAllocImageBuffer();
    ImageExpanded = FALSE;
  }
}

WORD Compand::GetWdith(void) {
  return (Codec->GetWidth());
}

WORD Compand::GetHeight(void) {

  return (Codec->GetHeight());
}

WORD Compand::GetColors(void) {
```

```
    return (Codec->GetNumOfColors());
}

WORD Compand::GetBitsPerPixel(void) {

  return (Codec->GetBitsPerPixel());
}

int Compand::GetError(void) {

  return(Codec->GetError());
}

// Return the filetype from the filename.
CompandType Compand::FileTypeFromName(LPSTR FileName) {

  if (FileName[0] == '\0')        // Return immediately for NULL filenames
    return NOTYPE;

  strupr(FileName);               // All chars of filename to upper case
  // Check file extension for file type
  if (strstr(FileName,(LPSTR) ".GIF"))
    return GIFTYPE;
  else
  if (strstr(FileName,(LPSTR) ".BMP"))
    return BMPTYPE;
  else
  if (strstr(FileName,(LPSTR) ".THM"))
    return THMTYPE;
  else
  if (strstr(FileName,(LPSTR) ".TIF"))
    return TIFTYPE;
  else
    return NOTYPE;
}

BOOL Compand::FileNameFromType(LPSTR FileName, CompandType Type) {

  // Append the proper file extension to the filename
  // If the filename has an extension, locate the position of the
  // period. No truncation of filename will take place if improper
  // type is specified.

  if (FileName[0] == '\0')        // Return immediately for NULL filenames
    return FALSE;

  LPSTR PeriodPtr = strchr(FileName,'.');

  // Now append the proper file extension
  switch(Type) {
    case BMPTYPE:
      if (PeriodPtr != NULL)      // Truncate filename at period
        *PeriodPtr = '\0';
      lstrcat(FileName, ".BMP");  // Append the file extension
```

```
            return TRUE;
        case THMTYPE:
          if (PeriodPtr != NULL)      // Truncate filename at period
            *PeriodPtr = '\0';
          lstrcat(FileName, ".THM");  // Append the file extension
          return TRUE;
        case TIFTYPE:
          if (PeriodPtr != NULL)      // Truncate filename at period
            *PeriodPtr = '\0';
          lstrcat(FileName, ".TIF");  // Append the file extension
          return TRUE;
        case GIFTYPE:
          if (PeriodPtr !=NULL)       // Truncate filename at period
            *PeriodPtr = '\0';
          lstrcat(FileName, ".GIF");  // Append the file extension
          return TRUE;
        default:
          return FALSE;
    }
}


// The following two functions are used for message output
// from the string table resource bound to this DLL.

char *String(WORD MsgNumber, WORD BufferIndex) {
  static char szBuffer[2][256];    // Room for two messages

  LoadString(DLLInstance, MsgNumber, (LPSTR) szBuffer[BufferIndex], 255);
  return ((LPSTR) szBuffer[BufferIndex]);
}

void ErrorMessage(WORD ErrorNumber) {
  MessageBox(NULL, String(ErrorNumber, 1),
                   String(IDS_ERROR, 0), MB_OK|MB_ICONEXCLAMATION);
}

#ifdef __WIN32__
// Entry point for Compand DLL
BOOL WINAPI DllEntryPoint (HINSTANCE hinstDLL, DWORD /*fdwReason*/, LPVOID
  /*lpvReserved*/) {

  // Just save the instance handle
  DLLInstance = hinstDLL;
  return TRUE;
}
#else

// Library entry point for initialization
int CALLBACK LibMain (HANDLE hInst, WORD, WORD wHeapSize, LPSTR) {

  DLLInstance = hInst;

  if (wHeapSize > 0)
    UnlockData (0);
```

```
  return 1;
}

int CALLBACK WEP(int) {

  return(1);
}
#endif
```

Figure 4.3 describes the member functions of the Image class, which is the base class that all Codecs inherit and use. Listings 4.3 and 4.4 show the Image class code for your reference. Finally, Figure 4.4 describes the member functions of the BMP classes while Listings 4.5 and 4.6 show the code. As mentioned, GIF and TIF classes are also provided in addition to the BMP classes, but they are not shown or discussed in the chapter.

Listing 4.3 The Image class interface definition.

```
/*********************************************************/
/***                    "image.hpp"                  ***/
/***            Image Class Definition File          ***/
/***                    written by                   ***/
/***                 Craig A. Lindley                ***/
/***                                                 ***/
/***      Revision: 2.0     Last Update: 11/11/94    ***/
/*********************************************************/

// Copyright (c) 1995 John Wiley & Sons, Inc. All rights reserved.

#ifndef IMAGE_HPP
#define IMAGE_HPP
#include "errors.h"      // Include the error codes

#ifdef __WIN32__
#define huge
#endif

#define MAX256PALETTECOLORS 256 // Number of colors expected.
#define ALIGN_DWORD(x) (((x)+3)/4 * 4) // Double word alignment macro

#ifndef __RGBCOLOR
#define __RGBCOLOR
typedef struct {
  BYTE Red;
  BYTE Green;
  BYTE Blue;
} RGBCOLOR;
#endif

enum ImgType {NOIMAGE, MONOCHROME, PALETTECOLOR, TRUECOLOR};

// Image base class definition
class Image {
  private:
```

```
      HGLOBAL         hRasterData;
      HGLOBAL         hPalette;
      BYTE huge       *hpRasterData;
      RGBCOLOR        *lpPalette;
      BYTE            FileBuf[5120];      // 10 sector file buffer
      int             nIndex;             // Used in ReadByte/WriteByte
      int             iDataBytes;         // functions

   protected:
      HFILE           hFile;              // Input/Output file handle
      char            FileName[256];      // Storage for filename
      int             iError;
      WORD            wWidth;             // Dimensions of image
      WORD            wHeight;
      WORD            wColors;            // Number of colors
      WORD            wBitsPerPixel;      // Number of bits per pixel in the image
      DWORD           lRasterSize;
      DWORD           dwAppRasterSize;    // Approx total size of image in bytes

   // Protected member functions
      BOOL AllocImageBuffer(WORD Width, WORD Height);
public:
   Image();
   virtual         ~Image();
   virtual         BOOL CompressImage(WORD Quality, enum ImgType Type);
   virtual         BOOL ExpandImage(void);
   void            DeAllocImageBuffer(void);
   POINT           GetSize(void);
   void            SetSize(POINT Pt)          { wWidth = (WORD) Pt.x; wHeight =
                                                  (WORD) Pt.y; }
   WORD            GetWidth(void)             { return wWidth; }
   void            SetWidth(WORD Width)       { wWidth = Width; }
   WORD            GetHeight(void)            { return wHeight; }
   void            SetHeight(WORD Height)     { wHeight = Height; }
   WORD            GetNumOfColors(void)       { return wColors; }
   void            SetNumOfColors(WORD Colors) { wColors = Colors; }
   WORD            GetBitsPerPixel(void)      { return wBitsPerPixel; }
   void            SetBitsPerPixel(WORD BPP)  { wBitsPerPixel = BPP; }
   BYTE huge       *GetImageDataPtr(void)     { return hpRasterData; }
   void            SetDataPtr(BYTE huge *Ptr) { hpRasterData = Ptr; }
   DWORD           GetAppRasterSize(void)     { return dwAppRasterSize; }
   RGBCOLOR        *GetImagePalettePtr(void)  { return lpPalette; }
   void            SetPalettePtr(RGBCOLOR *Ptr) { lpPalette = Ptr; }
   int             GetError(void)             { return iError; }

   // File I/O functions
   BOOL            OpenReadFile(LPSTR FileName);
   BOOL            OpenWriteFile(LPSTR FileName);
   BOOL            CloseFile(void);
   BYTE            ReadByte(void);
   BOOL            ReadMBytes(BYTE huge *Buffer, DWORD Number);
   BOOL            WriteByte(BYTE TheByte);
   BOOL            WriteMBytes(BYTE huge *Buffer, DWORD Number);
   BOOL            FlushWriteFile(void);
};
#endif
```

The Image class

Purpose

The Image class is the base class from which all Codecs (*Coders/Decoders*) for the various graphic file formats are derived. This class encapsulates all of the information about a image file necessary for its management. In addition, this class contains a collection of buffered, low-level file input and output code that may optionally be used during the processing of graphic image files.

Member Functions

Image.   This is the class constructor. Its function is to initialize all of the class variables to known values and to allocate memory for a 256-color palette structure. This constructor is called automatically whenever an object derived from this class is instantiated.

~Image.   This class destructor frees any memory associated with this image instance and releases the memory allocated by the constructor for the 256-color palette.

AllocImageBuffer.   This function allocates and locks a block of memory for image storage. Parameters to this function include Width (which in this case is the number of bytes of image data per row, taking into consideration the number of bits per pixel) and Height, which is the number of rows of image data. The actual size of the allocated memory block is the calculated required size plus a 256-byte pad just for good measure. This function returns TRUE if the image memory was allocated successfully and FALSE if not.

DeAllocImageBuffer.   This function unlocks and frees any memory allocated by the earlier function. If no memory has been allocated, this function does nothing.

CompressImage.   This virtual function is a placeholder for a function of the same name in a derived class. C++ polymorphism is used to execute the actual **CompressImage** function (in the Codec being used for image file compression) at runtime when this function is called.

ExpandImage.   This virtual function is a placeholder for a function of the same name in a derived class. C++ polymorphism is used to execute the actual **ExpandImage** function (in the Codec being used for image file expansion) at runtime when this function is called.

GetSize.   This function returns the size in pixels of the image contained within the Image object. The value is returned in a POINT structure with the x member being the image width and the y member being the image height.

SetSize.   This function is used to set the dimensions of the image within the Image object.

GetWidth.   This function returns the width in pixels of the image contained within the Image object.

SetWidth.   This function sets the width in pixels of the image contained within the Image object.

GetHeight.   This function returns the height in pixels of the image contained within the Image object.

FIGURE 4.3 The Image class.

SetHeight.   This function sets the height in pixels of the image contained within the Image object.

GetNumOfColors.   This function returns the number of colors used by the image contained within the Image object.

SetNumOfColors.   This function sets the number of colors to be used by the image contained within the Image object.

GetBitsPerPixel.   This function returns the number of bits per pixel being used by the image contained within the Image object.

SetBitsPerPixel.   This function sets the number of bits per pixel to be used by the image contained within the Image object.

GetImageDataPtr.   This function returns a pointer to the memory allocated for the image's raster data.

SetDataPtr.   This function sets the pointer to be returned when the previous function is called.

GetAppRasterSize.   This function returns the size of the block of memory allocated for holding the image's raster data.

GetImagePalettePtr.   This function returns a pointer to the memory allocated for storage of the image's palette. The palette memory was allocated by the constructor of this class.

SetPalettePtr.   This function sets the pointer to be returned when the previous function is called.

GetError.   Calling this function returns an error code for the last error encountered by the Image class code.

The functions that follow provide buffered low-level file I/O support for classes derived from Image. Use of these functions is not mandatory and are provided within the Image class for convenience only. See Listing 4.6 for example of their usage.

OpenReadFile.   This function opens the file whose name was passed as a parameter in preparation for reading data from the file.

OpenWriteFile.   This function opens the file whose name was passed as a parameter in preparation for writing data to the file. If a file by the specified name already exists, it will be overwritten.

CloseFile.   This function is called to close a file that was opened for reading or writing.

ReadByte.   This function reads the next byte of image data from the read file. This function provides buffered I/O in that the next byte will be read from memory if it is contained in the buffer FileBuf. If all of the data within FileBuf has already been read, FileBuf will be refilled by reading from the image file, allowing the next byte of the image data to be returned.

ReadMBytes.   This function reads a specified number of bytes from the read file into the buffer location specified. This function also supported buffered I/O because it calls **ReadByte** during its operation. This function is useful for reading whole structures from an image file into memory at one time.

WriteByte.   This function writes a byte of image data to the write file. This function provides buffered I/O in that the byte will not actually be written to the output file until the buffer, FileBuf, is completely full. At that time, all of the data in FileBuf is

FIGURE 4.3   *(Continued)*

written to disk in one operation. The **FlushWriteFile** function is necessary to guarantee that all image data destined for the write file actually gets there.

WriteMBytes.   This function writes a specified number of bytes from a specified buffer location to the write file. This function also supports buffered I/O because it calls **WriteByte** during its operation. This function is useful for writing whole structures to an image file at one time.

FlushWriteFile.   A call to this function guarantees that all image data contained in FileBuf is written to the write file. If this function is not called after writing all of the image data, the last portion of the data may be left behind in memory.

FIGURE 4.3 *(Continued)*

The BMP classes

Purpose

Two classes, ExpandBMP and CompressBMP, make up the BMP classes. The ExpandBMP class is instantiated as the Codec whenever the Compand class must expand a BMP graphic image file. The CompressBMP class is the Codec when BMP image file compression is required. Both of these classes are derived from the Image base class.

ExpandBMP Class Member Functions

ExpandBMP.   This is the class constructor. It expects a filename of an already existent BMP file. This function opens the file, verifies that the file is a BMP file by checking the type entry in the BITMAPFILEHEADER structure, reads the BITMAPINFOHEADER into a class variable, and then extracts the image parameters such as width, height, number of colors, and bits per pixel from the BITMAP-INFOHEADER. If an error occurs in parsing the BMP file information, an error message will be displayed in a Windows message box.

ExpandImage.   This function actually decodes the BMP file. It first allocates a block of memory by calling the function **AllocImageBuffer** in the base class, for holding the image raster data once it is read from the file. Next, this function reads the RGBQUAD color table entries from the BMP file and stores them into the palette storage area maintained in the base class. Finally, each row of image data is read from the file and stored in the memory allocated for image data storage. Win16 Note: Because raster data in a BMP file is stored upside down and because DIB image data in memory must be stored the same way, the image data can be moved directly from the file to memory without requiring the data inversion that all other graphic file formats require.

CompressBMP Class Member Functions

CompressBMP.   This class constructor is called in preparation for compressing a BMP graphic image file. For parameters, it requires a filename that is to be

FIGURE 4.4 The BMP classes.

assigned to the BMP file; a pointer to the image's DIB raster data; a pointer to the palette to be stored with the image; and the width, height, bits per pixel, and the number of colors to be assigned to the image.

WriteBMPHdr. This private member function is called by **CompressImage** to write all of the non-raster image information required in a valid BMP file. Specifically, the write file is opened, the BITMAPFILEHEADER structure is initialized with size and offset information, and is then written to the file. Next, a BITMAPINFOHEADER is filled with the specifications of the image to be stored, and it is written to disk. Finally, if the image being stored is palettized, an array of RGBQUAD color table entries are initialized with information from the image's palette. The color table entries are then written to the disk file following the BITMAPINFOHEADER. If the image is true color, no color table entries are made. This function returns NoError if all went well.

CompressImage. This function performs the actual writing of the BMP file to disk. In essence, this function performs a conversion from a DIB image and palette in memory to a BMP file on disk. First, it calls **WriteBMPHdr** to write all of the non-image data information to the file and then enters a loop writing each and every row of image data to the file.

FIGURE 4.4 *(Continued)*

Listing 4.4 The Image class member functions.

```
/***************************************************************/
/***                    "image.cpp"                      ***/
/***              Image Class Functions                  ***/
/***                   written by                        ***/
/***               Craig A. Lindley                      ***/
/***                                                     ***/
/***      Revision: 2.0     Last Update: 11/11/94        ***/
/***************************************************************/

// Copyright (c) 1995 John Wiley & Sons, Inc. All rights reserved.

#include <windows.h>
#include <io.h>
#include <mem.h>
#include "image.hpp"
#include "defines.h"

extern void ErrorMessage(WORD ErrorNumber);

/*
All other member functions are inline and contained in the
"image.hpp"file.
*/

/* Constructor for the image class */
Image::Image() {

  memset(FileName, 0, sizeof(FileName));
  iError       = NoError;
```

```
  wWidth        = 0;
  wHeight       = 0;
  wColors       = 0;
  wBitsPerPixel = 0;
  hFile         = 0;
  hRasterData   = 0;
  hpRasterData  = NULL;
  nIndex        = 0;
  iDataBytes    = 0;
  // Allocate memory for the palette
  hPalette = GlobalAlloc(GHND, sizeof(RGBCOLOR) * MAX256PALETTECOLORS);
  lpPalette = (RGBCOLOR *) GlobalLock(hPalette);
}

/* Destructor for the image class */
Image::~Image() {

  DeAllocImageBuffer();
  // Free the palette memory
  GlobalUnlock(hPalette);
  GlobalFree(hPalette);
}

// Return the size of the image in a POINT structure
POINT Image::GetSize() {
  POINT pt = {wWidth,wHeight};
  return pt;
}
BOOL Image::OpenReadFile(LPSTR FileName) {

  hFile = _lopen(FileName, OF_READ);
  if (hFile == HFILE_ERROR) {
    ErrorMessage(IDS_OPENFILEERROR);
    iError = EFileNotFound;
  }
  return (hFile != HFILE_ERROR);
}

BOOL Image::OpenWriteFile(LPSTR FileName) {
  OFSTRUCT ofs;

  hFile = OpenFile(FileName, (LPOFSTRUCT) &ofs, OF_CREATE);
  if (hFile == HFILE_ERROR) {
    ErrorMessage(IDS_OPENFILEERROR);
    iError = EOpeningFile;
  }
  return (hFile != HFILE_ERROR);
}

BOOL Image::CloseFile(void) {

  HFILE hCFile = _lclose(hFile);
  if (hCFile != 0) {
    ErrorMessage(IDS_CLOSEFILEERROR);
    iError = EClosingFile;
  }
```

```
      return(hCFile == 0);
   }

   // Read the next byte from the file buffer. Read file if necessary
   BYTE Image::ReadByte(void) {

     if (iDataBytes == 0) {
       if ((iDataBytes = _lread(hFile, FileBuf, sizeof(FileBuf))) <= 0) {
         ErrorMessage(IDS_ERRORREADINGIMAGEDATA);
         iError = ECorrupt;
       }
       nIndex = 0;
     }
     --iDataBytes;
     return(*(FileBuf+(nIndex++)));
   }


   //Read multiple byte entities from the input file
   BOOL Image::ReadMBytes(BYTE huge *Buffer, register DWORD Number) {
     register DWORD Index;

     Index = 0L;

     while (Number--) {
       if (iDataBytes == 0) {
         if ((iDataBytes = _lread(hFile, FileBuf, sizeof(FileBuf))) <= 0) {
           ErrorMessage(IDS_ERRORREADINGIMAGEDATA);
           iError = ECorrupt;
           return FALSE;
         }
         nIndex = 0;
       }
       --iDataBytes;
       Buffer[Index++] = *(FileBuf+(nIndex++));
     }
     return TRUE;
   }
   BOOL Image::WriteByte(BYTE TheByte) {

     if (nIndex == sizeof(FileBuf)) {
       if (_lwrite(hFile, (LPSTR) FileBuf, sizeof(FileBuf)) <= 0) {
         ErrorMessage(IDS_ERRORWRITINGIMAGEDATA);
         iError = EWrtOutFile;
         return FALSE;
       }
       nIndex = 0;
     }
     *(FileBuf+(nIndex++)) = TheByte;
     return TRUE;
   }

   // Write multiple byte entities to the output file
   BOOL Image::WriteMBytes(BYTE huge *Buffer, DWORD Number) {
     register DWORD Index;
```

```
        Index = 0L;

        while (Number--)
          if (!WriteByte(Buffer[Index++]))
            return FALSE;
        return TRUE;
}
// Flush the output write file
BOOL Image::FlushWriteFile(void) {

        if (_lwrite(hFile, (LPSTR) FileBuf, nIndex) <= 0) {
          ErrorMessage(IDS_FLUSHFILEERROR);
          iError = EWrtOutFile;
          return FALSE;
        }
        return TRUE;
}


/*
This function is called when the image decoder has determined
the size of the raster image. This function allocates a block
of memory of the required size and initializes a class data
member with the long pointer.
*/

BOOL Image::AllocImageBuffer(WORD Width, WORD Height) {

        wWidth = Width;        // Store in local data base
        wHeight = Height;

        DWORD dwBytesPerLine = ALIGN_DWORD(Width);
        dwAppRasterSize = dwBytesPerLine * (DWORD) Height;

        dwAppRasterSize += 256;      // Add a pad for safety

        // Allocate memory for the image buffer and get a far ptr to it
        hRasterData = GlobalAlloc(GHND, dwAppRasterSize);
        if (!hRasterData) {
          ErrorMessage(IDS_NOMEMORYERROR);
          iError = ENoMemory;
          return FALSE;
        }
        hpRasterData = (BYTE *) GlobalLock(hRasterData);
        return TRUE;
}

void Image::DeAllocImageBuffer(void) {
        if (hRasterData) {
          GlobalUnlock(hRasterData);
          GlobalFree(hRasterData);
          hRasterData = 0;
        }
}
```

```
// Should never get to these classes
BOOL Image::CompressImage(WORD, enum ImgType) {

  ErrorMessage(IDS_OPSERROR);
  return FALSE;
}


BOOL Image::ExpandImage(void) {

  ErrorMessage(IDS_OPSERROR);
  return FALSE;
}
```

Listing 4.5 The BMP class interface definition.

```
/********************************************************/
/***                    "bmp.hpp"                 ***/
/***              BMP class include file          ***/
/***                   written by                 ***/
/***                Craig A. Lindley              ***/
/***                                              ***/
/***        Revision: 2.0     Last Update: 11/11/94    ***/
/********************************************************/

// Copyright (c) 1995 John Wiley & Sons, Inc. All rights reserved.

#ifndef BMP_HPP
#define BMP_HPP

#include "image.hpp"

/* BMP File Structures and Defines */

// Class for BMP expansion
class ExpandBMP: public Image {
  private:
    BITMAPFILEHEADER BitMapFileHeader;
    BITMAPINFOHEADER BitMapInfoHeader;
    RGBQUAD bmiColors[MAX256PALETTECOLORS];

  public:
    ExpandBMP(LPSTR FileName);
    BOOL ExpandImage(void);
};

// Class for BMP compression
class CompressBMP: public Image {
  private:
    BITMAPFILEHEADER BitMapFileHeader;
    BITMAPINFOHEADER BitMapInfoHeader;
    RGBQUAD bmiColors[MAX256PALETTECOLORS];
    DWORD BytesPerLine;
    // Private functions
    int WriteBMPHdr(void);
```

```
  public:
    CompressBMP(LPSTR Name, BOOL ABMPFile, BYTE huge *RasterDataPtr,
                RGBCOLOR *PalettePtr, WORD Width, WORD Height,
                WORD BitsPerPixel, WORD NumOfColors);
    BOOL CompressImage(WORD Quality, enum ImgType Type);
};
#endif
```

Listing 4.6 The BMP class member functions.

```
/**********************************************************/
/***                    "bmp.cpp"                    ***/
/***               BMP Class Functions               ***/
/***                   written by                    ***/
/***                 Craig A. Lindley                ***/
/***                                                 ***/
/***       Revision: 2.0    Last Update: 11/11/94    ***/
/**********************************************************/

// Copyright (c) 1995 John Wiley & Sons, Inc. All rights reserved.

#include <string.h>
#include <windows.h>
#include "image.hpp"
#include "bmp.hpp"
#include "defines.h"

extern void ErrorMessage(WORD ErrorNumber);

// BMP class based upon Image class. It opens an already known to
// exist BMP or THM file. This constructor initializes certain data members.
ExpandBMP::ExpandBMP(LPSTR FileName) {

  // Attempt to open the input file
  if (!OpenReadFile((LPSTR) FileName)) {
    ErrorMessage(IDS_OPENFILEERROR);
    return;
  }
  // Try to read the file header record
  if (!ReadMBytes((LPBYTE) &BitMapFileHeader, sizeof(BITMAPFILEHEADER))) {
    CloseFile();
    ErrorMessage(IDS_ERRORREADINGHEADER);
    return;
  }
  // Check to make sure its a BMP file
  if (strncmp((char *) &(BitMapFileHeader.bfType),"BM",2) != 0) {
    CloseFile();
    ErrorMessage(IDS_NOTBMPIMAGE);
    return;
  }
  // Try to read the BitMapInfo information
  if (!ReadMBytes((LPBYTE) &BitMapInfoHeader, sizeof(BITMAPINFOHEADER))) {
    CloseFile();
    ErrorMessage(IDS_ERRORREADINGBMIH);
```

```
        return;
    }

    // Calculate the number of colors used in the inclosed image
    WORD ColorsUsed;
    if ((ColorsUsed = (WORD) BitMapInfoHeader.biClrUsed) == 0)
        ColorsUsed = 1 << BitMapInfoHeader.biBitCount;
    // Now initialize data members from the BMP file information
    wWidth = (WORD) BitMapInfoHeader.biWidth;
    wHeight = (WORD) BitMapInfoHeader.biHeight;
    wColors = ColorsUsed;
    wBitsPerPixel = BitMapInfoHeader.biBitCount;
}

// Expand all varieties of BMP images

BOOL ExpandBMP::ExpandImage(void) {

    WORD BytesPerLine, SizeOfbmiColorArray;

    // Check to see if file is compressed. We cannot handle compressed
    // BMP images at this time.
    if (BitMapInfoHeader.biCompression != BI_RGB) {
        ErrorMessage(IDS_BMPCOMPRESSED);
        CloseFile();
        return FALSE;
    }

    switch(BitMapInfoHeader.biBitCount) {
        case 1: // 1 bit per pixel monochrome images
            BytesPerLine = (wWidth+7)/8;// Round up to nearest byte
            break;

        case 4: // 4 bits per pixel 16 color images
            BytesPerLine = (wWidth+1)/2;// Exactly two pixels in each byte
            break;

        case 8: // 8 bits per pixel 256 color images
            BytesPerLine = wWidth;       // Exactly one pixel in each byte
            break;

        case 24: // 24 bits per pixel image
            BytesPerLine = 3 * wWidth;  // Three bytes per pixel
            wColors = 0;   // Flag as true color image
            break;
    }
    BytesPerLine = ALIGN_DWORD(BytesPerLine);

    WORD ImageWidth = wWidth;
    // Now that image size is known allocate memory for it
    if (!AllocImageBuffer(BytesPerLine, wHeight)) {
        CloseFile();
        ErrorMessage(IDS_NOMEMORYERROR);
        return FALSE;
    }
```

```
      wWidth = ImageWidth;
      // Get a pointer to the Image palette structure
      RGBCOLOR * Palette = GetImagePalettePtr();

    if (wColors != 0) {              // If not a true color image
      // Calculate the number of bytes of color data to read
      SizeOfbmiColorArray = wColors*sizeof(RGBQUAD);

      // With the memory statically allocated, read bmiColor array
      if (!ReadMBytes((LPBYTE) bmiColors, SizeOfbmiColorArray)) {
        CloseFile();
        ErrorMessage(IDS_ERRORREADINGCOLORDATA);
        return FALSE;
      }
      // Now move the color data from the file into the palette structure
      // This is wasteful because the display class will move it back.
      for (int i=0; i < wColors; i++)  {
        Palette[i].Red   = bmiColors[i].rgbRed;
        Palette[i].Green = bmiColors[i].rgbGreen;
        Palette[i].Blue  = bmiColors[i].rgbBlue;
      }
    } else {                         // A true color image
      BYTE Red, Green, Blue;         // Create a spread of colors for the palette
      Red = Green = Blue = 0;        // See Guide to Programming pg 19-6
      for (int i=0; i < 256; i++) {
        Palette[i].Red = Red;
        Palette[i].Green = Green;
        Palette[i].Blue = Blue;
        if(!(Red += 32))
          if (!(Green += 32))
            Blue += 64;
      }
    }
    // Now read the bitmap data directly into the allocated memory
    BYTE huge *lpImage = GetImageDataPtr(); // Get a pointer to the buffer
    for (int h=0; h < wHeight; h++)
      if (!ReadMBytes(lpImage + ((LONG) h * BytesPerLine), BytesPerLine)) {
        CloseFile();
        ErrorMessage(IDS_ERRORREADINGIMAGEDATA);
        return FALSE;
      }

  CloseFile();
  return TRUE;
}


// The following functions deal with BMP image compression

CompressBMP::CompressBMP(LPSTR Name, BOOL ABMPFile, BYTE huge *RasterDataPtr,
                    RGBCOLOR *PalettePtr, WORD Width, WORD Height,
                    WORD BitsPerPixel, WORD NumOfColors) {

  // Concatenate the proper file extension to the file name
  if (ABMPFile)
    strcat(Name, ".BMP");
```

```
    else
      strcat(Name, ".THM");

    lstrcpy((LPSTR)FileName, Name);// Copy filename to local store

    SetDataPtr(RasterDataPtr);      // Save ptr in subclass
    SetPalettePtr(PalettePtr);      // Save ptr to palette

    wWidth       = Width;           // Log image attributes
    wHeight      = Height;
    wBitsPerPixel = BitsPerPixel;
    wColors      = NumOfColors;
    // Calculate raster size
    lRasterSize = (DWORD) wWidth * (DWORD) wHeight;

    if (BitsPerPixel == 24)         // If 24 bpp image, triple raster size
      lRasterSize *= 3;
}

// Write the BMP file header
int CompressBMP::WriteBMPHdr() {

  // Attempt to open the output file
  if (!OpenWriteFile(FileName))
    return(EOpeningFile);

  // Create and fill in the BITMAPFILEHEADER structure
  // First clear the storage area
  memset(&BitMapFileHeader, 0, sizeof(BitMapFileHeader));
  lstrcpy((LPSTR) &BitMapFileHeader.bfType, "BM"); // Write the BMP tag to
    header

  // Now calculate the total file size from the image attribute info
  switch (wBitsPerPixel) {
    case 1: // 1 bit per pixel monochrome images
      BytesPerLine = (wWidth+7)/8;// Round up to nearest byte
      break;

    case 4: // 4 bits per pixel 16 color images
      BytesPerLine = (wWidth+1)/2;// Exactly two pixels in each byte
      break;

    case 8: // 8 bits per pixel 256 color images
      BytesPerLine = wWidth;      // Exactly one pixel in each byte
      break;

    case 24: // 24 bits per pixel image
      BytesPerLine = 3 * wWidth;  // Three bytes per pixel
      wColors = 0;   // Flag as true color image
      break;

  }
  BytesPerLine = ALIGN_DWORD(BytesPerLine);
  // Calculate the entire file size for incorporation into header
  BitMapFileHeader.bfSize =
```

```
      (DWORD) sizeof(BitMapFileHeader)     +
      (DWORD) sizeof(BitMapInfoHeader)     +
      (DWORD) (wColors * sizeof(RGBQUAD)) +
     ((DWORD) BytesPerLine * wHeight);

// Now calculate the offset to the bitmap data in this BMP file
BitMapFileHeader.bfOffBits =
   (DWORD) sizeof(BitMapFileHeader)     +
   (DWORD) sizeof(BitMapInfoHeader)     +
   (DWORD) (wColors * sizeof(RGBQUAD));

// Attempt to write the BitMapFileHeader to the file
if (!WriteMBytes((LPBYTE) &BitMapFileHeader, sizeof(BitMapFileHeader))) {
  ErrorMessage(IDS_ERRORWRITINGBMFH);
  return(EWrtOutFile);
}

// Now build the BitMapInfoHeader for the file. Only important entries are
     filled in.
// The remaining entries are initialized to zeros.
// First clear the storage area
memset(&BitMapInfoHeader, 0, sizeof(BitMapInfoHeader));

BitMapInfoHeader.biSize      = sizeof(BitMapInfoHeader);
BitMapInfoHeader.biWidth     = wWidth;
BitMapInfoHeader.biHeight    = wHeight;
BitMapInfoHeader.biPlanes    = 1;
BitMapInfoHeader.biBitCount  = wBitsPerPixel;
BitMapInfoHeader.biSizeImage = BytesPerLine * (DWORD) wHeight;
BitMapInfoHeader.biClrUsed   = wColors;
// Attempt to write the BitMapInfoHeader to the file
if (!WriteMBytes((LPBYTE) &BitMapInfoHeader, sizeof(BitMapInfoHeader))) {
  ErrorMessage(IDS_ERRORWRITINGBMIH);
  return(EWrtOutFile);
}

// Now attempt to format and write the image palette if there is one.
if (wColors != 0)  {              // If not a 24 bpp image, there is a palette
  // First clear the palette storage area
  memset(&bmiColors, 0, sizeof(bmiColors));
  RGBCOLOR *Palette = GetImagePalettePtr(); // Get pointer to palette
  for (WORD Index=0; Index < wColors; Index++) {
    bmiColors[Index].rgbRed   = Palette[Index].Red;
    bmiColors[Index].rgbGreen = Palette[Index].Green;
    bmiColors[Index].rgbBlue  = Palette[Index].Blue;
    bmiColors[Index].rgbReserved = 0;

  }
  // With the palette prepared, attempt to write it to the file
  if (!WriteMBytes((LPBYTE) &bmiColors, wColors * sizeof(RGBQUAD))) {
    ErrorMessage(IDS_ERRORWRITINGCOLORDATA);
    return(EWrtExtPal);
  }
}
  // If we get here, all is well
```

```
      return(NoError);
   }

   // Do the actual image writing
   BOOL CompressBMP::CompressImage(WORD, enum ImgType) {

      // write out BMP header and palette
      if ((iError = WriteBMPHdr()) == NoError) {

         // Now read the bitmap data directly from the allocated memory
         BYTE huge *lpImage = GetImageDataPtr(); // Get a pointer to the buffer
         for (int h=0; h < wHeight; h++) {
            if (!WriteMBytes(lpImage + ((LONG) h * BytesPerLine), BytesPerLine)) {
               ErrorMessage(IDS_ERRORWRITINGIMAGEDATA);
               return FALSE;
            }
         }
      }
      // File has been written, flush the file and close up shop
      FlushWriteFile();
      CloseFile();
      return(iError == NoError);
   }
```

The BMP Graphic File Format

Note: The following discussion applies to both BMP files and THM files. For the sake of clarity in the discussion, only the term BMP file will be used.

The BMP file format is an encapsulation of a DIB (device-independent bitmap) and supporting image information stored within a disk file and is referred to as the device-independent bitmap file format within the Windows documentation. A BMP file always has a ".BMP" file extension, whereas a THM file always has a ".THM" file-name extension. To understand how the BMP Codec works within the graphic image file library architecture, you must first understand the format and contents of a BMP file as stored on disk. Much of the information used in this chapter is based on the discussions in Chapter 2. Please refer to those discussions if you come to a topic you do not understand.

The first item of information encountered when reading a BMP file from disk is a BITMAPFILEHEADER structure defined as follows:

```
typedef struct {
    UINT    bfType;
    DWORD   bfSize;
    UINT    bfReserved1;
    UINT    bfReserved2;
    DWORD   bfOffBits;
} BITMAPFILEHEADER;
```

The BITMAPFILEHEADER structure contains information about the type, size, and layout of a device-independent bitmap BMP file. The entry bfType specifies the type of file and must contain the two characters BM in a legitimate BMP file. The bfSize mem-

Error Indication	Error Code	Cause of Error
NoError	0	No errors detected
EFileNotFound	-1	Could not find file to open
EOpeningFile	-2	Error opening file
EClosingFile	-3	Error closing file
EReadFileHdr	-4	Error reading the file header
ECorrupt	-5	Error reading file data; possibly corrupt file
ENonSupported	-6	Graphics file type not supported
EWrtFileHdr	-7	Error writing header to graphics file
EWrtOutFile	-8	Error writing to graphics output file
EReadScanLine	-9	Error reading a row/scan line of image data
EWrtScanLine	-10	Error writing a row/scan line of image data
ENoMemory	-11	Not enough memory to perform operation
EWrtExtPal	-12	Error writing image palette to file
ENotGIFFile	-13	File violates GIF specification
EBadHandle	-14	Bad handle for cached image*
ETooManyOpenImages	-15	Too many cached images*
EEmptyFileName	-16	Null filename string*

* Error codes not used in "compand.dll." Error codes from "mycache.dll." See Chapter 10.

FIGURE 4.5 Compression/expansion error codes.

ber contains the size of the whole BMP file in bytes. The two reserved members must always be zeros, and the bfOffBits field specifies the offset (in bytes) from the BITMAP-FILEHEADER structure to the actual bitmap data stored in the file. A BITMAPINFO or BITMAPCOREINFO structure must immediately follow the BITMAPFILEHEADER structure in the BMP file. BITMAPCOREINFO structures are used in the OS/2 versions of BMP files and are not discussed further. The BMP files supported by the code in this chapter have a BITMAPFILEHEADER structure followed immediately by a BITMAP-INFO structure. The remainder of the information within a BMP file follows the DIB format described in Chapter 2. Please refer to the discussion of device-independent bitmaps in Chapter 2 if you require more information.

Using the Graphic Image File Library

Once the Compand DLL is available, it is very easy to use in conjunction with an application program. The following two requirements are placed upon an application program wishing to use the Compand DLL:

    1. The application must be made aware of the functions contained within the Compand DLL. It is recommended that this be accomplished by linking the application program with the import library file "compand.lib" created from "compand.dll" using the import library tool "implib.exe". Normally, the **LoadLibrary** Windows API function in conjunction with the **GetProc-Address** could also be used for accessing the functions within the DLL, but because of the name mangling performed on C++ classes, this is very difficult to do. For hints on how to use **LoadLibrary** with C++ classes, see the article entitled "Very Dynamic Linking in Windows" in the Dr. Dobb's Special Windows issue, Fall 1994.

2. The application must include the DLL's interface definition file "compand.hpp" to provide access to the member functions of the Compand class.

With these requirements satisfied, using a Compand object to expand a graphic image file is as simple as:

```
#include "compand.hpp"    // Include interface class definition

Compand Expander;         // Declare instance of Compand object

// Prepare the Compand object for expansion of the file FileName
if (!Expander.InitExpander(FileName))
  return FALSE; // Return error if problem with file or file type

// All went well, expand the image from the file
if (!Expander.DoExpansion())
  return FALSE; // Return error if problem with expansion

// Compand object now contains the image data in DIB format. The
// image data can now be processed as required
```

To compresses an image in memory in DIB format into a GIF file called "mygirl.gif" the following code segment could be used:

```
Compand Compressor;  // Declare an instance of Compand object

// Prepare the Compand object for compression of image file. All image
// parameters must be readily available including a pointer to the DIB image
// data and a pointer to a palette.
if (!Compressor.InitCompressor(GIFTYPE, "mygirl.gif",
                          ImageWidth, ImageHeight,
                          ImageBitsPerPixel, ImageNumberOfColors,
                          lpImageData, lpImagePalette))
  return FALSE;

  // Now inform the Compand object of the image type
if (ImageNumberOfColors == 0)
  Compressor.SetImageType(TRUECOLOR);
else if (ImageNumberOfColors > 2)
  Compressor.SetImageType(PALETTECOLOR);
else
  Compressor.SetImageType(MONOCHROME);

// Now compress the image into a GIF graphical image file.
if (Compressor.DoCompression())
  return TRUE;
else
  return FALSE;
```

   In the previous examples, an instance of a Compand object was created as a local variable. This is the preferred way of using a Compand object because when the object goes out of scope, any memory allocated within the object for image data and/or image palette storage is automatically released back to the system. Of course, Compand objects can also be created and destroyed dynamically using the C++ **new** and **delete** operators as follows:

```
Compand *CompandObjPtr = new Compand; // Create a Compand object

// Member functions of Compand class are called using CompandObjPtr->
// as shown below
if (!CompandObjPtr->Expander.InitExpander(FileName))
  return FALSE;                  // Return error if problem with file or file type
.
.
.
delete CompandObjPtr; // Destroy the Compand object when
                                // no longer required
```

   The TestApp program of Chapter 1 uses Compand objects exclusively for reading and writing graphic image files. Consult the file "tappchil.cpp" if further examples of the use of the Compand class are required.

   The Compand DLL could also be used for building a simple graphic image file conversion utility program for Windows. A small application program could be developed that would load a user specified graphic image file (say a BMP file) into memory and then write out the same image in a different user specified output file format (say TIF). The common dialog box classes described in Chapter 3 coupled with the earlier code would be all that is required for this simple application of the Compand DLL.

Conclusions

   Graphic image files play a very important role in all imaging programs. In fact, without the capability to read or write image files, an imaging program would be worthless regardless of what other functions it performed. In today's competitive environment, a professional imaging application should be able to read and write a great many file formats. For this reason, if you are contemplating developing a world class imaging application, I suggest you purchase a library of image file functions from a reputable software developer. If you wish to undertake the development of a library of your own, careful attention to its architecture is very important to the finished product. An object-oriented approach is recommended similar to what was presented here. The architecture embodied in the Compand DLL has been in use in a professional imaging application program for over three years and is used daily for all imaging work I do. It does what it was designed to do in a very efficient and easy to understand and use fashion.

Color Reduction Techniques for Images

In this chapter you will learn:
- Why color reduction is sometimes necessary for display of image data
- Why color reduction techniques are becoming a thing of the past
- The differences between uniform quantization with dithering and median cut quantization
- How dithering works and when it should be used
- Some of the techniques used for color quantization
- How median cut color quantization works

Introduction

It might seem that the display of the photographic quality imagery would be a trivial task in comparison to the technical difficulty in acquiring the image data in the first place. This initial thought turns out to be incorrect, at least at the present time. If photographic images always contained fewer colors than your computer graphics adapter and monitor (or other output devices) were capable of displaying, the display of these images would indeed be trivial. Unfortunately, given current graphics adapter technology, this is not yet true.

The ideal situation is, of course, if your computer's graphics adapter and monitor are capable of displaying the full gambit of colors contained in a typical photographic image. For this to be true, your graphics adapter and monitor would need to support "true color" capability. True color capability implies the ability to display 24 bits of color information per pixel on the screen: eight bits each of Red, Green, and Blue color data. This works out to be an impressive 16.8 million colors, which is far more than the human eye is capable of perceiving. True color display allows images to be displayed without any visible color artifacts caused by the image display process. The vast number of colors available on true color systems allows completely smooth color transitions to occur. As the number of simultaneously displayable colors is reduced color banding occurs. The banding occurs because the color transitions become drastic enough that visible edges are detectable by the human eye.

As of this writing, true color graphics adapters at reasonable resolutions (greater than 800×600) are still too expensive for most people, and for this reason are not yet universally available. Given the rapidly falling prices of computer hardware (and the rising value per dollar invested), it should not be long until most newly purchased personal computer systems have true color display capability. Until that time, however, we must maximize the use of what is available.

The problem with today's SuperVGA capable computers is that images produced by various devices such as color scanners and color video digitizers contain many more colors than can be displayed. Typical SuperVGA hardware is capable of displaying 256 colors in resolutions up to $1,024 \times 768$; 65,535 (64K) colors in resolutions up to 800×600; and true color with a resolution of 640×480. The shortage of colors becomes acute when we are required to display true color images that could contain a million colors (typically much fewer) on an output device capable of only 256 or 64K colors. Just how are the 256 (or 64K) most important colors in an image picked so that the displayed image looks like it is supposed to? This process is called *color quantization* or sometimes *color reduction*, and it deals with how the most important colors in an image are picked and with how the colors from the original image are mapped to these selected colors to represent the full range of colors necessary for accurate image display. In the future as display adapter hardware evolves to become more powerful, color quantization techniques will not be necessary. For now, however, they are standard equipment in every imaging tool box.

Many different algorithms exist for performing color quantization and reduction. Probably the best known algorithms are:

1. Uniform quantization. This technique divides the three dimensional RGB color space into equal volumes and uses the mean color values in these volumes to display an image. In other words, the image is displayed using a fixed, full range, color palette that was not derived from its content. Colors from the original image are displayed with the closest color found in the fixed palette.
2. Popularity quantization. The most frequently occurring colors in an image are used to display the image.
3. Median cut quantization. This technique chooses the colors for display of the image so that each color represents approximately the same number of pixels in the original image.
4. Octree quantization. This technique tries to maintain the full range of colors within an image by merging similar colors together and replacing them with their mean color value.

Each of these quantization methods solves the color reduction problem in a unique way. Some of these quantization techniques work well for some types of images but terribly for others. Some require massive amounts of memory for an effective implementation. Still others are slow in execution because of the computations involved in the reduction of colors. Two types of color reduction techniques will be described here: uniform quantization (which is the basis of the dithering technique to be presented) and median cut quantization. For readers interested in other quantization techniques, I refer you to my other books that are detailed in Appendix B "Further Reading."

Please note that the color reduction code presented here was developed for the display of photographic images, but its usefulness does not end there. Any type of true color imaging data available in DIB format or that can be converted into DIB format can be processed with this code. This means that images produced by ray tracers or fractal program can also be processed by the color reduction code described here. In keeping with the imaging architecture presented in Chapter 1, the code in this chapter accepts image data input in the form of a DIB and produces image output also in DIB format. Additionally, both color reduction techniques presented produce a palette with which to display the processed images.

When using the code presented here, it is gratifying to see accurate, full color images displayed on a computer system capable of only a limited number of simultaneously available colors, especially when the required data manipulation occurs so very quickly.

Uniform Quantization and Dithering

To reiterate, some form of color reduction is required when an image must be displayed that contains more colors than the display hardware is capable of displaying. This is typically the case when a true color (24 BPP) image must be displayed on a system having only 256-color capability. Color reduction can be performed in either a static or a dynamic sense. Static color reduction implies that a onetime color reduction process is performed on the true color image data to convert it permanently to fewer colors; that is, a new image data file is created that contains the image in the reduced color format. The converted image data are then used exclusively for manipulation and display. The true color image data may be completely discarded.

The term *dynamic color reduction,* as used here, implies that the image data is always kept in true color format (while on disk) but may be converted to fewer colors at runtime if required for its display. The color reduction process is applied dynamically to the image data on an as-needed basis.

The median cut color quantization code discussed later is one method of color reduction that is applied in a static manner throughout this book. Color quantization techniques such as this one extract the N most important colors from an image and convert less important colors in the image to the closest of the N important colors. Once a 24-BPP image is quantized in this manner, it can be displayed on 256-color VGA systems without any further specialized runtime processing being required. The downside to using static or permanent color reduction is that for those systems with more than 256-color capabilities, either they are forced to display the 256-color quantized images, or the original true color image must also be kept around for display on those systems capable of displaying them. Neither approach is optimum.

Before discussing median cut quantization, a dynamic color reduction technique that falls under the general category of uniform quantization is presented. As hinted at earlier, uniform quantization attempts to display an image using a fixed, full range palette of 256 colors that were selected for their coverage of the RGB color space and not for their presence in the image to be quantized. All images subjected to uniform quantization are displayed using the exact same palette of 256 colors. Uniform quantization alone, however, when applied to most images, results in unusable images. It is only when uniform quantization is coupled with an error diffusion technique such as dithering are the results usable in professional imaging applications. Throughout the remainder of this chapter I will refer to the combination of uniform quantization and error diffusion using the generic term *dithering*. The C++ code for dithering is shown in Listings 5.1 and 5.2 and is contained in the files "dither.hpp" and "dither.cpp" on the companion disk. Please refer to these code listings throughout the discussion to follow. Figure 5.1 gives a brief description of the member functions of the **UniformQuantWithDither** class.

Listing 5.1 The Dither class interface definition.

```
/***********************************************************/
/***                    "dither.hpp"                    ***/
/***        Uniform Quantization with Dithering         ***/
/***                  Class definition                  ***/
/***                                                    ***/
/***                    written by                      ***/
/***                  Craig A. Lindley                  ***/
/***                                                    ***/
/***      Revision: 2.0     Last Update: 11/11/94       ***/
/***********************************************************/

// Copyright (c) 1995 John Wiley & Sons, Inc. All rights reserved.

#ifndef DITHER_HPP
#define DITHER_HPP

#ifdef _WIN32_
#define huge
#define hmemcpy memcpy
#endif

#ifndef _RGBCOLOR
#define _RGBCOLOR
typedef struct {
BYTE Red;
BYTE Green;
BYTE Blue;
} RGBCOLOR;
#endif

#define ALIGN_DWORD(x) (((x)+3)/4 * 4) // Double word alignment macro
#define MAXPALETTEENTRIES 256     // Max number of quantized colors

// Uniform Quantization with Dithering class definition.
class UniformQuantWithDither {
  private:
    // Private data
```

```
        WORD ImageWidth;
        WORD ImageHeight;
        DWORD TotalPixels;
        WORD NumberOfColors;
        DWORD BytesPerLineS;
        DWORD BytesPerLineD;

        BYTE huge *lpSImage;
        BYTE huge *lpDImage;

        static RGBCOLOR DitherPalette[256];

        HGLOBAL hImageMemory;

        // Miscellaneous Variables used in dithering
        int  TRed, TGreen, TBlue;
        int  RedError, GreenError, BlueError;
        BYTE PaletteIndex;
        int  BlueOffset;
        BYTE near *PixelAddr;
        BYTE near *RPixelAddr;
        BYTE near *DPixelAddr;

        // Private Member functions
        void DeAllocImageMemory(void);
        BOOL AllocImageMemory(void);

        void DitherLine(BYTE near *pLine1, BYTE near *pLine2);
        BOOL DitherAnImage(void);

    public:
        UniformQuantWithDither(WORD Width, WORD Height, BYTE huge *lpImage);
        virtual ~UniformQuantWithDither();
        BOOL DitherImage(void);
        BYTE huge *GetImageDataPtr(void)    { return lpDImage; }
        RGBCOLOR *GetImagePalettePtr(void) { return DitherPalette; }
};

#endif
```

Listing 5.2 The Dither class member functions.

```
/***********************************************************/
/***                   "dither.cpp"                    ***/
/***      Uniform Quantization with Dithering Class    ***/
/***              produces 256 color images            ***/
/***           from 24 bit RGB data in memory          ***/
/***                        by                         ***/
/***                 Craig A. Lindley                  ***/
/***                                                   ***/
/***      Revision: 2.0    Last Update: 11/11/94       ***/
/***********************************************************/

// Copyright (c) 1995 John Wiley & Sons, Inc. All rights reserved.
```

```
#include <string.h>
#include <windows.h>
#include "dither.hpp"

// Macros used to facilitate RGB pixel access into DIB for dithering
#define GetRGBPixel(Addr, Red, Green, Blue) \
  Blue  = (int) *(Addr);          \
  Green = (int) *(Addr+1);        \
  Red   = (int) *(Addr+2);

#define PutRGBPixel(Addr, Red, Green, Blue) \
  Red = (Red < 0) ? 0:Red;                  \
  Red = (Red > 255) ? 255:Red;              \
  Green = (Green < 0) ? 0:Green;            \
  Green = (Green > 255) ? 255:Green;        \
  Blue = (Blue < 0) ? 0:Blue;               \
  Blue = (Blue > 255) ? 255:Blue;           \
  *(Addr) = (BYTE)Blue;                     \
  *(Addr+1) = (BYTE)Green;                  \
  *(Addr+2) = (BYTE)Red;


extern RGBCOLOR DitherPalette[256];

// Class Constructor
UniformQuantWithDither::UniformQuantWithDither(
                               WORD Width, WORD Height,
                               BYTE huge *lpImage) {

  // Record the parameter passed in
  ImageWidth = Width;
  ImageHeight = Height;
  lpSImage = lpImage;

  // Initialize some class variables
  BytesPerLineS = ALIGN_DWORD(Width * 3L); // Source image has 24 BPP
  BytesPerLineD = ALIGN_DWORD(Width);    // Dest image has 8 BPP

  hImageMemory = 0;              // No memory yet allocated for dithered
  lpDImage = NULL;               // image. Zero pointer and handle.
}

// Class Destructor. Get rid of dithered image memory when object
// goes out of scope.
UniformQuantWithDither::~UniformQuantWithDither(void) {

  DeAllocImageMemory();
}

// This function deallocates the global memory that was allocated
// for dithered image storage.
void UniformQuantWithDither::DeAllocImageMemory(void) {

  // If image memory was allocated, free it
  if (hImageMemory) {            // If memory allocated
```

```
      GlobalUnlock(hImageMemory);    // Unlock then free it
      GlobalFree(hImageMemory);
      hImageMemory = 0;
   }
}


// Allocate memory for the dithered image.
BOOL UniformQuantWithDither::AllocImageMemory(void) {

  hImageMemory = GlobalAlloc(GHND, BytesPerLineD * ImageHeight);
  if (hImageMemory == NULL)
    return FALSE;

  lpDImage = (BYTE huge *) GlobalLock(hImageMemory);
  return TRUE;
}


// Dither a single row of image data. Source of data is near buffer
// under Win16.
void UniformQuantWithDither::DitherLine(BYTE near *pLine1,
                                                  BYTE near *pLine2) {

  // Do for each pixel in row
  for (register WORD Pixel=0; Pixel < ImageWidth; Pixel++) {
    // Get the pixel of interest for the dither
    PixelAddr = pLine1 + (Pixel * 3);
    GetRGBPixel(PixelAddr, TRed, TGreen, TBlue);
     // Determine which blue entry from palette to use
     BlueOffset = (TBlue/85);
     if ((TBlue - (BlueOffset * 85)) > 43)
      BlueOffset += 1;

     // Calculate palette entry address from color
     // PaletteIndex = ((TRed/32)*32) + ((TGreen/32)*4) + BlueOffset;
     // For speed we will calculate the color index as follows
     PaletteIndex = (TRed & 0xE0) + ((TGreen >> 5) << 2) + BlueOffset;

     // Store the palette back into the same buffer
    *(pLine1 + Pixel) = PaletteIndex;
    /*
  Pixel is set, now distribute the error to adjacent pixels
  using a modified version of the Floyd-Steinberg algorithm.
   In this implementation the error is distributed as follows
                          Pixel
                                  o 1/2->o forward
                        1/4 |
                    down o
  The algorithm is modified to increase performance.

   Calculate errors between the desired color and color used
   for this pixel. Actual error / 4. Use near pointers for speed.
    */
    // pColor is near pointer to a palette color
    Byte near *pColor = (BYTE near *) &DitherPalette[PaletteIndex];
    RedError  = (TRed  - *(pColor))   >> 2;
```

```
      GreenError = (TGreen - *(pColor+1)) >> 2;
      BlueError  = (TBlue  - *(pColor+2)) >> 2;

        // Do the pixel directly below target pixel
      DPixelAddr = pLine2 + (Pixel * 3);
     GetRGBPixel(DPixelAddr, TRed, TGreen, TBlue);
      TRed   += RedError;                    // 1/4 error
    TGreen += GreenError;
    TBlue  += BlueError;
      PutRGBPixel(DPixelAddr, TRed, TGreen, TBlue);

        // Do the pixel directly to the right
      if (Pixel != ImageWidth - 1) {
        RPixelAddr = PixelAddr + 3;
       GetRGBPixel(RPixelAddr, TRed, TGreen, TBlue);
       TRed   += RedError   + RedError;        // 1/2 error
        TGreen += GreenError + GreenError;
       TBlue  += BlueError  + BlueError;
       PutRGBPixel(RPixelAddr, TRed, TGreen, TBlue);
      }
    }
}

// This function dithers the DIB image pointed at by lpSImage. It returns
// TRUE if successful and FALSE otherwise. The dithered image is written
// at lpDImage.
BOOL UniformQuantWithDither::DitherAnImage(void) {

  // Allocate two lines of RGB buffer for dithering
  HLOCAL hLine1Buffer = LocalAlloc(LMEM_MOVEABLE, (WORD) BytesPerLineS);
  if (!hLine1Buffer)
    return FALSE;

  HLOCAL hLine2Buffer = LocalAlloc(LMEM_MOVEABLE, (WORD) BytesPerLineS);
  if (!hLine2Buffer) {
    LocalFree(hLine1Buffer);
      return FALSE;
  }

  // Now lock the pointers for access
  BYTE near *Line1Buffer = (BYTE near *) LocalLock(hLine1Buffer);
  BYTE near *Line2Buffer = (BYTE near *) LocalLock(hLine2Buffer);

  // Move the first two lines of the source image to dither buffers
  hmemcpy(Line1Buffer, lpSImage, BytesPerLineS);
  hmemcpy(Line2Buffer, lpSImage + BytesPerLineS, BytesPerLineS);

  for (register WORD Row = 2; Row < ImageHeight; Row++) {
    DitherLine(Line1Buffer, Line2Buffer);

    // Copy the dithered data in Line1Buffer to destination
    hmemcpy(lpDImage + ((Row-2) * BytesPerLineD),
            Line1Buffer, BytesPerLineD);

    // Copy Line2Buffer to Line1Buffer so it can be dithered
    memcpy(Line1Buffer, Line2Buffer, (WORD) BytesPerLineS);
```

```
        // Move new data to Line2Buffer
        hmemcpy(Line2Buffer, lpSImage + (Row * BytesPerLineS),
                    BytesPerLineS);
    }
    // Must complete the last two rows in the line buffers
    DitherLine(Line1Buffer, Line2Buffer);

    // Copy the dithered data in Line1Buffer to destination
    hmemcpy(lpDImage + ((ImageHeight-2) * BytesPerLineD),
            Line1Buffer, BytesPerLineD);

    memcpy(Line1Buffer, Line2Buffer, (WORD) BytesPerLineS);

    DitherLine(Line1Buffer, Line2Buffer);
    // Copy the dithered data in Line1Buffer to destination
    hmemcpy(lpDImage + ((ImageHeight-1) * BytesPerLineD),
                Line1Buffer, BytesPerLineD);

    // Free the local line buffers
    LocalUnlock(hLine1Buffer);
    LocalFree(hLine1Buffer);
    LocalUnlock(hLine2Buffer);
    LocalFree(hLine2Buffer);

    // Signal all is well
    return TRUE;
}


// Perform Uniform Quantization with Dithering on the image
BOOL UniformQuantWithDither::DitherImage(void) {

    if (!AllocImageMemory())          // Allocate memory for dithered image
        return(FALSE);

    return DitherAnImage();          // Do the dithering of the image
}
// This is the palette against which all true color images will be
// displayed when Uniform Quantization is utilized.
RGBCOLOR UniformQuantWithDither::DitherPalette[256] = {
    {0,   0,   0}, {0,   0,  85}, {0,   0, 170}, {0,   0, 255},
    {0,  36,   0}, {0,  36,  85}, {0,  36, 170}, {0,  36, 255},
    {0,  73,   0}, {0,  73,  85}, {0,  73, 170}, {0,  73, 255},
    {0, 109,   0}, {0, 109,  85}, {0, 109, 170}, {0, 109, 255},
    {0, 146,   0}, {0, 146,  85}, {0, 146, 170}, {0, 146, 255},
    {0, 182,   0}, {0, 182,  85}, {0, 182, 170}, {0, 182, 255},
    {0, 219,   0}, {0, 219,  85}, {0, 219, 170}, {0, 219, 255},
    {0, 255,   0}, {0, 255,  85}, {0, 255, 170}, {0, 255, 255},

    {36,   0,   0}, {36,   0,  85}, {36,   0, 170}, {36,   0, 255},
    {36,  36,   0}, {36,  36,  85}, {36,  36, 170}, {36,  36, 255},
    {36,  73,   0}, {36,  73,  85}, {36,  73, 170}, {36,  73, 255},
    {36, 109,   0}, {36, 109,  85}, {36, 109, 170}, {36, 109, 255},
    {36, 146,   0}, {36, 146,  85}, {36, 146, 170}, {36, 146, 255},
    {36, 182,   0}, {36, 182,  85}, {36, 182, 170}, {36, 182, 255},
```

```
{36, 219,   0}, {36, 219,  85}, {36, 219, 170}, {36, 219, 255},
{36, 255,   0}, {36, 255,  85}, {36, 255, 170}, {36, 255, 255},

{73,   0,   0}, {73,   0,  85}, {73,   0, 170}, {73,   0, 255},
{73,  36,   0}, {73,  36,  85}, {73,  36, 170}, {73,  36, 255},
{73,  73,   0}, {73,  73,  85}, {73,  73, 170}, {73,  73, 255},
{73, 109,   0}, {73, 109,  85}; {73, 109, 170}, {73, 109, 255},
{73, 146,   0}, {73, 146,  85}, {73, 146, 170}, {73, 146, 255},
{73, 182,   0}, {73, 182,  85}, {73, 182, 170}, {73, 182, 255},
{73, 219,   0}, {73, 219,  85}, {73, 219, 170}, {73, 219, 255},
{73, 255,   0}, {73, 255,  85}, {73, 255, 170}, {73, 255, 255},

{109,   0,   0}, {109,   0,  85}, {109,   0, 170}, {109,   0, 255},
{109,  36,   0}, {109,  36,  85}, {109,  36, 170}, {109,  36, 255},
{109,  73,   0}, {109,  73,  85}, {109,  73, 170}, {109,  73, 255},
{109, 109,   0}, {109, 109,  85}, {109, 109, 170}, {109, 109, 255},
{109, 146,   0}, {109, 146,  85}, {109, 146, 170}, {109, 146, 255},
{109, 182,   0}, {109, 182,  85}, {109, 182, 170}, {109, 182, 255},
{109, 219,   0}, {109, 219,  85}, {109, 219, 170}, {109, 219, 255},
{109, 255,   0}, {109, 255,  85}, {109, 255, 170}, {109, 255, 255},

{146,   0,   0}, {146,   0,  85}, {146,   0, 170}, {146,   0, 255},
{146,  36,   0}, {146,  36,  85}, {146,  36, 170}, {146,  36, 255},
{146,  73,   0}, {146,  73,  85}, {146,  73, 170}, {146,  73, 255},
{146, 109,   0}, {146, 109,  85}, {146, 109, 170}, {146, 109, 255},
{146, 146,   0}, {146, 146,  85}, {146, 146, 170}, {146, 146, 255},
{146, 182,   0}, {146, 182,  85}, {146, 182, 170}, {146, 182, 255},
{146, 219,   0}, {146, 219,  85}, {146, 219, 170}, {146, 219, 255},
{146, 255,   0}, {146, 255,  85}, {146, 255, 170}, {146, 255, 255},

{182,   0,   0}, {182,   0,  85}, {182,   0, 170}, {182,   0, 255},
{182,  36,   0}, {182,  36,  85}, {182,  36, 170}, {182,  36, 255},
{182,  73,   0}, {182,  73,  85}, {182,  73, 170}, {182,  73, 255},
{182, 109,   0}, {182, 109,  85}, {182, 109, 170}, {182, 109, 255},
{182, 146,   0}, {182, 146,  85}, {182, 146, 170}, {182, 146, 255},
{182, 182,   0}, {182, 182,  85}, {182, 182, 170}, {182, 182, 255},
{182, 219,   0}, {182, 219,  85}, {182, 219, 170}, {182, 219, 255},
{182, 255,   0}, {182, 255,  85}, {182, 255, 170}, {182, 255, 255},

{219,   0,   0}, {219,   0,  85}, {219,   0, 170}, {219,   0, 255},
{219,  36,   0}, {219,  36,  85}, {219,  36, 170}, {219,  36, 255},
{219,  73,   0}, {219,  73,  85}, {219,  73, 170}, {219,  73, 255},
{219, 109,   0}, {219, 109,  85}, {219, 109, 170}, {219, 109, 255},
{219, 146,   0}, {219, 146,  85}, {219, 146, 170}, {219, 146, 255},
{219, 182,   0}, {219, 182,  85}, {219, 182, 170}, {219, 182, 255},
{219, 219,   0}, {219, 219,  85}, {219, 219, 170}, {219, 219, 255},
{219, 255,   0}, {219, 255,  85}, {219, 255, 170}, {219, 255, 255},

{255,   0,   0}, {255,   0,  85}, {255,   0, 170}, {255,   0, 255},
{255,  36,   0}, {255,  36,  85}, {255,  36, 170}, {255,  36, 255},
{255,  73,   0}, {255,  73,  85}, {255,  73, 170}, {255,  73, 255},
{255, 109,   0}, {255, 109,  85}, {255, 109, 170}, {255, 109, 255},
{255, 146,   0}, {255, 146,  85}, {255, 146, 170}, {255, 146, 255},
{255, 182,   0}, {255, 182,  85}, {255, 182, 170}, {255, 182, 255},
{255, 219,   0}, {255, 219,  85}, {255, 219, 170}, {255, 219, 255},
```

```
   {255, 255,   0}, {255, 255,  85}, {255, 255, 170}, {255, 255, 255}
};
```

Because dithering is usually a dynamic color reduction technique (dithering is used as a static color reduction technique for illustration purposes in the TestApp example program of Chapter 1), it is applied only when an image is displayed and only if the display hardware requires it. The upside of this technique is that an imaging program need only keep one copy of the image data (in 24-BPP format), regardless of the capabilities of the computer system on which images are to be displayed. If the same image is displayed on computer systems with different display capabilities, each system will display the image optimized for its capabilities. The downside of using dithering, of course, is the processing requirements necessary to manipulate the image data at display time. Techniques to maximize dithering performance will be presented later.

Even though I refer to the color reduction technique presented here as dithering, it is really much more than that. In truth, the technique presented is comprised of the following processes:

1. Palette selection
2. Image data to palette matching
3. Error diffusion

The term dithering really only refers to the error diffusion part of the process. I will, however, for expediency, continue to use the term dithering to describe the complete color reduction process presented here. Each of the above processes will be discussed shortly.

A general description of how dithering works follows. For the purpose of discussion, assume a 24-BPP image must be displayed on a system capable of only 256 colors. First, there must be a palette available that the image will be displayed against. This palette is called the dither palette. In this discussion, the dither palette will contain 256 colors because that is the number of colors we want to dither our 24-BPP image down to. If we were dithering an image down to 16 colors, the palette would contain just 16 entries.

The color content of the dither palette is extremely important. It should contain the widest possible range of colors for display of the widest range of images. Whereas median cut color quantization extracts the most important colors from the image for display, dithering does not use any knowledge of the colors contained in an image. Instead, dithering attempts to display an image as accurately as possible using whatever colors are available in the dithering palette. It is for this reason that the dithering palette must contain a wide spectrum of colors.

To dither the image, each RGB pixel of image data is compared against the RGB values of the entries in the dither palette. The dither palette entry that represents the closest color match is chosen for display of this pixel. In other words, the image RGB pixel value is replaced with the index into the dither palette of the closest matching color. Thus the 24-bit, three-byte, RGB value becomes a single byte palette index. The converted image pixel is then written to memory or the display, but the dithering process is not yet complete. If the dithering process ended here with the palette-matching step, the quality of the dithered image would be terrible and would not justify the

The UniformQuantWithDither class

Purpose

The purpose of this class is to encapsulate Uniform Quantization with dithering to provide an easy to understand and easy to use toolbox object for true color image dithering. Typically, only one object of this class is ever instantiated within a program. It is usually instantiated locally when needed and allowed to go out of scope when no longer required.

Member Functions

UniformQuantWithDither.   This is the class constructor. Parameters passed to this constructor include the dimensions of the image to be dithered and a pointer to the DIB image data in memory.

~UniformQuantWithDither.   This is the class destructor. Its only function is to free the memory associated with the dithered image when an object of this class goes out of scope. It is the programmer's responsibility to copy the dithered image data out of this object before allowing this destructor to run; otherwise, the image data will be lost when the object goes out of scope.

DeAllocImageMemory.   This function frees the memory associated with the dithered image contained in the UniformQuantWithDither object. It is called within the destructor of this class. When an UniformQuantWithDither object goes out of scope, the dithered image memory is automatically freed. For this reason, the dithered image data must be copied out of the UniformQuantWithDither object before the object is allowed to go out of scope or the object is deleted.

AllocImageMemory.   This function allocates the memory needed for storage of the dithered output image. It calculates the amount of memory required for the DIB output image from the image dimensions passed into the constructor of this class. A TRUE Boolean value is returned by this function if the required amount of memory is available and FALSE if not.

DitherLine.   This function performs a modified Floyd-Steinberg dithering on a single row (line) of image data. Within this function, a palette entry index is assigned to each pixel of the original image. Also, the error determination calculations and error diffusion processes are performed here.

DitherAnImage.   This function steps through a 24-BPP source image and converts it line by line to a dithered image by calling the **DitherLine** function. In addition, this function manages the buffers used during the dithering process.

DitherImage.   Execution of this function results in the uniform quantization and dithering operations being applied to the input image data. After execution of this member function, the dithered image data and a palette are available for further manipulation and display of the image.

GetImageDataPtr.   This function returns a pointer to the dithered image data. It should only be called after the **DitherImage** function has been called.

GetImagePalettePtr.   This function returns a pointer to the palette to be used in conjunction with the dithered image data. It should only be called after the **DitherImage** function has been called.

FIGURE 5.1 The UniformQuantWithDither class.

effort involved. (If you don't believe me, modify the dithering code presented here and try it; you'll quickly become a believer). To make dithering work, a process called *error diffusion* must be applied after the palette-matching step. Error diffusion diffuses the error between an image's RGB pixel value and the palette RGB value with which the pixel is to be displayed. The error value is diffused (distributed) to the pixels that surround the pixel just converted. The error diffusion process is what allows dithering to produce a decent image on color-limited systems. Error diffusion continually attempts to minimize the differences between the colors in an image and the colors in the dither palette. Many different error diffusion techniques are possible. I use my own modification of Floyd-Steinberg dithering in the code presented here. The modifications I made to the basic algorithm and the reasons I made them will be discussed.

To make dithering work in a professional quality imaging program requires attention to image quality as well as performance issues. The best looking dithered image in the world won't matter if it takes 10 minutes to produce. Conversely, a dithered image of terrible quality produced in 2 seconds won't be of much use either. A balance must be struck between quality and performance. I believe the code presented here does just that. With the trade-offs of image quality and performance in mind, let's discuss how the dithering code presented works and how it meets both, somewhat mutually exclusively, goals.

Palette Selection

It was mentioned that for image display quality reasons, dither palette colors must be selected carefully to contain the widest possible range of colors that the image will be rendered against. Once the palette colors are chosen, how they are organized within the palette is important in terms of performance. After all, each pixel of an image needing display will need to be associated with a dither palette entry. Numerous methods exist for organizing the colors within the palette, and each requires a different algorithm for color matching. As you might guess, any method that requires an RGB pixel value to be compared against one or more palette entries will be inefficient in terms of performance. In other words, if any type of searching must be performed to locate the closest palette entry given an RGB value, image dithering performance will suffer.

The 256-color dither palette used in this chapter is shown in Figure 5.2. The color values chosen for use in this palette were a result of much thought and experimentation. They were chosen for their wide range of color coverage and organized specifically for quick access. In fact, they are organized in such a manner that no palette searching is ever required. Instead, the RGB value of an image pixel can be used to directly compute the closest color's palette index. The result: speed. To understand how this bit of palette magic is accomplished, look closely at the arrangement of colors in Figure 5.2. As you can see, the 256 colors in the palette are broken up into eight groups of 32 entries each. You can also see that the red value (all entries are stored RGB) changes in each group once in every 32 entries, the green values change every four entries, and the blue values change each entry. If you think about this arrangement of colors and specifically about how the green and blue component colors cycle in value, you'll see that this palette indeed provides a very wide range of colors with the granularity dictated by the 256-color limit. Another way to think about how the palette is broken up is to consider that there are eight levels of red and green available but

The Dither Palette Color Selection and Organization

Index	R	G	B	Index	R	G	B	Index	R	G	B
0	0	0	0	32	36	0	0	64	73	0	0
1	0	0	85	33	36	0	85	65	73	0	85
2	0	0	170	34	36	0	170	66	73	0	170
3	0	0	255	35	36	0	255	67	73	0	255
4	0	36	0	36	36	36	0	68	73	36	0
5	0	36	85	37	36	36	85	69	73	36	85
6	0	36	170	38	36	36	170	70	73	36	170
7	0	36	255	39	36	36	255	71	73	36	255
8	0	73	0	40	36	73	0	72	73	73	0
9	0	73	85	41	36	73	85	73	73	73	85
10	0	73	170	42	36	73	170	74	73	73	170
11	0	73	255	43	36	73	255	75	73	73	255
12	0	109	0	44	36	109	0	76	73	109	0
13	0	109	85	45	36	109	85	77	73	109	85
14	0	109	170	46	36	109	170	78	73	109	170
15	0	109	255	47	36	109	255	79	73	109	255
16	0	146	0	48	36	146	0	80	73	146	0
17	0	146	85	49	36	146	85	81	73	146	85
18	0	146	170	50	36	146	170	82	73	146	170
19	0	146	255	51	36	146	255	83	73	146	255
20	0	182	0	52	36	182	0	84	73	182	0
21	0	182	85	53	36	182	85	85	73	182	85
22	0	182	170	54	36	182	170	86	73	182	170
23	0	182	255	55	36	182	255	87	73	182	255
24	0	219	0	56	36	219	0	88	73	219	0
25	0	219	85	57	36	219	85	89	73	219	85
26	0	219	170	58	36	219	170	90	73	219	170
27	0	219	255	59	36	219	255	91	73	219	255
28	0	255	0	60	36	255	0	92	73	255	0
29	0	255	85	61	36	255	85	93	73	255	85
30	0	255	170	62	36	255	170	94	73	255	170
31	0	255	255	63	36	255	255	95	73	255	255

FIGURE 5.2 The Dither palette.

The Dither Palette Color Selection and Organization

Index	R	G	B	Index	R	G	B	Index	R	G	B
96	109	0	0	128	146	0	0	160	182	0	0
97	109	0	85	129	146	0	85	161	182	0	85
98	109	0	170	130	146	0	170	162	182	0	170
99	109	0	255	131	146	0	255	163	182	0	255
100	109	36	0	132	146	36	0	164	182	36	0
101	109	36	85	133	146	36	85	165	182	36	85
102	109	36	170	134	146	36	170	166	182	36	170
103	109	36	255	135	146	36	255	167	182	36	255
104	109	73	0	136	146	73	0	168	182	73	0
105	109	73	85	137	146	73	85	169	182	73	85
106	109	73	170	138	146	73	170	170	182	73	170
107	109	73	255	139	146	73	255	171	182	73	255
108	109	109	0	140	146	109	0	172	182	109	0
109	109	109	85	141	146	109	85	173	182	109	85
110	109	109	170	142	146	109	170	174	182	109	170
111	109	109	255	143	146	109	255	175	182	109	255
112	109	146	0	144	146	146	0	176	182	146	0
113	109	146	85	145	146	146	85	177	182	146	85
114	109	146	170	146	146	146	170	178	182	146	170
115	109	146	255	147	146	146	255	179	182	146	255
116	109	182	0	148	146	182	0	180	182	182	0
117	109	182	85	149	146	182	85	181	182	182	85
118	109	182	170	150	146	182	170	182	182	182	170
119	109	182	255	151	146	182	255	183	182	182	255
120	109	219	0	152	146	219	0	184	182	219	0
121	109	219	85	153	146	219	85	185	182	219	85
122	109	219	170	154	146	219	170	186	182	219	170
123	109	219	255	155	146	219	255	187	182	219	255
124	109	255	0	156	146	255	0	188	182	255	0
125	109	255	85	157	146	255	85	189	182	255	85
126	109	255	170	158	146	255	170	190	182	255	170
127	109	255	255	159	146	255	255	191	182	255	255

FIGURE 5.2 (*Continued*)

The Dither Palette Color Selection and Organization

Index	R	G	B	Index	R	G	B	Index	R	G	B
192	219	0	0	214	219	182	170	235	255	73	255
193	219	0	85	215	219	182	255	236	255	109	0
194	219	0	170	216	219	219	0	237	255	109	85
195	219	0	255	217	219	219	85	238	255	109	170
196	219	36	0	218	219	219	170	239	255	109	255
197	219	36	85	219	219	219	255	240	255	146	0
198	219	36	170	220	219	255	0	241	255	146	85
199	219	36	255	221	219	255	85	242	255	146	170
200	219	73	0	222	219	255	170	243	255	146	255
201	219	73	85	223	219	255	255	244	255	182	0
202	219	73	170	224	255	0	0	245	255	182	85
203	219	73	255	225	255	0	85	246	255	182	170
204	219	109	0	226	255	0	170	247	255	182	255
205	219	109	85	227	255	0	255	248	255	219	0
206	219	109	170	228	255	36	0	249	255	219	85
207	219	109	255	229	255	36	85	250	255	219	170
208	219	146	0	230	255	36	170	251	255	219	255
209	219	146	85	231	255	36	255	252	255	255	0
210	219	146	170	232	255	73	0	253	255	255	85
211	219	146	255	233	255	73	85	254	255	255	170
212	219	182	0	234	255	73	170	255	255	255	255
213	219	182	85								

FIGURE 5.2 (*Continued*)

only four levels of blue. This compromise was chosen because the human eye is less sensitive to blues than to either reds or greens. More granularity is therefore given to the red and green color components than to the blue color component.

If you are wondering where some of the strange color numbers came from, consider this: To divide up the range of color values, 0 to 255, into eight equal segments you need to divide 255 by 7 (not 8), which results in a segment size of 36.43. The ideal values for each of the color increments would therefore be 0, 36.43, 72.86, 109.29, 145.71, 182.14, 218.57, and 255. However, since all color values within a palette must have integer values with no fractional parts, the values become 0, 36, 73, 109, 146, 182, 219, and 255 after appropriate rounding. Because the red and green entries in the palette colors vary with a period of eight, they use these values. Blue values, however, are different because they have a period of four. Calculation of the blue values is similar in that the color range, 0 to 255, must be broken up into four equal segments or 255 divided by 3 (not 4), which equals 85 exactly. The range of blue component values is therefore 0, 85, 170, and 255.

With the palette organized as described, an image's RGB pixel value can be used to directly calculate the closest dither palette index, thereby eliminating the need for any palette searching. If the variables Red, Green, and Blue contain the RGB value of a pixel, the color index is calculated as follows:

```
PaletteIndex = (Red / 32) * 32 + (Green / 32) * 4 + (Blue / 85)
```

To understand how this calculation works, consider the RGB value 120, 47, 200. Note: When performing the index calculations, remember that only integer arithmetic is used, and any fractional values are ignored (120/32 = 3, for example). The palette index calculated from this RGB value is therefore equal to 96 + 4 + 2 or 102. The RGB value of the color of the 102 entry in the dither palette is 109, 36, 170.

While this method for palette index calculation is quite fast, it can be sped up even further by judicious manipulation of the expression. Specifically, replacing the divide by 32 and subsequent multiply by 32 in the Red expression with a logical AND which accomplishes the same task. Further improvements can be had by replacing as many multiplies and divides as possible with shifts. Consider the following, further optimized palette index calculation:

```
PaletteIndex = (Red & 0xE0) + ((Green >> 5) << 2) + (Blue / 85)
```

Why this works is left as a thought exercise for the reader.

Error Diffusion

Before a pixel's error can be diffused to surrounding pixels, the error must be calculated. Error calculations must be performed on each of the three color components separately, resulting in three separate error terms. A first-pass approach is as follows:

```
int RedError    = Red   - DitherPalette[PaletteIndex].Red;
int GreenError  = Green - DitherPalette[PaletteIndex].Green;
int BlueError   = Blue  - DitherPalette[PaletteIndex].Blue;
```

The error term variables must be signed because the error can be positive or negative. More often than not, they are positive values. A more optimized approach to the error calculation would be to replace array access with pointer access. The near designation on the pointer, pColor, would only be applicable in Win16 applications where using near pointers instead of far pointers is an optimization. The near designation is irrelevant under Win32.

```
BYTE near *pColor = (BYTE near *) &DitherPalette[PaletteIndex];
int RedError    = (Red   - *(pColor));
int GreenError  = (Green - *(pColor+1));
int BlueError   = (Blue  - *(pColor+2));
```

With the error terms calculated, they need to be diffused to adjoining pixels. In the approach I have taken, I diffuse one-half of the error to the pixel directly to the right and one-quarter of the error to the pixel directly beneath. The actual Floyd-

Steinberg algorithm diffuses part of the total error in four different directions: the pixel directly to the right, the pixel to the lower left, the pixel directly beneath, and the pixel to the lower right. As you can see, the error terms are always diffused in a forward direction from the pixel being processed. The error is diffused by fetching the pixel into which the error is to be diffused, adding the error terms to it and storing it back again.

The reason for this deviation from the standard approach is again performance. The more pixels the error is diffused into, the slower the dithering process is going to be. I arrived at the error diffusion directions and the diffusion coefficients by subjective experimentation with a great many images. With the numbers chosen, I cannot tell the difference between an image dithered using the classic approach and my approach. My approach, however, is somewhat faster.

To see how dithering is actually performed, check out the functions **Dither-AnImage** and **DitherLine** shown in Listing 5.2. **DitherAnImage** manages the image dithering process on a line-by-line basis. Two local line buffers that help optimize the code for Win16 applications are allocated within this function. After this, each row of the image data is dithered by calling the **DitherLine** function. After a line of image data is dithered, it is transferred from the local buffers to the destination buffer allocated for holding the dithered data. After all of the rows of the image are dithered, the local buffers that are no longer needed are freed.

The **DitherLine** function is where the palette index calculations and the error diffusion processes are performed. As you can see, this function accepts pointers to the two local buffers that contain sequential rows of image data (these buffers are maintained by the **DitherAnImage** function) and is aware of the number of pixels that need to be dithered in the row of image data from the ImageWidth class variable. The process begins when a pixel from the line one buffer is fetched and its palette index calculated. The palette index is then written back into the same buffer that the RGB data was fetched from. Next, the error terms are calculated as described earlier except they are divided by four. This makes it easier to diffuse one-quarter and one-half of the error when required. In the next step of the process, the pixel directly beneath the pixel being processed is fetched from the line two buffer, and one-quarter of the error terms are added to that pixel's value. The pixel is subsequently placed back into the buffer from whence it came. The final step of the process involves adding twice the error terms to the pixel in line one buffer that is directly to the right of the pixel currently being processed. A check is made to see if the pixel being processed is the last one in the row of image data. If so, diffusion of the error to the next pixel to the right is prohibited. The **DitherLine** function returns when a whole row of image data has been dithered and line one buffer contains a full row of palette indexes. The **DitherAnImage** function transfers the dithered data to the destination buffer, copies line two buffer to line one buffer, copies the next row of RGB image data to line two buffer, and calls **DitherLine** again. This process continues until the whole RGB image has been dithered.

Astute readers may have realized that because the DIB data are stored in an inverted raster format, the dithering actually takes place from the bottom of the image to the top instead of the more traditional top to bottom. This has no discernible effect on the looks of the dithered image.

Using the dithering code is simple. The code snippet below shows the typical steps required.

```
// Instantiate a dithering object. Pass the width and height of the image in
// pixels and a pointer to the DIB formatted image in memory.

UniformQuantWithDither D(ImageWidth, ImageHeight, lpImageData);

// Perform the dithering
if (!D.DitherImage()) {
  MessageBox(NULL, "Error quantizing image. No memory", "User Advisory",  MB_OK );
  return;
}
// The image is now dithered. Get pointers to the palettized image data and
// the palette for further processing.
BYTE huge *lpImage = D.GetImageDataPtr();
RGBCOLOR *lpPalette = D.GetImagePalettePtr();
.
. Process the image data
.
// Note, the palettized image data block will be freed when the
// UniformQuantWithDither object goes out of scope.
```

Median Cut Color Quantization

The median cut color quantization algorithm is probably the most widely used quantization technique in the graphics and imaging industry, even though it is one of the most complex of the algorithms to implement. The reason for its popularity is the quality of the images it produces. This algorithm works remarkably well, regardless of the image content. Other color quantization algorithms may produce equal or better quality images for any given image, but none consistently produce the quality of images produced with the median cut algorithm. The median cut quantization technique was chosen for incorporation into this book for just that reason.

The code that performs median cut color quantization is shown in Listings 5.3 and 5.4 and is contained in the files, "mcquant.hpp" and "mcquant.cpp" on the companion disk. Please refer to these listings during the discussion to follow. Figure 5.3 provides a quick description of the member functions of the **MedianCutQuant** class.

Listing 5.3 The Mcquant class interface definition.

```
/***********************************************************/
/***                    "mcquant.hpp"                  ***/
/***   Median Cut Color Quantization Class Definition  ***/
/***                                                   ***/
/***                    written by                     ***/
/***                  Craig A. Lindley                 ***/
/***                                                   ***/
/***      Revision: 2.0    Last Update: 11/11/94       ***/
/***********************************************************/

// Copyright (c) 1995 John Wiley & Sons, Inc. All rights reserved.

#ifndef MCQUANT_HPP
#define MCQUANT_HPP

#ifdef _WIN32_
```

```
#define huge
#endif

#ifndef _RGBCOLOR
#define _RGBCOLOR
typedef struct {
  BYTE Red;
  BYTE Green;
  BYTE Blue;
} RGBCOLOR;
#endif

#define ALIGN_DWORD(x) (((x)+3)/4 * 4) // Double word alignment macro
#define SQUARE(x) ((x)*(x))            // Multiplies a number times itself
#define MAXPALETTEENTRIES 256          // Max number of quantized colors
#define COLLEVELS          64          // Number of brightness levels
#define NUMAXIS             3          // Num of axes in RGB cube

/*
BOX: Structure holding the unsorted generated color boxes. Includes the
low and high value along each axis of RGBCube, and the number of elements
in the box.
*/
typedef struct {                       // Basic data structure
  WORD Lo[3];
  WORD Hi[3];
  DWORD NumElements;
} BOX;

// Quantizer class definition. Note static definition of Palette, SPalette,
// Boxes and SBoxes. This makes the code a little easier.
class MedianCutQuant {
  private:
    // Private data
    WORD ImageWidth;
    WORD ImageHeight;
    DWORD TotalPixels;
    WORD NumberOfColors;
    DWORD BytesPerLineS;
    DWORD BytesPerLineD;

    BYTE huge *lpSImage;
    BYTE huge *lpDImage;
    RGBCOLOR Palette[MAXPALETTEENTRIES];
    RGBCOLOR SPalette[MAXPALETTEENTRIES];
    // RGBCube: A pointer to a three dimensional array of colors. The
    // indices into this array are the color components, RGB, normalized
    // to fit in the range defined by COLLEVELS. The values in the array
    // are frequency counts of the particular color.

    HGLOBAL hImageMemory;
    HGLOBAL hRGBCube;
    DWORD (huge *lpRGBCube) [COLLEVELS] [COLLEVELS];
```

```
        WORD NumBoxes;
        BOX Boxes[MAXPALETTEENTRIES];            // Main data structure
        BOX SBoxes[MAXPALETTEENTRIES];           // Sorted version of above

        // Private Member functions
        void DeAllocRGBCube(void);
        void DeAllocImageMemory(void);
        BOOL AllocRGBCube(void);
        BOOL AllocImageMemory(void);
        void BuildRGBCube(void);
        void OtherAxes(WORD MainAxis, WORD *Other1, WORD *Other2);
        void Shrink(WORD BoxIndex);
        void SelectColorBoxes(void);
        void CalculateColors(void);
        void MapImageData(void);
        void ScalePalette(void);

    public:
        MedianCutQuant(WORD NumColors, WORD Width, WORD Height,
                    BYTE huge *lpImage);
        virtual ~MedianCutQuant();
        BOOL QuantizeImage(void);
        BYTE huge *GetImageDataPtr(void)    { return lpDImage; }
        RGBCOLOR *GetImagePalettePtr(void) { return SPalette; }
};

#endif
```

Listing 5.4 The Mcquant class member functions.

```
/***********************************************************/
/***                   "mcquant.cpp"                    ***/
/***        Median Cut Color Quantization Class         ***/
/***              produces N color images               ***/
/***            from 24 bit RGB data in memory          ***/
/***                         by                         ***/
/***                 Craig A. Lindley                   ***/
/***                                                    ***/
/***        Revision: 2.0    Last Update: 11/11/94      ***/
/***********************************************************/

// Copyright (c) 1995 John Wiley & Sons, Inc. All rights reserved.

#include <string.h>
#include <windows.h>
#include "mcquant.hpp"

MedianCutQuant::MedianCutQuant(WORD NumColors, WORD Width, WORD Height,
                             BYTE huge *lpImage) {

  // Record the parameter passed in
  NumberOfColors = NumColors;
  ImageWidth = Width;
  ImageHeight = Height;
  lpSImage = lpImage;
```

```
  // Initialize some class variables
  TotalPixels = (DWORD) ImageWidth * (DWORD) ImageHeight;
  BytesPerLineS = ALIGN_DWORD(Width * 3L);
  BytesPerLineD = ALIGN_DWORD(Width);

  hRGBCube = 0;
  lpRGBCube = NULL;
  hImageMemory = 0;
  lpDImage = NULL;

  NumBoxes = 0;

  // Zero the storage areas
  memset(Palette,0, MAXPALETTEENTRIES * sizeof(RGBCOLOR));
  memset(Boxes,  0, sizeof(Boxes));
  memset(SBoxes, 0, sizeof(SBoxes));
}


MedianCutQuant::~MedianCutQuant(void) {

  DeAllocRGBCube();                 // Probably not necessary
  DeAllocImageMemory();
}


// This function deallocates all global memory that has been allocated
// for the RGBCube.
void MedianCutQuant::DeAllocRGBCube(void) {

  // If RGBCube memory was allocated, free it
  if (hRGBCube) {                   // If memory allocated
    GlobalUnlock(hRGBCube);         // Unlock then free it
    GlobalFree(hRGBCube);
    hRGBCube = 0;
  }
}


// This function deallocates all global memory that has been allocated
// for palettized image storage.
void MedianCutQuant::DeAllocImageMemory(void) {

  // If image memory was allocated, free it
  if (hImageMemory) {               // If memory allocated
    GlobalUnlock(hImageMemory);     // Unlock then free it
    GlobalFree(hImageMemory);
    hImageMemory = 0;
  }
}

// Allocate memory for the RGBCube.
BOOL MedianCutQuant::AllocRGBCube(void) {

  // Calculate the total amount of memory required by the RGBCube
  DWORD RGBCubeSize = ((DWORD) sizeof(DWORD)) * COLLEVELS * COLLEVELS * COLLEVELS;
```

```
    hRGBCube = GlobalAlloc(GHND, RGBCubeSize); // Now alloc what we need
    if (hRGBCube == NULL)
       return FALSE;

    lpRGBCube = (DWORD (huge *) [COLLEVELS][COLLEVELS]) GlobalLock(hRGBCube);
    return TRUE;
}


// Allocate memory for the palettized image.
BOOL MedianCutQuant::AllocImageMemory(void) {

    hImageMemory = GlobalAlloc(GHND, BytesPerLineD * ImageHeight);
    if (hImageMemory == NULL)
       return FALSE;

    lpDImage = (BYTE huge *) GlobalLock(hImageMemory);
    return TRUE;
}


// This function reads the true color image data, scales the
// data and builds the RGBCube.
void MedianCutQuant::BuildRGBCube(void) {
    BYTE huge *lpSLine;
    BYTE huge *lpSPixel;
    BYTE Red, Green, Blue;

    // Scan the complete image scaling the RGB values from
    // the range 0..FF to 0..3F by right shifting two bits.
    for (register int Row = 0; Row < ImageHeight; Row++) {
       // Calculate pointer to line of image data
       lpSLine = (BYTE huge *) (lpSImage + (Row * BytesPerLineS));
       for (register int Col = 0; Col < ImageWidth; Col++) {
          lpSPixel = (BYTE huge *) (lpSLine + (Col * 3L));
          Blue  = *lpSPixel++ >> 2;
          Green = *lpSPixel++ >> 2;
          Red   = *lpSPixel   >> 2;

          // Add one to the count of pixels with that color
          (lpRGBCube[Red][Green][Blue])++;
       }
    }
}


// This function sets the indices to the numbers of the other axis after
// a main axis has been selected.
void MedianCutQuant::OtherAxes(WORD MainAxis, WORD *Other1, WORD *Other2) {

    switch (MainAxis) {
      case 0:
        *Other1 = 1;
        *Other2 = 2;
        break;
      case 1:
        *Other1 = 0;
        *Other2 = 2;
```

```
          break;
      case 2:
        *Other1 = 0;
        *Other2 = 1;
  }
}

// This function takes a index value into the Boxes array, and shrinks the
// specified box to tightly fit around the input color frequency data (eg.
// there are no zero planes on the sides of the box).
void MedianCutQuant::Shrink(WORD BoxIndex) {

  WORD Axis,Aax1,Aax2;
  int Ind[3], Flag;

  // Along each axis:

  for (Axis=0; Axis < NUMAXIS; Axis++) {
        OtherAxes(Axis,&Aax1,&Aax2);

        // Scan off zero planes on from the low end of the axis
        Flag = 0;
        for (Ind[Axis]=Boxes[BoxIndex].Lo[Axis];
                        Ind[Axis] <= Boxes[BoxIndex].Hi[Axis]; Ind[Axis]++) {
                for (Ind[Aax1]=Boxes[BoxIndex].Lo[Aax1];
                            Ind[Aax1] <= Boxes[BoxIndex].Hi[Aax1]; Ind[Aax1]++) {
                    for (Ind[Aax2]=Boxes[BoxIndex].Lo[Aax2];
                            Ind[Aax2] <= Boxes[BoxIndex].Hi[Aax2]; Ind[Aax2]++)
                        if (lpRGBCube[Ind[0]][Ind[1]][Ind[2]]) {
                                Flag=1;
                break;
            }
          if (Flag) break;
        }
        if (Flag) break;
        }
        Boxes[BoxIndex].Lo[Axis] = Ind[Axis];

        // Scan off zero planes from the high end of the axis
        Flag = 0;
        for (Ind[Aax1]=Boxes[BoxIndex].Hi[Axis];
                    Ind[Axis]+1 >= Boxes[BoxIndex].Lo[Axis]+1; Ind[Axis]--) {
          for (Ind[Aax1]=Boxes[BoxIndex].Hi[Aax1];
                    Ind[Aax1]+1 >= Boxes[BoxIndex].Lo[Aax1]+1; Ind[Aax1]--) {
            for (Ind[Aax2]=Boxes[BoxIndex].Hi[Aax2];
                            Ind[Aax2]+1 >= Boxes[BoxIndex].Lo[Aax2]+1; Ind[Aax2]--)
              if (lpRGBCube[Ind[0]][Ind[1]][Ind[2]]) {
                 Flag = 1;
                 break;
              }
            if (Flag) break;
          }
          if (Flag) break;
    }
    Boxes[BoxIndex].Hi[Axis] = Ind[Axis];
```

```
   }
 }


 // This function selects the optimum colors from the color frequency data,
 // using the Median Cut algorithm.
 void MedianCutQuant::SelectColorBoxes(void) {

   WORD SelectedBox, c;
   WORD Ind[3], Max, Axis, TargetBox, k;
   WORD Aax1,Aax2;
   DWORD LongMax, PlaneSum, ElementSum;

   // Initialize the first and only box in the array to contain the
   // entire RGBCube, then discard unused zero planes surrounding it.
   for (c=0; c < NUMAXIS; c++) {
     Boxes[0].Lo[c] = 0;
     Boxes[0].Hi[c] = COLLEVELS-1;
   }
   Boxes[0].NumElements = TotalPixels;
   NumBoxes = 1;


   Shrink(0);


   // Perform the following until all color registers are used up
   while(NumBoxes < NumberOfColors) {
      // Pick the box with the maximum number of elements that is not
      // a single color. It will be the box that will be split.
      LongMax = 0;
     SelectedBox = 1000;
      for (c=0; c < NumBoxes; c++) {
         if ((Boxes[c].NumElements > LongMax) &&
             ((Boxes[c].Lo[0] < Boxes[c].Hi[0]) ||
              (Boxes[c].Lo[1] < Boxes[c].Hi[1]) ||
              (Boxes[c].Lo[2] < Boxes[c].Hi[2]))) {
           LongMax = Boxes[c].NumElements;
           SelectedBox = c;
         }
      }
      // If we couldn't find any box that was not a single color, we don't
      // need to assign any more colors, so we can terminate this loop.
      if (SelectedBox == 1000)
       break;

      // Choose the longest axis of the box to split it along
      Axis = 0;
      Max = Boxes[SelectedBox].Hi[Axis] - Boxes[SelectedBox].Lo[Axis];
       for (k=1; k < NUMAXIS; k++) {
          if (Max < (c=(Boxes[SelectedBox].Hi[k]-Boxes[SelectedBox].Lo[k]))) {
          Max = c;
          Axis = k;
        }
      }
       // Check to see if any of the previously assigned boxes have zero
       // elements which may happen in degenerate cases. If so, reuse them.
```

```
      // If not, use the next available box.
TargetBox = NumBoxes;
 for (c=0; c < NumBoxes; c++) {
    if (Boxes[c].NumElements == 0) {
    TargetBox = c;
    break;
  }
}
OtherAxes(Axis,&Aax1,&Aax2);
 if (Boxes[SelectedBox].Hi[Axis] != Boxes[SelectedBox].Lo[Axis]) {
    // Sum planes of box from low end until the sum exceeds half the
    // total number of elements in the box. That is the point where
    // the split will occur.
    ElementSum = 0;
    for (Ind[Axis]=Boxes[SelectedBox].Lo[Axis];
         Ind[Axis] <= Boxes[SelectedBox].Hi[Axis]; Ind[Axis]++) {
      PlaneSum = 0;
      for (Ind[Aax1]=Boxes[SelectedBox].Lo[Aax1];
           Ind[Aax1] <= Boxes[SelectedBox].Hi[Aax1]; Ind[Aax1]++)
        for (Ind[Aax2]=Boxes[SelectedBox].Lo[Aax2];
             Ind[Aax2] <= Boxes[SelectedBox].Hi[Aax2]; Ind[Aax2]++)
          PlaneSum += lpRGBCube[Ind[0]][Ind[1]][Ind[2]];

      ElementSum += PlaneSum;
      if (ElementSum > Boxes[SelectedBox].NumElements/2)
        break;
    }
    // If we did not exceed half the total until we added the last
    // plane (such as in a case where the last plane contains the bulk
    // of the data points), back up so we do not create the new box
    // as a degenerate box.
    if (Ind[Axis] == Boxes[SelectedBox].Hi[Axis]) {
    Ind[Axis]--;
    ElementSum -= PlaneSum;
  }
    // The new box has most of the data the same as the old box, but
    // its low extent is the index above the point where we needed to
    // split, and its number of elements is the total number of elements
    // in this whole box, minus the number in the planes we just summed.
    for (c=0; c < NUMAXIS; c++) {
    Boxes[TargetBox].Lo[c] = Boxes[SelectedBox].Lo[c];
    Boxes[TargetBox].Hi[c] = Boxes[SelectedBox].Hi[c];
  }
    Boxes[TargetBox].Lo[Axis] = Ind[Axis]+1;
    Boxes[TargetBox].NumElements = Boxes[SelectedBox].NumElements -
                                   ElementSum;
    // The high extent of our old box is now cut off at the plane just
    // split at and the number of elements in it is the number we just
    // summed.
    Boxes[SelectedBox].Hi[Axis] = Ind[Axis];
    Boxes[SelectedBox].NumElements = ElementSum;

    // Discard zero planes around both our new boxes
    Shrink(SelectedBox);
    Shrink(TargetBox);
```

138 *Chapter 5*

```
                        // If we used the top box in our list, we have to increment the
                        // total number of boxes used, to make ready for the use of the next
                        // free box.
                    if (TargetBox == NumBoxes)
                        NumBoxes++;
                }
            }
        }


// This function calculates the actual color register values for each box,
// based on the weighted distribution of data in the box.
void MedianCutQuant::CalculateColors(void) {

    WORD Index, R, G, B;
    DWORD RSum, GSum, BSum, Tmp;
    WORD Indices[MAXPALETTEENTRIES];
    DWORD WeightedColor[MAXPALETTEENTRIES];

    for (Index=0; Index < NumBoxes; Index++) {
        // Calculate a weighted sum of the color values in the box
        RSum = BSum = GSum = 0;
        for (R=Boxes[Index].Lo[0]; R<=Boxes[Index].Hi[0]; R++) {
            for (G=Boxes[Index].Lo[1]; G<=Boxes[Index].Hi[1]; G++) {
                for (B=Boxes[Index].Lo[2]; B<=Boxes[Index].Hi[2]; B++) {
                    Tmp = lpRGBCube[R] [G] [B];
                    RSum += R*Tmp;
                    GSum += G*Tmp;
                    BSum += B*Tmp;
                }
            }
        }
        // Pick the actual color for that box based on the weighted sum. Be
        // careful about overflow of byte values.
        Tmp = Boxes[Index].NumElements;
        RSum /= Tmp;
        Palette[Index].Red = (BYTE)((RSum > 255) ? 255:RSum);
        GSum /= Tmp;
        Palette[Index].Green = (BYTE)((GSum > 255) ? 255:GSum);
        BSum /= Tmp;
        Palette[Index].Blue = (BYTE)((BSum > 255) ? 255:BSum);
    }
    // Set up for an index sort of the brightness by first calculating the
    // weighted brightness of each color (based on the NTSC luminance
    // calculation.
    for (Index=0; Index < NumBoxes; Index++) {
        Indices[Index] = Index;
        WeightedColor[Index] = Palette[Index].Red * 30 +
                                Palette[Index].Blue  * 11 +
                                Palette[Index].Green * 59;
    }
    // Do a bubble sort of the weighted colors via indices. Sort is done in
    // ascending order.
    BOOL Flag = 1;
    while (Flag) {
        Flag = 0;
```

```
            for (Index=0; Index < NumBoxes-1; Index++) {
               if (WeightedColor[Indices[Index]] > WeightedColor[Indices[Index+1]]) {
               Tmp = Indices[Index];
               Indices[Index] = Indices[Index+1];
                 Indices[Index+1] = (WORD) Tmp;
               Flag = 1;
               }
            }
         }
      // Remap the boxes and the color registers into SBoxes and SPalette
      // via the sorted indices found above.
      for (Index=0; Index < NumBoxes; Index++) {
        SPalette[Index].Red   = Palette[Indices[Index]].Red;
        SPalette[Index].Blue  = Palette[Indices[Index]].Blue;
        SPalette[Index].Green = Palette[Indices[Index]].Green;
        SBoxes[Index].NumElements = Boxes[Indices[Index]].NumElements;
         for (WORD c=0; c < NUMAXIS; c++) {
          SBoxes[Index].Hi[c] = Boxes[Indices[Index]].Hi[c];
          SBoxes[Index].Lo[c] = Boxes[Indices[Index]].Lo[c];
       }
     }
   }
}


// This function maps the raw image data into the new color map we've
// come up with in the SPalette array.
void MedianCutQuant::MapImageData(void) {
  WORD Red, Green, Blue, Index;
  WORD GoodIndex;
  DWORD MinError,Error;

  // Set the RGBCube array to a value that can't be a color register index
  // (MAXPALETTEENTRIES*2) so we can detect when we hit on a part of the
  // array that is not included in a color box.
  for (Red=0; Red < COLLEVELS; Red++)
    for (Green=0; Green < COLLEVELS; Green++)
      for (Blue=0; Blue < COLLEVELS; Blue++)
        lpRGBCube[Red] [Green] [Blue] = MAXPALETTEENTRIES*2;

// Fill the boxes in the RGBCube array with the index number for that
// box, so we can tell which box a particular color index (into the
// RGBCube array) is in by a single access.
for (Index=0; Index < NumBoxes; Index++)
  for (Red=SBoxes[Index].Lo[0]; Red <= SBoxes[Index].Hi[0]; Red++)
    for (Green=SBoxes[Index].Lo[1]; Green <= SBoxes[Index].Hi[1]; Green++)
      for (Blue=SBoxes[Index].Lo[2]; Blue <= SBoxes[Index].Hi[2]; Blue++)
        lpRGBCube[Red] [Green] [Blue] = Index;

// Rescan the image data so that it can be quantized and stored.
BYTE huge *lpSLine;
BYTE huge *lpSPixel;
BYTE huge *lpDLine;
BYTE huge *lpDPixel;

// Scan the complete image scaling the RGB values from
// the range 0..FF to 0..3F by right shifting two bits. Lookup
```

```
// the appropriate index and store it in the destination image.
for (register int Row = 0; Row < ImageHeight; Row++) {
   // Calculate pointer to line of image data
   lpSLine = (BYTE huge *) (lpSImage + (Row * BytesPerLineS));
   lpDLine = (BYTE huge *) (lpDImage + (Row * BytesPerLineD));
   for (register int Col = 0; Col < ImageWidth; Col++) {
      lpSPixel = (BYTE huge *) (lpSLine + (Col * 3L));
      lpDPixel = (BYTE huge *) (lpDLine + Col);

      Blue  = *lpSPixel++ >> 2;
      Green = *lpSPixel++ >> 2;
      Red   = *lpSPixel   >> 2;

      // If this particular color is inside one of the boxes,
      // assign the color index for this pixel to the value at that
      //spot in the cube.
      if (lpRGBCube[Red] [Green] [Blue] != MAXPALETTEENTRIES*2)
        *lpDPixel = (BYTE) lpRGBCube[Red] [Green] [Blue];
      else {
        // Otherwise, we need to scan the array of colors to find which is
        // the closest to our prospective color.
        GoodIndex = 0;
        MinError = SQUARE(Red - SPalette[GoodIndex].Red) +
                      SQUARE(Green - SPalette[GoodIndex].Green) +
                      SQUARE(Blue - SPalette[GoodIndex].Blue);
        // Scan all color registers to find which has the smallest error
        // when it is used for this pixel.
        for (Index=1; Index < NumBoxes; Index++) {
           Error = SQUARE(Red - SPalette[Index].Red) +
                      SQUARE(Green - SPalette[Index].Green) +
                      SQUARE(Blue  - SPalette[Index].Blue);
           if (Error < MinError) {
              MinError = Error;
              GoodIndex = Index;
           }
        }
        // Assign that register to this pixel
      *lpDPixel = GoodIndex;
    }
   }
  }
}

// The purpose of this function is to partially make up
// for the normalization of pixel values performed previously.
// The values in the color registers are scaled upwards toward
// the maximum value of 255 to increase image brightness.
  void MedianCutQuant::ScalePalette(void) {

   // Find the maximum value of any RGB color in the palette
   BYTE Red, Green, Blue;
   WORD MaxValue = 0;
   for (register int Index = 0; Index < MAXPALETTEENTRIES; Index++) {
      Red   = SPalette[Index].Red;
      Green = SPalette[Index].Green;
```

```
      Blue  = SPalette[Index].Blue;
    if (Red > MaxValue)
      MaxValue = Red;
    if (Green > MaxValue)
      MaxValue = Green;
    if (Blue > MaxValue)
      MaxValue = Blue;
  }
  // Scale all of the palette entries accordingly
  // Max color component value is 255
  WORD Temp;
  for (Index = 0; Index < MAXPALETTEENTRIES; Index++) {
    Temp = (WORD) SPalette[Index].Red * ((WORD) 255);
    Temp /= MaxValue;
    SPalette[Index].Red = Temp;

    Temp = (WORD) SPalette[Index].Green * ((WORD) 255);
    Temp /= MaxValue;
    SPalette[Index].Green = Temp;

    Temp = (WORD) SPalette[Index].Blue * ((WORD) 255);
    Temp /= MaxValue;
    SPalette[Index].Blue = Temp;
  }
}


// Perform the, in memory, image quantization
BOOL MedianCutQuant::QuantizeImage(void) {

  if (!AllocRGBCube())         // Allocate memory for the RGBCube
    return(FALSE);

  if (!AllocImageMemory())     // Allocate memory for palettized image
    return(FALSE);

  BuildRGBCube();              // Color quantize the image
  SelectColorBoxes();
  CalculateColors();           // Calculate weighted colors for each box
  MapImageData();
  ScalePalette();
  DeAllocRGBCube();            // Free RGB Cube memory and go home
  return TRUE;                 // Return no error code
}
```

The Median Cut Algorithm and Implementation

The median cut algorithm is the brain child of Paul Heckbert and was first published in *Computer Graphics Magazine* in 1982. See Appendix B "Further Reading" for the specifics of this article.

During the color quantization process, the median cut algorithm tries to assign colors so that each assigned color represents approximately the same number of pixels in the original image. Intuitively, this provides an explanation of why this algorithm seems to be universally applicable. (In the discussion to follow, *N* refers to the number of colors an image is to be quantized down to. For systems capable of 256-

---

The MedianCutQuant class

Purpose

The purpose of this class is to encapsulate the Median Cut quantization algorithm to provide an easy to understand and easy to use toolbox object for true color image quantization. Typically, only one object of this class is ever instantiated within a program. It is usually instantiated locally when needed and allowed to go out of scope when no longer required.

Member Functions

MedianCutQuant. This is the constructor for this class. Parameters passed to this constructor include the number of colors the image should be quantized down to, the dimensions of the image to be quantized, and a pointer to the DIB image data in memory.

~MedianCutQuant. The destructor for this class. Its only function is to free the memory associated with the palettized image when an object of this class goes out of scope. It is the programmer's responsibility to copy the palettized image data out of this object before allowing this destructor to run; otherwise, the image data will be lost when the object goes out of scope.

DeAllocRGBCube. This function frees the approximate 1Mb of memory associated with the RGBCube. It is called after the quantization operation is performed when the RGBCube is no longer needed.

DeAllocImageMemory. This function frees the memory associated with the palettized image contained in the MedianCutQuant object. It is called within the destructor of this class. When the MedianCutQuant object goes out of scope, the palettized image memory is automatically freed. For this reason, the palletized image data must be copied out of the MedianCutQuant object before the object is allowed to go out of scope or the object is deleted.

AllocRGBCube. This function allocates the memory to be used for the RGBCube. In the current implementation, the RGBCube requires about 1Mb of memory. The memory allocated by this function is manipulated as a three-dimensional array of unsigned long values.

FIGURE 5.3 The Median Cut Color Quantization class.

color display, *N* is typically 256.) The median cut algorithm searches for and finds *N* regions within the total color space defined by an image that represents approximately the same number of pixels. Regions within the color space with lots of clustered pixels are assigned many, unique color values. Regions that contain few pixels are gathered together and assigned a single color value. This makes sense in that regions of the color space that contain only a few pixels are not that important in the display of the image. Regions that contain lots of pixels are important, and the use of accurate colors for display of these pixels is much more important to the resultant image quality.

To quantify the colors contained in an image, as required for the quantization process, a three-dimensional color histogram is used. Because each color component

AllocImageMemory. This function allocates the memory needed for storage of the palettized output image. It calculates the amount of memory required for the DIB output image from the image dimensions passed into the constructor of this class. A TRUE Boolean value is returned by this function if the required amount of memory is available and FALSE if not.

BuildRGBCube. This function builds the three-dimensional histogram from the image data. Each non-zero entry in the RGBCube represents a unique color in the original image.

OtherAxes. This function sets the indexes to the other axes after a main axis has been selected.

Shrink. This function takes an index value into the Boxes array and shrinks the specified box to tightly fit around the input color frequency data.

SelectColorBoxes. This function identifies the color boxes that optimally divide the image color space into approximately equal pixel counts.

CalculateColors. This function calculates the color value to use for each box. The color is calculated as the mean value of all colors contained in the box.

MapImageData. This function maps each pixel of the RGB input data to the palette index to be used for display of the pixel.

ScalePalette. This function attempts to reverse the effects of color data scaling used during RGBCube generation by scaling the quantized palette color values toward the maximum value of 255.

QuantizeImage. Execution of this function results in the quantization operation being applied to the input image data. After execution of this member function, the palettized image data and a palette are available for further manipulation and display of the image.

GetImageDataPtr. This function returns a pointer to the palettized image data. It should only be called after the **QuantizeImage** function has been called.

GetImagePalettePtr. This function returns a pointer to the palette to be used in conjunction with the palettized image data. It should only be called after the **QuantizeImage** function has been called.

FIGURE 5.3 (*Continued*)

value can range from 0 to 255, an ideal three-dimensional histogram could be implemented as a three-dimensional array (with Red, Green, and Blue indexes) declared as follows:

```
unsigned long RGBCube[256] [256] [256];
```

The data stored in each array entry is the count of pixels within the original image that had the specific RGB color value; for example, if a Red pixel value (RGB = 1,0,0) were detected, the entry in the RGBCube array corresponding to that value would be incremented as follows:

```
RGBCube[1] [0] [0]++;
```

Unfortunately, an array of this type would require over 67Mb of memory to implement. An array type of unsigned long (requiring four bytes for each entry) is required to count the number of pixels within the image that had the color specified by the array indexes. A data type of unsigned short (maximum value of 65,535) might not be sufficient because there could be more pixels than that in an image with the same value, black (RGB = 0, 0, 0) for instance. This is especially true for images acquired at high resolution from a scanner.

Typically, images produced by a scanner or color digitizer contain less than 10,000 unique colors (depending on content of course). In this case, the RGBCube declared earlier would have 10,000 or fewer nonzero entries. These entries, when totaled, would equal the number of pixels within the image. Once it is realized that the RGBCube is a rather sparse array, various techniques can be used to reduce its voracious appetite for memory.

The method chosen for this implementation is to prescale the RGB data so that each color component occupies the range from 0 to 63 instead of 0 to 255. This is done by shifting the color component values two bits to the right. This scaling, in effect, groups the four closest shades of each color together. This causes distortion in the color quantization process as a trade-off for reduced memory consumption. The bottom line is that we are attempting to reduce images with vast numbers of colors down to N colors. This color reduction causes considerable amounts of color distortion. The additional amount of distortion we are introducing as a side effect of this implementation is negligible by comparison. The new declaration of the RGBCube could then become:

```
unsigned long RGBCube [64] [64] [64];
```

which would require a mere 1Mb of memory to implement and is in the realm of practicality for Windows software. To access a single entry within the RGBCube, the following mechanism is used:

```
RGBCube [Red] [Green] [Blue]
```

The function, **BuildRGBCube,** in Listing 5.4, shows how the three-dimensional color histogram, RGBCube is built. Basically, as the RGB components of each pixel's value are identified, they are used as the indexes into the RGBCube. The value in the RGBCube at these indexes is incremented each time a pixel of this color is found. After the complete image is read and processed, each non-zero entry in the RGBCube represents a unique color in the original image. If the non-zero entries in the RGBCube were to be counted, the result would be the number of unique colors contained in the image.

Once the RGBCube is built, the median cut algorithm can be applied to the color data contained within it. To do this, a data structure called a "Box" is used. A Box is defined as follows:

```
struct Box  {
    unsigned short Lo[3];
    unsigned short Hi[3];
    unsigned long NumElements;
};
```

One Box exists for each color in the final image. In this case, an array of N Boxes will be used. The array "Lo" within the Box contains the lower extremes of the RGB color component values contained within this Box, while "Hi" contains the upper extreme. "NumElements" contains the number of image pixels that fall within this Box, that is, within the range of the RGB values contained within the Box. The median cut algorithm then attempts to divide the RGBCube into *N* regions (Boxes) of nearly equal pixel counts. This function is performed within the "SelectColorBoxes" function. Initially, a single Box, Box[0] is created that spans the complete RGBCube. This is accomplished by setting the "Lo" entries to zero, the "Hi" entries to 63 (COLLEVELS-1), and the "NumElements" to the total number of pixels in the image being quantized. Then for each of the *N* Boxes, a search is made through the currently used Boxes for the Box that contains the highest "NumElements" count. Within this Box, the Hi and Lo values of each color component are subtracted to determine the color that has the largest spread of values. The color with the largest delta is considered the major axis. This is the axis along which this Box will be split. Next, the number of pixels contained within this Box is summed from the low to the high end of the Box along the major axis. The process is stopped when the sum exceeds one-half the total number of pixels in this Box (NumElements/2). This Box is then split into two boxes along the major axis at the point where one-half the pixel count was detected. Thus, Box[0] is split into Box[0] and Box[1], with each containing approximately the same number of pixels. In this case, they each would contain one-half the total number of image pixels. This process continues until *N* Boxes of approximately equal pixel counts are identified.

Once all the Boxes are identified, it is necessary to determine the single color that will be used for display of the pixel values that fall within the region of the color space defined by each Box. The **CalculateColors** function performs this operation. The single color used for each Box is the weighted average of the color component values multiplied by the color counts (from RGBCube) divided by the total number of pixels contained within this Box. Once a single color is identified for each Box, the luminance (or brightness) value of these colors is calculated. The luminance values (calculated from the simple formula shown in Listing 5.4) of each color are used to sort the color values by increasing brightness. The result of this process is that the **SPalette** array that contains the *N* sorted color values is created. These color values, after scaling, will be used as the palette that the image will be displayed against.

The final process that needs to be performed is to establish a mapping between the original pixels' RGB values and the new palette index values to be used for image display. This is the operation performed by the **MapImageData** function. Here, the RGBCube is reused. Its initial function has been fulfilled and therefore the color histogram data that it contains is no longer required. The RGBCube will be reused for our mapping function. The RGB color components of a pixel from the original image will be used as indexes into the RGBCube. The value fetched from the RGBCube will be the color index value to display the pixel with, thus the mapping.

Before this can be done, however, the RGBCube must be prepared with the mapping function. The first step in this process is to initialize every entry in the RGBCube to some out-of-range value so that we can determine if we hit a portion of the RGBCube not contained within a Box (not a very common occurrence). Next, nested loops access each Box, assigning a single, unique color index value to all colors encompassed by the Box. Now that the mapping function has been established, pass two over the image data is performed. As each pixel in the original data is identified, its RGB components are scaled (shifted right by two, as previously discussed), applied as indexes to the RGBCube, and a color index is returned. If the index is valid, the pixel will be displayed with the color described by this color index (into the palette of N colors previously produced). If, however, the index is not valid (the out-of-range initialization value was returned), a search is made through the palette values to determine the closest color with which to display this pixel. The color that exhibits the smallest error is that used for the display of the pixel.

At a very high level, the process of quantizing image data from true color to palettized image format with N colors can be described by a four-step process. The first step is the sampling of the image to determine its color distribution. The result of this step is a three-dimensional color histogram (the RGBCube in our implementation) that is needed in step two.

The second step in this process is "colormap selection." Here, the optimal N colors required to display the color image are extracted from the input color distribution (or histogram) provided in step one. This color distribution is the content of the original image.

In the third step, a mapping is established between all colors that made up the original image and the closest colors contained in the extracted color map. The mapping function is usually stored in a quantization table (the RGBCube is reused in this implementation) to speed the processing in step four that follows. In other words, the mapping between the many thousands of colors in the original image and the N colors that will be used to display the image is developed.

After the colormap or palette has been selected in step two and the quantization table is created in step three, the fourth and final step of the process is image quantization. In this step, each pixel of the original image is passed through the quantization table (thereby mapping it to the corresponding palette entry required for display), and its mapped value is written into a new DIB memory block allocated for storage of the output image. In other words, the net result of the application of this quantization code is a block of memory in DIB format that contains the quantized image and a palette for displaying the image against.

Detailed Algorithm Operation

The following steps illustrate the actual steps that the median cut code goes through to process full color images. As you will see, many more steps are required in practice than were described earlier.

1. The constructor for the Median Cut Quantization Class, when instantiated, records the parameters passed into it. Parameters include **NumColors,** which determines the number of colors, N, the image should be quantized down to; **Width,** which is the width of the image in pixels; **Height,** which is the number of rows of image data in pixels; and **IpImage,** which points at the true color image data in DIB format somewhere in memory. After the parameters are recorded, the member function, **QuantizeImage,** is called to quantize the image.
2. Memory is next allocated for the RGBCube.
3. Memory is allocated for a DIB that will contain the quantized, 8-BPP palletized image on completion of the color quantization process.
4. A color histogram is built from the DIB image data and stored in the RGBCube.
5. The median cut algorithm is applied to the RGBCube data to divide the color space into N regions of approximately equal pixel counts.

6. A single color value is calculated for display of all RGB colors mapped into a single region. This calculation is repeated for the *N* regions.
7. Color mapping is then applied to the image data. Each pixel of RGB data from the original image is passed through the color map (within the RGBCube) and converted into a palette index to be used for display. This index is stored in the output DIB image memory at the row, column location defined for the pixel.
8. The palette produced by the application of quantization is then manipulated to reverse the effect of data scaling used in building the original RGBCube.
9. The memory used by the RGBCube is then freed because it is no longer needed.

On completion of image quantization, the median cut quantization object contains a block of memory that contains the quantized image in DIB format. The quantization object also contains a palette containing *N* colors for displaying the quantized image. Member functions are available in the MedianCutQuant class for providing access to the quantized image data and quantized image palette. See Figure 5.3 for the description of the member functions of the MedianCutQuant class.

As you can see from the code listings, the production of median cut quantized color images is not a trivial task. In fact, the code for performing this algorithm is probably the most complex presented in this book. Thankfully, the encapsulation of the code into a C++ class makes it extremely easy to use whether or not you understand the underlying algorithm. The best part is that the results, for the most part, are quite spectacular in terms of color quality and color selection.

As was the case with the dithering code, using the median cut class code is simplicity in itself. The following code snippet shows the typical steps required:

```
// Instantiate a quantizer object. Pass the desired number of colors, the width
// and height of the image in pixels and a pointer to the DIB formatted image
// in memory.

MedianCutQuant Q(NumberOfColors, ImageWidth, ImageHeight, lpImageData);

// Perform the quantization to the user specified number of colors
if (!Q.QuantizeImage()) {
  MessageBox(NULL, "Error quantizing image. No memory", "User Advisory", MB_OK );
  return;
}
// The image is now quantized. Get pointers to the palettized image data and
// the palette for further processing.
BYTE huge   *lpImage = Q.GetImageDataPtr();
RGBCOLOR *lpPalette = Q.GetImagePalettePtr();
.
. Process the image data
.
// Note, the palettized image data block will be freed when the
// MedianCutQuant object goes out of scope.
```

Although a stand-alone demonstration program could have been developed in this chapter for exercising the dithering and median cut quantization code, I decided that it was more trouble than it was worth. Instead, the reader is directed to the TestApp imaging example program of Chapter 1 to see how the quantization code is used. The TestApp program is an ideal vehicle for investigating dithering and median cut color quantization because:

1. It allows side-by-side comparison of true color versus quantized color images. This allows you to see and compare the quality of the quantized images to that of the original true color image (assuming your graphics adapter supports true color image display). I think you will be surprised by these comparisons.

2. It allows side-by-side comparisons between images that are dithered and images that are quantized. Within the TestApp program, true color images will automatically be dithered if your VGA graphics adapter is running in a 256-color mode.

3. Finally, the user can select the number of colors for Median Cut color quantization. For example, the original true color image can be displayed alongside quantized versions of the same image at 20, 32, 64, 128, and 256 colors. The results are, in most cases, illuminating.

Conclusions

Information on color reduction techniques and code for implementing these techniques has been presented here. Three different color quantization algorithms have been discussed, and two have been implemented: uniform quantization (using dithering) and the median cut algorithm. The code in this chapter has been implemented as stand-alone C++ classes. Both of these color reduction techniques should find application in many areas of computer graphics in addition to photographic imaging as described and used in this book. Additional information on dithering will be presented in Chapter 6 when the topic of image display is taken up.

Displaying Images in Windows

In this chapter you will learn about:
- How DIB images are displayed
- How different image display operations are performed including:
  1. Panning
  2. Zooming
  3. Displaying to scale
  4. Displaying to fit a window
  5. Aspect ratio protection
- Why two types of dithering are necessary
- How the Display class works
- How the Display class is used in application programs

Introduction

The display of images is arguably the most important aspect of any imaging system and is the most frequent operation performed by any imaging software. As such, the information and code presented in this chapter may be the most important in this book. After all, you can possess the most complete collection of image processing algorithms available but they're not worth a hill of beans unless the results of the image processing operations can be displayed for viewing.

On first thought, image display may be considered a rather mundane exercise in Windows programming. After all, Windows is a visual environment that offers device independence, right? How difficult can the display of images be? On further inspection, however, it becomes apparent that a well-thought-out image display philosophy must combine the ideas of device independence and performance with that of maximum flexibility. A couple of examples will help illustrate this point. Consider first the display of a true color image on a computer only capable of displaying 256 colors. If Windows 3.1 is asked to display this image under these circumstances, it will require approximately three to four minutes to display the image (depending on image size), and the displayed result will be terrible. This is because Windows 3.1 does not know how to correctly manipulate (dither) the image data for display. Using Windows 95 under similar circumstances, the image will be displayed immediately, but it will be converted from full color into black and white. Don't ask me why.

As a second example, consider a network of computers with various types of display hardware (256-color and true color SuperVGA systems) all trying to view a true color image. Any of the computer systems with true color image display capability will have no trouble viewing the image. All systems without true color capability will get Windows interpretation (a slow, terrible display) of the image as described earlier. This arrangement is not very useful in the majority of nonhomogeneous systems that make up typical computer networks. An alternative is for the imaging software to convert all images to the lowest common denominator necessary for display by all systems; that is, convert all true color images to 256-color format so that every system on the network can view them. Although this technique works, its drawback is that the systems that have true color display capability are handicapped by this approach, and as anyone who has seen the difference between 256-color and true color images will attest, true color images are generally much better to look at and to interpret.

The optimum solution to this networked scenario is to have the imaging software running on each computer system smart enough to process the true color image data into whatever form necessary for display on the local display hardware. If true color display hardware is available, the image data are passed through to the hardware unprocessed. If the display hardware is only capable of 256-color display, the true color image data are converted to 256 colors for display. The important point here is that the display software must be flexible enough to make display decisions automatically on an image by image basis for the local computer without much involvement of the user.

I present here a C++ class called **Display** that satisfies the display requirements of most professional imaging applications. By this I mean that the class provides flexible, locally adaptive support for image display on most SuperVGA display devices. In addition, it was designed with performance in mind and, as a result, is quite fast considering that it is written entirely in C++. Finally, it hides the complexity of Windows device-independent bitmaps from the programmer, making it very easy to use in any application.

In a nutshell, the **Display** class is used to display device-independent bitmaps (DIBs) in the Windows environment. This class implements the display functions of the imaging system architecture portrayed in Figure 1.1 of Chapter 1. Once an instance of the Display class is instantiated and given information about an image needing display, various member functions of the class can be called to display the image is different ways. One scenario for use of the Display class follows:

```
#include "display.hpp" // Included for the class definition

Display DisplayObj;          // Declare an object of the class for use

// Tell the display object about the image needing display. Besides providing
// the width, height and number of colors in the image, a pointer to the
// raster data and a pointer to a palette must be provided.
```

```
DisplayObj.InitForDisplay(Width, Height, Colors, lpImageData, lpPalette, FALSE);
// Display the image in window
DisplayObj.DisplayImage(hWindow, Pt, FALSE);
```

With four statements similar to the ones shown, an application program can display a DIB image. It doesn't get much easier than that.

How DIB Images Are Traditionally Displayed in Windows

The following discussion is in a large part based on the information provided in Chapter 2 concerning device-independent bitmaps. If you are unfamiliar with DIBs or need more information than is presented here, you are encouraged to read or reread the appropriate sections of Chapter 2.

The basic steps required to display a device-independent bitmap image in Windows are as follows:

1. First, a BITMAPINFO structure, which consists of a BITMAPINFOHEADER structure and an array of RGBQUAD values describing the image colors, must be allocated and initialized with values pertinent to the image to be displayed.
2. Next, a logical palette is created from the image color values. Logical palettes are the vehicles used to inform the Windows palette manager about the colors to use when displaying the image.
3. The handle of the original palette associated with the device context on which the image will be displayed is saved for later restoration.
4. The logical palette associated with the image is selected and realized into the device context of the display device. This is true regardless of the device type: screen, film recorder, or printer. The concepts of selecting a logical palette and realizing a logical palette are discussed in Chapter 2 in the discussion of the Windows treatment of color.
5. The image data in its inverted raster format are then bit blit (moved) into the device context. If the display device is the screen (actually a window on the screen), the image becomes visible at this point in the process.
6. Finally, the original palette associated with the display device context is restored.

As you can see there are a fair number of steps required to display a DIB image. The step-by-step process is the same in Windows 95 as it is in Windows 3.1. An application programmer has the option of repeating the earlier steps whenever an image needs to be displayed in his or her program or can use the much simpler and more versatile approach of incorporating the Display class described in the next section.

The Display Class

The Display class encapsulates the knowledge required for the display of device-independent bitmaps into a single, easy to use class. The Display class consists of 21 member functions that are briefly described in Figure 6.1. The interface specification for the Display class is contained in the file "display.hpp" and is shown in Listing 6.1. Listing 6.2 shows the implementation of the class functions contained in the file "display.cpp." Both files "display.hpp" and "display.cpp" are available for your perusal and use on the companion disk.

Listing 6.1 The Display class interface definition.

```
/*********************************************************/
/***                   "display.hpp"                 ***/
/***            Display Class Definition File         ***/
/***                                                  ***/
/***                    written by                    ***/
/***                 Craig A. Lindley                 ***/
/***                                                  ***/
/***      Revision: 2.0     Last Update: 11/11/94     ***/
/*********************************************************/

// Copyright (c) 1995 John Wiley & Sons, Inc. All rights reserved.

#ifndef DISPLAY_HPP
#define DISPLAY_HPP

#ifdef _WIN32_
#define huge
#endif

#ifndef _RGBCOLOR
#define _RGBCOLOR
typedef struct {
BYTE Red;
BYTE Green;
BYTE Blue;
} RGBCOLOR;
#endif

class Display {
  private:
    // Private Member Functions
    BOOL DisplayDIB(HDC hDevice, POINT& SrcPosition, RECT& DestRect, BOOL fClip);
    HPALETTE MakePalette(RGBQUAD* pColors, WORD NumOfColors);

    // Added for dithering
    HGLOBAL hDitheredImage;          // Handle to dithered image memory
    HGLOBAL DecimateImage(BYTE huge *lpImage,
                    WORD ImageWidth, WORD ImageHeight,
                    WORD DisplayWidth, WORD DisplayHeight);

    // Private Data
    HGLOBAL hBmi;                    // Handle to memory for BitMapInfo structure
    LPBITMAPINFO lpBmi;              // Long ptr to BitMapInfo structure
    // The next two values are for returning a 24 BPP BitMapInfo structure
    // when a 24 BPP image has been dithered to 8 bits.
    HGLOBAL hBmi24;                  // Handle to memory for BitMapInfo structure
    LPBITMAPINFO lpBmi24;            // Long ptr to BitMapInfo structure

    WORD    wWidth;                  // Dimensions of image raster NOT window
    WORD    wHeight;
```

```
   WORD      wColors;             // Number of image colors
   WORD      wBPP;                // Number of bits/pixel in image
   WORD      ZoomFactor;          // Zoom factor for horiz and vertical
   BYTE huge *lpRasterData;       // Ptr to image data
   HPALETTE hPalette;             // Palette handle
   BOOL      fClipFlag;           // Clipping flag
   BOOL      EightBitColorMode;   // TRUE if 8 bit graphics adapter
   WORD      BytesPerLine;        // Number of bytes in one row of image data
   BOOL      DitherFullSize;      // TRUE if full size dither is desired
   BOOL      DitheringRequired;   // TRUE if dithering is required
 public:
   Display();
  ~Display();
   BOOL IsDisplayHwdTrueColor(void);
   void SetImageDataPtr(BYTE huge *Ptr);
   WORD GetNumOfColors(void);
   HPALETTE GetPalette(void);
   WORD GetWidth(void);
   WORD GetHeight(void);
   WORD GetBPP(void);
   void UpdateAllColors(HWND hWindow);
   BOOL InitForDisplay(WORD Width, WORD Height, WORD NumOfColors,
                        BYTE huge *RasterData, RGBCOLOR far *Palette,
                        BOOL FullSizeDither);
   BOOL DisplayImageNative(HDC hDC, RECT& Rect, POINT& Pt, BOOL BGFlag);
   BOOL DisplayImage(HWND hWindow, POINT& Pt, BOOL BGFlag);
   BOOL DisplayImageInWindowRect(HWND hWindow, RECT& Area, BOOL BGFlag);
   BOOL DisplayImageWithAspect(HWND hWindow, BOOL BGFlag);
   void SetClipMode(void);
   void SetStretchMode(void);
   BOOL IsClipMode(void);
   void SetZoom(WORD TheZoom);
   WORD GetZoom(void);
   LPBITMAPINFO GetPtrToBITMAPINFO(void);
   void ErrorMessage(PSTR message);
};

inline void Display::ErrorMessage(PSTR message) {
  MessageBox(NULL, (LPSTR) message, (LPSTR) "Error", MB_OK|
    MB_ICONEXCLAMATION |MB_TASKMODAL);
}


#endif
```

Listing 6.2 The Display class member functions.

```
/********************************************************/
/***                "display.cpp"               ***/
/***            Display Class Functions          ***/
/***                 written by                  ***/
/***              Craig A. Lindley               ***/
/***                                             ***/
/***    Revision: 2.0    Last Update: 11/11/94   ***/
/********************************************************/

// Copyright (c) 1995 John Wiley & Sons, Inc. All rights reserved.
```

```
#include <windows.h>
#include <mem.h>
#include "display.hpp"

#ifdef _WIN32_
#define huge
#define hmemcpy memcpy
#endif

#define ALIGN_DWORD(x)  (((x)+3)/4 * 4) // Double word alignment macro

// Macros used to facilitate RGB pixel access for dithering
#define GetRGBPixel(Addr, Red, Green, Blue) \
  Blue  = (int) *(Addr);           \
  Green = (int) *(Addr+1);         \
  Red   = (int) *(Addr+2);

#define PutRGBPixel(Addr, Red, Green, Blue)   \
  Red = (Red < 0) ? 0:Red;             \
  Red = (Red > 255) ? 255:Red;         \
  Green = (Green < 0) ? 0:Green;       \
  Green = (Green > 255) ? 255:Green;   \
  Blue = (Blue < 0) ? 0:Blue;          \
  Blue = (Blue > 255) ? 255:Blue;      \
  *(Addr)   = (BYTE)Blue;              \
  *(Addr+1) = (BYTE)Green;             \
  *(Addr+2) = (BYTE)Red;

extern RGBCOLOR DitherPalette[256];

/* Constructor for the display class */
Display::Display() {

  lpBmi     = NULL;
  hBmi      = 0;
  hPalette  = 0;
  wWidth    = 0;
  wHeight   = 0;
  wColors   = 0;
  ZoomFactor = 0;                    // No zooming
  fClipFlag = TRUE;
  lpBmi24   = NULL;                  // Ptr to 24 BPP Bmi for dithered image
  hBmi24    = 0;
  hDitheredImage  = 0;               // Handle to dithered image if any

  DitheringRequired = FALSE;      // Assume no dithering required
  DitherFullSize = TRUE;          // Assume a full size image dither
  // Determine what video mode we are running in
  HDC hIC = CreateIC("DISPLAY", NULL, NULL, NULL);
  EightBitColorMode = GetDeviceCaps(hIC, BITSPIXEL) == 8;
  DeleteDC(hIC);
}


/* Destructor for the display class */
Display::~Display() {
```

```
  if (lpBmi != NULL) {              // If a BITMAPINFO structure exists
    GlobalUnlock(hBmi);             // Free the memory it occupies
    GlobalFree(hBmi);
  }

  if (hPalette) {                   // If a logical palette exists
    DeleteObject(hPalette);         // Free the memory it occupies
    hPalette = 0;
  }

  // If 24BPP BMI structure has been used, free it
  if (lpBmi24 != NULL) {
    GlobalUnlock(hBmi24);
    GlobalFree(hBmi24);
  }

  if (hDitheredImage) {             // If object contained a dithered image
    GlobalFree(hDitheredImage);     // Free the memory it occupies
    hDitheredImage = 0;
  }
}

// These functions were inline but sometimes failed to work
void Display::SetClipMode(void)      { fClipFlag = TRUE; }
void Display::SetStretchMode(void)   { fClipFlag = FALSE; }
BOOL Display::IsClipMode(void)       { return fClipFlag; }
void Display::SetImageDataPtr(BYTE huge *Ptr)    { lpRasterData = Ptr; }
WORD Display::GetNumOfColors(void)   { return wColors; }
HPALETTE Display::GetPalette(void)   { return hPalette; }
WORD Display::GetWidth(void)         { return wWidth; }
WORD Display::GetHeight(void)        { return wHeight; }
WORD Display::GetBPP(void)           { return wBPP; }
WORD Display::GetZoom(void)          { return 1 << ZoomFactor; }

// This function returns a pointer to a Bmi structure built for display
// of the image by the code in InitForDisplay. If this display object
// contains a 24 BPP image dithered to 8 bits, the original structure is
// copied and modified before a pointer is returned.
LPBITMAPINFO Display::GetPtrToBITMAPINFO(void) {

  if (hDitheredImage) {             // If this object contains a dithered image
    // We will never get here unless a 24 BPP image has been dithered
    if (hBmi24 == 0) {              // If the 24BPP Bmi has not been allocated
      hBmi24 = GlobalAlloc(GHND, sizeof(BITMAPINFOHEADER) + 256 * sizeof(RGBQUAD));
      if (!hBmi24)  {
        ErrorMessage("Out of memory");
        return NULL;
      }
      // Get a ptr to the allocated memory
      lpBmi24 = (LPBITMAPINFO) GlobalLock(hBmi24);
      // Copy the dithered image's Bmi to this new structure
      *lpBmi24 = *lpBmi;
      // Modify the Bmi to reflect the 24 BPP image's true nature
      LPBITMAPINFOHEADER pBi = &lpBmi24->bmiHeader;
      pBi->biBitCount = 24;
```

```
        pBi->biClrUsed = 0;
        pBi->biSizeImage = ALIGN_DWORD((DWORD) wWidth * 3) * (DWORD) wHeight;
    }
    return lpBmi24;                      // Return the modified structure ptr
  } else
    return lpBmi;                        // Return the original structure ptr
}


// This function returns true if display hwd is capable of direct display
// of true color images. This function returns TRUE when the display
// adapter supports more than 8 BPP.
BOOL Display::IsDisplayHwdTrueColor(void) {

  // Determine what video mode we are running in
  HDC hIC = CreateIC("DISPLAY", NULL, NULL, NULL);
  int BitsPerPixel = GetDeviceCaps(hIC, BITSPIXEL);
  DeleteDC(hIC);
  if (BitsPerPixel > 8)
    return TRUE;
  else
    return FALSE;
}


// These declared here so they will not be stack variables accessed
// by offset from SP. This, hopefully, helps performance.
int   TRed, TGreen, TBlue;
int   RedError, GreenError, BlueError;
BYTE  PaletteIndex;
int   BlueOffset;
BYTE near *PixelAddr;
BYTE near *RPixelAddr;
BYTE near *DPixelAddr;


// Dither a single row of image data
void DitherLine(WORD Width, BYTE near *pLine1, BYTE near *pLine2) {

  for (register WORD Pixel=0; Pixel < Width; Pixel++) {
    // Get the pixel of interest for the dither
    PixelAddr = pLine1 + (Pixel * 3);
    GetRGBPixel(PixelAddr, TRed, TGreen, TBlue);
     // Determine which blue entry from palette to use
     BlueOffset = (TBlue/85);
     if ((TBlue - (BlueOffset * 85)) > 43)
      BlueOffset += 1;
     // Calculate palette entry address from color
     // PaletteIndex = ((TRed/32)*32) + ((TGreen/32)*4) + BlueOffset;
    // For speed we will calculate the color index as follows
     PaletteIndex = (TRed & 0xE0) + ((TGreen >> 5) << 2) + BlueOffset;
     // Store the palette back into the same buffer
    *(pLine1 + Pixel) = PaletteIndex;
     /*
    Pixel is set, now distribute the error to adjacent pixels
    using a modified version of the Floyd-Steinberg algorithm.
```

```
            In this implementation the error is distributed as follows
                              Pixel
                                        o 1/2->o
                                  1/4  |
                                  o
        The algorithm is modified to increase performance.
         */
        // Calculate errors between the desired color and color used
        // for this pixel. Actual error / 4. Use near pointers for speed.

        BYTE near *pColor = (BYTE near *) &DitherPalette[PaletteIndex]; // Ptr to color
        RedError = (TRed - *(pColor)) >> 2;
         GreenError = (TGreen - *(pColor+1)) >> 2;
        BlueError = (TBlue - *(pColor+2)) >> 2;
         // Do the pixel directly below target pixel
        DPixelAddr = pLine2 + (Pixel * 3);
        GetRGBPixel(DPixelAddr, TRed, TGreen, TBlue);
         TRed  += RedError;                  // 1/4 error
        TGreen += GreenError;
        TBlue  += BlueError;
         PutRGBPixel(DPixelAddr, TRed, TGreen, TBlue);
         // Do the pixel directly to the right
         if (Pixel != Width - 1) {
            RPixelAddr = PixelAddr + 3;
          GetRGBPixel(RPixelAddr, TRed, TGreen, TBlue);
          TRed  += RedError  + RedError;   // 1/2 error
            TGreen += GreenError + GreenError;
          TBlue  += BlueError  + BlueError;
          PutRGBPixel(RPixelAddr, TRed, TGreen, TBlue);
         }
   }
}


// This function dithers the image contained in this object. It returns
// a handle to a global memory block containing the dithered data.
HGLOBAL DitherAnImage(BYTE huge *lpImageData,
                       WORD Width, WORD Height) {

  // Calculate width in bytes of a row of RGB data
  WORD BytesPerLine = ALIGN_DWORD(Width * 3); // Source 24 BPP image
  // Calculate width in bytes of a row of palettized data
  WORD BytesPerLineDest = ALIGN_DWORD(Width); // Dest 8 BPP image


  // Allocate two lines of RGB buffer for dithering
  HLOCAL hLine1Buffer = LocalAlloc(LMEM_MOVEABLE, BytesPerLine);
  if (!hLine1Buffer)
     return NULL;

  HLOCAL hLine2Buffer = LocalAlloc(LMEM_MOVEABLE, BytesPerLine);
  if (!hLine2Buffer) {
    LocalFree(hLine1Buffer);
    return NULL;
  }
```

```
    // Allocate the destination dither buffer
    HGLOBAL hMem = GlobalAlloc(GHND, (DWORD) BytesPerLineDest * Height);
    if (!hMEM) {
      LocalFree(hLine1Buffer);
       LocalFree(hLine2Buffer);
       return NULL;
    }

    // Now lock the pointers for access
    BYTE near *Line1Buffer = (BYTE near *) LocalLock(hLine1Buffer);
    BYTE near *Line2Buffer = (BYTE near *) LocalLock(hLine2Buffer);
    BYTE huge *lpDitheredRasterData = (BYTE huge *) GlobalLock(hMem);

    // Move the first two lines of the source image to dither buffers
    hmemcpy(Line1Buffer, lpImageData, BytesPerLine);
    hmemcpy(Line2Buffer, lpImageData + BytesPerLine, BytesPerLine);

    for (register WORD Row = 2; Row < Height; Row++) {
      DitherLine(Width, Line1Buffer, Line2Buffer);
        // Copy the dithered data in Line1Buffer to destination
      hmemcpy(lpDitheredRasterData + ((Row-2) * (DWORD) BytesPerLineDest),
              Line1Buffer, BytesPerLineDest);
        // Copy Line2Buffer to Line1Buffer so it can be dithered
      memcpy(Line1Buffer, Line2Buffer, BytesPerLine);

        // Move new data to Line2Buffer
      hmemcpy(Line2Buffer, lpImageData + (Row * (DWORD) BytesPerLine),
              BytesPerLine);
    }
    // Must complete the two rows in the line buffers
    DitherLine(Width, Line1Buffer, Line2Buffer);
    // Copy the dithered data in Line1Buffer to destination
    hmemcpy(lpDitheredRasterData + ((Height-2) * (DWORD) BytesPerLineDest),
            Line1Buffer, BytesPerLineDest);
    memcpy(Line1Buffer, Line2Buffer, BytesPerLine);

    DitherLine(Width, Line1Buffer, Line2Buffer);
    // Copy the dithered data in Line1Buffer to destination
    hmemcpy(lpDitheredRasterData + ((Height-1) * (DWORD) BytesPerLineDest),
            Line1Buffer, BytesPerLineDest);

    // Free the local line buffers
    LocalUnlock(hLine1Buffer);
    LocalFree(hLine1Buffer);
    LocalUnlock(hLine2Buffer);
    LocalFree(hLine2Buffer);

    // Signal all is well
    GlobalUnlock(hMem);                     // Unlock the dithered raster data
    return hMem;                            // Return the handle of the data
}

// This function sets the zoom factor. Valid parameters are
// 1, 2, 4 or 8. Any invalid parameter sets the zoom to 1 or no zoom.
void Display::SetZoom(WORD TheZoom) {
```

```
    switch (TheZoom) {
      case 1: ZoomFactor = 0;
        break;
      case 2: ZoomFactor = 1;
        break;
      case 4: ZoomFactor = 2;
        break;
      case 8: ZoomFactor = 3;
        break;
      default:
        ZoomFactor = 0;
        break;
    }
}


/*
This function displays a DIB on the device specified by the handle to the device
context hDevice. This function returns TRUE if the DIB was displayed and FALSE
otherwise. If fClip is TRUE, the image is clipped, if necessary, to display in
the specified context (probably a window). If cClip is FALSE, StretchBlt is used
to fit the whole image into the destination context. This function works in
MM_TEXT mapping mode only. The point SrcPosition determines the position in the
bit map to begin display and the rect DestRect provides information about the
size of the display area on the destination context.
*/
BOOL Display::DisplayDIB(HDC hDevice, POINT& SrcPosition, RECT& DestRect,
                         BOOL fClip) {
  WORD ScanLines;
  BOOL DispOk;
  BYTE huge *lpImageData = lpRasterData;

  // This mode seems to work best for color and monochrome images
#ifdef _WIN32_
  SetStretchBltMode(hDevice, COLORONCOLOR);
#else
  SetStretchBltMode(hDevice, STRETCH_DELETESCANS);
#endif
  if (fClip) {
    // This moves a portion of the image to the window depending
    // upon the size of the window. This code supports scrolling
    // and zooming but only supports full size dithering.

    if (!DitheringRequired) {     // If dithering is not required
      ScanLines = StretchDIBits(hDevice, 0, 0,
                                DestRect.right, DestRect.bottom,
                                SrcPosition.x >> ZoomFactor,
                                wHeight - (DestRect.bottom >> ZoomFactor)
                                  (SrcPosition.y >> ZoomFactor),
                                DestRect.right >> ZoomFactor,
                                DestRect.bottom >> ZoomFactor,
                                lpImageData, lpBmi, DIB_RGB_COLORS, SRCCOPY);

      // See if the complete image was displayed
      DispOk = (ScanLines == (DestRect.bottom >> ZoomFactor));
    } else {                      // Dithering is required
```

```
        if (DitherFullSize) {        // Dither image in already in dither buffer
          // Get a pointer to the dither image data.
          lpImageData = (BYTE huge *) GlobalLock(hDitheredImage);

          // Blit the 8 BPP dithered image to device context
          ScanLines = StretchDIBits(hDevice, 0, 0,
                                    DestRect.right, DestRect.bottom,
                                    SrcPosition.x >> ZoomFactor,
                                    wHeight - (DestRect.bottom >> ZoomFactor) -
                                      (SrcPosition.y >> ZoomFactor),
                                    DestRect.right >> ZoomFactor,
                                    DestRect.bottom >> ZoomFactor,
                                    lpImageData, lpBmi, DIB_RGB_COLORS, SRCCOPY);
          GlobalUnlock(hDitheredImage); // Unlock pointer

          // See if the complete image was displayed
          DispOk = (ScanLines == (DestRect.bottom >> ZoomFactor));
        } else {
          DispOk = FALSE;                // Dithering on demand not supported
        }
      }
    } else {                             // Stretch mode
      // This stretches the bitmap to the window regardless of size.
      // NOTE: this code does not support zooming or panning but does support
      // both full size and dithering on demand.

      if (!DitheringRequired) {          // Dithering is not required
        ScanLines = StretchDIBits(hDevice, DestRect.left, DestRect.top,
                                  DestRect.right - DestRect.left,
                                  DestRect.bottom - DestRect.top,
                                  0, 0, wWidth, wHeight,
                                  lpImageData, lpBmi, DIB_RGB_COLORS, SRCCOPY);

        // See if the complete image was displayed
        DispOk = (ScanLines == wHeight);
      } else {                           // Dithering is required
        if (DitherFullSize) {            // Dither image in already in dither buffer
          // Get a pointer to the dither image data.
          lpImageData = (BYTE huge *) GlobalLock(hDitheredImage);

          ScanLines = StretchDIBits(hDevice, DestRect.left, DestRect.top,
                                    DestRect.right - DestRect.left,
                                    DestRect.bottom - DestRect.top,
                                    0, 0, wWidth, wHeight,
                                    lpImageData, lpBmi, DIB_RGB_COLORS, SRC COPY);
          GlobalUnlock(hDitheredImage); // Unlock pointer

          // See if the complete image was displayed
          DispOk = (ScanLines == wHeight);
        } else {                             // Perform dithering on demand
          // Calculate displayed dimensions of image in pixels
          WORD DisplayWidth = DestRect.right - DestRect.left + 1;
          WORD DisplayHeight = DestRect.bottom - DestRect.top + 1;
          // Decimate image to displayed dimensions
```

```
HGLOBAL hMem = DecimateImage(lpRasterData, wWidth, wHeight,
                             DisplayWidth, DisplayHeight);
if (!hMem)
  return FALSE;

// When we get here, the image has been decimated
BYTE huge *lpImage = (BYTE huge *) GlobalLock(hMem);
HGLOBAL hDitherMem = DitherAnImage(lpImage, DisplayWidth, DisplayHeight);
// Decimated image data can now be freed regardless of whether
// the image dithered successfully.
GlobalUnlock(hMem);
GlobalFree(hMem);

if (!hDitherMem)               // Did image dither ?
  return FALSE;

// When we get here the image has been decimated and dithered
// Now prepare a BITMAPINFO structure with which to display it.
HGLOBAL hBmi = GlobalAlloc(GHND, sizeof(BITMAPINFOHEADER) +
                           256 * sizeof(RGBQUAD));
if (!hBmi) {
  GlobalFree(hDitherMem);
  return FALSE;
}
LPBITMAPINFO lpBmi = (LPBITMAPINFO) GlobalLock(hBmi);

LPBITMAPINFOHEADER pBi = &lpBmi->bmiHeader;
pBi->biSize     = sizeof(BITMAPINFOHEADER);
pBi->biWidth    = DisplayWidth;
pBi->biHeight   = DisplayHeight;
pBi->biPlanes   = 1;
pBi->biBitCount = 8;
pBi->biSizeImage = ALIGN_DWORD((DWORD) DisplayWidth * 3) * (DWORD)
                   DisplayHeight;
pBi->biClrUsed  = 256;
// Copy palette to DIB color table
for (register int i = 0; i < 256; i++) {
  lpBmi->bmiColors[i].rgbRed   = DitherPalett[i].Red;
  lpBmi->bmiColors[i].rgbGreen = DitherPalette[i].Green;
  lpBmi->bmiColors[i].rgbBlue  = DitherPalette[i].Blue;
  lpBmi->bmiColors[i].rgbReserved = 0;
}
// Get a pointer to the dithered data
lpImage = (BYTE huge *) GlobalLock(hDitherMem);

// Blt the data to the device
ScanLines = StretchDIBits(hDevice, DestRect.left, DestRect.top,
                          DisplayWidth, DisplayHeight,
                          0, 0, DisplayWidth, DisplayHeight,
                          lpImage, lpBmi, DIB_RGB_COLORS, SRCCOPY);

// Free up the dithering image memory
GlobalUnlock(hDitherMem);
GlobalFree(hDitherMem);
```

```
            // Free up BITMAPINFO memory
            GlobalUnlock(hBmi);
            GlobalFree(hBmi);
            // See if the complete image was displayed
            DispOk = (ScanLines == DisplayHeight);
        }
    }
}
    return DispOk;
}


/*
This function builds a logical palette. This palette is made up of wColors number
of colors. It returns a handle to the palette if successful and NULL otherwise.
*/
HPALETTE Display::MakePalette(RGBQUAD* pColors, WORD NumOfColors) {
    HGLOBAL hPaletteMem;

    if (!pColors || NumOfColors == 0)
        return NULL;

    WORD ColorsInPalette = (NumOfColors > 16) ? 256:NumOfColors;

    hPaletteMem = GlobalAlloc(GHND, sizeof(LOGPALETTE) + ColorsInPalette *
        sizeof(PALETTEENTRY));
    if (!hPaletteMem)
        return NULL;

    LPLOGPALETTE pPal = (LPLOGPALETTE) GlobalLock(hPaletteMem);

    pPal->palNumEntries = NumOfColors;
    pPal->palVersion = 0x300;

    for (int i=0, i < NumOfColors; i++) {
        pPal->palPalEntry[i].peRed   = pColors[i].rgbRed;
        pPal->palPalEntry[i].peGreen = pColors[i].rgbGreen;
        pPal->palPalEntry[i].peBlue  = pColors[i].rgbBlue;
        pPal->palPalEntry[i].peFlags = 0;
    }
    HPALETTE hPal = CreatePalette(pPal);
    GlobalUnlock(hPaletteMem);
    GlobalFree(hPaletteMem);
    return hPal;
}

BOOL Display::InitForDisplay(WORD Width, WORD Height, WORD NumOfColors,
                             BYTE huge *RasterData, RGBCOLOR far *Palette,
                             BOOL FullSizeDither) {

    // Store the important values
    wWidth       = Width;
    wHeight      = Height;
    wColors      = NumOfColors;
    lpRasterData = RasterData;

    // Save the state of the dither flag passed in. Assume dithering won't
    // be required.
```

```
DitherFullSize = FullSizeDither;
DitheringRequired = FALSE;

HCURSOR hOldCursor = SetCursor(LoadCursor(NULL, IDC_WAIT));

if (hDitheredImage) {              // If object contained a dithered image
  GlobalFree(hDitheredImage);     // free up the memory
  hDitheredImage = 0;
}

// Create the DIB header
if (lpBmi != NULL) {
  GlobalUnlock(hBmi);
  GlobalFree(hBmi);
}

// If this image is a true color image, set NumOfColors to 256 for the
    allocation
if (NumOfColors == 0)
  NumOfColors = 256;

WORD ColorsInPalette = (NumOfColors > 16) ? 256:NumOfColors;

hBmi = GlobalAlloc(GHND, sizeof(BITMAPINFOHEADER) + ColorsInPalette *
  sizeof(RGBQUAD));
if (!hBmi) {
  ErrorMessage("Out of memory");
  return FALSE;
}

lpBmi = (LPBITMAPINFO) GlobalLock(hBmi);

// If this image was a true color image, set NumOfColors back to 0 for
    processing
if (wColors == 0)
  NumOfColors = 0;

// The following setup is independent of the # of colors
LPBITMAPINFOHEADER pBi = &lpBmi->bmiHeader;
pBi->biSize          = sizeof(BITMAPINFOHEADER);
pBi->biWidth         = wWidth;
pBi->biHeight        = wHeight;
pBi->biPlanes        = 1;
pBi->biCompression   = 0L;
pBi->biXPelsPerMeter = 0L;
pBi->biYPelsPerMeter = 0L;
pBi->biClrImportant  = 0L;

// The remainder of the processing is dependent upon the number of colors

WORD ActualNumOfColors = NumOfColors;
if (NumOfColors > 16)
  NumOfColors = 256;

register int Index;

switch(NumOfColors) {
  case 2:
```

```
      pBi->biBitCount = 1;
      pBi->biClrUsed = 2L;
      // Copy PCX Palette into DIB color table
      lpBmi->bmiColors[0].rgbRed      = Palette[0].Red;
      lpBmi->bmiColors[0].rgbGreen    = Palette[0].Green;
      lpBmi->bmiColors[0].rgbBlue     = Palette[0].Blue;
      lpBmi->bmiColors[0].rgbReserved = 0;
      lpBmi->bmiColors[1].rgbRed      = Palette[1].Red;
      lpBmi->bmiColors[1].rgbGreen    = Palette[1].Green;
      lpBmi->bmiColors[1].rgbBlue     = Palette[1].Blue;
      lpBmi->bmiColors[1].rgbReserved = 0;
      break;

case 4:
  pBi->biBitCount = 4;
  pBi->biClrUsed  = 4L;
  // Copy palette to DIB color table
    for (Index=0; Index < NumOfColors; Index++) {
      lpBmi->bmiColors[Index].rgbRed      = Palette[Index].Red;
      lpBmi->bmiColors[Index].rgbGreen = Palette[Index].Green;
      lpBmi->bmiColors[Index].rgbBlue  = Palette[Index].Blue;
      lpBmi->bmiColors[Index].rgbReserved = 0;
    }
    break;

    case 16:
     pBi->biBitCount = 4;
     pBi->biClrUsed  = 16L;
     // Copy palette to DIB color table
    for (Index=0; Index < NumOfColors; Index++) {
      lpBmi->bmiColors[Index].rgbRed      = Palette[Index].Red;
      lpBmi->bmiColors[Index].rgbGreen = Palette[Index].Green;
      lpBmi->bmiColors[Index].rgbBlue  = Palette[Index].Blue;
      lpBmi->bmiColors[Index].rgbReserved = 0;
    }
  break;

case 256:
  pBi->biBitCount = 8;
  pBi->biClrUsed  = (DWORD) ActualNumOfColors;
  // Copy palette to DIB color table
    for (Index=0; Index < ActualNumOfColors; Index++) {
      lpBmi->bmiColors[Index].rgbRed      = Palette[Index].Red;
      lpBmi->bmiColors[Index].rgbGreen = Palette[Index].Green;
      lpBmi->bmiColors[Index].rgbBlue  = Palette[Index].Blue;
      lpBmi->bmiColors[Index].rgbReserved = 0;
    }
  NumOfColors = ActualNumOfColors;
  break;

case 0:                              // 24 BPP image
  /*
  When we get here an image contains more than 256 colors and is
  therefore considered a true color image. How true color images
  are displayed depends upon the display hardware available and
```

```
the display mode being used. Windows cannot accurately display
a true color image when an 8 bit (256 color) display mode is
being utilized. A true color image must be dithered to be
displayable in a 256 color mode.

If a HiColor or True Color display mode is being utilized,
this discussion is mute because the VGA card and driver can
display the true color image directly.
*/

  pBi->biBitCount = 24;         // Indicate 24 BPP image in data structure

  // Determine if we are running in 8 bit color mode or greater
  if (!EightBitColorMode) {    // Display is capable of true color
    pBi->biClrUsed = 0;         // No palette manipulation is required
    NumOfColors = 256;          // but a palette must be created anyway.
  } else {
    // The VGA card itself is not capable of true color display. The
    // image will be dithered. Move dither palette into place.
    DitheringRequired = TRUE;   // Indicate dithering is required

    pBi->biClrUsed = NumOfColors = 256;
    // Copy palette to DIB color table and to main palette
    for (Index=0; Index < NumOfColors; Index++) {
      lpBmi->bmiColors[Index].rgbRed   = DitherPalette[Index].Red;
      lpBmi->bmiColors[Index].rgbGreen = DitherPalette[Index].Green;
      lpBmi->bmiColors[Index].rgbBlue  = DitherPalette[Index].Blue;
      lpBmi->bmiColors[Index].rgbReserved = 0;
    }
    if (DitherFullSize) { // If dithering full size
      // We must now prepare to dither the image and in the process
      // convert the copy of the image in memory to 256 color format
      pBi->biBitCount = 8; // Make Windows think image is 8 BPP

      // Do the full size dithering of the image
      hDitheredImage = DitherAnImage(lpRasterData, wWidth, wHeight);
      if (!hDitheredImage) {
        MessageBox(NULL, "No memory to dither image", NULL, MB_OK |
          MB_TASKMODAL);
        return FALSE;
      }
    }
  }
  break;
}
// Now calculate the size of the image
switch(pBi->biBitCount) {
  case 1:   // 1 bit per pixel monochrome images
    BytesPerLine = (wWidth+7)/8; // Round up to nearest byte
    break;

  case 4:   // 4 bits per pixel 16 color images
    BytesPerLine = (wWidth+1)/2; // Exactly two pixels in each byte
    break;
```

```
        case 8:   // 8 bits per pixel 256 color images
          BytesPerLine = wWidth;         // Exactly one pixel in each byte
          break;

        case 24:  // 24 bits per pixel image
          BytesPerLine = 3 * wWidth;     // Three bytes per pixel
          break;
    }
    // If the biSizeImage member is going to be set to a non-zero value
    // the number of bits/pixel must be taken into consideration
    // for its calculation.
    BytesPerLine = ALIGN_DWORD(BytesPerLine);

    // Store bits/pixel in image
    wBPP = pBi->biBitCount;
    // Calculate image size
    pBi->biSizeImage = (DWORD) BytesPerLine * (DWORD) wHeight;

    // Create and set logical palette
    if (hPalette)
      DeleteObject(hPalette);

    if ((hPalette = MakePalette(lpBmi->bmiColors, NumOfColors)) == NULL)
      ErrorMessage("Cannot create logical palette");

    SetCursor(hOldCursor);
    return TRUE;
}

// This function displays the image with the aspect ratio intact.
BOOL Display::DisplayImageWithAspect(HWND hWindow, BOOL BGFlag) {

    // Calculate the dimensions of the display window to force
    // correct aspect ratio.
    BOOL VertFit;                    // True if image is taller than wide
    if (wHeight > wWidth)
      VertFit = TRUE;
    else
      VertFit = FALSE;

    RECT Rect;
    // Get the dimensions of display window. These are the dimensions from
    // the layout.
    GetClientRect(hWindow, &Rect);
    // Modify the dimensions of the display window so StretchBlt does not
    // affect the aspect ratio.
    WORD HOffset = Rect.right;   // In preparation for centering grab the
    WORD VOffset = Rect.bottom;  // width and height of the display area.

    if (VertFit) {               // Make the image fit vertically
      WORD NewWidth = Rect.right + 1;
      while (NewWidth > Rect.right)
          NewWidth = (WORD) ((Rect.bottom-- * (DWORD) wWidth) / wHeight);
      Rect.bottom++;
      Rect.left   = HOffset = (HOffset - NewWidth) / 2;
      Rect.right  = NewWidth + HOffset;
```

```
      Rect.top    = VOffset = (VOffset - Rect.bottom) / 2;
      Rect.bottom = Rect.bottom + VOffset;
   } else {
      WORD NewHeight = Rect.bottom + 1;
      while (NewHeight > Rect.bottom)
         NewHeight = (WORD)((Rect.right-- * (DWORD) wHeight) / wWidth);
      Rect.right++;
      Rect.left  = HOffset = (HOffset - Rect.right) / 2;
      Rect.right = HOffset + Rect.right;
       Rect.top    = VOffset = (VOffset - NewHeight) / 2;
       Rect.bottom = NewHeight + VOffset;
   }
   // Now display the image in the modified display window
   return (DisplayImageInWindowRect(hWindow, Rect, BGFlag));
}


// This function is called to display an entire image which does not
// necessarily fill up the entire window area.
BOOL Display::DisplayImageInWindowRect(HWND hWindow, RECT& Area, BOOL BGFlag) {
   HPALETTE hOldPalette;
   HCURSOR hOldCursor;
   POINT Position;

   Position.x = Position.y = 0;
   BOOL Result;

   if (lpBmi == NULL)         // if InitForDisplay has not yet been called
      return FALSE;           // exit because there is no image to display

   if (GetPalette()) {        // Only display if palette is available
      hOldCursor = SetCursor(LoadCursor(NULL, IDC_WAIT));
      HDC hdc = GetDC(hWindow);    // Get a DC for the window

      // Now draw the bitmap into the device context
      hOldPalette = SelectPalette(hdc, GetPalette(), BGFlag);
      RealizePalette(hdc);
      Result = DisplayDIB(hdc, Position, Area, FALSE);

      // Put the old palette back
      SelectPalette(hdc, hOldPalette, TRUE);
      ReleaseDC(hWindow, hdc);
      SetCursor(hOldCursor);

      return Result;
   }
   return FALSE;
}


// This function is called to display an image which absolutely
// fills up the entire window area.
BOOL Display::DisplayImage(HWND hWindow, POINT& Position, BOOL BGFlag) {
   HPALETTE hOldPalette;
   HCURSOR hOldCursor;
   RECT Area;
   BOOL Result;
```

```
    if (lpBmi == NULL)              // if InitForDisplay has not yet been called
      return FALSE;                 // exit because there is no image to display

    if (GetPalette()) {             // Only display if palette is available
      hOldCursor = SetCursor(LoadCursor(NULL, IDC_WAIT));
      GetClientRect(hWindow, (LPRECT) &Area);// Get size of window to display into
      HDC hdc = GetDC(hWindow);     // Get a DC for the window
       // Now draw the bitmap into the device context
      hOldPalette = SelectPalette(hdc, GetPalette(), BGFlag);
      RealizePalette(hdc);
      Result = DisplayDIB(hdc, Position, Area, fClipFlag);

      // Put the old palette back. Force old palette to background.
      SelectPalette(hdc, hOldPalette, TRUE);
      ReleaseDC(hWindow, hdc);
      SetCursor(hOldCursor);

      return Result;
    }
    return FALSE;
}

// Update colors of bitmap without repainting the screen
void Display::UpdateAllColors(HWND hWindow) {
  WORD UpdatedEntries;

  if (GetPalette()) {               // If a palette to install
    HDC hdc = GetDC(hWindow);
    HPALETTE hOldPalette = SelectPalette(hdc, GetPalette(), 0);
    UpdatedEntries = RealizePalette(hdc);

    if (UpdatedEntries)             // If entries in palette have changed
      UpdateColors(hdc);            // Update the colors in bitmap
    // Put the old palette back
    SelectPalette(hdc, hOldPalette, TRUE);
    ReleaseDC(hWindow, hdc);
  }
}

// This function is called to decimate an RGB image. It decimates the full size
// RGB into a buffer (that it allocates), the size needed for display of the
// image. The decimated data is in RGB format also. This function returns a
// handle to the decimated data buffer if successful and NULL if not. NULL means
// no memory for the buffer was available.
HGLOBAL Display::DecimateImage(BYTE huge *lpRasterData,
                                    WORD ImageWidth, WORD ImageHeight,
                                    WORD DisplayWidth, WORD DisplayHeight) {

    DWORD BytesPerLineSource = ALIGN_DWORD(ImageWidth * 3);
    DWORD BytesPerLineDest   = ALIGN_DWORD(DisplayWidth * 3);

    // Allocate memory for the decimated data. Pad by 100 bytes
    HGLOBAL hMem = GlobalAlloc(GHND, (BytesPerLineDest * DisplayHeight) + 100);
    if (!hMem)
        return NULL;
```

```
// If we get here, there was enough memory for the decimated image.
// Lock a pointer to the decimated image data buffer.
BYTE huge *lpDecimatedImage = (BYTE huge *) GlobalLock(hMem);


DWORD SPixelY, SPixelX;
BYTE huge *lpSPixelRow;
BYTE huge *lpDPixelRow;
BYTE huge *lpSPixel;
BYTE huge *lpDPixel;


// Traverse destination image looking back at source image.
for (register int Row=0; Row < DisplayHeight; Row++) {
  // Calculate which row of source image to fetch
  SPixelY = ((DWORD) ImageHeight * Row) / (DWORD) DisplayHeight;
  lpSPixelRow = (BYTE huge *)(lpRasterData + (SPixelY * BytesPerLineSource));
  lpDPixelRow = (BYTE huge *)(lpDecimatedImage + (Row * BytesPerLineDest));
  for (register int Col=0; Col < DisplayWidth; Col++) {
    // Do calculations required for each col of destination image
    SPixelX = ((DWORD) ImageWidth * Col) / (DWORD) DisplayWidth;
    lpSPixel = (BYTE huge *)(lpSPixelRow + (SPixelX * 3L));
    lpDPixel = (BYTE huge *)(lpDPixelRow + (Col * 3L));


    // Fetch and Store image data as BYTEs
    *lpDPixel++ = *lpSPixel++;    // Move blue data
    *lpDPixel++ = *lpSPixel++;    // Move green data
    *lpDPixel = *lpSPixel;        // Move red data
  }
}
// Return handle to decimated image data
GlobalUnlock(hMem);              // Unlock the data
return hMem;
}


// This is the palette with which all true color images will be
// displayed when hardware support is unavailable.
RGBCOLOR DitherPalette[256] = {
    {0,   0,   0},  {0,   0,  85},  {0,   0, 170},  {0,   0, 255},
    {0,  36,   0},  {0,  36,  85},  {0,  36, 170},  {0,  36, 255},
    {0,  73,   0},  {0,  73,  85},  {0,  73, 170},  {0,  73, 255},
    {0, 109,   0},  {0, 109,  85},  {0, 109, 170},  {0, 109, 255},
    {0, 146,   0},  {0, 146,  85},  {0, 146, 170},  {0, 146, 255},
    {0, 182,   0},  {0, 182,  85},  {0, 182, 170},  {0, 182, 255},
    {0, 219,   0},  {0, 219,  85},  {0, 219, 170},  {0, 219, 255},
    {0, 255,   0},  {0, 255,  85},  {0, 255, 170},  {0, 255, 255},

    {36,   0,   0}, {36,   0,  85}, {36,   0, 170}, {36,   0, 255},
    {36,  36,   0}, {36,  36,  85}, {36,  36, 170}, {36,  36, 255},
    {36,  73,   0}, {36,  73,  85}, {36,  73, 170}, {36,  73, 255},
    {36, 109,   0}, {36, 109,  85}, {36, 109, 170}, {36, 109, 255},
    {36, 146,   0}, {36, 146,  85}, {36, 146, 170}, {36, 146, 255},
    {36, 182,   0}, {36, 182,  85}, {36, 182, 170}, {36, 182, 255},
    {36, 219,   0}, {36, 219,  85}, {36, 219, 170}, {36, 219, 255},
    {36, 255,   0}, {36, 255,  85}, {36, 255, 170}, {36, 255, 255},
```

```
    {73,    0,    0},  {73,    0,  85},  {73,    0,  170},  {73,    0,  255},
    {73,   36,    0},  {73,   36,  85},  {73,   36,  170},  {73,   36,  255},
    {73,   73,    0},  {73,   73,  85},  {73,   73,  170},  {73,   73,  255},
    {73,  109,    0},  {73,  109,  85},  {73,  109,  170},  {73,  109,  255},
    {73,  146,    0},  {73,  146,  85},  {73,  146,  170},  {73,  146,  255},
    {73,  182,    0},  {73,  182,  85},  {73,  182,  170},  {73,  182,  255},
    {73,  219,    0},  {73,  219,  85},  {73,  219,  170},  {73,  219,  255},
    {73,  255,    0},  {73,  255,  85},  {73,  255,  170},  {73,  255,  255},

    {109,    0,    0},  {109,    0,  85},  {109,    0,  170},  {109,    0,  255},
    {109,   36,    0},  {109,   36,  85},  {109,   36,  170},  {109,   36,  255},
    {109,   73,    0},  {109,   73,  85},  {109,   73,  170},  {109,   73,  255},
    {109,  109,    0},  {109,  109,  85},  {109,  109,  170},  {109,  109,  255},
    {109,  146,    0},  {109,  146,  85},  {109,  146,  170},  {109,  146,  255},
    {109,  182,    0},  {109,  182,  85},  {109,  182,  170},  {109,  182,  255},
    {109,  219,    0},  {109,  219,  85},  {109,  219,  170},  {109,  219,  255},
    {109,  255,    0},  {109,  255,  85},  {109,  255,  170},  {109,  255,  255},

    {146,    0,    0},  {146,    0,  85},  {146,    0,  170},  {146,    0,  255},
    {146,   36,    0},  {146,   36,  85},  {146,   36,  170},  {146,   36,  255},
    {146,   73,    0},  {146,   73,  85},  {146,   73,  170},  {146,   73,  255},
    {146,  109,    0},  {146,  109,  85},  {146,  109,  170},  {146,  109,  255},
    {146,  146,    0},  {146,  146,  85},  {146,  146,  170},  {146,  146,  255},
    {146,  182,    0},  {146,  182,  85},  {146,  182,  170},  {146,  182,  255},
    {146,  219,    0},  {146,  219,  85},  {146,  219,  170},  {146,  219,  255},
    {146,  255,    0},  {146,  255,  85},  {146,  255,  170},  {146,  255,  255},

    {182,    0,    0},  {182,    0,  85},  {182,    0,  170},  {182,    0,  255},
    {182,   36,    0},  {182,   36,  85},  {182,   36,  170},  {182,   36,  255},
    {182,   73,    0},  {182,   73,  85},  {182,   73,  170},  {182,   73,  255},
    {182,  109,    0},  {182,  109,  85},  {182,  109,  170},  {182,  109,  255},
    {182,  146,    0},  {182,  146,  85},  {182,  146,  170},  {182,  146,  255},
    {182,  182,    0},  {182,  182,  85},  {182,  182,  170},  {182,  182,  255},
    {182,  219,    0},  {182,  219,  85},  {182,  219,  170},  {182,  219,  255},
    {182,  255,    0},  {182,  255,  85},  {182,  255,  170},  {182,  255,  255},

    {219,    0,    0},  {219,    0,  85},  {219,    0,  170},  {219,    0,  255},
    {219,   36,    0},  {219,   36,  85},  {219,   36,  170},  {219,   36,  255},
    {219,   73,    0},  {219,   73,  85},  {219,   73,  170},  {219,   73,  255},
    {219,  109,    0},  {219,  109,  85},  {219,  109,  170},  {219,  109,  255},
    {219,  146,    0},  {219,  146,  85},  {219,  146,  170},  {219,  146,  255},
    {219,  182,    0},  {219,  182,  85},  {219,  182,  170},  {219,  182,  255},
    {219,  219,    0},  {219,  219,  85},  {219,  219,  170},  {219,  219,  255},
    {219,  255,    0},  {219,  255,  85},  {219,  255,  170},  {219,  255,  255},

    {255,    0,    0},  {255,    0,  85},  {255,    0,  170},  {255,    0,  255},
    {255,   36,    0},  {255,   36,  85},  {255,   36,  170},  {255,   36,  255},
    {255,   73,    0},  {255,   73,  85},  {255,   73,  170},  {255,   73,  255},
    {255,  109,    0},  {255,  109,  85},  {255,  109,  170},  {255,  109,  255},
    {255,  146,    0},  {255,  146,  85},  {255,  146,  170},  {255,  146,  255},
    {255,  182,    0},  {255,  182,  85},  {255,  182,  170},  {255,  182,  255},
    {255,  219,    0},  {255,  219,  85},  {255,  219,  170},  {255,  219,  255},
    {255,  255,    0},  {255,  255,  85},  {255,  255,  170},  {255,  255,  255}
};
```

The Display class

Purpose

The purpose of this class is for display of device-independent bitmap images on SuperVGA display devices.

Member Functions

Display.   This is the class constructor. It initialized all class variables in preparation for image display. The class variable, EightBitColorMode, will be set TRUE if the display device only supports 256 colors.

~Display.   This is the class destructor. It frees any memory, miscellaneous structures, and logical palette used internally by the Display class.

IsDisplayHwdTrueColor.   This function returns TRUE if the display hardware is true color capable. Once an object of the Display class is instantiated, an application program can call this member function if it needs to know whether the display hardware is capable of true color image display.

SetImageDataPtr.   This function is called to change the pointer to the image raster data maintained by this class. The function, **InitForDisplay,** is the preferred method for setting the pointer to the raster data. The raster data pointer points at an inverted format DIB image somewhere in memory. This function accepts a huge pointer to an image in Win16 applications.

GetNumOfColors.   This function returns the number of colors in the image. In actuality, it returns the number that was passed into the **InitForDisplay** function. In the case of true color images, this function returns a zero. This function should not be called until after **InitForDisplay.**

GetPalette.   This function returns a handle to the logical palette that was created during the execution of the **InitForDisplay** function. The logical palette is created from the palette information passed to the Display class. For valid results, this function should not be called until after **InitForDisplay.**

GetWidth.   This function returns the width, in pixels, of the image being managed by this instance of the Display class. For valid results, this function should not be called until after **InitForDisplay.**

GetHeight.   This function returns the height, in rows, of the image being managed by this instance of the Display class. For valid results, this function should not be called until after **InitForDisplay.**

GetBPP.   This function returns the number of bits per pixel of the image being managed by this instance of the Display class. An 8-bit image would return a value of eight while a true color image would return 24. For valid results, this function should not be called until after **InitForDisplay.**

UpdateAllColors.   This function updates an image displayed in a window by remapping the image colors to the currently realized logical palette. This function typically updates an image displayed in a window faster than redrawing the image using the other imaging displaying functions in this class. However, because this function performs the color translation based on the color of each pixel before the system palette changed, each call to this function results in the loss of some color

FIGURE 6.1 The Display class.

accuracy. For this reason, I rarely use this function. It is included in the Display class for completeness only.

InitForDisplay.   This function configures an object of the Display class in preparation for image display. Parameters needed to configure a Display object include the width, in pixels, of the image to be displayed; the height; the number of colors contained in the image (zero for a true color image); a pointer to the images' raster data; a pointer to an array of **RGBCOLOR** entries that describe a palette to display the image against; and a flag that controls how dithering should be applied if dithering is required to display the image. Once this function is called, any of the display image member functions in this class can be called to display the image in a window. Note: This function must be called before most of the other member functions of this class can return valid data.

DisplayImage.   This is the first of the image display functions. When called, this function displays all or part of an image within a window. If *clip mode* is in effect, this function will only display the portion of the image that fits within the window; that is, if the image is larger than the window, only the upper left part of the image that fits within the boundaries of the window will be displayed. If *stretch mode* is in effect, the image will be stretched or shrunk to fit fully within the window. In other words, in stretch mode the complete image is always visible. Parameters to this function include a handle to the window in which to display the image, a reference to a **POINT** structure that determines which pixel of the image should be placed in the upper left corner of the display window. This parameter is only used if clip mode is in effect and is ignored in stretch mode. The final parameter determines if the palette associated with the image should be rendered as foreground (FALSE) or background (TRUE). In almost all cases, a foreground palette should be indicated. See Chapter 2 for details of foreground and background palettes.

DisplayImageInWindowRect.   This image display function is used whenever a complete image must be displayed in only part of a window instead of in the whole window. A RECT parameter is passed into this function that controls the area of the window to display the image in. If the area specified is the complete client area of display window, this function works like the function discussed earlier.

FIGURE 6.1 (*Continued*)

The Display class incorporates and expands upon the traditional method of image display in Windows, as described in the previous section. The most important extension to the traditional method is the incorporation of image dithering *whenever needed for image display.* As you will recall from discussions in Chapter 5, dithering or some other form of color reduction must be applied to an image if it contains more colors than the output device is capable of displaying. This is the case when a true color image is to be displayed on a SuperVGA display adapter only capable of 256 colors. Dithering will prevent Windows from attempting to display an image it is not well equipped to handle. Of course, if the image is of a format that Windows can deal with directly, no dithering will be required and none will be performed. The subject of dithering is so important to the Display class that it will be touched upon many times throughout this chapter. In addition to a discussion of dithering, how the Display

DisplayImageWithAspect. This final image display function also displays an image within a window, but it does so while keeping the aspect ratio of the image intact. For our use here, aspect ratio can be defined as the ratio of height to width of an image. Note: This function will only work properly when displaying images that were acquired on devices that have square pixels, in other words, on devices whose pixels have the same physical width and height. On such images, as long as the ratio of display dimensions is kept the same as the ratio of image dimensions, no aspect ratio distortion will occur. The **DisplayImageWithAspect** function modifies the area into which an image will be displayed so that the display area has the same height to width ratio as the dimensions of the image. This function also has a palette flag that determines whether the image's palette should be rendered in the foreground or background.

SetClipMode. Execution of this function puts the display object into *clip mode.* All subsequent image display will be clipped into the display window instead of being stretched into it.

SetStretchMode. Execution of this function puts the display object into *stretch mode.* All subsequent image display will stretch the complete image into the display window instead of displaying only the portion of the image that would normally fit in the window.

IsClipMode. This inquiry function returns TRUE if the display object in currently in clip mode and FALSE if not.

SetZoom. This function controls the zoom factor to be applied during the display of an image. Valid zooms are one, two, four, or eight. Zooming can only be used when the display object is in clip mode.

GetZoom. Execution of this function returns the current zoom value. Valid returned values are one, two, four, or eight.

GetPtrToBITMAPINFO. This function is used to return a pointer to the bitmap information structure (BITMAPINFO) built for the display object by the **InitForDisplay** function. Since the BITMAPINFO structure contains a concise definition of the image, it is sometimes useful to have access to it. This is true, for example, when the image needs to be printed.

ErrorMessage. This function formats a error message into a Windows message box for display. It accepts a pointer to a error message string.

FIGURE 6.1 (*Continued*)

class implements various image display operations such as stretching, clipping, panning, zooming, and aspect ratio protection will be described in detail.

Preparation for Image Display

Once an object of the Display class is instantiated, it must be told about the image it is to display. The **InitForDisplay** member function performs the Display object's configuration. All of the parameters passed to this function are used to build a BITMAPINFO structure that describes the image to be displayed. A pointer to this structure will be required by the bit blit functions, described later, used to actually display the image data. In addition to setting up the BITMAPINFOHEADER portion of the BITMAPINFO structure, the **InitForDisplay** function copies the colors from the supplied palette into memory directly following the BITMAPINFOHEADER.

Why Two Types of Dithering Are Necessary

For reasons of flexibility, the Display class supports two different methods of applying dithering to images that require it. I call these methods *full-size dither* and *dither on demand*. When full-size dither mode is in effect and dithering is required, a full-size dithered copy of the original true color image will be generated and maintained within the Display class object. Whenever the image needs to be displayed, the dithered version of the image will be sent to the output device instead of the true color original. The pros and cons of this dithering method can be summarized as follows:

Pros

- Because a full-size dithered version of the image is available in memory at all times, the image can be displayed very quickly once the initial dithering operation has been performed.
- Because a full-size dithered version of the image is available in memory, display operations such as panning and zooming can be performed on the dithered image without a performance penalty.

Cons

- Large images require a lot of time to dither.
- Carrying around a dithered image one-third the size of the original true color image (dithered image has 8 BPP instead of 24) consumes lots of memory especially for large images such as those generated by a scanner or video digitizer.
- Large dithered images reduced to a small size for display generally look grainy because lots of rows and columns of the dithered image data have to be thrown away to fit the image into the allotted display space.

In contrast, the second dithering method, dither on demand, dithers an image each time it is to be displayed instead of dithering it all at once as in the previous method. More importantly, the image data are decimated in memory to the size required for display prior to being dithered. In other words, the image's RGB data are reduced in size by throwing away rows and columns of the data until the image will fit into the area available for display. The reduced size RGB image data are then subjected to dithering. Pros and cons of this technique follow:

Pros

- The display of images is very quick because the number of pixels dithered is usually small.
- No long-term or large amounts of memory are required because the image is redithered every time it needs to be displayed. The memory required for performing image decimation and dithering comes and goes quickly.
- Because the image data are decimated before it is dithered instead of afterward, the dithered images tend to look better.

Cons

- Whenever the image display area is large, the dithering operation can take a considerable amount of time because there are more pixels to dither.

- Dither on demand cannot be used in applications where image panning is to be performed because the image would need to be redithered each time the scroll bars were moved. Image display performance, under these conditions, would suffer greatly.

As you can see, there are pros and cons to consider when deciding which dithering technique to use in an application program. I use the dither on demand technique whenever possible because it has proven to be generally the most useful of the techniques presented. There are times, however, when full-size dithering is required and must be used.

The final parameter to the **InitForDisplay** function in Display class controls which dithering technique a Display object will use. If the Boolean value is TRUE, full-size dithering will be used. If FALSE, dithering will be performed on demand for those images that require dithering.

How the Various Image Display Operations Are Performed

All of the image display operations discussed here including image stretching, clipping, panning, zooming, and aspect ratio protection are all performed by careful application of the device-independent bitmap bit blit function, **StretchDIBits.** The prototype for this function follows:

```
int StretchDIBits(hDC, XDest, YDest, nDestWidth, nDestHeight, XSrc, YSrc,
                nSrcWidth, nSrcHeight, lpBits, lpBitsInfo, iUsage, dwRop);
```

where **hDC** is the handle of the device context on which the image is to be displayed, **XDest** is the logical x-coordinate of upper left corner of the destination rectangle on the device context, **YDest** is the logical y-coordinate of upper left corner of the destination rectangle, **nDestWidth** is the logical width of the destination rectangle, **nDestHeight** is the logical height of the destination rectangle, **XSrc** is the x-coordinate (in pixels) of upper left corner of the source rectangle in memory, **YSrc** is the y-coordinate (in pixels) of upper left corner of the source rectangle, **nSrcWidth** is the width of the source rectangle in pixels, **nSrcHeight** is the height of the source rectangle in pixels, **lpBits** is a pointer to the DIB raster data in memory, **lpBitsInfo** is a pointer to the BITMAPINFO structure that defines the DIB image, and **iUsage** specifies how the color information contained in BITMAPINFO is to be interpreted. Here, this parameter is always equal to DIB_RGB_COLORS, meaning that the color values are explicit RGB values instead of indexes into the currently realized logical palette. The final parameter to the **StretchDIBits** function is **dwRop** that controls which raster operation is to be applied in the transfer of image data from memory to the device context. In this code **dwRop** is always equal to SRCCOPY because we are only concerned about moving image data from one point to another; other raster operations are not required here.

To implement the various image display operations, the position and dimension parameters used in the calls to **StretchDIBits** are manipulated. All of the display operations supported by the Display class with the exclusion of the one dealing with aspect ratio are performed within the **DisplayDIB** function. The various calls to **StretchDIBits** shown in the following text were extracted from the **DisplayDIB** function. The simplest operation, which I refer to as image stretching, is where an image is stretched (or shrunk if larger than the window) as necessary to fit completely within the display window. In this case, XDest and YDest are set equal to zero because the upper left corner of the image should reside in the upper left corner of the window's client area during display. The parameters, nDestWidth and nDestHeight, are set equal to the dimensions of the window's client area so that the image will be displayed filling the entire area. XSrc and YSrc are set to zero because all of the image data are to be displayed, and these coordinates represent the upper left corner of the image data in memory. Finally, nSrcWidth and nSrcHeight are set equal to the image dimensions. When **StretchDIBits** is called, the image will be displayed, filling the entire client area of the window identified by hDC. Note that if the dimensions of the display area are not in the same ratio as the dimensions of the image, aspect ratio distortion will occur. In other words, the spatial relationships of the items in the image will be modified. Under these circumstances, if a circular object happened to be a part of the image, its dimensions will be modified so that it appears as an ellipse instead of a circle. Techniques for defeating aspect ratio distortion will be discussed shortly. The Display class is said to be in *stretch mode* (more on this later) when images are being stretched to fit the display area. A typical stretch mode call to StretchDIBits would be as follows:

```
StretchDIBits(hDC, 0, 0,
              DestRect.right,
              DestRect.bottom,
              0, 0, ImageWidth, ImageHeight,
              lpImageData, lpBmi, DIB_RGB_COLORS, SRCCOPY);
```

Panning (sometimes referred to as *image scrolling*) is required when an image that is larger than the display window is to be displayed and stretching or shrinking of the image is not appropriate because of aspect ratio distortion or other considerations. Panning is a term that refers to moving a set sized window over a larger image surface and viewing that portion of the image that can be seen through the window. Most people who have used some sort of paint program should be familiar with panning. Generally, scroll bars are used for positioning within the image. As a vertical scroll bar is moved down, the image appears to scroll upward. Along the same vein, as a horizontal scroll bar is moved to the right, the image scrolls left. I sometimes refer to this image display technique as displaying an image to scale because there is a one for one correspondence between a pixel of image data and a pixel of the display surface. (The TestApp imaging example program of Chapter 1 uses this terminology.) Since all SuperVGA display modes use square pixels (pixels whose dimensions represent the same physical distance), no aspect ratio distortion will result when displaying an image to scale. The Display class is said to be in *clip mode* when images are being displayed to scale because images will be clipped to the dimensions of the display area instead of being shrunk to fit into it.

A typical clip mode call to **StretchDIBits** that supports image panning is as follows:

```
StretchDIBits(hDC, 0, 0, DestRect.right, DestRect.bottom,
              SrcPosition.x,
              ImageWidth - DestRect.bottom - SrcPosition.y,
              DestRect.right,
              DestRect.bottom,
              lpImageData, lpBmi, DIB_RGB_COLORS, SRCCOPY);
```

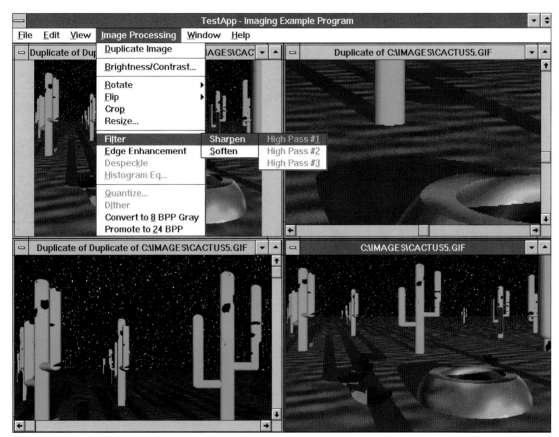

PLATE 1 TestApp program's user interface—see Chapter 1.

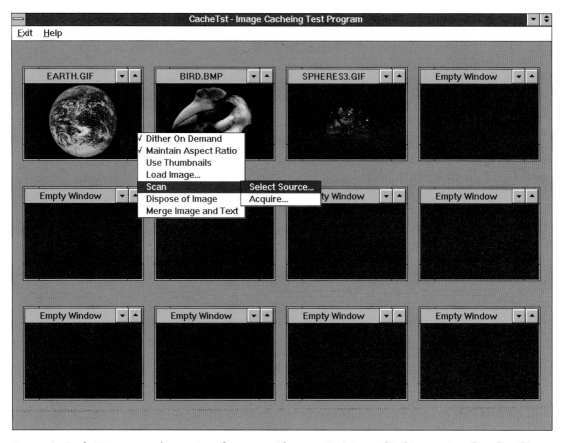

PLATE 2 CacheTst program's user interface—see Chapter 10. (Note: Third image is a thumbnail.)

PLATE 3 A true color image.

PLATE 4 A dithered image—see Chapter 5.

PLATE 5 A quantized image—see Chapter 5.

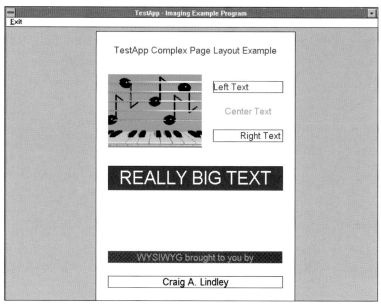

PLATE 6 The print preview operation in progress—see Chapter 7.

PLATE 7 An image annotated with text—see Chapter 10.

The important aspects of this call to **StretchDIBits** have to do with how the position and dimensions of the portion of the image (stored as DIB data in memory) to be displayed are calculated. For our purpose here, we assume the image is larger than the window it is to be displayed in; otherwise, panning would not be necessary. The specification of the destination rectangle for display is the same as discussed earlier because the displayed portion of the image will still fill the entire client area of the display window. A new POINT variable called SrcPosition is introduced and contains the location (upper left corner) within the image data that is to be the starting point for display. The X and Y values within SrcPosition would typically contain the positions of the scroll bars associated with the display window. SrcPosition values must be carefully chosen so that the display window over the image data always remains within the dimensions defined for the image. If care is not taken in these calculations, your imaging program is guaranteed to crash and burn the first time you touch a scroll bar. The valid range of values for SrcPosition.x is from 0 to ImageWidth − Rect.right + 1 and for SrcPosition.y, 0 to ImageHeight − Rect.bottom + 1.

Finally, instead of specifying the width and height of the entire image for the nSrcWidth and nSrcHeight parameters to the **StretchDIBits** call, the width and height of the client area are specified. This is required because only that many pixels of the image can be displayed when clip mode is in effect because of the one for one pixel relationship discussed previously.

Zooming into images requires further manipulation of StretchDIBits parameters, namely, the introduction of a zooming factor. To understand how image zooming works, you must think of an image zoomed at 2× as being equivalent to an image twice as large in each dimension as the actual image. Zooming is performed by reducing the area of the image to be displayed by the zoom factor (in this case two) while keeping the size of the display area constant. In short, the nSrcWidth and nSrcHeight parameters are divided by the zoom factor. If you think about what this accomplishes, it causes the display of a smaller portion of the image in the same size display area, hence the feeling of zooming into the image. The call to **StretchDIBits** that follows supports both zooming and panning of images. Notice how the calculations for XSrc and YSrc are impacted by the inclusion of zooming. These modifications are required because the values passed within ScrPosition are as if the image is zoom factor times as large as the actual image.

```
StretchDIBits(hDC, 0, 0,
              DestRect.right, DestRect.bottom,
              SrcPosition.x >> ZoomFactor,
              ImageHeight − (DestRect.bottom >> ZoomFactor) − (SrcPosition.y >>
              ZoomFactor),
              DestRect.right >> ZoomFactor,
              DestRect.bottom >> ZoomFactor,
              lpImageData, lpBmi, DIB_RGB_COLORS, SRCCOPY);
```

The code within the Display class supports 2×, 4×, and 8× zooming, although it could be made to support any zooming factor desired. The 2×, 4×, and 8× zooming was chosen so that shifts could be used instead of arithmetic divisions. This was a decision made purely for performance considerations. The function **SetZoom** within the Display class converts the zoom specification of one, two, four, or eight into the appropriate zoom shift factor of zero, one, two, and three, respectively.

The final image display operation, as implemented in the Display class member function **DisplayImageWithAspect,** displays an entire image within a window while keeping the aspect ratio of the image intact. In other words, the image will not be stretched or shrunk to fit the window; the dimensions of the display area within the window will be adjusted to fit the image instead. The code that performs this function can be seen in Listing 6.2 and is probably more complex than what you would imagine would be necessary. Please refer to the code at this time to understand why.

The **DisplayImageWithAspect** function performs two tasks. First, given the dimensions of the image to be displayed, it calculates the maximum dimensions of an area within the display window that has the same ratio of width to height as that of the image. By keeping the ratio of image dimensions to display area dimensions the same aspect ratio distortion is prevented. Second, this function calculates the horizontal and vertical offsets necessary to center the calculated display area within the display window. As you would expect, the dimensions of the image needing display must be taken into consideration. The variable, VertFit, will be set TRUE if the image is taller than it is wide and FALSE if the image is wider than it is tall. No assumptions are or can be made about the dimensions of the display window.

If an image is taller than it is wide, the height of the image will be scaled to fit the height of the display window, and the width of the display area will be calculated from the ratio of image width to image height. As you can see from the listing, the width calculation is performed iteratively instead of by using ratios. This is necessary because differences in the width to height of the image and that of the display area can necessitate reducing the length of the longest image dimension so that the shorter dimension can fit within the display window. If you take the time to sketch out some possible image dimensions and display window dimensions, you will understand why the iterative calculations are required.

Of course, if the image is wider than it is tall and VertFit is FALSE, a different set of calculations must be performed to fit the image within the display window. These calculations are governed by the same reasoning described earlier.

Whenever **DisplayImageWithAspect** is used to display an image within a window, the image is always sized to keep its aspect ratio intact. If the aspect ratio of the image matches that of the display window, no visible border will be seen around the image. As the aspect ratios of image and display window diverge, more and more border will be seen around the displayed image. This effect can be seen using the TestApp imaging example program of Chapter 1. If an image is displayed and the view mode for the image is set to *Display To Fit with Aspect,* the image will be displayed in its containing window with the aspect ratio intact. When you grab the corner of the display window and change its size and/or shape, the size and position of the image displayed within the window will change to compensate.

Using the Display Class in Application Programs

As simple and straightforward as the Display class is, it would require quite a large test application program to demonstrate its functionality appropriately. While preparing this chapter, I wrote such a demonstration program but soon figured out that to make the program short enough to print, I had to substantially reduce its functionality. The net result was a program that was not useful for anything other than to just demonstrate the Display class. I decided, therefore, not to include it in this chap-

ter but, instead, to point the interested reader to the TestApp imaging example program of Chapter 1 where the Display class is used extensively. Within the TestApp program, almost all functions of the Display class are exercised in a productive manner.
Within the TestApp program notice how:

- The Display class is used in conjunction with the Compand class (of Chapter
  Four) to display an image read from a graphics file
- The Display class is used to display an image with its aspect ratio intact
- The Display class provides zooming and panning within an image
- The Display class is used to display the results of the various image process-
  ing algorithms supported by the TestApp program.

I believe it is much more instructive to see how the Display class is used in a real
application than it would be to see it used in a contrived test program. I hope you
agree.

Conclusions

This chapter has concentrated on the display of device-independent bitmap images
within the Windows environment. The traditional approach to image display was discussed followed by a discussion of the Display class that incorporates and encapsulates the traditional approach into a very easy to use C++ class. The concept of
dithering, as used within the Display class, was discussed here because it is a necessary
part of any general purpose image display philosophy. Finally, the use of the Display
class within the TestApp program was discussed as a real-world application of this
technology.

7

Printing in Windows

In this chapter you will learn about:
- How printing in Windows is done
- Why printing is such a difficult undertaking for an application program
- Special treatment of images required for printing and previewing
- Scaling and font considerations
- Previewing printed output on the monitor to scale
- How the page layout process is performed

Introduction

Regardless of the pundits who say that we as a society are migrating toward a paperless world, I believe computers, directly and indirectly, cause the consumption of more paper than was ever used before the computer revolution. Some people must see facts and figures in printed form before they can grasp their significance. Even certain programmers I know must produce a program listing on paper in order to debug their code effectively. At this point in time, many people work better from a printed page than they do by viewing the same information online. This is probably a cultural bias that will disappear in the future as people get used to viewing and reading documents online and as computers themselves are better equipped to mimic a printed page of information on a display (when computers have greater display resolution and are portable).

For whatever reasons, at this time it is just as important for a computer application to be able to print images and text on a page as it is to display the same information on a computer's monitor. People want hard copy, we as application programmers must provide it. For this reason, this complete chapter is dedicated to the discussion of printed output in the Windows environment. More specifically, the ability to achieve What You See Is What You Get (WYSIWYG) printing of text and images on the printed page in a device-independent manner. As you will see in the upcoming discussions, WYSIWYG capability is harder to achieve than you might think. The techniques and code presented here were developed to simplify the unavoidable task of printing as much as possible by encapsulating all of the inane printer code into simple to use C++ class. By following a few simple guidelines, you will be able to develop, preview, and print page layouts as complex as you care to design. These layouts can include images, text, and/or tabular data. You'll have complete control of text, text placement, text fonts, text font size and effects, text justification, text framing, and text foreground and text background colors. In terms of images, you'll have complete control of image size and image placement on the page. In short, these techniques will provide you with maximum flexibility with minimum headaches.

Background

To design effective page layouts, one must have as much control as possible over the various attributes used for printing the page. The most basic of all attributes deals with the sizing and positioning of the material to be printed. To ease the layout process, it helps to be able to specify sizes and positions of printed items in units that are familiar and easy to use. In this way, a sketch of a page layout can be converted into actual code very quickly. In the code presented here, I have adopted the MM_LOENGLISH mapping mode for all page layouts. This sets the basic unit size to .01 inch. This means, for example, if you want an image to print in a 4- × 3-inch rectangle on the printed page, you would specify its dimensions as 400 × 300 units. This gives a layout resolution of .01 inch, which should be adequate for most imaging applications. Some desktop publishing applications may require greater resolution than this, but the .01 inch resolution provided by using the MM_LOENGLISH mapping mode is adequate for our uses here.

The use of the MM_LOENGLISH mapping mode has the additional benefit of being device independent. In other words, any page layout defined in this manner using the MM_LOENGLISH mapping mode should print correctly, regardless of the resolution of the printer or other output device. Windows itself will do the conversions necessary to map the .01-inch MM_LOENGLISH units to the physical pixels on the printer device.

An oddity of the MM_LOENGLISH mapping mode that must be kept in the front of one's mind during page layout is that the Y dimension becomes increasingly more negative the further down the page you go. For an 8.5- × 11-inch piece of paper, for instance, the coordinates of the upper left corner would be (0, 0). The coordinates of the lower right corner would be (850, −1,100). Actually, this last statement is not entirely true because of the way Windows print drivers work. Windows print drivers use the concept of printable area that reflects the physical limitations of the printer device. Printable area is that portion of the paper on which the printer can actually print. Coordinate (0, 0), from the printer's perspective, is the coordinate of the top left most printable pixel on the page. In most cases, this does not work out to be the actual corner of the paper since most printers cannot print there. When designing page layouts, one must be careful not to place printed items outside the printable area of your target printer. If you do, they will be truncated at the boundary of the printable area. This is one case where a preview of the printed page can differ in appearance from the actual printed page. Previews are not constrained by printable area as are most, if not all, actual printers. The concept of printable area will be taken up again later in this chapter when the Printer class is discussed.

Within the framework provided by the code here, font sizes to be used on page layouts are specified in terms of points, not .01-inch units. A point is ½ of an inch, which represents the actual physical size of the font when printed. A 10-point font therefore is approximately 0.14 inch tall. Fonts are specified using points in this manner because this is the standard in the typographic industry. If you desire to change how the font sizes are specified on a layout (from points to .01-inch units, for instance) have at it. That is the beauty of having the source code available to you; you can do with it as you please. A change such as this can be considered a minor academic exercise and as such be left to the reader (I just had to say that at least once in this book).

Handling a Printer in Windows

Because of Windows' device independence, anything you can display in a window on the screen can be sent to a printer and be printed. Windows takes care of many of the details involved in controlling a printer such as moving the paper, issuing the printer specific control sequences required for printing text and graphics, and loading the appropriate fonts. While this sounds like a lot of assistance, there is still a lot of work the programmer must do to making printing available in an applications program. The benefit of going to all of the trouble required for printing is that once the printing code works for one printer, it usually works for all printers. I say usually because in the real world, there are many small differences in how printers perform under Windows. This is mostly a result of print driver problems that are usually taken care of by getting the most current driver available for the printers you wish to work with.

The following list summarizes the typical steps a programmer must go through to print a single page within an application program. Most of the steps can be categorized as printing overhead. Only step 11 has anything at all to do with sending the information you want to print to the printer. What is not shown on this list is the extra programming effort required for error detection and recovery during the print process:

1. Read the WIN.INI file to retrieve the name of the currently selected printer, the name of the print driver for the printer, and the port to which the printer is attached to the computer.
2. Load the print driver into memory by calling **LoadLibrary** function.
3. Get the DeviceCapabilities entry point from the print driver for querying printer capabilities and functions.
4. Use the Windows function, **CreateDC,** to create a device context for the printer. This is the device context that will be used for all subsequent drawing operations.
5. Disable the main application window while the print operation proceeds.

6. Create an abort procedure (which will be called between printed pages) that may allow the user to abort printing.
7. Optionally put up a print abort dialog box to give user print status and to allow cancellation of the print job.
8. Use **MakeProcInstance** (in Win16) to get the address of the abort procedure and install it.
9. Issue a start document command to the printer.
10. Issue a start page command to the printer.
11. Issue all GDI commands necessary to print text and graphics on the page for each page of printed output.
12. Issue an end page command to the printer and return to step 10.
13. Issue an end document or abort document command to the printer.
14. Destroy the print abort dialog box.
15. Reenable the main application window.

The purpose of showing this list is to give you an idea of all that is involved in printing a single page when using the Windows API directly. As you will see, the C++ code provided here encapsulates (and takes care of) all of the required overhead steps and lets you concentrate instead on page layout and printing. In addition to facilitating printing, the code provides a print preview facility that allows you to see on screen exactly what the page will look like when printed. Print preview is a standard feature in most major application programs. If you use the code from this chapter, you get this feature essentially for free, and the preview feature will make your programs look more professional.

For the sake of completeness, the concept of printer banding should at least be mentioned. Banding is a technique that was used beginning with Window 3.0 to allow printing large and/or complex page layouts on printers without a lot of memory. It worked by sending text and graphics to the printer in rectangular chunks called *bands* instead of all at once, thereby overloading the printer's memory. In theory, as the printer printed the information contained in a band it had room in its memory and could therefore accept a new download of data: the next band. The problems with banding are that it had to be administered by the application program at a high level and that it is overly complex to implement. Luckily, most modern print drivers now handle banding directly, and the application program can safely ignore it. In addition, most modern printers are shipped with enough memory for simple to moderate page layouts. Very complex page layouts may necessitate increasing the memory in the printer. Banding is not used in the code here.

Page Layout Overview

Before getting into a detailed discussion of how the provided printing code works, I believe it is best to first provide a good understanding of how the page layout process works. How the code works will undoubtedly make more sense to you when you have an understanding of the page layout process. Actually, if you understand the page layout process, you needn't go further. It is unnecessary to completely understand how all of the provided printer code works to be able to use the code effectively. The operational details of the printer code are supplied for those people who, for example, want to modify the code for their purposes. The most important thing is to understand how printed pages are laid out. All the rest is gravy.

By way of example, I will use the rather contrived page layout used by the TestApp example program of Chapter 1. It is contrived because I tried to squeeze most of the available functionality provided by the printing code onto a single page. You should use more discretion in laying out your pages because the example page layout is rather garish. It serves well as an example, however. It is important to keep in mind that the layout is intended to be only a single page (FYI, multiple page layouts are supported by the code provided) and was meant for printing on 8.5- × 11-inch paper.

To begin the page layout process, you must define a new class that defines your new layout. Every layout requires a corresponding layout class definition. By design, all new layout classes must use the PageDefinitionBase class as its, or one of its base class(es). Listing 7.1 shows the class definition of a page layout called strangely enough *Layout1*. The layout class definition can have as many member functions as required but must have a member function called **PrintPage** with the parameter signature as shown on the listing. PrintPage is necessary because PageDefinitionBase is an abstract C++ class with PrintPage as a pure virtual function. All classes derived from an abstract class must override all pure virtual functions of the base class. Therefore a PrintPage function must be defined for all of your custom page layout classes. Also, as an abstract class an object of the class PageDefinitionBase cannot be instantiated on its own. This would not do any good anyway because an object of the class PageDefinitionBase would not know what to print anyway.

Listing 7.1 The Pglayout class interface definition.

```
/*****************************************************/
/***                                           ***/
/***                "pglayout.hpp"              ***/
/***         TestApp Imaging Example Program    ***/
/***         Printed Layout Page Definitions    ***/
/***                  written by                ***/
/***               Craig A. Lindley             ***/
/***                                           ***/
/***      Revision 2.0    Last Update: 11/11/94  ***/
/*****************************************************/

// Copyright (c) 1995 John Wiley & Sons, Inc. All rights reserved.

#ifndef PGLAYOUT_HPP
#define PGLAYOUT_HPP

#include <owlpch.h>
#pragma hdrstop

#include "printops.hpp"

// This file defines the example single page layout used for printing
// within the TestApp program.

// Page Definition. Printout contains both image and textual fields
class Layout1 : public PageDefinitionBase {
  private:
```

```
                IMAGEDESCRIPTOR ID;
                LPSTR lpImageTitle;

  public:

                Layout1(LPSTR PageName, LPSTR Text, IMAGEDESCRIPTOR& ImgDesc);
                virtual ~Layout1(void);

                virtual void PrintPage(HDC DC, WORD Page);
};

#endif
```

It is within the PrintPage function of your layout class that a page is formatted for printing. If your layout is a single page, the PrintPage function will be called once to print the page. If your layout requires multiple pages, your PrintPage function will be called once per page. The code within your PrintPage function must be prepared for this eventuality and must also be prepared to start printing your layout at the page number specified in the parameter passed in. A second requirement of multiple page layouts is that the **IsNextPage** virtual function in the PageDefinitionBase base class be overloaded to return TRUE as long is there is another page of the layout to print and FALSE when all pages have been printed. In short, one or possibly two functions written by you are all that is required to take advantage of the printing code provided here. To see how this works, let us discuss the code for the Layout1 class shown in Listing 7.2. As mentioned, this code produces the layout used in the TestApp example program and illustrates most all of the functionality provided by the printer code in this chapter.

Listing 7.2 The Pglayout class member functions.

```
/*********************************************************/
/***                 "pglayout.cpp"                   ***/
/***            Printed Layout Page Functions          ***/
/***                    written by                     ***/
/***                 Craig A. Lindley                  ***/
/***                                                   ***/
/***      Revision: 2.0    Last Update: 11/11/94       ***/
/*********************************************************/

// Copyright (c) 1995 John Wiley & Sons, Inc. All rights reserved.

#include "pglayout.hpp"

extern LPSTR StoreString(LPSTR String);

// This is a rather complex layout for illustration purposes only.
// It consists of seven text fields with various parameters and an
// image field.
Layout1::Layout1(LPSTR PageName, LPSTR lpText, IMAGEDESCRIPTOR& ImgDesc)
  : PageDefinitionBase(PageName){

  // Save IMAGEDESCRIPTOR passed in
  ID = ImgDesc;
```

```
      lpImageTitle = StoreString(lpText);
    }

  Layout1::~Layout1(void){

    if(lpImageTitle)
      delete lpImageTitle;
  }

  void Layout1::PrintPage(HDC hDC, WORD /*Page*/){
    RECT Rect;

    // Output the title field first
    SetRect(&Rect, 50, -50,800,-100);              // Set location
    SetJustificationFlags(DT_CENTER);              // Set justification
    SetFGColor(RGB(255, 0, 0));                    // Set foreground color
    PrintText(hDC, lpImageTitle, Rect);            // Output the text
    SetDefaults();                                 // Defaults back in place

    // Output the image field next
    SetRect(&Rect, 50, -150, 450, -500);           // Set location
    PrintImage(hDC, ID, Rect);                     // Output the image

    // Another text field left justified with red text.
    SetRect(&Rect, 500, -200, 800, -250);          // Set location
    SetFGColor(RGB(255, 0, 0));                    // Set foreground color
    SetFrameUse(TRUE);                             // Use a frame around text field
    PrintText(hDC, "Left Text", Rect);             // Output the text
    SetDefaults();                                 // Defaults back in place

    // Another text field center justified with green text.
    SetRect(&Rect, 500, -300, 800, -350);          // Set location
    SetJustificationFlags(DT_CENTER);              // Set justification
    SetFGColor(RGB(0, 255, 0));                    // Set foreground color
    PrintText(hDC, "Center Text", Rect);           // Output the text
    SetDefaults();                                 // Defaults back in place

    // Another text field right justified with blue text.
    SetRect(&Rect, 500, -400, 800, -450);          // Set location
    SetJustificationFlags(DT_RIGHT);               // Set justification
    SetFGColor(RGB(0, 0, 255));                    // Set foreground color
    SetFrameUse(TRUE);                             // Use a frame around text field
    PrintText(hDC, "Right Text", Rect);            // Output the text
    SetDefaults();                                 // Defaults back in place

    // Another text field center justified, large white text on blue
    // background drawn with a frame.
    SetRect(&Rect, 50, -550, 800, -650);           // Set location
    SetJustificationFlags(DT_CENTER);              // Set justification
    SetFGColor(RGB(255, 255, 255));                // Set foreground color
    SetBGColor(RGB( 0, 0, 255));                   // Set background color
    SetFontPointSize(55);                          // Set a font pt size
    SetFrameUse(TRUE);                             // Draw in a frame
    PrintText(hDC, "REALLY BIG TEXT", Rect);       // Output the text
    SetDefaults();                                 // Defaults back in place
```

```
    // Another text field center justified with green text on gray
    // background.
    SetRect(&Rect, 50, -900, 800, -950);              // Set location
    SetJustificationFlags(DT_CENTER);                 // Set justification
    SetFGColor(RGB( 0, 255, 0));                      // Set foreground color
    SetBGColor(RGB(64, 64, 64));                      // Set background color
    PrintText(hDC, "WYSIWYG brought to you by", Rect); // Output the text
    SetDefaults();                                    // Defaults back in place

    // Final text field center justified with frame.
    SetRect(&Rect, 50, -1000, 800, -1050);            // Set location
    SetJustificationFlags(DT_CENTER);                 // Set justification
    SetFontPointSize(30);                             // Set a font pt size
    SetFrameUse(TRUE);                                // Draw in a frame
    PrintText(hDC, "Craig A. Lindley", Rect);         // Output the text
}
```

The Layout1 class consists of three member functions. The class constructor that allocates space for and saves a title string to be used on the layout and makes a copy of an IMAGEDESCRIPTOR structure that defines the image to also be printed on the layout. The class destructor just frees the memory allocated for saving the layout title. The final function, PrintPage, is where the actual formatting of the layout is performed. Because Layout1 is a single page layout, the complication in handling multiple pages can be ignored. Layout1 consists of seven text fields and a single image field located at various locations across the page. What has not yet been mentioned is that the PageDefinitionBase class from which Layout1 was derived has built-in functions for handling the printing of textual fields and images on layouts. These functions are used extensively for formatting in the PrintPage function. Even though you have yet to see the code that provides the formatting functions, their functionality should be apparent from their names. Let us step through some of the PrintPage functions to show you how all of this works.

The first text field to be printed is the title string that was passed into the constructor of this class. The first item of business is to specify a rectangular area into which the string should be written (the rectangular area must be specified for use by the underlying **DrawText** Windows function). In this case, the rectangle is set to 50, −50, 800, −100 in the left, top, right, and bottom order. In MM_LOENGLISH .01-inch logical units, this refers to a rectangle 1 inch tall starting 0.5 inch from both the left and top edges of the page and stretching to within 0.5 inch of the right page boundary. Remember the top and bottom coordinates for the rectangle are negative because Y gets more negative the further down the page you go. With the location for the title string specified, other attributes for the printed text can be set. In this case, the text is to be center justified, and the foreground color is set to bright red. Finally the **PrintText** function is called to output the title string. The subsequent call to **SetDefaults** puts all the standard text attributes back to their default state. More on this later.

Next, the image is to be printed. In this case, the location and size of the image is set to the rectangle 50, −150, 450, −500. This places the upper left corner of the image ½ inch from the left border and 1.5 inch down from the top. The width and the height of the image is specified as 4 × 3.5 inches, respectively. Note: Because the image is always printed with aspect ratio intact, the actual size of the printed image may differ from that specified. It might be more accurate to say that the image will be printed centered in the specified rectangular area. The **PrintImage** function is the workhorse that actually performs the image printing operation. More on this function later also.

The other text output sequences within the PrintPage function follow a similar pattern. If you study the code closely, you will see that besides setting of the justification and foreground colors, functions exist for changing the default font, changing the default font size, changing the text background color, and for framing the text fields.

Using the Printing Capability

Once you have a layout defined for your printed output, only a very few steps are required to actually use it. These steps follow:

1. Instantiate an object of the PrintOp class for managing printer selection, printing, and/or the print preview operations.
2. Instantiate an object of your page layout class (which was derived from PageDefinitionBase).
3. Pass a pointer to the layout object to the PrintOp object by calling the **InitForPrintOp** member function of the PrintOp class. In addition to the page layout pointer, a pointer to the parent window is required along with the page number on which to start the printout or preview.
4. Call the **BeginPreview** function to preview the layout on the display. When finished with the preview display, call **EndPreview** to destroy the print preview window.
5. Call the **Print** member function of the PrintOp class to output the layout to the currently selected printer for printing.

In terms of code, the previous steps for printing resolve into the following code segment:

```
PrintObj = new PrintOp; // Instantiate an object of the PrintOp class
// Instantiate a page layout object. Pass layout name, layout title and
// an IMAGEDESCRIPTOR
lpPage = new Layout1("TestApp Layout Page", "TestApp Complex Page Layout
                     Example", ID);
if(lpPage){          // If page instantiated OK
 PrintObj->InitForPrintOp(this, lpPage, 1);
 PrintObj->Print();
 delete lpPage;
}
```

What could be simpler?

The Hierarchy of Print Support Classes

To help you understand the preview and printing code provided here, we will begin with a quick discussion of the C++ classes that make up the code. Figure 7.1 gives a pictorial overview of the classes used for printing while Figures 7.2 through 7.8 give

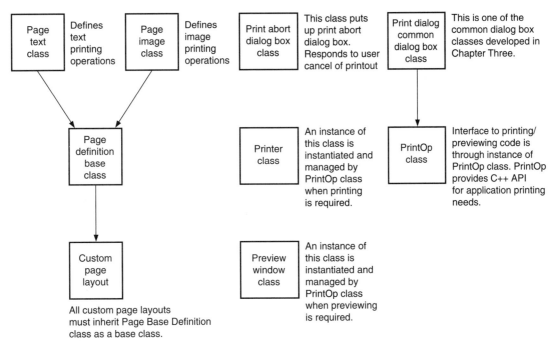

All custom page layouts
must inherit Page Base Definition
class as a base class.

FIGURE 7.1 The Printing class hierarchy.

a short description of all of the member functions provided in the print support classes. All printing support classes are defined in the file "printops.hpp" shown in Listing 7.3. Listing 7.4, the file "printops.cpp," shows the implementation of these C++ classes. As usual, both of these files are available on the companion disk described in Appendix A. The discussions to follow only touch on those parts of the code of special interest or that require further explanation to be understandable. It is hoped that, for the most part, the operations of these classes are understandable from the code listings with their extensive comments and from the descriptions of the member functions provided.

Listing 7.3 The Printops class interface definition.

```
/***********************************************************/
/***                   "printops.hpp"              ***/
/***    Printing and Print Preview Class Include File   ***/
/***                      by                       ***/
/***             Craig A. Lindley               ***/
/***                                              ***/
/***      Revision: 2.0    Last Update: 11/11/94   ***/
/***********************************************************/

// Copyright (c) 1995 John Wiley & Sons, Inc. All rights reserved.

#ifndef PRINTOPS_HPP
#define PRINTOPS_HPP
```

```
#include <owlpch.h>
#pragma hdrstop

#include <static.h>
#include "cdialogs.hpp"
#include "tappids.h"
#include "dialogs.hpp"

// Definitions of important data structures. Included only if necessary
#ifndef _RGBCOLOR
#define _RGBCOLOR
typedef struct {
  BYTE Red;
  BYTE Green;
  BYTE Blue;
} RGBCOLOR;
#endif

#ifndef _IMAGEDESCRIPTOR
#define _IMAGEDESCRIPTOR
// This structure is used for decribing an image.
typedef struct _IMAGEDESCRIPTOR {
  WORD Width;
  WORD Height;
  DWORD RasterSize;
  WORD BPP;
  WORD Colors;
  HGLOBAL hImageData;
  RGBCOLOR Palette[256];
} IMAGEDESCRIPTOR, *LPIMAGEDESCRIPTOR;
#endif

// PageText Class Definition
// This class is used for textual output on a printout
class PageText {
  private:
    BOOL UseFrame;
    WORD UseJustificationFlags;
    COLORREF UseFGColor;
    COLORREF UseBGColor;
    LOGFONT UseFont;
    int UseFontSizeInPoints;

  public:
    PageText(void);
    void PrintText(HDC hDC, LPSTR lpText, RECT& Rect, BOOL MultiLine = FALSE);

    void SetFrameUse(BOOL UseTheFrame)         { UseFrame = UseTheFrame; }
    BOOL IsFrameUsed(void)                     { return UseFrame; }

    void SetJustificationFlags(WORD Flags) { UseJustificationFlags = Flags; }
    WORD GetJustificationFlags(void)           { return UseJustificationFlags; }

    void SetFGColor (COLORREF Color)       { UseFGColor = Color; }
    COLORREF GetFGColor(void)                  { return UseFGColor; }
```

```
    void SetBGColor(COLORREF Color)          { UseBGColor = Color; }
     COLORREF GetBGColor(void)                { return UseBGColor; }

    void SetFont(LOGFONT& Font)              { UseFont = Font; }
    LOGFONT& GetFont(void)                   { return UseFont; }

     void SetFontPointSize(int Size)         { UseFontSizeInPoints = Size; }
     int GetFontPointSize(void)              { return UseFontSizeInPoints; }

    void SetDefaults(void);
};

// PageImage Class Definition
// This class is used for image output on a printout
class PageImage {
  private:
    // Private member functions
    HPALETTE CreateLogicalPalette(RGBCOLOR *lpColors, WORD NumOfColors);

  public:
    BOOL PrintImage(HDC hDC, IMAGEDESCRIPTOR& ID, RECT& Rect, BOOL IsPreview);
};

// PageDefinitionBase Class Definition
// This is the class that all printed page types are derived from. Every
// different printed page will require a definition class derived from
// this class.
class PageDefinitionBase : public PageText, public PageImage {
  protected:
    LPSTR lpPageName;
    WORD PageNumber;
    BOOL IsPreview;

  public:
    PageDefinitionBase(LPSTR PageName, WORD PgNum = 1);
     virtual ~PageDefinitionBase(void);
    virtual void PrintPage(HDC DC, WORD Page) = 0;
    virtual BOOL IsNextPage();
     LPSTR GetPageName(void)             { return lpPageName; }
     void SetPreview(void)               { IsPreview = TRUE; }
     void ResetPreview(void)             { IsPreview = FALSE; }

    BOOL PrintImage(HDC hDC, IMAGEDESCRIPTOR& ID, RECT& Rect) {
       return PageImage::PrintImage(hDC, ID, Rect, IsPreview);
    }
};

// PrintAbortDialog Class Definition
class PrintAbortDialog: public TCenteredDialog {
  private:
    LPSTR lpPageName;              // Storage for the various strings
    LPSTR lpPrinterName;
    LPSTR lpPortName;
    WORD PageNumber;
    TStatic *lpPageNameInd;
```

```
            TStatic *lpPrinterInd;
            TStatic *lpPortInd;
            TStatic *lpPageNumberInd;

    protected:
        virtual void CmCancel(void);

    public:
        PrintAbortDialog(TWindow *parent,
                            LPSTR PageName, LPSTR Printer, LPSTR Port, WORD PgNum,
                            TResId resID = IDD_PRINTABORT,
                            TModule *module = 0);
        virtual ~PrintAbortDialog();
        virtual void SetupWindow();
        void SetPageNumber(WORD PgNum);
};

// Printer Class Definition
// An object of this class represent the physical printer device.
// To print a document derived from PageDefinitionBase send a ptr
// to the document to Printer's Print function.
class Printer {
    private:
        HDC    hDC;                     // Local storage for printer hDC
        LPSTR  lpPrinterName;           // Ptr to storage for printer name
        LPSTR  lpPortName;              // Ptr to storage for printer port
        WORD   PageNumber;
        int    PaperWidth;              // Dimensions of printer paper
        int    PaperLength;

        virtual void ReportError(TWindow *Parent, int ErrorNumber);

    public:
        Printer(HDC hDC, LPSTR PrinterName, LPSTR PortName, WORD PgNum,
                    int WidthOfPaper, int LengthOfPaper);
        virtual ~Printer();
         BOOL Print(TWindow *Parent, PageDefinitionBase *lpPage);
};

// Preview Window Class Definition
#define BORDERPAD       10        // 0.1" gap surrounding preview window

class PreviewWindow : public TWindow {
    private:
        int PaperWidth;
        int PaperLength;
        WORD PageNumber;
        PageDefinitionBase *lpPage;

        // Response table
        DECLARE_RESPONSE_TABLE(PreviewWindow);

        // Window message processing functions
        virtual void Paint(TDC& hDC, BOOL Erase, TRect& Area);
      virtual void EvPaletteChanged(HWND hWindow);
```

```
    public:
        PreviewWindow(TWindow *Parent, int WidthOfPaper, int LengthOfPaper,
                        WORD PgNum, PageDefinitionBase *lpPage);
};


// The print operation class. All application programs deal with
// preview and printing via this class.
class PrintOp : public PrintDialog {
  private:
        TWindow *Parent;
        PreviewWindow *lpPreviewWindow;
        PageDefinitionBase *lpPageDefinition;
        WORD PageNumber;
        BOOL PrinterConfigured;

        WORD PaperWidth;                  // Currently selected paper
        WORD PaperLength;                 // specifications.
        int PaperOrientation;
        int PaperType;

        // Private member functions
        BOOL PaperSizeFromType(int PaperType,
                                WORD& PaperWidth, WORD& PaperLength);
        void GetCurrentPaperSpecification(void);

  public:
        PrintOp(void);
        virtual ~PrintOp(void);

        void DoPrinterSetupDialog(HWND hWindow);
        BOOL IsPrinterConfigured(void)      { return PrinterConfigured; }
        void InitForPrintOp(TWindow *Parent, PageDefinitionBase *lpPage,
                            WORD PgNum);
        BOOL Print(void);                   // Print the page definition to the printer
        BOOL BeginPreview(void);            // Display preview of page definition
                                            // in window
        BOOL EndPreview(void);              // Terminate display of preview
};
#endif
```

Listing 7.4 The Printops class member functions.

```
/*********************************************************/
/***                    "printops.cpp"              ***/
/***        Print and Print Preview Class Functions ***/
/***                        by                      ***/
/***                 Craig A. Lindley               ***/
/***                                                ***/
/***       Revision: 2.0     Last Update: 11/11/94  ***/
/*********************************************************/

// Copyright (c) 1995 John Wiley & Sons, Inc. All rights reserved.

// This file contains all of the classes necessary for previewing
// and printing.
```

```cpp
#include "printops.hpp"

// These functions are borrowed from display.cpp because they are
// needed for previewing true color images on 256 color displays.
extern HGLOBAL DitherAnImage(BYTE huge *lpImage, WORD Width, WORD Height);
extern RGBCOLOR DitherPalette[];

// Allocate storage and save a string
LPSTR StoreString(LPSTR String){

  LPSTR lpStorage = new char[Istrlen(String)+1];
  Istrcpy(lpStorage, String);
  return lpStorage;
}

// The Page Text Class Member Functions
// PageText Class Constructor
PageText::PageText(void){

  SetDefaults();      // Set all default values
}

void PageText::SetDefaults(void) {

  // Build a default LOGFONT structure for use. Font will be Arial
  // Bold and 28 points in size
  memset(&UseFont, 0, sizeof(LOGFONT));

  UseFont.IfWeight = 400;
  UseFont.IfOutPecision = 3;
  UseFont.IfClipPrecision = 2;
  UseFont.IfQuality = 1;
  UseFont.IfPitchAndFamily = 0x2;
  Istrcpy((LPSTR) &UseFont.IfFaceName, "Arial");

  UseFrame = FALSE;
  UseJustificationFlags = DT_LEFT;
  UseFGColor = RGB( 0, 0, 0);// Black text
  UseBGColor = RGB(255, 255, 255);// White background
  UseFontSizeInPoints = 28; // 28 pt font size
}

// Calls to this function print a line of text to the specified
// device context.
void PageText::PrintText(HDC hDC, LPSTR lpText, RECT& Rect, BOOL MultiLine){
  HPEN hOldPen;

  UNIT Format = DT_WORDBREAK | DT_NOPREFIX; // Force word wrap

  if(!MultiLine)
   Format |= DT_VCENTER | DT_SINGLELINE;

  // Merge in the specified justification
  Format |= UseJustificationFlags;
```

```
   // Move the string into temp buffer before printing. Alloc buffer
   // a little larger than absolutely required.
   WORD Length = Istrlen(lpText);
   HGLOBAL hBuf = GlobalAlloc(GHND, Length + 8);
   if(!hBuf)
    return;

   LPSTR lpBuf = (LPSTR) GlobalLock(hBuf);
   Istrcpy(lpBuf, lpText);

   if(Format & DT_RIGHT) // If right justified, add a space
    Istract(lpBuf,""); // so final char of text not cut off

   // Fill the window with background color
   HBRUSH hBrush = CreateSolidBrush(UseBGColor);
   HBRUSH hOldBrush = (HBRUSH) SelectObject(hDC, hBrush);
   HPEN hNullPen;
   if(!UseFrame){
    hNullPen = CreatePen(PS_NULL, 1, RGB(0, 0, 0));
    hOldPen = (HPEN) SelectObject(hDC, (HGDIOBJ) hNullPen);
   }
   // Draw an outlined rectangle filled with the background color
   Rectangle(hDC, Rect.left, Rect.top, Rect.right, Rect.bottom);
   // Now select the proper colors to display the text string
   SetBkMode(hDC, TRANSPARENT);
   SetTextColor(hDC, UseFGColor);

   // Now select the proper font size. Assume MM_LOENGLISH mapping mode
   // or equivalent extents. Specify text size directly in logical
   // units (.01 inch/unit). One point is 1/72 of an inch.
   UseFont.IfHeight = -((UseFontSizeInPoints * 100) / 72);

   HFONT hfont = CreateFontIndirect(&UseFont);
   HFONT hfontOld = (HFONT) SelectObject(hDC, hfont);

   // Draw the text into the device context
   DrawText(hDC, lpBuf, -1, (LPRECT) &Rect, Format); // Write the string with
     special font

   // Clean up the various objects: Font, Pen and Brush
   SelectObject(hDC, hfontOld);
   DeleteObject(hfont);
   if(!UseFrame){
    SelectObject(hDC, hOldPen);
    DeleteObject(hNullPen);
   }
   SelectObject(hDC, hOldBrush);
   DeleteObject(hBrush);

   GlobalUnlock(hBuf);
   GlobalFree(hBuf);
}


// The PageImage Class Member Functions
```

```
// This function builds a logical palette. This palette is made up of
// NumOfColors number of colors. It returns a handle to the palette if
// successful and NULL otherwise.
HPALETTE PageImage::CreateLogicalPalette(RGBCOLOR *lpPalette, WORD NumOfColors){
  HGLOBAL hPaletteMem;

  if(!lpPalette || NumOfColors == 0)
   return NULL;

  WORD ColorsInPalette = (NumOfColors > 16) ? 256:NumOfColors;

  hPaletteMem = GlobalAlloc(GHND, sizeof(LOGPALETTE) +
                 ColorsInPalette * sizeof(PALETTEENTRY));
  if(!hPaletteMem)
   return NULL;

  LPLOGPALETTE lpPal = (LPLOGPALETTE) GlobalLock(hPaletteMem);

  lpPal->palNumEntries = NumOfColors;
  lpPal->palVersion = 0x300;

  for (int i=0; i < NumOfColors; i++){
   lpPal->palPalEntry[i].peRed = lpPalette[i].Red;
   lpPal->palPalEntry[i].peGreen = lpPalette[i].Green;
   lpPal->palPalEntry[i].peBlue = lpPalette[i].Blue;
   lpPal->palPalEntry[i].peFlags = 0;
  }
  HPALETTE hPal = CreatePalette(lpPal);
  GlobalUnlock(hPaletteMem);
  GlobalFree(hPaletteMem);
  return hPal;
}


// Calls to this function print an image to the specified device
// context.
BOOL PageImage::PrintImage(HDC hDC, IMAGEDESCRIPTOR& ID,
         RECT& Rect, BOOL IsPreview){

// Because this can take awhile, put up hourglass
HCURSOR hOldCursor = SetCursor(LoadCursor(NULL, IDC_WAIT));

// Determine if dithering of image is necessary before output
BOOL DitheringRequired = FALSE;     // Assume not
if (IsPreview){                     // Only check if this output is a preview
  HDC hDC = GetDC(NULL);            // Get DC from screen
  // If screen is 8 BPP or less and image is true color dithering required
  if((GetDeviceCaps(hDC, BITSPIXEL) <= 8)&&(ID.BPP == 24))
   DitheringRequired = TRUE;        // I guess so
  ReleaseDC(NULL, hDC);             // Free up DC
}

// Build a BITMAPINFOHEADER to describe the image to be output. First
// calculate how many colors in image's palette
WORD ColorsInPalette = ((ID.Colors > 16) || DitheringRequired) ?
          256 : ID.Colors;
```

```
HGLOBAL hBmi = GlobalAlloc(GHND, sizeof(BITMAPINFOHEADER) +
            ColorsInPalette * sizeof(RGBQUAD));
if(!hBmi){
  SetCursor(hOldCursor);   // Put original cursor back
  return FALSE;
}
LPBITMAPINFO lpBmi = (LPBITMAPINFO) GlobalLock(hBmi);

// The following setup is independent of the # of colors
LPBITMAPINFOHEADER pBi = &lpBmi->bmiHeader;
pBi->biSize    = sizeof(BITMAPINFOHEADER);
pBi->biWidth  = ID.Width;
pBi->biHeight = ID.Height;
pBi->biPlanes = 1;
pBi->biCompression = 0L;
pBi->biXPelsPerMeter = 0L;
pBi->biYPelsPerMeter = 0L;
pBi->biClrImportant = 0L;


// The remainder of the processing is dependent upon the number of colors

// Copy palette to DIB color table. True color images will skip this
// code because ID.Colors == 0;
if(!DitheringRequired){   // Dithering is not required
  for (int i=0; i < ID.Colors; i++) {
    lpBmi->bmiColors[i].rgbRed = ID.Palette[i].Red;
    lpBmi->bmiColors[i].rgbGreen = ID.Palette[i].Green;
    lpBmi->bmiColors[i].rgbBlue = ID.Palette[i].Blue;
    lpBmi->bmiColors[i].rgbReserved = 0;
  }
} else {       // Dithering is required
  for (int i=0; i < 256; i++) {
    lpBmi->bmiColors[i].rgbRed = DitherPalette[i].Red;
    lpBmi->bmiColors[i].rgbGreen = DitherPalette[i].Green;
    lpBmi->bmiColors[i].rgbBlue = DitherPalette[i].Blue;
    lpBmi->bmiColors[i].rgbReserved = 0;
  }
}
switch(ColorsInPalette){
  case 2:
   pBi->biBitCount = 1;
    pBi->biClrUsed = 2L;
   break;

  case 4:
    pBi->biBitCount = 4;
   pBi->biClrUsed = 4L;
   break;

  case 16:
   pBi->biBitCount = 4;
   pBi->biClrUsed = ID.Colors;
   break;

  case 256:
   pBi->biBitCount = 8;
```

```
       pBi->biClrUsed = (DitheringRequired) ? 256 : ID.Colors;
       break;

     case 0:                  // 24 BPP image
       pBi->biBitCount = 24;  // Indicate 24 BPP image
       pBi->biClrUsed = 0;    // No color table entries
       break;
   }
   // Set the image size member
   if(!DitheringRequired)
     pBi->biSizeImage = ID.RasterSize;
   else
     pBi->biSizeImage = (DWORD) ALIGN_DWORD(ID.Width) * ID.Height;

   // Create a logical palette for this image. Where palette comes from
   // depends upon whether dithering is needed.
   HPALETTE hOldPalette;
   HPALETTE hNewPalette = CreateLogicalPalette(
                 (DitheringRequired) ? DitherPalette : ID.Palette,
                 (DitheringRequired) ? 256 : ID.Colors);

   // Install the image palette
   if (hNewPalette){
     hOldPalette = SelectPalette(hDC, hNewPalette, FALSE);
     RealizePalette(hDC);
   }

   // Prepare to adjust image display area for correct aspect ratio.
   BOOL VertFit;             // True if image is taller than wide
   if(ID.Height > ID.Width)
     VertFit = TRUE;
   else
     VertFit = FALSE;

   // Get dimensions of display area. Make Rect dimensions positive
   // because they are easier to work with that way. Mapping mode means
   // all Y dimensions negative.
   Rect.top *= -1;
   Rect.bottom *= -1;

   int DisplayWidth = Rect.right - Rect.left;
   int DisplayHeight = Rect.bottom - Rect.top;
   int DisplayLeft = Rect.left;
   int DisplayTop = Rect.top;

   // Adjust image display area for maintaining aspect ratio
   if (VertFit){              // Make the image fit vertically
     WORD NewWidth, VOffset;
     VOffset = DisplayHeight; // Save in case of vert centering
     NewWidth = DisplayWidth + 1;
     while (NewWidth > DisplayWidth)
       NewWidth = (WORD)(((DWORD) DisplayHeight--* ID.Width) / ID.Height);
     DisplayHeight++;
     DisplayLeft += (DisplayWidth - NewWidth) / 2;
```

```
    DisplayTop += (VOffset - DisplayHeight) / 2;
    DisplayWidth = NewWidth;
}else{          // Make the image fit horizontally
  WORD NewHeight, HOffset;
  HOffset = DisplayWidth; // Save in case of horz centering
  NewHeight = DisplayHeight + 1;
  while (NewHeight > DisplayHeight)
    NewHeight = (WORD)(((DWORD) DisplayWidth--* ID.Height)/ID.Width);
  DisplayWidth++;
  DisplayLeft += (HOffset - DisplayWidth) / 2;
  DisplayTop += (DisplayHeight - NewHeight) / 2;
  DisplayHeight = NewHeight;
}
// When we get here the dimensions of the display area have been
// modified to cause the image to be displayed with aspect ratio
// intact.
//
#ifdef_WIN32_
  SetStretchBltMode(hDC, COLORONCOLOR);
#else
  SetStretchBitMode(hDC, STRETCH_DELETESCANS);
#endif

  // Get a pointer to the image data. Either from IMAGEDESCRIPTOR or from
  // call to DitherAnImage depending upon whether dithering is necessary.
  HGLOBAL hDitheredImage = 0;
  BYTE huge *lpImageData = (BYTE huge *) GlobalLock(ID.hImageData);
  if(DitheringRequired){
    hDitheredImage = DitherAnImage(lpImageData, ID.Width, ID.Height);
    lpImageData = (BYTE huge *) GlobalLock(hDitheredImage);
  }

  // Bit the image to the output device
  BOOL Ok = (StretchDIBits(hDC,
        DisplayLeft, -DisplayTop,
            DisplayWidth, -DisplayHeight,
        0, 0, ID.Width, ID.Height, lpImageData,
            lpBmi, DIB_RGB_COLORS, SRCCOPY) == DisplayHeight);

  // Clean up and return
  if (hDitheredImage){                 // If a dithered image was used
    GlobalUnlock(hDitheredImage);      // Free memory it occupied
    GlobalFree(hDitheredImage);
  }
  GlobalUnlock(ID.hImageData);         // Unlock the image data
  if (hNewPalette){                    // If a new palette was used
    SelectPalette(hDC, hOldPalette, FALSE); // Select old palette back
    DeleteObject(hNewPalette);         // Delete the now unnecessary palette
  }
  GlobalUnlock(hBmi);                  // Unlock and free the BITMAPINFO memory
  GlobalFree(hBmi);
  SetCursor(hOldCursor);               // Put original cursor back
  return Ok;                           // Return status
}
```

```
// Global Flag used to indicate user wants to abort a printout
static BOOL UserAbort = FALSE;

// Abort procedure used for printing
BOOL FAR PASCAL_export AbortProc(HDC/*hDC*/, int/*Error*/){
  MSG Msg;

  while (!UserAbort && PeekMessage(&Msg, NULL, NULL, NULL, PM_REMOVE))
    if(!IsDialogMessage(GetFocus(), &Msg)){
    TranslateMessage(&Msg);
    DispatchMessage(&Msg);
    }
  return (!UserAbort);
}

// PageDefinitionBase class member functions
PageDefinitionBase::PageDefinitionBase(LPSTR PageName, WORD PgNum){

  // Store incoming parameters
  lpPageName = StoreString(PageName);
  PageNumber = PgNum;
  IsPreview = FALSE;      // Assume page will be printed
                         // not previewed.
}


PageDefinitionBase::~PageDefinitionBase(void){

  delete lpPageName;
}


BOOL PageDefinitionBase::IsNextPage(void){

  return FALSE;
}

// PrintAbortDialog class member functions. This is a modeless dialog box.
PrintAbortDialog::PrintAbortDialog(
                    TWindow *parent,
                    LPSTR PageName, LPSTR Printer, LPSTR Port, WORD PgNum,
                    TResId resId, TModule *module)
:TCenteredDialog(parent, resId, module){

lpPageName = StoreString(PageName);
lpPrinterName = StoreString(Printer);
lpPortName = StoreString(Port);
PageNumber = PgNum;
  // Instantiate all of the static text areas in abort dialog box
  lpPageNameInd = new TStatic(this, IDPRTABORTPAGENAMEIND, 40);
  lpPrintInd = new TStatic(this, IDPRTABORTPRINTERNAMEIND, 50);
  lpPortInd = new TStatic(this, IDPRTABORTPORTNAMEIND, 10);
  lpPageNumberInd = new TStatic(this, IDPRTABORTPAGENUMBERIND, 5);
}


PrintAbortDialog::~PrintAbortDialog(void){
```

```
    // Give up all of the local strings
    delete lpPageName;
    delete lpPrinterName;
    delete lpPortName;
}

void PrintAbortDialog::SetupWindow(void){
    char Buffer[10];

    // Do default processing
    TCenteredDialog::SetupWindow();

    // Write the text into the static areas
    lpPageNameInd->SetText(lpPageName);
    lpPrintInd->SetText(lpPrinterName);
    lpPortInd->SetText(lpPortName);
    // Convert the passed page number to ascii.
    Itoa(PageNumber, Buffer, 10);
    lpPageNumberInd->SetText((LPSTR) Buffer);
}

// Cancel button has been clicked. Terminate the printout
void PrintAbortDialog::CmCancel(void){

    UserAbort = TRUE;

    // Do default processing
    TCenteredDialog::CmCancel();
}

// This function sets the page number displayed in the print abort
// dialog box.
void PrintAbortDialog::SetPageNumber(WORD PgNum){
    char Buffer[10];

    PageNumber = PgNum;
    lpPageNumberInd->SetText(Itoa(PageNumber, Buffer, 10));
}

// Printer class functions. This object type is an encapsulation around
// the Windows printer device.

// Print Class Constructor
Printer::Printer(HDC PrintDC, LPSTR PrinterName, LPSTR PortName, WORD PgNum,
                 int WidthOfPaper, int LengthOfPaper){

    // Save incomming parameters
    hDC = PrintDC;
    lpPrinterName = StoreString(PrinterName);
    lpPortName = StoreString(PortName);
    PageNumber = PgNum;
    PaperWidth = WidthOfPaper;
    PaperLength = LengthOfPaper;
}
```

```
Printer::~Printer(void) {
  delete lpPrinterName;
  delete lpPortName;
}

typedef BOOL (FAR PASCAL_export *AbortProcFn)(HDC hDC, int Error);

BOOL Printer::Print(TWindow *Parent, PageDefinitionBase *lpPage){
  BOOL Result;
  AbortProcFn AbortProcFunction; // Address of AbortProc function

  Result = FALSE;                 // Assume printout was unsuccessful
  UserAbort = FALSE;              // User has not yet aborted the printout

  if(!Parent || !lpPage)          // Check parameters passed in
  return Result;                  // Must have valid non null pointers

    // Because this can take awhile, put up hourglass
    HCURSOR hOldCursor = SetCursor(LoadCursor(NULL, IDC_WAIT));

    // Put up the print abort dialog box
    PrintAbortDialog *lpDlg = new PrintAbortDialog(Parent,
                                  lpPage->GetPageName(),
                                  lpPrinterName, lpPortName;
                                  PageNumber);
if(lpDlg == NULL){              // Was instantiation successful?
  SetCursor(hOldCursor);        // Put original cursor back
  return Result;
}
lpDlg->Create();                // Make dialog visible

// Disable application program while printout occurs
EnableWindow(Parent->HWindow, FALSE);

// Get address of abort function
AbortProcFunction = (AbortProcFn)
            MakeProcInstance((FARPROC) AbortProc,
            Parent->GetModule()->GetInstance());

// Install the abort function. If error terminates
if (SetAbortProc(hDC, AbortProcFunction) < 0){
  SetCursor(hOldCursor);                 // Put original cursor back
  EnableWindow(Parent->HWindow, TRUE);   // Turn app back on
  return Result;                         // Return error indication
}
// Build a DOCINFO structure describing this print job
DOCINFO DI;
DI.cbSize = sizeof(DOCINFO);
DI.lpszDocName = lpPage->GetPageName();
DI.lpszOutput = NULL;

// Issue a StartDoc function call
if (StartDoc(hDC, &DI) < 0){
  SetCursor(hOldCursor);                              // Put original cursor back
```

```
    EnableWindow(Parent->HWindow, TRUE);            // Turn app back on
    FreeProcInstance((FARPROC) AbortProcFunction);  // Free abort instance
    return Result;                                   // Return error indication
  }
  SaveDC(hDC); // Save the device context
  // Calculate printable area in .01" units
  int PrintableWidth = (int)((GetDeviceCaps(hDC, HORZRES) * 100L)/
                        GetDeviceCaps(hDC, LOGPIXELSX));
  int PrintableHeight = (int)((GetDeviceCaps(hDC, VERTRES) * 100L)/
                        GetDeviceCaps(hDC, LOGPIXELSY));

  // Calculate offset from upper left corner of page to start of
  // printable area. Offsets in .01" units.
  int HorzOffset = (PaperWidth - PrintableWidth) / 2;
  int VertOffset = (PaperLength - PrintableHeight) / 2;

  SetMapMode(hDC, MM_LOENGLISH); // Set LOENGLISH mapping mode

  // The following change in window org is necessary because a printer
  // assumes its org at the corner of its printable area instead of
  // the corner of the page as would be expected.
  SetWindowOrgEx(hDC, HorzOffset, -VertOffset, NULL);

  // Now for each page of printout do the following
  int Error = 0;
  do {
    // Call the abort procedure between pages
    if (!(*AbortProcFunction)(hDC, 0))
      Error = SP_ERROR;              // If user aborted, set error indication

    if (Error >= 0)                  // If no error or user abort occurred
      Error = StartPage(hDC);        // Issue start page command

    if (Error >= 0){                 // If no error, do page printing
      // Print the page
      lpPage->PrintPage(hDC, PageNumber);
      Error = EndPage(hDC);          // Indicate page printing has ended
      PageNumber++;                  // Increment page number and send to dialog
      lpDlg->SetPageNumber(PageNumber);
    }
  } while ((Error >= 0) && (lpPage->IsNextPage())):

  // The document is now finished printing or an error has occurred.
  // Find out which.
  if (Error < 0)                     // If an error occurred
    Error = AbortDoc(hDC);           // Abort the document printing
  else
    Error = EndDoc(hDC);             // If successful call EndDoc

  RestoreDC(hDC, -1);                // Put original device context back

  // Free allocated resources
  FreeProcInstance((FARPROC) AbortProcFunction);
  EnableWindow(Parent->HWindow, TRUE);
```

```
  lpDlg->Destroy();
  delete lpDlg;

if (Error & SP_NOTREPORTED)
  ReportError(Parent, Error);

  SetCursor(hOldCursor);       // Put original cursor back

  return (Error > 0) && (!UserAbort);
}

void Printer::ReportError(TWindow *Parent, int Error){
  LPSTR ErrorMsgPtr;

  switch (Error){
    case SP_APPABORT:
      ErrorMsgPtr = "Application aborted";
      break;
    case SP_OUTOFDISK:
      ErrorMsgPtr = "Out of disk space";
      break;
    case SP_OUTOFMEMORY:
      ErrorMsgPtr = "Out of memory";
      break;
    case SP_USERABORT:
      ErrorMsgPtr = "Printing aborted from print manager";
      break;
    case SP_ERROR:
      ErrorMsgPtr = "General printing error or user abort";
      break;
    default:
      return;
  }
  MessageBox(Parent->HWindow, ErrorMsgPtr,
        "User Advisory - Printout Terminated",
        MB_OK | MB_ICONSTOP | MB_TASKMODAL);
}

// Previewer Window Member Functions

// Build a response table for all messages/commands handled
// by this window.
DEFINE_RESPONSE_TABLE1(PreviewWindow, TWindow)

  EV_WM_PALETTECHANGED,

END_RESPONSE_TABLE;

// Print preview window constructor
PreviewWindow::PreviewWindow(TWindow *Parent,
                     int WidthOfPaper, int LengthOfPaper,
                     WORD PgNum, PageDefinitionBase *lpPg)
  : TWindow(Parent){

  // Save the passed in parameters
  PaperWidth = WidthOfPaper;          // Paper dimensions
```

```
PaperLength = LengthOfPaper;
PageNumber = PgNum;                  // Save the page number
lpPage = lpPg;                       // Save ptr to page description

// Set the print preview window style
Attr.Style = WS_BORDER | WS_CHILD | WS_CLIPSIBLINGS | WS_VISIBLE;

// Get dimensions of window into which the preview will be displayed
RECT Rect;
::GetClientRect(Parent->HWindow, (LPRECT) &Rect);
HDC hDC = GetDC(Parent->HWindow);
SetMapMode(hDC, MM_LOENGLISH);

// Convert client dimensions in DP to logical dimensions
DPtoLP(hDC, (LPPOINT) &Rect, 2);

// From mapping mode we know this values will be negative. We make
// them positive now because they are easier to manipulate that way.
Rect.top *= -1;
Rect.bottom *= -1;

// Figure out the larger of the two dimensions of the page. VerticalFit
// is true if page is larger vertically than horizontally.
BOOL VerticalFit = (PaperLength > PaperWidth);
/*
NOTE: Care must be taken in calculating how to fit a page into the client area
of the window. If the page is to be vertically fit, there are no problems
because we squeeze the longer dimension of the page into the smaller vertical
client area dimension. When we scale the page to fit this way, we never have to
worry that the horizontal width of the page will exceed the width of the client
area. If the page is horizontally fit, however, meaning that the page's larger
dimension is it width. The scaling is more problematic. If we blindly scale the
page width to fit within the client area width, it is possible that the verti-
cal size of the page will be larger than the smaller vertical height of the
client area. To solve this problem, we must back off of the maximum client area
width repeatedly until the page height fits comfortably within the vertical
dimension of the client area.
*/

// Now calculate size of print preview based on longest dimension
DWORD TotalHeight, TotalWidth;
WORD Top, Left;
if (VerticalFit) {            // The simple case as noted above
  TotalHeight = Rect.bottom - Rect.top - (2 * BORDERPAD);
  Top = BORDERPAD;
  TotalWidth = (TotalHeight * PaperWidth) / PaperLength;
  Left = (WORD)(((Rect.right - Rect.left) / 2) - (TotalWidth / 2));
}else{                        // The more difficult case
  WORD N = 1;
  BOOL Done = FALSE;
  WORD ClientWidth = Rect.right - Rect.left;
  WORD MaxClientHeight = Rect.bottom - Rect.top - (2 * BORDERPAD);
  while (!Done) {
   TotalWidth = ClientWidth - (2 * N * BORDERPAD);
   TotalHeight = (TotalWidth * PaperLength) / PaperWidth;
    if (TotalHeight <= MaxClientHeight)
```

```
         Done = TRUE;
       else
         N++;
     }
     Left = (WORD)((ClientWidth / 2) - (TotalWidth / 2));
     Top = (WORD)(((Rect.bottom - Rect.top) / 2) - (TotalHeight / 2));
   }
   Rect.top = -Top;
   Rect.left = Left;
   Rect.bottom = -(Top + (WORD) TotalHeight);
   Rect.right = Left + (WORD) TotalWidth;
   // Convert logical coordinates back to device coordinates within client area
   LPtoDP(hDC, (LPPOINT) &Rect, 2);
   ReleaseDC(Parent->HWindow, hDC);
   Attr.X = Rect.left;
   Attr.Y = Rect.top;
   Attr.W = Rect.right - Rect.left;
   Attr.H = Rect.bottom - Rect.top;
}

void PreviewWindow::EvPaletteChanged(HWND hWindow){

   // If this window is NOT the window who caused the palette to
   // change, force this window to realize its logical palette.
   if (hWindow != HWindow)       // If this window did not change palette
     ::InvalidateRect(HWindow, NULL, FALSE); // cause repaint
}

// Process the paint message and display the page
void PreviewWindow::Paint(TDC& hDC, BOOL /*Erase*/, TRect&/*Area*/){

   // Get dimensions of window's client area
   RECT Rect;
   ::GetClientRect(HWindow, &Rect);     // Get size of window client area in DPs

   // Setup the ISOTROPIC mapping mode in this display context
   SaveDC(hDC);                         // Save the device context
   SetMapMode(hDC, MM_ISOTROPIC);
   SetWindowExtEx(hDC, PaperWidth, PaperLength, NULL);
   SetViewportExtEx(hDC, Rect.right - Rect.left, -(Rect.bottom - Rect.top), NULL);
   lpPage->PrintPage(hDC, PageNumber);
   RestoreDC(hDC, -1);                  // Put the DC back the way it was
}

// PrintOp class functions
PrintOp::PrintOp(void){

   lpPreviewWindow = NULL;              // No previewer window yet

   // Get info on default printer. PrinterConfigured will be false
   // if no printer is configured.
   PrinterConfigured = GetPrinterInformation();

   // Gather specs on currently selected paper in printer
   GetCurrentPaperSpecification();
}
```

```
PrintOp::~PrintOp(void){

  if (lpPreviewWindow)        // Destroy preview window if any
    EndPreview();
}


// Determine the dimensions of the paper from its paper type

typedef char PAPERNAMEENTRY[64];
typedef POINT PAPERSIZEENTRY;
typedef WORD PAPERIDENTRY;

BOOL PrintOp::PaperSizeFromType(int PaperType,
                     WORD& PaperWidth, WORD& PaperLength){

  // Get the number of supported paper types for current printer
  WORD NumOfEntries = (WORD) GetPrinterCapabilities(DC_PAPERS, NULL);

  // Allocate buffer for paper ID array
  HLOCAL hPaperIDArray = LocalAlloc(LHND, NumOfEntries *
    sizeof(PAPERIDENTRY));
  if (!hPaperIDArray){
    MessageBox(NULL, "No memory for paper ID array", "User Advisory",
          MB_ICONSTOP | MB_TASKMODAL);
    return FALSE;          // Return error indication
  }
  // Allocate buffer for paper size array
  HLOCAL hPaperSizeArray = LocalAlloc(LHND, NumOfEntries *sizeof(PAPERSIZEENTRY));
  if (!hPaperSizeArray) {
    LocalFree(hPaperIDArray);
    MessageBox(NULL, "No memory for paper size array", "User Advisory",
          MB_ICONSTOP | MB_TASKMODAL);
    return FALSE;           // Return error indication
  }

  // Get ptrs to the array storage locations
  PAPERIDENTRY *PaperIDs = (PAPERIDENTRY *) LocalLock(hPaperIDArray);
  PAPERSIZEENTRY *PaperSizes = (PAPERSIZEENTRY *) LocalLock(hPaperSizeArray);

  // Now that we have buffers to receive paper info, get the info
  GetPrinterCapabilities(DC_PAPERS, (LPSTR) PaperIDs);
  GetPrinterCapabilities(DC_PAPERSIZE,(LPSTR) PaperSizes);

  // Now determine which entry has the proper ID for the current paper
  // size.
  for (WORD Index=0; Index < NumOfEntries; Index++){
    if (PaperType == PaperIDs[Index])
      break;
  }
  // Paper sizes in 1/10 mm units
  PaperWidth = PaperSizes[Index].x;
  PaperLength = PaperSizes[Index].y;

  // Convert units to .01" units. Sizes assume portrait orientation.
  PaperWidth = (WORD)((PaperWidth * 100L) / 254L);
  PaperLength = (WORD)((PaperLength * 100L) / 254L);
```

```
    // Unlock and free the memory for the arrays
    LocalUnlock(hPaperIDArray);
    LocalFree(hPaperIDArray);
    LocalUnlock(hPaperSizeArray);
    LocalFree(hPaperSizeArray);
    return TRUE;
}

// Get the specifications for the currently selected paper on the
// printer. Class variables are updated with the results. Values
// returned in .01" units.
void PrintOp::GetCurrentPaperSpecification(void){

  // Get paper type and paper orientation
  PaperType = GetPaperType();
  PaperOrientation = GetPaperOrientation();

  // With the paper type known, get specifications on the currently
  // selected printer paper.
  PaperSizeFromType(PaperType, PaperWidth, PaperLength);

  // Paper dimensions must be reversed if in landscape mode
  int Temp;
  if (PaperOrientation == DMORIENT_LANDSCAPE){
    Temp = PaperWidth;
    PaperWidth = PaperLength;
    PaperLength = Temp;
  }
}

// This function must be called before a preview or printout can
// be performed
void PrintOp::InitForPrintOp(TWindow *TheParent,
                             PageDefinitionBase *lpPage,
                             WORD PgNum){

  Parent = TheParent;           // Store ptr to parent window

  if (lpPreviewWindow)          // Destroy preview window if any
    EndPreview();

  lpPageDefinition = lpPage;    // Store new page definition
  PageNumber = PgNum;           // Store starting page number
}

// Bring up the printer setup dialog box for the user
void PrintOp::DoPrinterSetupDialog(HWND hWindow){

  SelectPrintSetupDialog();
  DoDialog(hWindow);

  // Gather specs on currently selected paper for current printer
  GetCurrentPaperSpecification();
}
```

```
// Perform a user requested printout of document page
BOOL PrintOp::Print(void){
  BOOL Result = FALSE;

  // We can now perform a printout. Declare instance of printer class.
  Printer *lpMyPrinter = new
    Printer(GetPrtHDC(), GetPrinterName(), GetPortName(), PageNumber,
        PaperWidth, PaperLength);

  // If error instantiating the printer device, exit
  if (lpMyPrinter == NULL)
    return FALSE;

  if (lpPageDefinition){    // If page definition OK
    // Reset preview bit in page definition in case it was set
    lpPageDefinition->ResetPreview();
    // Print the page layout
    Result = lpMyPrinter->Print(Parent, lpPageDefinition);
  }

  delete lpMyPrinter;        // Get rid of printer device object
  return Result;             // Return results
}

// Perform a user requested preview of document page
BOOL PrintOp::BeginPreview(void){

  if (!lpPageDefinition)      // If page definition not OK
    return FALSE;

  // Set the preview bit in the page definition
  lpPageDefinition->SetPreview();

  // Instantiate a PreviewWindow object
  lpPreviewWindow = new PreviewWindow(Parent, PaperWidth, PaperLength,
                          PageNumber, lpPageDefinition);
  if (!lpPreviewWindow);
    return FALSE;

  // Make the window visible
  lpPreviewWindow->Create();

  return TRUE;
}

BOOL PrintOp::EndPreview(void){

  if (!lpPreviewWindow)      // Must have a PreviewWindow object
    return FALSE;

  lpPreviewWindow->Destroy();        // Destroy interface element
  delete lpPreviewWindow;            // Destroy interface object
  lpPreviewWindow = NULL;            // Set ptr to NULL
  return TRUE;
}
```

As has been previously mentioned, all custom page layout classes are derived from the PageDefinitionBase base class. PageDefinitionBase itself derives much of its functionality from the two classes it inherents: PageText and PageImage. As you can probably deduce from the name, the PageText class provides the PageDefinitionBase class with its text printing capabilities while the PageImage class does the same for images. Both of these functions help provide WYSIWYG functionality. Any extensions necessary for textual output should be added to the PageText class. Any imaging extensions should be added to the PageImage class. See Figure 7.2 for a short description of the member functions of the PageText class and Figure 7.3 for a description of the PageImage functions. Figure 7.4 describes the PageDefinitionBase class and its member functions.

Probably the most interesting (and complex) code in these classes, from an imaging point of view, is that found in the PrintImage member function of the PageImage class. This is the code that displays images during a preview operation or sends the image data to a printer during print operations. As you will see, a great deal of effort must be expended before images can be previewed or printed. Most of the effort is used to setup the **StretchDIBits** bit blit function that actually moves the data to the output device. Other interesting parts of this code include the use of dithering, if required, during a preview operation and the code that maintains the aspect ratio of the image. See Listing 7.4 for the implementation details.

The Printer class encapsulates all of the code required to send a page of output to the printer for printing. The use of this class insulates the programmer from dealing directly with the Windows API. The **Print** member function of this class does the actual printing. For the most part, it is a direct translation of Windows printing requirements into code. The only portion of the code that may appear somewhat obscure is that dealing with printable area. Printable area is that portion of a page onto which the printer is capable of writing pixels. Printable area dimensions vary from printer to printer, even if the printers are using the same paper size. Restrictions in printable area are usually due to some mechanical limitations of the printer. What does not vary from printer to printer is the fact that Windows offsets the coordinates on a printed page by the dimensions of the printable area. For example, the coordinates 0, 0 on a printed page do not represent the upper left corner of the paper as one might expect. Instead, they represent the upper left corner of the printable area of the page. If the dimensions of the printable area are not taken into consideration, all items drawn on a printed page will be offset toward the lower right by the dimensions of the printable area. To circumvent this offset, the code in the **Print** function shifts the window origin up and to the left by the dimensions of the printable area. That way page layouts designed to the dimensions of the paper will print centered on the page as expected.

The PreviewWindow class is called upon to preview a layout page within a window on the screen. The preview should be a nearly exact scaled down replica of what would be printed if the layout were to be submitted to a printer for printing. I say nearly exact because WYSIWYG technology under Windows (especially where fonts are concerned) is not yet perfect, but very close. The size of the displayed preview depends on the size of the window in which the preview is displayed. Small preview windows, although kind of cute, scale the displayed information so severely they are hardly usable. It is advisable to use the largest window possible for displaying a print preview.

The PageText class

Purpose

The purpose of this class is to provide textual output capability to the derived PageDefinitionBase class. In brief, this class encapsulates and extends the Windows **DrawText** function into an easy to use C++ class that provides complete control of almost all text formatting and printing attributes including font selection, font size, text justification, text color, and so on. A set of default text printing attributes are established that can be selectively changed by calling the various member functions of this class before text output is performed.

Member Functions

Page Text. This is the constructor for the class. The only action performed by this constructor is to call the function **SetDefaults** to establish the default text output attributes.

PrintText. This is the function that is called to output text to a specified device context (usually a printer). In addition to the handle to the device context, the parameters passed to this function include a pointer to the string to print, a reference to a RECT structure that specifies the position of the text on the printed page, and a Boolean that indicates whether the text should be printed in multiline as opposed to single-line format. See help on the Windows **DrawText** API function for further information on single and multiline text fields. Note: The position information contained in the RECT structure must be thought of in the MM_LOENGLISH mapping mode using the requisite .01-inch units.

SetFrameUse. This function controls whether the output text gets a frame drawn around it. A TRUE passed as a parameter causes a frame to be drawn. Frame drawing is off by default.

IsFrameUsed. This function returns TRUE if the frame drawing mode is currently being used and FALSE if not.

SetJustificationFlags. This function is used to set the text justification mode to be used for all subsequent text output functions. The justification flags passed to this function are the same as used for the Windows **DrawText** function. By default, the flag DT_LEFT is set, meaning that all text will be left justified within the specified rectangular area.

GetJustificationFlags. This function returns the justification flags currently in effect.

SetFGColor. This function is used to specify a foreground color to be used for the printed text. Colors within this class are specified by RGB values. The default foreground text color is black.

GetFGColor. This function returns the current foreground text color.

SetBGColor. This function is used to specify a background color to be used for the printed text. The default background color is white.

GetBGColor. This function returns the current background text color.

SetFont. This function is used to set the font to be used for all subsequent text output. By default, a 28-point bold, Arial font is used for all text unless changed by this

Figure 7.2 The PageText class.

function. A reference to a LOGFONT structure is passed to this function to define the text font.

GetFont. This function returns a reference to the LOGFONT structure that defines the font currently being used.

SetFontPointSize. This function is used to set the point size of the font used for text output. The default font size is 28 points. This function is used to change the default size. This function can change the size of the font regardless of the font type.

GetFontPointSize. This function returns the point size of the currently used font.

SetDefaults. This function establishes the defaults to be used for text output. The default font is set to Arial 28-point bold, the text framing function is turned off, left text justification is selected, the text foreground color is set to black, and the text background color is set to white. This function can be called after any text output operation to return the defaults to a known state.

FIGURE 7.2 *(Continued)*

The PageImage class

Purpose

The purpose of this class is to provide easy to use image output capability to the derived PageDefinitionBase class. This class encapsulates all of the code necessary to print images to a device context. This class operates differently depending on whether the device context represents an actual printer or a screen for previewing.

Member Functions

CreateLogicalPalette. This private function builds a logical palette for an image to be displayed. A logical palette is necessary for outputting the image to a device context.

PrintImage. This function performs all of the operations necessary to print an image into a device context. For parameters, this function requires a handle to the device context, a reference to an IMAGEDESCRIPTOR structure defining the image to be printed, a reference to a RECT structure containing the destination location of the image on the printed page (in MM_LOENGLISH units), and a Boolean that is to be TRUE only when a preview operation is requested and FALSE if an actual printout is to occur. This function must know whether a preview operation is being requested so it can dither a true color image, if necessary, for display on the computer's monitor.

The operations performed for printing an image include the following. Please refer back to Chapter 2 if you have any questions about why these operations are necessary for image output.

1. A BITMAPINFOHEADER structure is built describing the type of image to be displayed or printed.
2. A logical palette is created for display or printing of the image.

FIGURE 7.3 The PageImage class.

3. The new logical palette is selected into the device context and the new palette is realized.
4. The dimensions of the specified image display area are manipulated to maintain the aspect ratio of the image.
5. The image is bit blit into the device context.
6. The old palette is selected back into the device context.
7. Various housecleaning functions are performed to clean up resources no longer needed.

FIGURE 7.3 *(Continued)*

The PageDefinitionBase class

Purpose

This is the abstract class from which all custom page layouts are derived. As an abstract class, an object of this class type cannot be instantiated directly. This class inherits the PageText and PageImage classes, discussed previously, to give layouts derived from it basic text and image output capabilities.

Member Functions

PageDefinitionBase.   This is the class constructor. The only operation performed within the constructor is to save the parameters passed in. Parameters include the page (layout) name string and the page number (to begin printing from).

~PageDefinitionBase.   This is the class destructor. Its only function is to free the storage space allocated in the constructor for storage of the page name string.

PrintPage.   This is a pure virtual function that is nothing more than a placeholder for functions of the same name in derived classes. No code exists in this class for this function. The PrintPage function (in derived layout classes) will be called once for each page of a layout to be printed.

IsNextPage.   This is a virtual function that must be overridden in derived classes to permit multipage printout capability. By default, this function returns FALSE, indicating a single-page layout. Multipage layout classes must override this function and return TRUE as long as there is another page of the layout to be printed.

GetPageName.   This function returns a pointer to the page name string stored in this object.

SetPreview.   This function sets a Boolean in this object, indicating the layout derived from this class is involved in a preview operation.

ResetPreview.   This function sets a Boolean in this object, indicating the layout derived from this class is involved in a printing operation.

PrintImage.   This function provides an interface to a function of the same name in the PageImage base class whose function is printing images into a device context (which usually belongs to a printer). This function calls the base class function passing along all of its parameters but adds the IsPreview class Boolean to the parameter list. Passing of this parameter allows the base classes PrintImage function to know whether an image is actually being printed or is being used instead for a preview operation.

FIGURE 7.4 The PageDefinitionBase class.

213

The PrintAbortDialog class

Purpose

The purpose of this class is to provide a print dialog box that provides the user with print status and allows the user to cancel the print operation.

Member Functions

PrintAbortDialog.   This is the class constructor. It stores the strings for page (layout) name, printer name, and printer port, passed in as parameters, and instantiates the static text display objects used for displaying this information to the user.

~PrintAbortDialog.   This is the class destructor. Its only function is to free the string storage areas allocated in the constructor for the strings.

CmCancel.   This private function is called whenever the user clicks the cancel button in the print abort dialog box. Its only function is to set the variable UserAbort to TRUE, which subsequently causes the print operation to be aborted.

SetupWindow.   This function writes the stored strings into the appropriate fields of the print abort dialog box.

SetPageNumber.   This function sets the page number displayed in the print abort dialog box to that passed in as a parameter.

FIGURE 7.5 The PrintAbortDialog class.

Most of the work performed by the PreviewWindow class is done in the class constructor and in the **Paint** function for the PreviewWindow window. The function of the constructor is to size the PreviewWindow window to the scaled down dimensions of the paper on which the layout will be printed. The size calculations for the PreviewWindow are surprisingly non-intuitive and are given a thorough explanation on the listing. The **Paint** function for a PreviewWindow is where scaling is setup so that all items drawn in the preview window scale according to the size of the preview. Scaling requires the use of the MM_ISOTROPIC mapping mode in conjunction with setting both the window and the viewport extents correctly. (For readers needing more information about mapping mode and such, please see Chapter 2.) Here, the window extents are set equal to the dimensions of the paper on which the layout would be printed, and the viewport extents reflect the size of the client area of the preview window. With these quantities set up, a call is made to the PrintPage function of the layout class to actually render the information onto the preview window.

The PrintOp class manages printer selection and configuration, the print preview process, and the printing process. It gains much of its functionality from the PrintDialog (common dialog) class (see Chapter 3) it inherits. By combining these two classes, the PrintOp class becomes a one-stop shop for providing printer functionality to an applications program. Most of the functionality provided has been described earlier in this chapter and will not be reiterated here. It has not been mentioned that the PrintOp class also maintains information about the type of paper that is selected for use on the currently selected printer. This information is necessary for the print preview function to work correctly. Two private member functions of the PrintOp class **PaperSizeFromType** and **GetCurrentPaperSpecification** work together to keep a current record of the selected paper type, its dimensions, and the orientation in which the paper is to be used. This information is fed to the PreviewWindow class when a preview is to be performed.

The **PaperSizeFromType** function itself is a rather interesting piece of code. It uses the **GetPrinterCapabilities** function from the PrintDialog base class to ask the printer about the types and sizes of the paper the printer supports. From the paper type identifier passed as a parameter to this function, the size of the paper is first determined in metric units and is subsequently converted into .01-inch units and stored in the class variables PaperWidth and PaperLength. The function of

---

The Printer class

Purpose

The purpose of this class is to encapsulate all of the arcane code necessary for printing into a single class. The code deals with the printer or print driver directly by calling the appropriate Windows API functions. An object of a page layout class is sent to an object of the Printer class to be printed.

Member Functions

Printer. This is the class constructor. As parameters it requires a handle to the device context of the printer device, a printer name string, a port name string, the page number on which to begin printing, and the dimensions of the paper (in .01-inch units) that will be used. The only work actually performed by this constructor is to save the parameters passed into it.

~Printer. This is the class destructor. Its only function is to free the storage space allocated in the constructor for the storage of the various strings.

ReportError. This function displays any error messages that need to be displayed resulting from errors occurring during printing. A standard Windows message box is used for the display.

Print. This is the workhorse function in this class. It performs all of the interactions with Windows that are necessary to print single or multiple page layouts on the selected printer. It requires a pointer to a parent window and a pointer to an layout object derived from PageDefinitionBase. In essence, it performs all of the steps detailed in the section of this chapter called "Handling a Printer in Windows." Control returns to the code that called this function when the printing operation is complete, when a print operation is aborted by the user, or whenever a print error occurs that aborts the printing process. The code in this function is the core printing technology provided in this chapter. See Listing 7.4 for additional details of its operation.

FIGURE 7.6 The Printer class.

The PreviewWindow class

Purpose

This class implements the preview (print preview) functionality. It performs all of the magic necessary to display a scaled-down version of the printed output in a window on the screen giving a user an idea of what printed output will look like before printing. An object of a page layout class is sent to an object of the PreviewWindow class when previewing is necessary.

Member Functions

PreviewWindow. This is the class constructor. It performs most of the work necessary to provide the print preview capability. Specifically, it sets the style to be used for the preview window, and, more importantly, it calculates the size to make the preview window to emulate a specific size of printer paper. Because the calculation of the window size is somewhat complicated, you are directed to the comments in the listing for further details.

Paint. This private function is called whenever a PreviewWindow needs to be painted. This function is executed indirectly in response to a WM_PAINT message for a PreviewWindow. Internally, this function uses the MM_ISOTROPIC mapping mode and sets the window and viewport extents so that the size of the window reflects the paper size on which the layout would be printed. Use of the MM_ISOTROPIC mapping mode guarantees that everything shown in the preview window is drawn to scale. Fonts, text, images, and graphics scale directly. After all of the setup is performed, a call is made to the PrintPage function in the layout class (a pointer to the layout class was passed into the class constructor) for drawing the information on the simulated page.

EvPaletteChanged. If the PreviewWindow receives a palette changed message while a preview is being displayed, this private class function is called to cause a repaint. Repainting makes the palette for the preview window the foreground palette, thereby making its colors correct on limited color systems. See Chapter 2 for information on foreground and background palettes if further information is required.

FIGURE 7.7 The PreviewWindow class.

GetCurrentPaperSpecification beyond that mentioned earlier is to first ask the PrintDialog base class for the paper type and the paper orientation currently selected, call the **PaperSizeFromType** function to get the dimensions of the paper from the paper type, and to swap the paper dimensions if the orientation is landscape instead of the assumed portrait.

Because the PrintOp class provides the ability to select and configure printers via the **DoPrinterSetupDialog** member function, it is necessary to call the **GetCurrentPaperSpecification** function each time a change is made to a printer or its

The PrintOp class

Purpose

It is through this class that an application program controls the printer selection and configuration process, the print preview process, and the printing process. Instances of the other printer support classes as described in Figures 7.2 through 7.7 are rarely instantiated directly. Instead, these classes are used directly and indirectly by the PrintOp class for previewing or printing. Because this class has PrintDialog (described in Chapter 3) as its base class, it keeps track of the currently selected printer during its lifetime. For this reason, an object of the PrintOp class should be instantiated during program initialization and destroyed during program shutdown. If it is instantiated only as needed, it will forget information about the current printer between invocations.

Member Functions

PrintOp.   This is the class constructor. Its first operation is to call the **GetPrinter-Information** function in the PrintDialog base class to determine if a printer is configured for use. The class variable PrinterConfigured will be set TRUE if a printer is configured and FALSE if not. The other function of this constructor is to call the private member function **GetCurrentPaperSpecification** to ascertain the specifications of the paper selected for use by the current printer. Class variables for PaperType, PaperOrientation, PaperWidth, and PaperLength are set as a result.

~PrintOp.   This is the class destructor. Its only function is to destroy a Preview-Window if it still exists when this destructor is called. Good programming practice would dictate that the **EndPreview** member function be called to destroy any PreviewWindow long before this destructor would be called. The call to EndPreview here is just a precaution.

PaperSizeFromType.   This private member function returns the dimensions of a paper size in .01-inch units given the paper identifier. An 8.5- × 11-inch paper (paper type No. 1) would return the dimensions 850 × 1,100 units. The dimensions are returned as if the paper were going to be used in standard portrait mode. If the paper is going to be used in landscape mode, the paper width and paper length dimensions returned by this function would need to be reversed.

GetCurrentPaperSpecification.   The execution of this private member function causes the class variables for PaperType, PaperOrientation, PaperWidth, and PaperLength to be set. All of this information is obtained directly or indirectly by calling functions within the PrintDialog base class that reflects the values for the currently selected printer. If PaperOrientation indicates landscape mode is selected for the current printer, the PaperWidth and PaperLength values are automatically swapped.

DoPrinterSetupDialog.   When this function is called, the user is presented with the printer common dialog box by which a current printer can be selected and configured for use. This functionality is provided for the most part by the PrintDialog

FIGURE 7.8 The PrintOp class.

base class. The function **GetCurrentPaperSpecification** is called on return from the common dialog box to gather information about the current paper just in case the paper size or orientation were changed by the user.

IsPrinterConfigured. This function returns a Boolean TRUE if a printer has been configured for use in the Windows environment and FALSE otherwise. This function can be used to inform a user that he or she should configure a printer before attempting any print operations.

InitForPrintOp. This function is called to log the parameters for the next preview or print operation. A pointer to the parent window is saved as well as a pointer to a page layout object and a page number on which to begin the preview or print operation. If a preview operation was being performed when this function is called, it is terminated in preparation for the next PrintOp operation. If a preview is subsequently performed, it will be formatted to fit within the parent window whose pointer was passed to this function.

Print. This function is called when a printing operation is to be performed. It creates an instance of a Printer class object for the currently selected printer and passes the pointer to the page layout to it for printing. This function returns the result of the print process as a Boolean.

BeginPreview. This function works basically the same as the earlier function except instead of creating a Printer object, a PreviewWindow is created for a preview instead. An additional difference is that this function is called to begin the preview, and **EndPreview** must be called to end it. If a multiple page layout needs to be previewed, each page previewed must begin with an **InitForPrintOp** function call followed by **BeginPreview** and terminated with **EndPreview.**

EndPreview. This function is called to terminate a preview operation begun by **BeginPreview.**

FIGURE 7.8 *(Continued)*

configuration. This is because the user may have changed the selected paper type or the paper orientation. By calling **GetCurrentPaperSpecification** within the **DoPrinterSetupDialog** function the PrintOp class always has the latest information about the selected printer and the selected paper. To see this in action, use the TestApp program to preview the canned layout that was designed with 8.5- × 11-inch paper in mind. Next, change the orientation of the paper from portrait to landscape using the printer setup menu function. When you preview the layout again after the paper orientation change, you will see that the preview reflects the currently selected paper orientation.

The operation of the other PrintOp member functions should be obvious from the comments in the listings.

Conclusions

A lot of information about printing text and images has been presented in this chapter. As you have seen, there is a great deal going on behind the scenes to provide printing and preview WYSIWYG functionality on the screen and on the printed page. In addition to the discussion of techniques, a suite of printer support classes were provided and discussed that make printing within an application program much easier to accomplish. With the incorporation of these classes into your programs, you can forget about the complexities of the overhead printer code and concentrate on the all-important page layout process instead.

Image Acquisition from Scanners Using TWAIN

In this chapter you will learn about:
- The reasons why standard interfaces such as TWAIN are important
- The history of TWAIN
- Problems with "standard" TWAIN implementations
- How TWAIN works
- How to encapsulate the TWAIN API into a DLL for use in application programs
- How scanning was incorporated into the TestApp and CacheTst programs

Introduction

TWAIN defines a standard for control of, and acquisition of image data from, raster-generating devices. Raster-generating devices at this juncture mean scanners, but TWAIN compatible video digitizer boards, still video cameras, and other hardware devices are quickly appearing. The TWAIN specification is general enough to even allow imaging software such as an imaging database program to be TWAIN compliant and therefore accessible by any TWAIN compliant application just as if it were a data source itself. Almost all scanner manufacturers have jumped on the TWAIN bandwagon. This has allowed TWAIN to become a widely accepted industry standard in a relatively short period of time.

Standards in our industry are important because they allow different pieces of hardware and software from different vendors to plug together and play. They minimize the effort required by all parties involved while maximizing the return on engineering investment for everyone. Consider the control and acquisition of images from a scanner. Before TWAIN, to support a scanner within an application in a fully integrated fashion meant the application developer had to write separate drivers for each scanner supported. The alternative, nonintegrated approach to scanned image acquisition forced users to use whatever program came with their scanner for acquiring and saving images. The images could then be imported or cut and pasted into the end use application (a paint program, word processor, etc.).

In the first scenario, the acquisition of images could be fully integrated into the application at the cost of developing and maintaining a separate driver for each supported scanner. In some cases, the effort required for the drivers could exceed that required for the actual application. Further, it forced application developers to spend a great deal of their time doing something they may not have been particularly good at or wanted to do.

The second scenario posed fewer problems for application developers, but it made the user perform a many step process to get the desired image into the desired application. Aside from the large number of error prone steps required to acquire and then import the image, this process was cumbersome because the acquisition and use of scanned images took place in two separate programs. Shuffling of two separate applications under DOS was next to impossible, and the process is only marginally easier under Windows.

Today, thanks to TWAIN, acquisition of images can easily be built directly into an application with little work on the application developer's part. This is good news because:

- Application developers can spend the majority of their time developing their application, not worrying about low-level drivers for each supported device. These developers are assured of compatibility with a wide range of TWAIN compatible devices.
- Scanner, still digital camera, and video digitizer manufacturers write the TWAIN driver (called the Source in TWAIN parlance) for their device once, regardless of the end application. They, too are assured of compatibility with a wide range of applications without writing application-specific code or having to have custom applications written specifically for them.
- Application programs that are TWAIN compliant can be used with any TWAIN compliant Source. A TWAIN compliant Source can be used with any TWAIN compliant application. Thus both parties involved maximize their return on the engineering investment.

Please note that as good as TWAIN sounds and is, in practice there are many incompatibility issues that crop up between supposedly compliant TWAIN devices. Compatibility issues will be discussed later.

In this chapter, I will discuss what TWAIN is, how it evolved, and how it is used to facilitate image acquisition and use among TWAIN compliant applications and Sources. I will provide and discuss a C++ class, implemented as a Windows DLL (called mytwain.dll), that can be used to add image acquisition to any Windows application in almost no time at all. To illustrate how the DLL interface works, I will discuss how this code is integrated into the TestApp program. Although the focus here is on Windows applications and Windows program development, the code presented here along with that provided in the TWAIN tool kit (described later) could be used to make a Macintosh version of this code with not too much effort.

To use the code presented in this chapter requires access to a scanner or other raster image-generating device along with its TWAIN compliant Source. If you have an older device without a TWAIN Source, contact the manufacturer to see if there is a TWAIN Source available for it. To make matters worse, to use the Win32 TWAIN code presented in this chapter requires a 32-bit TWAIN Source for your imaging device and a 32-bit Source Manager (again discussed shortly but provided on the companion disk). Most of the available TWAIN code is written for 16-bit Windows at this time. This will change over time, however, as 32-bit operating systems such as Window NT and Windows 95 become more widely available.

Also at this time, the TWAIN code is architected so that all pieces (the application, the Source Manager, and the Source) must all be 16 bit or all be 32 bit with no mixing and matching allowed. The TWAIN working group has promised that this will be corrected in future TWAIN code releases. In other words, image acquisition from TWAIN compliant equipment will be allowed, regardless of whether 16- or 32-bit components are available.

Before delving into the code details, a short history of TWAIN might prove interesting.

From Whence It Came

The precursor to TWAIN can trace its roots back to 1990 with the formation of the Macintosh Scanner Roundtable. From these early activities, a consortium called the TWAIN working group was formed by representatives from major imaging product companies including Aldus, Caere, Kodak, Hewlett-Packard, and Logitech. Their primary goal was the creation of an easy to use image acquisition protocol and API and the education of the public as to its existence. The people in the working group represented both image producers (hardware manufacturers) and image consumers (application developers). Thus the eventual TWAIN specification embodied the concerns of both of these interest groups in a rational manner. The willingness of all companies involved to set aside their fiercely competitive natures to develop an open industry standard must be applauded.

In February of 1992, the TWAIN working group announced Release 1.0 of the TWAIN tool kit that defined "the protocol and API for generalized acquisition of raster data." As of this writing, Release 1.0 is still the current version of the tool kit. The tool kit is made available to all interested parties for a very low cost. Details will be provided later in this chapter.

Some of the goals of the published specification include:

- The provision of a well-thought-out and well-defined API that developers will embrace quickly
- The ability to support multiple platforms; that is, the ability to use the protocol described on many different operating system platforms. The current tool kit addresses the Windows and Macintosh environments. Extensions to UNIX and OS/2 should be forthcoming.

- The ability to support a broad range of raster image-generating devices. This includes, but is not limited to, flatbed document scanners, hand scanners, slide scanner, image digitizer boards, digital still frame cameras, and so on.
- The ease of implementation and integration
- The ability to support future unknown circumstances and/or devices without invalidating the existing specification and existing code

By the time you finish reading this chapter, you will have an appreciation of how well the TWAIN working group did in meeting their own design goals.

Getting Additional TWAIN Information

Information on TWAIN can be found in many different places. First and foremost, interested persons should obtain the TWAIN tool kit. The tool kit includes both a printed specification and a disk full of code to help the developer. Included in the tool kit is the Source Manager DLL. The tool kit can be ordered by calling 1-800-722-0379. The cost as of March 1992 was about $30.

The most recent versions of the tool kit code, the Source Manager, miscellaneous development files, tech notes, and so on can be obtained via CompuServe. Type GO HPPERIPH and look for the TWAIN library (#15). You can also post technical questions there that HP support personal will attempt to answer.

Phone and FAX technical support is available from any of the participating companies in the following list. Expect a significant delay in getting answers to your questions. Remember, these companies are volunteering their services; they are not making money on providing TWAIN support. Also, these telephone numbers may have changed by the time you read this book.

Company	Phone Number	FAX Number
Aldus	(206) 628-6593	(206) 343-4240
Caere	(408) 395-5148 x5600	(408) 354-2743
Hewlett-Packard	(303) 350-4830	(303) 350-4631
Logitech	(510) 713-5338	NA
Kodak	(716) 724-1682	NA

The TWAIN Architecture

Figure 8.1 shows a high-level diagram of the TWAIN architecture as embodied in Release 1.0 of the specification. As shown in this diagram, there are, in essence, three different entities involved in most TWAIN transactions. They are:

1. The portion of the application program that understands the TWAIN protocol, referred to in the diagram as the TWAIN Code.
2. The TWAIN Source Manager which is the go-between between the application and a Source. The Source Manager is a Windows DLL called "twain.dll" or "twain32.dll" under Windows and is located in the Windows directory. On the Macintosh, the Source Manager is called "Source Manager." Look for it in the Preferences folder.

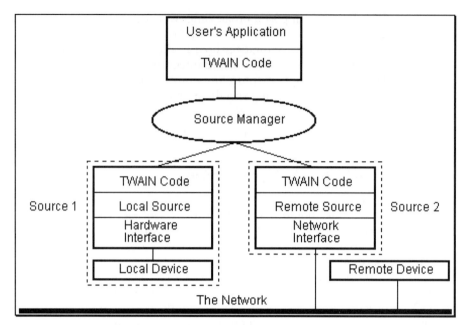

FIGURE 8.1 TWAIN architecture block diagram.

3. The Source (or device driver) for the imaging hardware. This, too, is a DLL under Windows (with a .DS file extension, however).

The application developer is responsible for developing item one from the previous list. Plenty of help is available, however, in the form of code provided within the TWAIN tool kit. Item two was developed by the TWAIN working group and is distributed free of charge for all to use. Item three in the previous list is written by the hardware vendor in support of their TWAIN compliant product. These three well-defined pieces work together to provide seamless acquisition of images from within an application program.

The application controls the acquisition process by making calls to the single entry point of the Source Manager called DSM_Entry. Parameters used in conjunction with these calls control the process. An application never calls a Source directly. As requests for service are made to the Source Manager (DSM), it acts on some directly and passes others to the selected Source as required. As image data is returned by the Source to the application, it is done so under the supervision and auspices of the Source Manager. Because the application knows nothing hardware-specific about the Source to which it is communicating, the Source can be a local device such as a SCSI connected scanner or a device located remotely and connected via a network. Only the developer of the Source must (or should) be aware of the hardware specifics. An application just requests connection to a specific Source and does not care how the connection is made.

Possibly the most interesting and certainly the most useful aspect of the TWAIN architecture is that the Source must provide a user interface (UI) for controlling its device. This releases application developers from having to develop a UI specific for each different device supported. Again, this makes great sense because the hardware manufacturer who developed the device and its Source should be the most capable of understanding how it should be controlled and how to maximize its functionality. If the incorporation of a UI is not enough icing on the cake, consider for a moment that the application can partially or, in some cases, completely control the presentation of the UI with a process called capability negotiation. More on this later.

The UI for the Polaroid CS-500i TWAIN compatible scanner is shown in Figure 8.2. Most scanners have a similar UI.

TWAIN Operational Overview

The TWAIN working group recommends two menu selections be added to an application program's user interface for control of TWAIN transactions. These are *Select Source . . .* and *Acquire . . .* , both preferably located in the *File* menu. The select source operation allows a user to determine which Source (if more than one are available in the system) is to be used for image acquisition. Once the user selects a Source, it is used for all subsequent image acquisitions until such time as another Source is

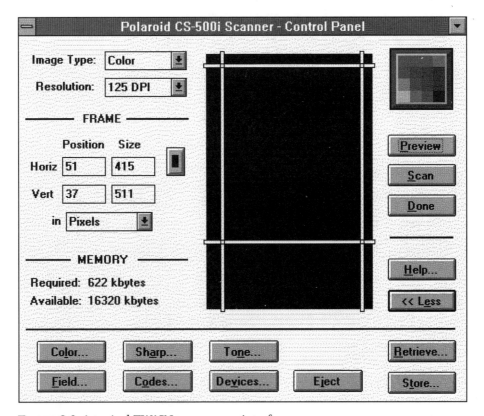

FIGURE 8.2 A typical TWAIN source user interface.

selected. The *Acquire* . . . operation typically brings up the UI of the selected Source for control of its corresponding device. Using the controls provided within the UI, the user decides what portion and how images are acquired for incorporation into the application.

As an aside, a Source's UI can be treated as modal or nonmodal under Windows, although it is inherently nonmodal in nature. A modal interface (as represented by the code in this chapter) restricts the user to dealing with the scanner until such time as the UI is closed down, typically after an image is acquired and transferred into the application. At that time, control is returned to the application program. Other applications, however, use the Source's UI in a nonmodal way, bringing up the UI and keeping it up as just another window of the application. This allows images to be acquired for as long as the UI is active. Which method to use is dictated entirely by the application.

The steps required in support of these menu operations are summarized in the following annotated list. Error detection and recovery are left out for the sake of brevity. Please consult Listings 8.1 and 8.2 during the discussion to follow.

Listing 8.1 The Twain class interface definition.

```
/**********************************************************/
/***                      "twain.hpp"                  ***/
/***          Interface class for TWAIN devices        ***/
/***                                                   ***/
/***                     written by                    ***/
/***                  Craig A. Lindley                 ***/
/***                                                   ***/
/***      Revision: 2.0     Last Update: 11/11/94      ***/
/**********************************************************/

// Copyright (c) 1995 John Wiley & Sons, Inc. All rights reserved.

// Check to see if this file already included
#ifndef TWAIN_HPP
#define TWAIN_HPP

#include "twain.h"
#include "containr.hpp"
#include "compand.hpp"

#ifndef _WIN32_                        // If 16 bit code
/*
The following is required when using a C++ class as an interface
for a DLL. It is required because this file will be included in
both the application compilation and the DLL compilation. Remember
that all members (functions and data) are far!
*/
#ifdef _DLL_
# define EXPORT _export
#else
# define EXPORT huge
#endif
```

```
#define SOURCEMANAGERNAME    "twain.dll"
#define DSMENTRY             "DSM_ENTRY"
#define WINDIRPATHSIZE       160

#else                             // If 32 bit code

#ifdef _DLL_
# define EXPORT _export
#else
# define EXPORT
#endif

#define SOURCEMANAGERNAME    "twain32.dll"
#define DSMENTRY             "DSM_Entry"
#define WINDIRPATHSIZE       260
#define huge
#define hmemcpy memcpy

#endif


#define MAXXFERSPERSESSION   1
#define WM_XFERDONE          WM_USER + 100

#ifndef _IMAGEDESCRIPTOR
#define _IMAGEDESCRIPTOR

// This structure is used for describing an image.
typedef struct _IMAGEDESCRIPTOR {
  WORD Width;
  WORD Height;
  DWORD RasterSize;
  WORD BPP;
  WORD Colors;
  HGLOBAL hImageData;
  RGBCOLOR Palette[256];
} IMAGEDESCRIPTOR, * LPIMAGEDESCRIPTOR;
#endif

enum TransferType {THRU_MEMORY, THRU_FILE, THRU_FILEANDMEMORY};

// The Twain Class Definition
class EXPORT Twain : public Containr {
  private:
    // Private Data
    LPSTR           lpFileName;

    TransferType TType;             // Type of the transfer

    LPIMAGEDESCRIPTOR lpID;
    TW_IDENTITY   AppIdentity;
    TW_IDENTITY   SourceIdentity;
    DSMENTRYPROC lpDSM_Entry;
    TW_IMAGEINFO ImageInfo;
    TW_PALETTE8  PaletteInfo;
    TW_USERINTERFACE dcUI;
```

```
    BOOL        DSMOpen;
    BOOL        DSOpen;
    BOOL        DSEnabled;
    HINSTANCE   hDSMDLL;
    HINSTANCE   hDLLInstance;
    HWND        hBackgroundWindow;
    HWND        hAppWindow;
    BOOL        ScanResults;

    HGLOBAL     hImageMemory;
    DWORD       BytesPerLine;
    DWORD       RequiredMemory;

    // Private Functions
    BOOL PaintMemoryMessage(HWND hWindow);
    BOOL ProcessImageData(LPSTR ImageFileName, CompandType CompType, WORD
      Quality);
    void TransferImage(HWND hWindow);
    BOOL GetCompleteImage (HWND hWindow);
    BOOL ProcessDCMessage(LPMSG lpMsg, HWND hWindow);
    void ExplainError(HWND hWnd, LPSTR lpText, int MsgNumber);
    BOOL SetPixelTypes(void);
    BOOL SetXferMechanism(TW_UINT16 Mechanism);
    BOOL SetupFileTransfer(LPSTR FileName);
    BOOL SetImageXferCount(int Count);
    BOOL OpenDSM(HWND hWindow);
    BOOL CloseDSM(void);
    BOOL OpenDS(void);
    BOOL CloseDS(void);
    BOOL EnableDS(void);
    BOOL DisableDS(void);
    BOOL SelectDS(void);

public:
  FAR Twain(void);                 // Class constructor/destructor
  FAR ~Twain(void);

  BOOL FAR SelectSource(HWND hWindow);

  // Three scan functions: transfer thru memory, thru file,
  // thru memory and file.
  BOOL FAR ScanImage(IMAGEDESCRIPTOR& ID);
  BOOL FAR ScanImage(LPSTR FileName, CompandType CompType, WORD Quality);
  BOOL FAR ScanImage(LPSTR FileName, CompandType CompType, WORD Quality);
                  IMAGEDESCRIPTOR& ID);

  static long CALLBACK _export
    BackDropWndProc(HWND hwnd, UINT message, WPARAM wParam, LPARAM lParam);

};

#endif
```

Listing 8.2 The Twain class member functions.

```
/*********************************************************/
/***                  "twain.cpp"                    ***/
/***           TWAIN Class Member Functions          ***/
/***                                                 ***/
/***                  written by                     ***/
/***                Craig A. Lindley                 ***/
/***                                                 ***/
/***         Revision: 2.0 Last Update: 11/11/94     ***/
/*********************************************************/

// Copyright (c) 1995 John Wiley & Sons, Inc. All rights reserved.

#include <string.h>
#include <windows.h>
#include "twainids.h"
#include "twain.h"
#include "twain.hpp"

// These numbers were arrived at by trial and error
#define SOURCEMEMORYOVERHEAD 1020000L
#define SOURCEBUFFEROVERHEAD 125000L
#define MINIMUMSCANNEDIMAGESIZE     20000L

// Variables global to this file only
static HINSTANCE hDLLInst;
static char szAppName [] = "TWAINBackDropWindow";
static Twain *lpTwain;

// Constructor for class
Twain::Twain(void) {

  lpTwain = this;                  // Save a ptr to this object
  hDLLInstance = hDLLInst;         // Store this DLLs' instance in class data
  TType = THRU_FILE;               // File transfer is normal mode

  // Clear the identity structure for application and source.
  memset (&AppIdentity,    0, sizeof(TW_IDENTITY));
  memset (&SourceIdentity, 0, sizeof(TW_IDENTITY));

  // Now set the fields of the structure appropriately. Some fields are
  // hardcoded, some are read as string resources.
  AppIdentity.Id = 0;              // Source Manager will assign real value
  AppIdentity.Version.MajorNum = 1;
  AppIdentity.Version.MinorNum = 0;
  AppIdentity.Version.Language = TWLG_USA;
  AppIdentity.Version.Country = TWCY_USA;
  AppIdentity.ProtocolMajor = TWON_PROTOCOLMAJOR;
  AppIdentity.ProtocolMinor = TWON_PROTOCOLMINOR;
  AppIdentity.SupportedGroups = DG_IMAGE | DG_CONTROL;

  // Read these strings from resource.
  LoadString(hDLLInstance, IDS_MANUFACTURE, (LPSTR) &AppIdentity.Manufacturer,
```

```
                   sizeof(TW_STR32));
      LoadString(hDLLInstance, IDS_PRODUCTFAMILY, (LPSTR) &AppIdentity.ProductFamily,
                   sizeof(TW_STR32));
      LoadString(hDLLInstance, IDS_PRODUCTNAME,    (LPSTR) &AppIdentity.ProductName,
                   sizeof(TW_STR32));
      LoadString(hDLLInstance, IDS_VERSIONINFO,    (LPSTR) &AppIdentity.Version.Info,
                   sizeof(TW_STR32));
      DSMOpen = FALSE;
      DSOpen = FALSE;
      DSEnabled = FALSE;
      hAppWindow = 0;
      hImageMemory = 0;
      RequiredMemory = 0L;
    }


    Twain::~Twain(void) {

      // Nothing yet to do

    }


    /*************************************************************************
    *FUNCTION:TransferImage
    *
    *ARGS:     hWindow Handle of window messages go to
    *
    *RETURNS: none
    *
    *NOTES:    1) Get information about image.
    *          2) Set up a loop to pull image(s) from the Source
    *          3) Call GetCompleteImage to get image
    *
    *NOTES: This function is called in response to a XFERREADY message.
    *************************************************************************/


    void Twain::TransferImage(HWND hWindow) {
      TW_PENDINGXFERS dcPendingXfer;
      TW_UINT16 Status;

      // Get the image information. It is nice to know a little about the
      // image the Source will be sending.
      Status = (*lpDSM_Entry) (&AppIdentity,
                               &SourceIdentity,
                               DG_IMAGE,
                               DAT_IMAGEINFO,
                               MSG_GET,
                               (TW_MEMREF) &ImageInfo);

      if (Status == TWRC_SUCCESS) {
        // When we get here, the ImageInfo call was successful. Now make sure
        // that the TWAIN device is buffer. We cannot support unbuffered
        // devices.
        if ((ImageInfo.ImageWidth == -1) ||
            (ImageInfo.ImageLength == -1)) {
```

```
    // When we get here, we have determined device is unbuffered.
    // Output error message and then attempt to recover. That is, attempt
    // to transition back to state 6 or 5.
    ExplainError(NULL, "TransferImage - ", IDS_NOBUFFERING);
    dcPendingXfer.Count = 0;
    Status = (*lpDSM_Entry) (&AppIdentity,
                             &SourceIdentity,
                             DG_CONTROL,
                             DAT_PENDINGXFERS,
                             MSG_ENDXFER,
                             (TW_MEMREF) &dcPendingXfer);
    return;
  }
// Determine how much memory will be required for the image
// we are about to transfer.
switch(ImageInfo.PixelType) {
  case TWPT_BW:           // BW image have 1 bit per pixel
    BytesPerLine = (ImageInfo.ImageWidth+7) / 8;   // Round up to
      nearest byte
    break;

  case TWPT_GRAY:         // Gray scale image can have 4 or 8 BPP
    if (ImageInfo.BitsPerPixel == 8)
      BytesPerLine = ImageInfo.ImageWidth;
    else                  // If 4 BPP exactly two pixels per byte
      BytesPerLine = (ImageInfo.ImageWidth+1) / 2;
    break;

  case TWPT_PALETTE:      // Palettized color images have 8 BPP
    BytesPerLine = ImageInfo.ImageWidth;// Exactly one pixel per byte
    break;

  case TWPT_RGB:          // RGB images have 24 BPP
    BytesPerLine = 3 * ImageInfo.ImageWidth; // Three bytes per pixel
    break;
}
// Make sure to align to double word boundary
BytesPerLine = ALIGN_DWORD(BytesPerLine);

RequiredMemory = BytesPerLine * ImageInfo.ImageLength;

// If memory was previously allocated, free it and alloc again.
if (hImageMemory) {
  GlobalUnlock(hImageMemory);
  GlobalFree(hImageMemory);
  hImageMemory = 0;
}

// Allocate the required shared memory for the DIB.
// Check for successful alloc.
hImageMemory = GlobalAlloc(GHND | GMEM_SHARE, RequiredMemory);
if (hImageMemory == NULL) {
  ExplainError(NULL, "TransferImage - ", IDS_LOWMEMORY);
  dcPendingXfer.Count = 0;
```

```
            Status = (*lpDSM_Entry) (&AppIdentity,
                                     &SourceIdentity,
                                     DG_CONTROL,
                                     DAT_PENDINGXFERS,
                                     MSG_ENDXFER,
                                     (TW_MEMREF)&dcPendingXfer);
        return;
    }

    // Now, get an image from the Source and then ask if more images are coming.
    // EV only supports one image per transfer. The do/while loop is
    // included for future expansion possibilities.

    // Explicitly initialize the count of images Source has for App.
    dcPendingXfer.Count = 0;
    do {
      GetCompleteImage (hWindow); // Transfer the image
      // Required for proper 7<->6 or 5 state transitions
      if ((Status = (*lpDSM_Entry) (&AppIdentity,
                       &SourceIdentity,
                       DG_CONTROL,
                       DAT_PENDINGXFERS,
                       MSG_ENDXFER,
                       (TW_MEMREF)&dcPendingXfer)) != TWRC_SUCCESS)

        dcPendingXfer.Count = 0; // trash remaining images

    } while (dcPendingXfer.Count != 0);
  }
}

/***********************************************************************
*FUNCTION:GetCompleteImage
*
*ARGS:    hWindow Handle to window messages go to
*
*RETURNS: TRUE if success.
*
*NOTES:   Asks the Source to start sending the pending image. We
*         were told about this by receipt of a XFERREADY message
*         from the Source.
*
*NOTES:   This function causes an image to be transferred through
*         memory in an unformatted, uncompressed fashion. The app must
*         ask the source about it preferences for buffer size and then
*         accept buffers of that size. The image is transferred from
*         top to bottom. As the image is transferred, it is inverted as
*         required for the DIB format.
*
*         For a file transfer only one operation is required
*         so a WHILE loop would not be required here. For memory
*         transfers which are slice/tile by slice/tile a loop is required.
*
*         A status of TWRC_CANCEL indicates the user cancelled an in
*         progress image transfer. TWRC_FAILURE indicates the transfer
*         crashed. TWRC_SUCCESS indicates a good transfer so continue.
***********************************************************************/
```

```
BOOL Twain::GetCompleteImage(HWND hWindow) {
  TW_SETUPMEMXFER dcSetupMemXfer;
  TW_IMAGEMEMXFER dcImageMemXfer;

  TW_UINT16 Status;
  BOOL Result = FALSE;
  BOOL Done = FALSE;

  WORD StoreAtImageRow = (WORD) (ImageInfo.ImageLength - 1);

  // Clear the data structures
  memset (&dcSetupMemXfer, 0, sizeof(TW_SETUPMEMXFER));
  memset(&dcImageMemXfer, 0, sizeof(TW_IMAGEMEMXFER));

  // Ask for Source for its buffer size preferences
  Status = (*lpDSM_Entry) (&AppIdentity,
                           &SourceIdentity,
                           DG_CONTROL,
                           DAT_SETUPMEMXFER,
                           MSG_GET,
                           (TW_MEMREF) &dcSetupMemXfer);
  if (Status != TWRC_SUCCESS)         // If error abort xfer
    return FALSE;
  // Source has written dcSetupMemXfer structure with its wishes. Try
  // to allocate memory for the buffer. If Source doesn't care about
  // the size of the allocation pick a value as shown. If preferred amount
  // of memory is not available, use minimum usable.
  DWORD SizeOfBuffer;

  if (dcSetupMemXfer.Preferred == TWON_DONTCARE32)
    SizeOfBuffer = SOURCEBUFFEROVERHEAD;

  else if (dcSetupMemXfer.Preferred > SOURCEBUFFEROVERHEAD)
    SizeOfBuffer = (dcSetupMemXfer.MinBufSize < SOURCEBUFFEROVERHEAD) ?
                   SOURCEBUFFEROVERHEAD:dcSetupMemXfer.MinBufSize;
  else
    SizeOfBuffer = dcSetupMemXfer.Preferred;

  HGLOBAL hImageBuffer = GlobalAlloc(GHND, SizeOfBuffer);
  if (hImageBuffer == NULL) {
  ExplainError(NULL, "GetCompleteImage - ", IDS_LOWMEMORY);
  return FALSE;
}
// Lock down ptrs to buffer and image memory
BYTE huge *ImageBufferPtr  = (BYTE huge *) GlobalLock(hImageBuffer);
BYTE huge *ImagePtr        = (BYTE huge *) GlobalLock(hImageMemory);

// When we get here a buffer has been allocated.
// Place a reference to it in dcImageMemXfer.
dcImageMemXfer.Memory.Length  = SizeOfBuffer;
dcImageMemXfer.Memory.TheMem  = (TW_MEMREF) ImageBufferPtr;
dcImageMemXfer.Memory.Flags   = TWMF_POINTER | TWMF_APPOWNS;

// Go into a loop to get all of the image data
while ((Status != TWRC_XFERDONE) && !Done) {
```

```
                   // Ask for thru memory image transfer
                   Status = (*lpDSM_Entry) (&AppIdentity,
                                        &SourceIdentity,
                                        DG_IMAGE,
                                        DAT_IMAGEMEMXFER,
                                        MSG_GET,
                                        (TW_MEMREF) &dcImageMemXfer);
                   // See what the returned status is
                   WORD Index;
                   switch (Status) {
                     case TWRC_SUCCESS:
                       // Buffer transfer completed. Now copy the data from buffer
                       // to storage a row at a time while inverting the image.
                       for (Index=0; Index < dcImageMemXfer.Rows; Index++)
                         hmemcpy((BYTE huge *) (ImagePtr + (StoreAtImageRow-- * BytesPerLine)),
                                 (BYTE huge *) (ImageBufferPtr + (Index *
                                   dcImageMemXfer.BytesPerRow)),
                         dcImageMemXfer.BytesPerRow);
                       break;

                     case TWRC_XFERDONE:
                   // Buffer transfer completed. Now copy the data from final buffer
                       // to storage a row at a time while inverting the image.
                   for (Index=0; Index < dcImageMemXfer.Rows; Index++)
                     hmemcpy(
                                 (BYTE huge *) (ImagePtr + (StoreAtImageRow-- * BytesPerLine)),
                                 (BYTE huge *) (ImageBufferPtr + (Index *
                                   dcImageMemXfer.BytesPerRow)),
                         dcImageMemXfer.BytesPerRow);

                   // Transfer is done. Free memory for buffer and then if image was
                   // palette type, get the palette from the device.
                       GlobalUnlock(hImageMemory);
                       GlobalUnlock(hImageBuffer);
                       GlobalFree(hImageBuffer);


                       if ((ImageInfo.PixelType == TWPT_PALETTE) ||
                               (ImageInfo.PixelType == TWPT_GRAY)) {
                         // Ask the Source for the image's palette
                         Status = (*lpDSM_Entry) (&AppIdentity,
                                               &SourceIdentity,
                                               DG_IMAGE,
                                               DAT_PALETTE8,
                                               MSG_GET,
                                               (TW_MEMREF) &PaletteInfo);
                         // See what the returned status is. If no current palette
                         // get the default palette.
                         if (Status != TWRC_SUCCESS) {
                           Status = (*lpDSM_Entry) (&AppIdentity,
                                                 &SourceIdentity,
                                                 DG_IMAGE,
                                                 DAT_PALETTE8,
                                                 MSG_GETDEFAULT,
                                                 (TW_MEMREF) &PaletteInfo);
                           if (Status != TWRC_SUCCESS) {
                             // If all else fails install our own palette
```

```
                    PaletteInfo.NumColors = MAX256PALETTECOLORS;
                    for (Index=0; Index < MAX256PALETTECOLORS; Index++) {
                      PaletteInfo.Colors[Index].Channel1 = (BYTE) Index;
                      PaletteInfo.Colors[Index].Channel2 = (BYTE) Index;
                      PaletteInfo.Colors[Index].Channel3 = (BYTE) Index;
                    }
                  }
                }
              }
              // Pass the completion acknowledgement back to App
              // thru message queue.
              SendMessage (hWindow, WM_XFERDONE, TRUE, 0);
              Result = TRUE;
              Done = TRUE;
              break;

          case TWRC_FAILURE:
              ExplainError(hAppWindow, "GetCompleteImage - ", 0);
              // NOTE: code falls through

          case TWRC_CANCEL:
          default:
              // Something wrong, free buffer memory and then pass a FALSE
              // back to App.
              GlobalUnlock(hImageMemory);
              GlobalFree(hImageMemory);
              hImageMemory = 0;
              GlobalUnlock(hImageBuffer);
              GlobalFree(hImageBuffer);
              SendMessage (hWindow, WM_XFERDONE, FALSE, 0);
              Result = FALSE;
              Done = TRUE;
      }
  }

  return Result;
}

/****************************************************************************
*FUNCTION:ProcessDCMessage
*
*ARGS:     lpMsg Pointer to Windows msg retrieved by GetMessage
*          hWnd   Application's main window handle
*
*RETURNS: TRUE  if application should process message as usual or FALSE
*               if application should skip processing of this message
*
*NOTES:
****************************************************************************/

BOOL Twain::ProcessDCMessage(LPMSG lpMsg, HWND hWindow) {
  TW_UINT16 Status = TWRC_NOTDSEVENT;
  TW_EVENT dcEvent;

  // Only ask Source Manager to process event if there is a Source connected.
  if (DSMOpen && DSOpen) {
```

```
/* A Source provides a modeless dialog box as its user interface.
 * The following call relays Windows messages down to the Source's
 * UI that were intended for its dialog box. It also retrieves TWAIN
 * messages sent from the Source to the App.
 */
dcEvent.pEvent = (TW_MEMREF) lpMsg;
Status = (*lpDSM_Entry) (&AppIdentity,
                         &SourceIdentity,
                         DG_CONTROL,
                         DAT_EVENT,
                         MSG_PROCESSEVENT,
                         (TW_MEMREF) &dcEvent);

switch (dcEvent.TWMessage) {
  case MSG_XFERREADY:            // Source has an image to xfer
    ScanResults = FALSE:         // Don't yet know if scan will be successful
    TransferImage(hWindow);
    if (dcUI.ModalUI) {          // If the Source is modal
      DisableDS();               // Close down UI after acquisition
      DestroyWindow(hBackgroundWindow);
      CloseDS();                 // Close the Source
      CloseDSM();                // Close the DSM
    }
    break;

  case MSG_CLOSEDSREQ:           // User requested close of UI
    DisableDS();                 // Close down UI
    DestroyWindow(hBackgroundWindow);
    CloseDS();                   // Close the Source
    CloseDSM();                  // Close the DSM
    break;

  case MSG NULL:                 // All other messages go here and
  default:                       // into the bit bucket
    break;
  }
}
// tell the caller what happened
return (Status == TWRC_DSEVENT);
}
```

```
/***************************************************************************
*FUNCTION:ProcessImageData
*
*ARGS:     ImageFileName is the name to be given to the acquired image.
*          CompType specifies the compression type to be applied to a
*          scanned image. Quality is the quality factor or compression
*          amount to be applied to JPEG compressed images. These parameter
*          are ignored if using a thru memory transfer to the application.
*
*RETURNS: TRUE if successful, FALSE if not
*
*NOTES:    This function manipulates the image data returned from the
*          scanning process. It builds a proper DIB format for the data
*          and then calls the Compand DLL to compress the newly acquired
```

```
*        image. When using a thru memory transfer to the application,
*        an image file is not written.
********************************************************************/

BOOL Twain::ProcessImageData(LPSTR ImageFileName,
                             CompandType CompType, WORD Quality) {
  RGBCOLOR Palette[MAX256PALETTECOLORS];

  // When we get here, the image data is in a buffer.
  // Set cursor to hourglass
  HCURSOR hOldCursor = SetCursor(LoadCursor(NULL, IDC_WAIT));

  // Clear the palette storage area.
  memset(Palette, 0, sizeof(Palette));
  // If the image is BW, set the first two palette entries
  // to black and white.
  if (ImageInfo.PixelType == TWPT_BW) {
    Palette[0].Red = Palette[0].Green = Palette[0].Blue = 0x00;
    Palette[1].Red = Palette[1].Green = Palette[1].Blue = 0xFF;
}

// If the image was palettized, convert TWAIN Palette8 into a
// normal palette.
if ((ImageInfo.PixelType == TWPT_PALETTE) ||
    (ImageInfo.PixelType == TWPT_GRAY)) {
  for (WORD Index = 0; Index < PaletteInfo.NumColors; Index++) {
    Palette[Index].Red   = PaletteInfo.Colors[Index].Channel1;
    Palette[Index].Green = PaletteInfo.Colors[Index].Channel2;
    Palette[Index].Blue  = PaletteInfo.Colors[Index].Channel3;
  }
}
// Now, if the image was an RGB type, convert the RGB data format
// in the image buffer to BGR as required for DIB. First, lock
// down a ptr to the image data.
BYTE huge *ImagePtr = (BYTE huge *) GlobalLock(hImageMemory);

BYTE huge *RowDataPtr;
BYTE huge *lpPixel;
BYTE Temp;

if (ImageInfo.PixelType == TWPT_RGB) {
  for (WORD Row=0; Row < ImageInfo.ImageLength; Row++) {
    // Calculate the address of row in image data
    RowDataPtr = (BYTE huge *) (ImagePtr + (Row * BytesPerLine));
    for (WORD Col=0; Col < ImageInfo.ImageWidth; Col++) {
      // Calculate the address of desired pixel in buffer
      lpPixel = (BYTE huge *)(RowDataPtr + (Col * 3L));
      // Swap values of R and B as required for DIB.
      Temp = *(lpPixel);           // Save red value
      *(lpPixel) = *(lpPixel+2);   // Store blue over red
      *(lpPixel+2) = Temp;         // Store red over blue
    }
  }
}
WORD NumOfColors;
```

```
      if (ImageInfo.BitsPerPixel == 24)
        NumOfColors = 0;
      else if (ImageInfo.BitsPerPixel > 1)
        NumOfColors = 1 << ImageInfo.BitsPerPixel;
      else
        NumOfColors = 2;


      // With all conversions complete, prepare to return the image data.
      // Image data can be returned in a file, thru memory or both
      if ((TType == THRU_FILE) || (TType == THRU_FILEANDMEMORY)) {
        // When we get here we know we must write an image file
        Compand C;

        C.InitCompressor(CompType, ImageFileName,
                         (WORD) ImageInfo.ImageWidth, (WORD) ImageInfo.ImageLength,
                         ImageInfo.BitsPerPixel, NumOfColors,
                         ImagePtr, Palette);

        if (ImageInfo.BitsPerPixel == 24)
          C.SetImageType(TRUECOLOR);
        else if (ImageInfo.BitsPerPixel > 1)
          C.SetImageType(PALETTECOLOR);
        else
          C.SetImageType(MONOCHROME);


        // Set the quality factor for compression in case of JPEG
        C.SetCompressionQuality(Quality);


        // Compress the new image into the TempFileName.
        C.DoCompression();
          if (TType == THRU_FILE) {     // Free the image memory as it is no longer
            required.
            GlobalUnlock(hImageMemory);
            GlobalFree(hImageMemory);
            hImageMemory = 0;
          }
      }
      // Check to see if image data must be passed thru memory.
      if ((TType == THRU_MEMORY) || (TType == THRU_FILEANDMEMORY)) {
        // When we get here we know we must return image data thru shared memory.
        // Fill in the ID structure
        lpID->Width      = (WORD) ImageInfo.ImageWidth;
        lpID->Height     = (WORD) ImageInfo.ImageLength;
        lpID->RasterSize = RequiredMemory;
        lpID->BPP        = ImageInfo.BitsPerPixel;
        lpID->Colors     = NumOfColors;
        // Copy the palette to the ID
        memcpy((LPSTR) lpID->Palette, (LPSTR) Palette, sizeof(Palette));
        // Now deal with the shared memory which contains the image.
        GlobalUnlock(hImageMemory);         // Unlock the image data
        lpID->hImageData = hImageMemory;    // Save the handle in ID
        hImageMemory = 0;                   // Set handle to zero because we are
                                            // done with this memory block here.
                                            // It is now shared memory and handled
                                            // by the cacheing code.
```

```
  }
  // Remove hourglass cursor.
  SetCursor(hOldCursor);
  return TRUE;
}


/*************************************************************************
*FUNCTION:ScanImage
*
*ARGS:     FileName   Path and FileName without extension to store the
*                     scanned image in.
*          CompType   Specifies the type of image to store
*          Quality    Specifies the quality factor if image type is JPEG
*RETURNS: TRUE if successful, FALSE if not
*
*NOTES:    This function interfaces to the TWAIN source for acquisition
*          of an image.
*************************************************************************/

BOOL Twain::ScanImage(LPSTR ImageFileName, CompandType CompType,
                      WORD Quality) {

  DSMOpen = FALSE;                    // Initialize class variables
  DSOpen = FALSE;
  DSEnabled = FALSE;
  hAppWindow = 0;
  hImageMemory = 0;
  RequiredMemory = 0L;


  TType = THRU_FILE;                  // Utilize a file transfer
  lpFileName = ImageFileName;         // Save ptr to filename
  ScanResults = FALSE;                // No image scanned yet


  // Create TWAIN backdrop window. It is parent to Source's UI dialog
  hBackgroundWindow = CreateWindow(szAppName, NULL,
                      WS_POPUP | WS_BORDER,
                      0, 0, CW_USEDEFAULT, CW_USEDEFAULT,
                      HWND_DESKTOP, NULL, hDLLInstance, NULL);


  ShowWindow(hBackgroundWindow, SW_SHOWMAXIMIZED);
  SendMessage(hBackgroundWindow, WM_SYSCOMMAND, SC_MAXIMIZE, 0L); // Expand
    parent window to full screen


  // The modeless Source UI window must be taken into consideration
  MSG Msg;
  while (GetMessage (&Msg, NULL, 0, 0)) {
    if ((!DSOpen) || (!ProcessDCMessage((LPMSG)&Msg, hBackgroundWindow))) {
      TranslateMessage (&Msg);
      DispatchMessage (&Msg);
    }
  }


  UpdateWindow(GetActiveWindow());// Update calling program
```

```
    // Process and store image data if scan was successful
    if (ScanResults == TRUE)
      if (!ProcessImageData(ImageFileName, CompType, Quality))
        return FALSE;

  return ScanResults;                    // Return result of scan
}

/**************************************************************************
*FUNCTION:ScanImage
*
*ARGS:     ID reference. This is a reference to a IMAGEDESCRIPTOR
*          which on return will be filled with the parameters of the
*          scanned image.
*RETURNS: TRUE if successful, FALSE if not
*
*NOTES:    This function interfaces to the TWAIN source for acquisition
*          of an image.
***************************************************************************/

BOOL Twain::ScanImage(IMAGEDESCRIPTOR& ID) {

  lpID = &ID;                          // Save ptr to descriptor

  DSMOpen = FALSE;                     // Initialize class variables
  DSOpen = FALSE;
  DSEnabled = FALSE;
  hAppWindow = 0;
  hImageMemory = 0;
  RequiredMemory = 0L;

  TType = THRU_MEMORY;                 // Utilize thru memory transfer to app
  ScanResults = FALSE;                 // No image scanned yet

  // Create TWAIN backdrop window. It is parent to Source's UI dialog
  hBackgroundWindow = CreateWindow(szAppName, NULL,
                    WS_POPUP | WS_BORDER,
                    0, 0, CW_USEDEFAULT, CW_USEDEFAULT,
                    HWND_DESKTOP, NULL, hDLLInstance, NULL);

  ShowWindow(hBackgroundWindow, SW_SHOWMAXIMIZED);
  SendMessage(hBackgroundWindow, WM_SYSCOMMAND, SC_MAXIMIZE, 0L); // Expand
    parent window to full screen

  // The modeless Source UI window must be taken into consideration
  MSG Msg;
  while (GetMessage (&Msg, NULL, 0, 0)) {
    if ((!DSOpen) || (!ProcessDCMessage((LPMSG)&Msg, hBackgroundWindow))) {
      TranslateMessage (&Msg);
      DispatchMessage (&Msg);
    }
  }

  UpdateWindow(GetActiveWindow());// Update calling program
```

```
  // Process and store image data if scan was successful
  if (ScanResults == TRUE)
    if (!ProcessImageData("", NOTYPE, 0))
      return FALSE;

  return ScanResults;                    // Return result of scan
}

/**************************************************************************
*FUNCTION:ScanImage
*
*ARGS:    FileName   Path and FileName without extension to store the
*                    scanned image in.
*         CompType   Specifies the type of image to store
*         Quality    Specifies the quality factor if image type is JPEG
*         ID         Reference to a IMAGEDESCRIPTOR which on return will
*                    be filled with the parameters of the scanned image.
*RETURNS: TRUE if successful, FALSE if not
*
*NOTES:   This function interfaces to the TWAIN source for acquisition
*         of an image. It stores the scanned image in the named file
*         and passes a copy of the image data through shared memory.
**************************************************************************/

BOOL Twain::ScanImage(LPSTR FileName, CompandType CompType, WORD Quality,
                      IMAGEDESCRIPTOR& ID) {
  lpID = &ID;                            // Save ptr to descriptor

  DSMOpen = FALSE;                       // Initialize class variables
  DSOpen = FALSE;
  DSEnabled = FALSE;
  hAppWindow = 0;
  hImageMemory = 0;
  RequiredMemory = 0L;

  TType = THRU_FILEANDMEMORY;            // Utilize thru memory transfer to app
  ScanResults = FALSE;                   // No image scanned yet

  // Create TWAIN backdrop window. It is parent to Source's UI dialog
  hBackgroundWindow = CreateWindow(szAppName, NULL,
                      WS_POPUP | WS_BORDER,
                      0, 0, CW_USEDEFAULT, CW_USEDEFAULT,
                      HWND_DESKTOP, NULL, hDLLInstance, NULL);

  ShowWindow(hBackgroundWindow, SW_SHOWMAXIMIZED);
  SendMessage(hBackgroundWindow, WM_SYSCOMMAND, SC_MAXIMIZE, 0L); // Expand
    parent window to full screen

  // The modeless Source UI window must be taken into consideration
  MSG Msg;
  while (GetMessage (&Msg, NULL, 0, 0)) {
    if ((!DSOpen) || (!ProcessDCMessage((LPMSG)&Msg, hBackgroundWindow)))) {
      TranslateMessage (&Msg);
      DispatchMessage (&Msg);
    }
  }
```

```
    UpdateWindow(GetActiveWindow()); // Update calling program

    // Process and store image data if scan was successful
    if (ScanResults == TRUE)
      if (!ProcessImageData(FileName, CompType, Quality))
        return FALSE;
    return ScanResults;              // Return result of scan
}


/***************************************************************************
 * FUNCTION: ExplainError
 *
 * ARGS:        hWnd       handle to a display window
 *              lpText     ptr to a character string which defines
 *                         these error strings.
 *              MsgNumber  if non zero it represents a message number
 *                         for direct output.
 * RETURNS:     none
 *
 ***************************************************************************/

void Twain::ExplainError(HWND hWnd, LPSTR lpText, int MsgNumber) {
  TW_STATUS dcStatus;
  TW_UINT16 Status;
  char Details [255];
  int ErrorCode;

  // Put in detail of current operation
  lstrcpy (Details, lpText);

  if (MsgNumber != 0)              // If MsgNumber non zero output specified
    ErrorCode = MsgNumber;         // error message directly without polling
  else {                           // SM.
    // determine details of failure from SM and/or Source
    if (*lpDSM_Entry) {
      Status = (*lpDSM_Entry) (&AppIdentity,
                               &SourceIdentity,
                               DG_CONTROL,
                               DAT_STATUS,
                               MSG_GET,
                               (TW_MEMREF)&dcStatus),

      if (Status == TWRC_SUCCESS) {
        switch(dcStatus.ConditionCode) {
          case TWCC_SUCCESS:
            ErrorCode = IDS_SUCCESS;
            break;

          default:
          case TWCC_BUMMER:
            ErrorCode = IDS_BUMMER;
            break;
```

```
            case TWCC_LOWMEMORY:
              ErrorCode = IDS_LOWMEMORY;
              break;

            case TWCC_NODS:
              ErrorCode = IDS_NODS;
              break;

            case TWCC_MAXCONNECTIONS:
              ErrorCode = IDS_MAXCONNECTIONS;
              break;

            case TWCC_OPERATIONERROR:
              // Error in the DS or DSM which was already reported to the user. The
              // App should not be redundant.
              goto NoErrorToDisplay;

            case TWCC_BADCAP:
              ErrorCode = IDS_BADCAP;
              break;

            case TWCC_BADPROTOCOL:
              ErrorCode = IDS_BADPROTOCOL;
              break;

            case TWCC_BADVALUE:
              ErrorCode = IDS_BADVALUE;
              break;

            case TWCC_SEQERROR:
              ErrorCode = IDS_SEQERROR;
              break;

            case TWCC_BADDEST:
              ErrorCode = IDS_BADDEST;
              break;

          }
        } else {
          ErrorCode = IDS_NODETAIL;
        }
      } else
        ErrorCode = IDS_NODSM;
  }
  // Now send out the text in a message box
  LoadString(hDLLInstance, ErrorCode, Details + lstrlen(Details),
    sizeof(Details));
  MessageBox(hWnd, Details, "TWAIN Error", MB_OK);

  // don't report error
NoErrorToDisplay:
  return;
}
```

```
// Negotiation Code Functions

/**************************************************************************
*FUNCTION:SetImageXferCount
*
*ARGS:     -1 means app can support any number of xfers from source per session
*           1 means app will support only a single xfer per session
*           N means app will support N xfers per session
*
*RETURNS: TRUE if set of xfer count was successful.
*
*NOTES:    This function sets up the number of image xfers the app can
*          accept from the source per session. Change MAXXFERSPERSESSION
*          for any N greater than 1.
**************************************************************************/


BOOL Twain::SetImageXferCount(int Count) {
  TW_CAPABILITY Caps;
  TW_INT16 Status;

  if ((Count < -1) || (Count > MAXXFERSPERSESSION)) // Verify parameter is
    not bogus
    return FALSE;


  // Check to see if scanner in Canon CJ10, if so do not negotiate
  // this capability.
  if (lstrcmpi(SourceIdentity.ProductName, "Canon CJ10 Scan") == 0)
    return TRUE;


  Caps.Cap = CAP_XFERCOUNT;          // Set this capability
  if (!BuildUpOneValue(&Caps, TWTY_INT16, Count))
    return FALSE;                    // False if no memory


  // Tell the source
  Status = (*lpDSM_Entry) (&AppIdentity,
                           &SourceIdentity,
                           DG_CONTROL,
                           DAT_CAPABILITY,
                           MSG_SET,
                           (TW_MEMREF)&Caps);


  GlobalFree(Caps.hContainer);       // Free up container memory

  if (Status != TWRC_SUCCESS) {      // If problem occured
    ExplainError(hAppWindow, "SetImageXferCount - ", 0);
    return FALSE;
  }
  return TRUE;                        // Everything OK
}
```

```
/*************************************************************************
*FUNCTION: SetPixelTypes
*
*ARGS:      None.
*
*RETURNS:   TRUE if set successful
*
*NOTES:     This function forces the TWAIN device to use a pixel type that
*           we can support. EnhancedView can support BW, Gray, Palettized
*           and RGB images. NOTE: all TWAIN devices are required to
*           negotiate this capability. Spec says only a ONEVALUE or ENUMERATION
*           container type will be returned.
*************************************************************************/

BOOL Twain::SetPixelTypes(void) {
  TW_CAPABILITY Caps;
  TW_INT16 Status;
  TW_UINT16 PixelTypes[10];         // 9 type defined in spec
  TW_UINT16 PixelTypesSupported[4]; // Only 4 types supported by app
  int Index;
  BOOL ResultCode;

  // Clear the PixelTypes array
  memset(PixelTypes,              0, sizeof(PixelTypes));
  memset(PixelTypesSupported,     0, sizeof(PixelTypesSupported));

  Caps.Cap = ICAP_PIXELTYPE;        // Get values for this ICAP

  // Ask the source for these values
  Status = (*lpDSM_Entry) (&AppIdentity,
                           &SourceIdentity,
                           DG_CONTROL,
                           DAT_CAPABILITY,
                           MSG_GET,
                           (TW_MEMREF)&Caps);
  if (Status != TWRC_SUCCESS) {     // If error occurred
    if (Caps.hContainer)            // If the container was allocated
      GlobalFree(Caps.hContainer);  // free up container memory
    return FALSE;                   // Return FALSE
  }
  // We have gotten the capability container
  switch(Caps.ConType) {            // Parse the returned container type
    case TWON_ONEVALUE:             // If its one value, extract it
      ExtractOneValue(&Caps, &PixelTypes[0]);
      if ((PixelTypes[0] == TWPT_BW) ||      // If the single value is one of
          (PixelTypes[0] == TWPT_GRAY) ||    // types we support, we're set,
          (PixelTypes[0] == TWPT_RGB) ||     // no negotiation to be done.
          (PixelTypes[0] == TWPT_PALETTE))   // If not, we're hosed because
        ResultCode = TRUE;                   // we cannot accept the single
      else                                   // type the scanner can produce.
        ResultCode = FALSE;
      GlobalFree(Caps.hContainer);           // Free container memory
      return ResultCode;                     // Return completion code
```

```
        case TWON_ENUMERATION:              // A ENUMERATION was returned
          Index = 0;                        // Index of enumerated value to return
          do {                              // read all values into array.
            if (!ExtractEnumerationValue(&Caps, &PixelTypes[Index], Index))
              break;                        // Index exceeded items in enumeration
            Index++;
          } while (TRUE);
          GlobalFree(Caps.hContainer);  // Free container memory
          break;

        default:                            // Any other container type is an error
          GlobalFree(Caps.hContainer);  // Free container memory
          return FALSE;
    }

    // When we get here, all PixelTypes supported by device are in array
    WORD NumSupported = 0;
    WORD NumEntries = Index;

    // Go through the device supported pixeltypes and save those that
    // our application supports.
    for (Index = 0; Index < NumEntries; Index++) {
      if ((PixelTypes[Index] == TWPT_BW)     ||
          (PixelTypes[Index] == TWPT_GRAY)   ||
          (PixelTypes[Index] == TWPT_RGB)    ||
          (PixelTypes[Index] == TWPT_PALETTE))
        PixelTypesSupported[NumSupported++] = PixelTypes[Index];
    }
    // PixelTypesSupported array now has all types the device and app can
    // support.

    // Now go back through the supported pixel types and log the indices
    // for the various types. This is done so that the app can select
    // the most appropriate type for use.
    int RGBIndex = -1;
    int PaletteIndex = -1;
    int GrayIndex = -1;
    int BWIndex = -1;

    for (Index = 0; Index < NumSupported; Index++) {
      if (PixelTypesSupported[Index]        == TWPT_BW)
        BWIndex = Index;
      else if (PixelTypesSupported[Index]   == TWPT_GRAY)
        GrayIndex = Index;
      else if (PixelTypesSupported[Index]   == TWPT_RGB)
        RGBIndex = Index;
      else
        PaletteIndex = Index;
    }

    // Select RGB, Palette, Gray and BW in that order.
    WORD CurrentIndex;
    if (RGBIndex != -1)
      CurrentIndex = RGBIndex;
```

```
      else if (PaletteIndex != -1)
        CurrentIndex = PaletteIndex;
      else if (GrayIndex != -1)
        CurrentIndex = GrayIndex;
      else
        CurrentIndex = BWIndex;

      Caps.Cap = ICAP_PIXELTYPE;        // Cap type is ICAP_PIXELTYPE
      Caps.ConType = TWON_ENUMERATION;  // Will use enumeration container
      TW_ENUMERATION Enum;              // Create enumeration data structure
      Enum.ItemType = TWTY_UINT16;      // Type of enum data is UINT16
      Enum.NumItems = NumSupported;     // The number of pixeltypes the app and
                                        // TWAIN device support.
      Enum.CurrentIndex = CurrentIndex; // The PixelType the App wants to use
      Enum.DefaultIndex = TWON_DONTCARE32; // Don't set default. Send DONTCARE.

      // Build up the container
      BuildUpEnumerationType(&Caps, &Enum, &PixelTypesSupported);

      // Ask the source to use only these pixel types
      Status = (*lpDSM_Entry) (&AppIdentity,
                                &SourceIdentity,
                                DG_CONTROL,
                                DAT_CAPABILITY,
                                MSG_SET,
                                (TW_MEMREF)&Caps);

    GlobalFree(Caps.hContainer);       // free up container memory
    // Check the return code
    if (Status != TWRC_SUCCESS) {      // If error occurred
      ExplainError(hAppWindow, "SetPixelTypes - ", 0);
      return FALSE;
    }
    return TRUE;                        // Everything OK
}


/************************************************************************
*FUNCTION: SetXferMechanism
*
*ARGS:     Image transfer mechanism. One of the following:
*          DCSX_NATIVE, DCSX_FILE, DCSX_MEMORY
*
*RETURNS:  TRUE if mechanism successfully set
*
*NOTES:    This function should check to see if Mechanism is supported
*          before forcing it.
************************************************************************/

BOOL Twain::SetXferMechanism(TW_UINT16 Mechanism) {
 TW_CAPABILITY Caps;
 TW_INT16 Status;

 Caps.Cap = ICAP_XFERMECH;       // Set this capability
 if (!BuildUpOneValue(&Caps, TWTY_UINT16, Mechanism))
   return FALSE;                 // False if no memory
```

```
    // Tell the source
    Status = (*lpDSM_Entry) (&AppIdentity,
                             &SourceIdentity,
                             DG_CONTROL,
                             DAT_CAPABILITY,
                             MSG_SET,
                             (TW_MEMREF)&Caps);

    GlobalFree(Caps.hContainer);        // Free up container memory

    if (Status != TWRC_SUCCESS) {       // If problem occured
      ExplainError(hAppWindow, "SetXferMechanism - ", 0);
      return FALSE;
    }
    return TRUE;                         // Everything OK
}


/***************************************************************************
*FUNCTION:SetUpFileTransfer
*
*ARGS:      FileName is the name to be given to the scanned image file.
*
*RETURNS: TRUE if setup was completed successfully. Also the FileName
*         is given a .TIF file extension.
*
*NOTES:    This function should check to see if TIFF is supported by the
*          TWAIN device before forcing it.
***************************************************************************/

BOOL Twain::SetupFileTransfer(LPSTR FileName) {
  TW_SETUPFILEXFER FileXfer;
  TW_INT16 Status;

  if (!SetXferMechanism(TWSX_FILE)) // Ask the device to use file xfer
    return FALSE;                    // If it says no, we're in trouble

  LPSTR PeriodPtr = strchr(FileName, '.');   // Search for period of extension
  if (PeriodPtr != NULL)              // If period found, truncate name there
    *PeriodPtr = '\0';
  lstract(FileName, ".tif");          // Add the TIF file extension.


  // Fill in the TW_SETUPFILEXFER structure with the info
  lstrcpy((LPSTR) &FileXfer.FileName, FileName); // Copy the filename to use
  FileXfer.Format = TWFF_TIFF;        // Ask for a TIFF file
  FileXfer.VRefNum = 0;               // This field is DONTCARE

  // Tell the source about the filename and type
  Status = (*lpDSM_Entry) (&AppIdentity,
                           &SourceIdentity,
                           DG_CONTROL,
                           DAT_SETUPFILEXFER,
                           MSG_SET,
                           (TW_MEMREF)&FileXfer);
```

```
    if (Status != TWRC_SUCCESS) {     // If error occurred
      ExplainError(hAppWindow, "SetupFileTransfer - ", 0);
      return FALSE;                    // Return FALSE
    }
    return TRUE;
}

/************************************************************************
*FUNCTION: OpenDSM
*
*ARGS:      none
*
*RETURNS:   current state of the Source Manager
*
*NOTES:     1) Makes sure SM is not already open
*           2) Explicitly loads the DLL for the Source Manager
*           3) Call Source Manager to:
*               - open SM
*               - pass the handle to the app's window to the SM
*               - Set the SM assigned AppIdentity.id field
************************************************************************/

BOOL Twain::OpenDSM(HWND hWindow) {
  TW_UINT16      Status;
  OFSTRUCT       OpenFiles;
  char           WinDir[WINDIRPATHSIZE];

  // Only open SM if currently closed
  if (!DSMOpen) {
    hAppWindow = hWindow;              // Save the App window handle
    // Find the path to the Windows directory and then attempt to open the SM.
    GetWindowsDirectory(WinDir, WINDIRPATHSIZE);
    if (WinDir[lstrlen(WinDir)]-1] != '\\')
      lstrcat (WinDir, "\\");

    // Get the name of the source manager and cat it to path
    lstrcat (WinDir, SOURCEMANAGERNAME);

    // Check to see if it exists. If so open library
    if ((OpenFile(WinDir, &OpenFiles, OF_EXIST) == HFILE_ERROR)  ||
      ((hDSMDLL = LoadLibrary(SOURCEMANAGERNAME)) == NULL)        ||
      ((lpDSM_Entry = (DSMENTRYPROC) GetProcAddress(hDSMDLL, DSMENTRY)) ==
        NULL)) {
      // NOTE: must pass error number here so ExplainError will not attempt
      // to ask DSM what the details of the error were. This is not possible
      // because the DSM could not be opened.
      ExplainError(hWindow, "OpenDSM - ", IDS_NODSM);
      return FALSE;
    }
    /*
    This call performs four important functions:
      - opens/loads the SM
      - passes the handle to the app's window to the SM
      - returns the SM assigned appID.id field
```

```
            - be sure to test the return code for SUCCESSful open of SM
        */
        Status = (*lpDSM_Entry) (&AppIdentity,
                            NULL,
                            DG_CONTROL,
                            DAT_PARENT,
                            MSG_OPENDSM,
                            (TW_MEMREF)&hWindow);

      switch (Status) {
        case TWRC_SUCCESS:
          // Open was a success
          DSMOpen = TRUE;
          break;

        case TWRC_FAILURE:
        default:
          // Trouble opening the SM, inform the user
          DSMOpen = FALSE;
          ExplainError(hWindow, "OpenDSM - ", 0);
          break;
      }
    }
    // Let the caller know what happened
    return (DSMOpen);
}

/***************************************************************************
*FUNCTION:  CloseDSM
*
*ARGS:       none
*
*RETURNS:    TRUE if DSM was closed or was already closed
*
*NOTES:     1) Makes sure SM is already open
*           2) calls Source Manager to request closure from this app.
****************************************************************************/

BOOL Twain::CloseDSM(void) {
  TW_UINT16 Status;
  // Only close something which is already open
  if (DSMOpen) {
      * This call performs one important function:
        - tells the SM which application, AppIdentity.id, is requesting SM to close
        - be sure to test return code, failure indicates SM did not close !!
      */
      Status = (*lpDSM_Entry) (&AppIdentity,
                            NULL,
                            DG_CONTROL,
                            DAT_PARENT,
                            MSG_CLOSEDSM,
                            &hAppWindow);

      if (Status != TWRC_SUCCESS) {
        ExplainError(hAppWindow, "CloseDSM - ", 0);
```

```
        return FALSE;
    } else {
      DSMOpen = FALSE;              // Set flag if close was successful
      // Explicitly free the SM library
      if (hDSMDLL) {
        FreeLibrary (hDSMDLL);
        hDSMDLL=0;
      }
      hAppWindow = 0;              // Clear handle to App window
    }
  }
  return TRUE;
}


/***********************************************************************
*FUNCTION:   OpenDS
*
*ARGS:       none
*
*RETURNS:    current state of select Source
*
*NOTES:
*           1) Only attempt to open a source if it is currently closed
*           2) Call Source Manager to:
*           - open the Source indicated by info in SourceIdentity
*           - SM will fill in the unique SourceIdentity.Id field
***********************************************************************/

BOOL Twain::OpenDS(void) {
  TW_UINT16 Status;

  // If a Source is not already open
  if (!DSOpen) {
    // This will open the specified Source and will give it a new ID
    // for this session. If this is called before SelectDS, the default
    // source will be opened.
    SourceIdentity.Id = 0;
    Status = (*lpDSM_Entry) (&AppIdentity,
                             NULL,
                             DG_CONTROL,
                             DAT_IDENTITY,
                             MSG_OPENDS,
                             &SourceIdentity);

    if (Status == TWRC_SUCCESS) {
      // Do not change flag unless we successfully open
      DSOpen = TRUE;
    } else {
      // Trouble opening the Source
      ExplainError (hAppWindow, "OpenDS - ", 0);
    }
  }
  return DSOpen;
}
```

```
/***************************************************************************
*FUNCTION:   CloseDS
*
*ARGS:       none
*
*RETURNS:    none
*
*NOTES:      1) only attempt to close an open Source
*            2) call Source Manager to ask identified Source to close itself
****************************************************************************/

BOOL Twain::CloseDS(void) {
  TW_UINT16 Status;

  if (DSOpen) {
    // Close an open Source
    Status = (*lpDSM_Entry) (&AppIdentity,
                             NULL,
                             DG_CONTROL,
                             DAT_IDENTITY,
                             MSG_CLOSEDS,
                             &SourceIdentity);

    if (Status != TWRC_SUCCESS) {
      ExplainError(hAppWindow, "CloseDS - ", 0);
      return FALSE;
    } else {
      DSOpen = FALSE;
    }
  }
  return TRUE;
}


/***************************************************************************
*FUNCTION:   EnableDS
*
*ARGS:       none
*
*RETURNS:    BOOL for TRUE=open; FALSE ot open/fail
*
*NOTES:      1) only enable an open Source
*            2) call the Source Manager to bring up the Source's User Interface
****************************************************************************/

BOOL Twain::EnableDS (void) {
  BOOL Result = FALSE;
  TW_UINT16 Status;

  // only enable an open Source
  if (DSOpen) {
    // This will display the Source User Interface. The Source should only
    // display a user interface that is compatible with the group defined
    // by AppIdentity.SupportedGroups (in our case DG_IMAGE | DG_CONTROL).
    dcUI.ShowUI = TRUE; // Initialize structure
```

```
      dcUI.ModalUI = TRUE;
      dcUI.hParent = hAppWindow;
      Status = (*lpDSM_Entry) (&AppIdentity,
                               &SourceIdentity,
                               DG_CONTROL,
                               DAT_USERINTERFACE,
                               MSG_ENABLEDS,
                               (TW_MEMREF)&dcUI);
      if (Status!=TWRC_SUCCESS)
        ExplainError (hAppWindow, "EnableDS - ", 0);
      else {
        Result = TRUE;
        DSEnabled = TRUE;
      }
   }
   return Result;
}


/*************************************************************************
*FUNCTION: DisableDS
*
*ARGS:     none
*
*RETURNS:  none
*
*NOTES:    1) Only disable an open Source
*          2) Call Source Manager to ask Source to hide it's User Interface
*************************************************************************/

BOOL Twain::DisableDS(void) {
  TW_UINT16 Status;
  BOOL Result = FALSE;

  // only disable open Source's
  if (DSOpen && DSEnabled) {
    // Hide the Source UI. Structure was initialized by EnableDS.
    dcUI.ShowUI = FALSE;

    Status = (*lpDSM_Entry) (&AppIdentity,
                             &SourceIdentity,
                             DG_CONTROL,
                             DAT_USERINTERFACE,
                             MSG_DISABLEDS,
                             (TW_MEMREF) &dcUI);

    if (Status!=TWRC_SUCCESS)
      ExplainError (hAppWindow, "DisableDS - ", 0);
    else {
      Result = TRUE;
      DSEnabled = FALSE;
    }
  }
  return Result;
}
```

```
/**************************************************************************
*FUNCTION:  SelectDS
*
*ARGS:      none
*
*RETURNS:   BOOL TRUE if successfull, FALSE if not
*
*NOTES:     1) Call the Source Manager to:
*                 - have the SM put up a list of the available Sources
*                 - get information about the user selected Source from
*                   NewDSIdentity, filled by Source
***************************************************************************/

BOOL Twain::SelectDS(void) {
  TW_UINT16 Status;
  TW_IDENTITY NewDSIdentity;
  BOOL Result = TRUE;

  if (DSOpen) {
  ExplainError(hAppWindow, "SelectDS - ", IDS_SOURCEOPEN);
  return FALSE;
}
// Get the system default Source
Status = (*lpDSM_Entry) (&AppIdentity,
                  NULL,
                  DG_CONTROL,
                  DAT_IDENTITY,
                  MSG_GETDEFAULT,
                  (TW_MEMREF)&NewDSIdentity);

/* This call performs one important function:
    - should cause SM to put up dialog box of available Source's
    - tells the SM which application, appID.id, is requesting, REQUIRED
    - returns the SM assigned NewDSIdentity.id field, you check if changed
      (needed to talk to a particular Data Source)
    - be sure to test return code, failure indicates SM did not close !!
*/
Status = (*lpDSM_Entry) (&AppIdentity,
                  NULL,
                  DG_CONTROL,
                  DAT_IDENTITY,
                  MSG_USERSELECT,
                  (TW_MEMREF)&NewDSIdentity);

 /* Check if the user changed the Source and react as apporpriate.
    - TWRC_SUCCESS,       log in new Source
    - TWRC_CANCEL,        keep the current Source
    - default,            check down the codes in a status message, display result
*/
switch (Status) {
  case TWRC_SUCCESS:
    SourceIdentity = NewDSIdentity;
    break;

  case TWRC_CANCEL:
    break;
```

```
    default:
    case TWRC_FAILURE:
      ExplainError(hAppWindow, "SelectDS - ", 0);
      Result = FALSE;
      break;
  }
  // Let the caller know what happened
  return (Result);
}

/************************************************************************
*FUNCTION: SelectSource
*
*ARGS:      hWindow is handle of window dialog box should come up in.
*
*RETURNS:  BOOL TRUE if successful, FALSE if not
*
*NOTES:     Opens Source Manager to put up a list of the available Sources
************************************************************************/

BOOL Twain::SelectSource(HWND hWindow) {

  if (OpenDSM(hWindow)) {         // Open the DSM
    SelectDS();                   // If successful ask it to display sources
    CloseDSM();                   // Close DSM before exit
    return TRUE;                  // Return TRUE for no error
  } else
    return FALSE;                 // FALSE means error occurred.
}


/*
This function calculates how much virtual memory is available and
advises the user on maximum scanned image size. It writes a message
at the bottom of the backdrop window with the information.
*/

#define ONEQUARTERMEGOFMEMORY 262144L

BOOL Twain::PaintMemoryMessage(HWND hWindow) {

  // Find out if we are running in 256 color mode
  HDC hIC = CreateIC("DISPLAY", NULL, NULL, NULL);
  BOOL EightBitColorMode = (GetDeviceCaps(hIC, BITSPIXEL) == 8);
  DeleteDC(hIC);

  // Find out how much free memory space is available by acquiring
  // progressively smaller blocks until the allocation is successful.
  // This causes the memory management system to discard and compact
  // as much as it can to return the largest block possible.
  BOOL Done = FALSE;
  LONG MaxMemoryAvailable = 63 * ONEQUARTERMEGOFMEMORY;   // Start near 16M
  HGLOBAL hMem;
  while (!Done) {
    hMem = GlobalAlloc(GMEM_MOVEABLE, MaxMemoryAvailable);
    if (hMem) {
```

```
      Done = TRUE;
      GlobalFree (hMem);
    } else
      MaxMemoryAvailable -= ONEQUARTERMEGOFMEMORY;// Lower block size
  }


  // Subtract the fixed requirements for the source and transfer buffer
  MaxMemoryAvailable -= SOURCEBUFFEROVERHEAD;
  MaxMemoryAvailable -= SOURCEMEMORYOVERHEAD;


  // Max scanned image size is calculated from the amount of memory
  // available and the requirements for the image. If the computer
  // is running in 256 color mode, the available memory is divided by
  // 2.33 because of the need for two memory images and the dither buffer
  // which is 1/3 the size of the image. When operating with more colors
  // only two memory images are required, no dither buffer. We therefore
  // divide the available memory by 2.
  if (EightBitColorMode)
    MaxMemoryAvailable = (MaxMemoryAvailable * 100) / 233;
  else
    MaxMemoryAvailable = MaxMemoryAvailable / 2;


  // See if there is enough memory for scanning
  if (MaxMemoryAvailable < MINIMUMSCANNEDIMAGESIZE) {
    // If we get here, not enough memory to allow scanning
    MessageBox(hWindow, "Not enough free memory for scanning. To free "
                        "additional memory, close open database records "
                        "and other Windows applications.",
                        "User Advisory", MB_OK | MB_ICONEXCLAMATION);
    return FALSE;
  }


  // Format number into message for display
  char Buffer[100];
  wsprintf(Buffer, "Due to database processing requirements, DO NOT "
                   "scan images larger than %ld kbytes.", MaxMemoryAvailable /
                    1024);


  // Prepare to write message on last line of window
  WORD TextHeight;
  RECT Rect;

  GetClientRect(hWindow, &Rect);    // Get size of client area
  HDC hDC = GetDC(hWindow);         // Get a DC for the area
  // Get size of text for display

#ifndef WIN32                       // If Win16
  DWORD TextSize = GetTextExtent(hDC, Buffer, sizeof(Buffer));
  TextHeight = HIWORD(TextSize);
#else                               // If Win 32
  SIZE Size;
  GetTextExtentPoint(hDC, Buffer, sizeof(Buffer), &Size);
  TextHeight = (WORD) Size.cy;
#endif
```

```
  // Calculate position of text string
  Rect.left = 0;
  Rect.top = Rect.bottom - (TextHeight + 12);

  // Now draw the message on the screen
  SetTextColor(hDC, RGB(255, 0, 0)); // Use this color for text
  DrawText(hDC, Buffer, -1, &Rect, DT_SINGLELINE | DT_CENTER);
  ReleaseDC(hWindow, hDC);

  return TRUE;
}

// Backdrop window Window Procedure
long CALLBACK _export Twain::BackDropWndProc(HWND hwnd, UINT message,
                                             WPARAM wParam, LPARAM lParam) {
  static BOOL FirstPaint;
  PAINTSTRUCT Ps;
  static HWND hUIWindow;

  switch (message) {

    case WM_CREATE:
      lpTwain->ScanResults = FALSE;    // No image yet scanned
      // Here is where the image scan is setup
      // Attempt to open the DSM
      if (!lpTwain->OpenDSM(hwnd))
        return -1L;

      // Attempt to open the source, if error close DSM
      if (!lpTwain->OpenDS()) {
        lpTwain->CloseDSM();
        return -1L;
      }

      // Set image transfer count to 1. A single image per session.
      if (!lpTwain->SetImageXferCount(1)) {
        lpTwain->CloseDS();
        lpTwain->CloseDSM();
        return -1L;
      }

      // Set up for thru memory, non compressed image xfers.
      if (!lpTwain->SetXferMechanism(TWSX_MEMORY)) {
        lpTwain->CloseDS();
        lpTwain->CloseDSM();
        return -1L;
      }                                // Restrict scanner to RGB images

      // Restrict pixel types to BW, Grey, Palette or RGB
      if (!lpTwain->SetPixelTypes()) {
        lpTwain->CloseDS();
        lpTwain->CloseDSM();
        return -1L;
      }
```

```
        hUIWindow = 0;                    // No handle yet for Source UI window
        FirstPaint = TRUE;                // Indicate window not yet painted


        // If we get here all is well
        return 0L;

    case WM_SETFOCUS:                     // Background window has been given focus
        if (hUIWindow)
            SetFocus(hUIWindow);          // Return focus to Source's UI
        return 0L;


    case WM_PAINT:
        BeginPaint(hwnd, &Ps);
        if (lpTwain->PaintMemoryMessage(hwnd)) {    // Output message to
            background window

            if (FirstPaint) {             // If first time window is painted
                FirstPaint = FALSE;       // Only bring up Source UI once
                if (!lpTwain->EnableDS()) {    // Bring up Source's UI
                    lpTwain->CloseDS();   // If error cleanup
                    lpTwain->CloseDSM();
                    DestroyWindow(hwnd);
                }
                InvalidateRect(hwnd, NULL, FALSE); // Force a repaint to get handle
            } else
                if (!hUIWindow)
                    hUIWindow = GetParent(GetFocus());// Get handle of Source's
                        window
        } else {
            lpTwain->CloseDS();
            lpTwain->CloseDSM();
            DestroyWindow(hwnd);          // If error cleanup
        }
        EndPaint(hwnd, &Ps);
        return 0L;


    case WM_SYSCOMMAND:
        if ((wParam & 0xFFF0) == SC_MOVE)// Don't allow background window to move
            return 0L;
        break;


    case WM_XFERDONE:                     // Source says it done xfering image
        if (wParam)                       // If the transfer was successful
            lpTwain->ScanResults = TRUE;// Indicate that an image was scanned
        // Indicate message has been processed
        return 0L;


    case WM_DESTROY:
        PostQuitMessage(0);
        return 0L;
    }
    return DefWindowProc (hwnd, message, wParam, lParam);
}
```

```
// Library entry point for initialization
#ifndef _WIN32_                    // If Win16

int CALLBACK LibMain(HINSTANCE hInstance, WORD, WORD wHeapSize,
                     LPSTR) {

  hDLLInst = hInstance;

  if (wHeapSize > 0)
    UnlockData (0);
  WNDCLASS wndclass;

  // Define the backdrop window class
  wndclass.style          = CS_HREDRAW | CS_VREDRAW | CS_BYTEALIGNWINDOW;
  wndclass.lpfnWndProc    = Twain::BackDropWndProc;
  wndclass.cbClsExtra     = 0;
  wndclass.cbWndExtra     = 0;
  wndclass.hInstance      = hInstance;
  wndclass.hIcon          = NULL;
  wndclass.hCursor        = LoadCursor (NULL, IDC_ARROW);
  wndclass.hbrBackground  = (HBRUSH) GetStockObject(WHITE_BRUSH);
  wndclass.lpszMenuName   = NULL;
  wndclass.lpszClassName  = szAppName;
  RegisterClass(&wndclass);

  return 1;
}

// Window's exit procedure for this DLL
int CALLBACK WEP(int nParameter) {

  if (nParameter == WEP_SYSTEM_EXIT) {
    // system shutdown in progress
    return(1);
  }
  else if (nParameter == WEP_FREE_DLL) {
    // Every application has freed this DLL
    // Free up memory for these items
    return(1);
  } else {
    // Undefined value -- ignor
    return(1);
  }
}

else                               // If Win32
BOOL WINAPI LibMain(HINSTANCE hinstDLL, DWORD fdwReason, LPVOID) {

  if (fdwReason == DLL_PROCESS_ATTACH) {
    hDLLInst = hinstDLL;

      WNDCLASS wndclass;

      // Define the backdrop window class
      wndclass.style                = CS_HREDRAW | CS_VREDRAW | CS_BYTEALIGNWINDOW;
```

```
        wndclass.lpfnWndProc    = Twain::BackDropWndProc;
        wndclass.cbClsExtra     = 0;
        wndclass.cbWndExtra     = 0;
        wndclass.hInstance      = hDLLInst;
        wndclass.hIcon          = NULL;
        wndclass.hCursor        = LoadCursor (NULL, IDC_ARROW);
        wndclass.hbrBackground  = (HBRUSH) GetStockObject(WHITE_BRUSH);
        wndclass.lpszMenuName   = NULL;
        wndclass.lpszClassName  = szAppName;
        RegisterClass(&wndclass);
    }
  return TRUE;                           // Return TRUE always
}

#endif
```

The Select Source Operation

1. Open the Source Manager if it is not already open. This step brings the Source Manager into memory and extracts the DSM_Entry point used for all subsequent TWAIN operations. This function is called **OpenDSM** in the code.
2. Select the data Source (called **SelectDS** Listing 8.2). The execution of this function causes the Source Manager to locate all Sources on the system and display a dialog box with a list box for selecting which Source to use. While the dialog box is visible, the F1 key can be pressed to get a description of the highlighted Source for your inspection. Similarly, the key sequence AltWG (hold the Alt key and type WG) will bring up the list of members of the working group for your inspection. Making a Source selection dismisses the dialog box.
3. Close the Source Manager (the **CloseDSM** function). This step may or may not be appropriate for a given application. In the code presented here, the Source Manager is unloaded after each operation, including this one. In other applications, the Source Manager might be brought up during program initialization and shut down when the application terminates.

The Acquire Operation

1. Open the Source Manager if it is not already open. This step brings the Source Manager into memory and extracts the DSM_Entry point used for all subsequent TWAIN operations. The function that opens the Source Manager is called **OpenDSM** in the code listing.
2. Open the specified Source, if it is not already open. This operation is embodied in the function **OpenDS** in the listing.
3. Negotiate with the Source for any capabilities required by the application. The functions **SetResolution, SetupFileTransfer,** and **RestrictToRGB** from the listing are all examples of capability negotiation between the application and the selected Source. Negotiation will be discussed in more detail later.
4. Enable the data Source (the **EnableDS** function). The execution of this function brings up the user interface supplied by the selected Source. The UI communicates with the application code by sending Windows messages to

it. Any negotiation performed before the UI was brought up should now be visible. A message, MSG_XFERREADY, will be sent to the application whenever there is an image to transfer. A message, MSG_CLOSEREQ, will be sent to the application whenever the user requests the UI to shut down. As part of the shutdown process, the following steps will be performed.

5. Disable the data Source (the **DisableDS** function). In response to the reception of the MSG_CLOSEREQ message, this function is called to close down the Source's UI.

6. Close the data Source (the **CloseDS** function). Again, this step may or may not be appropriate for a given application.

7. Close the Source Manager (the **CloseDSM** function). This step may or may not be appropriate for a given application as previously explained.

TWAIN Complexities

The discussion so far has probably left the impression that the TWAIN interface is extremely easy to understand, easy to use, and not extremely powerful. On the contrary, there is quite a bit of meat to be found within the specification, which will take some time to fully understand and appreciate. Just look at the include file TWAIN.H for an idea of what is involved. The approximately .75-inch-thick specification document is filled with information on controlling image transfers (native, through file, through memory, formatted, or not), capability negotiation, state transition diagrams, detailed message descriptions, JPEG compression issues, and more. The discussion in this chapter only scratches the surface. Anyone interested in truly understanding TWAIN should purchase the tool kit and plan to spend a few long days reading the documentation. After the second or third pass over the specification, things will begin to make sense. Seeing the code provided in the tool kit and in this chapter should speed the learning process substantially.

Containers

Containers are data structures used to hold structured information that is passed between an application and a Source. Specifically, containers are used for information exchange during capability negotiation. For this reason, they must be understood before capability negotiation can be fully appreciated. Listings 8.3 and 8.4 show the code that implements the Containr class. Four unique types of containers are defined by the specification and supported by this code. They are:

- **One Value Container.** This container type can hold one 32-bit value.
- **Array Container.** Array containers can contain an arbitrary number of values of any defined type. These values are accessed using an index value just as in an array in C.
- **Range Container.** Range containers contain information that describes a range of values of a specified type. Included in a range container are a minimum value, maximum value, a step size value, a default value, and a current value.

- **Enumeration Container.** Enumeration containers contain a list of values of a defined type from which to choose along with a current and default value.

There are 13 TWAIN defined data types that can show up in containers. These are shown in the following table:

Data Type	Description
TW_INT8	8-bit signed value
TW_INT16	16-bit signed value
TW_INT32	32-bit signed value
TW_UINT8	8-bit unsigned value
TW_UINT16	16-bit unsigned value
TW_UINT32	32-bit unsigned value
TW_BOOL	A Boolean value
TW_FIX32	A fixed point description of a floating point number
TW_FRAME	A data structure defining an area. Members include Left, Top, Right, and Bottom
TW_STR32	A string 32 bytes in length
TW_STR64	A string 64 bytes in length
TW_STR128	A string 128 bytes in length
TW_STR255	A string 255 bytes in length

The code for the container interface class "containr.hpp" is shown in Listing 8.3. The code implements the class functions in Listing 8.4. The "Containr" class has 10 public functions that are available for manipulation of containers. The Containr class is unusual in that it does not have an explicit constructor or destructor. These functions are grouped together into a C++ class only to take advantage of encapsulation, not for any other reasons. Therefore a constructor and destructor are not required. The Twain class, discussed shortly, inherits the Containr class for access to these functions. A short synopsis of each class member function is provided later. Their usage will become more apparent when viewed in the context in which they are used as shown in Listing 8.2. The functions will be discussed in the order they appear in Listing 8.4.

Listing 8.3 The Containr class interface definition.

```
/*********************************************************/
/***                   "containr.hpp"              ***/
/***        Interface class for TWAIN containers   ***/
/***                                               ***/
/***                   adapted by                  ***/
/***               Craig A. Lindley                ***/
/***                                               ***/
/***      Revision: 2.0   Last Update: 11/11/94    ***/
/*********************************************************/

// Copyright (c) 1995 John Wiley & Sons, Inc. All rights reserved.
```

```
// Check to see if this file already included
#ifndef CONTAINR_HPP
#define CONTAINR_HPP

#include "twain.h"

class _export Containr {

  private:
    void GetItem(TW_UINT16 Type, LPVOID lpSource, LPVOID lpDest,
                 int SourceIndex, int DestIndex);

  public:
    TW_FIX32 FloatToFIX32(float AFloat);
    float FIX32ToFloat(TW_FIX32 Fix32);

    BOOL BuildUpOneValue(pTW_CAPABILITY pCap, TW_UINT16 ItemType,
      TW_UINT32 Item);
    BOOL ExtractOneValue(pTW_CAPABILITY, pCap, LPVOID pVoid);

    BOOL BuildUpEnumerationType(pTW_CAPABILITY pCap, pTW_ENUMERATION pE,
                                LPVOID lpList);
    BOOL ExtractEnumerationValue(pTW_CAPABILITY pCap, LPVOID pVoid, UINT Index);

    BOOL BuildUpArrayType(pTW_CAPABILITY pCap, pTW_ARRAY pA, LPVOID lpList);
    BOOL ExtractArrayValue(pTW_CAPABILITY pCap, LPVOID pVoid, UINT Index);

    BOOL BuildUpRangeType(pTW_CAPABILITY pCap, pTW_RANGE lpRange);
    BOOL ExtractRange(pTW_CAPABILITY pCap, pTW_RANGE lpRange);
};

#endif
```

Listing 8.4 The Containr class member functions.

```
/***********************************************************/
/***                  "containr.cpp"               ***/
/***        Interface class for TWAIN containers   ***/
/***                                               ***/
/***                   written by                  ***/
/***               Craig A. Lindley                ***/
/***                                               ***/
/***      Revision: 2.0   Last Update: 11/11/94    ***/
/***********************************************************/

// Copyright (c) 1995 John Wiley & Sons, Inc. All rights reserved.

/*
This class contains routines to manipulate containers. Containers are
used in CAPability negotiations to exchange information about the input
device between the Source and the App. The information may define data
exchange or input device characteristics.
```

```
This code was originally provided as part of the TWAIN toolkit. It has been
substaintally modified and enhanced by Craig A. Lindley.
*/
#include <windows.h>
#include "containr.hpp"

// Array of type sizes in bytes
int DCItemSize[] = {
  sizeof(TW_INT8),
  sizeof(TW_INT16),
  sizeof(TW_INT32),
  sizeof(TW_UINT8),
  sizeof(TW_UINT16),
  sizeof(TW_UINT32),
  sizeof(TW_BOOL),
  sizeof(TW_FIX32),
  sizeof(TW_FRAME),
  sizeof(TW_STR32),
  sizeof(TW_STR64),
  sizeof(TW_STR128),
  sizeof(TW_STR255),
};

/***************************************************************************
* FloatToFIX32
*
* Convert a floating point value into a FIX32.
***************************************************************************/

TW_FIX32 Containr::FloatToFIX32(float AFloat) {

  TW_FIX32 Fix32_value;
  TW_INT32 Value = (TW_INT32) (AFloat * 65536.0 + 0.5);
  Fix32_value.Whole = (WORD) (Value >> 16);
  Fix32_value.Frac = (WORD) (Value & 0x0000ffffL);
  return(Fix32_value);
}

/***************************************************************************
* FIX32ToFloat
*
* Convert a FIX32 value into a floating point value
***************************************************************************/

float Containr::FIX32ToFloat(TW_FIX32 Fix32) {
  float AFloat;

  AFloat = (float) Fix32.Whole + ((float) Fix32.Frac / (float) 65536.0);
  return(AFloat);
}

/***************************************************************************
*GetItem
*
*Gets data item at lpSource[SIndex] of datatype Type
*and stores it at lpDest[DIndex].
***************************************************************************/
```

```
void Containr::GetItem(TW_UINT16 Type, LPVOID lpSource,
                       LPVOID lpDest, int SIndex, int DIndex) {

  switch (Type) {
    case TWTY_INT8:
      *((pTW_INT8)lpDest + DIndex) = * ((pTW_INT8)lpSource + SIndex);
      break;

    case TWTY_UINT8:
      *((pTW_UINT8)lpDest + DIndex) = *((pTW_UINT8)lpSource + SIndex);
      break;

    case TWTY_INT16:
    case 44:                    // TWTY_HANDLE
      *((pTW_INT16)lpDest + DIndex) = *((pTW_INT16)lpSource + SIndex);
      break;

    case TWTY_UINT16:
    case TWTY_BOOL:
      *((pTW_UINT16)lpDest + DIndex) = *((pTW_UINT16)lpSource + SIndex);
      break;

    case TWTY_INT32:
      *((pTW_INT32)lpDest + DIndex) = *((pTW_INT32)lpSource + SIndex);
      break;

    case TWTY_UINT32:
    case 43:                    // TWTY_MEMREF
      *((pTW_UINT32)lpDest + DIndex) = *((pTW_UINT32)lpSource + SIndex);
      break;

    case TWTY_FIX32:
      *((pTW_FIX32)lpDest + DIndex) = *((pTW_FIX32)lpSource + SIndex);
      break;

    case TWTY_STR32:
      lstrcpy((pTW_STR32)lpDest + DIndex, (pTW_STR32)lpSource + SIndex);
      break;

    case TWTY_STR64:
      lstrcpy((pTW_STR64)lpDest + DIndex, (pTW_STR64)lpSource + SIndex);
      break;

    case TWTY_STR128:
      lstrcpy((pTW_STR128)lpDest + DIndex, (pTW_STR128)lpSource + SIndex);
      break;

    case TWTY_STR255:
      lstrcpy((pTW_STR255)lpDest + DIndex, (pTW_STR255)lpSource + SIndex);
      break;
  }
}
```

```
/*********************************************************************
 * FUNCTION:      BuildUpOneValue
 *
 * ARGS:          pCap    pointer to a capability structure, details about
 *                        container
 *                ItemType constant that defines the type of the Item to follow
 *                Item    the data to put into the OneValue container
 *
 * RETURNS:       pData->hContainer set to address of the container handle, ptr is
 *                returned there. A TRUE BOOL is returned from this function if
 *                all is well and FALSE if container memory could not be allocated.
 *
 * NOTES:   This function creates a container of
 * type OneValue and returning with the hContainer value (excuse me)
 *"pointing" * to the container. The container is filled with the values
 *for ItemType * and Item requested by the caller.
 */


BOOL Containr::BuildUpOneValue(pTW_CAPABILITY pCap, TW_UINT16 ItemType,
  TW_UINT32 Item) {
  pTW_ONEVALUE pOneValue;

  if ((pCap->hContainer = (TW_HANDLE) GlobalAlloc(GHND,
    sizeof(TW_ONEVALUE))) != NULL) {
    // log the container type
    pCap->ConType = TWON_ONEVALUE;
    if ((pOneValue = (pTW_ONEVALUE)GlobalLock(pCap->hContainer)) != NULL) {
      pOneValue->ItemType = ItemType;       // TWTY_XXXX
      pOneValue->Item = Item;               // TWPT_XXXX...
      GlobalUnlock(pCap->hContainer);
      return TRUE;
    } else {                                // If lock error, free memory
      GlobalFree(pCap->hContainer);
      pCap->hContainer = 0;
    }
  }
  // Could not allocate or lock memory
  return FALSE;
}


/*********************************************************************
 * FUNCTION:  ExtractOneValue
 *
 * ARGS:      pCap   pointer to a capability structure, details about container
 *            pVoid  ptr will be set to point to the item on return
 *
 * RETURNS:   pVoid pts to extracted value.
 *
 * NOTES:   This routine will open a container and extract the Item. The Item
 * will be returned to the caller in pVoid. I will type cast the returned
 * value to that of ItemType.
 */
```

```
BOOL Containr::ExtractOneValue(pTW_CAPABILITY pCap, LPVOID pVoid) {
  pTW_ONEVALUE pOneValue;

  if ((pOneValue = (pTW_ONEVALUE)GlobalLock(pCap->hContainer)) != NULL) {
    // Extract the one value
    GetItem(pOneValue->ItemType, (LPVOID) &(pOneValue->Item), pVoid, 0, 0);
    GlobalUnlock(pCap->hContainer);
    return TRUE;
  }
  return FALSE;
}


/***********************************************************************
 * FUNCTION:  BuildUpEnumerationType
 *
 * ARGS:      pCap   pointer to a capability structure, details about container
 *            pE     ptr to struct that contains the other fields of
 *                   ENUM struct
 *            *pList ptr to array of elements to put into the ENUM array
 *
 * RETURNS:   pData->hContainer set to address of the container handle, ptr is
 *            returned here
 *
 * NOTES:   The routine dynamically allocates a chunk of memory large enough
 * to contain all the struct pTW_ENUMERATION as well as store it's ItemList
 * array INTERNAL to the struct. The array itself and it's elements must be
 * type cast to ItemType. I do not know how to dynamically cast elements
 * of an array to ItemType so it is time for a big static switch.>>>
 *
 * Protocol: Used by MSG_GET.. calls were Source allocates the container and the
 * APP uses and then frees the container.
 *
 */
BOOL Containr::BuildUpEnumerationType(pTW_CAPABILITY pCap, pTW_ENUMERATION pE,
                                      LPVOID lpList) {
  pTW_ENUMERATION pEnumeration;     // template for ENUM fields
  int Index;                        // anyone with more than 32K array elements
                                    // should crash. Could type on NumItems.
  LPVOID pVoid;

  // Allocate a block large enough for struct and complete enumeration array
  if ((pCap->hContainer = (TW_HANDLE) GlobalAlloc(GHND,
                        (sizeof(TW_ENUMERATION)-sizeof(TW_UINT8))+
                        pE->NumItems*DCItemSize[pE->ItemType])) == NULL)
    return FALSE;                   // return FALSE if memory error

  if ((pEnumeration = (pTW_ENUMERATION) GlobalLock(pCap->hContainer)) == NULL) {
    GlobalFree(pCap->hContainer); // return FALSE if memory error
    return FALSE;
  }

  pCap->ConType = TWON_ENUMERATION;                 // Fill in container type
  pEnumeration->ItemType = pE->ItemType;            // TWTY_XXXX
```

```
  pEnumeration->NumItems = pE->NumItems;              // TWPT_XXXX...
  pEnumeration->CurrentIndex = pE->CurrentIndex;      // current index setting
  pEnumeration->DefaultIndex = pE->DefaultIndex;      // default index setting
  // Assign base address of ItemList array to 'generic' pointer
  // i.e. reposition the struct pointer to overlay the allocated block
  pVoid = (LPVOID)pEnumeration->ItemList;
  // Now store the enumerated items
  for (Index=0; Index < (int)pE->NumItems; Index++)
    GetItem(pE->ItemType, (LPVOID) lpList, (LPVOID) pVoid, Index, Index);
  // Unlock the container
  GlobalUnlock(pCap->hContainer);
  return TRUE;
}

/***************************************************************************
 * FUNCTION: ExtractEnumerationValue
 *
 * ARGS:     pCap    pointer to a capability structure, details about container
 *           pVoid   ptr will be set to point to the item on return
 *           Index   requested index into the enumeration
 *
 * RETURNS: pVoid  is set to pointer to itemtype
 *
 * NOTES:   This routine will open a container and extract the Item. The
 * Item will be returned to the caller in pVoid. Returned value will
 * be type cast to that of ItemType.
 *
 * COMMENTS: only a single value is returned. It is referred to by the
 * indexed value.
 ***************************************************************************/

BOOL Containr::ExtractEnumerationValue(pTW_CAPABILITY pCap, LPVOID pVoid,
  UINT Index) {
  pTW_ENUMERATION pEnumeration;
  LPVOID pItemList;

  // Lock the container for access
  if ((pEnumeration = (pTW_ENUMERATION) GlobalLock(pCap->hContainer)) == NULL)
    return FALSE;

  // Check that Index is within range
  if (Index > pEnumeration->NumItems-1)
    return FALSE;

  // Assign base address of ItemList array to 'generic' pointer
  pItemList = (LPVOID) pEnumeration->ItemList;
  GetItem(pEnumeration->ItemType, pItemList, pVoid, Index, 0);
  GlobalUnlock(pCap->hContainer);
  return TRUE;
}

/***************************************************************************
 * FUNCTION:  BuildUpArrayType
 *
 * ARGS:      pCap    pointer to a capability structure, details about
 *                    container
```

```
*              pA      ptr to struct that contains the other fields of ARRAY struct
*              *pList  ptr to array of elements to put into the ARRAY struct
*
* RETURNS:   pData->hContainer set to address of the container handle, ptr is
            returned here
*
* NOTES: The routine dynamically allocates a chunk of memory large enough to
* contain all the struct pTW_ARRAY as well as store it's ItemList array
* INTERNAL to the struct. The array itself and it's elements must be
* type cast to ItemType.
*/

BOOL Containr::BuildUpArrayType(pTW_CAPABILITY pCap, pTW_ARRAY pA,
                                LPVOID lpList) {
  pTW_ARRAY pArray;
  int Index;                        // No more than 32K array elements
  LPVOID pVoid;

  // Allocate a block large enough for struct and complete array
  if ((pCap->hContainer = (TW_HANDLE) GlobalAlloc(GHND,
                      (sizeof(TW_ARRAY)-sizeof(TW_UINT8))+
                       pA->NumItems*DCItemSize[pA->ItemType])) == NULL)
    return FALSE;                   // Return FALSE if error

  // Lock the memory
  if ((pArray = (pTW_ARRAY) GlobalLock(pCap->hContainer)) == NULL) {
    GlobalFree(pCap->hContainer);
    return FALSE;                   // Return FALSE if error
  }
  pArray->ItemType = pA->ItemType;  // TWTY_XXXX
  pArray->NumItems = pA->NumItems;  // TWPT_XXXX...

  // Assign base address of ItemList array to 'generic' pointer
  // i.e. reposition the struct pointer to overlay the allocated block
  pVoid = (LPVOID)pArray->ItemList;
  // For each item of the array
  for (Index=0; Index < (int)pA->NumItems; Index++)
    GetItem(pA->ItemType, lpList, pVoid, Index, Index);

  // Unlock the memory
  GlobalUnlock(pCap->hContainer);
  return TRUE;
}

/*************************************************************************
* FUNCTION:      ExtractArrayValue
*
* ARGS:          pCap   pointer to a capability structure, details about
                        container
*                pVoid  ptr will be set to point to the item on return
*                Index  requested index into the array
*
* RETURNS:       pVoid  is set to pointer to itemtype
*
```

```
 * NOTES:          This routine will open a container and extract the Item. The
 * Item will be returned to the caller in pVoid. Returned value will
 * be type cast to that of ItemType.
 *
 * COMMENTS: only a single value is returned. It is referred to by the
 *   indexed value.
 */

BOOL Containr::ExtractArrayValue(pTW_CAPABILITY pCap, LPVOID pVoid, UINT Index) {
  pTW_ARRAY pArray;
  LPVOID pItemList;

  // Lock the container for access
  if ((pArray = (pTW_ARRAY) GlobalLock(pCap->hContainer)) == NULL)
    return FALSE;

  // Check that Index is within range
  if (Index > pArray->NumItems-1)
    return FALSE;

  // Assign base address of ItemList array to 'generic' pointer
  pItemList = (LPVOID) pArray->ItemList;
  GetItem(pArray->ItemType, pItemList, pVoid, Index, 0);
  GlobalUnlock(pCap->hContainer);
  return TRUE;
}


/****************************************************************************
 * FUNCTION:  BuildUpRangeType
 *
 * ARGS:     pCap     pointer to a capability structure, details about container
 *           lpRange ptr to RANGE struct
 *
 * RETURNS:  pCap->hContainer set to address of the container handle, ptr is
 *           returned here
 *
 * NOTES:    The routine dynamically allocates a chunk of memory large
 * enough to contain the RANGE struct.
 */

BOOL Containr::BuildUpRangeType(pTW_CAPABILITY pCap, pTW_RANGE lpRange) {

  pTW_RANGE pRange;

  // Allocate a block large enough for RANGE struct
  if ((pCap->hContainer = (TW_HANDLE) GlobalAlloc(GHND, sizeof(TW_RANGE))) ==
NULL)
    return FALSE;                    // Return FALSE if error
  // Lock the memory
  if ((pRange = (pTW_RANGE) GlobalLock(pCap->hContainer)) == NULL) {
    GlobalFree(pCap->hContainer);
    return FALSE;                    // Return FALSE if error
  }
  // Copy complete RANGE structure
  *pRange = *lpRange;
```

```
  // Unlock the memory
  GlobalUnlock(pCap->hContainer);
  return TRUE;
}

/***************************************************************************
 * FUNCTION: ExtractRange
 *
 * ARGS:      pCap    pointer to a capability structure, details about container
 *            lpRange ptr to RANGE struct for return
 *
 * NOTES:     This routine will open a container and extract the RANGE.
 *
 * COMMENTS: the complete RANGE struct is returned at lpRange.
 */

BOOL Containr::ExtractRange(pTW_CAPABILITY pCap, pTW_RANGE) lpRange) {
  pTW_RANGE pRange;

  // Lock the container for access
  if ((pRange = (pTW_RANGE) GlobalLock(pCap->hContainer)) == NULL)
    return FALSE;
  // Copy the complete structure
  *lpRange = *pRange;

  GlobalUnlock(pCap->hContainer);
  return TRUE;
}
```

The function **FloatToFIX32** converts a C floating point value into a TW_FIX32 value. Floating point values are passed to a TWAIN source from an application in 32-bit fixed point format as embodied in a TW_FIX32 number.

The function **FIX32ToFloat** performs the inverse conversion, from a fixed point TW_FIX32 number back into a C float. An application must convert TW_FIX32 numbers passed from a source into C floating point format before they can be manipulated by the application.

The private member function, **GetItem**, is used by many of the container functions for storage and retrieval of data. This function can move TWAIN data of any defined type from one place to another in memory. The incorporation of source and destination indexes, SIndex and DIndex, allows the code maximum flexibility when fetching and storing data. You'll note that there is a separate case for each data type implemented with a C switch statement.

The function **BuildUpOneValue** is the simplest of the container *build* functions. **BuildUpOneValue** constructs a one-value container object from the parameters passed to it. A block of global memory, the size required for storage of a one-value container, is first allocated using the Windows **GlobalAlloc** function. Next, the one-value container is labeled as to the type of data it contains, and finally it is filled with one item of data. If the function is successful, the global memory block is unlocked, and its handle is returned indirectly through a capability structure and the function returns a Boolean TRUE.

ExtractOneValue opens up a one-value container contained in a block of memory and extracts the one data value it contains. The data is stored at a location in memory passed in as a parameter to this function.

The function, **BuildUpEnumerationType**, is a bit more complex than **BuildUpOneValue** because of the inherent complexity of the enumeration data type. Within an enumeration container are an enumeration data structure and the enumerated data. The size of an enumeration container depends on the data type and the number of items included in the container. Building the container proceeds in a similar fashion to that previously described. Memory is allocated for the whole container, the enumeration data structure within the container is filled in with the appropriate values, the **GetItem** function is called to move the enumerated values into the container memory, and, finally, the memory is unlocked and the handle passed back to the calling function. TRUE is returned if all went well.

ExtractEnumerationValue retrieves a single value from an enumeration container as specified by an index. **GetItem** is used here to move data from the container's memory to a memory location specified for the returned value.

The functions **BuildUpArrayType** and **ExtractArrayValue** operate almost identically to the enumeration functions previously described and will therefore not be discussed. The functions **BuildUpRangeType** and **ExtractRange** are similar also except that they deal with range type containers. All data that can be contained in a range container is contained in the TW_RANGE data structure. Therefore, **BuildUpRangeType** requires a pointer to a TW_RANGE data structure to be stored into a container, and **ExtractRange** returns a complete TW_RANGE data structure from a range container.

It is extremely important to note that it is always the application program's responsibility to release any memory occupied by containers when finished with them. This is true whether the container memory was originally allocated by the Source or by the application.

Capability Negotiations

It is via capability negotiations that an application program informs a Source about the type of image(s) that it desires or that it can deal with. For example, if an application wants to handle only color images but is connected to a Source capable of both color and gray scale images the application would negotiate the ICAP_PIXELTYPE capability with the Source. (See the functions **SetPixelTypes** and **RestrictToRGB** in Listing 8.2 for exactly this type of negotiation.) A successful negotiation of this capability would result in the UI for the Source not allowing the selection of gray scale images. Therefore the Source could only acquire color images for the application.

Most negotiations that take place between an application and a Source are of a similar form. The application first asks the Source its abilities in a certain area (a capability). The Source returns a container describing its abilities. The application then chooses from what the Source said it could do and requests the Source to limit its ability to a certain subset of its capability. The Source will either agree or disagree to the application's request. Capability negotiations are made tricky by the fact that Sources are not required by the specification to negotiate on every conceivable capability. Some Sources will not even negotiate on capabilities the specification says they must negotiate. For these reasons, the application program must be ready for a refusal to negotiate at any point in the negotiation process.

To illustrate the process of negotiation, refer to the function **SetResolution** from Listing 8.2. This function accepts as a parameter a specification in dots per inch (DPI) for the maximum resolution the application wants the attached TWAIN device to acquire at. The negotiation performed results in the Source allowing acquisition in any resolution up to and including the specified DPI value. In terms a user will understand, the resolution selection function in the Source's UI will not show resolutions greater than the specified value.

To begin the negotiation, we must inquire of the Source which resolutions it supports. This is done by sending a GET message on the Source's ICAP_XRESOLUTION capability. The messaging is done by properly forming the parameters and calling the DSM_Entry point discussed previously. The TWAIN specification says that a container of One Value, Range, or Enumeration type can be used to return the XResolution capability data. For this reason, the code must be prepared to parse any of these returned container types. The returned data type for the XResolution capability is specified in the specification as TW_FIX32, a fixed point representation of a floating point number. So each possible container must contain at least one FIX32 value.

The various container types are processed using a switch statement on the returned container type. If a One-Value container type is returned, the Source is capable of only a single resolution, and therefore no negotiations are possible. If the Source returns a Range container, all values less than or equal to the requested resolution are stored for later use. The same is true of all values returned in an Enumeration container. Once all of the data in the returned container is parsed, the container memory is freed.

At this point, all resolutions supported by the Source and that meet our specification have been saved. The application must now tell the Source (ask the Source nicely?) which resolutions it is free to use. This is done by forming an Enumeration container containing the allowed values in FIX32 format and passing this to the Source via a SET message on the ICAP_XRESOLUTION capability. If the Source accepts the request, it will limit the resolution selections provided in its UI to just those specified values. It may, however, still refuse the negotiation.

Negotiation must take place within certain states of the TWAIN protocol; for example, to negotiate with a source, we must have first loaded and executed the Source Manager and then opened a Source. Only then will the Source be available for the negotiation of capabilities. Most capabilities must be negotiated in this state (state four according to the specification) although a mechanism exists within the specification for extended negotiation in other states. See the TWAIN document for the details.

The TWAIN Class Code

Listing 8.1, the file "twain.hpp", shows the interface specification for the Twain class and various assorted data structures needed for scanning. The most important of the ancillary data structure is IMAGEDESCRIPTOR, which is used to maintain information about a scanned image. Its use will be described shortly. The enumerated data type "TransferType" determines how image data is sourced by the "mytwain.dll". If a THRU_MEMORY transfer type is used, the image data from the TWAIN device are returned in an IMAGEDESCRIPTOR structure. If THRU_FILE is used, the data are written directly to a graphics file (using the Compand DLL described in Chapter 4), and no data are returned to the application through memory. Finally, if THRU_FILEANDMEMORY is specified, the data are returned in an IMAGEDESCRIPTOR structure and are also written to a graphics file.

The Twain class consists of 17 private member functions and 6 public ones. A brief synopsis of the member functions is provided subsequently.

The **PaintMemoryMessage** function is called during the processing of the Paint message of the background window. The background window is a window that obscures the application program's window and is the parent of the TWAIN Sources' UI. The **PaintMemoryMessage** function analyzes the amount of virtual memory available and prints a message at the bottom of the background window, suggesting the maximum size of the image that can be scanned given the amount of virtual memory available and the conditions under which the image is to be processed. This function will cause image scanning to be aborted if not enough memory is available for processing a scanned image.

The **ProcessImageData** function post processes the data returned from an image scan. First, it builds a palette for the image if the image is black and white or palettized. Next, if the image is a true color RGB image, the image data must be manipulated to convert the RGB (storage order red, then green, then blue) data returned by the scanner to BGR (storage order blue, then green, then red) as required for the Windows 24-bit DIB format. Finally, it compresses the image data into a graphics file if the specified transfer type is THRU_FILE or THRU_FILEANDMEMORY or fills in the IMAGEDESCRIPTOR structure with information about the image if the image data are to be passed back through memory.

TransferImage is called internally within the Twain class when an image is about to be transferred from the scanner to the application program. Within this function, information about the pending image transfer is requested from the Source, and, subsequently, the memory block required for storage of the scanned image data is allocated. The function **GetCompleteImage** is then called to actually perform the transfer of the image data through memory.

GetCompleteImage first asks the Source its preference for the size of buffer to use to perform the image data transfer. A buffer no larger than SOURCEBUFFEROVERHEAD is then allocated for moving image data between the Source and the memory block allocated by **TransferImage.** With the buffer size decided, a while loop is used to transfer the image data through memory one buffer at a time. Note: As the image data are read from the scanner, they are stored inverted in memory as is required by the Windows DIB format.

The function **ProcessDCMessage,** which is called within the message loop of the Background window, routes messages to and from the Source's modeless dialog UI when it is active. It traps two important events sent from the Source to the application program. The first, MSG_XFERREADY, is sent when the Source has an image ready to transfer. Reception of MSG_XFERREADY subsequently calls **TransferImage.** The second, MSG_CLOSEDSREQ, or close data source request is sent when the Source wants its data source closed. This can occur at the end of image data transfer or when the user clicks a cancel or close button in the Source's UI.

Whenever errors occur in a TWAIN transaction, the Source Manager provides a mechanism for ascertaining the root cause of the error. The function **ExplainError** encapsulates this mechanism for use within the DLL. Whenever an error is detected in any of the Twain class functions, a call to **ExplainError** is made to display a message box with an appropriate error message to the user. The error message strings are read from the resource to avoid cluttering up the DLL's data space.

The function **SetPixelTypes** limits the types of images that a TWAIN Source should provide to the application program. This code is an excellent example of capability negotiation between the application program (this DLL) and a TWAIN Source. When this function is called, the Source is instructed to provide only black and white, gray scale, palettized color, and RGB true color images. If your application wants to restrict the types of images a connected Source can deliver, your changes would probably go into this function.

SetXferMechanism informs the Source about the type of image data transfer to perform. For our use in the DLL, the Source is always instructed to use through memory transfer. Some Sources can write the images directly to disk in standard graphic file formats, and some even provide JPEG data compression. If you wish to use any of these advanced possibilities, you need to understand the capabilities provided by your scanner. Although not used in the DLL currently, the function **Setup-FileTransfer** illustrates how a scanner can be requested to write a scanned image directly to disk as a TIFF file.

The function **OpenDSM** opens the (data) Source Manager if it is not already open. The function **CloseDSM** obviously close the Source Manager if it is indeed open. The functions **OpenDS** and **CloseDS** perform the open and close operations on the currently selected Source. The functions **EnableDS** and **DisableDS** make the Source's user interface visible and invisible, respectively. The final private function, **SelectDS,** is called when the Source Manager needs to put up the Source selection dialog box for the user to interact with.

There are only five public member functions that a user of the Twain DLL needs to be concerned with. Of course, the class constructor is called whenever an object of the Twain class is instantiated. No parameters are required by the constructor. The function **SelectSource** would be called when the Source selection dialog box is to be presented to the user. Three **ScanImage** functions are provided to allow flexibility in how images are delivered to the application. The first **ScanImage** function returns the image data contained in shared memory and described by an IMAGEDESCRIP-TOR. The second function causes the image data to be written directly to a graphics file. The third and final **ScanImage** function causes the data to be written to a graphics file and returned in an IMAGEDESCRIPTOR. Which function you call in your application to scan an image is dictated by your application's needs.

The Twain code that implements the class member functions described earlier is somewhat complex, and Listing 8.2 will need some study to understand. The code is heavily commented to help with its understanding. This code was partially derived from the code provided in TWAIN tool kit. The code was intentionally structured as a series of small functions to keep the complexity down.

As is required for all 16-bit DLLs and some 32-bit DLLs, a **LibMain** procedure is declared. The only function performed by **LibMain** is the registration of the window that will be used as a backdrop for the Source's user interface. A backdrop window is required because I wanted the DLL to process all messages to and from the Source instead of having the application program window do it. Thus all of the required functionality of the Twain class is encapsulated within the DLL. To do otherwise would have complicated the DLL interface substantially, with no benefit increase in functionality.

When the Twain class is instantiated, the only action performed is the creation of the AppIdentity structure. This structure is used to tell the Source Manager and the Source about the application that is requesting service. This is the mechanism by which all of the players involved in a TWAIN transaction keep track of one another.

The only part of this code that might be difficult to understand is what happens when a **ScanImage** function is called. When this function is called, it sets in motion a whole series of events that results in the display of the Source's user interface for image acquisition. The sequence of events that result in an acquired image are summarized as follows:

1. The **ScanImage** function calls **CreateWindow** to create the backdrop window. This window is sent a message to maximize itself to full screen, thus obscuring the actual application program's window. Finally, a message loop (for the backdrop window) is entered. Control will not return from the **ScanImage** function call until the backdrop window is disposed of.

    The message loop for the background window is normal except that it calls the function **ProcessDCMessage** as long as a data source is open. This function is waiting for the Source to post a message indicating either an image is ready to transfer from the device or that the user has requested that the Source be closed. Processing of the background window messages is performed in the function **BackDropWndProc** shown in the listing.

2. When the WM_CREATE message from the backdrop window is processed by **BackDropWndProc,** the Source Manager is opened, the currently selected Source is opened for use, and all negotiations between the application and the Source are performed. These negotiations are in the form of functions that are called before processing of the WM_CREATE message is completed. If an error occurs during any of the subsequent negotiations, the WM_CREATE processing will return a –1, thereby aborting the creation of the backdrop window. The negotiations performed at this time are the image transfer count is set to one, the transfer mechanism to be used by the Source is set to through memory, and the acceptable image types are negotiated. If all of these negotiations were successful, a zero is returned, and the background window is allowed to become visible.

3. When the backdrop window receives its first WM_PAINT message, the function **EnableDS** is called to bring up the Source's UI over the backdrop window. When this happens, the user should see and be able to interact with the Source's user interface. In other words, the user should be able to scan an image. Once the UI is visible, a flag is set to prevent another call to **EnableDS.** Also, during processing of the paint message, the **PaintMemoryMessage** function is called to inform the user of the maximum size allowed for a scanned image. Finally, the handle of the Source's UI window is stored away for use in WM_SETFOCUS message processing. Notice that if any errors occur, the Source and the Source Manager are closed down and the backdrop window destroyed.

4. When the user instructs the Source to scan an image, a MSG_XFER-READY message is sent to the backdrop window and is processed by the **ProcessDCMessage** function previously discussed. As a result, the **TransferImage** function is called to facilitate the transfer of the image from the device. This function and **GetCompleteImage** should be studied to understand how an image gets transferred. When an image is transferred, a WM_XFERDONE message is sent to the backdrop window procedure, indicating an image was transferred. The wParam of this message is TRUE if the transfer was successful and FALSE if an error occurred or the user aborted the transfer. If success is indicated, the ScanResults flag is also set TRUE. This flag is returned as status to the function that called **ScanImage.**

5. When the user closes the Source's UI, a MSG_CLOSEREQ message is posted to the backdrop window and processed by the **ProcessDCMessage** function. This message calls **DisableDS** to get rid of the UI, calls **CloseDS** to close the data Source, calls **CloseDSM** to close the Source Manager, and then calls the Windows function **DestroyWindow** to break down the backdrop window. As soon as the backdrop window is destroyed, control is returned from the **ScanImage** function into the application program that called it. Thus, the acquisition of an image is complete.

From the previous summary discussion and the availability of the listings, you should be able to ascertain how images are acquired using this DLL.

Problems with "Standard" TWAIN Implementations

As great a standard as TWAIN is, there are still compatibility problems that arise between devices and applications that both claim to be "TWAIN compliant." One reason for these problems is that a compatibility test suite does not exist that developers can run on their Source or their application program to ascertain true compliance. The volumes of textual information presented in the written TWAIN specification is open to a certain amount of interpretation, hence the possibility of incompatibilities.

The 16-bit version of the code presented in this chapter has been tested with six different TWAIN devices from five different manufacturers. The 32-bit code was tested with only one device because of the lack of 32-bit Sources available at the time this book was written. Of all of the devices tested, about half experienced some form of incompatibility. This incompatibility meant that the code contained in the DLL had to be changed to make the devices work even though the devices were usually at fault (in my opinion). This is an unfortunate fact of life when you must make your product work in a short period of time with a great many different scanners. Because the scanner manufacturers cannot react fast enough to fix problems in their Source code, I had to add and/or change code in the DLL to make their product work. Fortunately, the structure of the TWAIN code is such that the code in the DLL can always find out which scanner it is connected to and change the protocol slightly to make the scanner work (famous last words). An example of this can be found in the function **SetImageXferCount** in Listing 8.2.

In testing this code with the Canon CJ-10 scanner/copier, it was determined that their TWAIN Source would not negotiate transfer count (CAP_XFERCOUNT) even though the TWAIN specification explicitly says that all devices must negotiate this. Their Source's failure to negotiate this basic capability caused my code to error, making it look like my code had a problem. The solution to this problem, until such time as the CJ10's Source is revised, was to not attempt the negotiation of the capability when the CJ10 was recognized as the data source. A quick check of the SourceIdentity structure maintained by TWAIN against the product name "Canon CJ10 Scan" allowed me to bypass the erred negotiation and make the Canon device work with my code. However kludgey this seems, at least the specification gives a documented way of identifying the currently selected Source and a way of reacting to it (read that as working around any problems it might have) in a structured manner.

Some of the other problems I encountered in making the DLL code presented here work with various TWAIN devices include:

1. The TWAIN specification indicates that memory references passed between application programs and Sources can be in the form of either handles or pointers. The application program indicates its preference by telling the Source which to use. The problem is that some TWAIN Sources ignore the preferences stated by the application. Luckily, all Sources encountered to date will accept a pointer to memory. Some, however, will not accept a handle to the same memory.

2. Some TWAIN Sources will not pass back a palette when palettized gray scale images are acquired. My code had to change to generate a default gray scale palette for these images.

3. Some TWAIN Sources are fussy about the order in which their UI is closed in relation to the closure of the Background window maintained in the DLL. The order now maintained in the function **ProcessDCMessage** works with most scanners.

Fortunately for you, I have had to work through these problems, and the fixes I put in place are embodied within the code presented. Do be advised, however, if you use this code with a scanner that has not previously been tested, you face the real possibility of an incompatibility surfacing. In those cases, you will need to read and understand the TWAIN specification in detail and will need to run through the code with a debugger to determine what is failing. Once you understand the problem, a fix should not be far behind.

How to Use the Code Presented

All of the code described in this chapter is available in the Chapter 8 archive file on the companion disc. Please see the instructions given in Appendix A for retrieving the Chapter 8 files. To use the code, the code must be compiled and linked into a Windows DLL called "mytwain.dll". This process is accomplished using the project files provided. After a DLL is built, an LIB file must be generated from it for inclusion into the application program. LIB files are built various ways, depending on the programming environment. Please consult your development tools documentation for instructions on building an LIB file from the DLL.

To use this DLL within your application program's code, you must link the LIB file (called "mytwain.lib") into your application. With that done, your application code will be able to instantiate an object of the class Twain for use. One approach follows:

```
#include "twain.hpp"  // Included for the class definition
Twain MyTwainObject;  // Instantiate object. No parameters to the constructor are
required

// To select a TWAIN Source for use
MyTwainObject.SelectSource(Parent Window's Handle);

// To scan an image and save it in the file "testing.bmp", use
MyTwainOBject.ScanImage("testimg.bmp", BMPTYPE, 0);
```

These are basically the actions performed within the TestApp program to implement scanning. It is important to note that an application program using this TWAIN code must be prepared for handling the amount of data that can be produced by a scanner; for example, a 3- × 5-inch photograph scanned at 500 dots per inch (DPI) can approach 18 megabytes in size. Obviously, a lot of thought must be given as to how these images are to be held in memory and manipulated if the results of a scan are to be observable to a user in his or her lifetime.

Conclusions

This chapter has attempted to shed light on the use of TWAIN for control of raster image-generating devices. A Windows DLL was discussed that can be used to add TWAIN capabilities to virtually any Windows application in short order. For those readers requiring more information, additional sources for TWAIN information were provided.

CHAPTER

9

Imaging Processing Techniques for Windows

> In this chapter you will learn about:
> - The science of Image Processing
> - The application of that science to practical imaging
> - The categories of image-processing algorithms
> - How the TProcessImage class encapsulates the provided image-processing algorithms
> - How various image-processing algorithms work including image brightness adjustment, contrast adjustment, cropping, rotation, filtering, despeckling, edge enhancement, histogram equalization, and much, much more

Introduction

Image processing is a science that deals with images and image data. Image processing covers a broad spectrum of techniques that are applicable to a wide range of applications and sciences. Image processing can be thought of as a special form of two-dimensional signal processing used to uncover information about images. In general, image-processing techniques are applied to images or image data when:

- Enhancement or modification of an image is necessary to improve appearance or to highlight some aspect of the information contained in the image.
- Elements within an image need to be categorized, classified, matched, or measured.

- Portions of images need to be combined or a reorganization of image elements needs to be performed.

The techniques of image processing can be applied to data even if it did not originate in visible image form. The manipulation of visible image data is just one of the many uses of image processing, though probably the most predominate one. Image processing can be used to produce a visible image of purely numerical data enhanced in some manner to highlight some aspect of the data. Examples of this kind of image processing can be found in magnetic resonant medical imaging equipment, sonar, radar, ultrasound equipment, heat-sensing equipment, fractals, and so on. Humans, after all, can understand and interpret data easier in visual as opposed to purely numerical form.

The result of applying an image-processing algorithm to an image is not always done with the appearance of the image in mind. Actually, the result might not be pleasing to look at. Aesthetics are not the only criteria on which to judge the effectiveness of the applied image-processing transformations. If the transformation is designed to bring out additional information and/or details not visible in the original image, the result can be considered successful even if not pleasing to look at.

The focus of this chapter is not on the science of image processing but rather on the application of that science to photographic imagery. A rigorous discussion of image processing will not be presented in this chapter, nor anywhere else in the book. Instead a discussion of the image-processing algorithms that have been incorporated into the TestApp imaging example program of Chapter 1 will be presented. The discussions will show how the specific image-processing algorithms have been integrated into the TestApp program, in addition to showing how the algorithmic processing is made to fit into the overall imaging architecture presented in Chapter 1.

The image-processing algorithms that are provided are given a detailed discussion. This discussion is, however, slanted toward implementation and usage issues and away from the rigorous math upon which the algorithms are based. The result of this approach is that the image-processing algorithms can be used in a cookbook manner without having to completely understand their mathematical underpinnings. Of course, the results obtained will be more controllable if the mathematics behind the transformations is fully understood and can therefore be manipulated. Throughout the technical explanations that follow, a basic understanding of algebra and trigonometry is assumed. Please note that the image-processing algorithms presented in this chapter are useful in programming environments other than Windows. There is nothing Windows specific about the algorithms themselves but only how they are implemented to fit within the Windows environment.

You may notice while experimenting (playing) with the TestApp example program of Chapter 1 that many of the image-processing operations take a considerable amount of time to perform. The reasons for this include:

1. High-resolution images with lots of pixels require a lot of calculations.
2. The image-processing algorithms are all coded in C++. No assembly language was used in an attempt to increase or optimize performance.
3. No coding tricks were used. The code is very straightforward and is written with clarity more than speed in mind.

For these reasons, the more powerful the computer you have at your disposal, the better. If performance becomes an issue, you might try rewriting some of the C++ image-processing support functions in assembly language. It should be possible to gain nearly an order of magnitude improvement in performance with this relatively minor modification.

Image-Processing Basics

Most image-processing algorithms fall into one of the following categories:

1. **Point Processes.** These are processes that alter pixel values in an image based only on the original value of the pixel and possibly its location within an image.
2. **Area Processes.** These are processes that alter a pixel value based on its original value and the values of the pixels that surround it.
3. **Frame Processes.** These processes alter pixel values within an image based on the pixel values present in one or more additional images.
4. **Geometric Processes.** These processes alter the arrangement or placement of pixels in an image based on some geometric transformation.

Examples of algorithms in each category (except Frame Processes) will be provided and discussed. These algorithms can be applied to an image individually or in conjunction with other algorithms either within the same category or of different categories. Please note that the application of image-processing algorithms are not commutative in nature; that is, the order of application is very important in achieving the effect you desire.

Before the discussion can begin, it is necessary to define a few terms that will be used throughout this chapter.

Spatial resolution is the number of samples used to define an image. Spatial, in the image-processing context, refers to space. The higher the spatial resolution, the higher quality the image. Spatial resolution is usually thought of as a two-dimensional quantity organized into columns and rows. The intersection of each column and row contains a digitized sample taken from an image.

Spatial frequency is the rate of change of image pixel intensity. Spatial frequency is a two-dimensional quantity because pixel intensity can and does change in both the horizontal and vertical directions simultaneously. Portions of images that have constant or nearly constant intensity pixel values are said to have low spatial frequency content. Images with wildly fluctuating pixel intensity values have high spatial frequency content.

Brightness resolution is the total number of unique values used to express pixel intensity values in an image. Brightness resolution is related to the number of bits used to store each image sample; for example, with eight bits for each pixel of a gray scale image, there is a total of 256 unique brightness levels possible.

The following table categorizes the image-processing operations provided by the TestApp program of Chapter 1. A miscellaneous category is provided for those operations that do not fall neatly into one of the classic categories but that can still be considered an image-processing operation. All of the operations except Quantize Image and Dither Image will be discussed in this chapter. Both Quantize Image and Dither Image were discussed in Chapter 5.

Image Process	*Point Process*	*Area Process*	*Geometric Process*	*Miscellaneous Process*
Copy/Paste Image				x
Duplicate Image				x
Brightness Adjustment	x			
Contrast Adjustment	x			
Rotate Image			x	
Flip Image			x	
Crop Image			x	
Resize Image			x	
Sharpen Image (High-Pass Filtering)		x		
Soften Image (Low-Pass Filtering)		x		
Edge Enhancement		x		
Despeckle Image (Median Filtering)		x		
Histogram Equalization	x			
Quantize Image				x
Dither Image				x
Convert to 8 BPP gray				x
Promote to 24 BPP				x

Almost all of the image-processing code described in this chapter is part of the TProcessImage class and is comprised of the files "imgproc.hpp" shown in Listing 9.1 and "imgproc.cpp" which is shown in Listing 9.2. The exceptions are:

1. The code for the Duplicate Image function is spread between the files "tappchil.cpp" and "tappcli.cpp".
2. The code for the Quantize Image function for the most part resides in the files "mcquan.hpp" and "mcquan.cpp". The quantization code is executed, however, by way of a call to the Quantize member function of TProcess-Image.
3. The code for the Dither Image function resides in the files "dither.hpp" and "dither.cpp". The dithering code is executed by way of a call to the Dither member function of TProcessImage.

Figure 9.1 provides a detailed description of the TProcessImage class member functions.

Listing 9.1 The TProcessImage class interface definition.

```
/**********************************************************/
/***                                                  ***/
/***                  "imgproc.hpp"                    ***/
/***          Image Processing Class Definitions       ***/
/***                   written by                      ***/
/***                 Craig A. Lindley                   ***/
/***                                                  ***/
/***     Revision: 2.0     Last Update: 11/11/94       ***/
/**********************************************************/
```

```
// Copyright (c) 1955 John Wiley & Sons, Inc. All rights reserved.

#ifndef IMGPROC_HPP
#define IMGPROC_HPP

#include <owlpch.h>
#pragma hdrstop

#include "tappchil.hpp"        // TestAppMDIChild class definitions

#define ALIGN_DWORD(x) (((x)+3)/4 * 4) // Double word alignment macro
#define MAXCOLORLEVELS 256             // Max colors in a 256 color palettized image

// Definitions required for convolution image filtering
#define KERNELCOLS 3
#define KERNELROWS 3
#define KERNELELEMENTS (KERNELCOLS * KERNELROWS)

typedef struct {
  int Element[KERNELELEMENTS];
  int Divisor;
} KERNEL;

// Process Image Class Definition
class TProcessImage {
  private:
     TestAppMDIChild *pMDIChild;
     int ContrastTbl [MAXCOLORLEVELS];
     int BriteAdjustValue;
     int ContrastAdjustValue;

     // These values are extracted from the IMAGEDESCRIPTOREXT in the
     // child MDI window. They are used throughout this class.
     WORD TPIWidth;
     WORD TPIHeight;
     DWORD TPIRasterSize;
     WORD TPIBPP;
     WORD TPIColors;
     HGLOBAL TPIhImageData;
     RGBCOLOR TPIPalette[256];
     BYTE huge *TPIlpImageData;
     HWND TPIhWindow;
     DWORD TPIBytesPerLine8BPP;
     DWORD TPIBytesPerLine24BPP;

     BOOL ConvoluteImage(KERNEL *, int DefaultStrength, LPSTR Desc);
     BOOL RotateImage(BOOL Clockwise);
        BOOL FlipImage(BOOL FlipHorizontally);
     void BuildNewDisplayObject (void);
     void CleanUp(HGLOBAL hMem, HPALETTE hPalette);

  public:
     TProcessImage(TestAppMDIChild *pTestAppMDIChild);
    ~TProcessImage(void);
```

```
    BOOL ImageToClipboard(void);
    BOOL ImageFromClipboard(IMAGEDESCRIPTOR& ID);

    void BeginCrop (void);
    void EndCrop(POINT& BegPt, POINT& EndPt);

    void AdjustBrightnessContrast(void);
    void RotateCW(void);
    void RotateCCW(void);
    void FlipHorz(void);
    void FlipVert(void);
    void Resize(void);
    void HighPass1(void);
    void HighPass2(void);
    void HighPass3(void);
    void LowPass1(void);
    void LowPass2(void);
    void LowPass3(void);
    void NorthEdges(void);
    void NorthEastEdges(void);
    void EastEdges(void);
    void SouthEastEdges(void);
    void SouthEdges(void);
    void SouthWestEdges(void);
    void WestEdges(void);
    void NorthWestEdges(void);
    void Despeckle(void);
    void HistogramEq(void);
    void Quantize(void);
    void Dither(void);
    void ConvertToGray(void);
    void PromoteTo24BPP(void);
};

#endif
```

Listing 9.2 The TProcessImage class member functions.

```
/********************************************************/
/***                 "imgproc.cpp"                  ***/
/***        Image Processing Class Functions        ***/
/***                  written by                    ***/
/***              Craig A. Lindley                   ***/
/***                                                 ***/
/***     Revision: 2.0    Last Update: 11/11/94      ***/
/********************************************************/

// Copyright (c) 1995 John Wiley & Sons, Inc. All rights reserved.

#include <math.h>
#include "imgproc.hpp"
#include "dialogs.hpp"          // Dialog box definitions and functions
#include "mcquant.hpp"
#include "dither.hpp"
```

```
#define MINCROPWIDTH    10        // Min size of cropping to allow
#define MINCROPHEIGHT   10

DWORD CalculateBytesPerLine(WORD Width, WORD BPP);

// The following kernel definitions are for convolution filtering.
// Kernel entries are specified with a divisor to get around the
// requirement for floating point numbers in the low pass filters.

KERNEL HP1 = {                    // HP filter #1
  {-1, -1, -1,
   -1,  9, -1,
   -1, -1, -1},
    1                             // Divisor = 1
};

KERNEL HP2 = {                    // HP filter #2
  { 0, -1,  0,
   -1,  5, -1,
    0, -1,  0},
    1                             // Divisor = 1
};

KERNEL HP3 = {                    // HP filter #3
  { 1, -2,  1,
   -2,  5, -2,
    1, -2,  1},
    1                             // Divisor = 1
};

KERNEL LP1 = {                    // LP filter #1
  { 1,  1,  1,
    1,  1,  1,
    1,  1,  1},
    9                             // Divisor = 9
};

KERNEL LP2 = {                    // LP filter #2
  { 1,  1,  1,
    1,  2,  1,
    1,  1,  1},
   10                             // Divisor = 10
};

KERNEL LP3 = {                    // LP filter #3
  { 1,  2,  1,
    2,  4,  2,
    1,  2,  1},
   16                             // Divisor = 16
};

KERNEL EdgeNorth = {              // North gradient
  { 1,  1,  1,
    1, -2,  1,
   -1, -1, -1},
    1                             // Divisor = 1
};
```

```
KERNEL EdgeNorthEast = {              // North East gradient
  { 1,   1,   1,
   -1,  -2,   1,
   -1,  -1,   1},
    1                                 // Divisor = 1
};

KERNEL EdgeEast = {                   // East gradient
  {-1,   1,   1,
   -1,  -2,   1,
   -1,   1,   1},
    1                                 // Divisor = 1
};

KERNEL EdgeSouthEast = {              // South East gradient
  {-1,  -1,   1,
   -1,  -2,   1,
    1,   1,   1},
    1                                 // Divisor = 1
};

KERNEL EdgeSouth = {                  // South gadient
  {-1,  -1,  -1,
    1,  -2,   1,
    1,   1,   1},
    1                                 // Divisor = 1
};

KERNEL EdgeSouthWest = {              // South West gradient
  { 1,  -1,  -1,
    1,  -2,  -1,
    1,   1,   1},
    1                                 // Divisor = 1
};

KERNEL EdgeWest = {                   // West gradient
  { 1,   1,  -1,
    1,  -2,  -1,
    1,   1,  -1},
    1                                 // Divisor = 1
};

KERNEL EdgeNorthWest = {              // North West gradient
  { 1,   1,   1,
    1,  -2,  -1,
    1,  -1,  -1},
    1                                 // Divisor = 1
};

// Masks for bit manipulation in PromoteTo24BPP function
BYTE Masks [] = {
  0x00,  // Unused
  0x01,  // Mask for 1 bits
  0x03,  // Mask for 2 bits
  0x00,  // Unused
  0x0F   // Mask for 4 bits
};
```

```
// ProcessImage Class Functions
// Class Constructor. This constructor is usually called with a valid
// child window pointer. However, it may be called with a NULL pointer
// when using the ImageFromClipboard function.
TProcessImage::TProcessImage(TestAppMDIChild *pTestAppMDIChild) {

   if (pTestAppMDIChild) {              // If ptr is valid
      // Store the pointer to the child window object
      pMDIChild = pTestAppMDIChild;

      // Extract important image parameters from the MDI child's
      // IMAGEDESCRIPTOREXT structure.

      TPIWidth      = pMDIChild->ID.ImgDesc.Width;
      TPIHeight     = pMDIChild->ID.ImgDesc.Height;
      TPIRasterSize = pMDIChild->ID.ImgDesc.RasterSize;
      TPIBPP        = pMDIChild->ID.ImgDesc.BPP;
      TPIColors     = pMDIChild->ID.ImgDesc.Colors;
      TPIhImageData = pMDIChild->ID.ImgDesc.hImageData;
      memcpy(TPIPalette, pMDIChild->ID.ImgDesc.Palette,
          sizeof(RGBCOLOR) * MAXCOLORLEVELS);
      TPIlpImageData = pMDIChild->ID.lpImageData;
      TPIhWindow = pMDIChild->HWindow;
      TPIBytesPerLine8BPP = CalculateBytesPerLine(TPIWidth, 8);
      TPIBytesPerLine24BPP = CalculateBytesPerLine(TPIWidth, 24);
   } else {                             // Pointer was null
      TPIWidth      = 0;
      TPIHeight     = 0;
      TPIRasterSize = 0;
      TPIBPP        = 0;
      TPIColors     = 0;
      TPIhImageData = 0;
      memset(TPIPalette, 0, sizeof(TPIPalette));
      TPIlpImageData = 0;
      TPIhWindow = 0;
      TPIBytesPerLine8BPP  = 0;
      TPIBytesPerLine24BPP = 0;
   }
}


// Class Destructor
TProcessImage::~TProcessImage(void) {

// Nothing yet to do
}


// This function builds a new display object for the MDI child
// from the information contained in its IMAGEDESCRIPTOREXT structure.
// It reinstates the display mode and zoom factor of the original
// display object. NOTE: the information in the child's
// IMAGEDESCRIPTOREXT structure must be up to date.
void TProcessImage::BuildNewDisplayObject(void) {

   // Breakdown and rebuild a display object for the child.
   // Gather information from the display object
```

```
      BOOL ClipMode = pMDIChild->DisplayObj->IsClipMode();
      WORD Zoom = pMDIChild->DisplayObj->GetZoom();
      // Now delete the old display object
      delete pMDIChild->DisplayObj;

      // Instantiate a new one
      pMDIChild->DisplayObj = new Display;

      // Prepare the DisplayObj for display of image
      pMDIChild->DisplayObj->InitForDisplay(
                                    pMDIChild->ID.ImgDesc.Width,
                                    pMDIChild->ID.ImgDesc.Height,
                                    pMDIChild->ID.ImgDesc.Colors,
                                    pMDIChild->ID.lpImageData,
                                    pMDIChild->ID.ImgDesc.Palette, TRUE);

      // Put display parameters back
      if (ClipMode)
         pMDIChild->DisplayObj->SetClipMode();
      else
         pMDIChild->DisplayObj->SetStretchMode();

         pMDIChild->DisplayObj->SetZoom(Zoom);

      // Cause a repaint
      ::InvalidateRect(TPIhWindow, NULL, TRUE);
}

// Perform brightness or contrast adjust to the image
void TProcessImage::AdjustBrightnessContrast(void) {

   // Now initialize the Contrast LUT to no adjust of image data.
   for (WORD Index=0; Index < MAXCOLORLEVELS; Index++)
      ContrastTbl[Index] = 0;

   // Initialize brightness and contrast adjustments to no adjust.
   BriteAdjustValue = ContrastAdjustValue = 0;

   // Show the modal brightness adjust dialog box to get user values
   if (BriteContrastAdjustDialog(pMDIChild, &BriteAdjustValue,
                                 &ContrastAdjustValue).Execute() == IDOK) {
      // If we get here the user has selected an adjust value
      UpdateWindow(TPIhWindow);    // Get rid of dialog box
      if (ContrastAdjustValue != 0) {
         // Build the Contrast LUT as a function of user value. See text for
         // details.
         for (int Index=0; Index < MAXCOLORLEVELS; Index++)
            ContrastTbl[Index] = ContrastAdjustValue * sin(0.0245 * Index - 3.14);
      }
      // Prepare to transform the image data.
      // This can take some time so set the cursor to hourglass
      HCURSOR hOldCursor = ::SetCursor(LoadCursor(NULL, IDC_WAIT));

      BYTE huge *lpLine;
      BYTE huge *lpPixel;
```

```
int AdjustValue;
int Red, Green, Blue;

if (TPIBPP == 24) { // If a true color image
    for (register int Row=0; Row < TPIHeight; Row++) {
      // Calculate the address of row in image data
      lpLine = (BYTE huge *) (TPIlpImageData + (Row * TPIBytesPerLine24BPP));
      for (register int Col=0; Col < TPIWidth; Col++) {
        // Calculate the address of desired pixel
        lpPixel = (BYTE huge *) (lpLine + (Col * 3L));
        // Fetch, modify and store image data. Data is in BGR format.
        // The green value is used to determine the contrast value to
        // be applied to the pixel.
        AdjustValue = ContrastTbl[*(lpPixel+1)] + BriteAdjustValue;
        // Fetch and adjust the pixel's RGB value
        Blue  = *(lpPixel    ) + AdjustValue;
        Green = *(lpPixel + 1) + AdjustValue;
        Red   = *(lpPixel + 2) + AdjustValue;
        // Range check calculated values
        Red = (Red <      0)     ?   0:Red;
        Red = (Red > 255)     ? 255:Red;
        Green = (Green <   0) ?   0:Green;
        Green = (Green > 255) ? 255:Green;
        Blue = (Blue <    0)  ?   0:Blue;
        Blue = (Blue > 255)   ? 255:Blue;
        // Store the new values back into the DIB
        *(lpPixel    ) = (BYTE)Blue;
        *(lpPixel + 1) = (BYTE)Green;
        *(lpPixel + 2) = (BYTE)Red;
      }
    }
} else { //                    Image is palettized
    for (register int Index-0; Index < TPIColors; Index++) {
      // The green value is used to determine the contrast value to
      // be applied to the pixel.
      AdjustValue = ContrastTbl[TPIPalette[Index].Green] + BriteAdjustValue;
      Red = TPIPalette[Index].Red + AdjustValue;
      Green = TPIPalette[Index].Green + AdjustValue;
      Blue = TPIPalette[Index].Blue + AdjustValue;
      // Range check calculated values
      Red = (Red <    0)    ?   0:Red;
      Red = (Red > 255)     ? 255:Red;
      Green = (Green <   0) ?   0:Green;
      Green = (Green > 255) ? 255:Green;
      Blue = (Blue <    0)  ?   0:Blue;
      Blue = (Blue > 255)   ? 255:Blue;
      // Store the new palette values back
      TPIPalette[Index].Red = Red;
      TPIPalette[Index].Green = Green;
      TPIPalette[Index].Blue = Blue;
    }
    // Copy PTIPalette back to MDI child
    memcpy(pMDIChild->ID.ImgDesc.Palette, TPIPalette, sizeof(TPIPalette));
}
BuildNewDisplayObject();      // Build new display object for child
```

```
      // Mark the image as modified
      pMDIChild->MakeImageDirty();

    // Replace original cursor
     ::SetCursor(hOldCursor);
  }
}

// Generic rotation direction function
BOOL TProcessImage::RotateImage(BOOL Clockwise) {
  DWORD BytesPerLineS, BytesPerLineD;
  BOOL ImageIsTrueColor;

  // Change cursor, this could take some time
  HCURSOR hOldCursor = ::SetCursor(LoadCursor(NULL, IDC_WAIT));

  // Begin the process
  WORD SImageWidth  = TPIWidth;
  WORD SImageHeight = TPIHeight;
  WORD DImageWidth  = SImageHeight;    // Destination parameters are rotation
  WORD DImageHeight = SImageWidth;     // of original parameters
  // Calculate BytesPerLine of source and destination (rotated) images
  BytesPerLineS = CalculateBytesPerLine(SImageWidth, TPIBPP);
  BytesPerLineD = CalculateBytesPerLine(DImageWidth, TPIBPP);

  // Determine if image is true color or palettized
  ImageIsTrueColor = (TPIBPP == 24);

  // Allocate memory for rotated image data
  HGLOBAL hRotatedImage = GlobalAlloc(GHND, BytesPerLineD * DImageHeight);
  if (!hRotatedImage) {
    ::MessageBox(NULL, "No memory available for image rotation",
                    "User Advisory", MB_OK | MB_TASKMODAL);
    ::SetCursor(hOldCursor);
    return FALSE;
  }
  // When we get here there is enough memory for rotation
  BYTE huge *lpDestImage = (BYTE huge *) GlobalLock(hRotatedImage);

  BYTE huge *lpSPixel;
  BYTE huge *lpDPixel;
  BYTE huge *lpSRowData;
  BYTE huge *lpDRowData;

  // Perform the image rotation
  if (ImageIsTrueColor) {        // A true color image ?
    if (Clockwise) {             // A clockwise rotation
    // Now traverse the dest image looking back at the source image
    // for the data.
      for (register int Row = 0; Row < DImageHeight; Row++) {
        lpDRowData = (BYTE huge *) (lpDestImage + (Row * BytesPerLineD));
          for (register int Col = 0; Col < DImageWidth; Col++) {
            lpSRowData = (BYTE huge *) (TPIlpImageData + ((SImageHeight - 1 - Col) *
BytesPerLineS));
            lpSPixel = (BYTE huge *) (lpSRowData + (Row * 3L));
```

```
            lpDPixel = (BYTE huge *) (lpDRowData + (Col * 3L));
            *lpDPixel++ = *lpSPixel++;    // Blue
            *lpDPixel++ = *lpSPixel++;    // Green
            *lpDPixel++ = *lpSPixel++;    // Red
            }
        }
    } else {                             // A counter clockwise rotation
    // Now traverse the dest image looking back at the source image
    // for the data.
        for (register int Row = 0; Row < DImageHeight; Row++) {
        lpDRowData = (BYTE huge *) (lpDestImage + (Row * BytesPerLineD));
            for (register int Col = 0; Col < DImageWidth; Col++) {
                lpSRowData = (BYTE huge *) (TPIlpImageData + (Col * BytesPerLineS));
            lpSPixel = (BYTE huge *) (lpSRowData + ((SImageHeight - 1 - Col) * 3L));

            lpDPixel = (BYTE huge *) (lpDRowData + (Col * 3L));
            *lpDPixel++ = *lpSPixel++;    // Blue
            *lpDPixel++ = *lpSPixel++;    // Green
                *lpDPixel++ = *lpSPixel++;    // Red
        }
        }
      }
    } else {                             // An 8 bit palettized image
      if (Clockwise) {                   // A clockwise rotation
      // Now traverse the dest image looking back at the source image
      // for the data.
        // Now traverse the dest image looking back at the source image
      // for the data.
        for (register int Row = 0; Row < DImageHeight; Row++) {
        lpDRowData = (BYTE huge *) (lpDestImage + (Row * BytesPerLineD));
            for (register int Col = 0; Col < DImageWidth; Col++) {
                lpSRowData = (BYTE huge *) (TPIlpImageData + ((SImageHeight -
                    1 - Col) *
BytesPerLineS));
            lpSPixel = (BYTE huge *) (lpSRowData + Row);

            lpDPixel = (BYTE huge *) (lpDRowData + Col);
            *lpDPixel++ = *lpSPixel++;    // Move data
        }
        }
      } else {                           // A counter clockwise rotation
      // Now traverse the dest image looking back at the source image
        // for the data.
        for (register int Row = 0; Row < DImageHeight; Row++) {
        lpDRowData = (BYTE huge *) (lpDestImage + (Row * BytesPerLineD));
        for (register int Col = 0; Col < DImageWidth; Col++) {
                lpSRowData = (BYTE huge *) (TPIlpImageData + (Col * BytesPerLineS));
            lpSPixel = (BYTE huge *) (lpSRowData + SImageWidth - 1 - Row);

            lpDPixel = (BYTE huge *) (lpDRowData + Col);
                *lpDPixel++ = *lpSPixel++; // Move data
        }
        }
      }
    }
  }
```

```
  // When we get here, a rotated image is available. Two things must be
  // done. First, the IMAGEDESCRIPTOREXT for the child window must be
  // altered to reflect the new image and second, a new display object
  // must be instantiated for display of the new image.

  // Change only those member which are affected by image rotation
  pMDIChild->ID.ImgDesc.Width = DImageWidth;
  pMDIChild->ID.ImgDesc.Height = DImageHeight;
  pMDIChild->ID.ImgDesc.RasterSize = BytesPerLineD * DImageHeight;

  // Free memory for child's image
  GlobalUnlock(TPIhImageData);
  GlobalFree(TPIhImageData);

  // Replace it with memory containing rotated image
  pMDIChild->ID.ImgDesc.hImageData = hRotatedImage;
  pMDIChild->ID.lpImageData = lpDestImage;

  BuildNewDisplayObject();          // Build new display object for child

  // Recalculate scroll parameters because they may have changed
  pMDIChild->CalculateScrollRange(pMDIChild->DisplayObj->GetZoom(),
                                        DImageWidth, DImageHeight);
  // Mark image as modified
  pMDIChild->MakeImageDirty();

  // Remove hourglass cursor.
  ::SetCursor(hOldCursor);
  return TRUE;
}

// Perform clockwise image rotation
void TProcessImage::RotateCW(void) {

  RotateImage(FALSE);
}

// Perform counter clockwise image rotation
void TProcessImage::RotateCCW(void) {

  RotateImage(TRUE);
}
BOOL TProcessImage::FlipImage(BOOL FlipHorizontally) {
  DWORD BytesPerLine;
  BOOL ImageIsTrueColor;

  // Change cursor, this could take some time
  HCURSOR hOldCursor = ::SetCursor(LoadCursor(NULL, IDC_WAIT));

  // Calculate BytesPerLine of source image
  BytesPerLine = CalculateBytesPerLine(TPIWidth, TPIBPP);

  // Determine if image is true color or palettized
  ImageIsTrueColor = (TPIBPP == 24);
```

```
// Allocate a buffer for one row of image data
HGLOBAL hBuffer = GlobalAlloc (GHND, BytesPerLine);
if (!hBuffer) {
  ::MessageBox(NULL, "No memory available for image flipping",
                     "User Advisory", MB_OK | MB_TASKMODAL);
  ::SetCursor(hOldCursor);
  return FALSE;
}


// When we get here there is enough memory for flipping
BYTE huge *lpBuffer = (BYTE huge *) GlobalLock(hBuffer);


// Perform the image flipping
if (!FlipHorizontally) { // A vertical flip
  // Vertical flips don't care whether image is true color or palettized
  // because whole rows of image data are moved at once.
   int LimitRow = TPIHeight / 2;
  BYTE huge *lpTopRow;
  BYTE huge *lpBottomRow;
  // Now traverse the image data buffer
  for (int Row = 0; Row < LimitRow; Row++) {
     lpTopRow = (BYTE huge *) (TPIlpImageData + (Row * BytesPerLine));
     lpBottomRow = (BYTE huge *) (TPIlpImageData + ((TPIHeight - 1 - Row)
       * BytesPerLine));
     // Perform three moves. Top row of data goes to buffer. Bottom row
   // of data goes to top row. Data in buffer goes to bottom row.
      hmemcpy(lpBuffer,    lpTopRow,    BytesPerLine);
    hmemcpy(lpTopRow,    lpBottomRow, BytesPerLine);
    hmemcpy(lpBottomRow, lpBuffer,    BytesPerLine);
  }
} else {                        // A horizontal flip
   int LimitCol = TPIWidth / 2;
  BYTE huge *lpLeftPixel;
  BYTE huge *lpRightPixel;
  BYTE huge *lpRow;
   BYTE Red, Green, Blue;


  if (ImageIsTrueColor) { // A true color image
     for (int Row = 0; Row < TPIHeight; Row++) {
       lpRow = (BYTE huge *) (TPIlpImageData + (Row * BytesPerLine));
      for (int Col = 0; Col < LimitCol; Col++) {
        lpLeftPixel = (BYTE huge *) (lpRow + (Col * 3L));
          lpRightPixel = (BYTE huge *) (lpRow + ((TPIWidth - 1 - Col) * 3L));
        // Move left most pixels to temp storage
        Blue = *(lpLeftPixel);
        Green = *(lpLeftPixel+1);
          Red = *(lpLeftPixel+2);
        // Move right most pixels to the left
          *(lpLeftPixel) = *(lpRight Pixel);
        *(lpLeftPixel+1) = *(lpRightPixel+1);
        *(lpLeftPixel+2) = *(lpRightPixel+2);
        // Store temp values at right
        *(lpRightPixel) = Blue;
        *(lpRightPixel+1) = Green;
```

```
                  *(lpRightPixel+2) = Red;
            }
         }
       } else {                         // A palettized image
         for (int Row = 0; Row < TPIHeight; Row++) {
           lpRow = (BYTE huge *) (TPIlpImageData + (Row * BytesPerLine));
         for (int Col = 0; Col < LimitCol; Col++) {
           lpLeftPixel = (BYTE huge *) (lpRow + Col);
             lpRightPixel = (BYTE huge *) (lpRow + (TPIWidth - 1 - Col));
             // Move left most pixels to temp storage
             Blue = *lpLeftPixel;
             // Move right most pixels to the left
             *lpLeftPixel = *lpRightPixel;
             // Store temp values at right
                *lpRightPixel = Blue;
         }
         }
     }
  }
  // Free buffer as it is no longer needed
  GlobalUnlock(hBuffer);
  GlobalFree(hBuffer);
  BuildNewDisplayObject();         // Build a new display object for child

  // Mark the image as modified
  pMDIChild->MakeImageDirty();

  // Put original cursor back
  ::SetCursor(hOldCursor);

  return TRUE;
}


// Flip image horizontally
void TProcessImage::FlipHorz(void) {

  FlipImage(TRUE);
}


// Flip image vertically
void TProcessImage::FlipVert(void) {

  FlipImage(FALSE);
}


// Crop an image to user defined size. BeginCrop is called by client
// window to begin the operation. It does little. EndCrop is called
// during the processing of the LBUTTONUP message in the child window.
// The majority of the cropping functionality is performed within this
// function.
void TProcessImage::BeginCrop(void) {

  // Tell the child window to begin the cropping operation
  pMDIChild->EnableCropping();
}
```

```
// This function accepts two points as input and will return them
// such that Pt1 is the upper left point and Pt2 is the lower
// right point.
void AdjustPoints(POINT& Pt1, POINT& Pt2) {
  POINT TPt1, TPt2;

  TPt1.x = (Pt1.x > Pt2.x) ? Pt2.x : Pt1.x;
  TPt1.y = (Pt1.y > Pt2.y) ? Pt2.y : Pt1.y;
  TPt2.x = (Pt1.x > Pt2.x) ? Pt1.x : Pt2.x;
  TPt2.y = (Pt1.y > Pt2.y) ? Pt1.y : Pt2.y;
  // Return the possibly rearranged values
  Pt1 = TPt1;
  Pt2 = TPt2;
}


// Coordinates passed to this function are relative to the upper
// left corner of child's client area.
void TProcessImage::EndCrop(POINT& BegPt, POINT& EndPt) {
  RECT Rect;

  // This can take some time so set the cursor to hourglass
  HCURSOR hOldCursor = ::SetCursor(LoadCursor(NULL, IDC_WAIT));

  AdjustPoints(BegPt, EndPt);      // Force BegPt to upper left of cropped
                                   // area.
  // First, calculate which pixels of image are included in the cropped area
  ::GetClientRect(TPIhWindow, &Rect); // Get dims of child's client area

  // Calculate cropped area in image dimensions
  WORD CroppedImageLeft = (WORD)(((DWORD) BegPt.x * TPIWidth) / Rect.right);
  CroppedImageLeft &= 0xFFF8; // Force start pixel to byte boundry
  WORD CroppedImageRight = (WORD)(((DWORD) EndPt.x * TPIWidth) / Rect.right);
  WORD CroppedImageTop = (WORD)(((DWORD) BegPt.y * TPIHeight) / Rect.bottom);
  WORD CroppedImageBottom = (WORD)(((DWORD) EndPt.y * TPIHeight) / Rect.bottom);
  WORD CroppedImageWidth = CroppedImageRight - CroppedImageLeft + 1;
  WORD CroppedImageHeight = CroppedImageBottom - CroppedImageTop + 1;

  // If cropped image is smaller than this, don't bother
  if ((CroppedImageWidth < MINCROPWIDTH) ||
      (CroppedImageHeight < MINCROPHEIGHT)) {
    ::InvalidateRect(TPIhWindow, NULL, FALSE); // Cause a repaint
    ::SetCursor(hOldCursor);
    return;
  }
  // Calculate BytesPerLine of original and cropped image
  DWORD BytesPerLineS, BytesPerLineD;
  switch(TPIBPP) {
    case 1:    // 1 bit per pixel monochrome images
      BytesPerLineS = (TPIWidth + 7) / 8;   // Eight pixels in each byte
      BytesPerLineD = (CroppedImageWidth + 7) / 8;
      break;

    case 2:    // 2 bits/sample    // Four pixels in each byte
      BytesPerLineS = (TPIWidth + 3) / 4;
```

```
            BytesPerLineD = (CroppedImageWidth + 3) / 4;
            break;

    case 4:    // 4 bits per pixel 16 color images
            BytesPerLineS = (TPIWidth + 1) / 2; // Two pixels in each byte
            BytesPerLineD = (CroppedImageWidth + 1) / 2;
            break;

    case 8:    // 8 bits per pixel 256 color images
            BytesPerLineS = TPIWidth;                  // One pixel in each byte
            BytesPerLineD = CroppedImageWidth;
            break;

    case 24:   // 24 bits per pixel image
            BytesPerLineS = 3 * TPIWidth;              // Three bytes per pixel
            BytesPerLineD = 3 * CroppedImageWidth;
            break;
}
// Make double word aligned
BytesPerLineS = ALIGN_DWORD(BytesPerLineS);     // BytesPerLine of source
BytesPerLineD = ALIGN_DWORD(BytesPerLineD);     // BytesPerLine of dest
BOOL ImageIsTrueColor = (TPIBPP == 24);         // Set flag
// Allocate memory for cropped image data
HGLOBAL hCroppedImage = GlobalAlloc(GHND, BytesPerLineD * CroppedImageHeight);
if (!hCroppedImage) {
    ::MessageBox(NULL, "No memory available for image cropping",
                 "User Advisory", MB_OK | MB_TASKMODAL);
    ::SetCursor(hOldCursor);
    return;
}
// When we get here there is enough memory for cropping
BYTE huge *lpDImage = (BYTE huge *) GlobalLock(hCroppedImage);

// Go ahead and crop the data out of the original image
BYTE huge *lpSLine;
BYTE huge *lpDLine;
BYTE huge *lpSPixel;
BYTE huge *lpDPixel;

// Calculate additional image parameters to make things easier
WORD RowOffset = TPIHeight - CroppedImageBottom - 1;
WORD ColOffset = CroppedImageLeft;

if (ImageIsTrueColor) {            // A true color image ?
    // Now traverse the dest image looking back at source image
    // for the cropped data.
    for (register int Row = 0; Row < CroppedImageHeight; Row++) {
        lpSLine = (BYTE huge *) (TPIlpImageData +
                    (Row + RowOffset) * BytesPerLineS);
        lpDLine = (BYTE huge *) (lpDImage + (Row * BytesPerLineD));
        for (register int Col = 0; Col < CroppedImageWidth; Col++) {
            lpSPixel = (BYTE huge *) (lpSLine + ((Col + ColOffset) * 3L));
            lpDPixel = (BYTE huge *) (lpDLine + (Col * 3L));
            *lpDPixel++ = *lpSPixel++;    // Blue
            *lpDPixel++ = *lpSPixel++;    // Green
```

```
                    *lpDPixel = *lpSPixel;        // Red
            }
        }
    } else {                           // A palettized image ?
        // Now traverse the dest image looking back at source image
        // for the cropped data.
        for (register int Row = 0; Row < CroppedImageHeight; Row++) {
            lpSLine = (BYTE huge *) (TPIlpImageData +
                            (Row + RowOffset) * BytesPerLineS);
            lpDLine = (BYTE huge *) (lpDImage + (Row * BytesPerLineD));

            lpSPixel = (BYTE huge *) (lpSLine + ((ColOffset * TPIBPP)/8));
            // Move the image data
            hmemcpy(lpDLine, lpSPixel, BytesPerLineD);
        }
    }
    // When we get here, a cropped image is available. Two things must be
    // done. First, the IMAGEDESCRIPTOREXT for the child window must be
    // altered to reflect the new image and second, a new display object
    // must be instantiated for display of the new image.

    pMDIChild->ID.ImgDesc.Width = CroppedImageWidth;
    pMDIChild->ID.ImgDesc.Height = CroppedImageHeight;
    pMDIChild->ID.ImgDesc.RasterSize = BytesPerLineD * CroppedImageHeight;

    // Free memory managed by IMAGEDESCRIPTOREXT in child window
    GlobalUnlock(TPIhImageData);
    GlobalFree(TPIhImageData);
    pMDIChild->ID.ImgDesc.hImageData = hCroppedImage;
    pMDIChild->ID.lpImageData = lpDImage;

    BuildNewDisplayObject();          // Build new display object for child

    // Mark the image as modified
    pMDIChild->MakeImageDirty();

    // Put original cursor back
    ::SetCursor(hOldCursor);
}

/*
This function accepts a positive or negative percentage value and
converts it into a scale factor. The results are illustrated below:
PerCentValue ScaleFactor
    -500%           .1
    -400%           .125
    -300%           .1667
    -200%           .25
    -100%           .5
     -50%           .67
       0%          1
     +50%          1.5
    +100%          2.0
    +200%          4.0
    +300%          6.0
```

```
        +400%           8.0
        +500%           10.0
        */

float CalculateScaleFactor(int PerCentValue) {

    float ScaleValue;
    int APCValue = abs(PerCentValue);

    if (APCValue == 0)               // 0% is a scale value of 1 or no change
        ScaleValue = 1.0;
    else if (APCValue < 100)         // If % less than 100
        ScaleValue = 1.0 + (APCValue / 100.0);
    else                             // Value >= 100
        ScaleValue = (APCValue * 2.0) / 100.0;

    if (PerCentValue >= 0)           // If percentage was positive
        return ScaleValue;           // return value directly
    else                             // Otherwise
        return 1.0 / ScaleValue;     // return fraction
}

// Resize image to user specification
void TProcessImage::Resize(void) {
    float ScaleFactor = 1.0;

    // Ask the user for scale factor to apply to the image.
    if (ResizeControlDialog(pMDIChild, TPIWidth, TPIHeight, &ScaleFactor).Execute()
        == IDCANCEL)
        return;

    UpdateWindow(TPIhWindow;          // Get rid of dialog box

    if (ScaleFactor == 1.0)           // If no scale change, nothing to do
        return;

    // This could take some time, put up hourglass
    HCURSOR hOldCursor = ::SetCursor(LoadCursor(NULL, IDC_WAIT));

    // Calculate size of new image
    WORD NewWidth = TPIWidth * ScaleFactor;
    WORD NewHeight = TPIHeight * ScaleFactor;

    DWORD BytesPerLineS = CalculateBytesPerLine(TPIWidth, TPIBPP);
    DWORD BytesPerLineD = CalculateBytesPerLine(NewWidth, TPIBPP);
    // Allocate memory for new image data
    HGLOBAL hResizedImage = GlobalAlloc(GHND, BytesPerLineD * NewHeight);
    if (!hResizedImage) {
        ::MessageBox(NULL, "No memory available for resizing image.",
                        "User Advisory", MB_OK | MB_TASKMODAL);
        ::SetCursor(hOldCursor);
        return;
    }
    // When we get here there is enough memory for resizing
    BYTE huge *lpDImage = (BYTE huge *) GlobalLock(hResizedImage);
    WORD SLine, SPixel;
```

```
          BYTE huge *lpSLine;
          BYTE huge *lpDLine;
          BYTE huge *lpSPixel;
          BYTE huge *lpDPixel;

          // Traverse destination image looking back at source image.
          if (TPIBPP == 24) {            // If a true color image
             for (register int Row=0; Row < NewHeight; Row++) {
                // Calculate which row of source image to fetch
                SLine = (WORD)(((DWORD) TPIHeight * Row) / (DWORD) NewHeight);
                lpSLine = (BYTE huge *) (TPIlpImageData + (SLine * BytesPerLineS));
                lpDLine = (BYTE huge *) (lpDImage + (Row * BytesPerLineD));
                for (register int Col=0; Col < NewWidth; Col++) {
                  // Do calculations required for each col of destination image
                  SPixel = (WORD)(((DWORD) TPIWidth * Col) / (DWORD) NewWidth);
                  lpSPixel = (BYTE huge *) (lpSLine + (lsSLine + (SPixel * 3L));
                  lpDPixel = (BYTE huge *) (lpDLine + (Col * 3L));

                  // Fetch and store image data
                  *lpDPixel++ = *lpSPixel++;    // Move blue data
                  *lpDPixel++ = *lpSPixel++;    // Move green data
                  *lpDPixel = *lpSPixel;        // Move red data
                }
             }
          } else {                       // Image is palettized
             for (register int Row=0; Row < NewHeight; Row++) {
                // Calculate which row of source image to fetch
                SLine = (WORD)(((DWORD) TPIHeight * Row) / (DWORD) NewHeight);
                lpSLine = (BYTE huge *) (TPIlpImageData + (SLine * BytesPerLineS));
                lpDLine = (BYTE huge *) (lpDImage + (Row * BytesPerLineD));
                for (register int Col=0; Col < NewWidth; Col++) {
                  // Do calculations required for each col of destination image
                  SPixel = (WORD)(((DWORD) TPIWidth * Col) / (DWORD) NewWidth);
                  lpSPixel = (BYTE huge *) (lpSLine + SPixel);
                  lpDPixel = (BYTE huge *) (lpDLine + Col);

                  // Fetch and store image data
                  *lpDPixel = *lpSPixel;        // Move pixel data
                }
             }
          }
          // When we get here, a resized image is available. Two things must be
          // done. First, the IMAGEDESCRIPTOREXT for the child window must be
          // altered to reflect the new image and second, a new display object
          // must be instantiated for display of the new image.

          pMDIChild->ID.ImgDesc.Width = NewWidth;
          pMDIChild->ID.ImgDesc.Height = NewHeight;
          pMDIChild->ID.ImgDesc.RasterSize = BytesPerLineD * NewHeight;

          // Free memory managed by IMAGEDESCRIPTOREXT in child window
          GlobalUnlock(TPIhImageData);
          GlobalFree(TPIhImageData);
          pMDIChild->ID.ImgDesc.hImageData = hResizedImage;
          pMDIChild->ID.lpImageData = lpDImage;
```

```
    BuildNewDisplayObject();              // Build new display object for child

    // Mark the image as modified
    pMDIChild->MakeImageDirty();

    // Put original cursor back
    ::SetCursor(hOldCursor);
}


// Generic convolution function. NOTE: only 24 BPP images are supported
// directly.
BOOL TProcessImage::ConvoluteImage(KERNEL *lpKernel,
                                   int DefaultStrength,
                                   LPSTR Desc) {
    // Ask the user for the strength factor to apply.
    int Strength = DefaultStrength; // Default filter strength
    if (FilterControlDialog(pMDIChild, &Strength, Desc).Execute() == IDCANCEL)
        return FALSE;

    UpdateWindow(TPIhWindow);          // Get rid of dialog box

    // User says it OK to continue, set cursor to hourglass
    HCURSOR hOldCursor = ::SetCursor(LoadCursor(NULL, IDC_WAIT));

    // Allocate and lock memory for filtered image data
    HGLOBAL hFilteredImage = GlobalAlloc(GHND, TPIBytesPerLine24BPP * TPIHeight);
    if (!hFilteredImage) {
        ::MessageBox(NULL, "No memory available for image filtering",
                     "User Advisory", MB_OK | MB_TASKMODAL);
        ::SetCursor(hOldCursor);
        return FALSE;
    }
    HLOCAL hBuf1 = LocalAlloc(LHND, (WORD) TPIBytesPerLine24BPP);
    if (!hBuf1) {
        ::MessageBox(NULL, "No memory available for image filtering",
                     "User Advisory", MB_OK | MB_TASKMODAL);
        GlobalFree(hFilteredImage);
        ::SetCursor(hOldCursor);
        return FALSE;
    }

    HLOCAL hBuf2 = LocalAlloc(LHND, (WORD) TPIBytesPerLine24BPP);
    if (!hBuf2) {
        ::MessageBox(NULL, "No memory available for image filtering",
                     "User Advisory", MB_OK | MB_TASKMODAL);
        GlobalFree(hFilteredImage);
        LocalFree(hBuf1);
        ::SetCursor(hOldCursor);
        return FALSE;
    }

    HLOCAL hBuf3 = LocalAlloc(LHND, (WORD) TPIBytesPerLine24BPP);
    if (!hBuf3) {
        ::MessageBox(NULL, "No memory available for image filtering",
                     "User Advisory", MB_OK | MB_TASKMODAL);
```

```
        GlobalFree(hFilteredImage);
        LocalFree(hBuf1);
        LocalFree(hBuf2);
        ::SetCursor(hOldCursor);
        return FALSE;
}
// When we get here there is enough memory for filtering
BYTE huge *lpDestImage = (BYTE huge *) GlobalLock(hFilteredImage);
BYTE near *pBuf1 = (BYTE near *) LocalLock(hBuf1);
BYTE near *pBuf2 = (BYTE near *) LocalLock(hBuf2);
BYTE near *pBuf3 = (BYTE near *) LocalLock(hBuf3);

// Prepare to perform the convolution
BYTE huge *lpDPixel;
BYTE huge *lpDRowData;

// Compensate for edge effects
WORD ColOffset = 1;
WORD RowOffset = 1;

WORD BegCol = ColOffset;
WORD BegRow = RowOffset;
WORD Width = TPIWidth - (KERNELCOLS - 1);
WORD Height= TPIHeight - (KERNELROWS - 1);

// Calculate new range of pixels to act upon
WORD ColExtent = BegCol + Width;
WORD RowExtent = BegRow + Height - 1;
int *lpElement;                    // Ptr element in kernel
int Element;

int RSum, GSum, BSum;
BYTE ORed, OGreen, OBlue;

for (register int Row = 0; Row < RowExtent; Row++) {
  // Get ptr to destination row data
  lpDRowData = (BYTE huge *) (lpDestImage + ((Row+1) * TPIBytesPerLine24BPP));

  // Copy three rows of data to near buffers
  hmemcpy(pBuf1,
    (BYTE huge *) (TPIlpImageData + (Row * TPIBytesPerLine24BPP)),
    TPIBytesPerLine24BPP);
  hmemcpy(pBuf2,
    (BYTE huge *) (TPIlpImageData + ((Row+1) * TPIBytesPerLine24BPP)),
    TPIBytesPerLine24BPP);
  hmemcpy(pBuf3,
    (BYTE huge *) (TPIlpImageData + ((Row+2) * TPIBytesPerLine24BPP)),
    TPIBytesPerLine24BPP);

  for (register int Col = BegCol; Col < ColExtent; Col++) {
    // Get ptrs to source and destination RGB pixel
    BYTE near *pSPixel = (BYTE near *) (pBuf2 + (Col * 3));
    lpDPixel = (BYTE huge *)(lpDRowData + (Col * 3L));

    // Get original source pixel RGB value
    OBlue = *pSPixel++;
```

```
OGreen = *pSPixel++;
ORed = *pSPixel;

register WORD ColAddr = Col * 3;
// Visit all of the pixels covered by the kernel
WORD ColMinusBlue  = ColAddr - 3;
WORD ColMinusGreen = ColAddr - 2;
WORD ColMinusRed   = ColAddr - 1;
WORD ColBlue       = ColAddr;
WORD ColGreen      = ColAddr + 1;
WORD ColRed        = ColAddr + 2;
WORD ColPlusBlue   = ColAddr + 3;
WORD ColPlusGreen  = ColAddr + 4;
WORD ColPlusRed    = ColAddr + 5;

// Point at first number in kernel
lpElement = lpKernel->Element;

Element = *lpElement++;
RSum = *(pBuf1 + ColMinusRed)    * Element;
GSum = *(pBuf1 + ColMinusGreen)  * Element;
BSum = *(pBuf1 + ColMinusBlue)   * Element;

Element = *lpElement++;
RSum += *(pBuf2 + ColMinusRed)    * Element;
GSum += *(pBuf2 + ColMinusGreen)  * Element;
BSum += *(pBuf2 + ColMinusBlue)   * Element;

Element = *lpElement++;
RSum += *(pBuf3 + ColMinusRed)    * Element;
GSum += *(pBuf3 + ColMinusGreen)  * Element;
BSum += *(pBuf3 + ColMinusBlue)   * Element;

Element = *lpElement++;
RSum += *(pBuf1 + ColRed)    * Element;
GSum += *(pBuf1 + ColGreen)  * Element;
BSum += *(pBuf1 + ColBlue)   * Element;

Element = *lpElement++;
RSum += *(pBuf2 + ColRed)    * Element;
GSum += *(pBuf2 + ColGreen)  * Element;
BSum += *(pBuf2 + ColBlue)   * Element;

Element = *lpElement++;
RSum += *(pBuf3 + ColRed)    * Element;
GSum += *(pBuf3 + ColGreen)  * Element;
BSum += *(pBuf3 + ColBlue)   * Element;

Element = *lpElement++;
RSum += *(pBuf1 + ColPlusRed)    * Element;
GSum += *(pBuf1 + ColPlusGreen)  * Element;
BSum += *(pBuf1 + ColPlusBlue)   * Element;

Element = *lpElement++;
RSum += *(pBuf2 + ColPlusRed)    * Element;
```

```
      GSum += *(pBuf2 + ColPlusGreen)      * Element;
      BSum += *(pBuf2 + ColPlusBlue)       * Element;

      Element = *lpElement++;
      RSum += *(pBuf3 + ColPlusRed)        * Element;
      GSum += *(pBuf3 + ColPlusGreen)      * Element;
      BSum += *(pBuf3 + ColPlusBlue)       * Element;

    if (lpKernel->Divisor != 1) {
      int Divisor = lpKernel->Divisor;
      RSum /= Divisor; // Divide if necessary
      GSum /= Divisor;
      BSum /= Divisor;
    }
    // When we get here, RSum, GSum and BSum have the new RGB value.
    if (Strength != 10) {
      // Linear interpolate pixel data
      RSum = ORed + (((RSum - ORed)   * Strength) / 10);
      GSum = OGreen + (((GSum - OGreen) * Strength) / 10);
      BSum = OBlue + (((BSum - OBlue)  * Strength) / 10);
    }
    // Range check the data before storing it in output buffer.
    RSum = (RSum > 255) ? 255:RSum;
    RSum = (RSum < 0) ? 0:RSum;
    GSum = (GSum > 255) ? 255:GSum;
    GSum = (GSum < 0) ? 0:GSum;
    BSum = (BSum > 255) ? 255:BSum;
    BSum = (BSum < 0) ? 0:BSum;
    // Now store the data
    *lpDPixel++ = BSum;
    *lpDPixel++ = GSum;
    *lpDPixel = RSum;
  }
}
// The temp buffers are no longer required and are freed.
LocalUnlock(hBuf1);
LocalFree(hBuf1);
LocalUnlock(hBuf2);
LocalFree(hBuf2);
LocalUnlock(hBuf3);
LocalFree(hBuf3);
```

```
// When we get here, a filtered image is available. Two things must be
// done. First, the IMAGEDESCRIPTOREXT for the child window must be
// altered to reflect the new image and second, a new display object
// must be instantiated for display of the new image.

// Free memory managed by IMAGEDESCRIPTOREXT in child window
GlobalUnlock(TPIhImageData);
GlobalFree(TPIhImageData);

// Replace with memory allocated in this routine. All other items in
// the IMAGEDESCRIPTOREXT remain the same.
pMDIChild->ID.ImgDesc.hImageData = hFilteredImage;
pMDIChild->ID.lpImageData = lpDestImage;
```

```
   BuildNewDisplayObject();            // Build new display object for child

   // Mark the image as modified
   pMDIChild->MakeImageDirty();

   return TRUE;
}

// The first high pass sharpening function
void TProcessImage::HighPass1(void) {

   // Call generic function for filtering with convolution.
   ConvoluteImage(&HP1, 3, "The sharpening filter tends to enhance image focus.");
}

void TProcessImage::HighPass2(void) {

   // Call generic function for filtering with convolution.
   ConvoluteImage(&HP2, 3, "The sharpening filter tends to enhance image focus.");
}

void TProcessImage::HighPass3(void) {

   // Call generic function for filtering with convolution.
   ConvoluteImage(&HP3, 3, "The sharpening filter tends to enhance image focus.");
}

void TProcessImage::LowPass1(void) {

   // Call generic function for filtering with convolution.
   ConvoluteImage(&LP1, 3, "The softening filter helps remove noise from
     images.");
}

void TProcessImage::LowPass2(void) {

   // Call generic function for filtering with convolution.
   ConvoluteImage(&LP2, 3, "The softening filter helps remove noise from
     images.");
}

void TProcessImage::LowPass3(void) {

   // Call generic function for filtering with convolution.
   ConvoluteImage(&LP3, 3, "The softening filter helps remove noise from
     images.");
}

void TProcessImage::NorthEdges(void) {

   // Call generic function for edge enhancement.
   ConvoluteImage(&EdgeNorth, 5,
     "This operation enhances image edges that are primarily vertical.");
}

void TProcessImage::NorthEastEdges(void) {
```

```
      // Call generic function for edge enhancement.
      ConvoluteImage(&EdgeNorthEast, 5,
         "This operation enhances north easterly image edges.");
   }

   void TProcessImage::EastEdges(void) {

      // Call generic function for edge enhancement.
      ConvoluteImage(&EdgeEast, 5,
         "This operation enhances image edges that are primarily horizontal.");
   }

   void TProcessImage::SouthEastEdges(void) {

      // Call generic function for edge enhancement.
      ConvoluteImage(&EdgeSouthEast, 5,
         "This operation enhances south easterly image edges.");
   }

   void TProcessImage::SouthEdges(void) {

      // Call generic function for edge enhancement.
      ConvoluteImage(&EdgeSouth, 5,
         "This operation enhances image edges that are primarily vertical.");
   }

   void TProcessImage::SouthWestEdges(void) {

      // Call generic function for edge enhancement.
      ConvoluteImage(&EdgeSouthWest, 5,
         "This operation enhances south westerly image edges.");
   }

   void TProcessImage::WestEdges(void) {

      // Call generic function for edge enhancement.
      ConvoluteImage(&EdgeWest, 5,
         "This operation enhances image edges that are primarily horizontal.");
   }

   void TProcessImage::NorthWestEdges(void) {

      // Call generic function for edge enhancement.
      ConvoluteImage(&EdgeNorthWest, 5,
         "This operation enhances north westerly image edges.");
   }

// Median filtering support definitions and functions
typedef struct {                    // Required for median filtering of
   BYTE Red;                        // color images
   BYTE Green;
   BYTE Blue;
   int Luminance;
} COLORVALUE;
```

```
// Compare two COLORVALUE elements. Used by qsort function.
int ColorValueCompare(COLORVALUE *lpEntry1, COLORVALUE *lpEntry2) {

  if (((*lpEntry1).Luminance) < ((*lpEntry2).Luminance))
    return -1;
  else if (((*lpEntry1).Luminance) > ((*lpEntry2).Luminance))
    return 1;
  else
    return 0;
}


typedef int (FAR * LPCOMPARE) (const void *, const void *);

// Perform median filtering on image
void TProcessImage::Despeckle(void) {

  // This could take some time, set cursor to hourglass
  HCURSOR hOldCursor = ::SetCursor(LoadCursor(NULL, IDC_WAIT));

  // Allocate and lock memory for filtered image data
  HGLOBAL hFilteredImage = GlobalAlloc(GHND, TPIBytesPerLine24BPP * TPIHeight);
  if (!hFilteredImage) {
    ::MessageBox(NULL, "No memory available for image despeckling",
                       "User Advisory", MB_OK | MB_TASKMODAL);
    ::SetCursor(hOldCursor);
    return;
  }

  HLOCAL hBuf1 = LocalAlloc(LHND, (WORD) TPIBytesPerLine24BPP);
  if (!hBuf1) {
    ::MessageBox(NULL, "No memory available for image despeckling",
                       "User Advisory", MB_OK | MB_TASKMODAL);
    GlobalFree(hFilteredImage);
    ::SetCursor(hOldCursor);
    return;
  }

  HLOCAL hBuf2 = LocalAlloc(LHND, (WORD) TPIBytesPerLine24BPP);
  if (!hBuf2) {
    ::MessageBox(NULL, "No memory available for image despeckling",
                       "User Advisory", MB_OK | MB_TASKMODAL);
    GlobalFree(hFilteredImage);
    LocalFree(hBuf1);
    LocalFree(hBuf2);
    ::SetCursor(hOldCursor);
    return;
  }

  HLOCAL hBuf3 = LocalAlloc(LHND, (WORD) TPIBytesPerLine24BPP);
  if (!hBuf3) {
    ::MessageBox(NULL, "No memory available for image despeckling",
                       "User Advisory", MB_OK | MB_TASKMODAL);
    GlobalFree(hFilteredImage);
    LocalFree(hBuf1);
    LocalFree(hBuf2);
```

```
            ::SetCursor(hOldCursor);
            return;
    }


    // When we get here there is enough memory for despeckling
    BYTE huge *lpDestImage = (BYTE huge *) GlobalLock(hFilteredImage);
    BYTE near *pBuf1 = (BYTE near *) LocalLock(hBuf1);
    BYTE near *pBuf2 = (BYTE near *) LocalLock(hBuf2);
    BYTE near *pBuf3 = (BYTE near *) LocalLock(hBuf3);


    // Prepare to perform the median filtering
    BYTE huge *lpDPixel;
    BYTE huge *lpDRowData;


    // Compensate for edge effects
    WORD ColOffset = 1;
    WORD RowOffset = 1;


    WORD BegCol = ColOffset;
    WORD BegRow = RowOffset;
    WORD Width = TPIWidth - (KERNELCOLS - 1);
    WORD Height= TPIHeight - (KERNELROWS - 1);


    // Calculate new range of pixels to act upon
    WORD ColExtent = BegCol + Width;
    WORD RowExtent = BegRow + Height -1;
    BYTE Red, Green, Blue;
    WORD Index;


    COLORVALUE MedianArray[KERNELELEMENTS];
    for (register int Row = BegRow; Row < RowExtent; Row++) {
       // Get ptr to destination row data
       lpDRowData = (BYTE huge *) (lpDestImage + ((Row+1) * TPIBytesPerLine24BPP));

       // Copy three rows of data to near buffers
       hmemcpy(pBuf1,
               (BYTE huge *) (TPIlpImageData + (Row * TPIBytesPerLine24BPP)),
                TPIBytesPerLine24BPP);
       hmemcpy(pBuf2,
               (BYTE huge *) (TPIlpImageData + ((Row+1) * TPIBytesPerLine24BPP)),
                TPIBytesPerLine24BPP);
       hmemcpy(pBuf3,
               (BYTE huge *) (TPIlpImageData + ((Row+2) *TPIBytesPerLine24BPP)),
                TPIBytesPerLine24BPP);

       for (register int Col = BegCol; Col < ColExtent; Col++) {
          // Get ptr to destination RGB pixel
          lpDPixel = (BYTE huge *) (lpDRowData + (Col * 3L));

          // Visit all of the pixels covered by the kernel
          register WORD ColAddr = Col * 3;
          WORD ColMinusBlue = ColAddr - 3;
          WORD ColMinusGreen = ColAddr - 2;
          WORD ColMinusRed = ColAddr - 1;
          WORD ColBlue = ColAddr;
```

```
WORD ColGreen = ColAddr + 1;
WORD ColRed = ColAddr + 2;
WORD ColPlusBlue = ColAddr + 3;
WORD ColPlusGreen = ColAddr + 4;
WORD ColPlusRed = ColAddr + 5;

Index = 0;
MedianArray[Index].Blue = Blue = *(pBuf1 + ColMinusBlue);
MedianArray[Index].Green = Green = *(pBuf1 + ColMinusGreen);
MedianArray[Index].Red = Red = *(pBuf1 + ColMinusRed);
MedianArray[Index++].Luminance =
   (30 * Red) + (59 * Green) + (11 * Blue);

MedianArray[Index].Blue = Blue = *(pBuf2 + ColMinusBlue);
MedianArray[Index].Green = Green = *(pBuf2 + ColMinusGreen);
MedianArray[Index].Red = Red = *(pBuf2 + ColMinusRed);
MedianArray[Index++].Luminance =
   (30 * Red) + (59 * Green) + (11 * Blue);

MedianArray[Index].Blue = Blue = *(pBuf3 + ColMinusBlue);
MedianArray[Index].Green = Green = *(pBuf3 + ColMinusGreen);
MedianArray[Index].Red = Red = *(pBuf3 + ColMinusRed);
MedianArray[Index++].Luminance =
   (30 * Red) + (59 * Green) + (11 * Blue);

MedianArray[Index].Blue = Blue = *(pBuf1 + ColBlue);
MedianArray[Index].Green = Green = *(pBuf1 + ColGreen);
MedianArray[Index].Red = Red = *(pBuf1 + ColRed);
MedianArray[Index++].Luminance =
   (30 * Red) + (59 * Green) + (11 * Blue);

MedianArray[Index].Blue = Blue = *(pBuf2 + ColBlue);
MedianArray[Index].Green = Green = *(pBuf2 + ColGreen);
MedianArray[Index].Red = Red = *(pBuf2 + ColRed);
MedianArray[Index++].Luminance =
   (30 * Red) + (59 * Green) + (11 * Blue);

MedianArray[Index].Blue = Blue = *(pBuf3 + ColBlue);
MedianArray[Index].Green = Green = *(pBuf3 + ColGreen);
MedianArray[Index].Red = Red = *(pBuf3 + ColRed);
MedianArray[Index++].Luminance =
   (30 * Red) + (59 * Green) + (11 * Blue);

MedianArray[Index].Blue = Blue = *(pBuf1 + ColPlusBlue);
MedianArray[Index].Green = Green = *(pBuf1 + ColPlusGreen);
MedianArray[Index].Red = Red = *(pBuf1 + ColPlusRed);
MedianArray[Index++].Luminance =
   (30 * Red) + (59 * Green) + (11 * Blue);

MedianArray[Index].Blue = Blue = *(pBuf2 + ColPlusBlue);
MedianArray[Index].Green = Green = *(pBuf2 + ColPlusGreen);
MedianArray[Index].Red = Red = *(pBuf2 + ColPlusRed);
MedianArray[Index++].Luminance =
   (30 * Red) + (59 * Green) + (11 * Blue);
```

```
            MedianArray[Index].Blue = Blue = *(pBuf3 + ColPlusBlue);
            MedianArray[Index].Green = Green = *(pBuf3 + ColPlusGreen);
            MedianArray[Index].Red = Red = *(pBuf3 + ColPlusRed);
            MedianArray[Index].Luminance =
              (30 * Red) + (59 * Green) + (11 * Blue);

            qsort(MedianArray, KERNELELEMENTS, sizeof(COLORVALUE), (LPCOMPARE)
              ColorValueCompare);

            // Now store the data from the middle element in the array
            *lpDPixel++ = MedianArray[4].Blue;
            *lpDPixel++ = MedianArray[4].Green;
            *lpDPixel = MedianArray[4].Red;
        }
    }
    // The temp buffers are no longer required and are freed.
    LocalUnlock(hBuf1);
    LocalFree(hBuf1);
    LocalUnlock(hBuf2);
    LocalFree(hBuf2);
    LocalUnlock(hBuf3);
    LocalFree(hBuf3);

    // When we get here, a filtered image is available. Two things must be
    // done. First, the IMAGEDESCRIPTOREXT for the child window must be
    // altered to reflect the new image and second, a new display object
    // must be instantiated for display of the new image.
      // Free memory managed by IMAGEDESCRIPTOREXT in child window
      GlobalUnlock(TPIhImageData);
      GlobalFree(TPIhImageData);

      // Replace with memory allocated in this routine. All other items in
      // the IMAGEDESCRIPTOREXT remain the same.
      pMDIChild->ID.ImgDesc.hImageData = hFilteredImage;
      pMDIChild->ID.lpImageData = lpDestImage;

      BuildNewDisplayObject();          // Build new display object for child

      // Mark the image as modified
      pMDIChild->MakeImageDirty();

      // Put original cursor back
      ::SetCursor(hOldCursor);
}

// Perform histogram equalization on 24 BPP images.
void TProcessImage::HistogramEq(void) {

    // Ask the user for the strength factor to apply.
    int Strength = 1;                 // Default filter strength
    LPSTR Desc = "Histogram equalization attempts to correct images that "
                 "are either too bright or too dark.";
    if (FilterControlDialog(pMDIChild, &Strength, Desc).Execute() == IDCANCEL)
      return;
```

```
UpdateWindow(TPIhWindow);          // Get rid of dialog box

// User says it OK to continue, set cursor to hourglass
HCURSOR hOldCursor = ::SetCursor(LoadCursor(NULL, IDC_WAIT));

// Allocate memory for storage of histogram data
HGLOBAL hHistogram = GlobalAlloc(GHND, MAXCOLORLEVELS * sizeof(DWORD));
if (!hHistogram) {
   ::MessageBox(NULL, "No memory available for histogram eq.",
                "User Advisory", MB_OK | MB_TASKMODAL);
   ::SetCursor(hOldCursor);
   return;
}

// Allocate memory for storage of histogram sum values
HGLOBAL hHistogramSum = GlobalAlloc(GHND, MAXCOLORLEVELS * sizeof(DWORD));
if (!hHistogram) {
   GlobalFree(hHistogram);         // Free storage for histogram values
   ::MessageBox(NULL, "No memory available for histogram eq.",
                "User Advisory", MB_OK | MB_TASKMODAL);
   ::SetCursor(hOldCursor);
   return;
}
// When we get here, we have memory for the histogram and the histogram
// sum arrays. Get their pointers.
DWORD *lpHistogram = (DWORD *) GlobalLock(hHistogram);
DWORD *lpHistogramSum = (DWORD *) GlobalLock(hHistogramSum);

// Create the histogram of the green channel data
BYTE huge * lpLine;
BYTE huge * lpPixel;
int Red, Green, Blue, PGreen, Delta;

for (register int Row = 0; Row < TPIHeight; Row++) {
   // Get ptr to source row data
   lpLine = (BYTE huge *) (TPIlpImageData + (Row * TPIBytesPerLine24BPP));
   for (register int Col = 0; Col < TPIWidth; Col++) {
     // Get ptr to source RGB pixel. Data stored B, G, R.
     lpPixel = (BYTE huge *) (lpLine + (Col * 3L));
     Green = *lpPixel++;            // Toss blue data away
     Green = *lpPixel;              // Retain the green data
     lpHistogram[Green] += 1;       // Increment count for this index
   }
}
// Now calculate the area under the histogram.
DWORD Sum = 0;                      // Initial area or sum is zero
for (register int Index = 0; Index < MAXCOLORLEVELS; Index++) {
   Sum += lpHistogram[Index];
   lpHistogramSum[Index] = Sum;
}
// Now go back throught the image data and transform it.
DWORD TotalArea = (DWORD) TPIWidth * TPIHeight;

for (Row = 0; Row < TPIHeight; Row++) {
   // Get ptr to source (and destination) row data
```

```
            lpLine = (BYTE huge *) (TPIlpImageData + (Row * TPIBytesPerLine24BPP));
            for (register int Col = 0; Col < TPIWidth; Col++) {
                // Get ptrs to source (and destination) RGB pixel. Data stored B, G, R.
                lpPixel = (BYTE huge *) (lpLine + (Col * 3L));

                Blue  = *(lpPixel    );        // Get RGB data from source image
                Green = *(lpPixel + 1);
                Red   = *(lpPixel + 2);

                // Calculate new value for green and delta for difference
                PGreen = (int) ((MAXCOLORLEVELS * lpHistogramSum[Green]) / TotalArea);
                Delta = ((PGreen - Green) * Strength) / 10;

                Red   += Delta;
                Green += Delta;
                Blue  += Delta;

                // Range check the data before storing it in output buffer.
                Red   = (Red   > 255) ? 255:Red;
                Red   = (Red   <   0) ?   0:Red;
                Green = (Green > 255) ? 255:Green;
                Green = (Green <   0) ?   0:Green;
                Blue  = (Blue  > 255) ? 255:Blue;
                Blue  = (Blue  <   0) ?   0:Blue;

                // Store new pixel value
                *lpPixel++ = Blue;
                *lpPixel++ = Green;
                *lpPixel   = Red;
            }
        }
        // Release memory for histogram storage
        GlobalUnlock(hHistogramSum);
        GlobalFree(hHistogramSum);
        GlobalUnlock(hHistogram);
        GlobalFree(hHistogram);

        BuildNewDisplayObject();        // Build new display object for child

        // Mark the image as modified
        pMDIChild->MakeImageDirty();

        // Put original cursor back
        ::SetCursor(hOldCursor);
    }

// Quantize the image into user specified number of colors
void TProcessImage::Quantize(void) {
    int NumberOfColors = 256;
    if (QuantizeControlDialog(pMDIChild, &NumberOfColors).Execute() == IDCANCEL)
        return;

    UpdateWindow(TPIhWindow);        // Get rid of dialog box

    // This could take some time, put up hourglass
    HCURSOR hOldCursor = ::SetCursor(LoadCursor(NULL, IDC_WAIT));
```

```
      // Instantiate a quantizer object
      MedianCutQuant Q(NumberOfColors, TPIWidth, TPIHeight, TPIlpImageData);

      // Perform the quantization to user specified number of colors
      if (!Q.QuantizeImage()) {
         ::MessageBox(NULL, "Error quantizing image.",
                        "User Advisory", MB_OK | MB_TASKMODAL);
         ::SetCursor(hOldCursor);
         return;
      }
      // Allocate memory for the quantized image
      DWORD RasterSize = TPIBytesPerLine8BPP * TPIHeight;
      HGLOBAL hQuantizedImage = GlobalAlloc(GHND, RasterSize);
      if (!hQuantizedImage) {
         ::MessageBox(NULL, "No memory for copying quantized image.",
                        "User Advisory", MB_OK | MB_TASKMODAL);
         ::SetCursor(hOldCursor);
         return;
      }

      // If we get here, the image has been quantized and memory exists for
      // the copy of the quantized image. Two more things must be
      // done. First, the IMAGEDESCRIPTOREXT for the child window must be
      // altered to reflect the new image and second, a new display object
      // must be instantiated for display of the new image.

      pMDIChild->ID.ImgDesc.RasterSize = RasterSize;
      pMDIChild->ID.ImgDesc.BPP = 8;
      pMDIChild->ID.ImgDesc.Colors = NumberOfColors;

      // Free memory managed by IMAGEDESCRIPTOREXT in child window
      GlobalUnlock(TPIhImageData);
      GlobalFree(TPIhImageData);
      pMDIChild->ID.ImgDesc.hImageData = hQuantizedImage;
      // Copy the new palette
      memcpy(pMDIChild->ID.ImgDesc.Palette, Q.GetImagePalettePtr(),
                sizeof(TPIPalette));
      pMDIChild->ID.lpImageData = (BYTE huge *) GlobalLock(hQuantizedImage);

      // Copy the image data from the quantizer object to storage
      hmemcpy(pMDIChild->ID.lpImageData, Q.GetImageDataPtr(), RasterSize);

      BuildNewDisplayObject();        // Build new display object for child

      // Mark the image as modified
      pMDIChild->MakeImageDirty();

      // Inform the client menu of the change in image type to 8 BPP
      pMDIChild->MU.MUBPP = 8;
      pMDIChild->SendMenuUpdateToClient();

      // Put original cursor back
      ::SetCursor(hOldCursor);
}

// Dither the image
void TProcessImage::Dither(void) {
```

```
    // This could take some time, put up hourglass
    HCURSOR hOldCursor = ::SetCursor(LoadCursor(NULL, IDC_WAIT));

    // Instantiate a quantizer object
    UniformQuantWithDither D(TPIWidth, TPIHeight, TPIlpImageData);

    // Perform the quantization to user specified number of colors
    if (!D.DitherImage()) {
        ::MessageBox(NULL, "Error quantizing image.",
                        "User Advisory", MB_OK | MB_TASKMODAL);
        ::SetCursor(hOldCursor);
        return;
    }
    // Allocate memory for the quantized image
    DWORD RasterSize = TPIBytesPerLine8BPP * TPIHeight;
    HGLOBAL hQuantizedImage = GlobalAlloc(GHND, RasterSize);
    if (!hQuantizedImage) {
        ::MessageBox(NULL, "No memory for copying quantized image.",
                        "User Advisory", MB_OK | MB_TASKMODAL);
        ::SetCursor(hOldCursor);
        return;
    }

    // If we get here, the image has been quantized and memory exists for
    // the copy of the quantized image. Two more things must be
    // done. First, the IMAGEDESCRIPTOREXT for the child window must be
    // altered to reflect the new image and second, a new display object
    // must be instantiated for display of the new image.

    pMDIChild->ID.ImgDesc.RasterSize = RasterSize;
    pMDIChild->ID.ImgDesc.BPP = 8;
    pMDIChild->ID.ImgDesc.Colors = MAXCOLORLEVELS;

    // Free memory managed by IMAGEDESCRIPTOREXT in child window
    GlobalUnlock(TPIhImageData);
    GlobalFree(TPIhImageData);
    pMDIChild->ID.ImgDesc.hImageData = hQuantizedImage;
    // Copy the new palette
    memcpy(pMDIChild->ID.ImgDesc.Palette, D.GetImagePalettePtr(),
            sizeof(TPIPalette));
    pMDIChild->ID.lpImageData = (BYTE huge *) GlobalLock(hQuantizedImage);

    // Copy the image data from the quantizer object to storage
    hmemcpy(pMDIChild->ID.lpImageData, D.GetImageDataPtr(), RasterSize);

    BuildNewDisplayObject();            // Build new display object for child

    // Mark the image as modified
    pMDIChild->MakeImageDirty();

    // Inform the client menu of the change in image type to 8 BPP
    pMDIChild->MU.MUBPP = 8;
    pMDIChild->SendMenuUpdateToClient();

    // Put original cursor back
    ::SetCursor(hOldCursor);
}
```

```
// Convert 8 BPP palettized images and 24 BPP true color images into 8 BPP
// gray scale images.
void TProcessImage::ConvertToGray(void) {

  // This could take some time, put up hourglass
  HCURSOR hOldCursor = ::SetCursor(LoadCursor(NULL, IDC_WAIT));


  // Processing is different depending upon image type
  if (TPIBPP == 24) {               // If image is true color
  // Allocate memory for new gray scale image
  HGLOBAL hGrayImage = GlobalAlloc(GHND, TPIBytesPerLine24BPP * TPIHeight);
  if (!hGrayImage) {
     ::MessageBox(NULL, "No memory available for image conversion to gray.",
                     "User Advisory", MB_OK | MB_TASKMODAL);
     ::SetCursor(hOldCursor);
     return;
  }
  // When we get here there is enough memory for conversion. Get pointers
  // to the source and destination images.
  BYTE huge *lpDImage = (BYTE huge *) GlobalLock(hGrayImage);
  BYTE huge *lpSLine;
  BYTE huge *lpDLine;
  BYTE huge *lpSPixel;
  BYTE huge *lpDPixel;
  int  Red, Green, Blue;
  int  Luminance;


  // Go through the source RGB image data, convert RGB to gray
  // and store in destination image memory.
  for (register int Row = 0; Row < TPIHeight; Row++) {
     lpSLine = (BYTE huge *) (TPIlpImageData + (Row * TPIBytesPerLine24BPP));
     lpDLine = (BYTE huge *) (lpDImage + (Row * TPIBytesPerLine8BPP));
     for (register int Col = 0; Col < TPIWidth; Col++) {
       lpSPixel = (BYTE huge *) (lpSLine + (Col * 3L));
       lpDPixel = (BYTE huge *) (lpDLine + Col);
       Blue  = *lpSPixel++;       // Fetch the RGB data for the pixel
       Green = *lpSPixel++;
       Red   = *lpSPixel;
       Luminance = ((30 * Red) + (59 * Green) + (11 * Blue)) / 100;
       *lpDPixel = Luminance;
     }
  }
  // Image data is converted, now change palette
  for (register int Index = 0; Index < MAXCOLORLEVELS; Index++) {
     TPIPalette[Index].Red   = Index;
     TPIPalette[Index].Green = Index;
     TPIPalette[Index].Blue  = Index;
  }
  // The IMAGEDESCRIPTOREXT for the child window must be
  // altered to reflect the new image. Change only those
  // members which are affected by the conversion.
  pMDIChild->ID.ImgDesc.RasterSize = TPIBytesPerLine8BPP * TPIHeight;
  pMDIChild->ID.ImgDesc.BPP = 8;
  pMDIChild->ID.ImgDesc.Colors = MAXCOLORLEVELS;
  GlobalUnlock(TPIhImageData);
```

```
        GlobalFree(TPIhImageData);
        pMDIChild->ID.ImgDesc.hImageData = hGrayImage;
        pMDIChild->ID.lpImageData = lpDImage;
    } else {                           // Image is palettized
        int Red, Green, Blue, Luminance;
        // Image is palettized, convert color values in the palette
        for (register int Index = 0; Index < TPIColors; Index++) {
            // Get color from the palette
            Red = TPIPalette[Index].Red;
            Green = TPIPalette[Index].Green;
            Blue = TPIPalette[Index].Blue;
            // Calculate luminance of palette color value
            Luminance = ((30 * Red) + (59 * Green) + (11 * Blue)) / 100;
        // Store luminance as RGB color of palette entry
            TPIPalette[Index].Red =
            TPIPalette[Index].Green =
            TPIPalette[Index].Blue = Luminance;
        }
    }
    // Copy the modified TPIPalette back to child
    memcpy(pMDIChild->ID.ImgDesc.Palette, TPIPalette, sizeof(TPIPalette));
        BuildNewDisplayObject();       // Build new display object for child

        // Mark the image as modified
        pMDIChild->MakeImageDirty();

        // Inform the client menu of the change in image type to 8 BPP
        pMDIChild->MU.MUBPP = 8;
        pMDIChild->SendMenuUpdateToClient();

        // Put original cursor back
        ::SetCursor(hOldCursor);
    }


// This function will convert DIB images with less than 24 BPP into images
// of 24 BPP.
void TProcessImage::PromoteTo24BPP(void) {
    DWORD PixelsPerByte, BytesPerLineS;

    // This could take some time, set cursor to hourglass
    HCURSOR hOldCursor = ::SetCursor(LoadCursor(NULL, IDC_WAIT));

    // Allocate and lock memory for filtered image data
    HGLOBAL hPromotedImage = GlobalAlloc(GHND, TPIBytesPerLine24BPP *
        TPIHeight);
    if (!hPromoteImage) {
        ::MessageBox(NULL, "No memory available for promotion of image to 24 BPP.",
                        "User Advisory", MB_OK | MB_TASKMODAL);
        ::SetCursor(hOldCursor);
        return;
    }
    // Calculate PixelsPerByte and BytesPerLine.
    switch(TPIBPP) {
        case 1:
                    BytesPerLineS = (TPIWidth+7)/8; // Exactly 8 pixels in each byte
```

```
                PixelsPerByte = 8;
                break;

        case 2:
        BytesPerLineS = (TPIWidth+3)/4; // Exactly 4 pixels in each byte
        PixelsPerByte = 4;
        break;

      case 4:
        BytesPerLineS = (TPIWidth+1)/2; // Exactly two pixels in each byte
        PixelsPerByte = 2;
        break;

      case 8:
        BytesPerLineS = TPIWidth;        // Exactly one pixel in each byte
        PixelsPerByte = 1;
        break;
}
BytesPerLineS = ALIGN_DWORD(BytesPerLineS);

BYTE huge *lpDImage = (BYTE huge *) GlobalLock(hPromotedImage);

BYTE huge *lpLineS;
BYTE huge *lpLineD;
BYTE huge *lpByteS;
BYTE huge *lpByteD;
BYTE TheByte, GrpNum, ShiftCount;

// Now pick apart the packed pixel data and store in 24 BPP DIB
for (register int Row=0; Row < TPIHeight; Row++) {
   lpLineS = (BYTE huge *) (TPIlpImageData + (Row * BytesPerLineS));
   lpLineD = (BYTE huge *) (lpDImageData + (Row * TPIBytesPerLine24BPP));
   for (register int Col=0; Col < TPIWidth; Col++) {
     lpByteS = (BYTE huge *) (lpLineS + (Col/PixelsPerByte));
     lpByteD = (BYTE huge *) (lpLineD + (Col * 3L));
     TheByte = *lpByteS;
     if (TPIBPP != 8) {
       GrpNum = (WORD) ((PixelsPerByte-1) - (Col % PixelsPerByte));
       ShiftCount = GrpNum * TPIBPP;
       TheByte = (TheByte & (Masks[TPIBPP] << ShiftCount)) >> ShiftCount;
     }
     // When we get here, TheByte contains the palette index of the
     // pixel of interest. Now, look up the palette entry and move
     // the palette's RGB value into the destination image buffer
     *(lpByteD    ) = TPIPalette[TheByte].Blue;
     *(lpByteD + 1) = TPIPalette[TheByte].Green;
     *(lpByteD + 2) = TPIPalette[TheByte].Red;
   }
}
// When we get here, a 24 BPP image is available. Two things must be
// done. First, the IMAGEDESCRIPTOREXT for the child window must be
// altered to reflect the new image and second, a new display object
// must be instantiated for display of the new image.
pMDIChild->ID.ImgDesc.BPP = 24;
pMDIChild->ID.ImgDesc.Colors = 0;
pMDIChild->ID.ImgDesc.RasterSize = TPIBytesPerLine24BPP * TPIHeight;
```

```
         // Free memory managed by IMAGEDESCRIPTOREXT in child window
         GlobalUnlock(TPIhImageData);
         GlobalFree(TPIhImageData);

         // Replace with memory allocated in this routine. All other items in
         // the IMAGEDESCRIPTOREXT remain the same.
         pMDIChild->ID.ImgDesc.hImageData = hPromotedImage;
         pMDIChild->ID.lpImageData = lpDImage;

         BuildNewDisplayObject();          // Build new display object for child

         // Mark the image as modified
         pMDIChild->MakeImageDirty();

         // Inform the client menu of the change in image type to 24 BPP
         pMDIChild->MU.MUBPP = 24;
         pMDIChild->SendMenuUpdateToClient();

         // Put original cursor back
         ::SetCursor(hOldCursor);
    }

    // This function calculates the number of bytes of image data per
    // line given the line width and the number of bits per pixel.
    DWORD CalculateBytesPerLine(WORD Width, WORD BPP) {

         DWORD BytesPerLine;

         // Calculate BytesPerLine
         switch(BPP) {
             case 1:
               BytesPerLine = (Width+7)/8; // Exactly 8 pixels in each byte
               break;

             case 2:
               BytesPerLine = (Width+3)/4; // Exactly 4 pixels in each byte
               break;

             case 4:
               BytesPerLine = (Width+1)/2; // Exactly two pixels in each byte
               break;

             case 8:
               BytesPerLine = Width;        // Exactly one pixel in each byte
               break;

             case 24:
               BytesPerLine = Width * 3;    // Exactly three bytes per pixel
               break;
         }
         BytesPerLine = ALIGN_DWORD(BytesPerLine);
         return BytesPerLine;
    }

    // This function is called to clean up in the event that a clipboard
    // error occurs.
    void TProcessImage::CleanUp(HGLOBAL hMem, HPALETTE hPalette) {
```

```
  if (hMem) {                    // If image memory allocated
    GlobalFree(hMem);            // free it and clear handle
    hMem = 0;
  }
  if (hPalette) {                // If palette created
    DeleteObject(hPalette);      // delete it and clear handle
    hPalette = 0;
  }
}


// This function sends the specified image to the clipboard using CF_DIB
// format. If the image is 8 BPP or less a CF_PALETTE entry is also made
// to the clipboard which contains the palette for the image. 24 BPP images
// do not set a CF_PALETTE entry.
BOOL TProcessImage::ImageToClipboard(void) {

  // This operation can take awhile, put up hourglass
  HCURSOR hOldCursor = ::SetCursor(LoadCursor(NULL, IDC_WAIT));

  // Calculate the number of bytes in a line of image data
  DWORD BytesPerLine = CalculateBytesPerLine(TPIWidth, TPIBPP);

  // Calculate color table size. If image is true color, the BITMAPINFO
  // structure doesn't contains any RGBQUAD entries. If the image is less
  // than 24 BPP, Colors number of RGBQUAD entries are required.
  WORD ColorTableSize = (TPIBPP == 24) ? 0 : TPIColors * sizeof(RGBQUAD);

  // Calculate total memory required to contain BITMAPINFOHEADER,
  // the bmiColor table and the image data.
  DWORD TotalMemoryRequired = sizeof(BITMAPINFOHEADER) + ColorTableSize +
                              BytesPerLine * TPIHeight;

  // Allocate the memory block
  HGLOBAL hBmi = GlobalAlloc(GHND, TotalMemoryRequired);
  if (!hBmi) {
      ::SetCursor(hOldCursor);      // Put cursor back to normal
      return FALSE;
  }
  // Make the memory block pointer into a pointer to a BITMAPINFO structure
  LPBITMAPINFO lpBmi = (LPBITMAPINFO) GlobalLock(hBmi);

  // The following setup is independent of the # of colors
  LPBITMAPINFOHEADER pBi = &lpBmi->bmiHeader;
  pBi->biSize          = sizeof(BITMAPINFOHEADER);
  pBi->biWidth         = TPIWidth;
  pBi->biHeight        = TPIHeight;
  pBi->biPlanes        = 1;
  pBi->biCompression   = 0L;
  pBi->biXPelsPerMeter = 0L;
  pBi->biYPelsPerMeter = 0L;
  pBi->biClrImportant  = 0L;
  // The remainder of the processing is dependent upon the number of colors
  if (TPIColors != 0) {            // If a palettized image
     pBi->biBitCount = TPIBPP;     // Store bits per pixel
     pBi->biClrUsed = TPIColors;   // Store actual number of color used
```

```
      // Copy palette to DIB color table
      for (register int Index = 0; Index < TPIColors; Index++) {
        lpBmi->bmiColors[Index].rgbRed = TPIPalette[Index].Red;
        lpBmi->bmiColors[Index].rgbGreen = TPIPalette[Index].Green;
        lpBmi->bmiColors[Index].rgbBlue = TPIPalette[Index].Blue;
        lpBmi->bmiColors[Index].rgbReserved = 0;
      }
    } else {                        // A true color image
      pBi->biBitCount = 24;         // True color images have 24 BPP
      pBi->biClrUsed = 0;           // Colors used is zero
    }

    // Calculate image size
    pBi->biSizeImage = BytesPerLine * (DWORD) TPIHeight;

    // Calculate where to store the image data in memory block.
    BYTE huge *lpImageStorage = (BYTE huge *)
                          ((BYTE huge *) lpBmi + (DWORD) sizeof(BITMAPINFOHEADER) +
                            ColorTableSize);
    // Now move the image data into the memory block
    hmemcpy(lpImageStorage, TPIlpImageData, pBi->biSizeImage);

    // Now the image is completely contained in the memory block.
    // Unlock the memory
    GlobalUnlock(hBmi);

    HPALETTE hPalette = 0;          // Assume no palette to be used

    // Now create a logical palette if the image is less than 24 BPP
    if (TPIBPP < 24) {
      HGLOBAL hPaletteMem = GlobalAlloc(GHND, sizeof(LOGPALETTE) +
      TPIColors * sizeof(PALETTEENTRY));
      if (!hPaletteMem) {           // If error, free image memory
        GlobalFree(hBmi);           // and return error indication
        ::SetCursor(hOldCursor);    // Put cursor back to normal also
        return FALSE;
      }
      // Get pointer to palette memory block
      LPLOGPALETTE pPal = (LPLOGPALETTE) GlobalLock(hPaletteMem);
      // Initialize entries
      pPal->palNumEntries = TPIColors;
      pPal->palVersion = 0x300;

      // Move the color values into place
      for (register int Index = 0; Index < TPIColors; Index++) {
        pPal->palPalEntry[Index].peRed   = TPIPalette[Index].Red;
        pPal->palPalEntry[Index].peGreen = TPIPalette[Index].Green;
        pPal->palPalEntry[Index].peBlue  = TPIPalette[Index].Blue;
        pPal->palPalEntry[Index].peFlags = 0;
      }
      hPalette = CreatePalette(pPal);// Create the logical palette
      GlobalUnlock(hPaletteMem);      // Free Memory
      GlobalFree(hPaletteMem);
    }
    // Now move the image data block and the palette (if required) to
```

```
    // the clipboard.
    if (!OpenClipboard(TPIhWindow)) {  // Attempt to open the clipboard
      CleanUp(hBmi, hPalette);          // If error, cleanup
      ::SetCursor(hOldCursor);          // Put cursor back to normal
      return FALSE;
    // Clipboard opened successfully, now clear it of its contents
    if (!EmptyClipboard()) {
      CloseClipboard();                 // If error cleanup and leave
      CleanUp(hBmi, hPalette);
       ::SetCursor(hOldCursor);         // Put cursor back to normal
       return FALSE;
    }
    // Clipboard is empty, now write the image data
    if (!SetClipboardData(CF_DIB, hBmi)) {
      CloseClipboard();                 // If error cleanup and leave
      CleanUp(hBmi, hPalette);
       ::SetCursor(hOldCursor);         // Put cursor back to normal
       return FALSE;
    }
    // Image data written successfully, now write palette if required
    if (hPalette) {
      if (!SetClipboardData (CF_PALETTE, hPalette)) {
        CloseClipboard();               // If error cleanup and leave
        CleanUp(0, hPalette);
        ::SetCursor(hOldCursor);        // Put cursor back to normal
        return FALSE;
      }
    }
    // Image and palette written to clipboard. Now close it
    ::SetCursor(hOldCursor);            // Put cursor back to normal
    if (!CloseClipboard())
      return FALSE;
    else
      return TRUE;
}


// Paste an image from the clipboard
BOOL TProcessImage::ImageFromClipboard(IMAGEDESCRIPTOR& ID) {

  // Check if DIB format data available on clipboard
  if (!IsClipboardFormatAvailable(CF_DIB))
    return FALSE;                       // return FALSE if not

  // There is a DIB on the clipboard. Attempt to open the clipboard
  if (!OpenClipboard(TPIhWindow)) // If error, bail out
    return FALSE;                       // and return error indication

  // Now attempt to get a handle to the clipboard data
  HGLOBAL hBmi = GetClipboardData(CF_DIB);
  if (!hBmi) {
    CloseClipboard();
    return FALSE;
  }
}
```

```
// Check to see if a palette is also available. If so load it.
HPALETTE hPalette = 0;
if (IsClipboardFormatAvailable(CF_PALETTE)) {
  // Now attempt to get a handle to the clipboard data
   hPalette = (HPALETTE) GetClipboardData(CF_PALETTE);
   if (!hPalette) {
      CloseClipboard();
    return FALSE;
   }
}
CloseClipboard();                 // Clipboard is no longer required

// We now have a handle to the image data, get pointers to its info
// so it can be decoded.
LPBITMAPINFO lpBmi = (LPBITMAPINFO) GlobalLock(hBmi);
LPBITMAPINFOHEADER pBi = &lpBmi->bmiHeader;
// Make sure we understand the format of the image data. Check the
// size field to see if it is what we expect.

// NOTE: The handle to the image data and palette should not be freed by
// the application under any circumstances. It belongs to the clipboard.

if (pBi->biSize != sizeof(BITMAPINFOHEADER)) {
  GlobalUnlock(hBmi);
   return FALSE;
}

// Read the information into the IMAGEDESCRIPTOR
ID.Width      = (WORD) pBi->biWidth;
ID.Height     = (WORD) pBi->biHeight;
ID.RasterSize = pBi->biSizeImage;
ID.BPP        = pBi->biBitCount;

// If app did not initialize RasterSize, do it ourselves.
if (ID.RasterSize == 0)
  ID.RasterSize = CalculateBytesPerLine(ID.Width, ID.BPP) * (DWORD) ID.Height;

// Figure out how to set the Color entry in ID
if (pBi->biClrUsed != 0)           // If number of colors are specified
  ID.Colors = (WORD) pBi->biClrUsed; // use them. Otherwise colors are max
else {                             // for the given image BPP.
  if (pBi->biBitCount != 24)       // If not a true color image
    ID.Colors = 1 << pBi->biBitCount;// Calculate max colors
  else                             // If true color image
    ID.Colors = 0;                 // Set to zero
}
// Calculate color table size. There are no RGBQUAD entries in BITMAPINFO
// if the image is true color (24 BPP).
WORD ColorTableSize =
     (ID.BPP == 24) ? 0 : ID.Colors * sizeof(RGBQUAD);

// Now allocate a block of memory which will contain the image DIB
// data.
HGLOBAL hImage = GlobalAlloc(GHND, ID.RasterSize);
```

```
if (!hImage) {                      // Check for low memory
  GlobalUnlock(hBmi);               // If error, unlock clipboard data
  return FALSE;                     // and return indication
}
// We have enough memory to copy the image data
ID.hImageData = hImage;             // Copy the handle into the ID

// Get a pointer to the memory
BYTE huge *lpImage = (BYTE huge *) GlobalLock(hImage);

// Calculate where to store the image data in memory block.
BYTE huge *lpImageData = (BYTE huge *)
                  ((BYTE huge *) lpBmi + (DWORD) sizeof(BITMAPINFOHEADER) +
                  ColorTableSize);
// Now move the image data into the memory block
hmemcpy(lpImage, lpImageData, ID.RasterSize);

// Now process the palette if there is one
PALETTEENTRY PaletteEntries[256];    // Storage for palette entries

if (!hPalette) {                    // If no palette for this image
  // Extract a palette from the DIB color table
  memcpy(PaletteEntries, lpBmi->bmiColors, ColorTableSize);
} else {
  // Process palette passed in from clipboard
  GetPaletteEntries(hPalette, 0, 256, (LPPALETTEENTRY) &PaletteEntries);
}
// Unlock the clipboard memory as it is no longer required. Unlock
// also the storage for the DIB image.
GlobalUnlock(hBmi);
GlobalUnlock(hImage);

// When we get here, PaletteEntries contains a palette. Parse out
// and store palette in ID.
for (register int Index = 0; Index < 256; Index++) {
  ID.Palette[Index].Red = PaletteEntries[Index].peRed;
  ID.Palette[Index].Green = PaletteEntries[Index].peGreen;
  ID.Palette[Index].Blue = PaletteEntries[Index].peBlue;
}
return TRUE;                        // All is well with the world
}
```

Image Processing Gray Scale and Color Images

Most books and articles dealing with image processing concentrate on the manipulation of gray scale or black and white images only. One reason for this is that one of the most prominent uses of image processing is as a part of machine vision where color images only complicate matters. Whenever computers are called upon to perform quantitative analysis of an image, the image must be simplified as much as possible (read that as colors eliminated). The human eye/brain system, however, is assisted in its analysis of images by the incorporation of image details and color. Because the focus of this book is photographic imaging and not machine vision, many of the algorithms presented have been extended into the realm of color. When image-processing

The TProcessImage class

Purpose

The TProcessImage class is a shell that binds together all of the image-processing algorithms presented in this chapter (and available in the TestApp example program of Chapter 1). In addition to its function as a shell, the constructor of this class extracts important information about the image to be processed and makes the information available to member function via class variables.

Member Functions

TProcessImage.   This is the class constructor. It accepts a pointer to an MDI child window that it uses to extract and store important image information that becomes available to all member functions of this class.

~TProcessImage.   This is the class destructor. It has no functionality at this time but is included as a place holder in case it is needed in the future.

ConvoluteImage.   This private member function performs convolution on an image. See text for details. As parameters, it expects a pointer to a convolution kernel, an integer in the range 1 to 10 that indicates the strength with which to apply the convolution to the image and a pointer to a descriptive string used in the filter control dialog box to identify the type of convolution to be performed.

RotateImage.   This private member function is called to rotate an image. It requires a Boolean parameter to determine rotation direction. TRUE indicates a clockwise rotation, whereas FALSE indicates a counterclockwise rotation. The public member functions **RotateCW** and **RotateCCW** call this function to perform their work.

FlipImage.   This private member function is called to flip an image either horizontally or vertically depending on the parameter. TRUE indicates a horizontal flip, FALSE a vertical flip. The public member functions **FlipHorz** and **FlipVert** call this function to perform their work.

BuildNewDisplayObject.   This private member function is called by many of the image-processing functions to tear down and rebuild a Display object for the MDI child window image being processed. A new Display object is usually required when the image parameters have been radically altered as a result of an image-processing operation; for example, when a 24-BPP image is converted into an 8-BPP image by quantization, a new Display object would be required to display the 8-BPP version of the image.

This function builds a new Display object from the information contained in the IMAGEDESCRIPTOR of the child window. For this reason, the child window's information must be updated with the results of the image-processing operation before this function is called.

CleanUp.   This private function is only used to clean up whenever a clipboard operation fails. This function has no general purpose utility.

ImageToClipboard.   This member function is called to place a copy of the image in the child window onto the clipboard. The image data are placed onto the clipboard in DIB format and are therefore tagged with CF_DIB. If the image placed on the clipboard is palettized, a CF_PALETTE entry is placed on the clipboard in addition to the image data.

FIGURE 9.1 The TProcessImage class.

ImageFromClipboard.   This function is called to retrieve an image placed onto the clipboard by another application or by a previous call to the **ImageToClipboard** function. This function returns TRUE if the image was retrieved successfully and FALSE otherwise. If successful, this function initializes an IMAGEDESCRIPTOR structure with information about the retrieved image so a child window can be created for display of the image.

BeginCrop.   This function is called to begin the image-cropping operation within a child window. When called, this function changes how the child window processes mouse messages (the left button down message, the mouse move message, and the left button up message) involved with cropping. When cropping is not being performed, mouse messages are ignored. After **BeginCrop** is called, the mouse messages generated within the child window are processed so that the user is given the ability to position and size a rectangular box over the portion of the image to crop. When the user releases the left mouse button (resulting in a left mouse button up message), **EndCrop** is automatically called to perform the image-cropping process.

EndCrop.   This function is called (within the left mouse button up message processing code in the child window) to terminate the cropping mode of operation. This function figures out the size of the cropped image area and prepares a new DIB that contains the new, reduced size, image data. It then updates the IMAGEDESCRIPTOR information in the child window to reflect the size of the new image and causes a new Display object to be built for image display.

AdjustBrightnessContrast.   When this function is called, the user is presented with a dialog box with which to control image brightness and contrast. A scroll bar control is provided for each adjustment. After any adjustments are made and the OK button is clicked, the image is processed, and the result is displayed over the original image in the child window. See the text for details of how image contrast and brightness adjustments are performed.

RotateCW.   Execution of this function causes the image in the child window to be rotated 90° in the clockwise direction.

RotateCCW.   Execution of this function causes the image in the child window to be rotated 90° in the counterclockwise direction.

FlipHorz.   Execution of this function causes the image in the child window to be flipped horizontally. This swaps image left with image right.

FlipVert.   Execution of this function causes the image in the child window to be flipped vertically. This swaps image top with image bottom.

HighPass1, HighPass2, HighPass3, LowPass1, LowPass2, LowPass3.   These functions cause convolution operations to be performed on the image in the child window. They differ in the convolution kernel used for the filter operation. See the text for details. The high-pass functions attenuate the low spatial frequency information in an image while allowing the high-frequency information to pass. The low-pass filters do just the opposite.

NorthEdges, NorthEastEdges, EastEdges, SouthEastEdges, SouthEdges, SouthWestEdges, WestEdges, NorthWestEdges.   These functions cause convolution operations to be performed on the image in the child window. They differ in the convolution kernel used for the edge enhancement operation. See the text for details. Each of these functions enhanced image edges in the direction indicated by the function names.

FIGURE 9.1 *(Continued)*

Despeckle.   The execution of this member function causes a Median Filter operation to be performed on the image data. Median filtering is used to remove random noise contained in an image. Repeated application of despeckling results in image blurring.

HistogramEq.   Execution of this function causes the histogram equalization algorithm to be applied to the image data. Histogram equalization is used to improve contrast in low-contrast images, that is, images that do not use the full range of pixel intensity values available. Histogram equalization smoothes out the clusters of pixel intensity values to more evenly use the entire range of values available. Application of this algorithm can sometimes bring out details in a low-contrast image that were never visible before.

Quantize.   Execution of this function results in the true color image in a child window being quantized to a user-selectible number of colors using the Median Cut algorithm. The code to perform the quantization is not actually in the TProcessImage class. The **Quantize** function is used merely as a surrogate to call the median cut code. This allows the TProcessImage class to present a consistent interface to any application program using it.

Dither.   Execution of this function results in the true color image in a child window being processed using the Uniform Quantization with Dithering algorithm. The code to perform the processing is not actually in the TProcessImage class. The **Dither** function is used merely as a surrogate to call the dithering code. This allows the TProcessImage class to present a consistent interface to any application program using it.

ConvertToGray.   This function converts a palettized color or true color image displayed in a child window to a palettized gray scale image. The gray scale value used for a pixel represents the luminance of the color as calculated by the following formula:

$$\text{Luminance} = \frac{((30 * \text{Red}) + (59 * \text{Green}) + (11 * \text{Blue}))}{100}$$

True color images are converted to 8 BPP, 256 shades of gray images. The RGB color component values of the palette used to display the gray scale images all have equal values. In other words, R = G = B. As an aside, all colors that have equal color components can be considered a shade of white beginning at black, through the various shades of gray, to white.

PromoteTo24BPP.   This function converts an image with less than 24 BPP into 24-BPP format. Since many of the image-processing algorithms within this class are only usable with 24-BPP images, this function is provided to perform the conversion so that any image can be processed. Note: Images converted into 24-BPP format will be considerably larger than the original image.

FIGURE 9.1 *(Continued)*

techniques are used for photographic imaging, the algorithmic accuracy is not as important as the aesthetic affect. In other words, the effects that are being sought are qualitative not quantitative, and a human judges the result, not a computer.

Many of the algorithms have a direct translation from the gray scale realm into color. Brightening an image is one example. Instead of adding some brightness adjustment value to a single gray scale pixel value, the same adjustment value is added to all three RGB components of the color pixel. Some algorithms such as contrast enhancement and histogram equalization work differently. These algorithms do their work solely on the green color component of an image. The red and blue components are adjusted using the same values to keep color shifts to a minimum.

Another complication that comes into play has to do with the type of image needing processing. As you will recall from Chapter 1, most images fall naturally into one of two unique types: palettized images (which includes black-and-white and gray scale images) where a pixel's value represents an index into an array of colors (the palette) and true color images whose pixel values (typically an RGB value) completely describes the color of the pixel (no palette is used). To brighten a palettized image requires that the brightening adjustment value be applied to the color values stored in the palette; the image's pixel data do not change. To brighten a true color image, as mentioned earlier, requires that the brightening adjustment value be added to all three of the color components that make up each pixel of the image. As I hope you realize, these are two entirely different methods of processing the image data.

In extending the image-processing algorithms for photographic imaging, I used the following guidelines:

- The human eye is most sensitive to the green area of the color spectrum.
- If an equal adjustment value is added to each color component of a pixel, the result will be a new color value that is brighter than the original but retains the basic hue.
- If different values are added to each color component of a pixel, the result will also be a new color value but with a shifted hue and/or brightness.
- Palettized images require manipulation of the palette values, whereas true color images require direct manipulation of the image data.
- When operating under Win16, huge pointers must be used to manipulate image data because most images contain more data than can fit in a single 16-bit segment. Under Win32, all pointers are 32 bits and the segment size is set at 2 gigabytes. This alleviates the need for any special treatment of pointers.
- RGB color data stored in DIB format is physically stored in memory in BGR order, opposite of what would be expected.

Specific algorithmic details will be provided in this chapter when each of the individual image-processing operations are described. Many of the books listed in Appendix B "Further Reading" contain more information on image-processing algorithms. Interested readers are encouraged to consult these references as needed.

The TProcessImage Class

The TProcessImage class provides the framework within which all of the image-processing algorithms described in this chapter work. The TProcessImage class itself provides very little functionality of its own, other than as a shell to bind the algorithms together. The TProcessImage class constructor requires a pointer to the MDI child window (which contains the image to be processed) when an object of this class is instantiated. On first thought, this may seem like a odd way to organize a class of image-processing algorithms that typically do not need any Windows specific information. This organization was adopted for the following reasons:

1. By having a pointer to the MDI child window, the members of the TProcessImage class are granted access to the IMAGEDESCRIPTOREXT structure within the child that completely describes the image within the window that is going to be processed.
2. By having a pointer to the MDI child window, the members of the TProcessImage class are granted access to the Display object within the child. This is required because most of the image-processing algorithms change the images in such a manner that the original Display object must be destroyed and a new one created for display of the processed image data.

When an object of the TProcessImage class is instantiated, the class constructor extracts pertinent information about the image to be processed from the IMAGE-DESCRIPTOREXT structure (of the MDI child window) and stores it in class variables. These variables are prefixed with a TPI designation and include image width (TPIWidth), image height (TPIHeight), and so on. This is done to make access to the image parameters faster and to make the image-processing code easier to read because image width can be referenced as TPIWidth instead of pMDIChild->ID.ImgDesc.Width. In addition, two quantities TPIBytesPerLine8BPP and TPIBytesPerLine24BPP are calculated by the constructor. These variables contain the number of bytes per line (row) of image data assuming 8 bits per pixel and 24 bits per pixel, respectively. These are useful quantities that are used by many of the image-processing algorithms.

If you have looked at the constructor code shown in Listing 9.2, you have probably noticed that a NULL pointer to a child window is also acceptable as a parameter. The code was implemented in this way only because image clipboard code is included within this class. The only time the child window pointer can be NULL is when using the **ImageFromClipboard** function. If any of the other member functions are used under these conditions, you are guaranteed a spectacular crash of your computer system. The reason for allowing a NULL child window pointer when using the **ImageFromClipboard** function is because when extracting an image from the clipboard no child window yet exists. A child window is created later after the image data is successfully extracted from the clipboard.

Point Processes

Point processes are fundamental image-processing operations. They are the simplest and yet probably the most frequently used of the image-processing algorithms. They are useful by themselves or in conjunction with the other categories of algorithms. Being less complex than other image-processing algorithms, they are a natural starting place for our discussion.

As mentioned, point processes are algorithms that modify a pixel's value in an image based on that pixel's value and sometimes its location. No other pixel values are involved in the transformation. Individual pixels are replaced with new values that are algorithmically related to their original value. As a result of the algorithmic relationship between the original and the new pixel value, point processes can generally be reversed. Point process algorithms scan through an image, pixel by pixel, performing the pixel transformation. If the transformation is dependent only on the original pixel value, the transformation process can be performed with the help of a Look Up Table (LUT). LUTs will be discussed shortly. If the point process transformation also takes into consideration the location of a pixel, a formula or a formula in conjunction with a LUT can be used to transform the pixel values. In general, point processes do not modify the spatial relationships within an image. For this reason, point processes cannot modify the detail contained in an image.

Look Up Tables

Look Up Tables are devices that provide a mapping between an input and an output value. As such, LUTs are a convenient implementation method for many point-processing algorithms—so convenient, in fact, that many manufacturers of image acquisition equipment provide LUTs in hardware for use with image-processing software. Providing LUTs in hardware maximizes the speed of the image-processing algorithms. We do not have hardware LUTs to toy with, but we can emulate them using arrays in software. The basic idea is the same.

A software LUT uses a pixel's value as an index into an array to return a new pixel value to be used in place of the original. The array will of course have been filled previously with values that represent the transformation or mapping to be performed on the image data ran through the LUT. In other words, a LUT must be initialized before being used; otherwise, the data coming out of the LUT will not have a definite relationship to the data going in. For most image-processing operations, a LUT is an array of 256 integers declared as follows:

```
int LUT[256];
```

An identity function can be mapped into a LUT by storing the value of its index into each LUT location; that is, location zero is loaded with zero, location one with a one up to location 255, which is loaded with 255 as shown below.

```
#define MINSAMPLEVALUE 0
#define MAXSAMPLEVALUE 255

int LUT [MAXSAMPLEVALUE + 1];

for (Index = MINSAMPLEVALUE; Index < MAXSAMPLEVALUE + 1; Index++)
  LUT [Index] = Index;
```

With the LUT initialized in this manner, data coming out of the LUT are the same as the data going in. In other words, no transformation is applied to the data. If this mapping were applied to an image, the result would be exactly nil, nothing, zip. The image would not be changed because what went in came out exactly the same. Said another way in terms of code,

```
int InPixelValue = GetPixelValue (Row, Col); // Fetch pixel value from image
int OutPixelValue = LUT[InPixelValue];       // Use value as index into identity
                                             // LUT
InPixelValue == OutPixelValue;               // OutPixelValue equals InPixelValue
```

Of course, LUTs are not usually used to perform nil transforms such as this. Instead, a LUT would be initialized with a transformation or mapping function to be applied to the image data. By way of example, let us discuss the process of brightening a gray scale image.

Brightening is a point process that adds (or subtracts) a constant value to (from) pixels in an image. Expressed algebraically, a pixel with intensity value V is transformed as follows:

$$V' = V + b$$

where b is the brightness adjustment constant that can be positive or negative and V' is the new brightness adjusted pixel value. If b is positive, the brightness of the pixels increases. If b is negative, the brightness is decreased. Applying a brightness adjustment to an image can be as easy as the direct application of the formula shown earlier to each affected pixel. Another way to implement the brightness adjustment, however, is to use a LUT to transform the data. The brightness transformation is computed and stored in the LUT and then the gray scale image data are run through it. The following code segment shows how a LUT might be initialized for this transformation.

```
#define MINSAMPLEVALUE 0
#define MAXSAMPLEVALUE 255

int LUT[MAXSAMPLEVALUE + 1];

for (Index = MINSAMPLEVALUE; Index < MAXSAMPLEVALUE + 1; Index++) {
  NewValue = Index + BrightnessAdjustValue;
  NewValue = (NewValue < MINSAMPLEVALUE) ?
                  MINSAMPLEVALUE : NewValue;
  NewValue = (NewValue > MAXSAMPLEVALUE) ?
                  MAXSAMPLEVALUE : NewValue;
  LUT[Index] = NewValue;
}
```

A complication that must be taken into consideration is pixel value overflow or underflow. If, for example, a positive brightness adjustment factor is added to a pixel's value and the result exceeds the maximum value of 255 (MAXSAMPLEVALUE), the overflow condition has just been experienced. Further, if a negative brightness adjustment is added to a small pixel value, the result may become negative. This is pixel value underflow. For these reasons, the LUT initialization code shown previously clamps the values placed in the LUT to the range 0 to 255. Setting up the LUT in this manner guarantees all pixels transformed with this LUT will be within legal limits. Because the clamping operations are only applied to the 256 entries in the LUT instead of to each pixel of the brightened image, performance is greatly enhanced.

You might be telling yourself at this point that using a LUT for such a simple transform is overkill, and you may be right. In terms of performance, it is obviously much faster to fetch a byte of data directly from an image, add the brightness factor to it, and store it back than it is to initialize the LUT array with the transfer function and then pass each pixel value through it. The elegance of LUT-based transforms only becomes obvious with more complex transfer functions. Performance of LUT-based transforms can be increased substantially by precomputing the LUTs and storing them in memory until required. The performance of the precomputed LUT transform when later applied to an image will be constant regardless of the complexity of the transfer function. This is because all the time-consuming math went into initializing the LUT. Application of the LUT is thus a direct array lookup. Another advantage of using LUTs for point process transforms is the consistent structure of the resultant algorithms. Once you understand how LUTs operate and have coded an algorithm using one, you'll never want to go back to other, seemingly brute force techniques. The use of a LUT for contrast adjustments will be discussed shortly.

Histograms

Histograms are another tool that finds use in image processing. A histogram is the distribution of pixel intensity values for an image or portion of an image. The distribution data contained within a histogram is used directly by some image-processing algorithms such as histogram equalization. The histogram data can also be plotted for visual inspection and analysis. Histograms indicate a lot about the overall brightness and contrast of an image. Further, the dynamic range of the pixel values that make up an image is readily apparent. As such, histograms are valuable tools for image processing both qualitatively and quantitatively.

A typical histogram plot is a two-dimensional graph of the number of occurrences of a pixel value versus pixel value. Figure 9.2 shows a typical histogram plot. Although the histogram shown in Figure 9.2 was fabricated for purposes of discussion, it shows the kind of information that can be conveyed about an image; for example, it shows that the whole range of possible pixel values is not being fully used. Pixel values between 42 to 62 are nonexistent in the image. If this were a histogram of a real image, the appearance of the real image might be improved by the application of histogram equalization. This would transform the image so that it would occupy the complete range of pixel values. This usually results in a more pleasing displayed image.

The point processes that are included in the TestApp program and discussed in this chapter are:

1. Image Brightness Adjustment
2. Image Contrast Adjustment
3. Histogram Equalization

Image Brightness and Contrast Adjustments

Within the TProcessImage class, the code for adjusting image brightness and contrast are combined into a single member function called **AdjustBrightnessContrast.** Image brightness and contrast adjustments are available for palettized and true color images. Upon execution of this function, the user is presented with a dialog box with scroll bar controls for the adjustment of image brightness and image contrast. Once the user's input are gathered, the algorithmic processing is performed. The brightness adjust value read from the scroll bar adjustment control is used directly for manipulation of the image data in a manner similar to what has already been discussed. The user's contrast adjustment value, however, must be preprocessed before it can be used to manipulate the image data. The user's data are, in fact, used to create a LUT for manipulating the image contrast.

Many algorithms exist for manipulation of image contrast. The method I chose for implementation in the TProcessImage class is one of the simplest and fastest because it does not require the precalculation of an image histogram before processing can be performed. For the sake of common understanding, when the contrast of an image is increased, lighter colors get lighter while the darker colors become darker. Conversely, when contrast is reduced, the lighter colors in the image get darker while the darker colors get lighter. Colors between light and dark are not impacted or are impacted very little by contrast adjustments. Understanding the concept of contrast is the key to understanding how contrast enhancement works.

The algorithm used in the TProcessImage class for contrast adjustment is based on the sin math function. To understand how this works, consider the graph of the sin function from 0 to 2 π radians as shown in Figure 9.3a. The sin function has a positive and a negative peak, and its value passes through zero in between the peaks. If we manipulate the sin function by first shifting it by negative π radians (Figure 9.3b) and then mapping it to the pixel value range 0 to 255, we end up with a sin curve suitable for manipulating image contrast. The graph of the manipulated sin function is shown in Figure 9.3c. The mathematical equation for this graph is:

$$-\text{ContrastAdjustValue} * \sin (0.0245 * \text{Index} - 3.14)$$

where

$$0.0245 = \frac{(2 * \pi)}{256} \text{ and } 0 \leq \text{Index and Index} < 256$$

Consider the attributes of this function that make it suitable for manipulating image contrast. First, midrange image pixel values (near 128 or 256/2) are unaffected or affected little by the adjustment. Second and most importantly, with ContrastAdjustValue positive (−ContrastAdjustValue negative) image pixel values below the midrange value are lowered in value, whereas pixels above the midrange value are raised in value. With ContrastAdjustValue negative, just the opposite occurs, which is exactly the scenario described earlier. Since the range of values that ContrastAdjustValue can have is limited to ±48, the maximum increase in value any pixel can be given is +48 and the maximum decrease is −48.

The manipulated sin function data are stored into a LUT that will be used to adjust the value of the image pixels. The following code segment, extracted from Listing 9.2, shows the initialization of the LUT in preparation for use:

```
for (Index = 0; Index < 256; Index++)
  ContrastTlb[Index] = ContrastAdjustValue * sin(0.0245 * Index - 3.14);
```

With a value for the brightness adjustment and an initialized LUT for the contrast adjustment, the processing of the image data is easy. For true color images the steps are as follows:

1. An RGB pixel value is fetched from the DIB image.

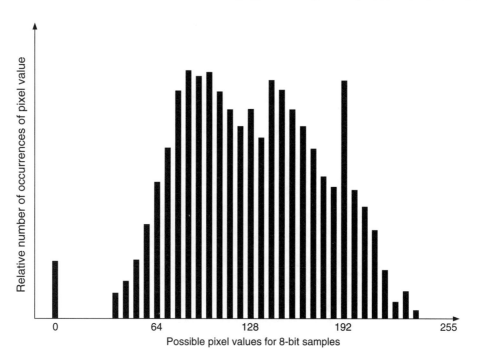

NOTE: The summation of pixel intensity values and occurrences equals the total number of pixels in image.

FIGURE 9.2 A typical histogram plot.

2. The value to be used to adjust each color component of the pixel is calculated using the following formula: AdjustValue = ContrastTbl[Green] + BriteAdjustValue. Notice the use of the green color component to look up the contrast adjustment value.
3. AdjustValue is added to each color component of the pixel, and the result is range checked to be sure the value of each of the color components remains in the range 0 to 255.
4. The modified RGB pixel value is stored back into the DIB image.

Palettized images are treated differently in that the color components of the palette entries are subjected to the previous four-step process. The palettized image data do not need to be manipulated at all.

Histogram Equalization

Histogram equalization is a point process also used for adjusting image contrast. As has been stated, histogram equalization attempts to spread out clusters of pixel values in low contrast images in an attempt to use the full range of pixel values available. In terms of a histogram plot, this algorithm equalizes the area under the histogram across the full spectrum of pixel intensity values. The application of this algorithm can make low-contrast features in an image more visible because after pixel value

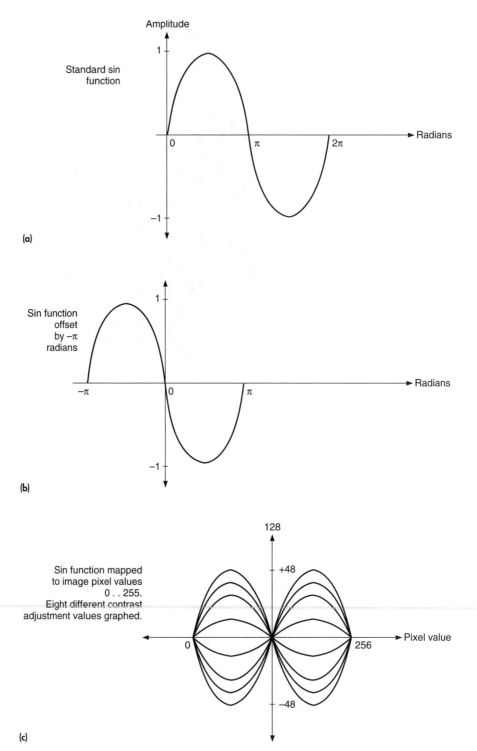

FIGURE 9.3 Using the sin function for manipulating image contrast.

spreading, these features may occupy a unique range of pixel intensity values not shared with the rest of the image. Histogram equalization is a vastly different technique for image contrast manipulation than that discussed earlier in that it requires a histogram of the image data before any processing occurs. In this implementation, a histogram of the green component of an image is built, and the results are used to manipulate the image data. Histogram equalization can only be used with 24-BPP images.

The steps required for histogram equalization can be summarized as follows:

1. A pass is made over the true color image data and a histogram (called lpHistogram on the listing) of the green color component is built.
2. The area under the histogram data curve is then calculated and stored in the array lpHistogramSum.
3. A final pass is made over the image data and for each pixel of the image a delta value is calculated, which reflects, first, the difference between the green value of the original image pixel and the idealized green value after spreading and, second, the strength of application the user specified. The calculated delta is added to the RGB value of the original pixel, the color components are clamped to the range 0 to 255, and the new pixel's value is stored back into the image's DIB.

See Listing 9.2 for further details if required.

Area Processes

Area processes, also referred to in some texts as *group processes,* use groups of pixels to extract information from an image. This is different from point processes, which use only a single pixel's information for performing the point process. The group of pixels used in area processes is referred to as the "neighborhood." The neighborhood is generally a two-dimensional matrix of pixel values with each dimension having an odd number of elements. The *pixel of interest* (the pixel whose old value is being replaced by its new value as a result of an algorithmic computation) resides at the center of the neighborhood. Having a cluster of pixels in the neighborhood around the pixel of interest furnishes brightness trend information (in two dimensions) that is used by most area processes. Another, more proper, term for brightness trend information is spatial frequency.

Spatial frequency is defined as the rate of change of pixel brightness or intensity divided by the distance over which the change occurred. Spatial frequency has components in both the horizontal and vertical directions in an image. An image with high spatial frequency content contains large, closely spaced changes in pixel values. An image of a black-and-white checkerboard would contain a high spatial frequency content. The smaller the squares, the higher the frequency content. An image with low spatial frequency contains large areas of constant or slowly changing pixel values. Images of clouds generally have a low spatial frequency content.

Having access to the spatial frequency information allows area processes to act as filters for removing or enhancing selective frequency components found in an image. Thus, many area processes fall into the general category of spatial filters.

Spatial filters, like their cousins in electronic engineering, have a firm basis in mathematics. In our treatment of spatial filters in this section, we will give examples of how spatial filters are used without delving into the mathematics involved. The reader is encouraged to consult any good book on digital signal processing (some are listed in Appendix B "Further Reading" if the mathematical proofs of these algorithms are of interest or are necessary. It is interesting to note that the complex mathematical underpinnings of the algorithms presented in this section have remarkably intuitive explanations. These explanations will be provided accordingly.

Spatial filtering has many applications in image processing. It can be used, for example, for extraction of image features (edge enhancement and detection), for sharpening an image, for smoothing an image, for blurring an image, and for removal of random noise present in an image. Many aspects of spatial filtering can be demonstrated using the TestApp example program of Chapter 1.

In this portion of the chapter, two area process algorithms will be discussed: *convolution* and *median filtering*. The median filter algorithm has a single specific use, whereas the convolution algorithm, being more general in nature, has many uses. The application of both of these algorithms to image data is similar to that used for point processes, specifically:

1. A single pass is made over the input image on a pixel-by-pixel basis.
2. Each pixel in the input image is processed via a transformation into a new value.
3. The new value for the pixel is placed into the output image buffer at the same row, column location it was taken from in the input image buffer.

The difference between a point process and an area process is the second item. A point process uses the value of, and sometimes the location of, the input pixel in the generation of the output pixel. An area process uses the value of each pixel in the neighborhood of the input pixel to generate the output pixel.

From the previous discussion, it should be apparent that more pixels are involved in the transformation calculation for an area process than are involved for a point process. In a typical three-by-three pixel neighborhood with nine total pixels, you might expect an area process to require roughly nine times as much processing than a point process. In actuality, the processing time can be much worse. The net result is that area processes take a relatively long period of time to complete, and the time increases dramatically with the size of the neighborhood. Area processes involving floating point numbers can take even longer and for this reason they are avoided here.

Convolution

Convolution is a general purpose algorithm that can be used in performing a variety of area process transformations. As complex as convolution might sound, it is actually quite easy to understand and implement. Figure 9.4 has been prepared to illustrate the convolution process.

The best way to understand a convolution is to think of it as a weighted summation process. Each pixel in the neighborhood (assumed to be three by three) is multiplied by a similarly dimensioned convolution kernel, and the sum that results replaces the value of the center pixel of interest. Each element of the convolution kernel is a weighting factor (also called a *convolution coefficient*). The size and the arrangement of the weighting factors contained in a convolution kernel determine the type of area transformation that will be applied to the image data. Changing a weighting factor within a convolution kernel influences the magnitude and possibly the sign of the overall sum and therefore affects the value given to the pixel of interest. Figure 9.5 shows various convolution kernels and the transfer functions they represent. As you can see, most kernels are three by three, and all have odd numbers of rows and columns. This format of convolution coefficients within the kernel has been accepted by industry as a standard. A larger kernel size, however, increases the flexibility of the convolution process. Although some rather complex mathematics went into the design of these convolution kernels (see references given in Appendix B), feel free to experiment with kernels of your own making. The results you produce may surprise you.

Unfortunately, the simple weighted sum convolution calculation has some implementation details that complicate its realization. First and foremost has to do with the edges of an image. As we move the convolution kernel (with the pixel of interest under the center of the kernel) across an image a pixel at a time, we will have problems with our calculations whenever we come to the borders of an image. That is because the weighting coefficients in the kernel are no longer positioned over nine pixels of the source image. In other words, the convolution kernel is, in effect, hanging over the edge of the image. This annoyance happens at the top, left, right, and bottom borders of an image. Several methods can be used to cope with this situation; the two most straightforward solutions are:

1. To ignore completely the data at the edges of the image or
2. To replicate data at the edges of the image to have data at the edges to process

The first method is used in the code provided in this chapter.

The second implementation complication has to do with the dynamic range and sign of the new value calculated for the pixel of interest. For most kernels, the calculated value for the pixel of interest is within the valid range 0 to 255. Some kernels, unfortunately, will produce values that are out of range or even negative. The strategy taken in this code is to clamp pixel values into the valid range of values. This may or may not be the strategy to take for other application programs.

The convolution function within the TProcessImage class is implemented somewhat differently than usual and in such a manner as to eliminate the need for floating point numbers in the calculations. This is done purely for performance considerations because floating point arithmetic is typically slow, especially on machines without a floating point coprocessor. The use of integer arithmetic is made possible by the addition of a divisor to the convolution kernel used to divide the convolution sums after they are calculated. So instead of a convolution kernel having 9 entries (three rows by three columns), the extended kernels used here have 10. After the convolution sums for each pixel of interest are calculated, they are divided by the divisor member of the kernel (as long as the divisor is not 1, in which case no division is performed). To illustrate how the addition of a divisor eliminates the need for floating point arithmetic consider the following convolution kernel:

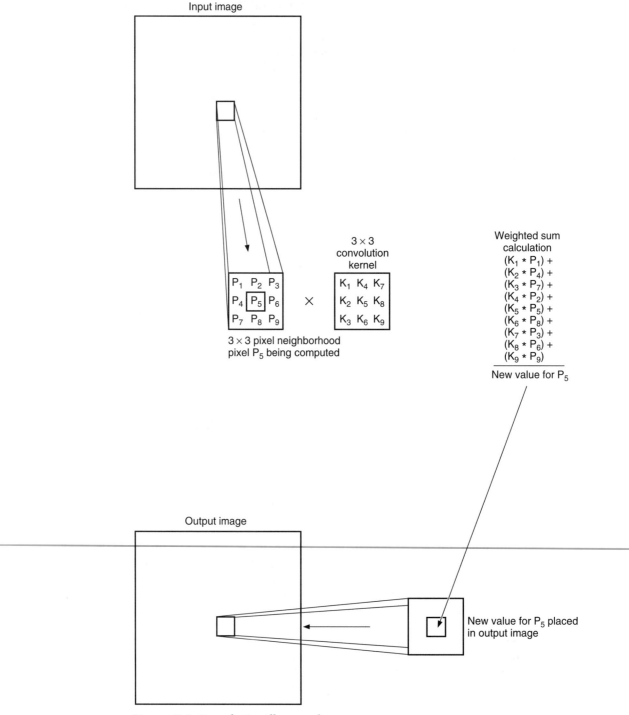

Figure 9.4 Convolution illustrated.

$$\begin{array}{ccc} \frac{1}{16} & \frac{1}{8} & \frac{1}{16} \\ \frac{1}{8} & \frac{1}{4} & \frac{1}{8} \\ \frac{1}{16} & \frac{1}{8} & \frac{1}{16} \end{array}$$

Without the change to the implementation used here, this kernel would have to be specified in terms of floating point numbers as follows:

$$\begin{array}{ccc} 0.0625 & 0.125 & 0.0625 \\ 0.125 & 0.25 & 0.125 \\ 0.0625 & 0.125 & 0.0625 \end{array}$$

and this would mean that floating point math would have to be used throughout the convolution calculations, thereby slowing them down. This same kernel in the extended format used in this implementation would be specified as follows:

$$\begin{array}{ccc} 1 & 2 & 1 \\ 2 & 4 & 2 \\ 1 & 2 & 1 \\ & 16 & \end{array}$$

where the number 16 is the divisor. As you can see, only integer coefficients are specified and therefore only integer arithmetic need be used in the convolution calculations.

The area processes that are included in the TestApp program and discussed here are:

1. Image sharpening (high-pass filtering using convolution)
2. Image softening (low-pass filtering using convolution)
3. Image edge enhancement (using convolution)
4. Image despeckling (using median filtering)

Image Sharpening (High-Pass Filtering Using Convolution)

High-pass filters accentuate the high-frequency details of an image while leaving the low-frequency content intact. Relative to the high-frequency content, the low-frequency content is attenuated. High-pass filtering is used whenever objects with high spatial frequency content need to be examined. The higher frequency portions of an image will be highlighted (become brighter), whereas the lower frequency portions become black. Image sharpness (subjectively equated to focus) is sometimes enhanced with high-pass filtering at the expense of accentuated image noise. Edge enhancement of an image is also possible with the application of high-pass filtering.

The large center kernel coefficient (see Figure 9.5) holds the key to the operation of high-pass filters. As the large center coefficient moves across a portion of an image with high spatial frequency content (meaning a large step change in pixel intensity), the new value of the pixel of interest is multiplied many times in value. The smaller negative coefficients in the kernel clustered around the large center value work to reduce the effect of the large weighting factor. The net effect is that large changes in pixel intensity are intensified while areas of constant pixel intensity are left alone. In other words, areas of constant pixel intensity (low spatial frequency areas) are not affected by this transformation.

Image Softening (Low-Pass Filtering Using Convolution)

In contrast to high-pass filters, low-pass spatial filters leave the low-frequency content of an image intact while attenuating the high-frequency content. Low-pass filters are good at reducing the visual noise contained in an image. They are also used to remove the high-frequency content of an image so the low-frequency content can be examined more closely. With the high frequencies gone, more subtle low-frequency changes can be identified. The cutoff frequency of a low-pass filter is determined by the size of the convolution kernel and the kernel coefficients. Three different low-pass filters (provided by three different convolution kernels) are available within the TestApp program. All convolution kernels used for filtering can be seen in Figure 9.5 and in Listing 9.2. Notice that the sum of the kernel values for all of the low-pass filters is 1 (after dividing by the divisor). This fact is important for understanding how low-pass filters operate.

Consider a portion of an image without high-frequency content. This means that the pixel values are of constant value or that they change slowly. As a low-pass kernel is passed over this portion of the image, the new value for the pixel of interest (the pixel centered under the kernel) is calculated as the sum of the kernel coefficients times the neighborhood pixel values. If all of the neighborhood pixel values are the same (constant), the new pixel value is the same as the old value. This is the reason the sum of the coefficients is chosen to be one. Low-frequency content has been preserved. As the kernel is moved over a portion of the image with high-frequency content, any rapid changes in intensity get averaged out with the remaining pixels in the neighborhood, thereby lowering the high-frequency content. The visual result of low-pass filtering is a slight blur of the image. This blur results because any sharp pixel transitions are averaged with their surroundings as the high-frequency content is attenuated.

Low-pass filtering can, as contrary as it sounds, be used to sharpen the appearance of an image. If a low-pass filtered image is subtracted from the original image, the result is a relative increase in high-frequency informational content without an increase in image noise. Subjectively, the resultant image appears sharper than the original. This could be used to highlight portions of an image that are obscured by haze or clouds. This technique might even be able to make an image of Los Angeles look good on a smoggy day.

Image Edge Enhancement (Using Convolution)

Another area process that can be performed using convolution is edge enhancement. Edge enhancement is used as a preliminary step in image feature extraction and is typically followed by a thresholding point process. Edge enhancement algorithms reduce an image into just edges; the image content is reduced and in many cases completely eliminated. For this reason, the processed image may not closely resemble the original image. The brightness of an edge after enhancement is proportional to the change in brightness surrounding the edge in the original image.

Although edge enhancement is used mainly for machine vision, it does have other uses as well; for example, the edge information provided by an edge enhancement process can be added back into the original image to sharpen it. Edge enhancement can also be used as an artistic tool to produce striking outlined

Low-Pass Spatial Filters

LP$_1$				LP$_2$				LP$_3$			
1	1	1		1	1	1		1	2	1	
1	1	1		1	2	1		2	4	2	$\Sigma = 1$
1	1	1		1	1	1		1	2	1	
Divisor = 9				Divisor = 10				Divisor = 16			

High-Pass Spatial Filters

HP1				HP2				HP3			
−1	−1	−1		0	−1	0		1	−2	1	
−1	9	−1		−1	5	−1		−2	5	−2	$\Sigma = 1$
−1	−1	−1		0	−1	0		1	−2	1	
Divisor = 1				Divisor = 1				Divisor = 1			

Shift and Difference Edge Enhancements

Vertical Edges				Horizontal Edges				Horizontal & Vertical Edges			
0	0	0		0	−1	0		−1	0	0	
−1	1	0		0	1	0		0	1	0	$\Sigma = 0$
0	0	0		0	0	0		0	0	0	
Divisor = 1				Divisor = 1				Divisor = 1			

Laplace Edge Enhancements

LAP1			LAP2			LAP3			LAP4			
0	1	0	−1	−1	−1	−1	−1	−1	1	−2	1	Σ normally $= 0$
1	−4	1	−1	8	−1	−1	9	−1	−2	4	−2	except LAP3
0	1	0	−1	−1	−1	−1	−1	−1	1	−2	1	
Divisor = 1			Divisor = 1			Divisor = 1			Divisor = 1			

Gradient Directional Edge Enhancements

North			NorthEast			East			SouthEast			
1	1	1	1	1	1	−1	1	1	−1	−1	1	
1	−2	1	−1	−2	1	−1	−2	1	−1	−2	1	$\Sigma = 0$
−1	−1	−1	−1	−1	1	−1	1	1	1	1	1	
Divisor = 1			Divisor = 1			Divisor = 1			Divisor = 1			

South			SouthWest			West			NorthWest		
−1	−1	−1	1	−1	−1	1	1	−1	1	1	1
1	−2	1	1	−2	−1	1	−2	−1	1	−2	−1
1	1	1	1	1	1	1	1	−1	1	−1	−1
Divisor = 1			Divisor = 1			Divisor = 1			Divisor = 1		

Figure 9.5 Various convolution kernels.

images. These images can then be touched up with a paint program to produce a work of art.

All edge enhancement methods work by analyzing the intensity of pixels contained in the pixel of interest's neighborhood. Again, the brightness trends in a pixel's neighborhood are used to find and accent the edges contained in an image. An *edge*, by definition, is a large change in intensity. All edge enhancement algorithms that use convolution are linear. That is, they are made up of the sum of first-degree products. Other edge detection algorithms exist (but are not described in this book) that use derivatives to detect edges. These nonlinear methods do a better job of detecting edges than the simple method described here. The interested reader is directed to Appendix B "Further Reading" for other books that describe edge enhancement and detection in a more rigorous manner.

The edge enhancements built into the TestApp example program use gradient directional edge enhancement kernels. The use of these kernels allows control over the direction of the image edges that are enhanced because it is sometimes necessary to highlight edges in an image that are other than strictly vertical or horizontal. Diagonal edges of parts during a machine inspection operation may be important, for example. Selectively highlighting edges in different directions can be used to give a computer an overall idea of what it is looking at. In our application in this book, however, edge enhancement is really just an artistic tool. The gradient directional edge enhancement method specifies eight different convolution kernels for the highlighting of edges in each of eight different directions. The directions are called out as points on a compass. The eight kernels are North, North East, East, South East, South, South West, West, and North West.

If a positive slope exists in the direction of the kernel, a light-colored pixel will be placed in the output image. The intensity of the output pixel will depend on the slope of the brightness. The larger the slope the brighter the pixel; for example, the east gradient kernel will enhance edges that transition from black to white from left to right. We also know that since the summation of the kernel coefficients equals zero, regions of constant brightness (low spatial frequency) will be attenuated. In other words, constant brightness areas will result in black pixels being output.

Image Despeckling (Using Median Filtering)

Median filtering is an area process that does not use convolution. Some people consider median filtering to be more a point process than an area process because of the way in which it works. Median filtering is considered an area process for our purposes.

Median filtering uses the values of the pixels contained in the pixel neighborhood to determine the new value given to the pixel of interest. It does not, however, algorithmically calculate the new pixel value from the pixels in the neighborhood. Instead, it sorts the pixels in the neighborhood into ascending numerical order and picks the middle or median pixel value as the new value for the pixel of interest. The median filter algorithm is illustrated pictorially in Figure 9.6. The result of median filtering is that any random noise contained in an image will be effectively eliminated. This is because any random, abrupt change in pixel intensity within a pixel neighborhood will be sorted out; that is, it will be placed at either the top or the bottom of the sorted neighborhood values and will be ignored because the median value (the value at the center of the sorted values) is always picked for the new pixel value. Multiple applications of median filtering to an image can result in rather pleasing visual effects similar to that of oil painting. To see this effect, you are encouraged to experiment with the TestApp program of Chapter 1.

Geometric Image-Processing Algorithms

Geometric processes change the number, spatial positioning, and/or arrangement of pixels within an image based on some geometric transformation. Geometric transformations do not necessarily alter pixel values. Instead, they alter the position of the pixels. In other words, the color and/or intensity value for a given pixel (the information contained in the pixel) is moved to a new location. This makes geometric processes quite different from the point and area processes we have discussed up to this point. Each of these other classes of image-processing algorithms intentionally altered the value of pixels (not the position), based on a specified transformation. Examples of geometric processes include image rotation, image scaling, mirror image production, and so on.

Geometric transformations have many uses both industrial and artistic. For example, they can be used:

1. To correct for some defect inherent in an imaging system, spatial aberrations in an image sensor or aspect ratio problems, for example
2. To prepare an image for subsequent point, area, or frame processing
3. To provide precise image registration between images that will be compared
4. To prepare for display or hard copy output, for example, the production of collage images
5. To provide a variety of special effects with images.

This list is by no means exhaustive; many more applications of geometric processes exist than are listed here.

Geometric processes, like the other forms of image processing already discussed, are not without their own set of technical and implementation difficulties. When images are altered using geometric transformations, the result might turn out differently than expected, unless the concepts of pixel value interpolation and aspect ratio are well understood and duly applied. The geometric algorithms provided within the TProcessImage class skirt these complications by making the following assumptions:

1. All images processed are assumed to have square pixels; that is, pixels with the same width and height dimensions. This is a valid assumption because most all modern photographic imaging equipment is designed for production of images with square pixels.
2. Rotations are performed only in 90 degree increments, therefore interpolation of pixel values is not necessary.
3. No non-linear geometric processes are provided by the code.

For a detailed discussion of pixel interpolation and aspect ratio correction, the reader is directed to another of my books entitled *Practical Image Processing in C* in which these topics are covered in gruesome detail.

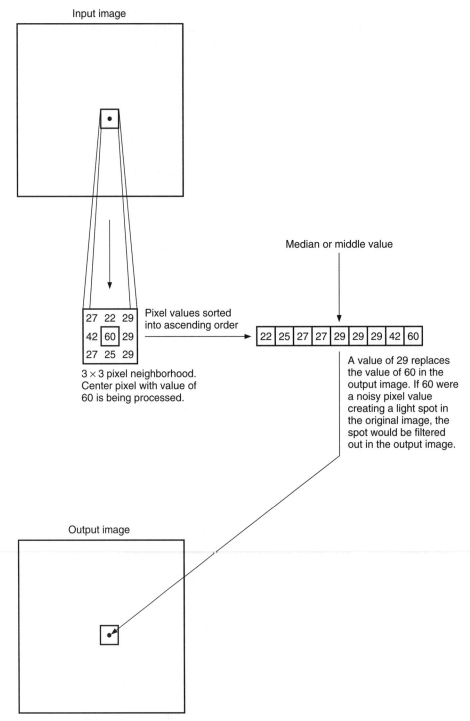

Input image

Median or middle value

27 22 29
42 60 29
27 25 29

Pixel values sorted
into ascending order

22 | 25 | 27 | 27 | 29 | 29 | 29 | 42 | 60

3 × 3 pixel neighborhood.
Center pixel with value of
60 is being processed.

A value of 29 replaces
the value of 60 in the
output image. If 60 were
a noisy pixel value
creating a light spot in
the original image, the
spot would be filtered
out in the output image.

Output image

FIGURE 9.6 The median filter operation.

Geometric transformations, in general, are performed from the destination image's perspective instead of from the source image perspective. Although seemingly backward, this reverse mapping is required to guarantee that every pixel in the destination image is given a value. Reverse mapping traverses the destination image space a pixel at a time and calculates via the designated transformation which pixels of the source image would be involved in the production of the destination pixel. When the value of the destination pixel is calculated in this manner and placed into the destination image, complete coverage of the destination image is guaranteed. If reverse mapping is not used, voids in the destination are possible, depending on the geometric transformation being applied.

The geometric processes that are included in the TestApp program and discussed here are:

1. Image rotation
2. Image flipping
3. Image cropping
4. Image resizing

The operation of these geometric processes is relatively straightforward so the discussions will be kept short.

Image Rotation

Image rotation, as provided by the **RotateImage** function within TProcessImage, is a very simple process because only rotations by 90° clockwise and counterclockwise are supported. Rotations by arbitrary angles would require pixel interpolation and special treatment of aspect ratio to be performed correctly and would subsequently be a slow process. Rotations by 90° are supported to correct for images that are scanned in with the wrong orientation. This can happen when using picture scanners and slide scanners.

If you'll look at the rotation code in Listing 9.2, you will see that a block of memory is allocated for the rotated image data. How the data are placed into the memory depends on whether the image being rotated is true color or palettized and whether a clockwise or counterclockwise rotation is to be performed. The operation of the code should be obvious from the listing.

Image Flipping

Flipping an image is similar to rotation of an image except that mirror images are obtained. When an image is flipped horizontally, image left is swapped with image right and vice versa. Vertical flipping swaps image top with image bottom. Again, how the image data are manipulated depends on the image type, true color or palettized, and the direction of the flip.

Image Cropping

As simple as it is to perform, image cropping is a much more complex process than either image rotation or image flipping. As implemented in the TestApp program, cropping is really made up of two distinct processes: a user interface process that allows the user to draw a rectangular rubber-banded box around the portion of an image to be saved and an image data extraction process that reaches into a DIB (which defines the image before cropping) and extracts the portion of the image identified by the user for saving. The extracted image data must be converted into DIB format for subsequent manipulation and storage.

The user interface portion of the cropping task is managed by the TProcess-Image class but is actually performed by code in the MDI child window (located in the file "tappchil.cpp"). Upon selection of cropping from the *Image Processing* menu in the TestApp program, the **BeginCrop** member of TProcessImage is called. This function changes how the MDI child window processes the left button down, the mouse move, and the left button up mouse messages. When cropping is not being performed, these mouse messages are ignored. After **BeginCrop** is called, a bit in the child window is set that changes how the mouse messages are processed in the child window. While in cropping mode, depressing the left mouse button and moving the mouse allows the user to position and size a rectangular box over the portion of the image to crop. When the user releases the left mouse button (resulting in a left mouse button up message), the **EndCrop** member of TProcessImage is called to perform the data extraction portion of the cropping process and to return the processing of mouse messages by the child window to normal.

The **EndCrop** function is called with two POINT reference parameters that mark the beginning and ending corners of the cropping rectangle. These points are converted internally to the upper left and lower right corners of the cropping rectangle. Since cropping is available for user selection only when an image is being displayed to fit entirely within the display window, the coordinates passed to this function can be used to calculate the portion of the image data to be extracted. A new DIB for the cropped data is produced, which has the same number of bits per pixel as the original image but which contains only the cropped portion of the image data. **EndCrop** then updates the IMAGEDESCRIPTOR information in the child window to reflect the size of the new image and causes a new Display object to be built for display of the cropped image.

Image Resizing

The **Resize** member function of the TProcessImage class is used to manipulate the dimensions (in pixels) of an image. The correct term for data reduction is *decimation*. With this function an image displayed in a child window can be reduced in size (decimated) or increased in size while keeping its aspect ratio constant and correct. Image size reduction is important when images are captured in high resolution, but only a low-resolution image is required for an application. High-resolution images require more memory to process and are much slower to access. As an example take, for instance, a 4- × 5-inch true color scanned image acquired at 500 DPI. This image requires some 15 Mb of memory when displayed and/or processed. If this image is always to be displayed on a monitor running in 640 × 480 format in a window that is 4- × 3-inch, most of the data contained in the image will be thrown away every time the image is displayed. Having the image in such high resolution will not make it look better when displayed, and, in addition, the high-resolution image will make the display of the image extremely slow on even the most powerful computer. The solution? Decimate the image data to something more reasonable for the application. In the image-processing realm, more is not always better.

Increasing the size of an image is of limited usefulness in serious image-processing applications but abounds with artistic possibilities. Whenever an image is increased in size, pixel replication occurs; that is, image pixels are copied to create the image data necessary to increase the image size. It must be understood that no new image data are actually generated; old data are just copied. The informational content of an image processed in this fashion remains the same.

Interesting artistic effects can be produced by first decimating an image to reduce image data and then increasing the size of the reduced image. Depending on the ratios chosen for image reduction and expansion, an interesting pixelizing special effect occurs. Try this using the TestApp program and you'll see what I mean.

The **Resize** function has the ability to resize images up to ±500 percent. Actually, the code can modify the image size by any percentage; it is the Resize dialog box user interface that limits the range of values. You should use **Resize's** ability to increase image size sparingly. You can create huge images if you are not cognizant of what you are doing.

Miscellaneous Image-Processing Functions

The image-processing functions described in this section do not fit into the classic categories of point, area, frame, or geometric processes that have been discussed to this point. However, each of the functions is involved with the manipulation of image data, in some way or another. The miscellaneous processes that are included in the TestApp program and discussed here are:

1. Image copying and pasting via the clipboard
2. Image duplication
3. Image color quantization
4. Image dithering
5. Image conversion to 8 BPP
6. Image promotion to 24 BPP

Image Copying and Pasting via the Clipboard

Two functions exist in the TProcessImage class for dealing with images and the Windows clipboard. These functions are **ImageToClipboard** and **ImageFrom-Clipboard.** The names of these functions imply their function. **ImageToClipboard** sends the image displayed in a child window to the clipboard (the copy function), and **ImageFromClipboard** retrieves image information from the clipboard (the paste function) in preparation for creating a new child window for its display. Let's talk about placing images on the clipboard first.

From a high level, placing images onto the clipboard can be viewed as a two-step process. First, the image data must be manipulated into a format suitable for placing onto the clipboard (the DIB format is used exclusively here), and second, an interaction must take place between the provider of the image data and the clipboard, which results in the image data being moved to and managed by the clipboard. Once the clipboard takes possession of the image data, it belongs to the clipboard, not the application that put it there. An application program should never attempt to access the image data again after it has been given over to the clipboard.

To place image data onto the clipboard using the CF_DIB Windows standard format requires that the data be contained in a single memory block and be of a specific format. Specifically, the block of image data should begin with a BITMAPINFO structure (which comprises a BITMAPINFOHEADER structure and zero or more RGBQUAD color table entries) and be followed by the image data (with each row zero padded to a double word boundary). See Chapter 2 if you need more general information on DIB format. As usual, the type of image, palettized or true color, controls to a large extent how the BITMAPINFOHEADER is filled in, whether any RGBQUAD color table entries are required and whether a palette will also need to be placed onto the clipboard along with the image. Suffice it to say that true color images do not need color table entries or a palette, whereas palettized images require both.

Most of the code within **ImageToClipboard** deals with getting the image into the CF_DIB format. After the image type has been determined, a block of memory is allocated for storage of the image data structures and image data. Once all of the image data are moved into the allotted memory block, the block is unlocked but not freed. It is the handle of the unlocked block of memory containing the image information that will be passed to the clipboard. If it is determined that the image requires a palette to be placed onto the clipboard in addition to the image data, a logical palette for the image is created using the Windows **CreatePalette** function. With the image data properly formatted and an optional logical palette available, the interaction with the clipboard can begin.

Before an application program can use the clipboard, the clipboard must be opened for use. The **OpenClipboard** Windows API function is called with a handle to the window that is to own the clipboard during subsequent interaction. The handle provided is that of the child window that contains the image being moved to the clipboard. If the clipboard opened successfully, it is cleared of any previous contents by a call to **EmptyClipboard.** Next, **SetClipboardData** is used to place the image data onto the clipboard. This function accepts two parameters, a specifier for the clipboard data format (in this case CF_DIB) and a handle to the memory block containing the image information. Next, a check is made to see if a palette is also required for the image whose data is already on the clipboard. If so, the **SetClipboardData** function is called again, this time with a CF_PALETTE format specifier and a handle to the logical palette (created earlier in the code) for the image. Finally, the **CloseClipboard** function is called to terminate communication between this code and the clipboard and to relinquish ownership of the clipboard. With these steps performed, the interaction with the clipboard is complete. The clipboard contains all of the information necessary to paste the image we just copied to it into any application that can accept it.

The other half of the clipboard support for images in the TProcessImage class, that of retrieving images from the clipboard, is provided by the **ImageFromClipboard** function. As one might expect, this code works backwards from the code discussed immediately preceding; that is, it conducts the interaction with the clipboard first to retrieve the image data block and possibly a palette from the clipboard and then manipulates the returned information into a format suitable for displaying in a child window opened specifically for that purpose. To wit . . .

The **ImageFromClipboard** function is called within the TestApp program as a result of the user selecting the *Paste* operation within the *Edit* menu. The first thing this code does is to check if an image in CF_DIB format is available on the clipboard by calling the Windows function **IsClipboardFormatAvailable.** This function will return TRUE if a DIB image is available on the clipboard and FALSE if not. A FALSE response terminates the **ImageFromClipboard** function because either there isn't an image on the clipboard or the image on the clipboard is in a format that this code does not understand. Once having detected the presence of a DIB image on the clipboard, the code opens the clipboard (as explained earlier) and calls **GetClipboardData** to retrieve a handle to the image data. Next, a check is made to see if a logical palette for the image is also available on the clipboard. **IsClipboardFormatAvailable** is called again with a format specifier of CF_PALETTE to make this determination. If a palette is detected, **GetClipboardData** is called again to get the handle of the logical palette with which to display the image.

With the memory block containing the image and an optional palette available, we have all the information that is needed to process the image into a form suitable for our use. Specifically, the information describing the image (from the BITMAP-HEADERINFO structure), the image palette (if any), and the image data are extracted from the provided clipboard data, manipulated appropriately, and then stored into an IMAGEDESCRIPTOR structure for use by the TestApp program. As you will hopefully recall, an IMAGEDESCRIPTOR contains all of the information necessary to completely describe an image. See Chapter 1 for specific details.

Please note that although the clipboard provided handles to the image data and the palette, the clipboard still owns these items. The application should copy the data items immediately, instead of relying on their data handles for long-term use. An application program does not need to worry about freeing these items when finished with them; the clipboard will free them when it deems necessary and appropriate. Neither should the application program leave the data item handles locked for any longer than necessary.

That which began with a click on the *Paste* menu item within the TestApp program results in a fully initialized IMAGEDESCRIPTOR structure containing the image data along with image specifications. The following code segment, extracted from the file "tappcli.cpp," shows the whole process for retrieving an image from the clipboard. As you can see, a new child window is created for display of the image pasted from the clipboard.

```
// This function is called when the user clicks Paste from the Edit menu
void TestAppMDIClient::CmEditPaste(void) {
  IMAGEDESCRIPTOR ID;           // An instance of an descriptor

  TProcessImage PI(NULL);       // Instantiate image processing object
  if (PI.ImageFromClipboard(ID)) {   // Copy image from clipboard
    // Create a new child window for display of image from clipboard
    new TestAppMDIChild(*this, ID)->Create();
    ChildCount++;
  }
}
```

Image Duplication

Image duplication is described here because it should be mentioned somewhere, and this seemed to be the most appropriate place. *Duplicate* is an operation available from within the *Image Processing* menu of the TestApp program. Its one function is to create a new child window that contains an exact copy of the image in the window duplicated; that is, the image duplicated is contained within the child window that currently has focus. The *Duplicate* function is so handy it is the first operation available in the *Image Processing* menu. It is handy because it allows multiple independent copies of an image to be brought up simultaneously and processed separately. If this functionality were not provided, multiple copies of an image would have to be loaded individually from disk—a painful and time-consuming operation. Image duplication also provides a sort of undo facility for images. Consider the following scenario. You want to experiment with image sharpening to see which strength setting gives the desired result. You bring up an image and apply a sharpening process to it. The original image is then gone because it has been processed. To go back and try another sharpening strength requires that the original image be loaded again from disk. A better way to accomplish this is to first bring up the original image and use the *Duplicate* facility to clone it. Process the cloned image with the sharpening operation and if not satisfied, delete the cloned (processed) image, clone a new one from the original image that is still available, and try the sharpening operation again. As you can see, this would be a much faster and easier way to experiment with the various image-processing algorithms provided by the TestApp example program.

It should be noted that the *Duplicate* function is not a member of the TProcessImage class. Actually, this functionality is provided entirely within the files "tappcli.cpp" (MDI client window code) and "tappchil.cpp" (MDI child window code) using the following code segment. In this code, an image is duplicated by passing a pointer (pChild) to the current child window with focus to a special constructor of the TestAppMDIChild class. The special constructor actually clones the image data in preparation for display.

```
// Image Duplication function. Called when the user click Duplicate on the
// Image Processing Menu
void TestAppMDIClient::CmImgProcDuplicate (void) {

  TestAppMDIChild * pChild =
     TYPESAFE_DOWNCAST(GetActiveMDIChild(), TestAppMDIChild);

  // Create a new child window for display of duplicated image

  new TestAppMDIChild(*this, pChild)->Create();

  ChildCount++;
```

Image Color Quantization

When the user of the TestApp program selects the *Quantize* operation from the *Image Processing* menu, control passes to the **Quantize** member function of the TProcessImage class described here. The first operation performed by this code is to bring up a dialog box for user selection of the number of colors to quantize the true color image down to. The valid range of colors is from 18 to 256. With the number of colors specified, an object of the MedianCutQuant class (described in detail in Chapter 5) is instantiated to perform the image color quantization. If the quantization is successful, the remainder of the code within **Quantize** busies itself with extracting the quantized image data from the MedianCutQuant object and preparing both an IMAGEDESCRIPTOR and a Display object to display the quantized image within the child window.

Image Dithering

When the user of the TestApp program selects the *Dither* operation from the *Image Processing* menu, control passes to the *Dither* member function of the TProcessImage class. The **Dither** function is identical to the **Quantize** function described earlier, except an object of the UniformQuantWithDither class (described in Chapter 5) is instantiated to process the image data. In all other respects these two function calls are identical.

Image Conversion to 8 BPP

The **ConvertToGray** member function of the TProcessImage class is used to convert a true color or palettized color image displayed within a child window into a gray scale image. The gray scale value used for a pixel represents the luminance (brightness) of the color as calculated by the following formula:

$$\text{Luminance} = \frac{((30*\text{Red}) + (59 *\text{Green}) + (11 * \text{Blue}))}{100}$$

where Luminance can range from 0 to 255.

True color images are converted into eight bits per pixel images with 256 shades of gray by plugging the RGB value of each pixel into the previous formula. In addition to the data conversion, a palette must be built for use in displaying these converted true color images. The palette consists of 256 RGBCOLOR values initialized as follows:

```
for (int Index = 0; Index < 256; Index++) {
    Palette[Index].Red = Index;
    Palette[Index].Green = Index;
    Palette[Index].Blue = Index;
}
```

With the data converted and stored and a palette available for the converted image, the IMAGEDESCRIPTOR for the child window can be updated, and a new Display object can be built for display of the gray scale image.

In contrast, palettized color images are processed into gray scale images by calculating the luminance of each palette color entry and subsequently replacing the palette entry with a color that has Red = Green = Blue = Luminance. No processing of the actual image data is required when converting palettized color images into palettized gray scale images. Just as explained earlier, after the palette has been converted, the IMAGEDESCRIPTOR for the child window must be updated and a new Display object built for display of the gray scale image.

The code that performs the color to gray scale conversion is very simple and should be understandable from the comments shown in Listing 9.2.

Image Promotion to 24 BPP

Many of the member functions of the TProcessImage class convert 24-BPP true color images into 8-BPP palettized images. Examples of these functions include **Quantize, Dither,** and **ConvertToGray.** However, it is sometimes necessary to perform the reverse conversion and convert a palettized image into a 24-BPP color image. This is necessary in the TestApp program because many of the image-processing algorithms provided will only work on true color images. Without this conversion capability, images with fewer than 24 BPP could not be processed with many of the algorithms provided.

Please understand that whenever images are converted to 24 BPP, their size will increase dramatically. Consider a black-and-white image with 1 BPP. If the resolution of the image were 640 × 480, the total size of the image's raster data would be 38,400 bytes. If that same image were converted into 24 BPP, the size of the raster data would balloon to 921,600 bytes—a 1,200 percent increase in size.

The promotion of palettized images to 24 BPP is a relatively simple process that is best described by the following steps:

1. A buffer is allocated for storage of the true color 24-BPP image data. The size of the buffer is calculated from the width and height of the image being converted.
2. A pixel is extracted from the DIB image data. Extraction of pixel values must take into consideration that eight, four, two, or one pixels may be stored in each byte of image data depending on the number of bits per pixel of the image. The pixel extraction code used within this function is rather interesting and can be studied in Listing 9.2.
3. The pixel value, once isolated, is used to locate the palette entry that describes the color of the pixel.
4. The RGB color components of the palette entry are extracted and written into the output 24-BPP DIB buffer in the required BGR format.
5. Steps 2 through 4 are repeated for each pixel of the source image.

When the data conversion is completed, the IMAGEDESCRIPTOR for the child window is updated to reflect the change in image type (to 24 BPP), and a new Display object is built for display of the now true color image. Note: Images promoted to 24 BPP have the same color fidelity as the original image. Said another way, there are no losses in color quality as a result of this conversion process. However, converted images may look worse when displayed alongside their palettized progenitor because they may now need to be dithered for display. As you will recall, 24-BPP images are automatically dithered for display if the display hardware is incapable of displaying them directly because of the video mode it is currently running in. If you are running your SuperVGA card in a 64K or true color video mode, a promoted image should be indistinguishable from its palettized cousin.

Conclusions

In this chapter, a lot was said about various types of image-processing algorithms and how they are combined into the TProcessImage class for use within application programs. Point processes, area processes, geometric processes, and a handful of miscellaneous processes are all described and implemented within this chapter. In keeping with the theme of this book, it was shown how these algorithms are made to fit into the imaging architecture presented in the first chapter and embodied in the TestApp example imaging program. With the inclusion of the TProcessImage class functionally, the TestApp program provides you with a vehicle for experimenting with the image-processing algorithms provided and with those algorithms you might want to add on your own.

Although the image-processing code was implemented with Windows in mind, with a little effort the TProcessImage class and its image-processing algorithms can easily be adapted for use in other programming environments. The general applicability of the imaging architecture presented is discussed in Chapter 1.

CHAPTER

10

Miscellaneous
Imaging Topics

In this chapter you will learn about:
- How images can be cached for maximum display performance
- How thumbnail images can be generated and used
- Textual annotation of images
- Other miscellaneous imaging topics of interest

Introduction

The purpose of this last chapter is to present some miscellaneous imaging topics that did not find a place in other parts of this book. Specifically, the topic of image cacheing for improved display performance is first discussed. Next, the generation and usage of thumbnail images will be presented. Following that, image annotation via image and text merging will be given a quick discussion. Finally, a test program called CacheTst (not Crash Test) is presented to tie all of these topics together in a demonstrable form. Because of the length of some of the code listing presented, there is more code in this chapter than textual description. The code is very well commented and should therefore be easy to understand in most cases without long-winded discussion.

The implementation given for the code presented in this chapter was driven somewhat by the needs of the CacheTst program used to demonstrate it. Some of the code is written in C and some in C++ classes. As presented, the code may or may not be in a form that will fit easily into programs of your design. The beauty of having all

354

of the source code available on the companion disk is that you can extract a piece of code here and there to make up the functionality you require. What is more important than the implementation issues are the concepts presented. Image cacheing, generation, and use of thumbnail images, and image and text merging are all concepts that come into play in professional imaging application programs. So without further ado, let's get into the meat of the matter.

Image Cacheing

A cache is defined in the dictionary as: (1) a hiding place for provision, treasures, and so on and (2) anything hidden or stored. The operative words here are hiding and storage. Image cacheing can be then construed to mean storage of images to hide them from direct access. Said another way, image cacheing is to store images in such a manner as to hide the complexities of their storage, access, and display from the programmer. In addition, cacheing implies fast access to those things stored away. Disk cacheing, for example, speeds access to information read from a disk, especially when the information is accessed multiple times. Image cacheing, as described here, has the same attribute; that is, it provides very high speed access to images once they have been stored in the cache.

You might be asking yourself why image cacheing is important. To that question, I provide the following answers that are specific to the implementation of cacheing described in this chapter:

- Image cacheing hides all of the complexities of reading graphic image files, storing the images in memory, and displaying those images on the screen or other device context (such as a printer) from the programmer. In fact, by using the code presented, a programmer does not need to know anything about images to add them to a program.
- Image cacheing is implemented as a single Windows DLL called "mycache.dll" for easy integration into any application program. This DLL does require the presence of another DLL called "compand.dll" described in Chapter 4, however.
- Image cacheing allows better management of system memory because the cache only allows 10 images (the number is easily changed) in memory simultaneously. When an eleventh image is requested by an application program, the image in the cache that was least recently used is removed from memory, and the new image is automatically loaded in its place.
- After an image is loaded into the cache, all subsequent requests for access to that image are satisfied immediately without the need to reread the image from disk. There is one and only one copy of the image's data in memory at a time, regardless of the number of clients of that data. Image cacheing is extremely important whenever images are used in a network environment. As you probably realize, reading images over a network can be a very time-consuming operation, and you therefore do not want to reread images very often if it can be avoided. Here, image cacheing comes to the rescue because once an image is loaded into the cache, it is stored on the local computer (in semiconductor memory [RAM] or virtual memory) and can therefore be accessed much faster than by rereading it over a network.

- *Least Recently Used* (LRU) algorithm is used for management of the images in the cache. This means images that are referenced often are more likely to remain in the cache while images that are used infrequently will be flushed out. This improves image access times and as a result improves performance of image-intensive application programs.
- Although not actually associated with image cacheing, the "mycache.dll" also supports the generation and display of thumbnail images (to be described later in this chapter). This design decision was made because in applications where image cacheing is required, thumbnail images generally are also.

The CacheTst program described later in this chapter was developed to put the image-cacheing DLL through its paces. The user interface for the CacheTst program is shown pictorially in Figure 10.1. You can use this program to see image cacheing in operation by attempting to display more than 10 images simultaneously. You will notice that as the eleventh image is loaded, the first image that was loaded becomes unavailable for repainting. The first image, the least recently used, has been swapped out to make room for the new image. If you click your mouse on the first image window, however, the image will automatically be loaded back into the cache and will be displayed correctly. More information concerning the operation of the CacheTst program will be presented toward the end of this chapter.

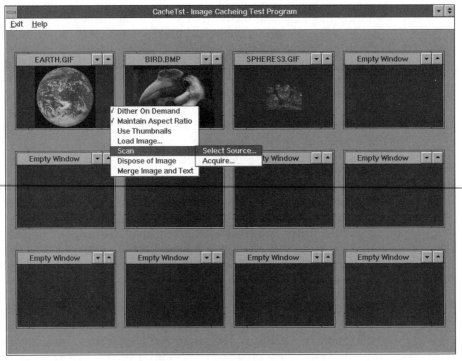

FIGURE 10.1 The CacheTst program main window.

A Short Description of the Cache Code

During the discussion to follow, please refer to Listing 10.1, the listing of the file "cache.hpp" and Listing 10.2, the file "cache.cpp". In addition, Figure 10.2 gives a short description of some of the pertinent functions that provide the cacheing functionality. The cacheing code is clearly complex, but since it resides in a DLL, it can be used without complete knowledge of its internal operation. The C++ interface to the cacheing code, shown in Listing 10.1 is typical of other DLLs described in this book. For information about building Windows DLLs, see Chapter 2.

Listing 10.1 The Cache class interface definition.

```
/*******************************************************/
/***                 "cache.hpp"                  ***/
/***      Image Cacheing and Display Subsystem     ***/
/***        utilizing LRU caching of images        ***/
/***                 written by                    ***/
/***              Craig A. Lindley                 ***/
/***                                               ***/
/***     Revision: 2.0    Last Update: 11/11/94    ***/
/*******************************************************/

// Copyright (c) 1995 John Wiley & Sons, Inc. All rights reserved.

// Check to see if this file already included
#ifndef CACHE_HPP
#define CACHE_HPP

#include "errors.h"
#include "display.hpp"

/*
The following is required when using a C++ class as an interface
for a DLL. It is required because this file will be included in
both the application compilation and the DLL compilation. Remember
that all members (functions and data) are far!
*/

#ifndef _WIN32_                    // If 16 bit code

#ifdef _DLL_
#  define EXPORT _export
#else
#  define EXPORT huge
#endif

#else                              // If 32 bit code

#ifdef _DLL_
#  define EXPORT _export
#else
#  define EXPORT
#endif

#endif
```

```
#ifndef _RGBCOLOR
#define _RGBCOLOR
typedef struct {
  BYTE Red;
  BYTE Green;
  BYTE Blue;
} RGBCOLOR;
#endif

#ifndef _IMAGEDESCRIPTOR
#define _IMAGEDESCRIPTOR
// This structure is used for describing a scanned image.
typedef struct _IMAGEDESCRIPTOR {
  WORD   Width;
  WORD   Height;
  DWORD  RasterSize;
  WORD   BPP;
  WORD   Colors;
  HGLOBAL hImageData;
  RGBCOLOR Palette[256];
} IMAGEDESCRIPTOR, * LPIMAGEDESCRIPTOR;
#endif

// Define the high and low level cache entry handles
typedef int LLHANDLE;
typedef int HLHANDLE;

#define MAXSIMULTANEOUSIMAGES 10 // Total simultaneous images

// Low level Cache class definition
class EXPORT LLCache {
  private:
    // Private data
    WORD NumOfImages;

    struct {                     // Image Descriptor array
      IMAGEDESCRIPTOR ImgDesc;   // Image Descriptor data structure
      Display *DisplayObject;    // Ptr to display object
    } ImageDesc[MAXSIMULTANEOUSIMAGES];

    // Private member functions
    WORD FindFreeDescriptor(void);

  public:
    LLCache(void);               // Class constructor/destructor
    ~LLCache(void);

    LLHANDLE OpenImage(LPSTR FileName, BOOL FullSizeDither);// Read compressed
image from a file
    LLHANDLE CacheImage(LPSTR FileName, LPIMAGEDESCRIPTOR lpImgDesc,
                        BOOL FullSizeDither);     // Cache an image
    BOOL DisplayImage(LLHANDLE hImage, HWND hWindow, POINT& Pt, BOOL BGFlag);//
Display Read/Acq image
    BOOL DisplayImageinWindowRect(LLHANDLE hImage, HWND hWindow, RECT& Area, BOOL
BGFlag); // Display Read/Acq image
```

```
    BOOL DisplayImageWithAspect(LLHANDLE hImage, HWND hWindow, BOOL BGFlag);//
Display Read/Acq image
    LPIMAGEDESCRIPTOR GetImageDescriptorPtr(LLHANDLE hImage);
    BOOL SetDisplayStretchMode(LLHANDLE hImage); // Make image stretch to fit
window
    BOOL SetDisplayClipMode(LLHANDLE hImage);    // Clip image at window bound-
ries
    HPALETTE GetHandleOfImagePalette(LLHANDLE hImage);// Return handle to palette
of specified image
    HGLOBAL GetHandleOfImageData(LLHANDLE hImage);    // Returns handle of image
data for image
    LPBITMAPINFO GetLPBITMAPINFO(LLHANDLE hImage);    // Return ptr to BMI struc-
ture for image

    BOOL DisposeofImage(LLHANDLE hImage);   // Free up desc for another image
    void DisposeOfAllImages(void);          // Free all descriptors


    int GetError(void);                     // Return overall error condition
};                                          // Must be read immediately after
operation


// High level Cache class utilizing LRU image management

#define MAXIMAGESMANAGED   50    // Up to this many images can be managed
#define ENTRYUSEDBIT        1    // Bit in Flags in LRUDesc indicating entry used
                                 // 0 = unused entry 1 = used entry
#define ENTRYPRESENTBIT     2    // Bit in Flags indicating image present in cache
                                 // 0 = Image on disk 1 = Image present in cache
class EXPORT Cache : public LLCache {
  private:
    // Private data
    // Descriptor array of LRU managed images
    struct LRUDesc {
      BYTE Flags;                // Status is entry used/image present in cache
      BYTE References;           // Number of tasks using this image
      BOOL FullSizeDither;       // Dither preference for image
      char FileName[256];        // Filename of image
      LLHANDLE LLHandle;         // Low level image handle
    } HandleArray[MAXIMAGESMANAGED+1];
    typedef LRUDesc far * PLRUDesc;

    HLHANDLE LRUArray [MAXSIMULTANEOUSIMAGES+1];    // Holds order of image
access
                                 // First entry = MR used image
                                 // Last entry = LR used image
    WORD NumOfCachedImages;      // Number of images in LL cache


    // Private member functions
    int FindFreeHandle(void);                // Find free LRUDesc in HandleArray
    void DeleteReference(HLHANDLE hImage);   // Delete reference to hImage in
LRUArray
    void ReferenceImage(HLHANDLE hImage);    // Make hImage MRU image
    LLHANDLE MakeImagePresent(HLHANDLE hImage, BOOL MakeMRU); // Make image
accessible in 11 cache
```

```
    public:
       FAR Cache(void);              // Class constructor/destructor
       FAR ~Cache(void);


       HLHANDLE FAR OpenImage(LPSTR FileName, BOOL FullSizeDither);    // Read com-
pressed image from a file
       HLHANDLE FAR CacheImage(LPSTR FileName, LPIMAGEDESCRIPTOR lpImgDesc,
                        BOOL FullSizeDither);// Cache an image
       BOOL FAR DisplayImage(HLHANDLE hImage, HWND hWindow, POINT& Pt, BOOL BGFlag);
// Display Read/Acq image
       BOOL FAR DisplayImageinWindowRect(HLHANDLE hImage, HWND hWindow, RECT& Area,
BOOL BGFlag); // Display Read/Acq image
       BOOL FAR DisplayImageWithAspect(HLHANDLE hImage, HWND hWindow, BOOL BGFlag);
// Display Read/Acq image
       BOOL FAR MakeRoomForNImages(WORD NumOfImages); // Free up this main LL cache
entries
       LPIMAGEDESCRIPTOR FAR GetImageDescriptorPtr(HLHANDLE hImage); // Get dimen-
sions of image
       BOOL FAR SetDisplayStretchMode(HLHANDLE hImage); // Make image stretch to fit
window
       BOOL FAR SetDisplayClipMode(HLHANDLE hImage);    // Clip image at window
boundries
       HPALETTE FAR GetHandleOfImagePalette(HLHANDLE hImage); // Return handle to
palette of specified image
       HGLOBAL FAR GetHandleOfImageData(HLHANDLE hImage); // Returns handle of image
data for image
       LPBITMAPINFO FAR GetLPBITMAPINFO(HLHANDLE hImage); // Return ptr to BMI
structure for image
       BOOL FAR DisposeOfImage(HLHANDLE hImage); // Free up desc for another image
       void FAR DisposeOfAllImages(void);        // Free all descriptors


       // Thumbnail functions
       BOOL FAR DisplayThumbnail(LPSTR FileName, HWND hWindow, BOOL BGFlag);
       BOOL FAR MakeThumbnail(LPSTR FileName);


       int FAR GetError(void);
    };


    #endif
```

Listing 10.2 The Cache class member functions.

```
/********************************************************/
/***                  "mycache.cpp"              ***/
/***        Image Cacheing and Display Subsystem      ***/
/***           utilizing LRU caching of images        ***/
/***                  written by                 ***/
/***              Craig A. Lindley                ***/
/***                                             ***/
/***     Revision: 2.0    Last Update: 11/11/94    ***/
/********************************************************/

// Copyright (c) 1995 John Wiley & Sons, Inc. All rights reserved.
```

```
#include <string.h>
#include <windows.h>
#include "display.hpp"
#include "cache.hpp"
#include "compand.hpp"
#include "thnails.hpp"
#include "errors.h"

#ifdef _WIN32_
#define hmemcpy memcpy
#endif

// Global data for the image acquisiton process.
HANDLE hDLLInstance;
int OverAllError;

DWORD CalculateBytesPerLine(WORD Width, WORD BPP);    // Forward reference

// The functions to follow are the interface routines for the LRU Cache class in
the DLL

// Class Constructor
Cache::Cache(void) {

  // Clear data structures used to manage images in LRU fashion
  memset(HandleArray, 0, sizeof(HandleArray));
  memset(LRUArray,    0, sizeof(LRUArray));
  NumOfCachedImages = 0;            // No images currently in 11 cache
}

// Class Destructor
Cache::~Cache(void) {

  // Nothing to do yet
}

// Return any errors detected during Cacheing operation
int Cache::GetError(void) {
return(LLCache::GetError());
}

/*
This function searches the HandleArray for a free LRUDesc entry. If one
is found its index is returned. If none available, which should be a
very rare occurrence -1 is returned.
*/
int Cache::FindFreeHandle(void) {
  int Index;

  for (Index = 0; Index < MAXIMAGESMANAGED; Index++)
    if ((HandleArray[Index].Flags & ENTRYUSEDBIT) == 0) // If entry is free
        return Index;               // Return its index
  return -1;                        // Should never get here
}
```

```
/*
This function searches the LRUArray for any reference to hImage. One
and only one reference can exist. A reference may not exist if
referenced image is not in the low level cache. If a reference is found,
it is deleted and the LRUArray is condensed. This function does not
dispose of images that are referenced, however.
*/
void Cache::DeleteReference(HLHANDLE hImage) {
  int Index, ImageIndex = -1;

  for (Index=0; Index < MAXSIMULTANEOUSIMAGES; Index++) {
    if (LRUArray[Index] == hImage) {
      ImageIndex = Index;
      break;
    }
  }
  if (ImageIndex == -1)              // If a reference not found to hImage
    return;                         // in LRUArray no need to continue.
  // A reference was found, delete it by condensing LRUArray
  for (Index=ImageIndex; Index < MAXSIMULTANEOUSIMAGES; Index++)
    LRUArray[Index] = LRUArray[Index+1];
}


/*
This function first deletes any references to hImage in LRUArray and then
places hImage at the beginning of LRUArray making this image the most
recently used image.
*/
void Cache::ReferenceImage(HLHANDLE hImage) {
  int Index;

  DeleteReference(hImage);          // Delete any older reference to hImage
  // Move all entries in LRUArray down one to make room for MRU image handle
  for (Index = NumOfCachedImages; Index > 0; Index--)
    LRUArray[Index] = LRUArray[Index-1];
  // Now indicate hImage is MRU image and clear entry past end of array
  LRUArray[0] = hImage;
  LRUArray[MAXSIMULTANEOUSIMAGES] = 0;
}


/*
This function guarantees the specified image is in the low level cache.
If the image was already there, no work needs to be performed. However,
if the image is currently swapped out, it is reloaded from disk. The
image is also made the MRU image in LRUArray.
*/
LLHANDLE Cache::MakeImagePresent(HLHANDLE hImage, BOOL MakeMRU) {

  if (hImage == 0) {                // A zero handle is not allowed
    OverAllError = EBadHandle;      // return error if so
    return 0;
  }

  PLRUDesc Ptr = &(HandleArray[hImage-1]);  // Get ptr to LRUDesc of image being
referenced
```

```
    if ((Ptr->Flags & ENTRYUSEDBIT) == 0) {   // Is entry used ?
      OverAllError = EBadHandle;    // If not then hImage is a bad handle
      return 0;                     // so return error handle of 0.
    }
    if ((Ptr->Flags & ENTRYPRESENTBIT) != 0) {// If image is currently in 11 cache
      if (MakeMRU) ReferenceImage(hImage);    // Make image MRU if told to
      return (Ptr->LLHandle);                 // and return the low level handle
    }
    // When we get here we know hImage is not in low level cache. Must read
    // it from disk. Is there room in low level cache for a new image ?
    if (NumOfCachedImages == MAXSIMULTANEOUSIMAGES) { // If not then LRU is swapped
out
      HLHANDLE Handle = LRUArray[MAXSIMULTANEOUSIMAGES-1]; // Get HL handle of LRU
image
      LRUArray[MAXSIMULTANEOUSIMAGES-1] = 0;  // Clear the entry for safety
      Ptr = &(HandleArray[Handle-1]);         // Get ptr to its LRUDesc
      LLCache::DisposeOfImage(Ptr->LLHandle); // Dispose of it
      Ptr->Flags &= ~ENTRYPRESENTBIT;         // Reset entry present bit
      Ptr->LLHandle = 0;
      NumOfCachedImages--;          // One less image in cache
    }
    // When we get here we know there is room in the cache for a new image
    // and that we must read that image from disk.
    Ptr = &(HandleArray[hImage-1]); // Get ptr to LRUDesc of image being referenced
    // Now attempt to bring image into the 11 cache
    LLHANDLE LLHandle = LLCache::OpenImage(Ptr->FileName, Ptr->FullSizeDither);
    if (LLHandle != 0) {            // If successful, get ptr to LRUDesc
      Ptr->Flags |= ENTRYPRESENTBIT;// Indicate image is in 11 cache
      Ptr->LLHandle = LLHandle;     // Saves its 11 handle
      NumOfCachedImages++;          // One more image in cache
      ReferenceImage(hImage);       // Make image MRU
    }                               // return the low level image handle
    return LLHandle;
}


/*
This function attempts to free up the LL cache. If possible, NumOfImages
of empty cache slots are produced. Images that were in the LL cache
are disposed of. Rarely is this function ever needed because the cache
usually takes care of itself.
*/
BOOL Cache::MakeRoomForNImages(WORD NumOfImages) {
  WORD Index;

  // Can only preempt the whole LL cache, no more
  if (NumOfImages > MAXSIMULTANEOUSIMAGES)
    return FALSE;
  // The request is reasonable if we get here. How many free cache
  // slots are there ?
  WORD FreeCacheEntries = MAXSIMULTANEOUSIMAGES - NumOfCachedImages;
  if (FreeCacheEntries >= NumOfImages)
    return TRUE;
  // When we get here, some LL cache images must be disposed of.
  WORD NumberToFree = NumOfImages - FreeCacheEntries;
  while (NumberToFree--) {
```

```
        Index = MAXSIMULTANEOUSIMAGES -1; // Start at last entry in LRUArray
        while (LRUArray[Index] == 0) // Search toward most recent images
          Index--;                   // until a non zero entry is found
        // We have found the oldest cached image in LRUArray
        HLHANDLE Handle = LRUArray[Index];   // Get handle from LRUArray
        LRUArray[Index] = 0;            // Clear the entry
        PLRUDesc Ptr = &(HandleArray[Handle-1]);     // Get ptr to its LRUDesc
        LLCache::DisposeOfImage(Ptr->LLHandle);   // Dispose of it
        Ptr->Flags &= ~ENTRYPRESENTBIT;     // Reset entry present bit
        Ptr->LLHandle = 0;
        NumOfCachedImages--;                 // One less image in cache
    }
  return TRUE;                          // Indicate all is well
}

// Bring image into the cache and call LLCache function to perform
// operation.
LPIMAGEDESCRIPTOR Cache::GetImageDescriptorPtr(HLHANDLE hImage) {

  return (LLCache::GetImageDescriptorPtr(MakeImagePresent(hImage, FALSE)));
}
BOOL Cache::SetDisplayClipMode(HLHANDLE hImage) {

  return (LLCache::SetDisplayClipMode(MakeImagePresent(hImage, FALSE)));
}


BOOL Cache::SetDisplayStretchMode(HLHANDLE hImage) {

  return (LLCache::SetDisplayStretchMode(MakeImagePresent(hImage, FALSE)));
}


LPBITMAPINFO Cache::GetLPBITMAPINFO(HLHANDLE hImage) {

  return (LLCache::GetLPBITMAPINFO(MakeImagePresent(hImage, FALSE)));
}


HPALETTE Cache::GetHandleOfImagePalette(HLHANDLE hImage) {

  return (LLCache::GetHandleOfImagePalette(MakeImagePresent(hImage, FALSE)));
}


HGLOBAL Cache::GetHandleOfImageData(HLHANDLE hImage) {

  return (LLCache::GetHandleOfImageData(MakeImagePresent(hImage, FALSE)));
}

// Dispose of an image.
BOOL Cache::DisposeOfImage(HLHANDLE hImage) {

  PLRUDesc Ptr = &(HandleArray[hImage-1]);   // Get ptr to LRUDesc of image to
dispose of
  if ((Ptr->Flags & ENTRYUSEDBIT) == 0)     // Is entry used ?
    return FALSE;                           // If not then error has occurred
```

```
   Ptr->References -= 1;                         // Decrement reference count for this
image
  if (Ptr->References == 0) {                    // If no more references, delete all
traces of image
    if ((Ptr->Flags & ENTRYPRESENTBIT) != 0) {   // If image is currently in 11
cache
      LLCache::DisposeOfImage(Ptr->LLHandle); // dispose of it
      DeleteReference(hImage);                 // Delete any reference to this image
in LRUArray
      NumOfCachedImages--;                     // One less image in cache
    }
    memset(Ptr, 0, sizeof(LRUDesc));           // Clear the descriptor
  }
  return TRUE;
}

// Dispose of all images contained in the cache
void Cache::DisposeOfAllImages(void) {

  // First clear out the low level image cache
  LLCache::DisposeOfAllImages();
  // Then clear data structures used to manage images in LRU fashion
  memset(HandleArray, 0, sizeof(HandleArray));
  memset(LRUArray,    0, sizeof(LRUArray));
  NumOfCachedImages = 0;            // No images currently in 11 cache
}

/*
This function caches an image. NOTE: image memory must be allocated as
shared before calling this function. Image memory block is dropped directly
into the cache, it is not copied and then freed.
*/
HLHANDLE Cache::CacheImage(LPSTR FileName, LPIMAGEDESCRIPTOR lpImgDesc,
                           BOOL FullSizeDither) {
  PLRUDesc Ptr;
  BOOL ImageSwappedOut = FALSE;

  // Is there room in low level cache for a new image ?
  if (NumOfCachedImages == MAXSIMULTANEOUSIMAGES) { // If not then LRU is swapped
out
    HLHANDLE Handle = LRUArray[MAXSIMULTANEOUSIMAGES-1]; // Get HL handle of LRU
image
    LRUArray[MAXSIMULTANEOUSIMAGES-1] = 0;  // Clear the entry for safety
    Ptr = &(HandleArray[Handle-1]);          // Get ptr to its LRUDesc
    LLCache::DisposeOfImage(Ptr->LLHandle); // Dispose of it
    Ptr->Flags &= ~ENTRYPRESENTBIT;          // Reset entry present bit
    Ptr->LLHandle = 0;
    ImageSwappedOut = TRUE;       // Indicate image has been swapped
  }
  LLHANDLE LLHandle = LLCache::CacheImage(FileName, lpImgDesc, FullSizeDither);

  if (LLHandle == 0) {           // If image not cached return 0 handle
    if (ImageSwappedOut)         // Also fix count of cached images
      NumOfCachedImages--;       // One less image in cache
```

```
      return 0;
  }
  // Image has been cached. Use FileName to search the list of
  // managed images to see if a match exists
  int Index, IIndex = -1;
  for (Index = 0; Index < MAXIMAGESMANAGED; Index++) {
     if ((HandleArray[Index].Flags & ENTRYUSEDBIT) &&
        (lstrcmp((LPSTR) &(HandleArray[Index].FileName), FileName) == 0)) {
        IIndex = Index;
        break;
     }
  }
  if (IIndex != -1) {              // If filename does exist, use that entry after
     Index = IIndex;               // Disposing of it in the ll cache
     Ptr = &(HandleArray[Index]); // Get ptr to image's LRUDesc
     if ((Ptr->Flags & ENTRYPRESENTBIT) != 0) { // If image is currently in ll
cache
        LLCache::DisposeOfImage(Ptr->LLHandle); // dispose of it
        NumOfCachedImages--;       // One less image in cache
     }
  } else {                         // Otherwise create a LRUDesc for new image
     if ((Index = FindFreeHandle()) == -1) { // Is there an image handle to use to
reference image
?

        OverAllError = ETooManyOpenImages;    // If not then set error indicator
        return 0;                  // and return error handle of 0. This should be
rare.
     }
  }
  // Index has the index into HandleArray to use for the LRUDesc
  if (!ImageSwappedOut)            // If image was swapped before then no need to
inc
     NumOfCachedImages++;          // One more image in cache
  Ptr = &(HandleArray[Index]);     // Get ptr to free LRUDesc
  Ptr->Flags = ENTRYUSEDBIT | ENTRYPRESENTBIT; // Indicate entry is no longer
free and image is cached
  Ptr->FullSizeDither = FullSizeDither;// Record dithering preference
  lstrcpy(Ptr->FileName, FileName);    // Copy filename to LRUDesc
  Ptr->LLHandle = LLHandle;        // Save the low level image handle
  if (Ptr->References == 0)        // If this LRUDesc was empty references will be
zero.
     Ptr->References = 1;          // in this case make it a one. If LRUDesc
reused, add
  else                             // one to current reference count
     Ptr->References++;
  return (Index+1);                // Return the high level handle with is index
plus one
}

// This function attempts to display an image with its correct aspect
// ratio.
BOOL Cache::DisplayImageWithAspect(HLHANDLE hImage, HWND hWindow, BOOL BGFlag) {

  // If the image to be painted is a background image and the cache is full
  // and this image is not in the cache, don't reload image. This causes
```

```
    // a continuous circle of image loading to repaint images.
    if (BGFlag &&
        (NumOfCachedImages == MAXSIMULTANEOUSIMAGES) &&
        ((HandleArray[hImage-1].Flags & ENTRYPRESENTBIT) == 0))
      return FALSE;
    else
      return(LLCache::DisplayImageWithAspect(MakeImagePresent(hImage, !BGFlag),
hWindow, BGFlag));
}


BOOL Cache::DisplayImageinWindowRect(HLHANDLE hImage, HWND hWindow, RECT& Area,
BOOL BGFlag) {

    // If the image to be painted is a background image and the cache is full
    // and this image is not in the cache, don't reload image. This causes
    // a continuous circle of image loading to repaint images.
    if (BGFlag &&
        (NumOfCachedImages == MAXSIMULTANEOUSIMAGES) &&
        ((HandleArray[hImage-1].Flags & ENTRYPRESENTBIT) == 0))
      return FALSE;
    else
      return(LLCache::DisplayImageinWindowRect(MakeImagePresent(hImage, !BGFlag),
hWindow, Area, BGFlag));
}


BOOL Cache::DisplayImage(HLHANDLE hImage, HWND hWindow, POINT& Pt, BOOL BGFlag) {

    // If the image to be painted is a background image and the cache is full
    // and this image is not in the cache, don't reload image. This causes
    // a continuous circle of imaging loading to repaint images.
    if (BGFlag &&
        (NumOfCachedImages == MAXSIMULTANEOUSIMAGES) &&
        ((HandleArray[hImage-1].Flags & ENTRYPRESENTBIT) == 0))
      return FALSE;
    else
      return(LLCache::DisplayImage(MakeImagePresent(hImage, !BGFlag), hWindow, Pt,
BGFlag));
}


// Begin the open image process. Note image is not actually read from disk
// until it is accessed.
HLHANDLE Cache::OpenImage(LPSTR FileName, BOOL FullSizeDither) {
    int Index;

    // Check to see if specified image is already known
    for (Index=0; Index > MAXIMAGESMANAGED; Index++) {
      // If filename matches one in HandleArray, just return the known handle
      // after bumping reference count.
      if (lstrcmp((LPSTR) &(HandleArray[Index].FileName), FileName) == 0) {
        HandleArray[Index].References++;
        return (Index+1);
      }
    }
    // When we get here we know there are no previous references to image
    if ((Index = FindFreeHandle()) == -1) { // Is there an image handle ?
      OverAllError = ETooManyOpenImages; // If not then set error indicator
```

```
      return 0;                         // and return error handle of 0. This should be
  rare.
    }
    PLRUDesc Ptr = &(HandleArray[Index]);// Get ptr to free LRUDesc
    Ptr->Flags = ENTRYUSEDBIT;         // Indicate entry is no longer free
    Ptr->References = 1;               // One and only one reference to this image
    Ptr->FullSizeDither = FullSizeDither;// Record dithering preference
    lstrcpy(Ptr->FileName, FileName);    // Copy filename to LRUDesc
    Ptr->LLHandle = 0;                 // Set low level handle to zero just in case
    return (Index+1);                  // Return the high level handle with is index
  plus one
  }

  // LLCache class functions follow

  // Constructor and destructor for the Low Level Cache Interface class
  LLCache::LLCache(void) {

    OverAllError = NoError;      // No errors yet
    NumOfImages = 0;             // No images yet
    memset((LPSTR) ImageDesc, 0, sizeof(ImageDesc)); // Clear descriptors
  }


  LLCache::~LLCache(void) {

    DisposeOfAllImages();
  }

  // Set clipping mode in display object
  BOOL LLCache::SetDisplayClipMode(LLHANDLE hImage) {
    Display *DispObj;

    OverAllError = NoError;
    if ((hImage >= 1) && (hImage <= MAXSIMULTANEOUSIMAGES) &&
        (ImageDesc[hImage-1].ImgDesc.hImageData != 0)) {
      // When we get here, we know the handle is valid and is assigned an image
      hImage--;                  // Index into ImageDesc is one less than handle
      DispObj = ImageDesc[hImage].DisplayObject; // Get ptr to display obj
      DispObj->SetClipMode();  // Set clip mode
      return TRUE;
    } else {
      OverAllError = EBadHandle;
      return FALSE;
    }
  }

  // Set stretch mode (default) in display object
  BOOL LLCache::SetDisplayStretchMode(LLHANDLE hImage) {
    Display *DispObj;

    OverAllError = NoError;
    if ((hImage >= 1) && (hImage <= MAXSIMULTANEOUSIMAGES) &&
        (ImageDesc[hImage-1].ImgDesc.hImageData != 0)) {
      // When we get here, we know the handle is valid and is assigned an image
      hImage--;                      // Index into ImageDesc is one less than handle
```

```
      DispObj = ImageDesc[hImage].DisplayObject; // Get ptr to display obj
      DispObj->SetStretchMode();     // Set stretch mode
      return TRUE;
   } else {
      OverAllError = EBadHandle;
      return FALSE;
   }
}


// Return image descriptor with all image specs
LPIMAGEDESCRIPTOR LLCache::GetImageDescriptorPtr(LLHANDLE hImage) {

   OverAllError = NoError;
   if ((hImage >= 1) && (hImage <= MAXSIMULTANEOUSIMAGES) &&
       (ImageDesc[hImage-1].ImgDesc.hImageData != 0)) {
      // When we get here, we know the handle is valid and is assigned an image
      hImage--;                  // Index into ImageDesc is one less than handle
      return &ImageDesc[hImage].ImgDesc;
   } else {
      OverAllError = EBadHandle;
      return NULL;
   }
}


// Return LPBITMAPINFO structure, needed for image printing functions
LPBITMAPINFO LLCache::GetLPBITMAPINFO(LLHANDLE hImage) {
   Display *DispObj;

   OverAllError = NoError;
   if ((hImage >= 1) && (hImage <= MAXSIMULTANEOUSIMAGES) &&
       (ImageDesc[hImage-1].ImgDesc.hImageData != 0)) {
      // When we get here, we know the handle is valid and is assigned an image
      hImage--;                  // Index into ImageDesc is one less than handle
      DispObj = ImageDesc[hImage].DisplayObject;   // Get ptr to display obj
      return (DispObj->GetPtrToBITMAPINFO());
   } else {
      OverAllError = EBadHandle;
      return NULL;
   }
}


// Return handle to logical palette of specified image
HPALETTE LLCache::GetHandleOfImagePalette(LLHANDLE hImage) {
   Display *DispObj;

   OverAllError = NoError;
   if ((hImage >= 1) && (hImage <= MAXSIMULTANEOUSIMAGES) &&
       (ImageDesc[hImage-1].ImgDesc.hImageData != 0)) {
      // When we get here, we know the handle is valid and is assigned an image
      hImage--;                  // Index into ImageDesc is one less than handle
      DispObj = ImageDesc[hImage].DisplayObject;   // Get ptr to display obj
      return (DispObj->GetPalette());
   } else {
      OverAllError = EBadHandle;
      return NULL;
```

```
      }
  }

  // Returns handle of image data for image
  HGLOBAL LLCache::GetHandleOfImageData(LLHANDLE hImage) {

    OverAllError = NoError;
    if ((hImage >= 1) && (hImage <= MAXSIMULTANEOUSIMAGES) &&
        (ImageDesc[hImage-1].ImgDesc.hImageData != 0)) {
      // When we get here, we know the handle is valid and is assigned an image
      hImage--;                         // Index into ImageDesc is one less than handle
      return (ImageDesc[hImage].ImgDesc.hImageData);
    } else {
      OverAllError = EBadHandle;
      return NULL;
    }
  }


  /*
  This function returns the index into the ImageDesc array of a free
  descriptor. This function should never be called unless it is known
  a free descriptor exists.
  */
  WORD LLCache::FindFreeDescriptor(void) {

    for (WORD Index = 0; Index < MAXSIMULTANEOUSIMAGES; Index++)
      if (ImageDesc[Index].ImgDesc.hImageData == 0)     // if entry is free
        return Index;           // Return its index
    return 0;                   // Should never get here
  }


  /*
  This function disposes of the image specified by the handle. A call to this
  function is necessary to free up an image descriptor for use by a new
  image either acquired from scanner or read from disk.
  */
  BOOL LLCache::DisposeOfImage(LLHANDLE hImage) {

    OverAllError = NoError;
    if ((hImage >= 1) && (hImage <= MAXSIMULTANEOUSIMAGES) &&
        (ImageDesc[hImage-1].ImgDesc.hImageData != 0)) {
      // When we get here, we know the handle is valid and is assigned an image
      hImage--;                         // Index into ImageDesc is one less than handle
      NumOfImages--;                    // One less image after dispose
      GlobalFree(ImageDesc[hImage].ImgDesc.hImageData); // Free memory
      memset(&(ImageDesc[hImage].ImgDesc), 0, sizeof(IMAGEDESCRIPTOR));
      Display *DispObj = ImageDesc[hImage].DisplayObject;    // Get ptr to display
object
      delete DispObj;                   // Finally delete the display object
      return TRUE;                      // Return all is well
    } else {
      OverAllError = EBadHandle;
      return FALSE;                     // Invalid handle
    }
  }
```

```
/*
This function gets rid of all of the allocated images.
*/
void LLCache::DisposeOfAllImages(void) {

  for (WORD Index = 0; Index < MAXSIMULTANEOUSIMAGES; Index++)
    DisposeOfImage(Index+1);        // Handle is Index plus one
  NumOfImages = 0;                  // Not necessary, but just in case
  OverAllError = NoError;           // Necessary because of implementation of this
function
}


/*
Low level portion of CacheImage functionality
*/
LLHANDLE LLCache::CacheImage(LPSTR FileName, LPIMAGEDESCRIPTOR lpImgDesc,
                            BOOL FullSizeDither) {

  OverAllError = NoError;

  if ((FileName == NULL) || (FileName[0] == '\0')) {
    OverAllError = EEmptyFileName;
    GlobalFree(lpImgDesc->hImageData);       // Free shared memory
    return 0;
  }

  // We got a proper filename, continue.
  if (NumOfImages < MAXSIMULTANEOUSIMAGES) {// Is there room for a new image ?
    // Insert the shared memory for the image into the cache.
    WORD Index = FindFreeDescriptor();// Find the next free image descriptor

    // Copy all of ID into ImageDesc entry
    ImageDesc[Index].ImgDesc = *lpImgDesc; // Save contents of ID

    // Get ptr to image memory.
    BYTE huge *lpCacheMemory = (BYTE huge *)
                          GlobalLock(lpImgDesc->hImageData);

    // Create new display object for image
    ImageDesc[Index].DisplayObject = new Display;     // Spawn a new display object
    (ImageDesc[Index].DisplayObject)->           // Init the display object
      InitForDisplay(lpImgDesc->Width, lpImgDesc->Height,
                     lpImgDesc->Colors, lpCacheMemory,
                     lpImgDesc->Palette, FullSizeDither);
    (ImageDesc[Index].DisplayObject)->SetStretchMode();

    GlobalUnlock(lpImgDesc->hImageData);     // Unlock the memory for now
    NumOfImages++;                   // One more image to manage
    return(Index+1);                 // Handle is one more than index into table
  } else {
    OverAllError = ETooManyOpenImages;
    GlobalFree(lpImgDesc->hImageData);
    return 0;
  }
}
```

```
// This function displays an image with the specified handle using
// the correct aspect ratio.
BOOL LLCache::DisplayImageWithAspect(LLHANDLE hImage, HWND hWindow,
                                               BOOL BGFlag) {

   Display *DispObj;

   OverAllError = NoError;
   if ((hImage >= 1) && (hImage <= MAXSIMULTANEOUSIMAGES) &&
       (ImageDesc[hImage-1].ImgDesc.hImageData != 0)) {
     // When we get here, we know the handle is valid and is assigned an image
     hImage--;                    // Index into ImageDesc is one less than handle
     DispObj = ImageDesc[hImage].DisplayObject; // Get ptr to display obj
     BYTE huge *ImageData = (BYTE huge *)
                            GlobalLock(ImageDesc[hImage].ImgDesc.hImageData);
     DispObj->SetImageDataPtr(ImageData);
     // Now display the image in aspect ratio intact
     DispObj->DisplayImageWithAspect(hWindow, BGFlag);
     GlobalUnlock(ImageDesc[hImage].ImgDesc.hImageData);
     return TRUE;
   } else {
     OverAllError = EBadHandle;
     return FALSE;
   }
}

// This function displays an image with the specified handle in a portion
// of a window.
BOOL LLCache::DisplayImageinWindowRect(LLHANDLE hImage, HWND hWindow,
                                               RECT& Area, BOOL BGFlag) {
   Display *DispObj;

   OverAllError = NoError;
   if ((hImage >= 1) && (hImage <= MAXSIMULTANEOUSIMAGES) &&
       (ImageDesc[hImage-1].ImgDesc.hImageData != 0)) {
     // When we get here, we know the handle is valid and is assigned an image
     hImage--;                    // Index into ImageDesc is one less than handle
     DispObj = ImageDesc[hImage].DisplayObject; // Get ptr to display obj
     BYTE huge *ImageData = (BYTE huge *)
                            GlobalLock(ImageDesc[hImage].ImgDesc.hImageData);
     DispObj->SetImageDataPtr(ImageData);
     // Display the image in rect
     DispObj->DisplayImageInWindowRect(hWindow, Area, BGFlag);
     GlobalUnlock(ImageDesc[hImage].ImgDesc.hImageData);
     return TRUE;
   } else {
     OverAllError = EBadHandle;
     return FALSE;
   }
}

// This function displays an image with the specified handle in a window
BOOL LLCache::DisplayImage(LLHANDLE hImage, HWND hWindow, POINT& Pt,
                              BOOL BGFlag) {
   Display *DispObj;
```

```
      OverAllError = NoError;
      if ((hImage >= 1) && (hImage <= MAXSIMULTANEOUSIMAGES) &&
          (ImageDesc[hImage-1].ImgDesc.hImageData != 0)) {
        // When we get here, we know the handle is valid and is assigned an image
        hImage--;                    // Index into ImageDesc is one less than handle
        DispObj = ImageDesc[hImage].DisplayObject; // Get ptr to display obj
        BYTE huge *ImageData = (BYTE huge *)
                               GlobalLock(ImageDesc[hImage].ImgDesc.hImageData);
        DispObj->SetImageDataPtr(ImageData);
        // Display the image
        DispObj->DisplayImage(hWindow, Pt, BGFlag);
        GlobalUnlock(ImageDesc[hImage].ImgDesc.hImageData);
        return TRUE;
      } else {
        OverAllError = EBadHandle;
        return FALSE;
      }
    }


LLHANDLE LLCache::OpenImage(LPSTR FileName, BOOL FullSizeDither) {
    HWND hWindowWithCurrentFocus;

    OverAllError = NoError;

    if ((FileName == NULL) || (FileName[0] == '\0')) {
      OverAllError = EEmptyFileName;
      return 0;
    }


    if (NumOfImages < MAXSIMULTANEOUSIMAGES) {// Is there room for a new image ?
      hWindowWithCurrentFocus = GetFocus();
      Compand C;                 // New compander instance
      HCURSOR hOldCursor = SetCursor(LoadCursor(NULL, IDC_WAIT));
      // See if compand understand the image type
      if (!C.InitExpander(FileNamme)) {
        OverAllError = EFileNotFound;
        SetCursor(hOldCursor);
        SetFocus(hWindowWithCurrentFocus);// Put focus back
        return 0;
      }
      // File found we can continue
      if (!C.DoExpansion()) {
        OverAllError = C.GetError();
        SetCursor(hOldCursor);
        SetFocus(hWindowWithCurrentFocus);// Put focus back
        return 0;
      }
      // Expansion when ok - cache the image
      // Allocate memory for the image data
      DWORD RasterSize =
        CalculateBytesPerLine(C.GetWidth(), C.GetBitsPerPixel()) *
                              C.GetHeight();

      HGLOBAL hMemory = GlobalAlloc(GMEM_MOVEABLE, RasterSize);
      if (!hMemory) {
```

```
        OverAllError = ENoMemory;
        SetCursor(hOldCursor);
        SetFocus(hWindowWithCurrentFocus);// Put focus back
        return 0;
    }
    // Memory has been allocated, we can continue
    // Find the next free image descriptor
    WORD Index = FindFreeDescriptor();

    // Fill ImageDesc data structure with image info from Compand object
    ImageDesc[Index].ImgDesc.Width = C.GetWidth();
    ImageDesc[Index.ImgDesc.Height = C.GetHeight();
    ImageDesc[Index].ImgDesc.RasterSize = RasterSize;
    ImageDesc[Index].ImgDesc.BPP = C.GetBitsPerPixel();
    ImageDesc[Index].ImgDesc.Colors = C.GetColors();
    ImageDesc[Index].ImgDesc.hImageData = hMemory; // Save handle to memory
    memcpy(ImageDesc[Index].ImgDesc.Palette, C.GetPalettePtr(),
            C.GetColors() * sizeof(RGBCOLOR));
    BYTE huge *lpImageData = (BYTE huge *) GlobalLock(hMemory);
    // Move the raster data to its new home
    hmemcpy(lpImageData, C.GetDataPtr(), RasterSize);

     ImageDesc[Index].DisplayObject = new Display;      // Spawn a new display
object
    (ImageDesc[Index].DisplayObject)->         // Init the display object
       InitForDisplay(C.GetWidth(), C.GetHeight(), C.GetColors(),
                   lpImageData, C.GetPalettePtr(), FullSizeDither);
    (ImageDesc[Index].DisplayObject)->SetStretchMode();

    GlobalUnlock(hMemory);           // Unlock the global memory for now
    NumOfImages++;                   // One more image to manage
    SetCursor(LoadCursor(NULL, IDC_ARROW));
    SetFocus(hWindowWithCurrentFocus);// Put focus back
    return(Index+1);                 // Handle is one more than index into table
  } else {
    OverAllError = ETooManyOpenImages;
    return 0;
  }
}


// Cache class thumbnail functions
BOOL Cache::DisplayThumbnail(LPSTR FileName, HWND hWindow, BOOL BGFlag) {
  Thumbnails THM;                    // Instantiate the class to do the work

  return(THM.DisplayThumbnail(FileName, hWindow, BGFlag));
}

BOOL Cache::MakeThumbnail(LPSTR FileName) {
  Thumbnails THM;                    // Instantiate the class to do the work

  return(THM.MakeThumbnail(FileName));
}

// Return the current error, if any.
int LLCache::GetError(void) {
  int ErrorRet;
```

```
    ErrorREt = OverAllError;
    OverAllError = NoError;
    return ErrorRet;
}

// This function calculates the number of bytes of image data per
// line given the line width and the number of bits per pixel.
DWORD CalculateBytesPerLine(WORD Width, WORD BPP) {

    DWORD BytesPerLine;

    // Calculate BytesPerLine
    switch(BPP) {
        case 1:
            BytesPerLine = (Width+7)/8;        // Exactly 8 pixels in each byte
            break;

        case 2:
            BytesPerLine = (Width+3)/4;        // Exactly 4 pixels in each byte
            break;

        case 4:
            BytesPerLine = (Width+1)/2;        // Exactly two pixels in each byte
            break;

        case 8:
            BytesPerLine = Width;              // Exactly one pixel in each byte
            break;

        case 24:
            BytesPerLine = Width * 3;          // Exactly three bytes per pixel
            break;
    }
    BytesPerLine = ALIGN_DWORD(BytesPerLine);
    return BytesPerLine;
}

#ifdef_WIN32_
// Entry point for Compand DLL
BOOL WINAPI DllEntryPoint(HINSTANCE hinstDLL, DWORD /*fdwReason*/, LPVOID
/*lpvReserved*/) {

    // Just save the instance handle
    hDLLInstance = hinstDLL;
    return TRUE;
}
#else

// Library entry point for initialization
int CALLBACK LibMain (HANDLE hInst, WORD, WORD wHeapSize, LPSTR) {

    hDLLInstance = hInst;

    if (wHeapSize > 0)
        UnlockData (0);

    return 1;
}
```

```
int CALLBACK WEP(int) {

  return(1);
}
#endif
```

Image cacheing is implemented on two distinctly different levels by two different C++ classes. The level on which an application program interacts is referred to as *high-level cacheing* and is implemented by the *Cache* class. The Cache class provides the interface to "mycache.dll." Underneath the high-level cacheing code is *low-level cacheing* code, which is implemented by a class appropriately called *LL Cache.*

The high-level cacheing code keeps track of various bits of information about the images stored in the cache. This information is maintained in a structure called a LRUDesc and includes:

1. Flags. A series of flags that indicate the LRUDesc is valid and whether this image is contained in the low-level cache at the present time.
2. References. This is the count of the number of times this image has been referenced, in essence, the count of the number of clients for this image.
3. FullSizeDither. A Boolean indicating the dithering preference for the image. If TRUE, a full-size dither of the image data will be performed if required for image display. If FALSE, the image will be dithered on demand, if required for image display. See Chapters 5 and 6 for more information on dithering.
4. FileName. The full path and filename of the image.
5. LLHandle. This is a handle for referencing the image in the low-level cache.

The information in LRUDesc is recorded the first time an image is cached by a call to the high-level cacheing functions **OpenImage** or **CacheImage.** The LRUDesc information is maintained from that point on automatically by the cacheing code. If the image must be swapped out of the cache, a bit in Flags is reset to indicate the image is no longer in the low-level cache and the LLHandle member is reset to zero. Filename information maintained in the LRUDesc is not deleted, however, when the image is swapped out of the low-level cache. This is because the filename is needed to reload the image the next time the image is referenced. If the cache function **Dispose-OfImage** is called and if the reference count for the image is one, then all traces of image information are removed from the high-level cache, including the filename. If **DisposeOfImage** is called and the reference count is greater than one, the reference count is decremented by one, but no other actions occur.

Both the **OpenImage** or **CacheImage** functions return a handle (a short integer value greater than one) when they are called to cache an image. It is via this handle that a image in the cache is accessed. All of the high-level cache functions that can be called by an application program require a handle in addition to the other parameters they require. It is an application's responsibility to save the handle returned from the cacheing code for all subsequent access to images.

It is interesting to note that when **OpenImage** is called to load a graphic image file into the cache, this function returns immediately to the calling application with a handle but does not actually load the image (images are loaded into the low-level cache). The image will not be loaded into the cache until the image is referenced by the application program, that is, the first time the image is to be displayed or the image data accessed. Up to MAXIMAGEMANAGED (50) images could be cached in this way in preparation for use but only the images that were actually accessed (via the handle) would ever be loaded into the low-level cache.

Finally, it is in the high-level caching code that a record of image accesses is maintained for implementation of the least recently used algorithm. The array LRUArray keeps track of which images have been accessed by the order in which the handles to the images are stored. The most recently accessed image's handle is stored in the first entry of LRUArray followed by the handles of the images accessed earlier. Every time an image is accessed (as a foreground image), it becomes the most recently used image, and its handle is placed at the front of LRUArray. As long as an image continues to be accessed, it will remain in the LRUArray, and its data will remain in memory in the low-level cache. However, once an image moves to the end of LRUArray, meaning that it is the least recently used image, and a request is made for access to a new image (not already in the cache), the image data of the least recently used image will be disposed of and the new image will take its place in the low-level cache. So you see why this cache management technique is referred to as the least recently used or LRU algorithm.

As hinted at earlier, the low-level cache actually manages image data. Whereas the high-level cache can contain information about 50 images simultaneously, the low-level cache can contain the image data for at most MAXSIMULTANEOUSIMAGES (10) images at one time. Image data are managed within the LLCache class using an ImageDesc data structure. This structure contains the following items:

1. ImgDesc. This is an IMAGEDESCRIPTOR structure (see description in Chapter 1) that contains the images' specifications and the images' raster data. All information needed about the image contained in a low-level cache entry is available in ImgDesc.

2. DisplayObject. This is a pointer to a Display object (see Chapter 6) used to display the image in the cache into a window or other device context. Because of the intelligence built into the Display class object, the display of the image will be dealt with according to the facilities of the display hardware and current Windows video mode.

When an image is said to be swapped out of the cache, its image data and display object are actually removed from the low-level cache. In other words, the memory occupied by the image is returned to the system, and the display object is deleted. For all intents and purposes, no trace of the image remains.

Using the Cache DLL

A concrete example of using the Cache code in an application program can be seen in the CacheTst program shown in Listing 10.3. The important points to glean from the code presented are that an application needs to include the file "cache.hpp" for gaining access to the function provided in the cacheing DLL "mycache.dll", that the application must be linked with a lib file, "mycache.lib", produced from the DLL, that only a single object of the Cache class is ever needed in an application program, and that all access to cached images are via handles. Understanding these four points is the key to using the cacheing DLL with your application program.

The LLCache and Cache classes

Purpose

The Cache class is the C++ interface between the image-cacheing code contained in the "mycache.dll" and an application program. All interaction between the cacheing DLL and an application program is by way of member functions of the Cache class. The Cache class inherits the LLCache class, although none of the member functions of LLCache are meant to be called directly. The cache code is rather complex so a thorough examination of Listings 10.1 and 10.2 is recommended if you wish to understand how image caching works at the lowest level. The low-level cacheing code manages the images in the low-level cache. The high-level cacheing code manages images that may or may not actually be in the low-level cache.

LLCache Member Functions

LLCache. This is the constructor for the low-level cache class. It sets the class variable OverAllError to NoError, it initializes the count of the number of images (NumOfImages) contained in the low-level cache to zero, and clears the ImageDesc array in preparation for use.

~LLCache. All this destructor of the LLCache does is to call the member function **DisposeOfAllImages** that frees the memory associated with all images contained in the low-level cache.

FindFreeDescriptor. This function searches the ImageDesc array in the low-level cache to find a free entry that can be used for cacheing a new image. See the text for a description of the ImageDesc data structure. This function returns an array index between zero and **MAXSIMULTANEOUSIMAGES**. This function should never be called unless a free entry is known to exist.

OpenImage. This function is called when a graphic image file is to be read into and subsequently managed by the low-level cache. Required parameters include the filename of the image to load and a Boolean, indicating a dithering preference. An object of the Compand class (see Chapter 4) is instantiated to read the image file into memory in DIB format. Next, memory is allocated for holding the image data while in the cache. **FindFreeDescriptor** is called next to find an empty ImageDesc for holding the image information. The IMAGEDESCRIPTOR within ImageDesc is then initialized with information about the image taken from the Compand object. Finally, a Display object (see Chapter 6) is instantiated and initialized for displaying the image contained in this cache entry. A pointer to this Display object is stored within ImageDesc. The dither Boolean preference passed into **Open-Image** is passed on to the Display object. If all went well, the class variable NumOfImages is incremented by one because the low-level cache contains one more image under its control.

CacheImage. This member function is used when an image (and its IMAGE-DESCRIPTOR) already exists and the image needs to be placed in the low-level cache for management. This is typically the situation when an image is retrieved from a scanner and needs to be cached. Internally, this function operates almost identically to the **OpenImage** function described earlier. Parameters to this function include the filename of the graphic image file that contains the image to be

FIGURE 10.2 The LLCache and Cache classes.

cached (this is necessary in case the image is swapped out and must be reloaded), a pointer to an IMAGEDESCRIPTOR that describes (and contains) the image data, and a Boolean indicating dithering preference.

DisplayImage. This member function causes a specified image, identified by a handle, to be displayed within a window. Parameters to this function are the same as to the **DisplayImage** member function of the Display class (see Chapter 6) except that a handle to an image is also required.

DisplayImageinWindowRect. This member function causes a specified image, identified by a handle, to be displayed within a window or portion of a window. Parameters to this function are the same as to the **DisplayImageinWindowRect** member function of the Display class (see Chapter 6) except that a handle to an image is also required.

DisplayImageWithAspect. This member function causes a specified image, identified by a handle, to be displayed with correct aspect ratio in a window. Parameters to this function are the same as to the **DisplayImageWithAspect** member function of the Display class (see Chapter 6) except that a handle to an image is also required.

GetImageDescriptorPtr. This member function returns a pointer to the IMAGEDESCRIPTOR of an image identified by a handle.

SetDisplayStretchMode. Execution of this member function places the Display object for the image contained in the low-level cache, and identified by a handle, into stretch mode. See Chapter 6 for information about stretch mode.

SetDisplayClipMode. Execution of this member function places the Display object for the image contained in the low-level cache, and identified by a handle, into clip mode. Again, see Chapter 6 for information about clip mode.

GetHandleOfImagePalette. This function returns a handle to the logical palette used to display the image identified by a handle.

GetHandleOfImageData. This function returns a handle to the block of global memory that contains the image data for the image identified by a handle. The handle is extracted from the IMAGEDESCRIPTOR stored in the ImageDesc structure for the specified image.

GetLPBITMAPINFO. This function returns a pointer to the BITMAPINFO structure used by the Display object for display of the image identified by a handle. Again, see Chapter 6.

DisposeOfImage. This function disposes of the image specified by a handle by flushing the image out of the low-level cache. Specifically, the memory occupied by the image is returned to Windows, the ImageDesc entry for the image is zeroed, the Display object for the image is deleted, and the variable, NumOfImages, is decreased by one because there is one less image in the low-level cache.

DisposeOfAllImages. This function calls **DisposeOfImage** for all images in the low-level cache. In other words, it empties the low-level cache completely.

GetError. This function returns the code of the last error that occurred during the operation of the low-level cache. If no error has occurred, this call returns NoError.

The Cache Member Functions

Cache. This is the class constructor. It functions to initialize an object of this class in preparation for cacheing images. Specifically, it zeroes the HandleArray and the

FIGURE 10.2 (*Continued*)

LRUArray in addition to setting the NumOfCachedImages to zero. See text for details.

~Cache. This is the class destructor. At this time, this function does nothing. It is just a place holder for future functionality.

FindFreeHandle. This function looks through the HandleArray for an entry that can be used for a new image. A value between zero and MAXIMAGESMANAGED is returned from this function. If −1 is returned, all high-level cache entries are being used. This happens very rarely.

DeleteReference. This function searches the LRUArray for any reference to the image specified by a high-level handle. One and only one reference can exist in LRUArray for an image. A reference may not exist if the referenced image is not in the low-level cache. If a reference is found, it is deleted and the LRUArray is condensed. This function does not dispose of images that are dereferenced, however.

ReferenceImage. This function first deletes any references in LRUArray to the image identified by the handle and then places the handle to the image at the beginning of LRUArray, making this image the most recently used image.

MakeImagePresent. It is within this function that cacheing magic is performed. This function accepts as parameters a handle to the image to make present (that is to load into the low-level cache) and a Boolean flag, indicating whether to mark the image as most recently used. If the referenced image is already in the low-level cache, no work needs to be done, and the low-level handle is returned from this function. If, however, the image is currently swapped out, it is reloaded from disk. If the low-level cache is full when this function is called, an image in the cache will be swapped out to make a cache entry available for swapping in the referenced image. If the parameter MakeMRU (*Most Recently Used*) is TRUE, the referenced image will be marked as most recently used (its handle is moved to the front of the LRUArray). If it is FALSE, no reference to the image in the LRUArray will be made. Only images that are displayed as foreground images (BGFlag = FALSE) will be marked as MRU. Background images are never marked as MRU because of their limited importance.

OpenImage. This high-level cacheing function requires a filename of the image to load and a Boolean, indicating a dithering preference. Its first order of business is to check whether the specified filename exists in the HandleArray and if so, to increment the reference count of the image (because there is more than one client for the image) and return the already assigned handle. In this manner, multiple references to an image are satisfied very quickly. If the filename does not already exist, the function **FindFreeHandle** is called to find a free entry in the HandleArray into which the information about the image file can be stored. The HandleArray entry is marked as used, the image reference count is set to one, the dither preference is stored, and the filename is copied into the HandleArray entry. On completion, a handle for referencing the image is returned from **OpenImage.** The handle's value is one greater than the index into the HandleArray. A handle with zero as its value is illegal. Note: Execution of this function does not actually cause an image to be loaded from disk. Image loading will not occur until a reference is made to the image via its handle. For this reason, there does not need to be a check within **OpenImage** to see whether a low-level cache entry is available for the image.

FIGURE 10.2 (*Continued*)

CacheImage. This member function is used to insert an image already in memory directly into the low-level cache for management. This member function is available for performance reasons. If an image already exists in memory, as in the case of a scanned-in image, it can be transferred directly into the cache for management instead of having to be loaded from a disk file. Hence, the performance improvement. Because an image is to be forced into the low-level cache, code within **CacheImage** must take care of providing a a low-level cache entry for the image. In providing a low-level cache entry for the new image, the LRU image in the cache may be swapped out. See the code in the listing for the gruesome details.

DisplayImage, DisplayImageinWindowRect, and **DisplayImageWithAspect.** These member functions call **MakeImagePresent** to bring the image referenced by a handle into the low-level cache in preparation for display and then call a function of their same name in the LLCache class for actually performing the display. If the image is to be displayed as a background image and the low-level cache is already full and the referenced image is not in the low-level cache, these functions will return a Boolean FALSE and refuse to display the image. If this were not done, background images would continuously swap foreground images out of the cache and a continuous circle of image painting and repainting would occur.

MakeRoomForNImages. This function swaps out however many images in the low-level cache necessary to make room for *N* new images. *N* is a parameter to this function. Rarely is this function ever needed because the LRU mechanism of the cache usually takes care of itself. This function is provided for completeness only.

GetImageDescriptorPtr, SetDisplayStretchMode, SetDisplayClipMode, GetHandleOfImagePalette, GetHandleOfImageData, GetLPBITMAPINFO. All of these functions work by calling **MakeImagePresent** to bring the image referenced by a handle into the low-level cache in preparation for access and then calling their low-level cacheing counterparts. See the previous discussion of members of the LLCache class for details.

DisposeOfImage. This function not only disposes of the image specified by a handle by flushing the image out of the low-level cache, but it also removes all information about the image from the HandleArray. In other words, all information about the image is removed from the high- and the low-level caches.

DisposeOfAllImages. This function calls **LLCache::DisposeOfAllImages** to get rid of all images in the low-level cache and then clears out all of the high-level cache data structures. In other words, it empties both the high- and low-level caches completely.

DisplayThumbnail. This function provides an interface to the thumbnail code for displaying a thumbnail image. See the discussion in the text on thumbnail images in this chapter for details.

MakeThumbnail. This function provides an interface to the thumbnail code for making a thumbnail image. See the discussion in the text on thumbnail images in this chapter for details.

GetError. This function returns the code of the last error that occurred during the operation of the cache. If no error has occurred, this call returns NoError. This member function calls **LLCache::GetError()** to return the error indication.

FIGURE 10.2 (*Continued*)

Listing 10.3 The Cachetst class member functions.

```
/********************************************************/
/***                  "cachetst.cpp"              ***/
/***             Image Cache Test Program         ***/
/***                   written by                 ***/
/***                Craig A. Lindley              ***/
/***                                              ***/
/***      Revision: 2.0    Last Update: 11/11/94  ***/
/********************************************************/

// Copyright (c) 1995 John Wiley & Sons, Inc. All rights reserved.

#include <owl\owlpch.h>
#pragma hdrstop

#include "cachetst.hpp"
#include "cchtstad.h"            // Definition of about dialog.
#include "dialogs.hpp"

#define NUMBEROFWINDOWS     12     // Number of image display windows
#define HORIZSCREENCOVERAGE 90     // Percentage of screen to cover

// Macros to make access to Twain and Cache object in TMainWindow easier
#define CACHEPTR TYPESAFE_DOWNCAST(Parent, TMainWindow)->CacheObjPtr
#define TWAINPTR TYPESAFE_DOWNCAST(Parent, TMainWindow)->TwainObjPtr

static HLHANDLE hImages [NUMBEROFWINDOWS];
static HWND     hWindow [NUMBEROFWINDOWS];

// Declaration of function in "merge.cpp" to merge image and text
extern BOOL MergeImageAndText(LPSTR InFileName, LPSTR OutFileName,
                    LPSTR lpLine1, LPSTR lpLine2,
                    LPSTR lpLine3, LPSTR lpLine4);

// Application Class Constructor
CacheTestApp::CacheTestApp(void) :
  TApplication("CacheTst - Image Cacheing Test Program") {

  // Nothing yet to do
}

// Application Class Destructor
CacheTestApp::~CacheTestApp(void) {

  // Nothing yet to do
}

// Main Window Intialization.
void CacheTestApp::InitMainWindow(void) {

  // Instantiate the FrameWindow and TMainWindow client
  TFrameWindow *Frame = new TFrameWindow(NULL, GetName(), new TMainWindow(NULL));

  nCmdShow = SW_SHOWMAXIMIZED;
```

```
  // Assign application icon
  Frame->SetIcon(this, IDI_APPLICATIONICON);

  // Assign menu
  Frame->AssignMenu(IDM_CMDMENU);
  SetMainWindow(Frame);
}

// Relay WM_PALETTECHANGED message to all child windows
void CacheTestApp::EvPaletteChanged(HWND hWindow) {

  TYPESAFE_DOWNCAST(MainWindow->GetClientWindow(), TMainWindow)->
    SendPaletteChanged(hWindow);
}

// Program Entry Point
int OwlMain(int , char* []) {
  CacheTestApp App;
  int Result;

  Result = App.Run();
  return Result;
}

// TMainWindow Class Constructor
TMainWindow::TMainWindow(TWindow* parent, const char far* title,
                         TModule* module) :
  TWindow(parent, title, module) {

  SetBkgndColor(RGB(160, 160, 160));

  CacheObjPtr = new Cache;        // Instantiate instance of Cache Object
  TwainObjPtr = new Twain;        // Instantiate the Twain Object
}

// TMainWindow Class Destructor
TMainWindow::~TMainWindow(void) {

  delete TwainObjPtr;             // Delete the Twain Object
  delete CacheObjPtr;             // Delete Cache Object
}

void TMainWindow::SetupWindow(void) {

  TWindow::SetupWindow();         // Do default setup

  WORD XPos, YPos, Window;
  TChildWindow *pChild;

  // Now calculate the location of and create the child windows
  HDC hDC = GetDC(NULL);
  WORD ScreenWidth = GetDeviceCaps(hDC, HORZRES);
  WORD ScreenHeight = GetDeviceCaps(hDC, VERTRES);
  ReleaseDC(NULL, hDC);
```

```
DWORD WindowCoverage = ((DWORD) ScreenWidth * HORIZSCREENCOVERAGE) / 100L;
WORD WindowWidth = (WORD) (WindowCoverage / 4);
WORD WindowHeight = (WindowWidth * 3) / 4;
WORD HorizSpacing = (ScreenWidth - (WindowWidth*4)) / 5;
WORD VertSpacing = (ScreenHeight - (WindowHeight*3)) / 4;
VertSpacing = (VertSpacing * 75) / 100;

// Create the child windows
for (Window=0; Window < NUMBEROFWINDOWS; Window++) {

  hImages[Window] = 0;        // Zero the image handle
  switch(Window) {            // Calculate position
    case 0:
      XPos = HorizSpacing;
      YPos = VertSpacing;
      break;
    case 1:
      XPos = (2*HorizSpacing) + WindowWidth;
      YPos = VertSpacing;
      break;
    case 2:
      XPos = (3*HorizSpacing) + WindowWidth*2;
      YPos = VertSpacing;
      break;
    case 3:
      XPos = (4*HorizSpacing) + WindowWidth*3;
      YPos = VertSpacing;
      break;

    case 4:
      XPos = HorizSpacing;
      YPos = (2*VertSpacing) + WindowHeight;
      break;
    case 5:
      XPos = (2*HorizSpacing) + WindowWidth;
      YPos = (2*VertSpacing) + WindowHeight;
      break;
    case 6:
      XPos = (3*HorizSpacing) + WindowWidth*2;
      YPos = (2*VertSpacing) + WindowHeight;
      break;
    case 7:
      XPos = (4*HorizSpacing) + WindowWidth*3;
      YPos = (2*VertSpacing) + WindowHeight;
      break;

    case 8:
      XPos = HorizSpacing;
      YPos = (3*VertSpacing) + WindowHeight*2;
      break;
    case 9:
      XPos = (2*HorizSpacing) + WindowWidth;
      YPos = (3*VertSpacing) + WindowHeight*2;
      break;
    case 10:
      XPos = (3*HorizSpacing) + WindowWidth*2;
```

```
            YPos = (3*VertSpacing) + WindowHeight*2;
            break;
        case 11:
            XPos = (4*HorizSpacing) + WindowWidth*3;
            YPos = (3*VertSpacing) + WindowHeight*2;
            break;
    }
    // Now create the child windows
    pChild = new TChildWindow(this, "Empty Window");
    pChild->Attr.Style = (WS_OVERLAPPEDWINDOW | WS_CLIPSIBLINGS | WS_VISIBLE |
WS_CHILD) & ~WS_SYSMENU;
    pChild->Attr.X = XPos;
    pChild->Attr.Y = YPos;
    pChild->Attr.W = WindowWidth;
    pChild->Attr.H = WindowHeight;
    pChild->ChildWindowNumber = Window;
    pChild->Create();
    hWindow[Window] = pChild->HWindow;
  }
}


// This non class function sends a custom palette changed message
// to each child window. It is envoked for each child window.
void SendPaletteChangedMessage(TWindow * P, LPVOID Parm) {

  ::SendMessage(P->HWindow, CTA_WM_PALETTECHANGED, 0, (LPARAM) Parm);
}
// This function sends a simulated palette changed message to each
// child window.
void TMainWindow::SendPaletteChanged(HWND hWindow) {

  ForEach((TActionFunc) SendPaletteChangedMessage, (LPVOID) hWindow);
}


// Menu Help About
void TMainWindow::CmAboutHelp(void) {

  // Show the modal dialog.
  AboutDialog(this).Execute();
}


// Child window class member functions
int TChildWindow::WindowNumberWithFocus = -1;

// TChildWindow Class Constructor
TChildWindow::TChildWindow(TWindow* parent, const char far* title,
                           TModule* module) :
  TWindow(parent, title, module) {

  // Initialize class variables
  memset(FileName, 0, sizeof(FileName));
  hMenu = 0;
  DitherOnDemand = TRUE;
  MaintainAspectRatio = TRUE;
  UseThumbnails = FALSE;
```

```
    SetBkgndColor(RGB(0, 0, 90));    // Set window background color

    OFD = new OpenFileDialog;         // Instantiate open file dialog box
    OFD->AddToFilter("All Files|*.*|BMP Files|*.bmp|GIF Files|*.gif|");
    OFD->AddToFilter("TIF Files|*.tif|");
    OFD->SetDialogBoxName("Select an Image File");

    SFD = new SaveFileDialog;         // Instantiate save file dialog box
    SFD->AddToFilter("All files (*.*)|*.*|");
}

// TChildWindow Class Destructor
TChildWindow::~TChildWindow(void) {

    if (hMenu)                        // If window had menu, which it should
      DestroyMenu(hMenu);             // Destroy menu associated with window

    delete OFD;                       // Delete the open file dialog box
    delete SFD;                       // Delete the save file dialog box
}

void TChildWindow::SetupWindow(void) {

    TWindow::SetupWindow();           // Do default processing

    // Now load the floating popup menu
    hMenu = LoadMenu(GetApplication()->GetInstance(),
                        MAKEINTRESOURCE(IDM_POPUPMENU));
    hMenu = GetSubMenu(hMenu, 0);
}

// Conditional window closing
BOOL TChildWindow::CanClose(void) {

    // If window contained an image, dispose of it
    if (hImages[ChildWindowNumber])
      CACHEPTR->DisposeOfImage(hImages[ChildWindowNumber]);
    return TRUE;
}

// Handle Mouse Left Button Down. Give this window focus, repaint if
// necessary. Store handle to window
void TChildWindow::EvLButtonDown(UINT modKeys, TPoint& point) {

    TWindow::EvLButtonDown(modKeys, point);   // Default processing

    if (WindowNumberWithFocus != ChildWindowNumber) {
      WindowNumberWithFocus = ChildWindowNumber;
      ::InvalidateRect(HWindow, NULL, FALSE);
    }
}

// Handle Mouse Right Button Down. Popup menu.
void TChildWindow::EvRButtonDown(UINT modKeys, TPoint& point) {

    TWindow::EvRButtonDown(modKeys, point);   // Default processing
```

```
    WindowNumberWithFocus = ChildWindowNumber;
    ::ClientToScreen(HWindow, (LPPOINT) &point);
    TrackPopupMenu(hMenu, TPM_CENTERALIGN, point.x, point.y, 0, HWindow, NULL);
}

// Sent to window whenever the system palette has been changed. If this
// was not the window which caused the palette to change, it should
// repaint itself.
LRESULT TChildWindow::EvPaletteChanged(WPARAM, LPARAM lParam) {

  HWND hWnd = (HWND) lParam;

  if (hWnd != HWindow)
     ::InvalidateRect(HWindow, NULL, FALSE);

  return 0;
}

// Process WM_SIZE message
void TChildWindow::EvSize(UINT sizeType, TSize& size) {

  TWindow::EvSize(sizeType, size);// Do default processing

  WindowNumberWithFocus = ChildWindowNumber;
   ::InvalidateRect(HWindow, NULL, FALSE);
}

// Process WM_MOVE message
void TChildWindow::EvMove(TPoint& clientOrigin) {

  TWindow::EvMove(clientOrigin); // Do default processing

  WindowNumberWithFocus = ChildWindowNumber;
   ::InvalidateRect(HWindow, NULL, FALSE);
}

// Paint Routine for Child Window
void TChildWindow::Paint(TDC&, BOOL, TRect&) {
  POINT Pt;

  BOOL BGFlag = (WindowNumberWithFocus == ChildWindowNumber) ? FALSE:TRUE;
  Pt.x = Pt.y = 0;

  if (hImages[ChildWindowNumber]) {     // If there is an image to display
    if (UseThumbnails && (OFD->GetPathNamePtr() != NULL))
      CACHEPTR->DisplayThumbnail(OFD->GetPathNamePtr(), HWindow, BGFlag);
    else if (!MaintainAspectRatio)
      CACHEPTR->DisplayImage(hImages[ChildWindowNumber], HWindow, Pt, BGFlag);
    else
      CACHEPTR->DisplayImageWithAspect(hImages[ChildWindowNumber], HWindow,
BGFlag);
  }
}

// Toggle the Dither on Demand Menu Item
void TChildWindow::PmDither(void) {
```

```
    DitherOnDemand = (DitherOnDemand) ? FALSE:TRUE;
    CheckMenuItem(hMenu, PM_DITHERONDEMAND,
      MF_BYCOMMAND | (DitherOnDemand) ? MF_CHECKED:MF_UNCHECKED);
}


// Toggle the Display With Aspect Menu Item
void TChildWindow::PmAspect(void) {

  MaintainAspectRatio = (MaintainAspectRatio) ? FALSE:TRUE;
  CheckMenuItem(hMenu, PM_ASPECT,
    MF_BYCOMMAND | (MaintainAspectRatio) ? MF_CHECKED:MF_UNCHECKED);
  ::InvalidateRect(HWindow, NULL, TRUE);
}


// Toggle the Use Thumbnails Menu Item
void TChildWindow::PmThumbnails(void) {

  UseThumbnails = (UseThumbnails) ? FALSE:TRUE;
  CheckMenuItem(hMenu, PM_USETHUMBNAILS,
    MF_BYCOMMAND | (UseThumbnails) ? MF_CHECKED:MF_UNCHECKED);
  ::InvalidateRect(HWindow, NULL, TRUE);
}


// Load an Image File Menu Item
void TChildWindow::PmLoadImage(void) {
// IMAGEDESCRIPTOR ID;

  if (hImages[ChildWindowNumber]) {
    CACHEPTR->DisposeOfImage(hImages[ChildWindowNumber]);
    hImages[ChildWindowNumber] = 0;
    ::SetWindowText(HWindow, "Empty Window");
  }

  if (OFD->DoDialog(HWindow)) {
    hImages[ChildWindowNumber] =
      CACHEPTR->OpenImage((LPSTR) OFD->GetPathNamePtr(), !DitherOnDemand);
    if (hImages[ChildWindowNumber]) {
      ::SetWindowText(HWindow, OFD->GetFileNamePtr());
      // Get image specs as a test
      // ID = *(CACHEPTR->GetImageDescriptorPtr(hImages[ChildWindowNumber]));
    }
  }
  ::InvalidateRect(HWindow, NULL, FALSE);
}


// Select a TWAIN Source Menu Item
void TChildWindow::PmSelectSource(void) {

  TWAINPTR->SelectSource(HWindow);
}


// Scan an Image Menu Item
void TChildWindow::PmScanImage(void) {
  IMAGEDESCRIPTOR ID;
```

```
    if (hImages[ChildWindowNumber]) {
        CACHEPTR->DisposeOfImage(hImages[ChildWindowNumber]);
     hImages[ChildWindowNumber] = 0;
      ::SetWindowText(HWindow, "Empty Window");
    }
    if (SFD->DoDialog(HWindow)) {
      // We must make a copy because acquisition will modify the
      // memory for storage directly.
      lstrcpy((LPSTR) FileName, SFD->GetPathNamePtr());
      if (TWAINPTR->ScanImage((LPSTR) FileName, BMPTYPE, 50, ID)) {
        hImages[ChildWindowNumber] =
          CACHEPTR->CacheImage((LPSTR) FileName, &ID, !DitherOnDemand);
        if (hImages[ChildWindowNumber]) {
          ::SetWindowText(HWindow, FileName);
          // Get image specs as a test
          ID = *(CACHEPTR->GetImageDescriptorPtr(hImages[ChildWindowNumber]));
        }
      }
    }
    ::InvalidateRect(HWindow, NULL, FALSE);
}

// Dispose of Image Menu Item
void TChildWindow::PmDisposeOfImage(void) {

  if (hImages[ChildWindowNumber]) {
    CACHEPTR->DisposeOfImage(hImages[ChildWindowNumber]);
    hImages[ChildWindowNumber] = 0;
    ::SetWindowText(HWindow, "Empty Window");
    ::InvalidateRect(HWindow, NULL, TRUE);
  }
}

void TChildWindow::PmMergeImageAndText(void) {

  // Ask user for what image to merge the text onto
  if (OFD->DoDialog(HWindow)) {
    // If we get here, the user has selected an image file to merge
    MergeImageAndText(OFD->GetPathNamePtr(),       // InFileName
                      "merge.XXX",                 // OutFileName
                      "Image and Text Merging Example",
                      "from the book",
                      "Imaging Techniques for Windows",
                      "(c) 1994, Craig A. Lindley. All Rights Reserved.");
  }
}
```

A Possible Enhancement to the Cacheing Code

While this cacheing code proves very usable for a professional imaging application, there is still an enhancement that could be made to make it even better. Currently, the number of images that can be cached in memory at one time is statically limited to MAXSIMULTANEOUSIMAGES or 10 images. This limit, which can easily be changed, was intentionally put in place to limit the amount of memory that could be consumed in an application program for image storage. After all, other (less important) parts of an application program probably need some memory to run in, also. For this reason, it would not be wise to let the imaging portion of the application consume all available memory. Hence the limit.

Instead of statically limiting the number of cached entries, in retrospect a more reasonable approach would have been to limit the number of low-level cache entries according to the amount of available memory. That way, possibly a hundred small images could be cached at one time if memory allowed. If large images were cached, maybe only five cache entries would be available, depending on memory. As you might expect, there are some complications with the cacheing code as presented, which would need to be overcome in implementing this limiting technique. If it is worth your trouble, have at it. When you get it to work, send me a copy of the code.

Final Thoughts on Cacheing

The cacheing code presented in this chapter will dramatically improve imaging performance in image-intensive application programs. If your application only needs to display one or two small images, the integration of the cacheing code might be overkill; you will have to be the judge. You have probably realized by now that the caching code was not used in the TestApp imaging example program of Chapter 1. The reason for this omission was to keep the TestApp example program as clean and uncluttered as possible so that understanding would be easier for the reader (you). The TestApp of Chapter 1 is an excellent example of an application program that could benefit by the incorporation of image cacheing. A professional version of the TestApp program would definitely incorporate the image-cacheing code presented in this chapter.

Thumbnail Images

The speed of image display (or user interaction in general) has a direct impact on how users feel about a program or product. Of course, there is no such thing as displaying images too quickly. The problem is with slow image display resulting in slow user interactivity. Unfortunately, slow image display will eventually gripe even the most patient user. For this reason, many techniques have evolved for mediating user irritation with slow image display. Some techniques attack the speed of image display directly, while others use psychological means for pacifying a user until the image is available (note the proliferation of progress meters to give the user something to look at until a lengthy operation is completed). And some, like the incorporation of thumbnail images, lie somewhere between the two extremes.

Thumbnail images, as defined here, are a smaller version of a larger or much larger image that can be displayed much faster than the image it represents. Although of much coarser resolution and color than the image it replaces, a thumbnail can quickly give a user the ability to see an image providing the near instant gratification that users demand. Users will generally put up with the display of thumbnail images in a program as long as they display quickly and as long as the full resolution image can be retrieved when needed. The use of thumbnail images is a virtual requirement in networked imaging application where image data must be moved across a network. It is much faster to move a thumbnail image across a network to represent a full resolution image than it would be to move the full-resolution, multimegabyte image in its entirety.

The thumbnail images generated and displayed by the code provided in this chapter have the following characteristics:

- Thumbnail images are a maximum of 80 × 80 pixels in size. The actual size of the thumbnail is determined from the aspect ratio of the original image; for example, if the original image was 640 × 480 pixels, the thumbnail generated from the image would have dimensions of 80 × 60. Thumbnail images maintain the same aspect ratio as the original image.
- A thumbnail image file is approximately 7,500 bytes maximum, regardless of the size of the original image. Some thumbnails files are smaller, depending on the aspect ratio of the original image as discussed earlier.
- All thumbnails are in 8-BPP, 256-color format. If the original image was true color, the image data are dithered down to 256-color format before the thumbnail is generated. Since all true color images are dithered against the same palette, all thumbnail images derived from true color images use an identical palette. This means that palette shifts will not be noticeable when displaying the thumbnails in 256-color video modes. See the discussion of foreground and background palettes in Chapter 2 for more information.
- Thumbnail images are stored in BMP file format (see Chapter 4) but are given a THM filename extension. This is necessary for thumbnail file management reasons but more on this later. The "compand.dll" has special support built in for reading and writing THM files.
- Thumbnail images are read from disk and displayed in a single operation every time a thumbnail image needs to be drawn in a window.

All of the code for generating and displaying thumbnail images is contained in the files "thnails.hpp" shown in Listing 10.4 and "thnails.cpp" shown in Listing 10.5. Figure 10.3 details the member functions of the Thumbnails class. The thumbnail code can be instantiated and used directly as presented or if "mycache.dll" image cacheing code is used in an application program, the thumbnail functions can be accessed through the interface to the Cache class. See Figure 10.2 for the definition of the Cache class interface functions. Please note that although the thumbnail code is integrated into the cacheing code, no cacheing of thumbnail images is performed. Thumbnail images are read from a file and displayed every time the thumbnail is painted in a window.

Listing 10.4 The Thnails class interface definition.

```
/*********************************************************/
/***                  "thnails.hpp"                  ***/
/***        Interface class for thumbnail support    ***/
/***                   written by                    ***/
/***               Craig A. Lindley                  ***/
/***                                                 ***/
/***      Revision: 2.0    Last Update: 11/11/94     ***/
/*********************************************************/

// Copyright (c) 1995 John Wiley & Sons, Inc. All rights reserved.
```

```
#ifndef THNAILS_HPP
#define THNAILS_HPP

#include <windows.h>
#include <dir.h>

#ifdef _WIN32_
#define huge
#endif

#define THUMBNAILWIDTH          80  // Max dimensions of thumbnail in pixels
#define THUMBNAILHEIGHT         80

// Thumbnails class
class Thumbnails {
  private:
    char TNFileName[MAXPATH];
    HGLOBAL hPromoteDIB;
    BYTE huge * DImagePtr;

    // Private Functions
    BOOL ValidateThumbnail(LPSTR FileName);
    BOOL PromoteTo8Bits(BYTE huge *ImagePtr, WORD Width, WORD Height, WORD BPP);

  public;
    Thumbnails();
    virtual ~Thumbnails();

    BOOL DisplayThumbnail(LPSTR FileName, HWND hWindow, BOOL BGFlag);
    BOOL MakeThumbnail(LPSTR FileName);
};

#endif
```

Listing 10.5 The Thnails class member functions.

```
/**********************************************************/
/***                "thnails.cpp"                      ***/
/***           Thumbnail Class Functions               ***/
/***                 written by                        ***/
/***              Craig A. Lindley                      ***/
/***                                                   ***/
/***      Revision: 2.0     Last Update: 11/11/94       ***/
/**********************************************************/

// Copyright (c) 1995 John Wiley & Sons, Inc. All rights reserved.

#include <math.h>
#include <string.h>
#include <time.h>
#include <sys\stat.h>
#include <io.h>
#include "thnails.hpp"
#include "compand.hpp"
#include "display.hpp"
```

```
extern HANDLE hDLLInstance;

// This function borrowed from "display.cpp"
extern HGLOBAL DitherAnImage(BYTE huge *lpImageData,
                             WORD Width, WORD Height);
extern RGBCOLOR DitherPalette[256];


/*
Two display object at the file level are required to prevent
oscillation of thumbnails due to continuous repaints.

The problem boils down to this:

A handle to a palette used to display an image cannot be deleted
until another palette has been realized as the foreground palette
even though the palette has been selected out of the device context.
This is important for thumbnails because the Display objects originally
came and went and the destructor for the Display object deletes
the contained palette; causing the oscillation.

The global Display objects prevent this from happening because
the foreground display object is never deleted (and therefore the
handle to the palette never destroyed) until a new foreground
palette is realized.
*/
static Display D[2];                    // Array of two display objects
                                        // One for foreground one for background

#ifdef _WIN32_
// Necessary because this function does not exist in Win32 API
LPSTR lstrcpyn(LPSTR lpszString1, LPCSTR lpszString2, int cChars) {

  if (lstrlen(lpszString2) <= cChars) {// If String2 shorter than cChars
    // Go ahead and copy String2 to String1 storage
    return lstrcpy(lpszString1, lpszString2);
  } else {                             // String1 longer than cChars
    LPSTR lpS1 = lpszString1;
    LPSTR lpS2 = (LPSTR) lpszString2;
    char S2Char = *lpS2++;
    while (S2Char && cChars--) {
      *lpS1++ = S2Char;
      S2Char = *lpS2++;
    }
    *lpS1 = '\0';
    return lpszString1;
  }
}
#endif
// Masks for bit manipulation in PromoteTo8Bits function
BYTE Masks[] = {
  0x00,  // Unused
  0x01,  // Mask for 1 bits
  0x03,  // Mask for 2 bits
  0x00,  // Unused
```

```
  0x0F    // Mask for 4 bits
};

// Thumbnail Class Constructor
Thumbnails::Thumbnails(void) {

  hPromoteDIB = NULL;
  DImagePtr = NULL;
}

// Thumbnail Class Destructor
Thumbnails::~Thumbnails(void) {

  if (hPromoteDIB) {
    GlobalUnlock(hPromoteDIB);
    GlobalFree(hPromoteDIB);
    hPromoteDIB = NULL;
  }
}

// This function builds a thumbnail image from an image file.
BOOL Thumbnails::MakeThumbnail(LPSTR FileName) {
  HGLOBAL hMem = 0;                 // Handle of dithered image data memory

  // Check to be sure filename is not NULL and that the image file exists.
  if ((FileName[0] == '\0') || (access(FileName, 0) != 0))
    return FALSE;                   // Return FALSE if not found or NULL

  // Since image file exists copy the filename to local storage
  lstrcpyn(TNFileName, FileName, MAXPATH);

  // Now attempt to expand the image file into memory
  Compand E;                        // Make an instance of the Compander

  // Change cursor to hourglass
  HCURSOR hOldCursor = SetCursor(LoadCursor(NULL, IDC_WAIT));

  if (!E.InitExpander(FileName)) {// Initialize the expander
    SetCursor(hOldCursor);
    return FALSE;
  }
  if (!E.DoExpansion()) {          // Attempt to expand the image
    SetCursor(hOldCursor);
    return FALSE;
  }

  // When we get here, the image file has been expanded.
  // Record the image parameters at this point. They will be changed
  // if the image is dithered.
  BYTE huge *ImageDataPtr = E.GetDataPtr();
  RGBCOLOR *ImagePalettePtr = E.GetPalettePtr();

  // Use the function DitherImage from "display.cpp" to dither a
  // 24 BPP image.
  if (E.GetBitsPerPixel() == 24) {// Image is true color, dither it
```

```
      // Image must be dithered.
      hMem = DitherAnImage(E.GetDataPtr(), E.GetWidth(), E.GetHeight());
      if (!hMem) {
        MessageBox(NULL, "Not enough memory to dither image.",
                         "Error Building Thumbnail",
                         MB_OK | MB_TASKMODAL | MB_ICONEXCLAMATION);

        SetCursor(hOldCursor);
        return FALSE;
      }
      // When we get here, the image is 256 colors.
      // Record the new image parameters for use in blting.
      ImageDataPtr    = (BYTE huge *) GlobalLock(hMem);
      ImagePalettePtr = DitherPalette;

  } else if (E.GetBitsPerPixel() < 8) {
      if (!PromoteTo8Bits(ImageDataPtr, E.GetWidth(), E.GetHeight(),
E.GetBitsPerPixel())) {
        SetCursor(hOldCursor);
        return FALSE;
      }
      ImageDataPtr = DImagePtr;   // New ptr to image data
  }
  // When we get here we have an 8BPP DIB

  // Now scale the image such that its aspect ratio is maintained and
  // it fits into a box no more than THUMBNAILWIDTH x THUMBNAILHEIGHT
  // pixels.
  BOOL VertFit;                   // True if image is taller than wide
  DWORD Width = E.GetWidth();     // Get original image dimensions
  DWORD Height = E.GetHeight();
  DWORD NewWidth = Width;
  DWORD NewHeight = Height;

  // Calculate size of image for thumbnail, leaving aspect ratio
  // intact.
  if (Height > Width)             // Determine which dimension to fit
    VertFit = TRUE;
  else
    VertFit = FALSE;

  if (VertFit) {                  // Make the image fit vertically
    NewWidth = THUMBNAILWIDTH + 1;
    NewHeight = THUMBNAILHEIGHT;
    while (NewWidth > THUMBNAILWIDTH)
      NewWidth = (NewHeight-- * Width) / Height;
    NewHeight++;
  } else {                        // Make the image fit horizontally
    NewWidth = THUMBNAILWIDTH;
    NewHeight = THUMBNAILHEIGHT + 1;
    while (NewHeight > THUMBNAILHEIGHT)
      NewHeight = (NewWidth-- * Height) / Width;
    NewWidth++;
  }
  // NewWidth and NewHeight now contain the thumbnail dimensions.
```

```
// Allocate memory for the thumbnail bitmap
DWORD RequiredMemory = ALIGN_DWORD(NewWidth) * NewHeight;
HGLOBAL hTNImageMemory = GlobalAlloc(GHND, RequiredMemory);
if (hTNImageMemory == NULL) {
  MessageBox(NULL, "Not enough memory for thumbnail image.",
                   "Error Building Thumbnail",
                   MB_OK | MB_TASKMODAL | MB_ICONEXCLAMATION);

  SetCursor(hOldCursor);
  return FALSE;
}
// Lock down a ptr to the thumbnail memory
BYTE huge *TNImageData = (BYTE huge *) GlobalLock (hTNImageMemory);

DWORD BytesPerLineS = ALIGN_DWORD(E.GetWidth());
DWORD BytesPerLineD = ALIGN_DWORD(NewWidth);

WORD SLine, SPixel;
BYTE huge *lpSLine;
BYTE huge *lpDLine;
BYTE huge *lpSPixel;
BYTE huge *lpDPixel;

// Do calculations required for each row of destination image.
// DIB is copied upside down as usual.
for (int Row = 0; Row < NewHeight; Row++) {
  // Calculate which row of source image to fetch
  SLine = (WORD) (((DWORD) Height * Row) / (DWORD) NewHeight);
  lpSLine = (BYTE huge *) (ImageDataPtr + (SLine * BytesPerLineS));
  lpDLine = (BYTE huge *) (TNImageData + (Row * BytesPerLineD));
  for (int Col = 0; Col < NewWidth; Col++) {
    // Do calculations required for each col of destination image
  SPixel = (WORD) (((DWORD) Width * Col) / (DWORD) NewWidth);
    lpSPixel = (BYTE huge *) (lpSLine + SPixel);
    lpDPixel = (BYTE huge *) (lpDLine + Col);
    // Fetch and store image data to thumbnail bitmap
    *lpDPixel = *lpSPixel;
  }
}
// When we get here, the thumbnail memory contains the thumbnail
// bitmap. Compress the new image to a THM file
Compand C;
C.InitCompressor(THMTYPE, TNFileName,
                 (WORD) NewWidth, (WORD) NewHeight,
                 8, 256,
                 TNImageData, ImagePalettePtr);

C.SetImageType(PALETTECOLOR);

// Compress the new image into the file TNFileName.
C.DoCompression();

// Free up the memory for the thumbnail bitmap.
GlobalUnLock(hTNImageMemory);
GlobalFree(hTNImageMemory);
if (hMem) {                      // If dithering was utilized
```

```
      GlobalUnlock(hMem);               // Free dithered memory block
      GlobalFree(hMem);
   }
   // Remove hourglass cursor.
   SetCursor(hOldCursor);
   return TRUE;
}


// This function promotes DIB images with less than 8 BPP to 8 BPP
// by splitting apart the bits.
BOOL Thumbnails::PromoteTo8Bits(BYTE huge *SImagePtr,
                               WORD Width, WORD Height, WORD BPP) {
   WORD PixelsPerByte;
   WORD BytesPerLineS, BytesPerLineD;

   // Calculate PixelsPerByte and BytesPerLine
   switch(BPP) {
     case 1:
       BytesPerLineS = (Width+7)/8;// Exactly 8 pixels in each byte
       PixelsPerByte = 8;
       break;
     case 2:
       BytesPerLineS = (Width+3)/4;// Exactly 4 pixels in each byte
       PixelsPerByte = 4;
       break;

     case 4:
       BytesPerLineS = (Width+1)/2;// Exactly two pixels in each byte
       PixelsPerByte = 2;
       break;

   }
   BytesPerLineS = ALIGN_DWORD(BytesPerLineS);
   BytesPerLineS = ALIGN_DWORD(Width);

   // Allocate memory for new 8BPP bitmap
   DWORD RequiredMemory = (DWORD) BytesPerLineD * Height;
   hPromoteDIB = GlobalAlloc(GHND, RequiredMemory);
   if (hPromoteDIB == NULL) {
     MessageBox(NULL, "Not enough memory for thumbnail image.",
                      "Error Building Thumbnail",
                      MB_OK | MB_TASKMODAL | MB_ICONEXCLAMATION);
     return FALSE;
   }
   // Lock down a ptr to the 8BPP image memory
   DImagePtr = (BYTE huge *) GlobalLock(hPromoteDIB);

   BYTE huge *lpLineS;
   BYTE huge *lpLineD;
   BYTE huge *lpByteS;
   BYTE huge *lpByteD;
   BYTE TheByte, GrpNum, ShiftCount, SPixel;

   // Now pick apart the packed pixel data and store in 8BPP DIB
   for (DWORD Row=0; Row < Height; Row++) {
     lpLineS = (BYTE huge *) (SImagePtr + (Row * BytesPerLineS));
```

```
      lpLineD = (BYTE huge *) (DImagePtr + (Row * BytesPerLineD));
      for (DWORD Col=0; Col < Width; Col++) {
        lpByteS = (BYTE huge *) (lpLineS + (Col/PixelsPerByte));
        lpByteD = (BYTE huge *) (lpLineD + (Col));
        TheByte = *lpByteS;
        GrpNum = (BYTE) ((PixelsPerByte-1) - (Col % PixelsPerByte));
        ShiftCount = GrpNum * BPP;
        SPixel = (TheByte & (Masks[BPP] << ShiftCount)) >> ShiftCount;
        *lpByteD = SPixel;
      }
    }
  return TRUE;
}

// This function checks for the existence of a thumbnail and builds a
// new one dynamically if necessary.
BOOL Thumbnails::ValidateThumbnail(LPSTR FileName) {
  struct stat StatBuf;
  long ImageTime, ThumbnailTime;
  BOOL BuildNewThumbnail = FALSE;

  // Check to be sure filename is not NULL and that the image file exists.
  if ((FileName[0] == '\0') || (access(FileName, 0) != 0))
  return FALSE;                        // Return FALSE if not found or NULL

  // Get the time when the image file was last modified.
  stat(FileName, &StatBuf);
  ImageTime = StatBuf.st_ctime;

  // Since image file exists copy the filename to local storage
  lstrcpyn(TNFileName, FileName, MAXPATH);
  LPSTR PeriodPtr = strchr(TNFileName,'.'); // Search for . of extension
  if (PeriodPtr != NULL)               // Truncate the filename there
    *PeriodPtr = '\0';
    lstrcat(TNFileName, ".THM");  // Add thumbnail ext ".THM"

  // Check to see if thumbnail exists
  if (access(TNFileName, 0) == -1)// Check for existence of thumbnail
    BuildNewThumbnail = TRUE;      // If not found set build flag
  else {                          // If found, get time of last modification
    stat(TNFileName, &StatBuf);
    ThumbnailTime = StatBuf.st_ctime;
  }
  // Compare the times. If the image is newer than the thumbnail
  // create a new thumbnail.
  if (!BuildNewThumbnail && (ImageTime > ThumbnailTime))
    BuildNewThumbnail = TRUE;    // Set build flag

  // Now build a new thumbnail if necessary
  if (BuildNewThumbnail)
    return (MakeThumbnail(FileName));
  else
    return TRUE;
}
```

```
// This function displays (and possibly builds) a thumbnail in a window.
BOOL Thumbnails::DisplayThumbnail(LPSTR FileName, HWND hWindow, BOOL BGFlag) {
  RECT Rect;

  // Check and possibly build a new thumbnail for the specified image.
  if (!ValidateThumbnail(FileName))
    return FALSE;

  // Now attempt to expand the thumbnail image
  Compand E;                              // Make an instance of the Compander

  // Change cursor to hourglass
  HCURSOR hOldCursor = SetCursor(LoadCursor(NULL, IDC_WAIT));

  if (!E.InitExpander(TNFileName)) {// Initialize the expander
    SetCursor(hOldCursor);
    return FALSE;
  }
  if (!E.DoExpansion()) {            // Attempt to expand the image
    SetCursor(hOldCursor);
    return FALSE;
  }
  // Image is now expanded, prepare for display
  WORD Width  = E.GetWidth();      // Get image dimensions
  WORD Height = E.GetHeight();     // width and height
  WORD HalfWidth =  Width  >> 1;   // Find middle of image
  WORD HalfHeight = Height >> 1;

  // Get the dimensions of display window. These are the dimensions from
  // the layout.
  GetClientRect(hWindow, &Rect);

  WORD HCenter = Rect.right >> 1;// Find middle of window
  WORD VCenter = Rect.bottom >> 1;
  Rect.left    = HCenter - HalfWidth;
  Rect.top     = VCenter - HalfHeight;
  Rect.right   = Rect.left + Width;
  Rect.bottom  = Rect.top + Height;

  // Use the display object indicated by the index.
  // Foreground images uses index 0.
  WORD DisplayObjectIndex = (BGFlag) ? 1:0;
  D[DisplayObjectIndex].InitForDisplay(E.GetWidth(), E.GetHeight(), E.GetColors(),
                              E.GetDataPtr(), E.GetPalettePtr(), TRUE);
  D[DisplayObjectIndex].SetStretchMode();

  // Call on Windows to display the image in the HDC. Use the display
  // object indicated by the index.
  D[DisplayObjectIndex].DisplayImageInWindowRect(hWindow, Rect, BGFlag);

  SetCursor(hOldCursor);

  return TRUE;
}
```

Thumbnail Image Management

The management of thumbnail images in an application program really consists of three separate tasks: the generation, the validation, and the display of the thumbnail images. All three tasks must be tightly coordinated for thumbnails to work effectively within an application program. All three tasks are discussed subsequently.

Thumbnail images are generated by calling **MakeThumbnail** within the Thumbnails class. The sole parameter to this function is a filename for the image for which a thumbnail is to be made. **MakeThumbnail** massages the image data into an 8-BPP, 256-color image (regardless of its original format) and writes the reduced size image to a file of the same name as the input file but with a ".THM" file extension. Two images now exist: the unaltered original image and a thumbnail version of same with a ".THM" file extension. Between these two image files a date and time correlation exits. In all cases, the date and time of the thumbnail image is newer than that of the original image. This correlation will remain true until such time that the original images are updated by some external process. This is where the thumbnail image validation code built into the Thumbnails class comes into play. As long as the date and time of the thumbnail image is newer than the original image, the thumbnail can be displayed in place of the original image because the thumbnail represents the original image. If, however, the thumbnail software detects that the image is more recent than the thumbnail image, a new thumbnail will be generated automatically before the thumbnail is displayed. Thumbnail validation guarantees that a displayed thumbnail always reflects the current content of the image file it is meant to represent. Of course, for this technique to work, thumbnail images must be stored in the same directory as the image files.

Thumbnail images are displayed within a window by a call to the **DisplayThumbnail** function of the Thumbnails class. This function requires three parameters: the filename of the image to be displayed (the original image filename not the thumbnail filename); a handle to the window the thumbnail is to be displayed centered within; and a Boolean indicating whether the thumbnail should be displayed with a foreground or background palette. The first operation performed within **DisplayThumbnail** is to perform thumbnail validation as described earlier. A call will be made to **MakeThumbnail** (from within **DisplayThumbnail**) if no thumbnail exists for the specified image or if the image is newer than the thumbnail. Once validation is completed, the thumbnail image will be displayed centered within the window. A call to **DisplayThumbnail** is generally placed within the paint routine of a window so the thumbnail image will be redrawn every time the window requires it.

Display of a thumbnail image is relatively straightforward. First, a local object of the Compand class (see Chapter 4) is instantiated to load the thumbnail image file from disk into memory. Next, calculations are performed for centering the thumbnail image in the client area of the containing window. Finally, a global Display object (see Chapter 6) is initialized and then used for display of the thumbnail image. Note: The thumbnail code is structured in such a way as to avoid problems with color oscillations that were experienced during the development of the code. Two static Display objects were needed to prevent the problem. See the comments in Listing 10.5 for more information.

Textual Annotation of Images

Annotation refers to the process of overlaying an image with text and/or graphics in some manner to point out or highlight the information contained in the image. The discussion here is limited to textual annotation, but the concepts presented could easily be extended to other types of graphic annotations as well.

Annotation of images is many times performed manually using a paint program. In general, the process consists of the following steps:

1. The image to be annotated is loaded into the paint program.
2. The text drawing tool is then selected.
3. The user optionally selects the font type (Arial, Times Roman, Black Forest, etc.), the font style (normal, bold, italic, bold and italic), the font size (10, 18, 32 points), and the foreground and background colors to use for the text.
4. The user clicks on the portion of the image where the text is to be placed.
5. The user is prompted for the text to place on the image. After the text is input, it usually shows up in the window displaying the image.
6. When the image is subsequently saved, it contains the text *merged* with the image.

As simple as the manual annotation process is, sometimes it is necessary to annotate an image under program control instead of user control. Possible applications of automated image annotation range from adding a simple caption to an image, to time and date stamping an image like a date back on a camera or the date display function on a camcorder, to the overlay of critical dimension information on an image of a defective part in a manufacturing environment or even to making personalized Christmas Cards using a scanned in picture of a snowy scene. As you can see, many real (and possibly imagined) applications exist for textual annotation of images.

In some cases, you may want to place the text directly over features in an image, and in other cases you may not want to obscure any part of the image, making it necessary to enlarge the image dimensions to hold both the (off image) annotation in addition to the image. With judicious application of the concepts presented in this chapter, either or both options can be accommodated.

The Annotation Process

Annotation is really the process of merging text with an image. If you think of the process at the pixel level, the pixels that make up the textual information are written over the pixels that make up the image. Luckily, with the GDI support provided by Windows, text and images can be merged without having to manipulate the individual pixels. Windows also takes care of the nasty details involved in using different types and sizes of fonts for the text.

The simplest form of annotation is where textual information is placed directly over the features of an image. Conceptually, this text and image merge operation can be broken down into the following series of steps:

1. Load the image to be annotated into memory in DIB format.
2. Set the text background color.
3. Set the text foreground color.

The Thumbnails classes

Purpose

The Thumbnails class provides thumbnail image capabilities to application programs. The functionality provided by this class is astonishing, especially considering the size of the class. An object of the Thumbnails class should be instantiated each time a thumbnail function or image is required, instead of instantiating an object once and reusing it.

Member Functions

Thumbnails.   This is the class constructor. Its only function is to initialize two class variables hPromoteDIB and DImagePtr to NULL.

~Thumbnails.   This is the class destructor. Its purpose is to free the memory, if any, used in promoting images with less than 8 BPP to 8 BPP in preparation for conversion into a thumbnail image.

ValidateThumbnail.   This function checks for the existence of a thumbnail and builds a new one dynamically if necessary. This function will cause a new thumbnail to be built (by calling **MakeThumbnail**) if a thumbnail image does not yet exist for the image whose filename was passed into this function, or if a thumbnail image does exist but the date and time of the thumbnail is older than the corresponding image. **ValidateThumbnail** guarantees that the thumbnail image always represents the original image by updating the thumbnail image whenever the corresponding image changes.

PromoteTo8Bits.   This function promotes DIB images with less than 8 BPP into 8-BPP format in preparation for conversion into a thumbnail image; for example, a monochrome image with 1 BPP would be converted into 8 BPP to allow the format of all thumbnail images to be the same. This is an interesting piece of code because it must pry apart multiple pixels stored within a single byte of image data and store them in one pixel/byte, 8-BPP format. Consult Listing 10.5 for details.

DisplayThumbnail.   This is the member function of the Thumbnails class that is called to display a thumbnail image. The first order of business is a call to **ValidateThumbnail** to validate and/or build a thumbnail image for display. Next, a Compand object (see Chapter 4) is used to expand the thumbnail image file into DIB format in memory. Next, the calculations are performed for centering the thumbnail image within the window it is to be displayed within. Finally, a global Display object is used to display the thumbnail image within the specified window. Short and to the point.

MakeThumbnail.   This is the most complex code in the Thumbnails class, and for this reason you should consult the text for the appropriate details. Basically, the generation of a thumbnail image from a graphic image file consists of the following steps. First, the graphic image must be loaded into memory. Next, the image must be dithered if it is in true color format, or it must be promoted to 8-BPP format if has less than 256 colors. Calculations are then performed to ascertain the size of the thumbnail image given the size and aspect ratio of the original image. Finally, the original image data is decimated into the dimensions of the thumbnail image, and the image is saved to disk with the name of the original image file and a ".THM" file extension. A Compand object is used to save the thumbnail image file.

Figure 10.3 The Thumbnails class.

4. Draw the text into the memory occupied by the DIB image.

5. Save the DIB image data out to disk as a DIB image.

In the case where annotation is to be placed off the image so that none of the image features are obscured, it is first necessary to add to the dimensions of the image by an amount required for holding the bit-mapped text. Say, for example, that four lines of text are to be added to the top of an image for annotation purposes. If the original image happened to be 640×480 pixels and each line of text needed to be 28 pixels high, the new dimensions of the image would become 640×592. With the new image dimensions known, the process of adding the text to the image conceptually breaks down as follows:

1. Allocate a buffer in memory large enough for a DIB image with the dimensions of 640×592.

2. Load the image to be annotated into memory in DIB format.

3. Copy the image data into the new buffer, leaving room for the text annotation at the top.

4. Fill the area at the top of the buffer with pixel values representing the background color you desire behind or beneath your text.

5. Set the text foreground color.

6. Draw the text into the buffer using the foreground color you selected.

7. Save the buffer out to disk as a DIB image.

As simple as these processes sound, they are complicated by restrictions Windows places on compatible bitmaps and on the types of images that are annotated. These complications will be discussed later. At this time, please refer to Listing 10.6, the file "merge.cpp," to help you understand how the image and text merging code provided in the chapter functions.

Listing 10.6 The Merge code.

```
/***********************************************************/
/***                                                    ***/
/***                   "merge.cpp"                      ***/
/***        Example Image/Text Merge Class Functions    ***/
/***                   written by                       ***/
/***                Craig A. Lindley                    ***/
/***                                                    ***/
/***        Revision: 2.0     Last Update: 11/11/94     ***/
/***********************************************************/

// Copyright (c) 1995 John Wiley & Sons, Inc. All rights reserved.

#include <string.h>
#include "dib8.hpp"
#include "compand.hpp"

// This function merges up to four lines of text onto image specified
// by InFileName and writes the resultant image to OutFileName.
BOOL MergeImageAndText(LPSTR InFileName, LPSTR OutFileName,
                LPSTR lpLine1, LPSTR lpLine2,
                LPSTR lpLine3, LPSTR lpLine4) {
```

```
HDC hDC = GetDC(NULL);          // Get DC from screen
// Find out how many bits/pixel the display device supports
WORD BitsPerPixel = GetDeviceCaps(hDC, BITSPIXEL);
ReleaseDC(NULL, hDC);           // Release the screen DC
if (BitsPerPixel < 8) {
  MessageBox(NULL, "Computer must be running in a 256 color video mode"
                   "at the very minimum for image/text merging to occur."
                   "Please change video modes and attempt merge"
                   "again.",
                   "Computer Requirements Error",
                   MB_OK | MB_TASKMODAL | MB_ICONEXCLAMATION);
  return FALSE;
}
// This can take awhile so put up hourglass
HCURSOR hOldCursor = SetCursor(LoadCursor(NULL, IDC_WAIT));

// Now attempt to expand the input file into memory
Compand E;
if (!E.InitExpander(InFileName)) {
  MessageBox(NULL, "Unsupported graphical image file specified."
                   "Cannot perform image/text merge.",
                   "User Advisory",
                   MB_OK | MB_TASKMODAL | MB_ICONEXCLAMATION);

  SetCursor(hOldCursor);
  return FALSE;
}

if (!E.DoExpansion()) {         // Expand the image
  MessageBox(NULL, "Error expanding graphical image file."
                   "File is possibly corrupt.",
                   "User Advisory",
                   MB_OK | MB_TASKMODAL | MB_ICONEXCLAMATION);

  SetCursor(hOldCursor);
  return FALSE;
}
// When we get here, the file has been expanded.
// Record the image parameters at this point. They will be changed
// if the image is dithered.
WORD ImageBPP = E.GetBitsPerPixel();
WORD ImageColors = E.GetColors();
BYTE huge *ImageDataPtr = E.GetDataPtr();
RGBCOLOR *ImagePalettePtr = E.GetPalettePtr();

// Declare a DIB8 object to dither the image if necessary
// It is declared outside of the conditional block to follow
// because it will contain the dithered data if dithering
// is necessary. If it were declared within the conditional it would go
// out of scope before we had access to the dithered data.
DIB8 D;
if ((E.GetColors() == 0) &&     // Image is true color
    (BitsPerPixel == 8)) {      // but hwd is 8 bit
  // Image must be dithered. Initialize the DIB8 object for dithering
```

```
    if (!D.InitDIB(E.GetWidth(), E.GetHeight(), E.GetColors(), E.GetDataPtr(),
                E.GetPalettePtr()))) {
        MessageBox(NULL, "Not enough memory to dither image.",
                   "User Advisory",
                   MB_OK | MB_TASKMODAL | MB_ICONEXCLAMATION);

        SetCursor(hOldCursor);
        return FALSE;
    }
    // When we get here, the image has been dithered. Record the new
    // image parameters.
    ImageBPP        = D.GetBPP();
    ImageColors     = D.GetNumberOfColors();
    ImageDataPtr    = D.GetImageDataPtr();
    ImagePalettePtr = D.GetPalettePtr();
}
SetCursor(hOldCursor);              // Put cursor back to normal for now

// Now calculate how much to add to the image height for the
// annotation. The first step is to pick a font point size
// for the text.
BOOL Done = FALSE;
HFONT hFont = 0;
HFONT hOldFont = 0;
hDC = GetDC(NULL);                  // Get a DC to work with
// Only allow text to take up this percent of image width
WORD PrintableWidth = (E.GetWidth() * 5)/8;
int TypePoints = 35;               // Begin with a 35 pt type

// Figure out which of the four lines of text is the longest
LPSTR lpLongestLine = lpLine1;
WORD LineLength, MaxLength = strlen(lpLine1);
WORD LinesToAdd = 1;

LineLength = strlen(lpLine2);
if (LineLength > 0)
  LinesToAdd++;
if (LineLength > MaxLength) {
  lpLongestLine = lpLine2;
  MaxLength = LineLength;
}

LineLength = strlen(lpLine3);
if (LineLength > 0)
  LinesToAdd++;
if (LineLength > MaxLength) {
  lpLongestLine = lpLine3;
  MaxLength = LineLength;
}

LineLength = strlen(lpLine4);
if (LineLength > 0)
  LinesToAdd++;
if (LineLength > MaxLength) {
```

```
      lpLongestLine = lpLine4;
      MaxLength = LineLength;
   }

   // Create a default font spec for use. Size will be filled in in
   // the loop below. The lfHeight is calculated from the required
   // point size and the resolution of the display.
   LOGFONT CurrentFont;

   int LogPixelsY = GetDeviceCaps(hDC, LOGPIXELSY);
   memset(&CurrentFont, 0, sizeof(LOGFONT)); // Clear the structure
   // Fill in the constant values
   CurrentFont.lfWeight = 700;
   CurrentFont.lfOutPrecision = 3;
   CurrentFont.lfClipPrecision = 2;
   CurrentFont.lfQuality = 1;
   CurrentFont.lfPitchAndFamily = 0x22;
   lstrcpy((LPSTR) &CurrentFont.lfFaceName, "Arial");

   int LogSize;
   // The font size must be determined interatively
   do {
      // Fill in the only variable portion of font spec
      LogSize = MulDiv(TypePoints, LogPixelsY, 72);
      CurrentFont.lfHeight = -1 * LogSize;
      if (hFont)                      // If a font exits, destroy it
        DeleteObject(SelectObject(hDC, hOldFont));
      // Create the new font and selected it into the DC
      hFont = CreateFontIndirect(&CurrentFont);
      hOldFont = (HFONT) SelectObject(hDC, hFont);// Select new font into DC
      // Get the width of the longest annotation string in the current font
      int TheTextSize;
#ifndef _WIN32_
      DWORD TextSize = GetTextExtent(hDC, lpLongestLine, lstrlen(lpLongestLine));
      TheTextSize = LOWORD(TextSize);
#else
      SIZE Size;
      GetTextExtentPoint(hDC, lpLongestLine, lstrlen(lpLongestLine), &Size);
      TheTextSize = (int) Size.cx;
#endif
      // If longest string will fit into printable area, we're done
      if (TheTextSize > PrintableWidth)
        TypePoints--;                 // Line doesn't fit reduce pt size
      else                            // and try for fit again
        Done = TRUE;
   } while (!Done);
   // When we get here the font size is picked. Determine the line height.
   TEXTMETRIC Tm;
   GetTextMetrics(hDC, &Tm);
   DeleteObject(SelectObject(hDC, hOldFont));
   WORD TextLineHeightinPixels = Tm.tmHeight + Tm.tmExternalLeading;

   // Calculate the amount of memory required to hold new image
   DWORD OldRasterSize =
      (DWORD) ALIGN_DWORD(E.GetWidth() * ((ImageColors == 0) ? 3:1)) *
```

```
     E.GetHeight();
DWORD NewRasterSize =
  (DWORD) ALIGN_DWORD(E.GetWidth() * ((ImageColors == 0) ? 3:1)) *
  (E.GetHeight() + (TextLineHeightinPixels * LinesToAdd));

HGLOBAL hImageMemory = GlobalAlloc(GHND, NewRasterSize);
if (!hImageMemory) {
  MessageBox(NULL, "Not enough memory to merge image and text.",
                   "User Advisory",
                   MB_OK | MB_TASKMODAL | MB_ICONEXCLAMATION);
  return FALSE;
}
// We got the memory to work with, lock it down and copy image
BYTE huge *ImageMemoryPtr = (BYTE huge *) GlobalLock(hImageMemory);
// Copy the image data into the new, larger buffer
hmemcpy(ImageMemoryPtr, ImageDataPtr, OldRasterSize);
ImageDataPtr = ImageMemoryPtr;

// Create another DIB object to build the BMI structure for the new image
DIB8 D2;
D2.InitDIB(E.GetWidth(), E.GetHeight() + (TextLineHeightinPixels * LinesToAdd),
          ImageColors, ImageDataPtr, ImagePalettePtr);
// Make the just expanded device independent bitmap to a device dependant one
// This call creates an uninitialized DDB from the DIB image
HBITMAP hBitmap = CreateDIBitmap(
                    hDC, (LPBITMAPINFOHEADER) D2.GetPtrToBITMAPINFO(),
                    0L, NULL, NULL, 0);

// When we get here, we have created a DDB bitmap of the image
// Now create a memory device context
HDC hMemDC = CreateCompatibleDC(hDC);
ReleaseDC(NULL, hDC);
// Select the bitmap into the memory device context. MemDC should
// take on the characteristics of the bitmap. That is, size and color
// organization.
HBITMAP hOldBitmap = (HBITMAP) SelectObject(hMemDC, hBitmap);
// Select the font into the MemDC
hFont = CreateFontIndirect(&CurrentFont);
hOldFont = (HFONT) SelectObject(hMemDC, hFont);

// Select the image's palette into the memory device context
HPALETTE hOldPalette = SelectPalette(hMemDC, D2.GetPaletteHandle(), FALSE);
RealizePalette(hMemDC);

// Blt the image into the MemDC
StretchDIBits(hMemDC,
              0, 0,
              E.GetWidth(), E.GetHeight() + TextLineHeightinPixels * LinesToAdd,
              0, 0,
              E.GetWidth(), E.GetHeight() + TextLineHeightinPixels * LinesToAdd,
              ImageDataPtr, D2.GetPtrToBITMAPINFO(),
              DIB_RGB_COLORS, SRCCOPY);

// Now draw the annotation onto the image bitmap in the memory
// device context.
```

```
RECT Area;
Area.top = 0;
Area.left = 0;
Area.right = E.GetWidth();
Area.bottom = TextLineHeightinPixels * LinesToAdd;

// First make the annotation area white
FillRect(hMemDC, &Area, (HBRUSH) GetStockObject(WHITE_BRUSH));

// We will use a red pen to annotate the image.
// Draw each line of the text onto the image in MemDC.
SetTextColor(hMemDC, RGB(255, 0, 0));
SetBkMode(hMemDC, TRANSPARENT);
Area.top = 0;
Area.left = 0;
Area.right = E.GetWidth();
Area.bottom = TextLineHeightinPixels;
// Draw the text of line 1
if (lpLine1)
  DrawText(hMemDC, lpLine1, lstrlen(lpLine1), &Area,
          DT_SINGLELINE | DT_CENTER);

Area.top = TextLineHeightinPixels;
Area.bottom = TextLineHeightinPixels*2;
// Draw the text of line 2
if (lpLine2)
  DrawText(hMemDC, lpLine2, lstrlen(lpLine2), &Area,
          DT_SINGLELINE | DT_CENTER);

Area.top = TextLineHeightinPixels*2;
Area.bottom = TextLineHeightinPixels*3;
// Draw the text of line 3
if (lpLine3)
  DrawText(hMemDC, lpLine3, lstrlen(lpLine3), &Area,
          DT_SINGLELINE | DT_CENTER);

Area.top = TextLineHeightinPixels*3;
Area.bottom = TextLineHeightinPixels*4;
// Draw the text of line 4
if (lpLine4)
  DrawText(hMemDC, lpLine4, lstrlen(lpLine4), &Area,
          DT_SINGLELINE | DT_CENTER);

// Copy the modified bitmap data into a buffer. NOTE:
// the bitmap must not be selected into a DC when this
// function is called.
SelectObject(hMemDC, hOldBitmap);
GetDIBits(hMemDC, hBitmap, 0,
          E.GetHeight()+(TextLineHeightinPixels * LinesToAdd),
          ImageDataPtr,
          D2.GetPtrToBITMAPINFO(), DIB_RGB_COLORS);

// Clean up after the merge operation
DeleteObject(SelectObject(hMemDC, hOldFont));
SelectPalette(hMemDC, hOldPalette, FALSE);
```

```
    DeleteObject(hBitmap);
    DeleteDC(hMemDC);

    // Now copy the palette for storage from the DIB color table
    RGBCOLOR *lpRGBColor = ImagePalettePtr = E.GetPalettePtr();
    RGBQUAD *lpRGBQuad = D2.GetPtrToBITMAPINFO()->bmiColors;
    // Fetch new palette from DIB
    for (WORD Index=0; Index < ImageColors; Index++) {
      lpRGBColor[Index].Red   = lpRGBQuad[Index].rgbRed;
      lpRGBColor[Index].Green = lpRGBQuad[Index].rgbGreen;
      lpRGBColor[Index].Blue  = lpRGBQuad[Index].rgbBlue;
    }

    // When we get here, we are ready to write out the merge image file.
    // Prepare a new compand object to compress the image in BMP format.
    hOldCursor = SetCursor(LoadCursor(NULL, IDC_WAIT));
    Compand C;
    C.InitCompressor(C.FileTypeFromName(InFileName),
                     OutFileName,
                     E.GetWidth(),
                     E.GetHeight() + (TextLineHeightinPixels * LinesToAdd),
                     ImageBPP, ImageColors,
                     ImageDataPtr,
                     ImagePalettePtr);

    if (ImageColors == 0)
      C.SetImageType(TRUECOLOR);
    else if (ImageColors > 2)
      C.SetImageType(PALETTECOLOR);
    else
      C.SetImageType(MONOCHROME);

    // Compress the new image into the OutFileName.
    if (!C.DoCompression()) {
      MessageBox(NULL, "Error writing output file.",
                       "User Advisory",
                       MB_OK | MB_TASKMODAL | MB_ICONEXCLAMATION);

      // Give back the image memory
      GlobalUnlock(hImageMemory);
      GlobalFree(hImageMemory);
      SetCursor(hOldCursor);
      return FALSE;
    }
    SetCursor(hOldCursor);                    // Put back original cursor

    // Give back the image memory
    GlobalUnlock(hImageMemory);
    GlobalFree(hImageMemory);
    return TRUE;
}
```

How the Merge Code Works

The first thing to understand about the code shown in Listing 10.6 is that it is not general purpose C++ code typical of what has been presented throughout this book.

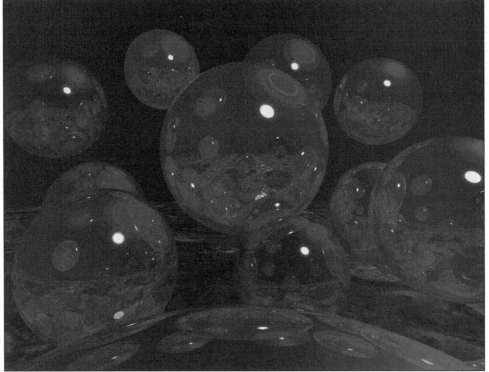

FIGURE 10.4 An annotated image.

Instead, the code presented is a hard-coded example of text and image merging included for illustration purposes only. A little later on some thoughts on how to make the code more general purpose will be provided. However, it is first necessary for the basic techniques of text and image merging to be discussed and understood before the concepts can be elaborated on.

The file "merge.cpp" shown in Listing 10.6 contains only a single function called **MergeImageAndText,** which we will discuss. This function performs off image annotation by allowing up to four lines of text to be added to an image without obscuring image features. The results of annotating a ray-traced image using this function is shown in Figure 10.4. The CacheTst program presented later in this chapter was used to drive the **MergeImageAndText** function in producing Figure 10.4. Consult Listing 10.7 to see how the **MergeImageAndText** function is set up and called within the CacheTst program.

Listing 10.7 The Cachetst class definition.

```
/***********************************************************/
/***                  "cachetst.hpp"                 ***/
/***             Image Cache Test Program            ***/
/***               Class Definition File             ***/
/***                    written by                   ***/
/***                 Craig A. Lindley                ***/
/***                                                 ***/
/***       Revision: 2.0    Last Update: 11/11/94    ***/
/***********************************************************/

// Copyright (c) 1995 John Wiley & Sons, Inc. All rights reserved.

#ifndef CACHETST_HPP
#define CACHETST_HPP

#include <owl\owlpch.h>
#pragma hdrstop

#include "cachetst.h"           // Definition of all resources.
#include "cdialogs.hpp"
#include "cache.hpp"
#include "twain.hpp"

// Application Definition
class CacheTestApp : public TApplication {
  private:
    virtual void InitMainWindow();
    void EvPaletteChanged(HWND hWindow);

    DECLARE_RESPONSE_TABLE(CacheTestApp);

  public:
    CacheTestApp();
    virtual ~CacheTestApp();
};

DEFINE_RESPONSE_TABLE1(CacheTestApp, TApplication)
  EV_WM_PALETTECHANGED,
END_RESPONSE_TABLE;

// Main Window Definition
class TMainWindow : public TWindow {
  protected:
    void SetupWindow(void);

    DECLARE_RESPONSE_TABLE(TMainWindow);

    void CmAboutHelp(void);        // Help Menu Operation

  public:
    Cache *CacheObjPtr;            // Cache Object Pointer
    Twain *TwainObjPtr;            // Twain Object Pointer
```

```
      void SendPaletteChanged(HWND hWindow);

      TMainWindow(TWindow* parent, const char far* title = 0,
                  TModule* module = 0);
      virtual ~TMainWindow(void);
};
DEFINE_RESPONSE_TABLE1(TMainWindow, TWindow)
  EV_COMMAND(CM_HELPABOUT, CmAboutHelp),
END_RESPONSE_TABLE;

// Child Window Definition
class TChildWindow : public TWindow {
  private:
    static int WindowNumberWithFocus;
    OpenFileDialog *OFD;
    SaveFileDialog *SFD;

    HMENU hMenu;

    char FileName[256];
    BOOL DitherOnDemand;
    BOOL MaintainAspectRatio;
    BOOL UseThumbnails;

  protected:
    void SetupWindow(void);
    BOOL CanClose(void);
    void Paint(TDC&, BOOL, TRect&);

    void EvLButtonDown(UINT modKeys, TPoint& point);
    void EvRButtonDown(UINT modKeys, TPoint& point);
    void EvSize(UINT sizeType, TSize& size);
    void EvMove(TPoint &clientOrigin);
    LRESULT EvPaletteChanged(WPARAM, LPARAM lParam);

    // Popup menu handlers
    void PmDither(void);
    void PmAspect(void);
    void PmThumbnails(void);
    void PmLoadImage(void);
    void PmSelectSource(void);
    void PmScanImage(void);
    void PmDisposeOfImage(void);
    void PmMergeImageAndText(void);

    // Response table
    DECLARE_RESPONSE_TABLE(TChildWindow);

  public:
    WORD ChildWindowNumber;

    TChildWindow(TWindow* parent, const char far* title = 0,
                 TModule* module = 0);
    virtual ~TChildWindow(void);
};
```

```
DEFINE_RESPONSE_TABLE1(TChildWindow, TWindow)
  EV_WM_LBUTTONDOWN,
  EV_WM_RBUTTONDOWN,
  EV_WM_SIZE,
  EV_WM_MOVE,

  EV_MESSAGE(CTA_WM_PALETTECHANGED, EvPaletteChanged),

  // Menu messages
  EV_COMMAND(PM_DITHERONDEMAND, PmDither),
  EV_COMMAND(PM_ASPECT, PmAspect),
  EV_COMMAND(PM_USETHUMBNAILS, PmThumbnails),
  EV_COMMAND(PM_LOADIMAGE, PmLoadImage),
  EV_COMMAND(PM_SELECTSOURCE, PmSelectSource),
  EV_COMMAND(PM_SCANIMAGE, PmScanImage),
  EV_COMMAND(PM_DISPOSEOFIMAGE, PmDisposeOfImage),
  EV_COMMAND(PM_MERGEIMAGEANDTEXT, PmMergeImageAndText),
END_RESPONSE_TABLE;

#endif
```

The **MergeImageAndText** function accepts six LPSTR parameters. The first parameter is the filename of the image to be annotated. The second parameter is the name to be given to the image file that contains the result of the annotation process. Note: The output file will be of the same type as the input file (e.g., if input file = BMP, output file = BMP). The remainder of the parameters are pointers to the lines of text to be merged with the image. These pointers can be NULL if less than four lines of annotation text are required. Then, up to four lines of text will be added to the top of the image and will be horizontally centered. The font type and size to be used for the text is hard coded as you shall see.

The first operation performed by the **MergeImageAndText** function is to determine how many bits per pixel (BPP) the video display device is currently running in. This information is required because we must use a memory device context later in the code, and the memory context must be made compatible with an existing device context (the display). If it is determined that the display device is running in less than a 256–color mode (less than 8 BPP), this code will abort because we are only interested in merging text with images that have at least 256 colors. Upon passing this first check, the input image is read into memory in DIB format using a Compand object. Next, the specifications of the newly expanded image are examined (and stored away) to determine if the image is in true color, 24-BPP format. If the image is true color and if the display device is only running in 8-BPP mode, an object of the DIB8 class is instantiated to dither the true color image into 8-BPP format. Again, this is necessary for the same memory device context reasons stated earlier. Code for the DIB8 class is not shown in this chapter but is included on the companion disk for those people who need it or want to look it over.

Next, some calculations are performed to determine the size of the font to be used for the textual annotation. To do this, the code must determine which of the four lines of text is the longest and pick the font size so that the longest line of text can fit on the image. Please note that the height of the annotated image will be extended to accommodate the lines of text; the image width, however, will not be increased to allow the text to fit. Font size will be reduced, instead, to allow the text to fit within the width dimension of the image.

The font type chosen for annotation is an Arial true type font. The font size is iteratively determined by starting at a 35-point font size and reducing the point size until the longest line of annotation text fits comfortably within about five-eighths of the image width. With the font point size determined, a call is made to **GetText-Metrics** so that the font size in pixels can be ascertained. The variable TextLine-HeightinPixels holds this information for later use. This is the vertical spacing that will be used between adjacent lines of the annotation text.

Next comes the allocation of a block of memory large enough to accommodate the original image and the lines of text for annotating the image. With the memory allocated, all of the image data are copied into it. Because the origin of DIB images is at the lower left (see Chapter 2) when the image data are copied into the new memory block, room is left at the top of the new memory block for the annotation. Conceptually, the image data are slid down to allow room for the annotation.

Now the interesting code begins. First a DIB8 object is used again to build a BITMAPINFO structure describing the image within the memory block. This is required for the call to **CreateDIBitmap** function that creates an uninitialized device-dependent bitmap for the device-independent image data. Next, a memory device context is generated for manipulation of the image data. The uninitialized bitmap is then selected into the memory context. The annotation font and the image palette are selected into the memory context as well. Next, the **StretchDIBits** bit blit function is called to move the image data into the memory device context. With the image data in place, the **FillRect** function is called to write the background color into the area of the memory context that will be occupied by the annotation text. Following that, the **DrawText** function is used to write the text strings into the memory context. With the text strings written, all of the image and textual information is then contained within the bitmap selected into the memory device context. To get access to the bitmap (and subsequently its data), it must first be selected out of the memory device context at the same time that the original bitmap is selected back in. The call to **GetDIBits** is used to extract the device-dependent image data from the bitmap and place it back into the memory block previously allocated. With this operation completed, a lot of house-cleaning must be performed in preparation for writing the DIB image in the memory block out to the specified output file. Most important is the extraction of the image palette from the BITMAPINFO structure. Naturally, a Compand object is employed to write the graphic image file that contains the merged image and text.

Because of the amount of effort required to produce it, you will probably look upon Figure 10.4 a little differently now that you understand how it was made.

Possible Extensions to the Merge Code

The image and text merge code provided in this chapter is, as mentioned, an application of the concepts discussed earlier and not a general purpose C++ class that can be used for image annotation. To make the code more general, you could change it to accept a list of annotation operations that could be a combination of both text and graphics. The annotation operations could be flagged as on or off of the image, and the code could react accordingly. Contained within a text annotation structure could be a font specification, foreground and background color specifications, and text position information. Contained within a graphic annotation structure could be a drawing operation (circle, square, line, etc.), position information for the graphic, and a color specification. With enough thought and appropriate motivation, the concepts presented in this code could be extended to provide all of the functionality of a paint program. Imagine the uses of a full paint program under program control.

The CacheTst Example Program

The CacheTst program was initially developed as a means of testing the image-cacheing code presented earlier in this chapter but has continuously grown in functionality since its inception. As presented, it not only is a vehicle for testing and/or demonstrating how image cacheing works, it allows side-by-side display of up to 12 different images simultaneously, in addition to supporting image scanning, thumbnail images, and image and text merging. In fact, I use the CacheTst program all of the time as a platform for testing out new imaging ideas. The screen layout for the CacheTst program is shown in Figure 10.1.

As you can see from Figure 10.1, in the CacheTst program the user is presented with 12 small, individual, fully independent windows for display of images. Each of the windows can be sized, maximized, or iconized by the user as needed. What you cannot see from Figure 10.1 is that the right mouse button is used to bring up a pop-up menu for interaction and control of each of the display windows. Clicking the left mouse button over a window selects it, whereas clicking the right mouse button brings up the pop-up menu. Menu operations are selected from the pop-up menu with a click of the left mouse button. The operations available from the pop-up menu are:

Dither On Demand
Maintain Aspect Ratio
Use Thumbnails
Load Image . . .
Scan->
   Select Source . . .
   Acquire . . .
Dispose Of Image
Merge Image and Text

The *Dither On Demand* menu operation controls the dithering preference for any image subsequently loaded or scanned into the display window. By default, this operation is checked, indicating dithering on demand is the one normally used. If unchecked, full-size dithering will be used instead. See Chapter 6 for more information of these two modes of operation. Please note that if an image has already been loaded into the display window, changing the state of this menu item will have no effect. The effect will be seen, however, when a new image is scanned into, or an graphic image file is loaded into, the display window.

The *Maintain Aspect Ratio* menu operation, also normally checked, means that images displayed within the window will have their aspect ratios protected; that is, they will not be stretched or crunched to fit within the client area of the window as is the case when this menu operation is unchecked. Click this menu item off and on to see the difference in the image display.

When the *Use Thumbnails* menu operation is checked, thumbnail images will be used for image display instead of full-resolution images. If a thumbnail does not exist for an image, it will be built automatically before being displayed. You can experiment with the thumbnail display mode to see the thumbnail code, described earlier in this chapter, in operation.

The *Load Image . . .* operation is used to load a graphic image file into the window for display. Once selected, the user will be prompted for a graphic image file using the common dialog box code of Chapter 3. After an image file is selected, it will be loaded into the cache and subsequently displayed in the window. Once an image is successfully loaded into a window for display, the window's caption changes from "Empty Window" to that of the filename of the image being displayed.

The *Scan* menu is two-level. Under *Scan* are two operations, *Select Source . . . ,* for selecting which TWAIN compatible device to acquire an image from and *Acquire . . .* for acquiring an image from the selected source. See Chapter 8 for a discussion of TWAIN and TWAIN image acquisition. When the *Acquire . . .* menu operation is selected, the user will be prompted for a filename to be assigned to the scanned image. Once the filename has been input, the user will be presented with the image acquisition interface provided by the selected TWAIN source. Once image scanning is completed, the image will stored in the cache and then shown in the display window.

The *Dispose Of Image* menu selection is used to flush the displayed image completely out of the cache. When the *Dispose Of Image* menu operation is used, the image is removed from the cache, the image is erased from the display window, and the window's title changes back to "Empty Window."

The final menu pick is *Merge Image and Text*. When this menu operation is selected, the user is prompted for the filename of an image that will be merged with the text hard coded into the call to the **MergeImageAndText** function described earlier in this chapter. The result of the text and image merging will be a new image file named "merge" with the same file extension as the user selected image file. To view the results of the merge process, the output file must be loaded into a window using the *Load Image . . .* menu operation.

The CacheTst program itself is fairly straightforward in its operation. The code for most of the program is contained in the file "cachetst.cpp" shown in Listing 10.3. The important things to notice from this listing are:

- The program consists of one main application window with two menu selections (Exit and Help) and 12 smaller image display windows that are children of the main window. The child windows are spread evenly throughout the client area of the main window.
- Each of the child windows is unique, is uniquely numbered, and each has its own pop-up menu.
- Only one instance of a Cache object is used by the program. The cache object is instantiated in the main window's constructor and deleted in its destructor. Child windows reference the Cache object via their Parent pointer.
- Only one instance of a Twain object is used by the program. The Twain object is instantiated in the main window's constructor and deleted in its destructor. Child windows reference the Twain object via their Parent pointer.

- Whenever a display window renders its image as a foreground image, a WM_PALETTECHANGED message is generated by Windows and is sent to all high-level windows. Since the WM_PALETTECHANGED message is delivered only to the application window of the CacheTst program, it must be sent down to each of the child windows for appropriate processing. This is accomplished by the application class calling **SetPaletteChanged** in the main window class whenever a WM_PALETTECHANGED message is received. The **SetPalette-Changed** function, in turn, sends a user-defined palette-changed message to each child window. The handle of the window that caused the palette to change is sent along to the child windows, allowing them to react accordingly. Within each child window, a repaint of the image data will occur on reception of the palette-changed message if and only if it was not this child window that caused the palette to change in the first place. If it was this child window that started the whole palette-changing process, it does not need to be repainted because it is the foreground image. See Chapter 2 for information on palettes and the other equally arcane subjects for foreground and background images.
- The CacheTst program uniquely numbers each child window as they are created and keeps track of which child window currently has focus by window number. The static class variable WindowNumberWithFocus always contains the number of the child window that has the user's attention. Clicking either the left or right mouse buttons over a display window causes it to become the window with focus and to have its window number recorded in Window-NumberWithFocus.
- The text that is merged into the user-selected image is hard coded into the call to **MergeImageAndText** found in the *PmMergeImageAndText* menu pick processing function.

Finally, the CacheTst program must have access to the DLL, "mycache.dll" described within this chapter, for providing the cacheing code; the DLL "mytwain.dll", described in Chapter 8, for use of image scanning; and finally to the DLL, "compand.dll", described in Chapter 4, for reading and writing graphic image files. These DLL files must exist in the same directory as the CacheTst program or be on the path or be located in the Windows or Windows\System directory for proper operation of the CacheTst program.

Conclusions

A lot of miscellaneous imaging information and code have been presented in this chapter. I think you will find that some of the code is usable in your application programs as designed while other portions will need serious massaging to work for you. I believe almost all programmers will find something in this chapter that is eminently usable.

As I have stated throughout this book, a lot of forethought must be given to an application program that is to support images. While the incorporation of the concepts presented in this book will not eliminate the forethought and planning that your world-class imaging application program requires, it can hopefully reduce the amount of effort to bring your application program to fruition. Having well-designed, reusable, tested, working, and well-documented imaging code at your disposal will allow you to produce imaging programs at a much faster rate than would otherwise be possible. Once you understand all of the imaging concepts presented in this book well enough to apply them, you will be able to consider yourself an imaging expert. Who knows, you might even find a date, get a better job, or get a raise. If any of these good things happen to you as a result of reading this book or you just want to chat, drop me a line. I'll be interested to hear about any clever applications that are derived from the concepts you found in this book.

Companion Disc

Computer Requirements for Imaging Software Use

Running any serious imaging software (like that provided in this book) on a PC requires a computer with a lot of processing power and a lot of free resources (read that as memory and free hard disk space). With the falling price of computer hardware, this is not as serious a problem as it once was. Computers that meet the minimum requirements for imaging can be purchased off the shelf for under $1,800 at the time of this writing. In fact, most computers that can be purchased at the neighborhood appliance store meet the majority of the requirements. As is usually the case, however, more is better in terms of processor speed, memory, and disk space. For these reasons, the computer requirement list that follows is broken up into two sections: minimum computer requirements and recommended computer requirements. If the computer you are using for your imaging software falls somewhere between these sets of requirements, you are set. If not, it may be time to upgrade your existing computer or bite the bullet and buy a new one.

Minimum Computer Requirements

- A 386 or 486 processor running at 20 MHz or faster
- Windows 3.1 running in enhanced 386 mode for 16-bit operation or
- Windows 95 for 32-bit operation. Running in 32-bit mode on Windows 3.1 using Win 32s is also possible.
- At least 6 Mb of RAM
- A VGA graphics adapter capable of at least 640 × 480 resolution with 256 colors. This also means an analog monitor for VGA display.

- At least 10 Mb of free disk space
- At least 15 Mb of virtual memory configured as permanent if possible. If you are not sure how to configure virtual memory consult your Windows documentation.
- A black and white laser printer similar to the Hewlett-Packard IIIP or equivalent

Recommended Computer Requirements

- A 486 or Pentium processor running at 66 MHz or faster
- Windows 95 or Windows NT. The speed of imaging software running in 32-bit mode is quite a bit faster, given the same processor speed, than when running in 16-bit mode.
- 16 Mb of RAM or more if you will be scanning very large images
- A VGA graphics adapter capable of at least 800×600 resolution with 64K colors
- At least 50 Mb of free disk space
- At least 50 Mb of virtual memory
- A color printer with true color capability. A Hewlett-Packard 1200C or an Epson Color Stylus are excellent choices as are most other modern true color printers.

Computer Requirements for Developing Imaging Software

To utilize the software provided in this book in imaging applications of your own you will need a computer capable of compiling, linking and running the software in the target environment. That is running Windows 3.1 for 16-bit development and running Win32s under Windows 3.1, Windows 95 or Windows NT for 32-bit development and execution. The computers used during the development of the code for this book were as follows:

For 16-bit code development:

- 486 processor running at 33 MHz
- 8 MB of RAM
- A SuperVGA card capable of 640×480 at 256 and 64K colors
- DOS 6.2 and Windows 3.1
- Borland C++ version 4.0. All code was developed using the Integrated Development Environment (IDE) using project files to control the build process.
- 50 MB of free disk space after all tools were loaded

For 32-bit code development:

- 486 processor running at 33 MHz
- 24 Mb of RAM
- A SuperVGA card capable of 640×480 at 256 and 64K colors
- Win32s for Windows 3.1 operation and Windows 95 for Win32 operation
- Borland C++ 4.0 for Win32s and Win32 development
- 100 Mb of free disk space after all tools were loaded.

Miscellaneous Notes about the Software
and the Software Installation

1. If you changed the name of the default install directory during the installation process from \lindley to something else you will also need to change the path to the include files in the IDE environment. Otherwise, the programs and DLLs will not compile correctly. To change the include file path within a project first open the project and then select Option/Project/Directories and change the Source Directories path entry for \lindley\include to \new_directory\include. Where new_directory is the name of the directory you specified during the install.
2. The TestApp program referred to in the text is delivered as two separate programs: tstapp16.exe and tstapp32.exe for the 16- and 32-bit environments respectively. The same is true for the Compand DLL which is delivered as compnd16.dll and compnd32.dll. The same is also true for the MyTwain DLL which comes in mtwain16.dll and mtwain32.dll flavors.
3. The CacheTst program comes in cactst16.exe and cactst32.exe. Finally the Cache DLL itself is supplied in both 16- and 32-bit versions which are called mcache16.dll and mcache32.dll respectively.
4. To utilize the source code provided for both 16- and 32-bit development, you must have access to the Borland BC++ 4.0 (or newer) development environment. Project files (*.ide) for the integrated development environment are provided in the appropriate directories on the CD-ROM.
5. All user interface code is based upon OWL 2.0 classes.
6. All filenames which have 16 as part of their name refer to 16-bit specific code. All filenames which have 32 as part of their name refer to 32-bit specific code.
7. To utilize the 16- or 32-bit programs provided (EXE files) requires that the \lindley\runtime directory (see note 1 above) be placed on the PATH or that the files in this directory are copied into the Windows directory of your computer.
8. The Win32s components are not supplied for running the 32-bit versions of the provided program under Windows 3.1. These components should be supplied by your development environment vendors.
9. To debug the supplied application programs and associated DLLs, the files will need to be recompiled with debugging information turned on. The files, as delivered, are stripped of all debugging information.

Installing the Software

To install the software, follow these simple steps:

1. Start Windows on your computer.
2. Place the CD-ROM into your CD-ROM drive.
3. From Program Manager, Select **File,Run**, and type **X:\INSTALL** (where **X** is the correct letter of your CD-ROM drive).
4. Follow the screen prompts to complete the installation.

List of Files

File	Description
chap1\ brite.bmp	Brightness (sun like) bitmap used in adjust brightness/contrast dialog box of TestApp program
chap1\contrast.bmp	Contrast (yin-yang like) bitmap used in adjust brightness/contrast dialog box of TestApp program
chap1\dialogs.cpp	Code for handling all of the dialog boxes in the TestApp program
chap1\dialogs.hpp	Interface definition for all of the dialog box classes in the TestApp program
chap1\messages.h	Various user-defined messages used in TestApp program
chap1\pglayout.cpp	Member functions for canned printed page layout in TestApp program
chap1\pglayout.hpp	Interface definition for canned printed page layout in TestApp program
chap1\saknife.ico	Swiss army knife icon
chap1\tappchil.cpp	Member functions for child windows in TestApp program
chap1\tappchil.hpp	Interface definition for child windows in TestApp program
chap1\tappcli.cpp	Member functions for client window in TestApp program
chap1\tappcli.hpp	Interface definition for client window in TestApp program
chap1\tappids.h	Menu and control Ids for the TestApp program
chap1\testapp.cpp	Member functions for TestApp application program
chap1\testapp.hpp	Interface definition for TestApp application program
chap1\testapp.rc	Resources for TestApp program
chap1\testapp.def	Module definition file for TestApp program
chap1\tstapp16.ide	16-bit project file for TestApp program
chap1\tstapp32.ide	32-bit project file for TestApp program
chap3\applsdi.ico	Borland icon for SDI application
chap3\cdialogs.cpp	Common dialog box class code
chap3\tstapp16.ide	16-bit project file for common dialog box driver program
chap3\tstapp32.ide	32-bit project file for common dialog box driver program
chap3\tstppabd.cpp	Common dialog box driver program code
chap3\tstppabd.h	Common dialog box driver program code
chap3\tstppapp.cpp	Common dialog box driver program code
chap3\tstppapp.h	Common dialog box driver program code
chap3\tstppapp.rc	Common dialog box driver program code
chap3\tstppapp.def	Common dialog box driver program code
chap4\compand.cpp	Compand class code
chap4\compand.rc	Compand DLL resource file
chap4\compnd16.ide	16-bit Compand DLL project file
chap4\compnd16.def	16-bit Compand DLL module definition file
chap4\compnd32.ide	32-bit Compand DLL project file
chap4\compnd32.def	32-bit Compand DLL module definition file
chap4\bmp\bmp.cpp	BMP Codec code
chap4\gif\gif.cpp	GIF Codec code
chap4\image\image.cpp	Base class for all graphical image file Codecs
chap4\tiff\mk2dtab.c	TIF Codec code
chap4\tiff\mkg3tab.c	TIF Codec code
chap4\tiff\mkspans.c	TIF Codec code
chap4\tiff\tif.cpp	TIF Codec class code
chap4\tiff\tifclose.c	TIF Codec code
chap4\tiff\tifcomp.c	TIF Codec code
chap4\tiff\tifcompr.c	TIF Codec code

File	Description
chap4\tiff\tifdir.c	TIF Codec code
chap4\tiff\tifdmpmo.c	TIF Codec code
chap4\tiff\tiferr.c	TIF Codec code
chap4\tiff\tiffax3.c	TIF Codec code
chap4\tiff\tiffax4.c	TIF Codec code
chap4\tiff\tifflush.c	TIF Codec code
chap4\tiff\tiflzw.c	TIF Codec code
chap4\tiff\tifopen.c	TIF Codec code
chap4\tiff\tifpkbit.c	TIF Codec code
chap4\tiff\tifread.c	TIF Codec code
chap4\tiff\tifrle.c	TIF Codec code
chap4\tiff\tifswap.c	TIF Codec code
chap4\tiff\tifwrite.c	TIF Codec code
chap5\dither.cpp	Uniform quantization with dither class code
chap5\mcquant.cpp	Median cut quantization class code
chap6\display.cpp	Display class code
chap7\printops.cpp	Printops class code
chap8\containr.cpp	Containr class code for MYTWAIN DLL
chap8\mtwain16.ide	16-bit project file for MTWAIN16 DLL
chap8\mtwain16.def	16-bit module definition file for MTWAIN16 DLL
chap8\mtwain32.ide	32-bit project file for MTWAIN32 DLL
chap8\mtwain32.def	32-bit module definition file for MTWAIN32 DLL
chap8\twain.cpp	TWAIN class code for MYTWAIN DLL
chap8\twain.rc	Resource file for MYTWAIN DLL
chap8\twainids.h	Misc. code for MYTWAIN DLL
chap9\imgproc.cpp	TProcessImage class code
chap10\dib8.cpp	DIB8 class code
chap10\mcache16.ide	16-bit project file for MCACHE16 DLL
chap10\mcache16.def	16-bit module definition file for MCACHE16 DLL
chap10\mcache32.ide	32-bit project file for MCACHE32 DLL
chap10\mcache32.def	32-bit module definition file for MCACHE32 DLL
chap10\merge.cpp	Image and Text merge code
chap10\mycache.cpp	MyCache class code
chap10\thnails.cpp	Thumbnails class code
chap10\test\cachetst.cpp	Code for CacheTst program
chap10\test\cachetst.h	Code for CacheTst program
chap10\test\cachetst.hpp	Code for CacheTst program
chap10\test\cachetst.rc	Code for CacheTst program
chap10\test\cachetst.def	Code for CacheTst program
chap10\test\cactst16.ide	16-bit project file for CacheTst program
chap10\test\cactst32.ide	32-bit project file for CacheTst program
chap10\test\cchtstad.cpp	Code for CacheTst program
chap10\test\cchtstad.h	Code for CacheTst program
chap10\test\dialogs.hpp	Code for CacheTst program
chap10\test\saknife.ico	Swiss army knife icon
include\bmp.hpp	Interface definition for BMP Codec
include\cache.hpp	Interface definition for image caching code
include\cdialogs.hpp	Interface definition for common dialog box classes
include\compand.hpp	Interface definition for Compand class
include\containr.hpp	interface definition for containr class
include\defines.h	Miscellaneous definitions
include\dib8.hpp	Interface definition for DIB8 class
include\display.hpp	Interface definition for Display class

File	Description
include\dither.hpp	Interface definition for Dither class
include\errors.h	Error code definitions
include\g3codes.h	Group 3 fax codes for TIF Codec
include\gif.hpp	Interface definition for GIF Codec
include\image.hpp	Interface definition for Codec base class
include\imgproc.hpp	Interface definition for TProcessImage class
include\machdep.h	Miscellaneous definitions
include\mcquant.hpp	Interface definition for Median Cut class
include\printops.hpp	Interface definition for Printops class
include\thnails.hpp	Interface definition for Thumbnails class
include\tif.hpp	Miscellaneous TIF code/definitions
include\tifcomp.h	Miscellaneous TIF code/definitions
include\tiff.h	Miscellaneous TIF code/definitions
include\tiff4.h	Miscellaneous TIF code/definitions
include\tiffax3.h	Miscellaneous TIF code/definitions
include\tiffio.h	Miscellaneous TIF code/definitions
include\twain.h	Miscellaneous TWAIN data structure definitions
include\twain.hpp	Miscellaneous TWAIN data structure definitions
include\twainids.h	Miscellaneous TWAIN data structure definitions
testimgs\bird.bmp	BMP true color test image of a bird
testimgs\brake1.gif	GIF palettized test image of a ray traced brake assembly
testimgs\earth.gif	GIF palettized test image of the earth
testimgs\eyes.tif	TIF black and white test image of eyes
testimgs\land2.bmp	BMP test image of true color fractal landscape
testimgs\spheres3.gif	GIF palettized test image of ray traced spheres
runtime\compnd16.dll	16-bit Compand DLL
runtime\compnd32.dll	32-bit Compand DLL
runtime\mtwain16.dll	16-bit MyTwain DLL
runtime\mtwain32.dll	32-bit MyTwain DLL
runtime\mcache16.dll	16-bit MyCache DLL
runtime\mcache32.dll	32-bit MyCache DLL
runtime\bc402rtl.dll	Borland run time library
runtime\bwcc.dll	16-bit custom control library
runtime\bwcc32.dll	32-bit custom control library
runtime\tstapp16.exe	16-bit TestApp program
runtime\tstapp32.exe	32-bit TestApp program
runtime\cactst16.exe	16-bit MyCache program
runtime\cactst32.exe	32-bit MyCache program

NOTE: All of the TIFF code is copyright © 1988, 1990 by Sam Leffler with all rights reserved. Thank you, Sam, for allowing others to utilize your efforts.

User Assistance and Information

John Wiley & Sons, Inc., is pleased to provide assistance to users of this CD-ROM. Should you have questions regarding the installation or use of this package, please call our technical support number at 212-850-6194 weekdays between 9 A.M. and 4 P.M. Eastern Time.

To place orders for additional copies of this book, including the software, or to request information about other Wiley products, please call 800-879-4539.

Further Reading

Books

Baxes, Gregory A., *Digital Image Processing, A Practical Primer,* Prentice-Hall, N.J., 1984.

Castleman, Kenneth R., *Digital Image Processing,* Prentice-Hall, N.J., 1979.

CONRAC Division, CONRAC Corp., *Raster Graphics Handbook,* Covina, Calif., 1980.

Gonzalez and Wintz, *Digital Image Processing,* Addison-Wesley Publishing Company, Reading, Mass., 1977.

Holzmann, Gerald J. and AT&T Bell Labs Staff, *Beyond Photography: The Digital Darkroom,* Prentice-Hall, N.J., 1988.

Lindley, Craig A., *Practical Image Processing in C,* John Wiley and Sons, Inc., New York, N.Y., 1991.

Lindley, Craig A., *Practical Ray Tracing in C,* John Wiley and Sons, Inc., New York, N.Y., 1992.

Mattison, Phillip E., *Practical Digital Video with Programming Examples in C,* John Wiley and Sons, Inc., New York, N.Y., 1994.

Newman, W. M. and Sproull, R. F., *Principles of Interactive Computer Graphics,* McGraw-Hill, New York, N.Y., 1979.

Parker, J. R., *Practical Computer Vision Using C,* John Wiley and Sons, Inc., New York, N.Y., 1993.

Petzold, Charles, *Programming Windows,* Microsoft Press, 1990.

Rosenfeld, A. and Kak, A. C., *Digital Picture Processing,* 2ed, Vol. 1 and 2, Academic Press, New York, N.Y., 1982.

vanDam, A. and Foley, J. D., *Fundamentals of Interactive Computer Graphics,* Addison-Wesley Publishing Company, Reading, Mass., March 1983.

vanDam, A., Foley, J. D., Feiner, S. K. and Hughes, J. F., *Computer Graphics—Principles and Practice,* Addison-Wesley Publishing Company, Reading, Mass., March 1990.

Articles

Apiki, Steve, "Lossless Data Compression" from the column *"Some Assembly Required,"* *BYTE magazine,* March 1991.

Dawson, Benjamin M., "Introduction to Image Processing Algorithms," *BYTE magazine,* March 1987.

Edson, Dave, "Slay the Porting Beasties: Dave's Top Ten Tips for Migrating to Windows NT," *Microsoft System Journal,* September 1993.

Edson, Dave, "Seventeen Techniques for Preparing Your 16-bit Applications for Chicago," *Microsoft System Journal,* February 1994.

Gellock, Scot, "Porting Your 16-bit Applications to Windows NT Without Ripping Your Hair Out," *Microsoft Systems Journal,* August 1993.

Gervautz, Michael and Purgathofer, Werner, "A Simple Method for Color Quantization," *Graphic Gems,* Vol. 1, 1990.

Heckbert, Paul, "Color Image Quantization for Frame Buffer Display," *ACM Computer Graphics Journal,* Vol. 16, No. 3, July 1982.

Lindley, Craig A., "Very Dynamic Linking in Windows," *Dr. Dobb's Special Windows* issue, Fall 1994.

McManis, Charles, "Low-Cost Image Processing," *BYTE magazine,* March 1987.

Nelson, Mark R., "LZW Data Compression," *Dr. Dobb's Journal,* October 1989.

Pomerantz, Dave, "A Few Good Colors," *Computer Language magazine,* August 1990.

Regan, Shawn M., "LZW Revisited," *Dr. Dobb's Journal,* June 1990.

Schore, Michael, "Octree Method of Color Matching," *The C User's Journal,* August 1991.

Schulman, Andrew, "At Last-Write Bona Fide 32-bit Programs that Run on Windows 3.1 Using Win32s," *Microsoft Systems Journal,* April 1993.

Star, Jeffrey L., "Introduction to Image Processing," *BYTE magazine,* February 1985.

Welsh, Terry A., "A Technique for High Performance Data Compression," *Computer Magazine,* June 1984.

I N D E X

427